Dear Miss Nightingale

Dear Miss Nightingale

A selection of
Benjamin Jowett's Letters
to Florence Nightingale
1860–1893

EDITED BY

VINCENT QUINN AND JOHN PREST

CLARENDON PRESS · OXFORD
1987

Oxford University Press, Walton Street, Oxford OX2 6DP
Oxford New York Toronto
Delhi Bombay Calcutta Madras Karachi
Petaling Jaya Singapore Hong Kong Tokyo
Nairobi Dar es Salaam Cape Town
Melbourne Auckland
and associated companies in
Beirut Berlin Ibadan Nicosia

Oxford is a trade mark of Oxford University Press

Published in the United States
by Oxford University Press, New York

© V. Quinn and J. Prest, 1987

All rights reserved. No part of this publication may be reproduced,
stored in a retrieval system, or transmitted, in any form or by any means,
electronic, mechanical, photocopying, recording, or otherwise, without
the prior permission of Oxford University Press

British Library Cataloguing in Publication Data
Jowett, Benjamin
Dear Miss Nightingale: a selection of
Benjamin Jowett's letters to Florence
Nightingale 1860-1893.
1. Jowett, Benjamin   2. Balliol College–
Biography   3. Classicists–Great Britain
–Biography
I. Title   II. Nightingale, Florence
III. Prest, Colin   IV. Quinn, Vincent
880'.09   LF544.J7
ISBN 0-19-822953-4

Library of Congress Cataloging in Publication Data
Data available

Set by Joshua Associates Limited, Oxford
Printed in Great Britain
at the University Printing House, Oxford
by David Stanford
Printer to the University

ACKNOWLEDGEMENTS

WE would like to thank the Jowett Copyright Trustees for permission to publish Jowett's letters, and the Trustees of the British Library for permission to print extracts from the Nightingale Papers.

Among the many friends and colleagues who have helped us, we are particularly indebted to Dr R. J. Bingle at the India Office Library. Many others have answered one or several queries, or volunteered information: D. M. Abbott, Dr P. Adams, W. E. K. Anderson, Lord Annan, J. Barnes, Miss P. A. M. Bown, Dr R. J. Catto, Mrs J. Cormack, Dr R. D. H. Custance, Mrs C. Dalton, S. Gilley, J. Griffin, H. A. Hanley, the Revd E. Hayden, Canon P. B. Hinchliff, M. Holmes, Dr J. H. Howarth, Dr J. H. Jones, Dr A. J. P. Kenny, Dr R. H. Lonsdale, Dr R. O. A. M. Lyne, Dr J. McCaffrey, Dr P. Malekin, Dr J. F. A. Mason, Dr H. C. G. Matthew, A. C. R. G. Montefiore, Dr R. C. Ockenden, Dr F. Rosen, Professor A. S. Skinner, R. S. Smart, the Revd. P. J. Taylor, Sir Philip Ziegler.

Above all, we wish to thank the Librarian of Balliol College, Dr P. A. Bulloch, the Assistant Librarian, Alan Tadiello, and the Library Assistant, Rosemary Phizackerley, for their never-failing good humour in the face of our incessant requests for help, and Dr D. P. Waley and the staff at the British Library Department of Manuscripts for their welcoming courtesy and assistance.

V.Q.
J.P.

CONTENTS

References and Abbreviations	viii
Introduction	ix
Chapter 1. 1860–1862	1
Chapter 2. 1862–1866	21
Chapter 3. 1866–1870	103
Chapter 4. 1870–1875	197
Chapter 5. 1875–1893	269
Index of Letters from Florence Nightingale to Benjamin Jowett	325
General Index	327

ABBREVIATIONS AND CONVENTIONS

All the letters are in Balliol College Library unless otherwise stated.

All biographical information relating to names which appear in the text has been placed in the index.

Round brackets are printed as they appear in the letters.

Square brackets denote editorial insertions.

Comments added to BJ's letters by FN appear in square brackets and are initialled F.N.

Where FN herself employed square brackets in her drafts, these are printed as italicized square brackets.

AC	E. Abbott and L. Campbell (eds.), *The Life and Letters of Benjamin Jowett, MA, Master of Balliol College, Oxford* (2 vols., 1897).
Add. Jowett Papers	Additional Jowett Papers in Balliol College Library.
Add. MS	Additional Manuscript.
BCL	Balliol College Library.
BJ	Benjamin Jowett.
Boswell	G. Birkbeck Hill (ed.), *Boswell's Life of Johnson* . . . , rev. L. F. Powell (6 vols., 1934–50).
BL	British Library.
C	Conservative.
CM	Minutes of College Meeting.
Cook	Sir Edward Cook, *The Life of Florence Nightingale* (2 vols., 1913).
Faber	G. Faber, *Jowett. A Portrait with Background* (1957).
FN	Florence Nightingale.
Gell	P. L. Gell (ed.), 'Essays on Men and Manners by the late Benjamin Jowett . . .' (printed but never published).
JCE	J. M. Prest (ed.), 'Jowett's Correspondence on Education with Earl Russell in 1867', a Supplement to the *Balliol College Record* (1965).
L	Liberal.
Letters	A. Abbott and L. Campbell (eds.), *Letters of Benjamin Jowett, MA, Master of Balliol College, Oxford* (1899).
PD	Parliamentary Debates.
PP	Parliamentary Papers.
RSBJ	J. M. Prest (ed.), 'Robert Scott and Benjamin Jowett', a Supplement to the *Balliol College Record* (1966).
WS	C. Woodham-Smith, *Florence Nightingale, 1820-1910* (1950).

INTRODUCTION

BENJAMIN JOWETT was born in 1817.[1] He was educated at St Paul's School in the City of London, and in 1835 he won an open scholarship to Oxford, at Balliol College. He came into residence in 1836, and in 1838, while still an undergraduate, he was elected to a Fellowship. In Michaelmas Term 1839 he was placed in the First Class in *Literae Humaniores*. In 1842 he became a Master of Arts and was made a Tutor. In 1845 he was ordained, and in 1855 he was appointed Regius Professor of Greek—a position which it was possible for him to hold concurrently with his college Fellowship.

Behind this simple record of scholarly achievement lay an upbringing scarred by poverty. Jowett's parents, Benjamin Jowett (born 1788) and Isabella Langhorne (born 1790), were married in 1814, and lived in Peckham where they had a family of nine children (Benjamin was the third). The family background lay in Bradford and the Yorkshire wool trade, but the father was a furrier, burdened with a declining business in Bermondsey. Faced with a growing family and a contracting income, he tried his hand at printing. When that, too, failed, he turned to his, or Isabella's, Yorkshire relations, who found him occupation as a 'devil' or research assistant to John Wood, the factory reformer, and to Lord Ashley. As the family drew ever closer to the margin of existence the home in Peckham had to be given up. In 1829 Isabella took Benjamin's brothers and sisters to live with relatives in Bath, and left Benjamin himself behind to stay in lodgings in the City Road, and to get his education at St Paul's. From Bath the family moved in 1841 to Blackheath, where there were more relatives, and thence to Teignmouth (1842), to Paris where it was cheap (1846), to Bonn where they were safe from revolution (1848), to Paris again where it was no longer so cheap (1850), to Dover (1856), and to Tenby.

At each stage along the road there were casualties among the children. One daughter, Isabella, and one son, Francis, died in infancy. Frederick was mentally deficient. Agnes died of consumption in 1837, and Ellen in 1839. Alfred and William secured cadetships in India (through the influence of Lord Ashley), where William died in 1850 and Alfred in 1858. Only two children, Emily and Benjamin, the future Master of Balliol, reached middle age. Emily remained with her mother and father, became a Roman Catholic, and helped to mind a home where one parent spent the last years of a defeated life indulging himself in the composition of *A New Metrical Translation of the Book of Psalms, Accentuated for Chanting* (1858), while the other no doubt wrung her hands. Jowett had grown up in an atmosphere of paternal failure, offset, but emphasized by repeated applications to relatives on his mother's side for assistance. This left him with a distaste for lives and talents frittered away in

[1] Biographical information in *AC* and *Faber*.

ill-conceived and unsustained effort, a hatred of dependence, and a preference for success. As a young Fellow of Balliol, he kept his family, and even his cousins, at a distance, and there is no record of any of them being invited to Oxford until Emily was at last allowed to visit him towards the end of her life. Jowett's father died in 1859, and when this correspondence with Florence Nightingale begins Jowett appears to have been contributing £400 p.a. to support his mother and sister in their new residence at Torquay.[2]

From the time he came to Balliol in 1836, Jowett made the college his home. The foundations of the college's pre-eminence in the nineteenth century had already been laid before he came up.[3] The college Tutors took their teaching duties seriously, and the scholarships (or many of them) had been thrown open to competition in 1828 (in good time for the lonely and self-reliant youngster from St Paul's). Jowett himself, then, did not initiate these changes. But he understood their importance, and when he became a Tutor in 1842 he threw himself into the work, opened his door to every member of the college, and invented vacation reading-parties. Reacting against the futility of his father's downhill career, he led his pupils on, as *Lit. Hum.* Tutors still do, from the study of ancient philosophy to discussions about contemporary problems and mores.

The study of the Classics had to be shown to be of use. It was a philosophy in accordance with the spirit of the times, and in 1850, when Russell's Whig Government took up the question of university reform, Jowett's first close friend, A. P. Stanley, became the Secretary of the Commission of Inquiry. Jowett seized the opportunity to give evidence to the Commission, and to recommend that other colleges, too, should be required to adopt the open system.[4] His name became identified with the progressives' campaign to make the institutions of the country useful, and in 1853 he was consulted by the Aberdeen government about the best way of bringing in a system of competitive entry to the Home Civil Service.[5] He became a member of 'Macaulay's' Committee inquiring into the Indian cadetships, and he seems to have felt no trace of embarrassment in recommending that appointments to India, two of which had gone to his brothers at the instance of Lord Ashley, should in future be made upon the basis of an open competition.[6] At the same time he ventured to draft a Parliamentary Bill for the reform of Oxford University, and sent it to Gladstone, the Member for the University, who was at that time Chancellor of the Exchequer. Gladstone circulated Jowett's draft, together with another of his own, to the Cabinet (which preferred Gladstone's

---

[2] *AC* i. 144.

[3] John Jones, 'Sound Religion and Useful Learning: the rise of Balliol under John Parsons and Richard Jenkyns, 1798–1854', in J. Prest (ed.), *Balliol Studies* (1982).

[4] BJ's evidence is in *PP* (1852), xxii. 416–26.

[5] E. Hughes, 'Civil Service Reform 1853–55', in *History* (1942), and 'Sir Charles Trevelyan and Civil Service Reform', in *English Historical Review* (1949).

[6] R. J. Moore, 'Abolition of Patronage in the Indian Civil Service and the Closing of Haileybury College', in *Historical Journal* (1964); C. J. Dewey, 'The Education of a Ruling Caste: the Indian Civil Service in the Era of Competitive Examination', in *English Historical Review* (1973).

approach to Jowett's).[7] It seems to have been as a reward for public service, then, that Palmerston invited Jowett, in 1855, to become the Regius Professor of Greek.

As a college Fellow and Tutor Jowett was expected to proceed to ordination. At the family home in Peckham he had been exposed to evangelicals. Now, in Oxford, it was the Tractarians who were making the running. Caught between the two schools of enthusiasts, Jowett rejected both, the first because they took no account of historical circumstances, and the second because the account they took was blinkered and partial. The one group discounted, and the other betrayed the human intellect. Almost alone among the Tutors of his day, Jowett went abroad for inspiration, to Germany, and found it in Hegel's philosophy, Niebuhr's historical works, and Strauss's attempt to unravel the circumstances in which the Gospels were written. Jowett gravitated towards what came to be known as a 'Broad Church' position, and turned against the imposition of religious tests as a condition of admittance to the University. He found a kindred spirit in A. P. Stanley, and together they planned to bring all the resources of modern scholarship to bear upon a re-examination of St Paul's epistles.

For his part, Stanley took Corinthians: Jowett, Thessalonians, Galatians, and Romans. Their two volumes were published in 1855, and the freedom with which Jowett expressed questions about the doctrine of the Atonement[8] scandalized evangelicals, tractarians, and old-fashioned high and dry Anglicans alike. The Vice-chancellor, R. L. Cotton, summoned Jowett to his room to subscribe the 'Articles' of Religion. Jowett, as he said, took the meaner part and signed, and then went away to prepare a second edition of the work which was published in 1859. The second edition was longer than the first, but there was still one essay, which Jowett had written, which he was unable to find room for, and which he was reluctant to waste. He jumped, therefore, at an invitation to join other 'liberal' Anglicans and contribute to a volume which was published in 1860 under the title *Essays and Reviews*. To a twentieth-century eye Jowett's essay 'On the interpretation of scripture' appears reverent enough, but to many of his contemporaries his plea for the Bible to be studied like any other book,[9] confirmed the impression made five years earlier by the publication of his views on the Atonement, that he was abusing his position as a clergyman to propagate doctrines of 'free thought'.

When the 'old' Master of Balliol, Dr Jenkyns, died in 1854, Jowett was thought likely to succeed him. But Jowett had never concealed that he belonged to the reforming party which wanted to free the University 'from the predominance of ecclesiasticism, recall it to its proper work, and restore it to

---

[7] BJ's draft Bill is in BL Add. MS 44743 fos. 1–12, and his covering letter of 28 Dec. 1853 in BL Add. MS 44376 fos. 246–51.

[8] 'Was the spectacle real which was presented before God and the Angels on Mount Calvary?... If the greatest fact of the whole is an illusion, why not all else?', ii. 473.

[9] For the interpretation of this phrase, see James Barr, 'Jowett and the "original meaning" of Scripture', *Religious Studies* (1982).

the nation',[10] and Fellows of the college who did not share his opinions formed an opposition to him. In order to keep him out, they brought a former Tutor, Robert Scott, joint author of the best known of all Greek lexicons, back from his country rectory at Luffenham, and carried the election. The rebuff hurt Jowett deeply, and it was not entirely offset, the following year, by his appointment as the Regius Professor of Greek, not least because the Students of Christ Church had delayed carrying out an 'undertaking' given to the University Commission to raise the Professor's stipend above its traditional £40 p.a. In the mid-1850s Jowett could have been forgiven for thinking that everything was going wrong. He withdrew from high table, and for four years, Florence Nightingale later informed Evelyn Abbott, he took all his meals in his own room.[11] There is no confirmation of the story that he went to live in lodgings in Broad Street, in what is still called Jowett House, and nourished his indignation by gazing directly into the Master's Lodgings opposite, and it seems unlikely that the college would have tolerated it if he had. In the meantime, Scott continued, like the gentleman he was, to handle Jowett courteously and sympathetically.[12] In return, Jowett chafed under Scott's rule: there were only six years between the two men, and in 1860 it must have seemed that Scott would remain for ever, blocking Jowett's path.

It was at this point that Arthur Hugh Clough asked Jowett to read something for him and comment on it. Clough, the son of a Liverpool cotton merchant and a product of Arnold's Rugby, was one of Jowett's undergraduate contemporaries at Balliol. He had become a Fellow of Oriel, but he was restless, a great traveller, and a poet. In 1853 he took a post in the Education Office, and the next year he married Blanche Smith, who was a first cousin of Florence Nightingale. In 1856, when Florence Nightingale returned from the Crimea, Clough became her secretary. Although Clough concealed the name of the author whose work he was inviting Jowett to read, it seems inconceivable that her identity can have gone completely unsuspected. The work itself, which Florence Nightingale referred to as the 'Stuff', had been set up in type under the title 'Suggestions for Thought to the Searchers After Truth Among the Artizans of England'. It had been conceived, ten years earlier, under the impression that 'the most thinking and conscientious of the artizans have no religion at all'.[13] To supply that want she presented personal cleanliness and the provision of public health as practical exercises in religious worship. Simple actions like the cleaning out of a gutter were to be undertaken as being in accordance with the will of God.

Florence Nightingale had already sent copies to her father, to her uncle Sam Smith, to Monckton Milnes (the Nightingales' neighbour in Derbyshire), to Sir John McNeill, who had worked on the Commission of inquiry into the commissariat in the Crimea, and to John Stuart Mill. Unable to pick her way

---

[10] The words are Goldwin Smith's, *AC* i. 177.
[11] BL Add. MS 45785 fos. 228–29
[12] RSBJ.
[13] *Cook*, i. 120.

through their comments she now turned to Professor Jowett. Not surprisingly, the Professor felt himself flattered to have been asked. He wrote to Clough that he had received 'the impress of a new mind'.[14] Clough revealed the name of the author, and after July 1860 Jowett wrote to Miss Nightingale direct. Tactfully, he advised her against publication: her thoughts were original, but the presentation was marred by lack of order, and by 'antagonisms' which it would be better to soften.[15] Miss Nightingale wanted to know more. Jowett had given her an answer which made sure that the correspondence would continue.

In 1860 Florence Nightingale was forty.[16] She and her elder sister Parthenope were the two daughters of William Edward Shore, a Unitarian, who changed his name to Nightingale in 1815 in order to inherit a fortune from an uncle. Their mother was Fanny Smith, one of ten children of William Smith, MP, of Parndon Hall in Essex, who had been involved in the campaigns to abolish the slave trade and to emancipate the slaves. The family divided its time between the two estates of Embley in Hampshire and Lea Hurst in Derbyshire. In writing about, and interpreting the career of Florence Nightingale it is not easy even today to know whether to follow the hagiographers like Mrs Woodham Smith (1950), or the iconoclasts like F. B. Smith (1982).[17] Too much of the evidence comes from Florence herself, and too much of that was set down long after the events she was describing. The legend informs us that she had early premonitions of a life spent nursing the sick, and her first, and best, biographer, Sir Edward Cook, gave credence to her belief that she had received a call to the service of God on 7 February 1837.[18]

For many years she was thwarted in her desire to follow a career by her parents, who tried to distract her by sending her away to travel in Italy, Egypt, and Greece. But she was eventually allowed to visit the protestant Pastor Fliedner at Kaiserswerth in 1850 and to stay there in 1851, observing the work of the hospitals in which he trained volunteer nurses as deaconesses. In 1853 she followed this up with a second 'apprenticeship' among the Roman Catholic sisters of charity in the Faubourg St-Germain. Thereafter, she refused to allow her name to be associated with any religious party. Her God was neither Roman Catholic, nor Protestant; he was neither the God of the High Church nor the God of the Low. In the same year she received her first appointment as the Superintendent of the Invalid Gentlewomen's Institution in Harley Street, and it was from this address that she volunteered for service in the Crimean War. The letter of 14 October 1854 in which she offered her services was addressed to Mrs Sidney Herbert, whom she had met in Rome in the winter of 1847–8, and her offer was taken up enthusiastically by Sidney Herbert, the Secretary at War.

Florence Nightingale was not the first woman, or even the first lady, to go into nursing. Nor were she and her nurses the first women to accompany

---

[14] *Cook*, i. 471.   [15] *WS*, p. 350.   [16] Biographical information in *Cook*.
[17] *Florence Nightingale, 1820-1910* (1950); *Florence Nightingale, Reputation and Power* (1982).
[18] *Cook*, i. 15.

a British Army in the field—wives and camp followers had been doing that time out of mind, and doing a good deal of nursing too. But the Crimean campaign was the first in which female nurses were officially recognized and attached to the Army to assist the Army medical staff and the male orderlies with the care of the wounded. The campaign took place after the invention of the electric telegraph, in the full glare of the publicity provided by the war correspondents of the newspapers (*The Times* especially), at a time when 'there were in all branches of the public service broad-minded men', who were willing to talk about the affairs of their departments to outsiders,[19] and before the imposition of censorship and the invention of the Official Secrets Act. The deficiencies in the organization and supply of the Hospital services, and of the Army generally, made of Miss Nightingale, not just a pioneer of employment for women, but a champion of the suffering masses against bureaucracy and the self-satisfaction of the military and medical professions.

When Florence Nightingale returned from the Crimea, in August 1856, she was a national heroine. But she was exhausted, and shut herself away from the public gaze. Servants guarded her lodgings, which were changed frequently, and much of the remainder of her long life (she died in 1910) was passed tortured by insomnia at night and resting upon a sofa by day. From her sick bed, however, she began the second, and possibly more important phase of her career. Driven forward by her sense of mission and by a feeling that she had become the 'Mother' of the British soldier, she capitalized upon her prestige, and turned from the occasional needs of the Army in war to the everyday requirements of the Army in peace. It was not just the hospitals but the health and the accommodation of the Army which required to be attended to. It was 'as criminal to have a mortality of 17, 19 and 20 per 1,000 in the Line, Artillery and Guards in England, when that of Civil life is only 11 per 1,000, as it would be to take 1,100 men per annum out upon Salisbury Plain and shoot them'.[20] She pressed for the appointment of a Royal Commission under the Chairmanship of her old ally of Crimean War days, Sidney Herbert. Six months passed before Panmure, the Secretary for War, appointed the Commission.

In the meantime Florence Nightingale conducted her own investigations and compiled her own report, 'Notes affecting the Health, Efficiency, and Hospital Administration of the British Army', which, as her biographer says, is 'the most remarkable' of her works.[21] The 'Notes' were printed, and privately circulated, but never published. They went far beyond the need for better Hospitals, to the provision of a proper diet, washing facilities, and sanitation, and to the necessity for the collection of reliable statistics. And even when the Government had begun to implement the recommendations of the Royal Commission, Florence Nightingale took no rest. Instead she turned to the condition of the British Army in India. The time was ripe, for the Mutiny had concentrated the attention of the public wonderfully. In 1859 Florence Nightingale showed that the average annual death rate among British soldiers

[19] *Cook*, i. 348. [20] *Cook*, i. 316. [21] *Cook*, i. 343.

in India since 1817 had been 69 per thousand.[22] Lord Stanley, the Secretary of State for India, agreed to set up another Royal Commission. Once again Sidney Herbert took the Chair, and Miss Nightingale was still engaged upon this work when the correspondence with Jowett began.

In addition to her work on behalf of the British soldier, Miss Nightingale was much concerned with the development of nursing as a profession. Towards the end of the Crimean War a grateful public subscribed £45,000 to a fund for the establishment of a Nightingale Training School for Nurses. There were almost as many delays in carrying out this plan as there might have been if it had been administered by the War Office itself, but eventually a Nightingale School was established in connection with St Thomas's Hospital in June 1860, with Mrs Wardroper as Matron, and a training school for midwives at King's College Hospital.[23] By this time Florence Nightingale herself was feeling bruised. Her whole working life had involved her in conflict. She was the veteran of many campaigns, her experiences had left their mark upon her, and she had become a very partisan person. As a political head for the War Office she was for Sidney Herbert and against the dilatory Panmure. She had fallen out with Sir John Hall, the Head of the Army Medical Department in the Crimea, and she felt a deep antipathy to Sir Benjamin Hawes, the Permanent Under-secretary at the War Office from 1857–62. When it came to sanitation, she quarrelled about contagion with Sir John Simon, the Medical Officer to the Privy Council under the Public Health Act of 1858, and took the side of one of Simon's former subordinates, Dr John Sutherland. Miss Nightingale had achieved much, but nothing had been achieved without friction, combat, and distress. By 1860 she was becoming increasingly lonely. In 1858 her sister, Parthe, married Sir Harry Verney, and went to live at Claydon in Buckinghamshire. It was not that she and Parthe had ever been close, but the marriage was a reminder that Florence herself was forty and had chosen a different path.

The relationship between Benjamin Jowett and Florence Nightingale falls into five periods.

1. 1860–1862

Two years passed between the time Jowett began to comment on the 'Stuff' and his first meeting with Florence Nightingale. Throughout this period his letters to Miss Nightingale remain the work of a philosophy tutor at a correspondence college, explaining that the old paradoxes of freedom and necessity have been exploded, but that it is still intellectually respectable to combine the idea of law with that of free agency. He is deferential to the fame and sex of his pupil, and from time to time he ventures to try and entertain and lift the spirits

---

[22] Cook, ii. 18–19.
[23] This second institution was closed in 1864 after an outbreak of puerperal fever.

of an invalid by telling her about a visit to Tennyson[24] or a story he has picked up about her old enemy of War Office days, Panmure.[25] Did he ever think it strange, one wonders, that he should be writing like this to her? He had been born into a straitened home, and his fame as a tutor and as a victim of clerical intolerance was now bringing him invitations to pass the vacations at the homes of cultivated and broadminded families up and down the length and breadth of the land. She had been born into the world of the upper ten thousand, and had become a recluse, who despised ladies who drove in parks and young men who stared through the windows of the clubs in St James's Street.[26]

In the meantime Jowett was writing in a lighter and more intimate vein to Margaret Elliot, a daughter of Gilbert Elliot, the Whig Dean of Bristol, whom he had met at a party given in the Principal's garden in Brasenose. At this time Heads of Houses were free to marry, but Fellows of colleges who wished to marry, were obliged to vacate their Fellowships. In practice, for most of them marriage meant removal to a college living. Jowett was smarting under the Mastership of Scott, he was being 'persecuted' for his heterodoxy, he was feeling deserted by friends whom he had expected to 'rally round' him,[27] and he was denied a proper salary for performing his duties as the Professor of Greek. Marriage would provide a way out of his Oxford difficulties, but then he felt no call to take a country living. There was, however, just one exception allowed. Under the Balliol College Ordinances of 1857, one Fellow, provided he was a University Professor or Lecturer, might be allowed to marry and to retain his Fellowship.[28] To stay in Oxford, and enjoy the support and inspiration of a wife, would be quite another matter. Geoffrey Faber, whose biography of Jowett was published in 1957, believed that Jowett applied for this permission in 1862, or that, if he did not, he had intended to, and was beaten to it by Henry Wall, the Professor of Logic, who was elected at a special meeting on 7 June.[29] When the decision went against him, Jowett seems to have realized that there was no prospect of his being able to marry in the foreseeable future, and to have ceased to pay court to Miss Elliot.

While Jowett had been thinking of Miss Elliot, Florence Nightingale's position had changed. In 1861, soon after the correspondence with Jowett began, she was separated in rapid succession from her hero, Sidney Herbert, who died at the beginning of August, and from her secretary and the secretary of the Nightingale Fund, Arthur Hugh Clough, who died in November (in Florence where she had been born). She was lonely, she knew that malicious gossip accused her of having worn Clough out, and she was in need of support. Her mind turned to her new correspondent. Jowett appeared to be just her kind of no-nonsense clergyman, and she was alarmed by a report that he might be prosecuted for his part in *Essays and Reviews*. In October 1862 she invited him

---

[24] See below, No. 4.
[25] See below, No. 14.
[26] BL Add. MS 45783 fos. 62–4.
[27] BL Add. MS 45785 fo. 236.
[28] Clauses 14, 16.
[29] *Faber*, p. 299.

to come to London and give her the sacrament. Jowett secured permission to conduct a service of holy communion in another diocese from the Bishop of London (a former Balliol Tutor, Tait), and on 26 October the first meeting took place. The excitement of being invited to minister to someone so famous, and the privilege of being admitted secretly through barred doors, must have worked powerfully upon Jowett's emotions.

Religion thus lay at the foundation of the future relationship between Benjamin Jowett and Florence Nightingale. Jowett was a leader of the Broad Church movement (though he disliked the name). He took the view that God himself would not be found to be fussy about the creeds which had formed the battleground of religious parties throughout the centuries. Christ 'must be regarded as what in modern language would be called a *latitudinarian*',[30] and the trouble with religion was the clergy and their attempts to impose clerical discipline. A clergyman must look with 'unaverted eyes'[31] at everything that scholars had to say, and Jowett objected strongly to the fact that people had remonstrated with him for his part in *Essays and Reviews* on grounds of prudence rather than truth.[32] The Old Testament contained a great deal of beauty and moral greatness, but it was inconceivable that anyone who read it should still be willing 'to hang the life of man on the inspiration of scripture'.[33] He found it impossible to credit the miracles of feeding and healing described in the New Testament, and he had serious doubts about the resurrection, though he trusted in God for immortality.[34] The death, and not the resurrection, of Christ was the really consoling fact: it was that which showed that human nature really was divine.[35]

Christ had been a great reformer, and faith in Christ should not consist in 'niceties of doctrine but in a pure and holy life'.[36] In the nineteenth century, the good man would ignore the outward forms, and concentrate upon leading a life of Christian conduct.[37] The fact that Christ's ministry, which had changed the course of history and had transformed the world, had lasted no more than three years, served as a continuous inspiration both to him, and to Miss Nightingale, who longed for the coming of a female Christ.[38] Jowett did not share Miss Nightingale's view that clean wards and unblocked drains were of more value than the whole ecclesiastical establishment, but he, too, did look forward to a kind of 'millenium',[39] in which men's characters would have been strengthened by education, and civilization would be very different. Jowett was, in his way, a prophet. By stripping away outdated formularies, which so many of the more intelligent undergraduates found it impossible to subscribe to, it ought to be possible to convert Christianity from a past to a present fact.[40]

---

[30] BL Add. MS 45785 fo. 268.   [31] See below, No. 81.
[32] See below, No. 7.   [33] BL Add. MS 45785 fos. 256–7.
[34] See below, No. 4, and *AC* ii. 280, 449.
[35] See below, No. 51, specially noted by FN at BL Add. MS 45785 fo. 260.
[36] BL Add. MS 45785 fo. 268.   [37] *AC* ii. 453.
[38] See below, Nos. 4, 110, 139.   [39] See below, Nos. 38, 69, 74.
[40] See below, No. 2.

This meant that Jowett could be unaffectedly anti-clerical in the cause of Christ. It was an attitude which separated him from many of his fellow clergy. With every year that passed he drew further away from old friends like A. P. Stanley, Tait, and Temple, who seemed to him to be making compromises with their consciences, and he did not encourage undergraduates to go into the Church.[41] Increasingly, therefore, he tended to prefer the company of lawyers, who saved him from the persecution and vengeance of the Puseyites. In 1871 lawyers formed the largest professional group among old members of Balliol College attending the great dinner organized in London to celebrate his election as Master. In 1872 he enjoyed meeting Lord Westbury, who had given the final verdict in the case of Williams's and Wilson's essays in *Essays and Reviews*. In 1893 he died at the home of a High Court Judge, Sir Robert Wright.

2. 1862–1866

Friendship with Miss Nightingale offered the excitement of gallantry without the unnerving prospect of matrimony. Jowett had no alternative but to remain 'married' to his college, and he was still, for several years to come, unhappily married. Until 1866 Scott kept control of the college with the assistance of Woollcombe (the Senior Tutor) and Wall (the Bursar), and Jowett and his supporters were in a minority. There was little that he could do, except devote himself self-consciously and conscientiously to the undergraduates, so few of whom seemed to him to come to anything. Jowett assumed responsibility for them all, and none must be lost. As a tutor he took it for granted that education had as much to do with character as with intellect. Jowett believed almost as strongly as his opponent Pusey that tutors ought to exercise a moral influence over their charges. He could scarcely conceal his expectation that Balliol undergraduates would become as anti-clerical in religion and as strenuous in their efforts to involve themselves in the active life of the nation as himself, and was disconcerted if they did not.

Florence Nightingale, too, was 'married' to her work on behalf of the British soldier, especially the British soldier in India. At a time when Jowett could do nothing with Balliol, she could do little with the War Office, and less than she wished with the government of India. Like Jowett she was aware that time was passing, and lamented her impaired usefulness. Of the two, it was Jowett who never lost a night's sleep, and remained the more sanguine. But he was glad to find compensation for the frustrations of college and University life in writing to the nation's heroine, and exchanging with her opinions on politics, letters, and the personalities of the day. Their correspondence ranged very widely. For some years Florence Nightingale took precedence over all Jowett's other friends, and he administered the holy communion to her every month.

At first sight it might appear that this was a somewhat unchallenging time to be looking around one and to be writing. In 1862 Bismarck had not yet begun

[41] See below, No. 54.

to remake the map of Europe, and Britain was secure in her power and in the reverence accorded to the constitution. From their places in Parliament Palmerston and Russell read lectures on freedom to the Eastern European autocrats. The one great democracy, the United States of America, had sunk into civil war, and the United Kingdom's only rival in liberty, France, had lapsed into plebiscitary Bonapartism. British institutions, which were neither autocratic nor democratic, served as a model to the world. Like the climate, they were temperate. In Britain, the excitements of the Reform period, in which Jowett and Miss Nightingale had grown up, seemed to have come to an end. The Chartists' demands for universal suffrage and annual Parliaments had been refused, and the reformed representative system of 1832 appeared to have established itself and taken root. The House of Commons had opened its doors to the intelligent middle class, and the proceedings in Parliament were reported at length in a free press. Two decades of reform following the Great Reform Act had removed old abuses and restored confidence in the country's institutions. By the late 1850s the Reform party itself seemed to have run out of things to do, and the late 1850s and early 1860s have been memorably termed, by W. L. Burn, 'The age of equipoise'.

This is not a view that would have found much favour with Benjamin Jowett and Florence Nightingale. Jowett appreciated that more than half of what was called patriotism was really dislike of other nations,[42] and he feared that England was falling behind in the liberality of her institutions.[43] The great evil was routine and want of originality,[44] as Florence Nightingale had discovered during the Crimean War, and people always cunningly pretended that all the mischief in the world was done by radicalism, when really it was done by conservatism.[45] There was something fearfully wrong in the present state of society—in family relations especially, between husbands and wives, and between parents and children.[46] Both Jowett and Florence Nightingale saw the need for further 'movement'. In his eyes, the revolution being effected by 'the career open to talents through examination', in hers, a religious approach to social problems, still had a long way to run. Both looked forward to seeing women play a larger role in the active life of the nation. Not only this: there were two fields in which their views were certain to command respect, education and (in a much broader sense than the Health of Towns' movement of the 1840s) public health. Both topics were making their way to the top of the Parliamentary agenda, and the fact that the best-known of all college Tutors and the most famous of all nurses were in constant communication marks theirs out as an ideal friendship for the 1860s.

Education was the 'bore of politics',[47] but literacy and learning were becoming two of the most sought-after commodities of the industrial age. At every level of society, the provision of schools had become a matter of

---

[42] See below, No. 102.   [43] See below, No. 114.
[44] See below, No. 145.   [45] See below, No. 103.
[46] See below, Nos. 3, 8, 96.   [47] JCE, p. 10.

urgency, and the content of the curriculum a subject of debate. Among the labouring classes, the standard of living had risen to the point where it was possible to contemplate the cessation of child labour, and the Newcastle Commission appointed in 1858 recommended the establishment of local boards of education and the construction of elementary schools in every area. At the other end of the scale, the Clarendon Commission of 1862 looked into the affairs of the schools attended by the children of the wealthy, the nine great endowed public schools which supplied so many of the entrants to Oxford and Cambridge. In the middle, between the many and the rich, the Taunton Commission, appointed in 1864, investigated the condition of the remaining schools not already covered by the first two commissions—the middle-class schools and endowed grammar schools. The Taunton Commission adopted a generous interpretation of its brief, and paid attention to the demands of middle-class women to be allowed to receive an education, at school and university, just as their brothers did. At every level, from Robert Lowe's 'revised code', which instituted a system of payment by results for teachers in the elementary schools aided and inspected by the State, to the Oxford and Cambridge Schools' Examination Boards, established in 1857, with their 'Locals' and 'Highers', the reformers put their trust in examinations as a means of testing and measuring educational attainment.[48]

Jowett kept in close touch with these developments through his friend R. R. W. Lingen, the Secretary in the Education Office. In writing to Miss Nightingale, however, he never felt it necessary to volunteer a systematic explanation of his views about education. She would have understood that they were grounded in anti-clericalism. The problem in Jowett's opinion, was that, from one end of the educational system to the other, the church 'would not sacrifice an "iota" of power to educate the whole country'.[49] At Oxford, dissenters were still excluded from the MA degree and from Fellowships, and throughout the nineteenth century the provision of primary education by the state had been frustrated by 'the religious question'—the quarrels between churchmen and dissenters as to the nature of the religious instruction which was to be given. The practice of allocating Privy Council grants in aid of voluntary schools, which began in 1833, had been, according to Jowett, 'a temporary expedient' which was passed 'in the interests of the religious denominations against the interests of the nation'.[50] Church and Dissent were equipollent, but nine-tenths of the education grant ended up in the hands of the Church, and the system thus transferred 'the management of education to the Clergy instead of interesting the population generally in it'.[51]

Jowett held the view that no one had ever yet fought the education cause with 'the earnestness which wins great causes such as the Anti-slavery Cause or the Factory Bill or the Free Trade measures'.[52] But it was not until October

---

[48] D. W. Sylvester, *Robert Lowe and Education* (1974); J. Roach, *Public Examinations in England, 1850-1900* (1971).
[49] JCE, p. 10.   [50] JCE, p. 9.   [51] JCE, p. 9.   [52] JCE, p. 10.

1867, when Russell announced that he intended to make a move about education, that Jowett produced a comprehensive paper on '1. the education of the poor in primary schools: 2. the education of the Middle Classes in Grammar Schools and Commercial Schools: 3. the education of the Higher Classes and of the Clergy at the University'.[53] This document is the fullest statement of his views upon the education question, matured over many years, and it is scarcely out of order to refer to it at this point. His preferred solution to the religious problem was to impose a common secular education and to allow separate denominational instruction. He favoured the substitution of rate-maintained schools for voluntary ones. For the ten- to eighteen-year-olds age-group, there was, at that time, in Jowett's opinion, very little good schooling.[54] But in many places the funds already existed to provide it. The Grammar Schools were endowed, and it was not niggardliness on the part of ratepayers, so much as lack of interest and incompetence on the part of the Trustees which needed to be combated. The go-ahead men in the schools, Jowett thought, like the reformers in the Universities, required the aid of the legislature if they were to succeed in setting the tone of the establishments in which they served. The Taunton Commission's report led to the Endowed Schools Act of 1869, and in 1874 an educational department was established within the Charity Commission, to liven up the Trustees, exactly as Jowett himself suggested to Earl Russell.[55]

In writing about education, Jowett had the advantage that he was an 'expert' (for the whole system already focused upon the Universities, although a minute proportion only of the population ever went there), and that the tide was running his way. But, in corresponding with Miss Nightingale, he was tempted beyond his own sphere and into her realm of 'public health'. Jowett became interested in soldiers—whether they should be allowed to marry, and how they spent their spare time. At a surprisingly early stage in their relationship Jowett found himself considering how soldiers (and others) were to be saved from the ravages of venereal disease. For over twenty years from the time the first regulatory statute was passed in 1864, to 1886, when the last statute was repealed at the instance of Josephine Butler, the Contagious Diseases Acts were a lively political issue.[56] They were also one where, as Jowett and Florence Nightingale were compelled to recognize, it was not possible to identify a clear 'liberal' line, and both preferred to concentrate upon the need to recruit a better class of soldiery, and the provision of reading rooms and other educational and recreational facilities.[57]

The Contagious Diseases Acts were an important, but also a somewhat specialized aspect of public health. Throughout the 1860s Florence Nightingale's interests were shifting from the needs of the Army to the condition of the

---

[53] JCE. [54] JCE, p. 7. [55] JCE, p. 7.
[56] See especially, J. R. Walkowitz, *Prostitution and Victorian Society, Women, Class, and the State* (1980).
[57] FN, 'Note on the Supposed Protection Afforded against Venereal Disease by Recognizing Prostitution and Putting it under Police Regulation' (privately printed, 1863).

population as a whole. The nurses trained in the Nightingale School at St Thomas's were not expected to take private work. Instead, they were sent out as missionaries for cleanliness to the great London teaching hospitals and to workhouse infirmaries in the big cities. In the nineteenth century hospitals were dangerous places for patients.[58] The rich kept well away from them, and it was the poor who received treatment in institutions. The stronger the sense of vocation a Nightingale nurse possessed, the more likely she was to be brought into contact with patients who could tell her what life was like at the bottom of society, in overcrowded houses, among men engaged in casual labour and women worn out by child-rearing. Nightingale nurses reported back to Miss Nightingale, who was disturbed by what she heard.

Florence Nightingale's life was predicated upon her faith in God, and the goodness of God could only be reconciled with the prevalence of poverty and squalor if the poverty and squalor were interpreted as signals in a divine plan to stir up the hearts of men. But which way did God intend men to turn? That was the question. The New Poor Law of 1834, with its workhouse test, had been intended to settle, if not to solve, 'the social problem'. By the early 1860s the New Poor Law had already been in operation for a generation: but the expansion of the economy had not put an end to poverty, and the 1834 Act had not eliminated pauperism. Even the most evangelical statesman could have been forgiven, at this period, for wondering whether God intended men to expand or to contract the scope of public provision for the poor. Florence Nightingale discussed this question with Jowett, and a large number of his letters written between 1862 and 1870 are concerned with the principles and administration of poor relief. Suggestions flowed from his pen, for political economy was a discipline which he taught, and believed he understood. But, in fact, he was unable to see far beyond the Metropolitan Poor Law Act of 1867, which transferred a little of the burden of the poor who crowded into the East End onto the wealth of the West End, and the 'organization' of charity (the Charity Organization Society was founded in 1869). In dealing with education, he held that 'no principle is violated by helping those who cannot help themselves'.[59] But, in this more fundamental area of work, wages, and the constitution of society, he was, like most of his contemporaries, afraid lest anything that smacked of 'socialism' might pauperize the entire working class. Comprehensive schemes of redistributive taxation, and the expansion of the Civil Service to the point where a centralized State could begin to alleviate the horrors of life among the poor, still lay beyond the leap even of a very liberal imagination. Beveridge did not come up to Balliol until four years after Jowett's death.

---

[58] F. B. Smith, *The People's Health, 1830-1910* (1979).
[59] JCE, p. 10.

3. 1866–1870

Things began to look up for Jowett when C. P. Ilbert was elected to a Fellowship at Balliol in 1864, but it was not until James Riddell died, and J. Purves and J. L. Strachan-Davidson were elected to Fellowships in 1866 that Jowett could be sure of a majority at a college meeting. When that time arrived he used his power decisively, and began to implement a systematic reform of the college along lines which had been germinating in his mind ever since the Commission of Inquiry in 1850–2. First he sought to open the remaining closed awards to competition.[60] Then he moved and carried resolutions to reduce the number of Clerical Fellowships,[61] to suppress the Catechetical Lectures,[62] and to employ Professor Max Müller to 'give a few lectures' on the religions of the East.[63] The Divinity Lectures were to be remodelled,[64] and undergraduates were no longer to be compelled to attend chapel on weekdays.[65]

None of these changes could be achieved without conflict, and several of the resolutions sponsored by Jowett led to appeals by the Master or the Senior Tutor to the Visitor. The Visitor disallowed the resolutions to reduce the number of Clerical Fellowships and suppress the Catechetical Lecturership.[66] But there can have been scant comfort for Scott in that, for Jowett's revenge was terrible, and none of his opponents escaped. He secured a ruling that undergraduates were to be allowed to choose their own lectures,[67] and when that led to a situation in which the Bursar (Wall) and the Senior Tutor (Woollcombe) had but a handful of pupils between them, Jowett took away their Lecturerships.[68] The 'rascal Bursar' was humiliated still further, and required to employ a professional accountant to help him with his work.[69] In 1868 Jowett attempted to strip the Master of his authority with a resolution granting the Governing Body a veto over the appointment of Tutors, but the Visitor disallowed that too.[70] Undismayed by this setback, Jowett seized the position of college preacher for the year in 1869, and retained it the following year.[71] Scott, as one observer said in his reminiscences of Oxford, had become 'a cipher' in Jowett's hands.[72] Jowett no longer felt frustrated, and Florence Nightingale must have been aware that he was in his element living in a world of ever-expanding vistas. Her own position, by contrast, was miserable. Her active life seemed, in retrospect, to have come to an end with the death of Sidney Herbert in 1861, and by the late 1860s it was becoming increasingly difficult to imagine how she would ever be able to start it up again. Jowett had a little less need of her support now, but he enjoyed inviting her to share in his enthusiasms and successes, and corresponded eagerly with her about the aspirations, needs, and

---

[60] CM, 17 Oct. 1866.
[61] CM, 30 Nov. 1867.
[62] Founded by Dr Richard Busby (1606–95). CM, 17–19 Oct. 1867.
[63] CM, 14–15 Oct. 1869.
[64] CM, 26 Apr. 1867. For details see below, No. 134, n. 2.
[65] CM, 17–18 Apr. 1868.
[66] CM, 15–17 Oct., 10 Nov. 1868.
[67] CM, 30 Nov. 1867.
[68] CM, 9–10 Apr., 8 June 1869.
[69] CM, 30 Nov. 1867.
[70] CM, 17–18 Apr. 1868, disallowed CM, 15–17 Oct. 1868.
[71] CM, 15 Jan. 1869, 28–9 Jan. 1870.
[72] W. Tuckwell, *Reminiscences of Oxford* (1900), pp. 202–3.

rights of women. Above all, perhaps, he still had the leisure to write, and if his letters were, on average, a little shorter than they had been, he wrote, if anything, more frequently. Throughout these years he continued to see her as often as possible.

There was one more reform which Jowett introduced, which was intended not just to improve the college, but to make a lasting impact upon the educational system as a whole. Jowett recognized that only an 'infinitesimal fraction of the talent of the nation' was at present reaching the universities. Boys, he thought, ought to be 'selected by merit from the parish schools', and promoted by means of 'a ladder' of bursaries formed 'from one end of society to the other' to enable them to reach the University.[73] In order to assist poor scholars when they arrived, the cost of a University education ought to be reduced. The thing to aim at, as he told a House of Commons' Select Committee on University Extension, was to graft a Scottish University onto Oxford, and to allow students to live in lodgings.[74] In October 1866 Jowett brought before the college a plan to allow undergraduates to live either 'in', or (cheaply) 'out' of college.[75] The college promoted a lodging-out statute: in 1867 a house was leased,[76] and in 1868 the Fellows agreed to award scholarships on the results of the Oxford Local Examinations.[77]

Jowett found little cause to quarrel with the class structure of society, and he was not above setting his cap at an aristocratic pupil. He had good reasons for this, because he took the view that there was 'one intellectual world with common ideas', and that 'the more permanent part of that was the world of the higher classes'.[78] But he also held that all education, even that offered to artisans, ought to be 'liberal as well as useful'.[79] Unlike most of his contemporaries, therefore (and unlike his favourite Plato), his thoughts turned readily to the idea of individuals rising up class by class through the social structure. The best-known of all the many stories connected with Jowett's views on education is, therefore, misleading. In *Jude the Obscure*, Hardy makes Jude write to the Master of 'Biblioll' to ask him how he can obtain a University education, and the Master (T. Tetuphenay) advises Jude that, as a working man, he will 'have a much better chance of success in life' by remaining in his own sphere and keeping to his trade.[80] If Jowett did ever return such an answer to such an inquiry, it cannot have been because he was indifferent to the aspirations of the Judes of this world, and must have been because he was concerned not to raise false hopes.

It was not only in college that Jowett reached the height of his influence at this period. He was never directly involved in politics, but he referred to the Liberals as his 'own' party.[81] He always voted Liberal at Parliamentary elections for Oxford University, and he was temperamentally sympathetic to Lord John (by then Earl) Russell. Throughout the 1860s he was also close to Robert

[73] JCE, p. 8.
[74] PP (1867), xiii. Qn. 2388, 'What I think you want is to retain Oxford in many respects as it is, and to add to it a Scotch University.'   [75] CM, 26–7 Oct. 1866.
[76] CM, 16 Mar. 1867.   [77] CM, 24 Jan. 1868.   [78] See below, No. 9; Cook, i. 478.
[79] JCE, p. 8.   [80] Bk. II, Chap. 6.   [81] See below, No. 123.

Lowe, who was Vice-president of the Privy Council Committee on Education from 1859–64. This was perhaps surprising, because Lowe was an outspokenly anti-democratic Liberal, whose defection destroyed Russell's and Gladstone's Reform Bill in 1866, and handed the Government of the country over to the Tories. But one result of Derby's and Disraeli's second Reform Act of 1867 was to ensure that the political parties would at last grasp the nettle, and legislate to provide a universal system of elementary education. In October 1867, as we have seen, Russell asked Jowett to draw him up a paper on education, and in November Jowett dined at Lord Russell's with the Liberal leaders, Granville, Coleridge, Bruce, Baines, and Lowe. Jowett had hesitated to accept the invitation because he had 'no real locus standi among these gentlemen',[82] but he must have enjoyed beginning his paper with a declaration that 'the great nation of the future will be that which has the best schools',[83] and ending with a passage which might almost have been inspired by Rousseau:

> When we think of what is and what might be—of the endless possibility of improvement in all human creatures during the first years of life, we feel that if there is such a thing as national guilt it is incurred in the neglect of education.[84]

The very next year, when Lowe became Chancellor of the Exchequer in Gladstone's first administration, Jowett had, for the first time, a close friend in the Cabinet. It was Lowe who acted as the intermediary between Gladstone and Jowett, and secured an ecclesiastical preferment for Scott which took him away from Balliol and cleared the path for his more dominating junior.[85] Year after year Jowett accepted Lowe's invitation, and went up to London to hear the budget speech.

4. 1870–1875

When Gladstone offered the Deanery of Rochester to the hapless Scott, Jowett became Master and occupied the place he felt he ought to have succeeded to sixteen years earlier. The status and the extra recognition were worth much, and brought him, for example, an invitation to give evidence before the Devonshire Commission inquiry into Scientific Instruction and the Advancement of Science.[86] But his new position imposed constraints too. Heads of Houses are placed under a stern necessity of appearing even-handed. Never again would Jowett feel able to speak out, and engage in theological controversy in quite the same way that he had done in 1855 and 1860. Perhaps the wounds had gone too deep, and he had already lost his appetite for this kind of battle. Perhaps he was perplexed by the way things were going, with the young men tending towards ritualism, positivism, or atheism. However that may be, his own opinions would henceforth have to be conveyed more guardedly, in places where they would not attract the attention of 'ordinary' Christians. Separated in this way

---

[82] JCE, p. 14. [83] JCE, p. 5. [84] JCE, p. 10. [85] RSBJ, p. 20.
[86] His evidence is in *PP* (1872), XXV. 250–6. See below, No. 248.

from the theological radicals, his past 'sins' still rendered him unacceptable to the establishment. He was not invited to participate in the revised translation of the Bible, and he can have found little real satisfaction in assisting his friend William Rogers to edit and abridge the Authorised Version to make a *School and Children's Bible* which was published in 1873. Nor could he any longer afford to appear quite so partisan in politics, and his direct political influence soon passed its peak. He had never been able to make much of Gladstone, who fascinated him but whom he did not trust, and his closest political friend of the 1860s, Lowe, was compelled to resign in 1873. With every year that passed Jowett held himself a little more aloof from the struggle of parties. He admired Disraeli, and later Balfour (but not Salisbury, the Chancellor of the University, who was too High Church), there was no telling where Gladstone would take the Liberal Party, and it seems likely that towards the end of his life he was at heart a Liberal Unionist.

In the meantime Jowett's prime concern remained what it had always been, the condition and future of Balliol. He was now able to run the college without the perpetual strife of previous years. But in several ways he must have found the Mastership a disappointment. It added little to his power. He had taken control in 1866, and it had been easier to run the college with the aid of a sustaining sense of moral outrage, against Scott, than it was when he became responsible for all the machinery himself. In the past four years, the college had passed through a heroic period of modernization: could Jowett now maintain the momentum? There was still some tidying up to be done: there were the Snell Exhibitions—could the college not make sure of a higher class of candidate by removing the restriction which confined them to graduates of Glasgow University and throwing them open to competition among the graduates of all the Scottish Universities?[87] There was the form of service at Morning and Evening Prayer to be modernized.[88] Then there were the causes which had been frustrated by Scott and Woollcombe's appeals and the Visitor's rulings. At the first opportunity Jowett renewed his assault upon the Clerical Fellowships and the Catechetical Lecturership.[89] The Visitor's ruling forbidding the college to dispense with the latter was circumvented by requiring the Lecturer not to enforce answers to the questions,[90] and the Visitor eventually consented to allow the Lecturership to be converted into a Theological Prize.[91] A committee was appointed to consider the revision of the Statutes.[92] Two of its recommendations—to make the Mastership terminable, and to remove the requirement for the Master to be in Holy Orders—smack of pursuing Scott beyond the bounds of the college.

Over and above all this, Jowett brought to the Master's Lodgings a vigorous intention of making Balliol into the model college of his dreams, a sort of

[87] CM, 13–15 Oct. 1871. He did not succeed.
[88] CM, 13 May 1871. See below, No. 263, n. 2.
[89] CM, 13–14 Oct. 1870.   [90] CM, 13–14 Oct. 1870.   [91] CM, 18 Apr. 1873.
[92] CM, 13–14 Oct. 1870. See below, No. 254, n. 4.

INTRODUCTION

heaven on earth, complementing his concept of Heaven as a kind of Balliol in the sky ('the education of after life').[93] Balliol College was to spread its influence over the whole world, and to this end he attracted to the college its first Siamese, and its first Japanese students. Success in this enterprise would depend upon the Fellows and Tutors. Henry Wall and W. L. Newman retired in 1871, and Jowett was able to make appointments of his own choosing in R. L. Nettleship (1870), R. G. Tatton and A. Goodwin (1872), and E. Abbott (1874). Hitherto, Tutors had been selected from among the Fellows. Now a new category of Tutorial Fellowships was created.[94]

To this body of Tutors much was to be offered, and from them much was to be expected. With his own experience in mind, Jowett turned to the removal of the restrictions upon Fellows marrying.[95] In future up to half the tutorial Fellows were to be allowed to marry.[96] Following this decision, some members of the Governing Body, at least, were in favour of selling off part or all of the college livings.[97] The college was converting itself from a part of the clerical establishment to a part of a new professional educational one, as described by A. J. Engel in *From Clergyman to Don* (1983). In order that these increasingly professional academics might keep up with their studies they were to be encouraged to take every fourth year off, as a year of 'grace', at two-thirds their normal salary.[98] In return Jowett expected them to accept stringent residence and lodging requirements, to devote themselves whole-heartedly to the undergraduates, and to participate in other schemes of educational reform. The 'out-resident' scheme was already established, and had added almost exactly one-third to the number of men studying at Balliol. In the next phase of 'University extension' Jowett's thoughts turned to the needs of the large towns, and to the possibility of the college sponsoring, and the Fellows of the college delivering, lectures out of Oxford.[99] The upshot was that the college, together with New College, gave £300 p.a. each for five years to what ultimately became Bristol University.[100] Jowett also turned the Tutors' minds to the admission of mature (or older) students.[101]

Jowett was never faced with a rebellion, and no new Fellow arose to challenge him as he had challenged Scott. But there are signs that he was not altogether satisfied with his achievement. On 19 February 1872 he wrote to Florence Nightingale that he felt more difficulty about the College than he used to do:

> ... men's characters are not easily trained or formed and I have not so much opportunity of influencing them as I had when I was only a Tutor. The tutors are very able men but they are not quite practical and vigorous. I take them out to walk and talk to them and they behave very well to me. Yet I doubt whether they are inspired with the real educational spirit.

---

[93] See below, No. 5.
[94] In the new Statutes of 1871.
[95] CM, 13–14 Oct. 1870, 20 Jan. 1871.
[96] 1871 Statutes, cl. 20.
[97] CM, 13 Apr. 1872, 11 Oct. 1873.
[98] CM, 24 Jan. 1873.
[99] CM, 19 Jan. 1872.
[100] CM, 19 Jan. 1872, *AC* ii. 57–8.
[101] CM, 23 Nov. 1874.

And it must come as something of a surprise that he felt obliged to secure a resolution

That every Tutor shall ... remain each day in College a sufficient time for the full performance of his Tutorial duties, it being understood that his arrangements shall always include a certain number of evening attendances.[102]

The philosophy Tutor, T. H. Green, had to be taken off lecturing, because he confused the undergraduates so badly[103] (Jowett would have been surprised by the reputation he has enjoyed in the twentieth century), and the Master was deeply hurt when Henry Smith, the mathematician, who had been a Fellow since 1850, abandoned Balliol for Corpus Christi College.[104] It is not clear why Smith went: he must have been familiar for many years with Jowett's prejudice in favour of classics, his bias against Comte and Darwin, and his tendency to scoff at 'mere' research.

After 1870 Jowett continued, as Master, to take a part in the teaching of the college. It might have been better had he stopped there, for there were now forty-seven men coming up on average every year in the 1870s, where there had been but twenty-eight in the 1860s. But at the first college meeting of the new era he stripped Wall of his duties, and in his enthusiasm, or his vanity, took over responsibility for the domestic side of the college himself.[105] This was an astonishing error of judgement: it was one thing for the Master to 'supervise' the domestic side of the college, as he was required to do by the Statutes, but quite another for him to undertake the management of it—even if only for one year. Within a few months Jowett began to feel the strain, and with every year that passed his success in making the college famous imposed new demands upon him. More rooms were needed to accommodate undergraduates, and a new Hall for them to eat in.[106] Single-handedly, the Master set about raising the money. Admirable as all this activity was, it meant that Jowett lost his way attending to administrative details, just when he ought to have risen clear of them. Florence Nightingale said that soon after he became Master, Jowett 'had a period of great depression'.[107] In 1873 he was seriously, perhaps desperately, ill. On 13 August he made a compact with Miss Nightingale in which he undertook not to work more than three hours a day and never more than one hour at a time.[108] That he, of all people, should have been reduced to this, strongly suggests that he had suffered a breakdown, and this loss of health was passed over very lightly by his biographers.[109] At all events, the result was to leave him with too little time for writing, either in his chosen field of Greek scholarship, or to an apprehensive Miss Nightingale. His letters became shorter, and fewer. Florence Nightingale can be excused for having felt that he had little time for her now, and although the correspondence never quite ceased (and more drafts of Florence Nightingale's letters to him survive from this period than from any

[102] CM, 13 Apr. 1872.
[103] See below, No. 297.
[104] See below, No. 316.
[105] CM, 13–14 Oct. 1870.
[106] CM, 8 Feb., 11 Oct. 1873.
[107] Letter of 23 Oct. 1894.
[108] BL Add. MS 45784 fo. 197.
[109] AC ii. 55–6.

other), it appears that by 1875 months might go by without a letter, and that the two friends were almost out of touch.

5. 1875–1893

The relationship survived and was re-established on a less ambitious and more stable basis which lasted until Jowett began to fail in 1891–3, when it ended on a note of deep affection and regard on both sides. In the late 1870s and 1880s Jowett was still bubbling over with schemes of educational improvement, and resolutions for making good use of the years that remained. In 1877 he gave evidence to the second Royal Commission of inquiry into the University, both in his capacity as Master of Balliol and as a Curator of the Bodleian Library[110] (though there is no reference to this in the surviving correspondence with Miss Nightingale). In 1882 he became Vice-chancellor, and held the post for the full term of four years. But there was a marked slackening of pace, and in any case, by the late 1870s, the University at large, and even, perhaps, the world, were beginning to move on beyond Jowett. He had never possessed a monopoly of the reforming spirit, and many of the things he contended for would have come to pass, and would have come to pass at about the same period, without him. It is too easy, reading a correspondence like this, to attribute too much to one man and to one woman. He was not the only person trying to change the face of the University, and Florence Nightingale was not the only person interested in the elevation of nursing as a career. In the 1870s and 1880s Jowett and Miss Nightingale still commanded respect, but like other ageing and slightly dated leading actors, they could no longer be sure of getting their own way. This was to become all too apparent in this final period, when Florence Nightingale raised a futile opposition to proposals for the registration of nurses, and Jowett was rebuffed over the age of the cadets chosen to staff the Civil Service in India.

India was a common bond between Jowett and Miss Nightingale (though neither of them ever went there). In the 1860s affectionate childhood memories of his two brothers, Alfred and William, had lain behind his support for Florence Nightingale's campaign to improve the health of the British Army in the East. Surveying the whole period since the mid-eighteenth century, Jowett came to the conclusion that Britain had given India little or nothing in return for the extinction of nationality.[111] Consequently, when Florence Nightingale pressed grand schemes of public works upon the Indian Government—schemes which would benefit not just the Europeans but also the natives, Jowett corresponded enthusiastically with her about the advantages of irrigation and the need to defend the peasant against the extortion of the tax collector. In all these affairs he was happy to accept that he was an amateur. But there was just one matter connected with India upon which he

[110] His evidence is in *PP* (1881), lvi. 152–9, 317–20.
[111] See below, No. 155.

did, with some reason, regard himself as an expert, and that was the Indian cadetships.

Jowett had been a member of Macaulay's committee in 1853-4, and he could never forget that the committee had made an eloquent plea for the competitive examinations for entry into the Indian Civil Service to be opened to university graduates:

> men who have been engaged up to one or two-and-twenty in studies which have no connexion with the business of any profession, and of which the effect is merely to open, to invigorate, and to enrich the mind, will generally be found, in the business of every profession, superior to men who have at eighteen or nineteen devoted themselves to the special studies of their calling.[112]

But this was never quite what came to pass. Candidates were selected at any age between seventeen and twenty-one, and the great majority went to London crammers before sitting the qualifying examinations which they had to pass before they were sent out to India. By the mid-1860s a very small minority, only, of those who reached India possessed a University degree.[113] Then, in 1874, the Secretary of State for India, Lord Salisbury, proposed to change the system, and to put an end to cramming. In future, candidates were to be selected when they left school, between seventeen and nineteen, and required to attend a University before they sat their qualifying examinations and were allowed to start their careers. Jowett had no objection to some candidates being selected when they left school, and sent to University, but he still wanted University graduates of twenty-two to be allowed to compete for selection (and to undergo a shorter period of training). Jowett returned to the issue time and again. Lord Salisbury listened to him, and in due course Viscount Cross, too, allowed him to press his case: both remained unconverted by what he had to say.[114] It was not until 1892 that changes were made.

Many other senior members of the University approved strongly of Lord Salisbury's proposals. A committee was set up under the chairmanship of Dean Liddell to see what facilities the University, which was already feeling its way towards a School of Oriental Studies, could provide for the candidates. As for Jowett himself, if the candidates were going to be selected when they left school, and sent to University, he was determined to have them. In 1875 he persuaded the college to open its doors to the Indian candidates, and to advertise to that effect. In 1878 he appointed a Tutor, Arnold Toynbee, to look after the 'Indian' students.[115] Jowett's actions gave the impression that he wanted to establish a monopoly and bring all the candidates to Balliol. If that was his aim, he was not completely successful, but he was very largely successful. Out of 255 candidates selected between 1878 and 1885, fifty-one went to Cambridge

---

[112] *AC* i. 186.
[113] C. J. Dewey, 'The Education of a Ruling Caste'.
[114] *AC* ii. 348-51.
[115] *AC* ii. 139.

and 161 to Oxford: of these 161, no fewer than 103 were attracted to Balliol.[116] This in its turn created another problem, because Jowett's eagerness to accommodate the Indian candidates, who were not normal undergraduates, and even to embark on another scheme to help 'Army' candidates,[117] threatened to unbalance the college.

In the 1850s Jowett had found himself in a position to tug at the sleeves of those who were senior to him in age and superior in social position. All his formative experiences suggested to him that Whig and Peelite administrations were approachable and impressible, and as late as 1867 he still found himself cultivated, as we have seen, by the Whig leaders. By that time, however, he was already looking to a longer future, and consciously grooming well-bred undergraduates, whom the social and political system would steer to places of great importance, to carry on his work after he was gone. Camperdown, who once contrived to leave Jowett and Gladstone closeted alone together for a whole day,[118] was one such pupil, and Lansdowne was another. From the day he came up to college in 1863, Lansdowne was marked out for distinction. Jowett thought of him as a future Governor-General, and Florence Nightingale said that she could '*see* the interest Sidney Herbert would have taken' in him.[119] Lansdowne received his first junior appointment in 1868, and in 1872 he became Under-secretary of State for War. In due course he became Governor-General of Canada, from 1883 to 1888, and then Viceroy of India from 1888 to 1893, where he bore many of Jowett's and Florence Nightingale's best hopes, as revealed in this fifth and final phase of their correspondence.

Finally, something must be said about one of the topics of the correspondence in this period—the proposal to found a Chair of Statistics, not so much for its obvious merits, as for its meaning to the two potential sponsors. As early as the 1860s Jowett had been struck by the lack of system in medicine, and appreciated some of the ways in which the collection of reliable statistics might advance understanding in medicine and public health. To Florence Nightingale, statistics were, as her biographer said, a passion,[120] and Jowett encouraged her to endow lectures, or a Chair of Statistics in her own name. The idea was first discussed between them in 1876,[121] but nothing came of it, and Jowett returned to the topic in 1890.[122] His proposal was that they should each contribute £2,000 to endow a Chair of Statistics. Miss Nightingale pointed to the enormous mass of statistics already collected by Government departments and left lying in pigeon holes. What was wanted was not so much 'an accumulation of facts ... but to teach the men who are to govern the country what are the *uses* of facts, of "Statistics"'.[123] She consulted Professor Galton, and together they drew up a list of the topics to which a Professor of Statistics might address himself. These were, in addition to matters of public health, the effects of the

---

[116] BCL, Additional Jowett Papers, 9b, and *Balliol College Register, 1833-1933* (1934).
[117] AC ii. 293-6.
[118] AC i. 406, 1 Oct. 1869.
[119] BL Add. MS 45784 fos. 86-9.
[120] Cook, ii. 395.
[121] See below, No. 362.
[122] See below, No. 422.
[123] BL Add. MS 45785 fos. 144-5.

Education Act of 1870, the action of punishment upon crime, the efficiency of workhouses, and the interpretation of statistics about India.[124] Jowett thought that it would be enough to start with one of these, and wanted the Chair to be established at Oxford.[125] Galton commented that, without a Final Honour School and without undergraduates, a Chair at Oxford would not prove very attractive to an able man, and recommended founding one at the Royal Institution instead.[126]

Cook suggested that Jowett entered into this scheme more from interest in Miss Nightingale than from interest in the subject.[127] Cook may have underestimated Jowett's interest in statistics, but he probably perceived the truth of the matter. The Chair would have been, it is tempting to suggest, a substitute for the lack of offspring of a marriage that never took place. It is not certain that Jowett ever wanted to marry Florence Nightingale. But he would have been free to do so at any time after he became Master in 1870 (when she was fifty), and Miss Sorabji, an Indian student in whom Jowett took an interest, recalled his saying that he had proposed to her (when?) and been refused.[128] What is certain is that Jowett regretted that 'the great want of life can never be supplied, and I must do without it'.[129] He was the survivor of nine children, all of whom died without issue. A Chair of Statistics, to which he and Florence Nightingale acted as joint 'parents', would have done something, however fanciful, to fill the gap. But it was not to be. Florence Nightingale could not make up her mind to do it, and in his latest alterations to his will, made less than a month before he died, Jowett recognized that there was 'no possibility of realizing the scheme'.[130] Florence Nightingale might regret afterwards that 'it is not done',[131] but she had never wanted to marry, and it was, perhaps, fitting that she never gave her name to this joint 'child' either.

Conclusion

Jowett's letters leave little room to doubt that throughout their relationship Florence Nightingale remained an invalid and a recluse. Not surprisingly, therefore, her influence tailed away after the mid-1860s. But what of Jowett himself? Here the last word must lie with Florence Nightingale, for she survived him and tried to jot down her impressions of their correspondence and of their relationship. She drew a sharp distinction between the period before Jowett became Master and the period after. She stressed 'the charm of character *before* his Mastership',[132] and found 'the letters before the Mastership ... so much better'.[133] The letters themselves 'were usually aphorisms or epigrams on conduct, because the ball was not given back to him as in conversation'.[134] Was his conversation, then, when he came to see her, better than his writing? Not

---

[124] BL Add. MS 45785 fos. 150–7. [125] BL Add. MS 45785 fos. 169–72. [126] Cook, ii. 397.
[127] Cook, ii. 397. [128] Verney family tradition. [129] AC ii. 175, 353.
[130] AC ii. 478. [131] BL Add. MS 45785 fo. 218. [132] BL Add. MS 45785 fo. 233.
[133] Letter of 23 Oct. 1894. [134] BL Add. MS 45785 fo. 244.

really, because 'I often felt extreme disappointment and exhaustion in conversation at *his* not giving back the ball'.[135] There is little point, then, in following Faber and defending Jowett against the charge that he sometimes talked to Florence Nightingale as though she were someone else.[136] He almost certainly did.

The ball which Jowett did not give back was, more than anything else, the theodicy. It was Florence Nightingale's 'Stuff' which had brought them together. Jowett had dissuaded her from publication, and she had always hoped that one day he would himself take up the task of explaining to the modern world the moral government of God. As she wrote to Abbott, 'the more I read his letters, the more sorry I feel that . . . he did not go deeper into some things of Theodike'.[137]

I used to bother him and remember once saying to him that the services of the Ch. of England and still more of the Ch. of Rome were like old clothes dropping off in rags bit by bit, and that soon, if he and others did not make haste, the Churches would be naked. Of course I only mention this because he always agreed, and would say: 'As soon as I have done "Plato" (and he would often add: which will be "in six months") I will set about it'.[138]

Perhaps Jowett really did believe that he might attempt it, for Abbott found a note, written after the Master had been reading the *De Imitatio Christi* in which he said, 'Could I, in ten years time, write a new Imitatio, adapted to our own days?'[139]

In the event, the Plato was never finished and was always being rewritten. Two things then happened. The first was, as Abbott put it, that 'as time went on and Jowett found that he could not accomplish the work which he had hoped to do, he put more and more of his thoughts into the Introductions to his Plato'.[140] The second was that Florence Nightingale did not accept that the Introductions to the successive editions of Plato were an acceptable substitute for the intended theodicy. She regretted very much that two men, Mohl and Jowett, 'who might have worked out the great Problem, the great Theodike', gave themselves to translation, 'a tragic end'.[141] And when Mohl offered her an escape from her difficulty, by assuring her that Plato had had the idea of a 'perfect God', she 'told this to Mr. Jowett, thinking to please him. But he did not take it up—I think he merely said that "perfect" was only a word and that we don't know what *is* perfect.'[142] When she remonstrated with him about his reluctance to embark upon the theodicy, Jowett replied that 'the truth is that *I am afraid of drawing too much upon another life* and assuming *a knowledge which we do not possess*':[143] 'God has not given me intellect enough' to write a definitive moral philosophy.[144] Florence Nightingale was left having to make the best of a bad job protesting that 'Mr. Jowett put as much of his genius into Plato as

---

[135] BL Add. MS 45785 fo. 244. [136] *Faber*, p. 310. [137] Letter of 8 Feb. 1895.
[138] Letter of 10 Nov. 1894. [139] BL Add. MS 45785 fos. 213–14.
[140] BL Add. MS 45785 fos. 209–10. [141] BL Add. MS 45785 fo. 244.
[142] BL Add. MS 45785 fo. 244. [143] BL Add. MS 45785 fo. 266. [144] BL Add. MS 45785 fo. 223.

Plato did into Mr. Jowett'.[145] Evelyn Abbott agreed with her (or was kind enough to agree with her) that 'Jowett saw more in Plato than is really there', and admitted that he sometimes wondered 'whether we might not find something better on which to train the thoughts of our "young men"'.[146]

The trouble with the translating of Plato was that it made Jowett too negative: '*He* used to say: "I am nothing if not critical" which of course was increased in him by the necessity of criticising the undergraduates' work ... and as he grew older it increased still more, encouraged too by the constant habit of polishing the translation of Plato.'[147] There was, after all, as Florence Nightingale said, 'nothing very inspiring in denying the Miracles, or denying a Moral governor, or in negation at all'.[148] She did sometimes wonder whether it was worth while shocking and wounding 'good people, who are really trying to be Christians', people 'to whom he offers nothing definite in the place of what he takes away'.[149] Jowett had helped to create a spiritual void which he was unwilling to refill. Pontius Pilate, she wrote, had not answered the question 'What is truth?' because he did not care, 'but Mr. Jowett should have answered because I did care'.[150] She found it strange that 'a man whose whole life was one enthusiasm' should have written such restrained, unimpassioned sermons.[151] She held it against him that 'he never had any pupil following up God's moral government',[152] but she conceded that the establishment of Toynbee Hall went some way to meet her lifelong ambition to be of practical assistance to the artisans.[153] She felt that, measured by her own religious standards, Jowett had deteriorated with age. 'You believed a great deal more than this when I first knew you, at least, My Lord you gave me cause to think so.'[154] And although she must have known how Jowett would have attempted to counter her sense of disappointment in him, she could never quite bring herself to accept the strength of his position and the force of his arguments.

Florence Nightingale herself, then, could be a severe critic and judge. But she would not have wanted this introduction to end on a peevish or negative note. In happier vein she described Jowett's letters as 'gems',[155] and wrote affectionately of his characteristics. He had a horror of 'singularity', of eccentricity, and of missing the train. His clothes were always neat and clean, and 'he never wrote and hardly ever spoke about this kind of thing'. He lived, she thought, like a monk, and 'never even kept any money *for himself*'.[156] She praised the extraordinary perseverance of his career from youth to age: 'Mr Jowett was always intent on improving his own character for the sake of his undergraduates. This is very rare in middle aged men and still more so in elderly and

---

[145] Letter of 8 Feb. 1895.
[146] BL Add. MS 45785 fos. 209–10.
[147] Letter of 10 Nov. 1894.
[148] BL Add. MS 45785 fo. 247.
[149] Letter of 10 Nov. 1894.
[150] BL Add. MS 45785 fo. 238.
[151] BL Add. MS 45785 fos. 219–21.
[152] BL Add. MS 45785 fo. 239.
[153] The East End settlement, founded in memory of Arnold Toynbee, who died in 1883. Asa Briggs, *Toynbee Hall: The First Hundred Years* (1984).
[154] BL Add. MS 45785 fos. 193–8.
[155] Letter of 8 Feb. 1895.
[156] BL Add MS 45785 fos. 219–21, 225, 228–9.

old men.'¹⁵⁷ Jowett, she concluded, possessed 'more character than any body I ever knew. . . . He mastered life, life did not master him: *that* was what the spirit of life was in him. He was master even when most depressed.'¹⁵⁸ She might well have added a tribute to the restless, eager, probing intellectual vitality of a man who kept the very words he used on the move (lest they become stereotyped like the formularies of the Church), and who, even in the last month of his life, could give a lift to a whole letter with a memorable phrase or an unexpected turn of thought.

The secret of Jowett's power over others was, Florence Nightingale thought, that 'he was always finding the better part of us'.¹⁵⁹ The extraordinary achievement of his teaching lay in 'connecting University education with a man's future career'.¹⁶⁰ 'Do you know', she asked Abbott, 'anyone with Mr. Jowett's power of making University the entrance to life?'¹⁶¹ In the days of Jowett's predecessors, 'the higher classes—the Ten Thousand' had been 'plastered on', while the poor had been 'dragged up'.¹⁶² Jowett had made room for both in Balliol and given them an education. He made a point of seeing every undergraduate every term. He held weekend parties, when he would ask the undergraduates in—not only Balliol men but Oxford men—and introduce them to the good and the great. 'He got scores of small posts under both Govts for men who then rose.'¹⁶³ In this way he came to hold an 'extraordinary unconscious influence over College, the University and the World',¹⁶⁴ and his life was an example: 'It stands alone. For it was more than the life of a Prophet, or of a Literary man or of a man of organization, tho' he prophesied, tho' he wrote, tho' he organized.'¹⁶⁵ He was, perhaps, the man who 'has lived the greatest life in this century. He created many a Statesman, many an Educator, many a devoted man and really religious man. And he did not feel, himself, the want of anything more definite, because as he always said: "The man is greater than the doctrine".'¹⁶⁶

The Text

Out of consideration for his correspondents Jowett was already destroying letters before his death, and in his will he left orders that his letters were to be burnt.¹⁶⁷ His executors, Evelyn Abbott and Sir William Markby, carried out his instructions, and the vast majority of the letters written by Florence Nightingale were lost in the holocaust. A small packet of her letters written at the time of the Master's illness in 1891 escaped notice, and survive in Balliol College Library, together with a single letter written by Florence Nightingale to Jowett's mother.

When Evelyn Abbott and Lewis Campbell were commissioned to write the

---

¹⁵⁷ BL Add. MS 45785 fo. 251.
¹⁵⁸ BL Add. MS 45785 fos. 224-5.
¹⁵⁹ BL Add. MS 45785 fos. 222-3.
¹⁶⁰ BL Add. MS 45785 fos. 222-3.
¹⁶¹ BL Add. MS 45785 fo. 229.
¹⁶² BL Add. MS 45785 fo. 241.
¹⁶³ BL Add. MS 45785 fos. 232-3.
¹⁶⁴ BL Add. MS 45785 fo. 271.
¹⁶⁵ Letter of 23 Oct. 1894.
¹⁶⁶ Letter of 10 Nov. 1894.
¹⁶⁷ AC ii. 476-8.

Life and Letters of Benjamin Jowett, Abbott sought access to Jowett's letters to Florence Nightingale. Miss Nightingale did not meet him with an outright refusal. But she declared that she was 'haunted by the feeling that ... what was written would not have been written but for the conviction that they were sacred to the receiver', and concluded that it seemed 'treacherous to show them even to you'.[168] She sent Abbott 'without selection or sorting a few letters of his of '70 and '71, and 2 letters of '64–'65', and added that it would cause her too much stress to look for more. Two weeks later she thought a little better of it and sent four packets of letters (one of which contained only one letter). Even then nothing was to be published without her consent, she insisted on being shown the extracts which Abbott made, and asked for certain passages to be omitted.[169] Whoever was responsible, many of the letters which were printed in the *Life and Letters* were condensed, though no indication of this was given in the text, and several were 'polished' or 'improved'. From start to finish Florence Nightingale made it a condition that her name was not to appear in the *Life*, and where Abbott and Campbell would have liked to have said that a letter was written to Miss Nightingale they were forced to substitute 'To a friend' or even a plain 'To ——'. No letter to Miss Nightingale was included in the supplementary *Letters of Benjamin Jowett* published in 1899.

After Florence Nightingale died in 1910, her papers were handed to Sir Edward Cook, who wrote the *Life* published in 1913. Cook quoted freely, but not extensively, from Jowett's letters, and when he had finished the biography he divided Jowett's letters into two groups. The great majority were returned to Balliol College, and a small minority, relating to Nightingale family affairs, which he judged to be too sensitive, were retained and ultimately deposited with the mass of Nightingale Papers in the British Library in 1941.

In the meantime Geoffrey Faber had expressed an interest in following up his highly successful book on the Oxford movement, *Oxford Apostles* (1933), with a new life of Jowett. All the letters held in Balliol College Library were carried over to All Souls College in the summer of 1935, where they remained throughout the Second World War. By 1947, the Master of Balliol, A. D. Lindsay, appears to have forgotten all about Faber, and when Guy Kendall, the author, who was looking for a subject, came to him, he suggested writing another life of Jowett. Kendall found out about Faber, and Sandy Lindsay had to excuse himself as best he could.[170] Faber's *Jowett. A Portrait with Background* was published in 1957. Faber made sparing use of Jowett's letters to Miss Nightingale, and all the extracts which appear in his biography had already been published either by Abbott and Campbell or by Cook. Faber himself looked forward delicately to 'this extraordinary correspondence' being published in its entirety by another hand.[171]

It has been public knowledge, then, for over seventy years, that Jowett was well acquainted with Miss Nightingale. No bar has ever been placed by the

[168] Letter of 23 Oct. 1894. [169] Letter of 10 Nov. 1894.
[170] Jowett Papers, BCL. [171] *Faber*, p. 18.

college upon scholars making use of the letters, and short extracts have from time to time appeared, notably in I. Ellis, *Seven Against Christ* (1980), F. B. Smith, *Florence Nightingale, Reputation and Power* (1982), and in Peter Hinchliff, 'Benjamin Jowett and the Church of England: or "Why Really Great Men are Never Clergymen"', in John Prest (ed.), *Balliol Studies* (1982). But the great bulk of the correspondence is printed here for the first time.

Although Jowett's letters to Florence Nightingale have, with a few exceptions, survived, and Florence Nightingale's letters to Jowett have, with a few exceptions, been destroyed, the correspondence, as printed here, is not entirely one-sided. Jowett wrote his letters straight off. His pen flew across the page, as the facsimiles in Abbott and Campbell suggest. He never crossed anything out and he never altered anything. He misspelt proper names, and he employed quotations without looking them up. He used punctuation sparingly, in the early letters especially. We have changed some of his dashes to commas and stops. But we have not corrected his spelling, nor have we spattered the text with editorial *sic*s. Florence Nightingale, on the other hand, composed her letters painstakingly, frequently writing draft after draft, and often taking copies (until the mid-1870s) or notes of what she had said. By choosing extracts from the drafts, copies, and notes which are preserved in the British Library, it is possible, if not to offer both sides of the correspondence, at least to give an impression of the kind of letters Florence Nightingale wrote.

In making a selection of about three-fifths from the great body of the correspondence we have omitted short notes written to suggest a visit or confirm an appointment. We have excluded accounts of the annual Scholarship examinations, which would seem to have too limited an interest. We have enormously reduced the many enquiries and exhortations which Jowett made as to Florence Nightingale's health. Representative examples can be found at pp. 28–9 and 208–9, and the reader can assume that these were being repeated time and again. We have dropped a number of passages which appear repetitive, and on several occasions we have omitted a sentence or two in order to speed up the flow of the narrative. Jowett was careless about dating, and we have accepted the dates (some of them placed on the letters by Florence Nightingale herself) attributed to the letters in the archives except where we have found evidence compelling us to change them.

Most of Jowett's letters were addressed to 'Dear Miss Nightingale'—a smaller number, to 'My dear Friend'. Flights of fancy were rare, and are printed. He used to end his letters 'ever your's truly', or 'ever your's sincerely', or just 'ever your's'. Florence Nightingale addressed him as 'Dear Mr. Jowett', and ended 'ever your's', or occasionally 'ever your's gratefully'.

CHAPTER 1

1860–1862

1   Oak Hill House   Hampstead
                                   [beginning of January 1861]

I am almost afraid to write to you any more upon the 'Stuff'[1] lest I should only weary you by repeating what I said before.

It seems to me that the differences between us are more in the mode of expressing certain ideas than in the ideas themselves.

I want the audience to be more considered. Truth in itself is independent of the state of public opinion, but truth as taught is in a great degree relative to it. Else everything gets misunderstood; reverence is conceived to be irreverence & the Christian life is supposed to be lost in health & science....

I hope I did not convey to you in my letter that I undervalued the 'Stuff'. It is true, I think, that very few persons will at first enter into that peculiar mixed sort of speculation or thought which attempts to unite science & religion. But that is no reason for abandoning it; or rather it is the greatest reason for continuing it & endeavouring to sew up the rents in the world & human knowledge. Any of us can do but little compared with what is to be done, but I am sure it is a duty to do what we can. I have no doubt that I see many things more clearly than I did for having attentively read your papers.

Please let me hear sometimes of the progress of the 'Stuff'; & also if I can be of any further use to you about it.

[*Postscript omitted*]

2   Jan. 11, 1861.
                                        Balliol College
                                        Oxford

I venture to write a line to thank you for the very kind note which you sent me about a fortnight since at Hampstead. It gave me great pleasure indeed.

I found it the reverse of a 'wearisome' task to read your work. Many things which are said in it were new to me & very striking. I think it may supply an important help in the direction to which we seem tending. I mean towards a Christianity, which is a present, not a past, fact.

At some future time, when you are well enough to see visitors, I hope to come & apologize for my impertinent criticisms.

Do not give up the hope of rewriting these papers—not now, nor, perhaps, for years. No one knows the possibilities of life & health with perfect rest. It is

---

[1] See above, p. xii. Vol. i: 'Suggestions for Thought to the Searchers after Truth among the Artizans of England', vols. ii and iii: 'Suggestions for Thought to Searchers after Religious Truth' (privately printed, 1860).

an absolute duty, especially in the case of a person who has the power of doing good to others, not to let the chance of returning health be impaired by the weakness & irritation of premature efforts. It sometimes appears to me that the mind has great power of curing the mischiefs which it has itself caused. Quietism is the true religion for illness.

(I hope you will excuse the liberty I take in saying these few words.)

I will not trouble you to answer this note. If you will entrust them to me I should like very much to see the remaining parts. Would you send them to Mrs Clough? . . .

3   April 6, 1861.
                                                          Balliol College
                                                                  Oxford

I write to thank you for the 'Stuff' to which I shall venture to add the epithet 'precious'. Indeed, I am very much overpaid by your expression of gratitude; the simple truth is that I found great pleasure & interest in reading your work. Pray let me do anything that I can for you at any time.

I forget what I may have said about irreverence, but I am sure that I did not intend it to apply to the writer, but to the effect on the reader. I agree in thinking that any attempt to enlarge religious ideas must appear irreverent to some minds but I would wish to make the appearance of irreverence as small as can be, consistently with regard for the truth.

I have read (hastily) in the last two days the second & third portions. I cannot deny that there is something fearfully wrong in the religious & social state of the world at present. And though it does not appear to me to be the whole truth I do not object to the evils of society being dwelt upon by one who feels them strongly, as an instrument of improvement. It will probably give great offence & at the same time be of real use. But I think it would add to the effect of what is said, 1) if the difficulties of the subject were more considered e.g. the extremely small number of women (or indeed of men) who are capable of fulfilling an ideal or carrying out an original walk of life;—the weakness which is often found precisely in the character most likely to form a sentimental ideal;—the dangers which women must incur unless they could be supposed to be quite impossible. 2)—if the reflections on the family took less the form of individual experience; this appears to me to lessen the weight of what is said & may, perhaps, lead to painful remarks.

Did it ever occur to you to write two or three pages (at the end of Cassandra[1] or in any other place) of what the Reviewers will probably say of the speculations of these papers about Society?

And do not let Cassandra die, but live & declare the works of God.

---

[1] A description, thinly disguised as fiction, of FN's upbringing and of her struggles to be allowed to follow a career, written in 1852, printed privately in 'Suggestions for Thought', ii. 374–411, published in Ray Strachey, *The Cause: A Short History of the Women's Movement in Great Britain* (1928), pp. 395–418.

4

May 11 [1861]
Freshwater[1]

It may seem a strange recreation to offer to a lady who is ill a discussion on metaphysics or theology. But I hear that you still feel interested in such subjects & therefore may I venture to try & entertain you? And I shall probably have the privilege which clergymen have enjoyed from time immemorial of not being answered.

 I have read over carefully the papers which you kindly entrusted to me. At some future time I will send some minute criticisms on them, if they are likely to be of any use. I shall always feel that I have learned a great deal from reading them. The three subjects in the papers on which I was going to offer a very few remarks are 1. Freedom & Necessity 2. M. Comte 3. the question of the position of women.

 1. That it is charming that the world should still be so young that any body should sit down to write on the first of these subjects is certainly a very natural thought. It seems to me on the other hand that although the old paradoxes of freedom & necessity are exploded, the concrete phase of the question, e.g. of the relation of morals to physics, of mind to body, of the will to circumstances, must ever remain one of the greatest of human enquiries. What I miss in your discussions on this subject is what I believe to be possible, the reconcilement of law with free agency. I am afraid that in some places you have tilted the machine over on the side of necessity. To take a coarse instance—a man feels an inclination to intemperance—a struggle ensues in his mind & the better principle prevails. Now, I want to make it as clear as the sun in the heavens, that this victory over self is a reality & not a mere illusion, although perfectly consistent with law & order & statistical averages. If the great struggle & the victory could all be resolved into material antecedents I should still desire & believe it true to maintain a real sense of freedom, though with our favourite antithesis of mind & matter, it might be difficult to do so. Some persons are greatly impressed with the possibility of material or mechanical agencies improving the world—(& certainly what may be done by their aid may be in the course of a century almost infinite). But I fear that human nature will also fall if it only follows the progress, however great, of Commercial or Sanitary improvement. Must it not have ideas & will & character unless it is to become the slave of the external world?

 II. About M. Comte I should like to say a few words. I observe many persons are beginning to talk of the three ages of the world—Polytheism, Monotheism, Atheism—& that people who have got tired of theology or philosophy fancy they find a rest in Positivism. It seems to me that Positivism is after all a kind of metaphysical dogma. To say that everything must be founded on fact is not new since Locke, & if by fact is meant mechanical fact it

---

[1] After Tennyson took up residence at Farringford in 1853, BJ made frequent visits to Freshwater, sometimes staying with the Tennysons and on other occasions lodging in their vicinity (AC i. 339).

is not true. Comte constantly asserts that morals & social science must rest on facts, but the whole point is really what are the facts on which they rest, towards the elucidation of which he contributes very little. The notion of Universal law is not his discovery but due to the growing sense & knowledge of the physical world. I think the same of his philosophy of history. Hegel had traced the sequence of ideas & nations forty years ago, with less violence to facts & with much greater metaphysical & poetical insight. To reduce morals to the type of physics is a mistaken wisdom: I would admit that they conform to the laws of nature but I want to have it shown how the moral & spiritual laws of nature rise above the material ones.

I feel & observe in reading Comte 1. excessive egotism (the very reverse of Socrates). 2. Vast generalization which is in fact a sort of metaphysical assumption. 3. an inverted Catholicism with God left out & the Saints left in. 4. a want of imagination & knowledge of human nature.

Shall I tell you what prompts me to make these sort of remarks? It arises from my finding that one of the best of my pupils has become possessed with the spirit of Comte so that he no longer believes in God or in a future state. And I find him as irrational & passionate in holding this negative faith, as some of those whom I have known formerly who determined to become Roman Catholics. Though I know that as in this case & in that of Comte himself, a person may become a Comtist and yet be a good & noble person, or (as theologians say) may be saved. I am very sorry to see younger men enamoured of such a truncated, imperfect system. I hope to see a Christianity which should include all that Comte has of truth, not be reduced to it.

I shall never give up the faith in immortality though I cannot determine or conceive the manner of another state of being. That Christ became a mass of clay again seems to me of all incredible things, the most incredible.

III. It is an old complaint among those who want to alter the position of women that they won't have it altered; as some say they have learned their duties so perfectly or as others they are such complete slaves that any agitation of the subject falls flat & dead with them. I feel with you that here is something fearfully wrong in the world as it is. But, how to remedy, or even to describe the evil without doing harm it is difficult to conceive. It seems to require a true woman or queen, a female Christ, as you say, to show the way. It seems to demand a nature which unites all feminine sympathies & in a certain sense, graces, with an heroic temper & firmness of soul. There are so many germs of nobleness in the characters of women that I cannot doubt a great deal might be done to ennoble them still more. But at present, the best women suffer more than any one from the degenerate state of religion & are fed or feed themselves on Methodistical or Catholic fancies. If a person were to attempt to raise their position or feeling about themselves, I think it would be necessary (if he is to succeed) that he should conceal his object. 'Why do you maintain this paradox?' some one will ask. Why?—because otherwise you could never work through the feeling of women & because the whole subject, if the veil be for a moment withdrawn from it, degenerates into vulgarity on the one side (Woman's mission &c) or sentimentalism on the other. Jean Paul,[2] who was certainly a great genius & had enough of the 'Coeur d'une femme', might have accomplished something great of this sort had he had a moral object & also if he had not been in the habit of falling in love about once a year.

Wretched Education of women, more solid information wanted, is a very common cry. But for the mass of women I doubt whether any change in the subjects of Education would do any good—a second rate mind intellectualized & crammed with information is very useless & disagreeable. The 'Sweet creature' who knows nothing is far preferable. With women even more than men it seems absolutely necessary that education should bear some proportion to original power.

(As some of my friends think that I have been rusticated from Oxford, I will just mention that I am staying at Freshwater to finish an Edition of the Republic of Plato,[3] which it was impossible to accomplish amid the routine of Oxford.)

I often see the poet & hear him talk about many things. He tells me that thirty years ago he formed the plan of a great poem on King Arthur, not an epic in 12 books but a sort of ideal or religious poem, veiling under the old legend the inner spiritual life of the world as it is. Arthur was to have been a hero Christ, who is at last driven from an evil world with the certainty that he is to return. He says that it often gives him pain to hear the Idylls[4] praised, because he thinks how unlike they are to what he intended. It would be a great possession for the world to have the real permanent religious truths embodied in a great poem. I have some hope that he may be got to resume the idea, which has so completely possessed him that I doubt whether he has left room for the plan of any other work.

One of his most favourite subjects of conversation is the immortality of the soul, of which he speaks in the most passionate manner again & again. (I like to hear him speak of it, especially when I think of "Polytheist, Monotheist, Atheist"). He seems to rest his faith in it on the Conscience, & also on a strange sense, that he himself has at certain times, of intense individuality & communion with a Supreme Being. His description of this last state is most extraordinary. He has told me of it several times & with strong asseverations, and any one who knows him, at once feels quite certain that it is true.

Other subjects that he is fond of talking about are the greatness of Christ, whom he can still less conceive than how Shakespear was a poet; also the perfectibility of the human species in long geological periods, a subject which greatly interests his imagination.

I tell you these things because I thought you would like to hear them in

[2] J. P. Richter. BJ possessed two copies of his *Life* published in 1849.

[3] The first edition of BJ's translation of *The Republic* was included in *The Dialogues of Plato* (4 vols., 1871).

[4] The first fragment of *Idylls of the King*, 'The Morte d'Arthur', was published in 1842, followed in 1859 by 'Enid', 'Vivien', 'Elaine', and 'Guinevere'.

confidence & because I believe he would not mind their being repeated to you. I need hardly say that as I have his friendship I do not wish any gossip about him to be spread through me. Notwithstanding some weaknesses on the surface, which makes it difficult if not impossible for the world in general to understand him, I always feel him to be in reality a noble character as well as a great poet.

I have inflicted on you a letter, I fear, which is a great deal too long. I will only add the most earnest wish that you may not want yourself the alleviation of suffering which you have been the means of imparting to numberless others.

[*Postscript omitted*]

5

Address until July 21st [1861]
Vicarage
Doncaster[1]
afterwards Oxford
to be forwarded

I write to thank you for your most kind letter which greatly interested me. You will never make me believe 1) that you have not a great deal of genius, or 2) that you are an egotist. About Cassandra[2] I see that I was mistaken. I did not exactly take Cassandra for yourself, but I thought that it represented more of your own feeling about the world than could have been the case. . . .

As you have shown me so much confidence I feel the strongest wish to help you in any way that I can, without intruding upon you. The difficulty seems to arise out of the form of the papers:

1) I think it is quite true that their value (as you imply) does depend in a great measure on the circumstance of their being a record of your own experience (who have worked in the world): on the other hand, the "disjecta membra" of the novel & imaginary conversations lead to a confusion & to very serious misunderstandings of another sort.

Shall I offer two or three suggestions about them? My object would be to give you the least labour possible.

(First of all there is the plan of abridging & rewriting them, but I set this aside because it appears to be impossible.) Secondly, suppose you were to publish the novel & imaginary conversations as they stood originally. I more incline to this about the imaginary conversations than about the novel. Yet the novel might also be published as far as the death of Cassandra. And this plan might be combined with 3) The publication of the remainder in fragments. . . .

'Thoughts or fragments' are not an ineffective mode of writing. And they impose no great obligation of connexion. . . .

---

[1] With C. J. Vaughan, who reacted to the publication of *Essays and Reviews* by reading the XXXIX Articles in public. BJ spoke humorously of imagining himself being burned in Doncaster churchyard. *The Times*, 10 Nov. 1860 (12d); *AC* i. 347.

[2] See above, No. 3, n. 1.

If I can help you to rearrange or reconstruct, I will gladly do so. The difficulty I should find would be to separate the part which expresses your own feelings & thoughts from those which belong to other characters.

There are some points which I should still like to see altered. I will mention one of those: 'Sin'. However right it is to preach on the one side, alter your circumstances & the sin which is the consequence of them will cease. On the other hand it must be admitted that any degree of sorrow or remorse which will tend to prevent the commission of the same sin is right. I *myself* have been guilty of many sins; I do not wish to horrify myself with the remembrance of them. Still I should regard it as a species of moral deterioration, against which I desire always to pray earnestly, if I were to acquiesce in these sins as a part of the order of the world, at least in any such sense as to make me irresponsible for them. . . .

When I am able I will venture to send you a few notes on the assertion of freewill in law—also on the education of after life—only heads without form, as I am going to be really egotistical, & ask you to read the last essay that I wrote in the 2nd vol. of the *2nd* Edition of my book on St Paul[3]—to save me the trouble of repeating what I said there—which though true, as I still think, seems to me an imperfect working out of the side of free will. . . .

[*Postscript omitted*]

6

For a month
7 Royal Crescent
Whitby[1]
[23 July 1861]

After reading your letter shall I try to put together the points of agreement that we may see where the difference begins (if there is any)?

I agree in the notion of Universal Law. Still it appears to me that laws are more or less complex, more or less known to us, admitting in a greater or less degree of motive or freedom in the individual. The law of attraction is not the type of physiological & still less of moral laws. Though it is true on the other hand that no freedom or choice in the individual can interfere with the reality of law in human actions, as well as in the workings of matter.

I do not object to admit that Socrates & Newton are the effects of law. But what that law is we are very far from knowing; the case is too exceptional & irregular to be made matter of knowledge. We should have to form averages of great men, & try to isolate them with their antecedents, before we could ascertain the causes which have produced them. This is the difficulty of tracing laws in history—we seem to require 'more worlds than one' before we could form a satisfactory induction about them.

---

[3] *The Epistles of St Paul to the Thessalonians, Galatians, Romans,* 1st edn. (1855), 2nd (rev.) edn. (1859).

[1] For BJ's holidays in the Long Vacations see *AC* i. 333.

I agree also about the power of external causes—(What you say of the drunkard is doubtless true)—But a free choice & absence of constraint must be admitted also in the use of these external causes. Suppose that the moral character, e.g. is chiefly affected by health. Still the care of the health is a duty which we may fulfill or neglect to fulfill. Free agency, to use the popular phraseology, still comes in. And it seems to me that you underrate this power of the will—not perhaps the power of the will of a drunkard shut up alone with a whisky bottle, but the power of the will when supported by sympathy & public opinion, e.g. in a temperance vow.

Whether we should trust most to external or internal influences is a question of experience which has really nothing to do with the controversy about free will. Neither is it always easy to separate what is to be regarded as external & what is internal—these two words having often a false opposition like that of necessity & free will.

I agree also in thinking that necessity & freewill are mere words by which we abstract under the form of opposites the phenomena of nature & of man. I should like to retain the last of these names & substitute for the other the idea of law.

You say 'that in one sense it is impossible to doubt that we are free agents: in another sense it is not true'.

I agree in this. But though no one is practically a fatalist it is also true that fatalistic aspects of human nature may insinuate themselves under the idea of law which may greatly impair the internal agency.

What appears to me untrue in your papers is not law—not the all importance of changing the circumstances of mankind for the sake of changing their characters—but an appearance of denying moral evil—wishing the individual to look back upon it *in his own case* as the result of law. This appears to me dangerous & antinomian. When I go into a particular room, move my hand &c it is not natural (though it is in a certain sense true) to consider all this as the effect of law. So if I steal, slander &c, it is quite true that this does not interfere with the moral order of nature, but neither is it a right or healthy thing to regard my own evil deeds as the effect of law.

I have no more paper, & sitting in the coffee room of an Inn is not the best place for discussing such matters—I will trespass on your patience once more at a future time.

7

7. Royal Crescent
Whitby
until Aug. 28 [1861]

. . . The Articles against Dr R. Williams were sent me the other day. They are preposterous.[1] On such questions hardly any one seems to have any sense

---

[1] Williams contributed a review of 'Bunsen's Biblical Researches' to *Essays and Reviews* (1860). Williams and H. B. Wilson, whose essay bore the title 'Séances historiques de Genève. The National

of truth or justice. Nothing has been more striking to me during the last six years than the circumstance that no one, even of the friends I respect most, has remonstrated with me on the ground that what I wrote was untrue, but always with arguments about prudence, public opinion & the like. In this recent discussion about Essays & Reviews the idea of truth has become childish, ridiculous, impertinent. Mr Carlyle says 'Seven sentinels—deserted their post—ought to be shot.' οὐδέν μοι μέλει.[2] It is impossible to think without amazement of the state into which the world has fallen in matters of religion: the conventionalities of both worlds—the religious & the other.

I hope you will not deem me impertinent if I express a fear that often occurs to me lest in your present state of health you should endanger or shorten life by mental exertion. (I know that this is one of those counsels which it is said to be impossible to follow.) Do not fail to take every chance of lengthened existence or, if possible, of recovery. For yourself I have no doubt that 'to depart & to be with Christ is far better' in the words of St Paul[3] but there are many things for you to do in this world & the only chance of doing them may be not to do them prematurely. As a stranger I ought not, perhaps, to write to you unasked on such a subject.

8

Address after Monday
Harehead
nr Selkirk
[about September 1861]

I write a line in haste to acknowledge your three enclosures. I shall always read letters from you with great pleasure & interest.

But don't let us discourage one another. I am very sensible how much you have to dispirit you in the weariness & solitude of illness and the late, real & great affliction of Lord Herbert's death. I am very sorry about it, if it would do any good to say so.

I shall not attempt to offer you "goodnatured" consolations. Consolers should be thrown out of the window. You know better than I do that it is useless to take any part either in speculation or action when the world is against you, without something of an heroic temper.

I don't think you are quite right about the 'jaw'. Though more distant the effect of writing is quite as great & not so limited as that of work. When a person has the capacity, some union of the two seems to me the right thing. The entire suppression of opinion on subjects which are very near to the hearts of all cripples the work; e.g., it seems to me that Dr Temple would make a great mistake if he suppressed his views & kept on good terms with the religious world (with which he really disagrees) and that the effect would be seen (in his

Church', were prosecuted in the Court of Arches under the Church Discipline Act of 1840 for infringing the formularies of the Church of England.

[2] Aristophanes, *The Frogs*, l. 655, 'Mind it? Not a bit.'   [3] Phil. 1: 23.

own rapid rise to the Episcopate—&) in the characters of his pupils in the next generation.[1]

It is, doubtless, true that sensible philanthropic persons implicitly agree in the greater part of what you say. If they could be made to recognize this they would work more surely & with fewer drawbacks. Therefore it is worthwhile to do much for the sake of conciliating them, by sympathy, by acknowledgement of the good & truth which they have, by omission of stray thoughts which would shock them, when they are not necessary to the argument. I don't think that all the bone & muscle of the book need be taken out.

Though there are not 20 people (in my opinion) who unite the strong consistent sense of law with reverence for Divine being, yet I do not doubt there is a real field & want which your book would supply: religious persons who will sympathize with the practical side—scientific people to whom religion (contrary to human nature) has become a blank. When I have considered your letters I will send you remarks on them, if any occur to me. But our controversy seems unlike other controversies to end in a nearer approach to agreement.

[*Postscript*]

Some things in your papers strike me as remarkably true to my own experience of life. 1) the unhappiness of families, which is generally, however, sealed & shrouded from the world. 2) the absolute want of discernment that parents have about the characters & tastes of their children; to which I should add their strong affection for them, & inversely the greater discernment that children have of the characters & wants of their parents together with a strong sense of duty towards them & yet a much feebler affection for them. 3) the waste of youthful talent for want of opportunity. Every year I am more & more impressed with the natural talents of young men. And I wish I could do more & more to prevent these good blossoms from falling—some from shyness, some from ignorance of the world & of the characters of others—some from fanaticism, religious or irreligious; others from worse causes yet none of them, while young, incurable. I know some persons will say 'You think young men able because they often take your opinions'. That is not, I think, the case; it is not difficult to distinguish between a young man following your opinions & his real capacity. From some young men I seem to learn more than from any older friends. But I fear this cannot be very interesting to others.

9

Balliol College
Oxford
Nov. 17 [1861]

A few more words:
1. I think there is no difficulty in getting rid of abstract terms, 'personality',

[1] Temple published 'The Education of the World' in *Essays and Reviews*. He became Bishop of Exeter in 1869.

'freedom', 'cause & effect' &c. so far as not to be, or to make others, the slave of them. . . .—to prevent the argument turning on the meaning of a word—to acknowledge, as Bacon would have done, the illusions of language. It often seems to me that no modern writer has carried the sense of this last so far as Bacon in the first Book of the Novum Organum. . . .[1]

3. I am glad you see the Artizans. Still let me add one thing that strikes me (I put down thoughts as they occur, knowing that you will not be offended at them though you may not think necessary to attend to them). A book cannot be written for the Artizans separated from the educated classes. It must embrace them both. There is one intellectual world with common ideas, & the more permanent part of that is the world of the higher classes. Therefore I would urge you not to write for the Artizans, but to write for everybody.

4. I should not much care if only a comparatively small part of your work is finished. Its greatest value will be that it comes from you who worked in the Crimea. Shall I say one odd & perhaps rather impertinent thing? You have a great advantage in writing on these subjects as a woman. Do not throw it away but use the advantage to the utmost. In writing against the world ('Athanasia contra mundum')[2] every feeling, every sympathy, should be made an ally so that with the clearest statement of the meaning there is the least friction & drawback possible. . . .

10   Balliol,[1]
                                                                                         Nov. 19 [1861]

Thank you for writing to me. I am very much grieved at the tidings which your letter brought me. I agree entirely in your estimate of our dear friend's character. It was in 1836 (the anniversary is next week) that I first saw him[2] when he was elected to the Balliol Scholarship. No one who only knew him in later life would imagine what a noble, striking-looking youth he was before he got worried with false views of religion and the world. I never met with any one who was more thoroughly high-minded: I believe he acted all through life simply from the feeling of what was right. He certainly had great genius, but some want of will or some want of harmony with things around him prevented his creating anything worthy of himself. I am glad he was married: life was dark to him, and his wife and children made him as happy as he was capable of being made. He was naturally very religious, and I think that he never recovered the rude shock which his religion received during his first years at Oxford. He did not see and yet he believed in the great belief of all—to do rightly. Did I quote to you ever an expression which Neander used to me of Blanco White: *einer Christ mehr in Unbewusstseyn als in Bewusstseyn*? It grieves me that you should

[1] *Novum Organum* (1620).
[2] St Athanasius (c. 298-373): *Athanasius contra mundum* was the definition of orthodoxy against Arianism.

[1] From *Cook*, ii. 12.   [2] A. H. Clough.

have lost so invaluable a friend. No earthly trial can be greater than to pursue without friends the work that you began with them. And yet it is the more needed because it rests on one only. If there be any way in this world to be like Christ it must be by pursuing in solitude and illness, without the support of sympathy or public opinion, works for the good of mankind....

11

Balliol College
Oxford
[about March 1862]

As I used to have the privilege of occasionally writing to you I hardly like to give up doing so altogether.

Is the 'Stuff' going on and can I assist you any further in sewing it together?

I should wish you every earthly good, if you were not past caring for such things. But now as years of suffering come & go & many of your friends are taken I cannot but wish you (as sincerely as I ever desired anything) unabated hope & trust & resolve to continue in your work to the end, & many rays of light to cheer the way. It is not the expedition to the Crimea so much as the patient, solitary, unknown toil which astonishes me & makes me feel grateful for your example.

Since I wrote to you last I have lost one of my best friends & pupils, Mr Luke of Ch. Ch., who was drowned at the age of 25.[1] He had great ability & the most indomitable will: I think that in the two years he was Tutor of Ch. Ch. he had done more for the place than any body else had done in the last 20. I wish you had known him; he was one of the men whose death is a real & great loss. He had very little religious belief but the strongest faith. One reason why I mention him to you is that on one of the last occasions on which I saw him he quoted to me a sentence of your letter to the Volunteers[2] (I never saw the letter & only know it from his descriptions): it was something about 'never having given an hour to friendship or amusement'. He did not know that I knew you, but he repeated this to me with great admiration; it seemed to be a model that he was proposing to himself. I thought you would like to hear of this.

I have seen most of our dear friend A. H. C.'s poems & am glad they are going to be published.[3] They don't do him justice, to those who knew him, but they cannot fail to raise his memory & reputation in the world. I feel in reading them that if he had had opportunities he would have been a really great poet....

[1] BJ wrote the obituary in *The Times*, 5 Mar. 1862 (12b): 'He understood perfectly the secret of success, as a college tutor. The secret is chiefly devotion to the work, and consideration for the characters of young men.'

[2] *The Standard*, 12 Oct. 1861 (3f).

[3] Clough's poems were printed for private circulation in 'Letters and Remains of Arthur Hugh Clough' in 1865, and published in 1869.

12 Address Oxford
[about July 1862]

I heard from M. Mohl that you would like me to write you some account of the Judgement in the matter of Essays & Reviews.[1] What shall I tell you about it? I will try as far as I can to avoid what you will have seen in the newspapers.

The general result is I think to extend considerably the borders of the Ch. of England. This judgement is to the 'Broad Church' (I hate that expression) what the judgement in the Gorham case was to the Evangelicals.[2] For 1) the Interpretation of Scripture is left entirely open; it may be literal, allegorical, ideological—what you please—provided there is no contradiction of the letter of some Article. To speculate whether there were two Isaiahs, whether the book of Daniel was written in the time of Antiochus Epiphanes &c. is no longer forbidden ground to a clergyman of the Ch. of England. Scripture is, or is supposed to be, the foundation of the C. of E. in popular opinion & therefore the value of this latitude can hardly be overrated.

2) wherabouts the law lies is now known. The region marked 'dangers', where you are liable to fall in, is in statements of doctrine which contradict the Articles.... The points which are decided in favour of the Essayists are final as the other party are not going to appeal; the points which are against them will have to go through a long process of refining and argument first on the readmission of the Articles; 2) when the Articles are admitted in the meaning of the accused parties' words; 3) after sentence is passed by Dr Lushington the whole suit (that is to say on the residuum of the charge) will have to begin over again before the Privy Council.[3] You will perceive that the points on which the accused are condemned are not the characteristic points of the case; also that their condemnation will certainly look like a condemnation (on two of the Articles at least) of the justice of God. Some of the judges' statements on these points appear to me very untenable & will scarcely be maintained when attention is minutely called to them.

There is something, doubtless, very unsatisfactory in trying such questions by a legal standard. 1) It is a mere fiction—Law applies definite facts to define words; here are indefinite & even contradictory words applied to the ever-changing shadows of opinion. 2) Lawyers don't seem to me aware that they

---

[1] Dr Lushington, the Dean of Arches 1858-67, ruled that general accusations were not acceptable. Neither scripture nor the traditions of centuries might be cited against the accused. But they did have an obligation not to teach anything contrary to the formularies they had voluntarily agreed to abide by. He therefore disallowed several of the articles of accusation, reformulated others, and left some standing. The reformulated articles were then resubmitted. *The Times*, 26 June 1862 (9def), 26 July (13d).

[2] The Bishop of Exeter considered G. C. Gorham 'unsound' on the doctrine of baptismal regeneration, and refused to institute him to the living of Brampford Speke. In 1850 the Privy Council ruled against the Bishop.

[3] On 15 Dec. 1862 Williams and Wilson were sentenced to be suspended from office and benefice for one year. Costs were awarded against the defendants, who later appealed successfully to the Privy Council. The Council's decision, announced on 8 Feb. 1864, immortalized the Lord Chancellor, Lord Westbury, as having dismissed hell with costs.

require to be theologians, even to be able to try words by their legal standard. Dr Lushington would say 'God forbid that I should get into the ocean of Theology or the meaning of Scripture', &c., &c. But the thing can't be avoided; a purely legal view of the case is not possible. 3) Again, there is a fiction of another sort in saying 'the Law knows only the literal & grammatical sense' when all the world has agreed that the Articles are not to be taken in their literal & grammatical sense.

There is something, as I was saying, very unsatisfactory & ludicrous in this legal fiction. Yet 1) what other body, or 2) what other rule of judgement can be proposed? 1) Convocation, the Bishops—2) Scripture, the Reformers, the Catholic Church. When I think of the other alternatives I am not disposed to complain. There are advantages on the other side: 1. The weight of a legal judgement makes people consider what they would otherwise never have considered. 2. The deliberation of the Court, & the respect Englishmen have for the very semblance of justice, serve as a sort of breakwater against public opinion. I do not regret on public grounds the personal remarks of the judge, which are otherwise very indefensible, because they show the world that the acquittal on the important points was wrung from the Court unwillingly. 'I would gladly convict him if I could, but the law will not allow me', appears to be the tone of them.

Dr Williams is a good & self denying man but he has the misfortune to be a Welshman & this, I believe, is the true explanation of his intemperate letter to the Daily News.[4] Mr Wilson is a very able & powerful man (did you ever see his Bampton Lectures):[5] if he had health & a little more knowledge of the world he would be very eminent, indeed.

The worst, I think, that can happen to either of them is to be admonished with costs. This, however, is a very serious matter and may involve £4000: they are neither of them men of fortune.

An important point in the case is the express statement of the Judge that no Clergyman can be called to account for anything but overt acts: 'The Court is not cognisant of mere opinions'.

Some one may say to the Essayists 'Why don't you leave the Church instead of endeavouring to reconcile your consciences to her teaching through all these legal processes?' A Unitarian may very naturally say this: no one can reply angrily to such a challenge. I never wish to conceal that there is great difficulty in the position of an intelligent clergyman. As to the matter of conscience I should be disposed to say: law & custom must settle that. As to freedom I believe that that there is upon the whole greater freedom in the balance of parties in the Ch. of England than there can be in any small

---

[4] Rounding on all his opponents, Williams accused *The Times* of misrepresenting the judgement delivered by Dr Lushington in 'an English court of law (I had almost written of justice)', the episcopate of taking up the position that 'every scholar who refuses to be corrupted as a critic, may be calumniated as a clergyman', and his prosecutor, the Bishop of Salisbury, of 'vindictive chicane': *Daily News*, 28 June 1862 (3f).

[5] *The Communion of Saints. An Attempt to Illustrate the true Principles of Christian Union* (1851).

community, even of Unitarians or free thinkers. As to unity there is no possibility even of the semblance of unity in any other body. I cannot give up the hope that this great organisation may be one day used for far higher purposes. (Do you know that the Calvinistic Church of Holland has entirely changed its character during the last 20 years?) At any rate I feel that I should be denationalized & sectarianized if I separated. It is a great misfortune socially, educationally, & in every way to belong to a sect; the forces which are entrusted for good become intensified in a struggle against one another. This way of regarding the subject is satisfactory to me—if any one likes to atack me for it they are welcome to do so.

[*Postscript*]

A word about the 'Stuff'. I hope you will some day make the world understand that it is not sentimentalism, Puseyism, or any other religious 'ism' which has enabled you to fulfill your great task.

FN to BJ [*copy*][1]

13 [16 July 1862]

... But what seemed to me deplorable in Dr Lushington's judgment was its *tendency*. I mean that it seemed to say 1. think what you please, provided you don't speak or preach it: as if I were to say, have the most distinct and correct idea you can upon the Nature of Cholera, but do nothing to cure or prevent cholera....

You are so good as to enquire after the 'stuff'. There has been nothing done to it (or about it) since you heard of it last.

But my War Office life is drawing to a close, and then, if I have any life left, I shall turn to the 'stuff', and if I do anything with it, it will be owing to your encouragement. (It is a year today since Sidney Herbert's resignation of office a fortnight before his death),[2] and in one short year Sir G. Lewis has dragged down the War Office to the position of contempt, out of wh. S.H. was 5 long years in dragging it up ... the War Office has never been at so low an ebb of intelligence, the Horse Guards at so high a flow of folly and insolence as now, at least not since the 8 years time I have worked in the W.O. Albert's death was a very great loss to us. He exercised a moral influence over the C. in Chief, keeping him in order, as S.H. excercised an administrative influence, and now that is all gone.

I have a few months more work to finish the Indian Commission,[3] wh. was to do for the Army in India what had been done for the Army at home—not that it will bear any fruit, for it will end in nothing but writing: the head and the heart are gone....

If I were what I was 8 years ago, I would have a Working Men's Children's

---

[1] BL Add. MS 45783 fos. 3–12, TS copy of an original now perished.
[2] Herbert resigned on 16 July and died on 2 Aug. 1861.
[3] The Commission, appointed by Lord Stanley in 1859, reported in 1863; see below, No. 19, n. 2.

School... to teach them all the laws of Nature (known) *upon this principle*, that it is a religious act to clean out a gutter and to prevent cholera, and that it is not a religious act to pray (in the sense of asking).

I have such a strong feeling that he who founds a Soldiers' Club (to keep them out of vice) is doing more than he who teaches abstract *religious truth*, that I would not teach the 'stuff' if I could do anything else practical—but I can't now.

...I could not go on for the sake of mankind, doing the immeasurably little I can for them, if I did not believe myself part of a plan by which God is doing the immeasurably much for them.... For otherwise it would seem as if I had been trying to work for God and he to thwart my work (I have often told him so). He brought about the most extraordinary combination—one wh. could hardly ever happen again, by which a woman obtains all the practical knowledge of Army organisation, and a Secretary of State is willing not only to listen to her, but to devote every instant of 5 years to it—and he breaks this up...

...I always am, believe me, yours most gratefully and ever lovingly, F.N.

14

Castleton
Braemar.
Address Oxford
[Summer 1862]

I need hardly tell you that I am greatly pleased at hearing that what I wrote was of any use or value to you.

I hope that you are not worse: believe that there is still work in the world for you to do & that God is willing that you should do it, even amid the trials of severe illness.

I agree with you about Sir G. Lewis & his book[1]—I felt the same disgust at Gladstone for writing nonsense about Homer[2] while the East India Bill[3] was passing through the house. Still he has in his hands to a great extent the fate of the soldier, & therefore I would never give up the attempt to influence him, however often repulsed. His sceptical & 'surtout point de zèle' nature is proof against enthusiasm & cannot be carried by force—but can he be altogether blind to the good effects of what Lord Herbert did, or to the universal popularity which followed his efforts? I wonder that politicians are not more often affected by their own interests in the higher sense of the term. Sir G. Lewis is a gentleman & a reasonable man; also not a jobber. Still he may possibly feel not perfectly at home in his work & therefore instinctively jealous of any one who presses a line of conduct upon him. Many interested persons are probably saying to him 'Have nothing to do with her', and it is only by great calmness that their efforts can be counteracted. While anything remains to be

---

[1] *Enquiry into the Credibility of the Early Roman History* (1855).
[2] *Studies on Homer and the Homeric Age* (1858).
[3] 21 and 22 Vict. c. 106, An Act for the better government of India.

done in the Sanitary department of the Army I would certainly not leave Sir G. Lewis, but 'hook on' & find new ways of approach to him. I am glad to hear what you say of Lord de Grey. Are you engaged about Indian Sanitary matters? I have a reason for being interested about them, which is that I lost my two brothers[4] in India & I think their lives would have been saved had there been better regulations about Furlough. The barracks at Calcutta I have heard described as a most fatal place. Is there any need for all this death & destruction? Might not India be as healthy as Europe (or almost so), if 1) the residences of Europeans were in healthy places; if 2) large bodies of men were kept upon the hills & 3) the regulations about furlough were made easier. Transporting barracks or even capitals is not so bad as shortening human life to half it's span—nor so expensive. As to the natives themselves, might they not be educated to cleanliness & health by the enforcement of sanitary regulations in the large towns? . . .

[*Postscript*]

I heard a day or two ago a story about your old enemy Lord Panmure. (It is always pleasant to hear a jest at the expense of an enemy.) Soon after he came to the title he met an old woman picking up sticks, as she had been accustomed to do in his woods. He spoke roughly to her and warned her off. She said 'I'm a thinking they buried the wrong Lord'.

15 Inglewood Abbey Park
Torquay[1] Oct. 3, 1862

I shall be very glad to give you the Sacrament: I am sure that many other clergymen would be equally glad.

I can come to you on Oct. 19 or any succeeding Sunday. Shall I fix the time 2 o'clock or, rather, will you fix any Sunday and hour which suits you?

Would you like Mr & Mrs Smith,[2] or any of their family, to join you?

I feel ashamed that you should speak of being 'grateful to me' for that or anything else. May the occasion be of good to both of us.

---

[4] Alfred and William.
[1] A private hotel where BJ's mother lived with his sister Emily.
[2] Mr Samuel Smith and Mrs Smith, FN's Aunt Mai who lived with FN and looked after her 1857-60.

CHAPTER 2

1862–1866

Private

Balliol College
Oxford
Oct. 28 [1862]

... I would much rather that you should preach to me than that I should seem to preach to you. Shall I tell you what struck me?—it seems natural, although perhaps presumptuous, to do so. I thought of your long solitude & suffering, & the extreme difficulty of keeping the mind altogether in the right place under such circumstances....

It seems to me very difficult to reconcile a public passion for the good of mankind with the ordinary course of daily life. The intense & universal sympathy with a class or with a public object is apt to become exacting or indifferent or antipathetic to all else, especially towards those who take no part in the object or are averse to it. In making a great & long-continued effort the balance of the feelings is apt to be disturbed. People are thought hard, & the real truth is that they are too soft, & have suffered so much pain that they are obliged to encase & encrust themselves. Did you ever think of this? I am the reverse of a forgiving nature yet I know alas that sympathy is strength & any degree of antipathy weakness.

You said to me in one of your letters that our dear friend Clough had not altogether found the right way: he did in one way but not in another.... But I think his view was too blank & dreary; too little of an identity of duty & the Will of God; too sceptical for strength or at least for happiness. I get to think more & more that we ought to have our minds resting in God & another world from which we should be let down to think (shall I say?) of Greek words & hospitals....

Dear Miss Nightingale, I shall always regard the circumstance of having given you the Communion as a solemn event in my life, which is a call to devote myself to the service of God & men (if He will give me the power to do so). Your example will often come before me, especially if I have occasion to continue my work under bodily suffering. There is something that I want to say to you which I hardly know how to express. I want you to feel that in the Communion you were really united not only to Christ, but to all mankind, especially to those whom you know and to your own family & friends. You cause more pain than you are aware of by isolating yourself from them. There are many sensibilities & irritations which are very natural in illness which must not be thought right or the Spirit of Christ. Forgive me: I am not finding fault—I am aware that difficulties of character & nervous states are very great; also that your public duties leave no time for gossip & friendships. Still it seems to me that Christian love should win a way over these obstacles, so far at least as to make people who love & care for you, understand that you love & care for them. If there is something terrible in the thought of passing away unreconciled to God, there is something sad & awful too, in passing away estranged from old companions & friends. The worldliness & weakness of many of them may be the reason of such an estrangement. Still the strong should find a place in their hearts for the weak. . . .

17

Coll. de Ball.
Oxon.[1]
Nov. 9 [1862]

I am thinking of coming to town on Sunday Nov. 29 [30] to bid Sir C. Trevelyan goodbye (he is an old acquaintance of mine), before he goes to India. I will gladly come and see you and if you would like will give you the Sacrament. . . .

You ask about Essays and Reviews. There is some talk of prosecuting me for my share of the work and an opinion of Sir R. Phillimore has been taken to the effect that for some things I have said I may be liable to prosecution. But I don't think it will come to much. If the prosecution is commenced I shall pay a lawyer to defend me and take no further trouble about the matter.

No one said anything unkind about you to me. Indeed, I am sure no one ever could say anything which could shake my faith or admiration. Mrs. Clough did not appear to me to entertain the painful impression to which you refer. . . .[2]

I consider you a sort of Royal personage, not to be gossiped about with any one.

[*Postscript omitted*]

18

Coll. de Ball.
Oxon.[1]
Dec. 3 [1862]

I had a very kind letter from Mr. Nightingale this morning in which, however, he makes severe reflections on me for having thrown on you a terrible load in your sufferings.

I am . . . extremely obliged to him for speaking what he thought quite plainly and straightforwardly. I don't answer his letter because he does not seem to wish that I should. Will you give my kind remembrances to him?

. . . I am very sorry that such painful and unjustifiable attacks should have

---

[1] BL Add. MS 45783 fos. 14–15.
[2] That FN had fagged Clough to his death.

---

[1] BL Add. MS 45783 fos. 16–18.

been made upon you. But what was the cause of these attacks? I do not know. But may they not have arisen in the common misery about the death of our dear friend?

I wish you would burn me or my letter, or expose me to some species of martyrdom: then I shall be more at rest. Still let me urge you to do all that may be to heal and reconcile matters. Only, as I don't know the circumstances, I do not venture to say that you have not done so already. I am sorry that you thought I was 'judging' you; indeed, nothing could be further from my intention; or that I spoke to you as one 'sinking into the grave'. There is certainly no one who had more sanguine hopes of your restoration to health and performance of many great things.

Please, 'be cheerful Madam'. I would give much to hear that you were so.

... To turn to other subjects. My prosecutors have not troubled me as yet and I rather hope they will not do so.[2] They have to set in motion a rusty old Court in which such a cause was never tried, and which has to proceed by the forms of Common Law. Then again the Statute seems expressly to say that they can only try me for what I have said as a Professor in lecturing, and not for any book and writing.

3. There is a statute of limitation of 2 years in the Ch. Discipline Act[3] which I am told will be held to apply.

4. The Delegates to whom the appeal has to be made are very liberal in their sentiments.[4] These are the chances of escape before the cause begins. So you see that I am a fortunate criminal. I keep all this dark here as I think they may as well try. There is some amusement, is there not, in fighting a battle?—at least I suppose there is no harm in trying to find amusement in doing so.

19

Balliol College
Oxford
Dec. 13 [1862]

I expect to be in London on Sunday week. May I hope to have the pleasure of coming to see you (at 2 o'clock) and would you like me to give you the Sacrament?

... The B. of London's charge[1] seems to me very good, especially the first

[2] In February 1863 BJ was prosecuted for his contribution 'On the Interpretation of Scripture' to *Essays and Reviews* in the Chancellor's Court by E. B. Pusey, C. A. Heurtley, and C. A. Ogilvie.

[3] 3 and 4 Vict. c. 86.

[4] In the Chancellor's Court the Vice-chancellor (J. P. Lightfoot, Rector of Exeter College) was the Presiding Judge. He appointed an assessor (Mountague Bernard) to act for him; see below, No. 21, n. 10. The two Proctors (James Riddell of Balliol College and Thomas Fowler of Lincoln College) might also sit if they wished.

[1] 'Shall we ... try to stifle [the unrestrained spirit of free inquiry]? This will do no good ... after all we are Protestants.... It will never do to lay down that a clergyman is bound not to inquire.... No man is bound by his ordination vow to turn a deaf ear to the whisperings of his conscience.... I do not look much to legal prosecutions ... for the preservation of orthodoxy in our clergy.' A. C. Tait, *A Charge Delivered in December 1862 to the Clergy of the Diocese of London*, pp. 6, 7, 17, 19, 20.

part—I shall tell him your opinion when I see him. He wrote very kindly when I had to write to him to ask his leave to celebrate the Communion.

[*Postscript*]

I should like very much to have the India Report.² Many thanks.

20 Jan. 22 [1863]

I send a line to thank you for the memoir about Lord Herbert,¹ which I read to day with great pleasure.

In the weary hours of wakefulness & pain I think you may have a real deep happiness in the work which he accomplished, & which is yours at least equally with his. . . .

21 *Private*

Balliol College
Oxford
[February 1863]

I promised to write & let you know about Bishop Colenso.¹ I shall hope to be in London & have the pleasure of coming to see you again in about a month's time.

There was a fierce conflict about Bp. Colenso which raged for three days, first at the Abp. of Canterbury's² & then at the Abp. of York's.³ (Please not to repeat all this, which is told me in confidence.) The extreme party among the Bps., led by S. Oxon.,⁴ wanted to issue a joint scrawl to their clergy prohibiting Bishop Colenso from preaching in any of their dioceses. The B. of London⁵ stoutly resisted this & was supported by the Abp. of York, the Bps. of St David's⁶ & Manchester.⁷ At last the debate closed by the B. of London threatening to issue a counter notice, which finally put an end to the proposal. A mild letter of remonstrance was at last agreed to.

In the Convocation the Bishops only carried by a majority of one (which one was St Asaph,⁸ who spoke on one side & voted on the other) the permis-

---

² Probably a draft of the *Report of the Royal Commission on the Sanitary State of the Army in India* (1863, Cmd. 3650-1).

¹ FN wrote a tribute to Lord Herbert in 1861. This was privately printed: it was revised and enlarged in 1862, when it was presented as 'Army Sanitary Administration, and its Reform under the late Lord Herbert' to the London meeting of the *Congrès International de Bienfaisance*. It was published in vol. ii of the *Mémoires, notices, et documents*, pp. 103–11, and also printed and published separately. W. J. Bishop and Sue Goldie, *A Bio-bibliography of Florence Nightingale* (1962), entries 118 and 54.

¹ Colenso had adapted Christian dogma to the circumstances and understanding of native Africans. In 1863 he was deposed and excommunicated by Robert Grey, the Archbishop of Cape Town, whose actions were declared null and void by the Privy Council in 1865.

² Longley. ³ Thomson. ⁴ Samuel Wilberforce. ⁵ Tait.
⁶ Thirlwall. ⁷ Lee. ⁸ Short.

sion to the lower house to have a Committee of Enquiry. The whole tone & aspect of matters appears to be very much changed since the denunciation of Essays & Reviews.

Have you seen B. Colenso's second part?[9] He is an able man but he has drawn the threads of his Criticism out too fine. He thinks that he can show that the name of Jehovah was introduced in the time of Samuel, & hence infers that the Pentateuch, or rather the Older part of the Pentateuch, was put together by Samuel after an earlier Elohistic writer. The arguments are two: (1) the absence of names compounded with Jehovah before Samuel. (2) the absence of the name in the earlier Psalms of David—The doubtful point is which are the earlier Psalms of David.

I hope you will get hold of Lord Stanley on some fitting opportunity. My impression of him is that he is a cold, ill-mannered Radical Aristocrat [by] nature, cut off from the religious world, & equally from the jolly world, but still a man with higher aims than any other politician. He will certainly have a great deal to do with governing this country during the next thirty years.

You may, perhaps, have observed that the doctrine of the Atonement is coming on for decision in the Small debts Court at Oxford.[10] However we hope to overthrow them on the question of the jurisdiction of the Court....

22

Balliol College
Oxford
April 22 [1863]

I wish you joy, and a new lease of life, health & 'office'.[1]

I don't think that a Minister requires great ability or eloquence to be useful & successful, but he requires great caution & reticence, a simple purpose, some degree of originality & intense perseverance. The gift of being invisible is much to be desired by any one who exercises a good influence over others. Though Deborah & Barak work together, Sisera, the Captain of the Host, must not suspect that he has been delivered into the hands of a woman.[2]

... The country clergy have been dragged up here today to overpower the residents in a matter of Education about which it is not too much to say that every sensible man was on one side & every fool on the other.[3]

---

[9] Of *Critical Examination of the Pentateuch* (1862–79).

[10] BJ's essay 'On the interpretation of scripture' was concerned with the atonement. The case of 'Dr. Pusey and others v. Professor Jowett' came before the Chancellor's Court on 15 Feb. 1863: on 27 Feb. the Assessor decided against continuing with the case.

[1] In Apr. 1863 Sir G. C. Lewis died and Earl de Grey succeeded him at the War Office.

[2] Judg. 4.

[3] The proposal not to require a Pass in Classics before candidates were allowed to sit for other Schools passed Congregation by 97 votes to 58, and was defeated in Convocation by 199 to 145. W. R. Ward, *Victorian Oxford* (1965), pp. 221–2.

23

High Force Inn
Middleton in Teesdale
Durham
[Summer 1863]

I read an article in 'The Times' of Thursday which I attribute to your inspiration.[1] Such things as you describe, in a civilized country ought to arouse the fiercest indignation. Although, perhaps, it may be more prudent to throw a politico-economical veil over the matter & persuade people that as an affair of business they ought to save human lives.

I think I told you of Gladstone saying to a friend of mine that he objected to war, because war implied armies, & armies implied a soldiery habitually living in an immoral state. I think this last is true, unless the soldier is allowed to have a second occupation which may fill up his vacant time & provide him with the means of marrying.

I do not see why the army, instead of being an immoral nuisance, should not be made as respectable as the police. A standing army gives just such an opportunity of training & education, as an Ancient Legislator would have rejoiced to use. The rifle movement & the militia show that we are not wholly dependent on the regular soldier. Might there not be industrial regiments, short terms of service: a second grade of militia more nearly approaching the regular troops?—fewer soldiers actually employed & more liable to be called out? Some one should write an essay on the theory of the English Army; its reserves, home & foreign service &c. I hardly see how the purchase system can be done away with unless at any rate the first Commissions were given by examination. This seems to imply more of the spirit of military Education than there is in this country, and would also tend (whether that be a good or evil) to destroy the 'gentlemen' character of the English Army. There are great advantages in the Aristocratic character of the army & the Church which persons in that class of life are never weary of dilating upon after Dinner—compared with an equal number of persons in any other class, the advantage is very considerable—but no doubt, if you included 10,00,000 [*ten hundred thousand*] you would find a much better pick of officers & Clergymen than out of the families of the 'Upper ten thousand'.

I write this not because I know anything about such matters, but because it interests me to think of them. I am staying at the head of Teesdale, at work on Plato. I wish you could be transplanted to have a sight of this beautiful country—I hear the soothing sound of the waterfall like the sea, about a hundred yards hence.

It troubles me sometimes to think of your solitary sufferings—you to whom

---

[1] Possibly a letter published on 13 Aug. 1863 (4c) in which 'AN OLD MADRASSY' referred to the Report of the Royal Commission on the Sanitary State of the Army in India, objected to troops being marched about in full kit under a hot sun, and drew attention to 'what this country pays for a single well-drilled soldier'.

others owe so much. I cannot think there is anything wrong in your desire for death: it seems to me quite natural & not in the least degree to be made a subject of self reproach. Only let me put the other side to you. It has pleased God to enable you to do great things for your fellow creatures. But far more may be done in the next ten years, if your life is spared, than has been already done. And you must not desert your post while anything remains to be done. Physical sufferings touch the springs of life & seem, in a manner, to destroy free agency. But, I think, that a blessed vision of those whose sufferings you have alleviated ought to hover around you by night or day, under the pressure of your own. And do not suppose, at least not as a permanent feeling, that the loss of Lord Herbert paralyzes the carrying out of your objects. It is a higher strain of faith to go on with them now when there is no human sympathy or friendship to assist in them, but God only....

24

Address Oxford
St Andrews
[1863]

Many thanks indeed for your very kind letter—I am always interested in hearing about the army which has such great opportunities for good or evil. But I hope you will not trouble yourself to write to me when you are either too unwell or have anything better to do.

It often seems to me monstrous that a railway or police force should live by morality & respectability & that an army should be just the opposite. The police are certainly to be included among the respectable classes: their 'business' & profession is to be honest & moral. Cannot this be made the business of the army also?

There seem to me to be chiefly four means of accomplishing an improvement in the Soldiers' condition:
 1. Military Colonization.
 2. Short periods of service.
 3. Work & amusements: trades.
 4. Localization.

I mean by the last keeping the Soldier at fixed stations, where he would be subject to the same influences of neighbourhood & society as the Civilian. Why is this impossible?

As to morality I should feel almost hopeless of this unless the soldier can marry. The level of morality which there is among agricultural labourers is very low—& what there is, chiefly maintained (I think) by three means: poverty, hard work, early marriages. None of these affect the soldier. If among agricultural labourers marriage were deferred as a rule until 30 there would be great vice & misery. And the soldier, though nominally serving only for ten years, cannot really find another employment: speaking generally he is hardly fitted either for skilled or unskilled labour. Therefore I think you cannot reckon that on the present system the soldier can marry at 30.

Clergymen have told me that the agricultural poor draw a strong distinction between the sin of drunkenness & other kinds of immorality *in favour of the latter*. I mention this to show that the public opinion of that class will give little help.

I am unwilling to give an opinion about the medical police regulations. If they are ineffectual wholly, & this can be clearly shown, no one would wish to enforce them. But I cannot think that you legalize sin by interfering to prevent disease. Suppose for example that the evil in question were ten-fold greater & the remedy proposed really effective. Would you think such interference evil or sinful? I believe the clergy might be very likely roused to take the other view of the subject, because they are always likely to be on the side of moral, rather than physical preventives—But I should be sorry to see the question argued on these grounds.

You must not suppose that I think lightly of sins of this class. By every means let us endeavour to preserve the young from them, & to raise the tone of society & the army about them. I dont think, however, that the moral principles of mankind will ever be really strengthened by the terrors of disease. And there seems to me a prior obligation to mitigate disease of so fearful a character which may affect the innocent quite as much as the vicious. I am far from saying that you are not right in thinking the attempt wholly ineffectual. But I should not feel any objections on moral grounds.

If I thought I could have any influence with you I should try to get you not to take any part in the controversy, beyond the statement that the medical police system is ineffectual. For several reasons.

First, because I don't think the proposal is likely to take effect; it is very difficult to carry out & what people call unenglish. It can hardly be applied to the army without being extended to the class generally. Secondly I fear that you may injure your influence for other objects. The public will not believe that you can understand the subject fully; they will think that you take the ground of female morality. And indeed there are horrors & evils connected with this subject of which statistical enquiries cannot give an adequate notion. Lastly the association is unpleasant. And although nothing painful or disgusting should be shrunk from on that ground only, the effect on the public ought to be considered for the sake of future efforts.

You will, I hope, forgive me for differing from you. I will not say with Sir J. Jebb that 'it would kill me if you were mistaken', but I can truly say that it would give me very great pain if you made a false step.

My idea would be that the right thing is to draw attention to the results of the enquiries & then leave the matter. Meanwhile never to leave all other possible efforts to raise the condition & morals of the soldier.

Did you ever talk over the subject with Dr Sutherland?

I have been at the Br. Association,[1] on the invitation of Sir W. Armstrong (whom I greatly like, he is a most simple & excellent man & a man of genius), where I saw signs of your labours in the shape of a serious debate about the health of the army in India. That was a great service, to have brought that question full in view before the public. I cannot help thinking that the morality of the army is a subject on which Gladstone is likely to be very impressible, if a way could be found of getting at him.

Our friend, Sir C. Trevelyan, has been making some suggestions about the Competition for Writerships.[2] They do not appear to me to be judicious. I think he is too fond of picking up the tree to see whether it is growing....

25

Private

Address Oxford
Sep. 15 [1863]

Thank you much for the paper which I have carefully read.[1] The disease appears to be wonderfully capricious, as well as destructive. I quite agree with you in thinking that the police system should not be introduced unless there is clear proof that this terrible scourge can be, if not suppressed, at least in a great degree alleviated by such measures. And I don't suppose there is such proof. But I don't think I agree in the moral objection—I cannot see that you legalize vice by bringing a vicious thing under the control of the law. About the medical part of the subject I never meant to express an opinion. The disease appears to be increasing terribly, and I believe we should err in expecting that, however it is to be met, it can be adequately met by an improvement in morality.

I know you think this 'hideous': and from a Clergyman? I am sure that will never alter my opinion of you & of your work. But I feel that as you write to me in great kindness & confidence I ought to say in reply exactly what I think: partly because there is use in hearing two sides of a question & also because I cannot do otherwise....

26

Sunday Dec. 6 [1863]

A young friend of mine, Mr R. S. Wright, Fellow of Oriel College, is employed by the Colonial Office to make a private report on Colonial Hospitals and Lunatic Asylums, to be extracted from certain voluminous returns. The report is, I believe, confidential & therefore not to be mentioned. He

---

[1] In 1863 the annual meeting took place at Newcastle-upon-Tyne, beginning on 27 Aug.

[2] Until 1833 the Civil Servants of the East India Company trained at Haileybury were described as 'Writers' when they were sent out to the Presidencies of Bengal, Madras, Bombay, etc. After 1858 the correct description of candidates chosen by the system of open competition, which BJ helped to establish in 1853-4, was 'Selected Candidates for the Civil Service of India'.

[1] 'Note on the Supposed Protection Afforded Against Venereal Disease by Recognizing Prostitution and Putting it Under Police Regulation' (privately printed, 1863).

describes their state as very bad. He is able & honest. His idea, which he has arrived at by the light of nature (as I don't suppose he ever considered the subject until the papers were brought to him), is that the great evils are the ventilation, drainage & situation of the hospitals: 2ndly their management by certain imaginary Boards instead of the medical men being made responsible for them.

What do you think of the last point? I should like to be able to tell him your opinions.

... He is a very able man who will one day be distinguished. . . .

...The week before last the Crown Princess came here[1] & I had a long interview with her. I was delighted with her kindness & sympathy, & her great intelligence. She talked chiefly about theology in which she seemed to have a great interest—I thought she was a genius—I will tell you more about her when we meet. No one here knows of this.

27 [February 1864]

... Do you take any interest in Oxford? We carried an important measure today, after a hard fight against Conservatives & High Churchmen.[1]

The effect of the measure is to release from the study of Classics &c., at the end of a year & a half, those who are willing to be candidates for honours in Modern History, Natural Science, or Mathematics.

The Education of this place is wonderfully altered & improved. The open fellowships & scholarships are reanimating the dullest colleges. On the other hand, there is a religious want which remains unsupplied, except in the worst way by confessions & Sunday Evenings at Dr Pusey's.

28

Balliol College
Oxford
[March 1864]

... I think the Oxford Convocation were quite right in not endowing the Greek Professorship,[1] as if I had got the money I intended to have done all the mischief that I could with it: (I had a plan for having subsidiary classes). I mean to do mischief still & to provide the means by writing. But this I only mention to you.

... I shall be glad to be rid of Plato (though he is a good friend to me). I have also got on hand the supervision of a new scheme for editing Greek Classics at

---

[1] Victoria. She came at the suggestion of A. P. Stanley and Morier; *AC* i. 342.

[1] The examination statute, see above, No. 22, n. 3. Convocation by 281 votes to 243; W. R. Ward, *Victorian Oxford* (1965), pp. 222–3.

[1] See above, p. xii. A proposal by Pusey that the University should endow the Chair with £400 p.a. on the understanding that it 'shall be held to have pronounced no judgement on his writings, in so far as they touch the Catholic Faith' passed Congregation, but was rejected in Convocation on 8 Mar. 1864 by 467 votes to 395.

the University Press.² This is a good thing, as I am enabled to set young men to work when they cease to be regular pupils.

[*Postscript*]

Have you seen 'the life of Blake'³
    'Pictor Ignotus'⁴
    very interesting
    or Froude's new volumes⁵
    or Kirke's Charles the Bold⁶
    or the life of Ulric von Hutten⁷

29   [*before* 17 April 1864]¹

... I think we may trust God to give us his own calmness and clearness on any great occasion, such as this is. I hope you will inspire G[aribaldi] for the future and not pain him too much about the past.² Ten years more of such a life as his might accomplish anything for Italy in the way of military organization and sanitary and moral improvement—if he could only see that his duty is not to break the yet immature strength of Italy against Austrian fortresses.

I think we must allow great men to be very different—Cavour for one use and Garibaldi for another—both of them almost enemies in life and yet both of them to be regarded from a higher point of view as carrying out a common work. I am not disappointed in Garibaldi for I do not expect from a man of genius who is impressible, a strong will. There are many ways and many instruments by which the world is carried on.

I should have been sorry if you had not seen him. I am sure you can do him good—if you can only make him see that more and something of a different kind is required of him in the remaining years of life. I sometimes think that in one point, the expedition to Naples, the foolishness of G. was wiser than the wisdom of Cavour.³

---

² In May 1863 the University Press set up a School Book Committee. P. H. Sutcliffe, *The Oxford University Press* (1978), pp. 19–20. As Vice-chancellor from 1882–6, BJ was still pursuing the plan 'for issuing a series of Greek texts which should take the place of the ill-printed books in use at school'; *AC* ii. 222.
³ Alexander Gilchrist, *Life of William Blake* (2 vols., 1863).
⁴ BJ is referring to Blake, and picking up the theme of Gilchrist's book.
⁵ J. A. Froude, *History of England from the Fall of Wolsey to the Death of Elizabeth* (12 vols., 1856–70), vols. vii and viii (1863).
⁶ J. F. Kirk, *History of Charles the Bold, Duke of Burgundy* (3 vols., 1863–8).
⁷ D. F. Strauss, *Ulrich von Hutten* (2 vols., 1858–60).

¹ BL Add. MS 45783 fos. 19–20.
² Garibaldi called on FN on 17 Apr. 1864; *Cook*, ii. 90 n.
³ A reference to the conquest of Sicily and Naples by Garibaldi's irregular Army in 1860, and their subsequent incorporation into the Kingdom of Piedmont.

30
                                                            Askrigg
                                                            nr Bedale
                                                            Yorkshire.
                                                            [July 1864]

    I am afraid that hardworking persons are very bad correspondents, at least I know that I am or I should have written to you long ago, which I have always a pleasure in doing. But Plato who is either my greatest friend or my greatest enemy, & has finally swelled into three large volumes (you will observe that I am proud of the size of my baby) is to blame for preventing me.[1] This place at which I shall be staying for about five weeks longer is at the head of Wensleydale, high among mountains in a most beautiful county & what I think adds greatly to the charm of the county, very pleasing for the simplicity & intelligence of the people. Among the enjoyments which I have here which, notwithstanding Plato, are really very great, I cannot help remembering you at 115 Park Street. I wish you could contrive to see something more of the sights & sounds of nature. You will never persuade me that your way of life is altogether the best for your health, any more than I could persuade you into Mr Gladstone's doctrine of the salubrity of living over a churchyard.

    ... What do you think of the great debate?[2] I read it with disgust—all these splendid orations are intended to gloss over the great mismanagement of the Ministry, which would have been still greater had the opposition been in office. I think that it is no use to deny that England is humiliated, but we shall soon recover our self complacency & time will heal the loss of prestige in Europe. The War would have been a Gunpowder plot which would have blown us all up. Also, I cannot bear that we should be spouting at the time when the Danes are dying. The neutrals in politics like Mr Cobden are the only people who have gained by this parliamentary battle. Yet they are not right. One good will probably result from this debate: we have been saved, so as by fire, from a war this time. But without this humiliation we could not have been saved another time—say, if Belgium falls to France, or some contingency of the sort occurs. The debate has enormously increased the sense of the responsibility of going to war. A friend of mine, in whose judgement I place confidence, assures me that one result of this war will be that France will *not* get the Rhine provinces. The reason is the strength of the Prussian Army, which is said to be as good an army as ever was seen, and could be raised in a short time to 700,000 men. ...

---

[1] *The Dialogues of Plato* finally appeared in 4 vols. in 1871.
[2] When Prussia and Austria invaded the Duchies of Schleswig and Holstein the British Government encouraged the Danes to resist, without, however, taking any effective action to help them. On 4 July Disraeli moved a vote of censure upon the Ministry, whose majority was reduced to eighteen.

31

Pitlochry N.B.
[September 1864]

... I perceive that you have effectually stirred the India Sanitary Commission[1]—Do you mean to do as much as that every year? I see no limit to what you may accomplish if life is spared. I am always very ambitious for you.

I don't know whether one colours objects with one's own vision, but I sometimes think that the state of religion in England gets worse & worse. The very idea of the truth is becoming ridiculous, & more & more, religious teaching is losing its moral character. The two great parties which really could say 'Rise up & walk' in the last generation, hardly have any moral purpose at all. The effervescence of their spirituality has passed away, & cunning & activity & political tactics have filled up the vacuum. Build Churches, fill them with Low Church Ministers, or set up the Authority of the Church—that is the great end. One healing word of the evils of mankind, one voice in behalf of truth among the so called orthodox clergy, I cannot hear. I am rather afraid that the Established Church, which has many advantages, rather increases the evil—you have not the chances of Dissent.

I often feel that I should like, if I could, to write about this. What seems to be wanted is a restoration of natural religion, not in the narrow, abstract sense, but as based on the past history of man, and as witnessed to by conscience & fact, & supported by our first notions of a Divine being. Natural religion should so leaven & penetrate Christianity (without the word natural religion ever appearing), that the doubtful points of fact & doctrine in Christianity should drop off of themselves. Unitarianism & German theology have both of them, in different ways, a zeal for Criticism & for truth which is very commendable. But neither of them have ever found a substitute for that which they were displacing. They have never got hold of the heart of the world. The attempt to show the true character of the Pentateuch & the Gospel History is very important negatively. But it does nothing towards reconstructing the religious life of the people.

This is a farm house in which I am writing (by the way the farmer told me this morning that the Corn Laws was one of the very worst acts ever passed. Does not that show intelligence in a small Scotch farmer—he puts his trust in beasts). I was going to say before this parenthesis that it is full of religious books of the worst & most unmeaning kind.... The people's ways seem to be honest enough, so I suppose that they are not much affected by them. Still a great opportunity seems to be utterly lost in the education of the common people. Half the books that are published are religious books, and perhaps 19/20 of those which have any moral or religious purpose—And what trash this

---

[1] In 1864 FN published *Suggestions in Regard to Sanitary Works Required for Improving Indian Stations, Prepared by the Barrack and Hospital Improvement Commission*. In leading articles on 24 Aug. (6ab), 27 Aug. (11bc), and 31 Aug. (12bcd) *The Times* gave prominence to the point that the death rate among soldiers was seventeen per thousand in the UK and sixty-nine per thousand in India.

religious literature is! Either formalisms or sentimentalisms about the Atonement, or denunciations of rational religion, or prophecies of the end of the world, explanations of the man of sin, the little horn, & the number of the beast[2]—even these last are no inconsiderable portion of English literature.

People sometimes say to me, 'Ah, you don't mind raising a blister occasionally, but you won't tell us what you think'. If you won't think me very egotistical I will tell you why I have as yet been able to do so little on these subjects. First of all because I know that it is very doubtful whether I could in any degree succeed in working them out, & I certainly could not succeed without entire health & rest, & a good deal of reading & thought. But then at present I have the translation & edition of Plato on hand, & besides this my pupils: in the last is a perfectly unlimited field, & when I see men passing through College or in the University, to whose course I might have given a twist in the right way if I had only had time or energy, I feel very strongly the responsibility of this. And the result is that I cannot possibly add a third object to the two which I have already. But when Plato is completed, if I live, I shall try schemes of another sort.

Have you got Tennyson's new volume?[3] Please to study, if in an hour of melancholy so much the better, 'The Northern Farmer'. It is one of the most humorous things ever written. 'Boadicea' is also very fine & wild—'Enoch Arden' is a beautiful thing—'Aylmer's Field' is very powerful & beautiful in parts, but it is obscure. Curiously enough he is perfectly unaware of his own obscurity & cannot be made to see it.

I wish you knew him. I consider him to be one of the best of friends—the most stubborn & faithful. I suppose some idea of him may be formed from his poetry, but there are other things about him of which no one would have any idea from his poetry—his great strength of will & common sense are very unlike the popular conception of a poet—of course he has the sensitive, irritable temperament also, with pains far greater than his pleasures. I think he has no pleasure at all from popularity, but the deepest sense of injustice when he is attacked.

The American War drags its length along—What a curious thing it is—A war, as I think justifiable almost on both sides, at any rate excusable, has become the most fatal & interminable of evils....

32

Balliol College
Oxford
[October 1864]

I send you some pamphlets which you may like to see, including a book of Polish travels which is written by a pupil of mine.[1] I don't think the book,

---

[2] 2 Thess. 2: 3, Dan. 7: 8, Rev. 13.
[3] *Idylls of the Hearth*, later called *Enoch Arden* (1864).

[1] W. H. Bullock, *Polish Experiences During the Insurrection of 1863–4* (1864).

though it contains some pathetic narratives, is worth your reading (too much gossip), but I want you to look at the poem of Krasinski[2] at the end—That touches a chord far deeper than ordinary poetry.

I sometimes wonder that a poet does not understand that he ought to be a prophet. But no English poets seem to have felt this. They have art & sentiment & imagination, but no moral force. Our dear friend Clough had a touch of something that might have been great had he been in other circumstances. There is no one whom I oftener wish for back again....

33   Balliol College
Oxford
Nov. 4 [1864]

I write a line to thank you for your most kind & welcome sympathy.

The vote to which you refer is of no real consequence to me.[1] It is now eight years since the question was first stirred, & nearly ten years since I began to work the Professorship. Latterly, I think I have spent nearly 100£ a year in getting assistance to do what I could not do myself. More money would not help to get rid of any other part of my work.

... I wonder whether you will be interested to hear what greatly interests me: that Newman is coming back to Oxford.[2] I am not sorry for this; it will make the battle a much more real one—though I fear that in the present excitable state of the Atmosphere many undergraduates will catch the Roman Epidemic.

34   Balliol College
Oxford
Nov. 20, 1864

I write to thank you for the paper on Indian Sanitary matters[1] which I read with great interest.

It is very good & very effective. May I make a criticism on the style (which is, perhaps, very impertinent)? I would not use 'stimulants' in writing: they don't give real strength.

[2] '*Resurrecturis*', a poem from the Polish of Sigismund Krasinski (1812–59).

[1] On 31 Oct. 1864 a new proposal to raise the stipend of the Regius Professor of Greek to £450 p.a. was defeated in the Hebdomadal Council.

[2] Soon after the publication of *Apologia Pro Vita Sua* (1864), Newman was offered a site running from St Giles to Walton Street and costing between eight and nine thousand pounds. 'Newman's idea was to secure it and re-sell for schools, a convent of teaching nuns and other charitable foundations, perhaps a Catholic College.... He had hopes of an Oratory, but no definite plans.' Meriol Trevor, *Newman, Light in Winter* (1962), p. 348.

[1] A reprint (Nov. 1864) with a new preface of FN's *How People May Live and Not Die in India*, a paper read at the Edinburgh meeting of the National Association for the Promotion of Social Science in 1863.

I send you one or two books: (I hope you have got Consalvi's Memoirs)²—I don't think the volume of Napoleon which I send looks so interesting as the account in the Times led me to expect.³ Will you let your servant return it to me (only the Napoleon) in a week or ten days?...

35

Balliol College
Oxford
Dec. 4 [1864]

Will you let your servant return me the Napoleon's Correspondence (nothing else)? The book comes from the Oxford Union which is so uncivil as to demand it.

I don't think I should agree with you about Napoleon I or Nap. III. I would rather not judge those sort of men by a moral standard, partly because they are really different, and also because their moral character is never present to me. I look upon them with a sort of awe as men who have done great evil, yet far greater good to their species—My feeling is expressed in the verse of Shakespeare:

> 'You are three men 'of sin'
> (if you like)
> whom destiny
> That hath to instrument this lower world'¹

But I don't expect you to agree with me.

Dizzy has been here talking about apes & angels,² & 'nebulous professors'— (I thought he meant me but the Record says that he means Mr Maurice),³ and Dizzy & Gladstone are, I am afraid, going to join in an attempt to alter the Judicial Committee. I believe they will fail, as the English people don't like clerical tribunals & the Evangelicals are beginning to be afraid of being delivered into the hands of the High Church....

---

² *Mémoires du Cardinal Consalvi* [1757-1824]... *avec une introduction et des notes par J. Crétineau-Joly* (2 vols., Paris, 1864).

³ Napoléon I, *Correspondance, publié par l'ordre de l'Empereur Napoléon III* (32 vols., 1858-70). Vol. xv was reviewed in *The Times* on 3 Aug. (10ab), and vol. xvi on 28 Nov. (8ab).

¹ 'You are three men of sin, whom destiny, / That hath to instrument this lower world / And what is in't, the never surfeited sea / Hath caused to belch up...' *The Tempest*, III. iii. 53-6.

² At a meeting of the 'Society for Increasing Endowments of Small Livings in the Diocese of Oxford', 25 Nov. 1864, Disraeli asked 'Is man an ape or an angel? Now I am on the side of the angels'. *Oxford Dictionary of Quotations*, 2nd edn. (1953), p. 180.

³ *The Record* (a Church of England newspaper first published in 1828 and incorporated in 1948 into *The Church of England Newspaper*), 30 Nov. 1864 (2b). But Disraeli's attack on 'the provincial arrogance and precipitate self-complacency which flash and glare in an essay or review' *was* taken to refer to Jowett.

36

Ockham Park,
Ripley, Surrey
until Wed. mg
[28 December 1864]

Shall I send you a happy Christmas, or New year, or something of that sort? I am afraid that there is something inappropriate in that, knowing, as I do, how very ill you are. Still you must allow me to say that in this joyful circle, in which we are keeping Christmas in the old fashioned way, I cannot help remembering you & wishing that, at this time, your labours for the good of others may be requited by happy thoughts & peace of mind, & the laying aside of all care, & good angels (whatever that means) watching over you....

My host here (Dr Lushington)[1] speaks with scorn of the idea of altering the Court[2]—Also, I gather from his tone, that Colenso is most likely, or rather certain, to win his appeal.[3]

What will the end be? That is a most curious question, which may well keep us thinking for the rest of our lives. The mere external roots of the Old Orthodoxy are so deep & tangled & knotted & widely spread, and the inner life so feeble; and so little of the appearance of a New Tree, under the shadow of which 'the birds of the air' may find shelter, that one can neither believe in the present, nor conjecture what is to come....

37

Balliol College
Oxford
Jan. 5, 1865

I send you a small parcel of books. Please not to trouble yourself to acknowledge them.

Will you look at the strange Easter Poem?[1]—quite aweful—& at the life of Spinoza?[2]

The Biglow papers[3] are only 'pour rire'.

I thought that you might like to see V's Poems (Mrs Clive).[4] She has certainly great genius, & it is a pity that she wasted her powers in trying to make a hero of a man who murdered his wife.

[1] Dr Stephen Lushington.
[2] Of Final Appeal in ecclesiastical causes.
[3] Colenso's appeal to the Judicial Committee of the House of Lords was heard between 14 and 21 Dec. 1864, and judgment was delivered in his favour on 20 Mar. 1865. P. B. Hinchliff, *John William Colenso* (1964), pp. 152–3.

[1] A. H. Clough's 'Easter Day, Naples 1849', the refrain of which is 'Christ is not risen'. The poem was printed in 'Letters and Remains of Arthur Hugh Clough' for private circulation in 1865.
[2] Probably K. Fischer, *Spinoza's Leben und Charakter* (1865).
[3] James Russell Lowell, *The Biglow Papers*, new edn., with pref. by T. Hughes (1861): 'two series of satirical verses in Yankee dialect', *Oxford Companion to American Literature*.
[4] Mrs Caroline Archer Clive published, under the initial 'V', *IX Poems*, 2nd edn. (1841); *Paul Ferroll: A Tale* (1855); *Why Paul Ferroll Killed his Wife* (1860).

Did you ever see Baur's Christenthum?[5] It is the best critical attempt, I think, that has been made to write the early history of Christianity, though exaggerated in the direction of the Tübingen school.

I have only looked at 'Samuel Vincent',[6] who was evidently a remarkable man....

38

Inglewood Abbey Park
Torquay
[January, 1865]

I see that you think I am hungering after the fleshpots of Egypt. But indeed that is not the case. I have long been aware that 'this head is so oddly constructed that, if mitres were to rain from heaven as thick as hail, not one of them would fit it': also I agree with Lord Melbourne, 'My dear fellow, would you wear such a dress as that for 10,000£ a year?'[1] Deaneries have more to be said for them. But, not having quite forgiven 'Anglicanus'[2] for deserting me, I am not going to give up the young life of Oxford (so full of hope) for the dead men's bones of a Cathedral town. Still I have difficulties; the greatest of them is perhaps Balliol College, which is to me 'the War Office', in which after all that I have done for them (forgive this boasting), I am only an inferior clerk, having to force along the inefficiency of others who hate me, & this will probably continue all my life. There is a trouble, as you get older, in having to do things by main force instead of by authority. Also, though I am aware of the great opportunity which has been given me at Oxford, & truly thankful to have such an opportunity, I feel often very uncertain whether I can use this, owing to my being tired in mind. Though I have the will, & am really not afraid, yet I believe that I never had the intellectual power which was needed for the task. These are the sort of impressions which made me 'speak as a fool' to you about sacrificing life. But I am not going to trouble you with any more such reflections. You treated me better than I deserved in replying to them. You know Carlyle's saying, 'Consume your own smoke', which perhaps has the advantage of increasing the internal heat.

I entirely agree with you about the Théodicée.[3] Instead of this sham religion, which is true neither to the facts of history nor to human nature, people must begin again and gather 1st from conscience, 2nd from experience, α) the nature of God; β) his manner of working in the world. There is a good deal of difficulty in reconciling these—not the old metaphysical difficulty but a practical one. For though conscience tells us that God is just & true & good, & though experience tells us that man has an indefinite power of turning evil into good,

---

[5] F. C. Baur, *Das Christenthum und die christliche Kirche der drei ersten Jahrhunderte* (1853).
[6] Jacques L. Samuel Vincent, *Du protestantisme en France*, with introd. by Prévost-Paradol (1860).

[1] Not traced, though the story has an authentic ring.
[2] A. P. Stanley.
[3] FN's projected work on 'the moral government of God'; *AC* i. 384.

both in himself & in the world—this hardly seems true for the mass of mankind; the stream of improvement is so narrow in the whole of the world & the whole of history, & such a mere rivulet, even in the improving countries, that instead of casting your eyes far & wide over the world, you have rather to look forward to some ideal future. And so far as religion has any dwelling place on earth, I suppose we should rather, like the Jewish prophets, get the habit of looking onwards to the future & not backwards to the past. This would be a new kind of Millenarianism founded on fact & not on the interpretation of prophecy. All countries & all individuals hang to the past, but they seem hardly to think of the future; & the tendency of the popular religion is to make us imagine that it will be at least as bad, if not worse than the present, & to be cured by the same fictitious remedies. The world are always being told that they are to make no progress in religion, & therefore they never do make any progress.

The danger in this Théodicée is the danger of being too abstract. There seems to be wanting intermediate ideas & associations to take the place of systems of doctrine in the human mind. 'God is just; God is true'. These are great 'types', as Plato would have said, in which to cast our ideas of God; but where are they to be found in nature, & how are they to be engraven in the human heart? The best chance seems to me to be through the old forms of religion, showing that this, more really & persistently than anything else, was what they meant, though often, as for example in their ideas of the divine justice, led from entertaining such an idea into a perversion of all justice in the popular doctrine of the Atonement. 'Whom ye ignorantly worship, him declare I unto you'.

The whole world & all things in it, instead of being secular & external to revelation, needs to be brought back within the sphere of revelation.

I have been staying with Tennyson, who is in great want of a subject for a poem. Can you think of one? It is worth while, if you can. I have given him one, 'the Grandmother', which has answered, & have been urging 'Galileo' upon him, but he is not inclined to this, nor to Sir J. Lawrence's Durbar. He has been amusing himself with translating passages of Homer & is not a little proud of his own immeasurable superiority to Lord Derby,[4] which indeed as poetry is poor stuff, but in facility & a sort of general ability (it was done in two summers) is as characteristic of the author as Gladstone's Book on Homer[5] is of him. The biographer of either of them may find their character in them. Gladstone reminds me of the Court of Appeal, the talk about altering which has begun to pass away.

[*Postscript omitted*]

---

[4] The fourteenth Earl's translation of the *Iliad* was dedicated to the Prince of Wales, printed and circulated privately in 1862, and published in 1864.
[5] *Studies on Homer and the Homeric Age* (1858).

39

Balliol College
Oxford
Feb. 9 [1865]

I perceive that you are truly honest, for you have returned me all my books. And I see that you know how to take care of books—and are the only person whom I know, who uses red tape.

I send you some more to be tasted only, & put aside if not agreeable. First that curious book, the Chronicle of Jocelyn.[1] Do look at this—the picture of a monastery in the reign of King John &, to a certain extent, of an Oxford College at the present day. Also two volumes of Lessing containing his paper on the education of the world, & another on eternal punishment;[2] a volume of Spinoza which has his book of criticism on the Old Testament,[3] & is a sort of anticipation of all modern criticism. Also Roper's Life of More,[4] which you probably know. I partly select my own favourites....

I sometimes wish that you would write more, or at least collect stray thoughts & materials for writing. Your writings appear to me to be very effective. Don't you think that if one has any true ideas—whether about the Army, the position of women, or about subjects of theology—it is a duty not to let them be lost?...

40

Balliol College
Oxford
[February, 1865]

I think you are the only person who encourages me about my work at Oxford. I cannot be too grateful for your words.

I write a line to say that M. Mohl is most welcome to the loan of the Persian poem[1] if he will return it in about a month. It was lent me by Tennyson, & the translation was made by Edward Fitzgerald, an unknown man of genius & one of his early friends. As he sets a fanciful value on the book, which is not to be purchased, I must insist on having it back. And in return I will ask M. Mohl to tell me the title of a French translation of some Chinese poems written by 'the Immortal who was given to Drink',[2] which Tennyson

---

[1] *Jocelinus de Brakelonda: Chronica de rebus gestis Samsonis abbatis*, Camden Society, vol. xiii (1840). The reference here is probably to BJ's own copy of *Monastic and Social Life in the Twelfth Century, as Exemplified in the Chronicles of Jocelin of Brakelond*, trans. and annot. by T. E. Tomlins (1844).
[2] G. E. Lessing, 'Die Erziehung des Menschengeschlechts', and 'Leibnitz von den ewigen Strafen'.
[3] Spinoza, *Tractatus theologico-politicus* 1st edn. (Hamburg, 1670).
[4] William Roper, *Life of Sir Thomas More* (1626).

[1] *Rubáiyát of Omar Khayyám* (1859).
[2] Hervey-Saint-Denys, *Poésies de l'époque des Thang (7e, 8e et 9e siècles de notre ère): tr. du Chinois avec une étude sur l'art poétique en Chine* (Paris, 1862). Li-Po (c. 700–62). 'He loved to loaf.... He liked to roam, and to climb mountains, but he also enjoyed the love of women, the gay company of friends, and especially the wine cup.'

has once seen & is always desirous to have—he does not know the name—nor do I.

I think that there is something strange in the atmosphere just at present. My servant came to me last night lamenting that his son had become a violent Puseyite,³ & some of our undergraduates have formed themselves into a society which they call 'the Brotherhood of the Holy Trinity'.⁴ And in another College they have a room fitted up as a chapel in which they smoke (not cigars, but) incense. Also a very fat undergraduate, who lives under me, performs his devotions about twelve o'clock at night by singing Gregorian chants. Is not this all very funny? The same epidemic which has seized Lady H. has taken my scout's boy—just as diseases attack indifferently high & low. I wonder whether this will go out like the influenza—(I heard of Lady Herbert the other day, as being at Palermo under the dominion of Catholic ideas, & devoted to good works). I hope she won't go over, for the sake of the memory of her husband & her children. . . .

I have been thinking a little about annuity schemes for the poor. They would have an indirect use as tending to break up the Trades Unions. I think you must make the scheme self-supporting, as the payment of money out of the Taxes for such a purpose seems hardly justifiable, especially when you consider that the class of annuitants would not generally be those who would, without the annuity, fall upon the Poor Rates. But might not the Government use their securities for the benefit of the poor, farming them out to bankers & money dealers, so as to obtain a higher rate of interest than is given in the funds—the Government, in short to become a dealer in money for the benefit of the poor? The times & terms of payment must be very easy—but there must be some. Perhaps any sum which had ever been paid in, if the payments were intermitted, might be allowed to accumulate at compound interest to be received so many years afterwards. I send you very crude thoughts on this subject.

41   Balliol College
                                                            Oxford
                                                            Feb. 19, 1865

I think you may like to hear that the Dean & Chapter of Ch. Ch. have agreed to give me 500£ a year.

I am very grateful to God for having given me this additional income, which I hope to make useful in some way. (I always intended to do more mischief

---

³ Presumably Knight, and his son, Matthew Knight.
⁴ The Brotherhood of the Holy Trinity was a High Church society of Oxford dons and undergraduates, which grew out of the Brotherhood of St Mary, founded in 1844. E. W. Urquhart, and W. E. Addis were members; Frederick Meyrick, *Memories of Life at Oxford and Elsewhere* (1905), pp. 173–5; F. L. Cross, *Darwell Stone* (1943), pp. 13–14; Humphry House (ed.), *The Journals and Papers of Gerard Manley Hopkins*, completed by Graham Storey, 2nd edn. (1966), p. 305.

when I got more money.) As I am very resentful against the Dean & Chapter of Ch. Ch., who voted this ten years ago, and then got this unvoted again, & now give me the money, not because I have a claim on them, but because Dr Pusey, having got himself & his party into a row by opposing the endowment by the University, gets them out again by reviving the obligation of Ch. Ch., & because the Dean is afraid of the hubbub of public opinion.

This is the last, as I believe, that you will ever hear of this matter. I am greatly indebted to some of my young friends Mr Wright & another, who, without my knowledge, hunted this matter out & assailed the Dean & Chapter in the newspapers.[1]

I hope you are pleased with the intended marriage of Miss Beatrice Smith and my friend Godfrey Lushington. He is a fine, manly, upright fellow with very considerable ability—one of whom any one might be proud, as a husband or a relative, (though grievously heterodox, both in political economy & in religion). He is certainly a man who lives for higher objects than the generality of the world, and also a man, I think, who may be safely trusted to take care of a wife.

42
                       Balliol College
                             Oxford
                       [26 February 1865]

I must write one line to thank you for your extremely kind letter, & also to say how pleased I am at your seven millions[1]—what large figures you deal in! You are quite a magnificent heiress. . . .

I was reading in Grote an account of an attempted Spartan revolution in the times of Agesilaus—one of the great objects of the Ephori was to keep the Spartan youth from getting under the influence of a woman (name unknown) who was stirring the rebellion.[2] Do you not think that woman may have been you in some former state of existence? Do you remember anything about it? . . .

FN to BJ [*drafts*][1]

43
                             [5 March 1865]

. . . My heart bleeds to see the sacrifice you have to make to 'prophecy' to Oxford. . . . I am afraid you feel as if she were wearing you out and as if you

---

[1] In response to an attack by the historian Edward Freeman, the Dean of Christ Church issued a formal statement on 18 Nov. 1864, saying that if it could be proved that the Chapter held lands specifically granted for the purpose of paying the Professor, he would himself propose to augment the salary. This challenge was taken up by C. Elton apparently assisted by R. S. Wright, in letters to *The Times* of 25 Nov. 1864 (5f) and 16 Jan. 1865 (5f).

[1] Seven millions sterling to be advanced through the Public Works Department in India for irrigation to reduce the risk of future famine.

[2] George Grote, *A History of Greece* (8 vols., 1846–56), 1862 edn., vi. 410–11: Kinadon's conspiracy.

[1] BL Add. MS 45783 fos. 21–6.

might perhaps do *more* good elsewhere, with a less amount of martyrdom. But whom has Oxford but you? And what would she do without you? It is very shocking to see a great Institution like that—the trainer of the best brains in England—actually behind the current ideas of those brains.

... I do assure you that, if I had not made myself 'intolerable' to the 'Kings' of the India Council, I never should have got my 7 millions.... Next time I want 7 millions, I shall give notice, as Lord Panmure does in the House of Lords, that I mean to make myself 'intolerable' to 'Kings', 'even pious ones', till I get it....

(Lord Panmure's motion tomorrow night is against Sidney Herbert's measures.[2] And he told a man privately (who told me), that he means 'not to spare S. Herbert's memory'. And we have no one but Lord de Grey to answer him!)

The 'irritator' of under-graduates—do you know I think that title quite Homeric? I wonder, if I were to direct to you by that title, whether it would reach you. (I have had letters from China and from native Hindoos... directed to me, the Queen of the Nurses, England.) ...

44

Inglewood
Torquay
March 5 [1865]

I think that you must be a very kind friend to wish me happier. And I *am* happier for your wish. But I must not trouble you with my troubles, & beg you not to bestow an ounce of care upon them. When I think that I have such friends as you & the Tennysons & many others I cannot reckon myself unhappy, & am determined not to be unhappy. I would like you to know that I consider no one has better friends than I have. I am quite proud of them.

Can we help one another to make life a higher & nobler sort of thing—more of a calm & peaceful & never ending service of God? ('I am quite aware that this is not the language of polite society')—Perhaps a little.

Your kind words came very opportunely to me, for I have come down here in consequence of the illness of my mother. Yesterday my sister thought she was dying & sent for me. She revived yesterday evg., but I am afraid that there is not much hope of her recovery.[1]

About what were you going to write to me? I am never too busy to read your letters, & here I have plenty of time to answer them.

---

[2] In the House of Lords, Panmure (Dalhousie) referred, on 6 Mar. 1865, to the military hospitals at Netley and Woolwich. The only fault he had found at Netley was that 'the quarters for the medical officers had been curtailed of certain appliances... all for a paltry saving of £4,000 or £5,000, which was struck off the Estimates by the late Lord Herbert'. At Woolwich he condemned the 'glass and glare' or 'pavilion' system of construction (which FN preferred to the 'corridor' system) used in what became known as 'The Herbert Hospital'; *PD*, clxxvii. 1099-107.

[1] She lived till 1869.

I don't think there is anything attractive in the book of Mormon (except here & there a passage like that 'Those who say that little infants who have not been baptized shall suffer eternal torments, shall themselves suffer eternal torments').[2] I suppose the attraction was in Joseph Smith, & temporal prosperity, & the belief that God could not have possibly left the Americans without a revelation. What a power 'fanaticism' is—which these people & some of the High Churchmen certainly have. I wish that I could be a 'rational fanatic'.

I think that you may be quite easy & very happy about Godfrey Lushington & Miss Beatrice. (I observe that you say in 'Notes for nurses' that the progress of a courtship gives great satisfaction to sick persons).[3] Godfrey's sisters & the whole family are excellent people. I think Miss Alice & Miss Fanny Lushington have really discovered in practice the secret of 'woman's mission'—They have kept a large school for many years, which they manage excellently.

45

Inglewood Torquay
March 8 [1865]

The books that are lent you produce such excellent fruit that I shall certainly send some more. When is Spinoza coming? Did I send you the Ethics? You should have them, as well as the Tractatus. . . .

I am grieved to hear of your sufferings. I am afraid that you hardly know what a good night's rest is (I hardly know the opposite, thank God). . . .

I think that you are quite right in getting rid of the fictions of the origin of evil, necessity & free will, those portentous abstractions which have ever been used to terrify the more intelligent part of the world into the belief of notions & articles of faith which have no connexion with them—'Pray, Sir, can you explain the Origin of Evil?'. 'Then why doubt the first chapter of Genesis?' When the 'ignorance of man' has only been exaggerated to the right point there is a vacuum in the mind that would be ready to receive anything—the immaculate conception or the incarnation of Vishnu. I think in your 'forthcoming Théodicée' there should be a head called 'Idola Templi', a new division of Bacon's idols. Among them I should place all the metaphysical puzzles of Theology, including the doctrine of the Trinity, & the real presence in the Sacraments. They must all dissolve before the questions: What do we know? Whence do they come? What is the fact?

To be true to human nature & to fact, Religion requires to be first:

I Spiritual—the religion of communion with God—reason to reason; heart to heart.

II Material, political, legal—the religion of Universal law in all it's gradations, moral & physical, or in transition from one to the other.

---

[2] *Moroni*, Chap. VIII, 'But little children are alive in Christ, even from the foundation of the world. . . .'

[3] 'A sick person does so enjoy hearing good news:—for instance, of a love and courtship, while in progress to a good ending.' *Notes on Nursing* (1860), p. 70.

Shall I break off with a sentence out of Jacob Behmen, which a friend of mine often quotes to me: "The place of the fish is the sea, the place of the bird is the air, the place of the salamander is the fire, the place of Jacob Behmen is the heart of God'.[1]

[*Postscript*]

My mother seems to be reviving though still in a dangerous state.

46

Inglewood
Torquay
[9 March 1865]

I think that the idea of law is traceable in all the Old Greek philosophers, Heraclitus & others. They seem to have had a sort of intuition of future knowledge—Were they not prophets as truly as the Hebrew ones, not anticipating the future of morality & religion but the future of philosophy & of knowledge?

I believe Socrates must have been the first who said distinctly that 'whatever is, is best', or, as Hegel phrases it:

> Was ist wirklich das ist vernunftig
> Was ist vernunftig das ist wirklich

and I think, as you say, that this is a very important notion & true, as you suppose, amid all the evil of the world....

I read through the Old Testament (begun Jan. 1 at the rate of 5 chapters a day, one of my tasks) with increasing wonder. 1. at its beauty & interest & moral greatness. 2nd at anybody being still willing to hang the life of man on the Inspiration of Scripture.

May I have the pleasure of coming to see you on Sunday week at 3 o'clock? My mother is getting better & I return to Oxford on Thursday.

I hope I was not intrusive about Lord Herbert & Netley Hospital. I fancy that, as you live alone, you may care to hear how matters strike a mere outsider, who has not the means of judging but only gives first impressions. Don't trouble yourself to answer this to me—in writing. You need never fear that Lord Dalhousie can seriously affect your usefullness, or damage among Englishmen the opinion of the great work which you have been able to do.[1] Please not to give yourself a thought about this, but just go on as if nothing had occurred at all—(I always like to look at things from the hateful side)—and therefore let me observe that this is far more provoking to your antagonists than the most successful answer (which may however be quite right at times).

---

[1] Jacob Böhmen (1575–1624), 'Im Wasser lebt der Fisch, die Pflanzen in der Erden, / Der Vogel in der Luft, die Sonn' im Firmament, / Der Salamander muss im Feu'r erhalten werden: / Und Gottes Herz ist Jakob Böhmen's Element.' Angelus Silesius, *Sämtliche poetische Werke* (Munich, 1949), vol. ii, p. 27. The lines are said to have stood 'unter einem Bildnis Jakob Böhmen's', but it is not clear what picture is meant. Information supplied by Dr Peter Malekin.

[1] See above, FN to BJ, No. 44, n. 2.

To say the truth, I only fear what effect in the way of excitement, a few words of the old ruffian may have upon you in your present state of health & not anything else.

Please to look at things sometimes from the comic side. This old lord is attacking a sick lady & a dead man. There is not much to be won in that encounter.

Do you ever use 'Soap'? I am afraid not enough.

[*Enclosure*]¹

1

Religion as identical with,
or as the opposite pole
of Science

2

Religion as identical with, or &c.
Morality

3

Freedom as obedience to Law

4

Faith as resignation to truth

5

The limitations imposed upon the
absolute idea of religion
α by a social state
β by differences of character,
intelligence, education

6

The ideal of Christ: 'a hidden Christ' (neither male nor female) in all purity & perfection, reconciled with the surface of things so as to work upon them within—supplemented by all modern knowledge—teaching the truth of the 19th as well as of the first century.

7

The Bible & History at sundry times, & in divers manners, the media of religious truth.

---

¹ In archival order, but may belong with No. 174 below.

47

My mother is certainly better
though terribly weak

Inglewood
Torquay
March 10, 1865

I am afraid that I am only a 'very little profit' if any, (you know the children's riddle about Samuel)—you should try 'the corrupter of the youth'—that would find me.

I should not trouble you with a second note, but I have been reading the debate in the House of Lords. Shall I tell you what strikes me?—not necessarily to impose my ideas upon you, for I do not suppose that I am able altogether to judge, & besides that, I do not know the facts.

(I am afraid this matter must pain you—partly for the animus against Lord Herbert & yourself, and for the unfairness; this is the sort of occasion on which one needs a calmness & composure, which in illness you can scarcely have).

1. I hope that you won't leave your incognito. It strikes me that would be the same sort of mistake as the Editor of the Times[1] made—It would seriously impede your influence, if you were known to have the influence.

(Did you know the Baron Stockmar, whom Sir R. Peel called one of the most influential persons in Europe? Hardly anyone in England, excepting kings & queens, knew of his existence—That was a model for that sort of life.)

2. A good deal depends on how the case really stands about Netley & Woolwich. The two important questions seem to be: Has Woolwich a bad foundation? Is Netley unhealthy? The question of expense altogether breaks down in the case of Woolwich. It must be remembered that Netley is a "fait accompli", & therefore no authorities can be expected to condemn it.

If you answer (as I hope anonymously, if at all) may I beg you to answer with facts only, & without a touch of feeling. A personal controversy would be most unfortunate.

3. About Lord Herbert may I say a word? You have the great happiness of knowing that his work would never [have] been carried out without your constant & active help. But this fact should be suppressed as much as possible. Now any defence of him by you tends to draw public attention to this, & would therefore have the effect which you would least desire. You need not fear for him: his fame will take care of itself. To adjust the proportions in which he & other Secretaries of War have, or have not cooperated, would lead to hopeless & endless personalities.

(You vex me in saying that you are worse than 5 years ago. Oh no! All that you mean is that bodily affliction at times clouds your mind—and takes away self control. May God bless you.)

[*Postscript*]

Did I ever tell you the sayings of three wise men that I have collected in the course of life?

[1] Delane.

1. My first wise man says 'Never quarrel'.
2. My second wise man says 'Never explain'.
3. My third wise man says 'Get it done & let them howl'.

No 1 is Dr Jeune, a most quarrelsome man; No 2 is Sir James Shuttleworth; No 3 is our acquaintance, Sir C. Trevelyan. I generally suppress the names....

48

Balliol College
Oxford
March 16 [1865]

... I am very sorry to hear of this event.[1] (I burnt your letter & have never mentioned Lady Herbert's name to any one. An old acquaintance of mine, Bishop Ewing, who is staying at Palermo for his health, told me about it, and, from what he said, I fear that his wife Lady Alice will go too). The great property & the family make the misfortune so very disastrous.

I like very much what you quote about prayer from Samuel Vincent.[2] Prayer, as at present conducted is an absurdity if it means praying for fair weather &c. (faith must snap in the face of universal, obvious facts), or an ambiguity of the worst kind if the theologian refuses to say, in reference to an action of everyday life, whether it is supposed to have this effect or not. There is nothing that more requires to be stated than that prayer is a mental, moral, spiritual process, a communion or conversation with God, or an aspiration after him & resignation to him, an anticipation of heaven, an identification of self with the highest law, the truest idea—the blending of true thought & true feeling, of the will & the understanding, containing also the recognition that we ask for nothing but to be better, stronger, truer, deeper than we are....

I think the human race is inspired—but how short the moments of inspiration have been. A little stream in Greece & Judea—dammed up after a century or two, is the original fountain. All other progress, or nearly all, is but the dilution of this 'water of life'. Great men like Luther & Bacon have been inspired, but how muddy the inspiration has been with the previous elements. Even Spinoza is a kind of schoolman warring against Scholasticism—(I mean in such things as his notion of substance & the importance that he attaches to mere logical demonstration)....

49

Balliol College
Oxford
March 22 [1865]

Though I hope to see you on Sunday I must have the pleasure of writing to thank you for the infinite pains which you have taken in getting me the curious book.[3] I have read some of the poems, which are very remarkable. When I have read them all I shall send the volume in triumph to Tennyson.

[1] *The Complete Peerage* gives 1865, Cook 1862, as the date of Lady Herbert's conversion to Rome.
[2] Samuel Vincent; see above, No. 37, n. 6.   [3] The poems of Li-Po; see above, No. 40, n. 2.

I would not have you grieve too much for Lady Herbert. There is no use in this. When there is so much to be done in the service of mankind, which is also the service of God, ought our feelings to be wasted in useless sorrow, especially when life is closing in upon us & the time of work is shortening & mere experience teaches us that painful things, like other things, fade into the distance? "But what is the use of prosing, amid real griefs & sorrows? 'Vacant chaff well meant for grain'". Well, perhaps: but if there is anything that will banish painful thoughts, I believe the sense that we are doing & have to do God's work is most likely to do so: "Heaven" as you once said.

The only thing worth considering is whether anything could be done to save *his* children. But, probably, these limers have caught them too. Would there be any use in trying to retain an influence over her or them with this object?

I hear that one of her Anglican perverters was Mr Liddon, a clergyman—She used to 'worship' him.

50

The Terrace
Freshwater
[April 1865]

... I am staying here with some of my undergraduates until Easter. Tennyson is delighting himself with Li-tai-pe.

I also sent a very dull packet of books of the most indigestible sort. If you are not disposed to read the Hegel, which, except perhaps to a regular student of philosophy, is not worth reading, will you look, when you have time, at the passages which I noted at the beginning (on the cover inside, I think). Hegel the Almighty Logician is a strange being—a good deal of the poet—strong, practical sense—yet conceiving all things in the form of categories, & believing the categories to be God—the first & only historian of philosophy—the great iconoclast of all metaphysical puzzles—limited to the world as it is, & finding the explanation of the present in the past, the strangest conservative-destructive, orthodox-heterodox, Christian-Antichristian system that ever was....

51

April 16 [1865]
Sir A. Grant's
Weston S. Mare
until Tues.
Inglewood, Torquay
Tues. to Thurs.
After Oxford

... I never knew any one so grateful as you are—and all for nothing. I am sure that I am the better & happier always for coming to see you.

I don't 'discredit' you about health—I wish I could. You know that any one who is in good health & has never an ache, must always seem rather 'brutal' to those who have long & weary days & nights of pain, saying 'Would God it were morning' & so on. . . .

So you think Hegel a mere 'pathological' metaphysician. I suppose that he would retort 'You must know the world first before you can act upon it'. And even very abstruse metaphysical questions are very near practice. His name is a symbol of every sort of mysticism: yet he certainly had great common sense— You know Coleridge's saying, that common sense was intolerable unless based on metaphysics.[1]

This is Easter Sunday. I don't suppose that we either have, or could by any possibility have, sufficient evidence of the resurrection to justify us in resting religion upon that, if we could be justified in resting upon anything of the sort. I sometimes think that the death, & not the resurrection of Christ, is the really strengthening & consoling fact—that human nature could have risen to that does show that it is divine. How curious it is that adversity & suffering should be the 'blessing of the New Testament', & this is probably the only Christian doctrine which is not to be found somewhere in Gentile anticipation of Christianity.

Please never to trouble yourself to answer a letter of mine when you have other things on hand or are tired.

52

Balliol College
Oxford
April 21 [1865]

Mr Wright's address is 4 Curzon St. If you feel able to write him a few lines I think he would value them & they would do him good.

He is engaged about Colonial Prisons. He says 'Does Miss Nightingale know anything about prisons?'

He is a remarkable young man—rather reckless, but with the most wonderful energy, & with uncommonly strong affection & attachment. He is a Fellow of Oriel College, & yesterday he put up & carried a motion for the admission of Roman Catholics at the College, without requiring attendance at Chapel &c.[1]

If these sort of young men can only be kept straight, they may do almost anything. Old staid Dons like the Provost of Oriel, whose repose they greatly

---

[1] '. . . for, from all we know of the *un*metaphysical Tribes of New Holland and elsewhere, a Common Sense not preceded by Metaphysics is no very enviable Concern'; *Aids to Reflection* (1825), p. 252 n.

[1] Wright proposed '"to allow persons not members of the Church of England to enter their names for admission to Oriel to become candidates for the Scholarships and Exhibitions" (so far as the Law allow of it) "and to make such relaxations of discipline in their favour as may be necessary"'; *Oriel College Archives*, II. K. 36, s.a. 1865. The clause in brackets was inserted at the instance of Provost Hawkins.

disturb, think them "wanting in reverence": that's the phrase. But without irreverence to a great many things in Oxford very little would be done.

53

Balliol College
Oxford
April 24 [1865]

I hesitate about undertaking the editorship of the printed papers which you irreverently call the 'Stuff', because I am doubtful whether they ought to appear in their present form at all. I read them with very great interest & caught up many new thoughts & notions from them. But they seem to me to be rather the preparation or materials of a book than the book itself. They show great power, but they are often unconnected; also in many passages, I think, maintaining philosophical positions, which are either untenable or require to be put in another way—e.g. the argument from a law to a lawgiver: also there are portions which either are or appear to be personal, & would give rise to great misconceptions.

I am afraid that these papers, unless greatly altered, would not do you or your opinions justice. And much as I wish & desire to help one of the kindest & noblest of friends, I think that I should be leading you into a mistake if I accepted your proposal. On the other hand, I don't like the notion of so much good & earnest thought being lost; or of no memorial of your life remaining for the encouragement of others: I think that would be a mistake also.

Could you write your thoughts or recollections on any subjects in a series of essays or memoranda? I hardly like to suggest this in your present state of torment, because it is adding another effort to tax the exhausted frame. Will you consider another proposal? You often write letters to me (& probably to Mr Mohl) on important subjects, which I very much value. What do you say to extending this a little, & writing your views a little more at length & with more of system—(not necessarily for publication—we might leave that). I would answer you, & we might let the thing follow the course of the winds. I think that I should have great pleasure in trying to carry on such a correspondence. Only, I am quite clear that in case of this or any other remains of your's being placed under my care, if I should outlive you (which is quite uncertain), they ought to appear anonymously or under the name of one of your own family. I make the proposal of the letters partly because that appears to me to be the easiest literary form & also not the least effective.

I am not at all desirous that you should give up your work, but only that you should work less painfully & more efficiently. And I am afraid that the increase of work & the giving up of opiates at the same time, has more than commonly overstrained you. This makes me recur once more to the suggestion of getting one of 'your pupils' to help you. (You are very good to let me talk to you in this way.) If you took an efficient lady away from her work for a time or for a part of the day, I think that you could far more than compensate for this by the impulse you might give her in life. She must be of the right sort, & have the right sort of quietness, temper, tact, sense. You might swear her to secrecy, but if you utterly distrust all women's powers of secrecy you might tell her no secrets. And indeed there are very few secrets in this world. How good that is at the end of 'Enoch Arden' when the woman is burning to run out into the street & tell the tale![1]

54

Balliol College
Oxford
[17 May 1865]

... I sometimes use *your* hints. A pupil of mine has a passion for public life, & having the means, is likely to get into parliament (he is a fine fellow). I turn to him, 'You are a fanatic. That cannot be helped, but you must try to be a "rational fanatic", & in time, if possible, get to be thought a "jolly fellow"'.

Did you ever know Sir Benjamin Brodie? I did, & therefore read with interest a little book[1] which his son[2] gave me, which I send. There is not, perhaps, much in it. But it has the usual merit of a genuine autobiography.

(I often try to get able young men here to go into medicine, & thus escape the perplexity of orders, & the hopeless (often) struggle of the Bar. But they are set against it. Men of ability seem to me almost as much wanting in medicine as in the Church. The great physiologist & philosopher hardly exists, nor does the progress seem to be great of natural philosophy, except in applications to the arts.)

I hope that you succeed in filling Sir John Lawrence with light & hopefulness. I wish that he saw his way to the improvement of the condition of the Services, civil as well as military. That would give him popularity, & without popularity he can do nothing. But that is not the chief reason for attending to the subject. Every year England is presenting more openings at the Universities, in Commerce, in secondary official positions, & every year India is becoming dearer & more expensive & less attractive. The consequence of this is that every year there will be a regular deterioration, both of Civil & military officers. It is not the competition, nor the age, but the character of the Service &, perhaps, in some degree, the 'cramming' manner in which the examinations are conducted, that is the cause of this.

---

[1] 'As the w⁓ ⁓an heard, / Fast flow'd the current of her easy tears / While in her heart she yearn'd incessantly / To rush abroad all round the little haven, / Proclaiming Enoch Arden and his woes.' *Enoch Arden* (1864), p. 47.

---

[1] *Autobiography of the late Sir Benjamin C. Brodie Bart.* (1865).
[2] Sir Benjamin Collins Brodie the younger.

55 [May 1865]¹

I thought you might like to hear from me after seeing Miss Carter.²

She seemed to be at peace, but she had suffered greatly. She said that her own sufferings made her think of what you must have gone through. Poor thing—she said that she had mental trial in past times and that she found had been alleviated by trusting in God, but she did not find that physical suffering could be similarly alleviated. I think that I shall always remember that pale, broken face. . . .

What shall I say to your last note? I think what Dr. Johnson said to a lady—'Madam, I think you will make a very complete rascal of me'.³ It is true that I try to do you a little kindness, and any one who knew you would think this a great privilege; you X 1000.

FN to BJ [*copy*]¹

56

34 South Street
Park Lane
London W
May 24, 1865

God bless you for what you have done for Hilary Carter.² It is the greatest comfort to her. She was so pleased with your letter. It does make a great difference to my life to know that you are in the world.

St Paul would be ashamed of me as a follower—to say nothing of our Lord. I am ashamed of myself.

But you do do me good. I wish I did you credit. I hope no one, except a Judas, will ever be as near despair as I have been.

I have not spoken to a hero of your calibre since Sidney Herbert's death and Mr Clough's and Albert's, except Sir John Lawrence.

And it is that which does me good—to know that you are in the world.

Ever yours gratefully
F. Nightingale

Are you going to turn out Mr Gladstone, by way of doing him good?³

---

¹ BL Add. MS 45783 fos. 27–8.
² Hilary Bonham Carter was suffering from cancer, and died on 6 Sept. 1865. *WS*, p. 437.
³ *Boswell*, iii. 1. '. . . as when he abruptly answered Mrs Thrale, who had asked him how he did, "Ready to become a scoundrel, Madam, with a little more spoiling you will, I think, make me a complete rascal"; he meant easy to become a capricious and self-indulgent valetudinarian.' BJ repeated this on 20 Aug.; see below, No. 69, n. 1.

---

¹ BL Add. MS 45783 fos. 29–30.
² A note on the copy says that BJ had taken Hilary Carter the sacrament.
³ There were two Members for Oxford University: at the general election of 1865, Sir William Heathcote (C) polled 3,236 votes, Mr Gathorne Hardy (C) 1,904, and Mr Gladstone (L) 1,724. The 3,850 voters polled was 'a number nearly double that polled on any former occasion'. *Annual Register* for 1865, p. 155.

57

Balliol College
Oxford
[28 May 1865]

I send you some books, one very good book among them, the works of a Saint,[1] & one very bad book, the Fable of the Bees[2]—one of those books which is condemned equally by the world & the Church; by the world because it is partly true, & by the Church because it is partly false, or vice versa—one of those books which delights in turning out the seamy side of society to the light. (Don't read it if you object to the coarseness of parts.) Dr Johnson says, 'Mandeville, Sir, never did me any harm, but he opened my views into life very much".[3] Nor do I think it a bad thing to read the book with patience & ask how much is true of ourselves (i.e. not of you but of me).

A clever & singular youth was talking to me about the "rights of women",[4] so I gave him the subject for an essay. Will you look at his production? I think it is interesting & worth reading. He does not, of course, know that I sent it to you.

Also I send you some of my translations of Plato. I have done the whole of Plato in that way. Do not read much of them for they are terribly interlined. But if you look at anything read the 'Crito' & the end of the 'Phaedo' & the 'Apology'.

The Bishop of Natal has made up his mind to return for a few years. This is clearly the right & courageous thing to do. As his income is withheld we are getting together a little money to assist him.

Plato has been a great labour. Yet I like being in such good company always. There is nothing better in style & manners, not even "in the first circles". I more & more wonder at the things which he saw & prophesied. Hardly anything important about law or natural religion which has ever been said may not be found in Plato. Mr Grote's book in 3 vols has just come out.[5] He is 70 years of age. He says "if the cerebral activity continues he means to go on to Aristotle".[6] I suspect that Lewes is right in maintaining that Aristotle's Physics have been greatly exaggerated.[7]

---

[1] Not identified.
[2] Bernard de Mandeville, *Fable of the Bees, or Private Vice, Public Benefits* (1714).
[3] 'I read Mandeville forty, or I believe fifty years ago. He did not puzzle me; he opened my views into real life very much', *Boswell*, iii. 292.
[4] Evidently Mr Williams; see below, No. 62. There was no Williams in residence at this time, and BJ is probably referring to P. T. Williams, who came up from Eton in 1867.
[5] *Plato and the other Companions of Socrates* (1865).
[6] He did go on to *Aristotle* (1872), and *Fragments on Ethical Subjects* (1876), both of which were published after his death.
[7] G. H. Lewes, *Aristotle: A Chapter from the History of Science, including Analysis of Aristotle's Scientific Writings* (1864): 'Aristotle and his followers ... failed in their attempts to establish the transcendental ideas of Physics.... Metaphysical disquisitions ... have furnished matter for centuries of idle speculation, but few beams of steady light to aid the groping endeavours of science.' (pp. 122, 127.)

[*Postscript*]

We are more doubtful about Mr Gladstone—constituency = 4000: he has 1400 promises, the others are said to have 1600, so that probably he may be thrown out—he will have had the hearty support of all liberals.

58

Balliol College
Oxford
[May 1865]

... Thank you for your letter about the Medical profession, which interested me greatly....

The Greek knew nothing of Anatomy. But somehow, by instinct or inspiration, he knew the whole man & made the most perfect forms that the world has ever seen. Is not something of this kind, or analogous to this, required in Medicine?

I think (besides the need of Statistics), that the proportion of the whole to the parts is not sufficiently considered in sciences which, like physiology, cannot rest wholly on experiment & observation. Medicine must be studied, I suppose, in minute details, but is the general idea sufficiently kept in view? I should think not, for two reasons 1. partly because physical science dreads general ideas as tending to vagueness & quackery, and 2. because to form a real general idea of a great science is an effort to which so few are equal.

The very little I have seen of doctors they seem to me neither to examine the symptoms with sufficient minuteness nor to form any general sympathetic notion of the temperament of the individual.

Might not more be done in the way of preventive medicine? I don't mean merely sanitary but in detecting & preventing the seeds of disease years before the diseases appear. At present, partly through the doctors, partly through the patients, no measures are taken until a person is found out to be in a consumption; to have a heart complaint &c.

An excellent friend of mine, Dr Symonds of Clifton,[1] who has a vast practice, says to me 'You know I am an impostor'. I don't think him the more impostor for saying this. I asked him what he thought about the general uncertainty of medicine. He said that in 9 cases out of 10 he could tell what was wanted, where an uneducated person would be utterly at sea, but in the 10th he was equally at fault. He also described to me very feelingly the difficulty which he had in dangerous cases, for he's obliged to prescribe a treatment such as the apothecary or nurse could be trusted to carry out.

I certainly think that Oxford might do a great deal more for the medical profession 1) The way to do so would be to get endowments for distinguished medical students: 2) to reduce the expenses for them & for all: 3) to adapt the

---

[1] J. A. Symonds the elder.

examinations for them. I suppose preliminary medical education is all that should be aimed at.

FN to BJ [*copy*]¹
59
                34 South Street
                Park Lane,
                London, W.
                June 1, 1865

... Is G. W. Bosanquet, now a subaltern in the 85th, a pupil of yours? He talks to his men about Plato & tells them they don't do what Plato would have them do, & don't realize Plato's ideal of what soldiers ought to be.²
 ... I should like, if you would let me, to send a little money towards the Bp of Natal's fund³—but should not like my name to be given. ...

60
                *Coll de Ball.*¹
                June, 1865

I ought to have thanked you for the £10 which I shall send under the signature of 'Libertas'.
 I believe that I was at a really happy marriage² on Saturday. The details may be left to ladies to tell. I thoroughly like & respect Godfrey, though I wish he were sounder on the subject of Political Economy. I am told that he has acquired a great deal of influence over the working men & that they have referred to him a dispute between them & Mr. Potter, the Secretary of the Trade Unions.
 I also saw poor Clough's children.³ The boy is a noble, gentle sort of boy & very intelligent. Would you like to see him some day, or would the pain of recollections be too great? If you would, I would bring him to see you, and I think they would be glad. But, of course, I said nothing about this at Combe Hurst.⁴ Never mind explaining, if you think better not. ...
 I was [a] good deal taken with Mazzini,⁵ who is a real fanatic. I sometimes think that the time will come when workmen will refuse to work except as their own employers. I cannot help hoping that there are ways in which

---
 ¹ BL Add. MS 45783 fos. 31–2.
 ² Capt. C. B. Brackenbury (ed.), *Essays and Stories by the late G. W. Bosanquet* (1870), contains something upon the education of Army officers, but does not refer to Plato.
 ³ The Trustees of the Colonial Bishoprics Fund were refusing to pay Colenso's episcopal salary.

---
 ¹ BL Add. MS 45783 fos. 33–4.
 ² Godfrey Lushington and Beatrice Smith.
 ³ Florence b. 1858, Arthur b. 1859, and Blanche Athena b. 1861 (whom Clough never saw) survived him.
 ⁴ Home of Samuel Smith and FN's Aunt Mai.
 ⁵ G. Mazzini, *The Duties of Man*, trans. Mrs E. A. Venturi (1862).

England, the Old Country, may raise the condition of the working classes as much as America the new one.

61

Balliol College
Oxford
June 12 [1865]

... I thought that I was getting too old to make a new friend, but I believe that I have made one—Mr Browning, the poet, who has been staying with me during the last few days.[1] It is impossible to speak without enthusiasm of his open, generous nature & his great ability & knowledge. I had no idea that there was a perfectly sensible poet in the world, entirely free from vanity, jealousy or any other littleness, & thinking no more of himself than if he were an ordinary man. His great energy is very remarkable & his determination to make the most of the remainder of life. Of personal objects he seems to have none, except the education of his son, in which I hope in some degree to assist him.

I can't help wishing (though I am afraid that it is a vain wish), that you would let me bring, as opportunity occurs, persons like him & Tennyson to see you. I am sure one is the better for knowing such persons & as there are not many of them, one need not fear being overcrowded with visitors. A singular one has returned to settle at Oxford, Thomas Arnold, the second son of Dr Arnold. 20 years ago he was one of the most prominent & distinguished Oxford undergraduates—then he took to social dislikes of domestic servants & other things—went to New Zealand in search of a Utopia—became a R. Catholic, which he remained for 10 years, & has now come back & is still a perfectly good & disinterested man, with a great deal of freshness & some genius. In former days he was intimate with Clough.

Oxford is convulsed by the opposition of the University to the Great Western scheme of locating 5000 people here as workmen in a factory which they are going to establish. My chief reason for objecting is that the new labourers are sure to be placed in a most unhealthy situation....

62

at M. Gaskell's Esq. M.P.
Stratford Place
June 27 [1865]

... I was very much amused with your criticisms on Mr Williams'[1] essay. I think your 'Octogamic' friend should be mentioned to Mr Froude,[2] for he certainly throws considerable light on the character of Henry VIII.

---

[1] After his wife's death at Florence in 1861, Robert Browning returned to England with his son, Robert Wiedemann Barrett Browning. In spite of BJ's interest, the younger Browning was not admitted to Balliol, and matriculated at Christ Church in 1869. The father was elected the first Honorary Fellow of Balliol in 1867.

[1] See above, No. 57, n. 4.
[2] J. A. Froude, *History of England from the Fall of Wolsey to the Death of Elizabeth* (12 vols., 1856–70).

As to 'the legal rights of women', could you not get some one to take up that cause? What ought they to be? Certainly a right to their own property, unless specially settled at the time of their marriage. A lesser measure of relief would be (in the case of the poor & it is the case of the poor which has to be mainly considered) a protecting order from a magistrate where the woman has supported her children for a year. People will say "Do you mean that the man should support his wife & that the wife should have besides, her own income?" I mean that they should come to an understanding, implied or understood, just as a brother & sister living together would do—there would be more affection if there were more independence.

It would require legal knowledge to say exactly what should be done. I merely mean to talk over the matter as one of interest. Before proposing any legal or social change one would always like to know what was the state of the law in other countries, especially in the United States. Mr Mill would have been the man to take up that question but I fear that philosopher is not likely to get in for Westminster.³ W. H. Smith & the public houses are too much for him, & I think that he is to blame for standing in a laissez faire way which makes success impossible.⁴

I talked to my dear old friend, Dr Lushington, on Sunday about Mr Forster—he thinks him quite one of the ablest men in the H. of Commons. Also he considers your friend, Mr Collins, to be 'an unconscionably idle dog'. I thought that these opinions from the outer world might interest you.

That Father of the Church, Lord Westbury, seems to be getting into trouble.⁵ I am sorry for it, for he is a much greater man than Sir Roundell Palmer, who will probably be his successor:⁶ the latter is of the straitest sect of High Churchmen, though a good man in private character, bigotted & hard....

63

Tummil Bridge
Pitlochry N.B.
July 9 [1865]

I am settled in the Highlands for the next six weeks at the above address. Will you write to me sometimes?

---

³ There were two Members for Westminster, and the result of the general election in 1865 was Hon. R. W. Grosvenor (L) 4,534, J. Stuart Mill (L) 4,525, W. H. Smith (C) 3,824. Smith (1825–91), the newsagent, was elected for Westminster in 1868.

⁴ Mill refused to canvass.

⁵ The Lord Chancellor resigned in 1865 after two irregularities were uncovered. (1) He had allowed the clerk to the patents, who had misappropriated public money, to retire with a pension, and replaced him by his own son, Mr Slingsby Bethell. House of Lords Select Committee report *PP* (1865), ix. 1, and xliii. 495. (2) He was supposed to have manœuvred in order to create a vacancy for his son, Hon. Richard Bethell, in the Court of Bankruptcy at Leeds. House of Commons Select Committee report *PP* (1865), ix. 413, and xliii. 465.

⁶ Westbury was succeeded by Lord Cranworth.

... I think it of great importance that you should retain any personal influence you can over Mr Gladstone or Mr Villiers or Lord Stanley: I am sure that Mr Gladstone or Lord Stanley would be very accessible to you. But you must not expect too much from them, or be too much worried or disappointed about them.

Having a sort of sympathy with clever rogues, I thought I would write and thank Lord Westbury for taking up my cause a year ago (which I had never done before). I send you his answer which is rather touching &, like himself, about half-sincere. 'Nothing in his life became him like the leaving of it'[1] as I hear people say. I believe he has a future still. I think the ministry wanted to get rid of him; their hangers-on abuse him, but the general public rather regret his fall, with the exception of the attorneys & the Clergy, who are chuckling over him. Lady Russell told me that he was such a liar that you could not believe a word he said, but as he signed a round-robin against Lord John after the Vienna Conferences,[2] probably the excellent lady is not perfectly impartial. People like Louis Napoleon & Lord Westbury can only be judged by their public acts; the lies that they tell, & the lies that are told about them, make any other criterion impossible.

FN TO BJ [*drafts*][1]
64

34 South Street,
Park Lane,
London, W.
July 12, 1865

My deepest reverence, my warmest sympathy are yours.

If you were happy, I could part good friends with life, after all—tho' that this world is hell; that is, the lowest place in God's universe, I do assure you—[on the best authority].

I thank you very much for the books—& especially for the sermons. I will keep Spinoza for a [n unreasonable] time—as you are so good as to wish it. But what is the use of making it mine? My heirs are the War Office clerks—Not even my "pupils" would take anything from me, if they knew I read Spinoza. One of them[2] wrote to me 12 pages beginning:—"How is it that while no one denies your philanthropy, every one doubts your Christianity?"—to which I answered, with the utmost sincerity, that she was quite right in thinking me a very poor follower of Christ. And we have been the best of friends—& she made me dispose of her life. And she is now Matron of one of the largest & poorest & hardest Nursing Establishments in the Kingdom. [Do your pupils

---

[1] 'Nothing in his life / Became him like the leaving it'; *Macbeth*, I. iv. 7–8.
[2] In 1855.

[1] BL Add. MS 45783 fos. 35–44.
[2] A note identifies Agnes Jones.

write to you in that way? Or is this exclusively feminine? Perhaps we have found out the "difference" between men & women.]

You are quite right in what you say of me. I mar the work of God by my impatience & discontent. I will try to take your advice. I have tried. But I am afraid it is too late. I lost my serenity some years ago—then I lost clearness of perception, so that sometimes I did not know whether I was doing right or wrong for two minutes together—the horrible loneliness—but I don't mean to waste your time. Only I would say that my life having been a fever, not even a fitful one, is not my own fault. Neck or nothing, has been all my public life. It has never been in my power to arrange my work. No more than I could help having to receive & provide for 4000 patients in 17 days (in the Crimean War, and how easy that was compared with what has happened since!). Could I help—in the two R. Commissions I have served, in the 9 years I have served the W.O.—exclusive of the Crimean War—my whole life being a hurry: if the thing were not done to the day it would not be done at all. Nursing was a good apprenticeship. Patients won't wait to die, or better, to be made to live, and operations won't wait till I am less in a hurry. And my whole W.O. work has been of the same kind. . . .

You can't think how pleased I was with poor Lord Westbury's letter. They have been very hard to him—a man with such an immense weight of responsibility, besides his Courts, & who has done so much good. He made a great mistake. But it was not what Hunt said it was. It was not what Bouverie said it was.[3] And now the Ho. of C. pass a vote of want of confidence in him. It was not for his vices but for his virtues they have "no confidence" in him. The religious question is at the bottom of their want of confidence—& the electioneering question at the top. The opposition wanted to shew with what pure hands they went to the poll. And then the Liberals had to bid against them for high mindedness. Only Ld Palmerston stuck firm. You say truly: Ld Westbury is but half sincere. But how many of the majority against him were even "half-sincere", do you suppose? Do you think they were really in a flame against "corruption"? One of them, a Liberal & one of the most high-minded was telegraphed up to London by a Q.C., his brother, who had returned Lord Westbury for Aylesbury[4] & was angry because the Chancellor had done nothing for him. [He told me this himself.]

In 6 or 8 months, I prophesy, the Ho. of C. will be ashamed & sorry for what it has done. And I don't believe but that nearly every Chancellor has been *worse* than Lord Westbury. And none of them but believe it too in their hearts. . . .

---

[3] G. W. Hunt, (C) Northants, came close to accusing Westbury of being personally corrupt, and E. Pleydell-Bouverie, (L) Kilmarnock, accused him of dereliction of duty and lack of discretion. *PD*, clxxx. 1045, 1116.

[4] The QC was F. Calvert, who was elected for Aylesbury in Dec. 1850. He was unseated, and was succeeded by Richard Bethell, later Lord Westbury, in Apr. 1851. Calvert was the brother of Sir Harry Verney.

65
                                                        Tummil Bridge
Pitlochry N.B.
July 23 [1865]

... I would not have you suppose that I am unhappy. I must fight a great deal more—that, as I think you will agree, is the sovereign remedy for all evils. I mean to have a real battle with the 'Hebrew Conservative'[1] when Plato is finished.[2] There is so much to be done, especially at Oxford, & life is so short.

    I am pleased with the Election: the new Parliament will certainly be a great improvement on the old one.[3] One election gives me individually great pleasure: my dear friend Arthur Peel has got in for Warwick.[4] He is the youngest son of Sir Robert Peel & almost, I suppose, unknown to the public. But I have always thought very highly of him. He has a sort of combination of simplicity & ability which is very rare. Also I am very glad that Mill has got in, & in general, that the Metropolitan districts are so well represented.

    I hardly know whether to rejoice or not at Gladstone's departure. I see the Hebrew Conservative is at him, trying to fling his toils round him, declaring 'that he is faithful to his Church & his God'. I suppose a great conflict of Romanism & Radicalism, Aristocracy & Plutocracy, Manchester & Oxford is going on in the mind of that distinguished man. They will tell him that now is the time to show that he is a true son of the Church. On the other hand, I see Mr Gladstone already begins to talk about Oxford 'enlarging her borders'. There is more, I think, to be said for the supporters of Mr Hardy than at first sight appears. They care little & know little about Commerce, but they say of Mr Gladstone—they neither want his Popery nor his Radicalism—nor his uncertainty....

    I don't think that there is any reason to fear that the Elections will be less disorderly when women are admitted to the franchise. An Irish friend of mine[5] said to me: 'I always go to Elections in a mackintosh'. I said 'Why'? 'Because the women spit at us.' (Excuse not a very nice story). I really think that Belfast & the county of Dublin ought to be disfranchised. The Orangemen are barbarians.

    I see that you are disposed to quarrel with me about L. Nap. My view about him is that, granting the criminality of the coup-d'état, the corruption of the Government, the profligacy of the Court, still we are indebted to him for having curbed Russia, for having liberated Italy, for having saved us from a war with Germany & from an invasion of England. Don't you feel some gratitude for all this? His Government presses hard upon the literary & bourgeois class, who have been used to talk & govern under Louis Philippe, but he has done

---

[1] Pusey.
[2] Plato was never 'finished', but was always being corrected and revised: 1st edn. 1871, 2nd edn. 1875, 3rd edn. 1892.
[3] Liberals 367, Conservatives 290, Liberal losses 33, gains 57; *Annual Register*.
[4] Warwick, two Members, G. W. J. Repton (C) 342, A. W. Peel (L) 315, E. Greaves (C) 297.
[5] Possibly J. Ffolliott, see *AC* i. 109, 136, and *Letters*, 219.

more than any previous government for the ouvrier class. I must add that he has given France an instalment of free trade & rebuilt Paris.

I don't think my pupils ever address me in the way that you describe. But some of them get wafted off to the Confessional & then no amount of personal kindness or obligation weighs a feather against their fanaticism. They lose all sense of loyalty or regard. This is one of the unpleasantnesses of Oxford at present. I think the best way is to ignore it & treat them as if I did not know that they go & repeat what I say to Pusey & Liddon. When they have thoroughly taken the disorder, they really are such fanatics that they know not what spirit they are of. Some of them will become Romanists & then, perhaps, they will become liberal. Any Catholic direction would be far better than they get in Oxford....

66

Tummil Bridge
Pitlochry N.B.
July 30 [1865]

Shall I make a few *ignorant* objections to your land house freehold scheme?

If I understand rightly the intention is α) to give an easy or parliamentary title to land in towns or the suburbs of towns which is used for the purposes of building: β) to prevent the ownership of the land & of the house from parting company.[1]

When you say 'for the future' I conclude that you only mean the plan to apply to fresh land which is taken in for building purposes. This of course, though necessary, enormously limits the operation of the plan, for the working man would only be able to buy land on the outskirts of large towns, & this would probably be too far from the place of his work.

1. I suppose the parliamentary title which is to make land for this purpose as easily marketable as the funds, means that you would limit the power of making settlements or other engagements on land of a certain description. You cannot say 'I will sweep away all these engagements';—and if you allow them to remain then the difficulties about title, except those artificial ones which the perversity of the lawyers may have made, will remain. The Irish Encumbered Estates[2] is a different case, because there you simply divided the property among the people who had claims upon it. And thus, even as to establishing the title until present engagements, entails, &c. were cleared off, the land which you want to except would be in the same difficulties as any other land.

2. I don't doubt the advantage of an English working man having a 'Castle of his own'. But do you think that the difference is very great between his having

---

[1] In the nineteenth century the ownership of the land on which a house was erected often remained in different hands from the ownership of the house itself.

[2] The Irish Encumbered Estates Act of 1849, 12 and 13 Vict. c. 77. See W. L. Burn, 'Free Trade in Land: An Aspect of the Irish Question', in *Transactions of the Royal Historical Society* (1949).

a lease for 99 years & his having the fee-simple? Is not that a long enough time to induce him to make any improvements, & the ground landlord will make him keep the house in repair. The bad, wretched tenements are those where there is no lease or, at least, where the occupant has no lease. . . .

It seems to me that this is a very entangled question. . . .

Why are you so hostile to the great Sir Roundell? I always think that "he is a prig, & a bad prig", as Dr Johnson said of Mr Harris who wrote the Hermes.³ But I have no reason for thinking this (except a strong impression that it is probably true), & therefore I wish you to have more Christian feelings towards him.

I hope you won't be discouraged at my objections to the land scheme, which are made in a good deal of ignorance & with as much experience as can be gathered from having been once College Bursar.⁴ There seems to be every chance, as I think, of considerable changes being made in the Poor Law next session⁵—Will you have a hand in this?

[*Postscript*]

Some years ago I persuaded the College to adopt a plan of insuring the servants' lives. The plan was simply that the College should pay half of the annual payments. I have given notice of a proposal to extend this to annuities to those I think who are above the age of 60.⁶ Will you kindly send me if you have them a paper of the government annuities? Merely the tables.

Should you want to get rid of my books, please send them to Oxford.

I must come & have a talk with you to clear my ideas about freehold land schemes when I come back from Scotland. There is no doubt that you could have a Parliamentary title but not without investigating all the claims on the land, which would be very expensive. You could not compel people to sell, & if their title was doubtful they would be unwilling to have it investigated. Also it must be remembered that you would be making a law not for poor freeholders, but for freeholders & freeholds of all sorts within a certain population. Rest assured that I will do all I can to help you in this or in any other matter.

The Established Church & the landed interest seem to me the two great puzzles of this country. One monopolizes the religion, & the other the power. I cannot see why the condition of the labouring classes in this country should not be as good as in America, for surely their labour is as valuable. The accident of their having boundless land ought not to make the difference in a well-ordered state of the world. I think a combination of Mr Mill, Mr Gladstone

---

³ James Harris, *Hermes, or A Philosophical Inquiry Concerning Universal Grammar* (1751). 'Harris, however, is a prig, and a bad prig', *Boswell*, iii. 245.

⁴ BJ was either Junior of Senior Bursar every year from 1846 to 1856. In 1857 the Bursarships were combined and Wall, who had been Senior Bursar, became Bursar.

⁵ He was probably thinking of what became the Metropolitan Poor Law Act of 1867, 30 and 31 Vict. c. 6, which introduced the 'Hospital and Asylum Rate' favoured by FN. *Cook*, ii. 123-39.

⁶ CM 12 Oct. 1865: 'That all Bedmakers hereafter appointed be required to subscribe one half of the annual sum necessary to purchase a Deferred Annuity of not less than Thirty Pounds a year, becoming payable at or about the age of Sixty years.' The object appears to have been not just to enable, but to compel them to retire.

& some expert conveyancer should take up the subject. I believe the landed interests are getting weaker—the farmers are beginning to sever from them as the late elections show: they are getting sulky about the Game Laws & want hares to be regarded as vermin. . . .[7]

67

Tummil Bridge
Pitlochry
Aug. 7 [1865]

. . . I have often felt what a wreck & ruin Lord Herbert's death must have been to you. You had done so much for him & he had grown so rapidly, in himself & in public estimation, that there seemed to be no limit to what he might have effected. He might have been one of the most popular & powerful prime ministers in this country—the man to carry us through the social & ecclesiastical questions that are springing up. And you would have had a great part in his work & filled him with every noble & useful ambition. Do not suppose that I don't feel & understand all this—(And you might have made me Dean of Ch. Ch., the only preferment that I would like to have, & I would have reformed the University & bullied the Canons). But it has pleased God that all this should not be & it must please us too, & we must carry on the struggle under greater difficulties, with more of hard & painful labour & less of success, still never flinching while life lasts.

Let me tell you two little things. About two years ago I was staying at Mrs Grote's. Mr Lowe was there talking about Lord Herbert & his administration. He said that he did not think that he had done altogether well in his use of patronage, but that he could not be too much praised for the improvements that he had introduced in the condition of the soldier. Mrs Grote said 'That was Miss Nightingale'.

I have a very kind & intelligent servant at Oxford[1] who sometimes takes parcels addressed to you. The other day he began talking to me: he said 'I should say, Sir, she was more of a man than most of the people who went to the Crimea'. These are but trifles; a hundred such things are said constantly about you, but I thought you might as well have them to remember on lonely days & weary nights. There is something very soothing in knowing that a great number of persons are attached to you. And the common people would be wonderfully attached to you if you could let them know of your existence a little more.

I am stupid about the land-scheme. I don't see how you can accomplish any important object without getting rid of leases or how this is possible: I know that you can have registration if you like. But is it not registration if you don't

---

[7] The game laws were not really modified until 1880, 43 and 44 Vict. c. 47, An Act for the better protection of Occupiers of Land against injury to their Crops from Ground Game.

[1] Presumably Knight the elder.

like, i.e. in doubtful cases, that you want? I will come & have a talk about it when I come back.

A friend was describing to me a day or two ago how the freehold system worked in America. He said that there was no inducement to have large landed properties in America because 1) they gave no power, & 2) they were a great loss, because you could not [find] a tenant who would give their annual value when he could get a freehold. There are no game laws; people shoot in a friendly manner over one another's ground.

I am here with Lord Kerry, Lord Lansdowne's son, in the remote Highlands; he reading Plato & fishing, & I also reading Plato & trying to catch him who is a great fish. He is very clever & has excellent taste, but a great want of will. I like having to do with fathers & mothers about their children; in that, at any rate, they are sincere.

FN to BJ [*draft*]¹
68 [*n.d.*]

There are a multitude of writers who try to prove that there is on the whole more happiness than misery in this world. . . . I conceive that this is the view of utter inexperience. I think the Evangelical view of utter corruption and the election of a few is more in accordance with the fact . . . must we not rather say that, if it is the wish of a good God, it is a dreadful mistake, and that it bears on the contrary the marks of being the work of a Devil? . . .

Indeed, I who have lived in Hospitals, should be far from saying that *these* impress me with the strongest idea of the misery of the world. On the contrary, I have seen more happiness in these than among people who drive in parks. It is not the inequality of conditions which strikes me so much.

If you look at the faces of Ladies who drive in parks or at those of the young men which you see thro' the windows in the Clubs of St James' Street, I think they convey to you a very opposite impression from that of happiness.

It is not that this world seems to me other than the perfection of beauty: I desire no other. I can imagine no place more beautiful in heaven or on earth than Scutari. And yet, what a hell it was!

It is that if you come really to live in the world as I have, in London, in Paris, in the Army, among the Fellahs of Egypt, among the peasantry of Prussia, among the Ragged Schools . . . among the struggling, breadwinning women of England, educated and uneducated, among the brutal beggars of Rome, it always strikes you—was this world worth creating after all?

¹ BL Add. MS 45783 fos. 62–4.

69

Tummil Bridge
Pitlochry N.B.
Aug. 20 [1865]

... I must tell you that you are under an equal delusion in imagining me better than I am as you are in imagining yourself worse. I am deeply grateful for your good opinion, which is anything but deserved. But then Madam, I also feel, as Dr Johnson says, 'that you are in a fair way to make me a very complete rascal'.[1]

(Do you read Boswell? Next to the Bible, I was going to say, I have read Boswell most of any book & can always take it up & read.—I am not sure whether I have not read it more. Though, indeed, I hardly know what one admires about Johnson except his strong English character & force of common sense; love of truth & philosophy in the higher sense he had none. But there is no book so rich in human life.)

... This place at which I am staying is wonderfully beautiful; under the shadow of two mountains, purple with heather & changing in colour & feature with every change of sun & cloud, with a torrent river connecting L. Rannoch to Loch Tummil. I have found rest here & done a good deal of work.

Yet I don't think that I do agree about Earth being a Hell, either in moral corruption or suffering. There is a great deal of moral corruption, no doubt, but there is a great deal more of mere custom, routine, eating & drinking &c., after the manners & ways of other people. The mere physical misery is a good deal alleviated by custom. And already, since the days of savagery there has been a good deal of mending in the world. People want to be shaken out of the great sin of keeping the world as it is. Perhaps, when this money making has gone on a little longer, people may get tired of it & begin to try something higher.

What will become of England & mankind in the next century—in the next 2, 3 centuries is a wonderful speculation—not altogether conjectural & very full of practical interest—and possibly under the old name of the Millenium might bear a new religious motive.

I think with you that there must be an utter fundamental change in religious teaching, or in a little while there will be none at all. The Christian Church will have as little relation to any real wants of men as the Paganism of the Emperors. But as far as I have anything to do in preaching it (which as yet is nothing) I don't think that I should preach it as a New Reformation, but as the truth of the Old, partly because this accidentally suits best with the position of a clergyman of the Church of England, & also because this appears to me the best way of avoiding the truth becoming sectarian.

I wrote last week my life of Plato, one of the chapters of my book. I like Mr Grote's book[2] but I doubt whether he is right about him. First, he seems to me

---

[1] See above, No. 55, n. 3.
[2] *Plato and the Other Companions of Socrates* (1865).

to be a bad critic of what authorities are trustworthy & what are not (I am surprized at his credulity & inconsistency in places). Secondly, that he reads Plato by the light of Mr John Stuart Mill's philosophy, which certainly prevents his seeing a great many things that are really there: this is a sort of dark lantern which he turns upon Plato. He does not seem to me quite to see the real relation of things, ancient & modern, & of this I find traces in his history....

FN to BJ [*draft*]¹

70 August, 1865

Don't make a joke about your being "Dean of Ch. Ch.". If I could have lived to see you Dean of Ch. Ch. (tho' Deans are a thing I can't abide) I should have thought life worth having—Whereas now?

... And this brings me to what you say: that it is all custom & routine, & eating & drinking like other people which does the mischief in the world. More than moral corruption. And so it is. But that is just what I complain of. It *is* the routine which brings about the moral corruption.... It is because Mr. Villiers eats & drinks "like other people" that the Workhouses are not reformed. It is because Lord Westminster & the other great London proprietors eat & drink & don't look after their London properties, "like other people", (tho' they *do* look after their country properties) that London dwellings are what they are. "*Well meaning*" people are, of all others, the people I detest. If you could but exchange them for *ill* meaning people, who will do the world's work, the world would be such a gainer....

I *must* hate "well meaning" people. Pray let me.

I was very much interested in what you told me about Plato. I always read Mr. Grote's books with the greatest respect—but in perfect ignorance....

I am rather glad to know that we need not read Plato by the light of Mr. J. S. Mill's philosophy, tho' I am Mr. Mill's profoundest admirer. If ever I open his Logic, the 2nd vol., I read straight through to the end, or as long as I can. It is so amusing.

[*Postscript*]

I thank you very much for your note just received. You know what I think about your preaching. /I won't deliver you up to the Bp. of London, who says, in his Charge, that as God made you & such as you, tho' God had much better not have done it, we must put up with you.²/ ...

---

¹ BL Add. MS 45783 fos. 45–9.
² FN is interpreting somewhat loosely A. C. Tait, *A Charge Delivered in December 1862 to the Clergy of the Diocese of London*.

71

Tummil Bridge
Pitlochry
until Aug. 31 [1865]

... I certainly mean when my Plato is finished to devote two or three years to preaching, giving up my whole mind to this & publishing the sermons. (You will help me a little with ideas, won't you?—& I try to collect "stock" for myself—that is the term which cooks give to their materials for soup). I have not told this design to any one but you, & I mean to go about it as quietly as I can, putting off the more heterodox aspect of things until I have gained (if I can) some hold. Though I regard the B. of London[1] as a friend, I don't feel certain that he would not silence me, that is to say if I succeeded—if I failed no one would care.

There are a great many other things that might be done—e.g. a commentary on the New Testament, at once true & practical. This should be the joint labour of many persons. Also tracts of another sort from those which are commonly circulated among the poor.

Any religious movement should be also, like that of the Jesuits, an educational movement. And this, I think, is to a considerable extent going on at the schools: e.g. Harrow, Rugby, Marlborough, & even Winchester. Eton is the stronghold of old fashioned notions among them. And there is a great change in education at the Universities, especially at Oxford. When I was an undergraduate we were fed upon Bp. Butler & Aristotle's 'Ethics' & almost all teaching leant to the support of doctrines of authority. Now there are new subjects, Modern History & Physical Science, & more important than this, perhaps, is the real study of metaphysics in the Literae Humaniores school; every man for the last ten years who goes in for honours has read Bacon, & probably Locke, Mill's 'Logic', Plato, Aristotle & the history of Ancient Philosophy. See how impossible this makes a return to the old doctrines of authority.

The "Hebrew Conservative" has just found this out, which he ought to have found out long ago, & is going to try & upset all this by appointing what he calls a Board of Studies, who would be nominated by himself & his friends. But I think that we can hinder him, as the Tutors are almost all on our side.

I was going to say when I made this digression, that I think something needs to be done for the educated, similar to what J. Wesley did for the poor. A real religious movement among the educated would be more permanent than any revival. What is wanted just now is not preaching for the poor, but teaching in schools, better & more of it, & preaching to the clergy & to the educated classes.

---

[1] Tait.

72

Sept. 7, 1865[1]

Thank you very much for writing to me about dear Miss Carter....

Don't look upon her life as lost or wasted. We cannot quite tell what is lost or wasted in this world. Very few persons can ever be expected to carry on their lives on a systematic plan, & persons who have great gifts least of all....

73

Professor Campbell's[1]
Sept. 8, 1865

... I don't know whether I ever told you that Miss Carter once made me a present which I greatly value & which is really a very nice work of art. It was a statuette of yourself. She used often to talk to me about you with great affection & interest....

I cannot think that any one could have done much more than you have, even with all the opportunities. Especially I value most what you have done since Lord Herbert's death: before that all was much easier & simpler. Considering what ministers are, instead of wondering at their not doing all you want, I wonder at their listening to a word you say. A poor sick lady sitting in a room by herself—they have only not to go near her, & never to read her letters, & there is an end of her. And yet you seem to draw them still by some silken cords—I am sometimes afraid that you let them see that you don't respect them. And then as you probably know—Goodbye influence!...

74

Professor Campbell's
St Andrews
N.B.
[9 Sept. 1865]

I should not trouble you with a letter to day but I can't help remembering that you are sitting alone, thinking sadly about your friend.

I am sure you are right in not looking back upon the past but only to the future & clinging to that; to a future not of castles in the air, but in which so much may be done, & in which we *will do much*, if God gives us health & strength. I often wonder that the idea of a millenium is not made more of in religion—so false when converted into a dreary notion of the personal reign of Christ on earth (a very bad time for us, when the saints will punish us), & so true when thought of in connexion with the real elements of the world already beginning to move towards God & better things & full of life & inspiration to us all....

---

[1] BL Add. MS 45783 fos. 51-2.

[1] BL Add. MS 45783 fos. 53-4.

I spent a day at Cortachy Castle[1] on my way here, where I met Bob Lowe—notwithstanding his cynicism & enmity to the people I was very favourably impressed with him. He is very able & quite honest & very liberal on other subjects but the suffrage.

[*Postscript omitted*]

75 [Sept. 1865]

I am very sorry that you should be troubled again about Lord Herbert....

It does not matter to him. Why should he or any of us have fame or justice, which in this world are mostly determined by accidents?...

I think the remark at the end of Lecky's book strikes one sadly: 'that we have lost the virtue of self-sacrifice in modern times'.[1] That is true & the world has hardly seen, even in individuals, the combination of self sacrifice with modern science & reason & material improvement. If that could be revived! Mere material improvement does much for peace & comfort &c., but it cannot be mere idealism to suppose that some other improvement is needed....

76

Professor Campbell's
St Andrews
until Tues. Sep. 26 [1865]

...I go on with Plato, writing 4 pages of the introduction; this I have done every day for 2 months, making up on Sundays for the two days which I spent at Cortachy & correcting ten pages of translation. This, with my pupil, is as much as I can manage. I don't find Mr Grote improves upon further acquaintance; for this I am sorry as I have the greatest regard & respect for him. But he ...is wholly unimaginative & unmetaphysical: two defects which spoil him as an expounder of Plato. He interprets the most comical things as if these were serious & is wholly ignorant of proportions. But if a person likes to say 'Ah, you are writing another book & therefore you don't do him justice', he is quite welcome to take such a view.

I have been reading the life of W. Napier,[1] a fine fellow but narrow & prejudiced. I like him for his admiration of Napoleon. I should like to have a good quarrel with you someday about the Duke of Wellington & Napoleon. I

---

[1] Home of Lord and Lady Airlie.

---

[1] W. E. H. Lecky, *History of the Rise and Influence of the Spirit of Rationalism in Europe* (2 vols., 1865), ends: 'but when we look back to the cheerful alacrity with which, in some former ages, men sacrificed all their material and intellectual interests to what they believed to be right, and when we realise the unclouded assurance that was their reward, it is impossible to deny that we have lost something in our progress'; ii. 375.

---

[1] H. A. Bruce, *Life of General Sir William Napier KCB* (2 vols., 1864).

cannot admire the Duke out of the camp or off the field of battle, & I believe Napoleon I and perhaps Napoleon III to be among the greatest of men—more than half honesty I do not claim for either of them, but besides genius they have the power of growth & adaptation to a changing world.

[*Postscript*]

I think that you are very contemptuous to me about the Statuette. When you came neatly packed in a box & offered yourself, could I refuse you? I own that I felt a little awkward at first, but I have put you in a place where nobody sees you. Had I known your disapproval a year ago, I would have had you broken in pieces, & called Nehushtan as Hezekiah (was it not?) did with the brazen serpent:[2] anything to please you. But now I must ever keep you as a memorial of the poor artist who is gone.

77 Balliol College
Oxford
[? October, 1865]

... You know that I never had any but petty troubles in life; never a great sorrow like your's, & therefore I may seem to pour out consolation too glibly. But I fancy that words of peace may sometimes do good, & I would rather write them than speak them.

I think I am happier than I used to be, seeing better where I am going & what I mean. I am now 48 years of age & I hope, if God wills, that I may live 20 years more, & am determined that they shall be years of energy. I know how little has been done as yet—how ragged & imperfect & dreary everything is that I have done. I shall do my best to improve this. One misfortune is that I have always been overworked, which is very fatal to growth or strength. I have been necessarily so much distracted....

78 Balliol College
Oxford
Oct. 16 [1865]

I know Lord Dufferin & his Mother, Lady Gifford, sufficiently, I think, to justify me in writing him a note requesting that he would call on you. I will gladly do this, if you wish, & if you will let me know when he is appointed. But I think I would rather advise you to write to him directly & without official intervention & ask him to call upon you as being interested in the Sanitary condition of India. That is the most complimentary way—if you are not

[2] 2 Kgs. 18: 4.

deterred by 'shyness': that I suspect is the word—and also I think that, like pickpockets in a crowd, we had better not be regarded as confederates.

I swore horribly at the Master & some of the Fellows of Balliol on Friday internally but fortunately no oath escaped me.[1] Having more room than I want, I offered to take a poor & distinguished scholar into my rooms who could not otherwise come up to the University. They objected, first that he would have 1/200 of the servants of the College gratuitiously waiting upon him at Dinner; 2ndly that he would pay nothing, not for coals but for having them carried to him. At last, after nearly an hour's discussion in which I said nothing, the majority graciously consented. Is there any red tape in the War Office worse than this?...

79
Balliol College
Oxford
[October 1865]

... I am truly glad that you have had the duty of consoling Lady Palmerston.[1] How naturally people's minds turn to you when they are in trouble....

May I come to see you next Sunday at 3 as usual?...

I wish that you would write an essay on the bourgeoisie of the highest classes. What you say is perfectly true. I am not very fond of the ideal of aristocracy because, necessarily, the gift of a very few. But the ideal of Aristocracy is never attained in these degenerate days: there are no Sir Philip Sidneys or Sir Walter Raleighs nowadays. There is bourgeoise Aristocracy, fashionable Aristocracy, insolent Aristocracy, exclusive Aristocracy, withered maiden Aristocracy (believing devoutly in the traditions of the caste to which marriage & every good of life have been sacrificed), but really gentle aristocracy, the freedom & kindness of a noble nature, is hardly to be found. Lord Lansdowne was thought to have superlative manners:[2] and they were certainly good, though not remarkable for dignity or grace. I think my dear old friend Dr Lushington is the best mannered person I have ever known. I suspect there were many such in the last generation.

So you are falling out already with Lord Russell.[3] Why should an old wrinkled statesman like him or Sir C. Wood trust an adventurer like you or me (not that I seriously mean to put you & myself on a level). I believe that you will beat them all in the long run as you always have done. But then you must be patient & crafty & not die in a passion: "the longest liver takes all".[4] 'Lord! sir' as an old fellow said to Mr Rogers, 'You & I, sir, will see them (i.e. the governors of Dulwich College) all out'.

[1] At College Meeting on 12 Oct. 1865.

[1] Palmerston died on 18 Oct. 1865.
[2] The third Marquess.   [3] Palmerston's successor.
[4] 'Be brisk a while, and the longer liver take all!' *Romeo and Juliet*, I. v. 13.

I ought not to have said that about Mr Gladstone which was only conjecture, grounded on the following disjunctive syllogism: 'Every one who is zealous about religion, is zealous either for Dissent, or the C. of E., or the R.C.C. But Mr Gladstone is not zealous for D. or C. of E. ∴ he is zealous for R.C.C.' Perhaps, you will think that this, like so many other things, is just a piece of illogical logic.

I agree, however, that he will probably be saved by casuistry, & was only speaking of his internal condition. Is not the casuistical statesman a new character in history (except a very poor attempt which M. Guizot made in the same direction when he said that 'the Spanish marriages should not take place together, meaning that one would be at 10 & the other at 1 o'clock)? But Mr Gladstone is the real master of the art. Nevertheless, I hope that you will 'make love to him'.

Indeed, I am a great hater, but my hatreds are so mean compared with yours. For I only hate people who have done me a wrong, whereas you pour out your wrath upon the public enemies. I should be ashamed to tell you whom I hate, or the reasons. . . .

[*Postscript*]

I send some books for you to try. Look at the vol. of the 'Lives of the poets', which is one of my favourite books—the 2nd best biography in the English language.[5] I will send more vols. if you like this.

80　　　　　　　　　　　　　　　　　　　　　　　　　　　　Balliol College
　　　　　　　　　　　　　　　　　　　　　　　　　　　　　　　Oxford
　　　　　　　　　　　　　　　　　　　　　　　　　　　　　　　Oct. 26 [1865]

I think you are a philosopher—Can you send me five or six questions on Ethical & Political Philosophy or Political Economy? They may be quite general. The reason is that I set so many that I am afraid of their all bearing the same impress & cast of thought & I want to put some originality into them. . . .

I suspect that the Ministry will want to do something & establish a reputation for useful reforms & therefore they will probably proceed with changes in the Poor Law.

What else can they do?

α Reform the small electoral Boroughs on the principle of a more equal distribution of seats—with a 6£ franchise; leave the counties to the effect of the Game Laws.
β Reform the Irish Church, i.e. abolish.
γ Abolish University Tests.

---

[5] BJ described Boswell's *Life of Samuel Johnson* as 'the foremost biography in the English language', and went on that 'I might without exaggeration add that there is no similar book in any literature ancient or modern' (Gell). The second best biography was probably Samuel Johnson's *Life of Mr Richard Savage* (1744), subsequently included in the *Lives of the Poets*, the affectionate record of a friend with whom he had shared extreme poverty.

δ Increase and equalize the Legacy duties & abolish the Income Tax which, as Mr Gladstone will then be able to prove, is a gigantic national immorality.
ε Reform the Grammar Schools, i.e. not in their studies but in their endowments.
ζ 'Come out' in the line of good appointments. They are more likely to do anything than this. I should think that the worst appointment Lord Palmerston ever made was probably his last—that of the Reg. Prof. of Divinity at Oxford.¹ Yet I agree in the main in your estimate of that departed 'hero'. He saved us in the Crimean War. That was the great fact of his life. Even his jests we shall miss now he is gone.

Gladstone is a great deal more mad than he is supposed to be. Everyone who wishes to understand him should read his Homer. I am afraid he is always in the hands of some confessor. Is he a Roman Catholic? I don't feel certain.

Lord Russell has much more, I think, of real philosophical notions than is commonly supposed. But he is shy, wanting in tact, & has the style of a man who has never been used to be contradicted in the days of his youth; quite honest but not magnanimous. She is a good woman but not popular even with her own family, & a bad minister's wife.

[*Postscript omitted*]

81

Balliol College
Oxford
November 15 [1865]

I send you the new translation of Strauss....¹

I believe ... that we ought to be ready to look with unaverted eyes at what Strauss or anybody else has to say & accept the truth as the condition of our life without fear.

I have had B. Lowe staying with me & was very much pleased with him & I think he was pleased with Oxford which he thought wonderfully changed since he resided here 25 years ago & took private pupils. He is a very honest man, & really full of liberal sentiments; as you say he has administrative indignation. He was reading Plato & abounded in talk about the Classics. Gladstone he despised as knowing nothing but Homer. I did not tell him that I was acquainted with you, on the 'pickpockets in a crowd' principle. (I never tell anyone, not exactly because I am ashamed of you.) If he ever becomes Minister at War I think you may do a good deal with him. He has the right sort of feeling about the Duke of Cambridge & all jobbing.² He offered to take up any

¹ R. P. Smith.

¹ *A New Life of Jesus* (2 vols., 1865), trans. from the rev. German edn., *Das Leben Jhesu für das deutsche Volk* (1864).

² Lowe did not become Secretary at War, but as Chancellor of the Exchequer he was a member of the cabinet which (1) passed the War Office Act of 1870, 33 and 34 Vict. c. 17, which enlarged the powers of the War Minister at the expense of the Duke of Cambridge, General Commanding in Chief, and (2) abolished the purchase of commissions in 1871.

matter connected with the University in the House of Commons for us—he thought that a Committee would be the right way of proceeding. When I have thought more of the matter I shall try to get him to move, not about tests—that he objects to as necessarily bringing on a party struggle,[3] but about University extension, which is at present stopped by the monopoly of the Colleges. Do you know why education is so expensive at Oxford? Because the Colleges are great eleemosynary institutions.

[*Postscript omitted*]

82   Balliol College
                                                                  Oxford
                                                                  Nov. 22 [1865]

... A few days ago I was at Eton & asked about Lord Pembroke. They gave a good account of him & said he was clever, but thought he was not of a character to withstand the influences of his mother &c.

Shall I tell you how I came to be at Eton? My good friend, the Crown Princess, sent for me to come & see her. She is a fine creature: frank, generous, warmhearted, imaginative, knowing heaps of books & full of observations on life & character. Also, she is quite free from royal or aristocratic prejudices, & devoted to the memory of her father. She has a great deal of ability & can understand (perhaps in a superficial way) anything. On the other hand, she is very rash & utterly devoid of reticence; she will astonish the royal circle of Prussia (they all dine together at a family party on Sunday though many of them hate one another) by expressing her peculiar regard for Jews. Is not this funny? She used to have a faithful Ahitophel, a curious silent man but one of the most sagacious of human beings, the younger Stockmar, who took care of her, & kept her from debt & other evils. But he has fallen ill & she is left to herself now. Whatever her faults may be I think she impresses you with real goodness & sincerity.

[*Postscript omitted*]

83   Private   Balliol College
                                                                  Oxford
                                                                  Dec. 5, 1865

What are the points which you would deem desirable that the Times should urge about the Poor Law? And where can information about them be obtained?

If you could answer this question quite shortly (& without much trouble to yourself), I will copy out your answers & send them to Mr Broderick,[1] who

---

[3] Bills were introduced annually from 1863 to abolish the remaining University tests, and in 1871 the Liberal Government passed an Act, 34 and 35 Vict. c. 26, which achieved this.

[1] Brodrick.

writes for the Times, & to another friend of mine,[2] who would not object to take up the subject in the Saturday Review. . . .

84

Balliol College
Oxford
Dec. 6 [1865]

Some points about the Poor Law seem to me worthy of consideration:

First as to the rate: There is great difficulty in shifting the burdens of one parish on to another. . . . But is this necessary? Might not the rate be apportioned to the parishes on the average of the last 7 or ten years, becoming either like the Land Tax a permanent fixed tax, or a tax of so much in the pound?—the excess only (if any) of the sum required over that obtained from all the parishes which are assessed on this principle, to be paid out of a common rate extending over the whole of London.

Secondly, as to the 1. sick, 2. aged, 3. incurable, 4. mad, 5. destitute children—I suppose that you must allow humanity to prevail over political economy. Still, political economy cries aloud 'that people will not take care of their parents & relatives if they are taken care of in asylums'. . . . How can this evil be minimized? Could a formal application be made to the relatives of such persons to assist in their support, giving them certain privileges of visiting &c., & taking their relations out of the category of paupers into that rather of patients in hospitals? Perhaps this is visionary. Are we then to give up the idea of the lowest class of the poor supporting their parents, & instead of this, committing them to the State, as their mother & nurse.

I suppose that the family tie is more broken up in the towns where people are lost than in the country where they are known. Looking at the matter in this point of view only, there would be less risk in extending the general system to the towns than to the country.

3. There are great difficulties about the law of settlement, which has such a bad effect on the dwellings of the poor & on the circulation of labour. What is the way out of this? I can see none but relief anywhere & everywhere (we are speaking now of the able-bodied poor) and an extremely severe workhouse test. The administration of the Poor Law would tend to become like that of a great mendicity society, supplemented by hard labour for all who remained in the workhouse more than a night—a sort of imprisonment for a few days.

For great casualties, such as the Manchester distress or a severe London winter, I would have another agency. One of the great evils & sources of expense in the Poor Law has been the confusion of the casual & permanent.

. . . I think one may learn something of principles, & a good deal of public opinion, by reading up debates on any political or social question in Hansard. Do you ever try this?

[*Postscript omitted*]

[2] Not identified.

85

Balliol College
Oxford
Dec. 24 [1865]

Let me have the pleasure of sending you my best & kindest wishes on Christmas Day.

... I have been reading the memoir of A.H.C. Did you ever see his 'Easter Day' or the drama called 'Dipsychus?'[1] I think that they are by far the most powerful things that he wrote. You will like the book, I think.

You will perceive by the last parcel of books which I sent that I am almost at the end of my entertaining reading. There are some little books which seem to me good & which I send chiefly because they are written by the wife of an Evangelical clergyman (Mrs Bowles)....[2]

Get a book called 'Ecce Homo',[3] which is beginning to make a stir. I have only seen accounts of the book but I guess that the defect of the book (which is very powerful) is the attempt to give a picture of an historical Christ without considering the nature of the materials.

... If you were to walk abroad you would be very much surprized to see the changes in our London Churches. There is a sort of esthetico-Catholic revival among them. I wonder how many more spurious forms of Christianity are to appear in these latter days. Muscular Christianity, which was upon the whole a better form is gone out. A sagacious High Churchman whom I know thinks that there will be an Evangelical Revival, which impresses me chiefly because he says it. How strange these 'toys in the blood' are! I find myself often wishing that the Established Church were either demolished or greatly enlarged. Certainly the tyranny is very great on Education & on opinion.

Do you see a statement of Dr Lankester that one woman in about every thirty in London is a child murderess? Is this credible? If this is true I almost think that we must begin to reconsider the orthodox opinion about foundling hospitals.

I am going to stay with Mr R. Lowe before returning to Oxford, who is much pleased at having invented a new phrase, 'We must bring the butcher to the ox, instead of taking the ox to the butcher'; also much more with having found people come round to his opinion about the cattle plague.[4] I like him & so would you, notwithstanding his open profession 'that he has a bad heart', which I don't believe....

---

[1] 'Letters and Remains of Arthur Hugh Clough' (privately printed, 1865). For 'Easter Day', see above, No. 37, n. 1. 'Dipsychus' was printed here for the first time.
[2] Possibly either Emily Bowles, *St Martha's Home: or, Work for Women* (1864), or Mrs George Cranley Bowles, *Life's Dissolving Views* (1865).
[3] By J. R. Seeley.
[4] Rinderpest, or steppe murrain, an Asiatic malady brought to London by foreign cattle and carried to all parts of the country by animals sold in Smithfield market. Stamped out by slaughter (with compensation).

86

Farringford
Dec. 31 [1865]

No matter about 'The Times'. I suspect you attribute to me more than I accomplished.[1]

I think you should pray for a hard frost. The sufferings of the poor from cold touch people's feelings far more than any other sufferings, which may be much more real.

"Hook on, hook on" as Falstaff says.[2] Imagine yourself an angler wanting to bring a great fish (Mr Villiers) to land. He is jumping about in all sorts of ways, but at last he comes tired into your net.

The Poor Law Board, I fancy, have always had an objection to taking up the Pauper Child. That, the demon of political economy within them says, is Education—another department &c., & not relief of the poor: and yet the pauper child is the grown up pauper. Could you get an array of statistics about this? More than any other children of the labouring classes the pauper child requires to be raised—he is never likely to become a real working man unless this is done. You are diminishing the local rates—say that you don't put him upon the general rate. Yet you ought to get something out of the parishes as an equivalent to this—there is no reason why a single penny should be taken off the landlords of Seven Dials without an equivalent—(do think of this)—& the equivalent might be a better organized system of pauper education, under the Poor Law Board or the Privy Council....

87

I stay at Farringford until Wed.

Wed.—Saturday
Dr Symonds Clifton Hill House
Bristol Dec. 31 [1865]

Enclosed is a note for Mr Broderick.[1] Will you run your eye over it, & see whether you approve? But I don't know his address: will you look in the Court Guide—he is in your neighbourhood....

I did not know that you were flirting with 4 gentlemen at once. Really that is too bad—and then you take on so terribly when you are disappointed in love. And you are always getting jilted by somebody.

I venture to send you some notes about pauper children. Whether you get the name of a school & hospital rate, it is essential that you should get the

---

[1] Presumably a reference to a Leader on the condition of the poor in sickness, 28 Dec. 1865 (6f), 'even when the mother is not the person attacked, the labour of nursing, in addition to her other work, is alone sufficient to prostrate her', advocated setting aside a cottage in every village as a 'hospital'.

[2] *2 Henry IV*, II. i. 156.

---

[1] Brodrick.

expense of them partly defrayed out of the general rate. This will give a reason for a better & central management....

[*Postscript*]

I had written another letter to you before I got yours this mg.

88   Balliol College
Oxford
Feb. 18, 1866

I hope you will write to me occasionally as I am afraid that I shall not be able to come & see you for a month or more; the chief reason is that I have to go to Edinburgh in order to give two lectures about Socrates.[1] (I am going to make Socrates going about cross-questioning different classes of persons: divines, lawyers &c.—tell me what he should say to the doctors.) I am going next Sunday or Monday.

I should be so glad to hear that you were suffering less than when I saw you. Sometimes I think that the Doctors ought to cure you: sometimes that you ought to cure yourself, or a combination of both. I wish you would try the latter process—though the age of miracles is past I think that something might be done....

I should like to have a talk with you about Strauss some day. I don't think it is all true as criticism. But I think about 2/3 is true & I would like to get the habit of looking that in the face & still retaining faith in God & in another world. I should not have sent you the book[2] if I had thought you would have been disturbed—the book is certainly not for a sick room—nor some of the other literature that I send you. But as there are some persons who are said to be able to eat anything I am accustomed to fancy that you can read anything.

89   Balliol College
Oxford
March 7, 1866

I write to tell you that I saw your Father at Lea Hirst about 10 days ago on my way to Edinburgh.... I think that I know you at home, now, as schoolboys say. What a lovely county that is!

I am disposed to take Strauss & Renan[1] with more patience, or less earnestness than you do. I am far from thinking that either of them have contributed much directly to the moral good of mankind. But they have contributed

---

[1] Delivered at the invitation of the Edinburgh Philosophical Institution in the Queen Street Hall on 27 Feb. and 2 Mar. 1866, *AC* i. 399. The first lecture on 'The Character of Socrates' was printed but never published in Gell; the second was entitled 'The Place of Socrates as a Philosopher'.

[2] See above, No. 81.

[1] E. Renan, *La Vie de Jésus* (1863).

(chiefly Strauss) a good deal to the cause of truth, & that indirectly & in a roundabout way works round into the moral good of men. And they have undergone, especially Strauss, as much contradiction of liars as a saint or a martyr.

What is to be the result of Monday?[2] Is Gladstone going to shipwreck himself on an inanity, harping back to the old reminiscences of his Conservative & High Church Youth. I sometimes wonder how Gladstone, having his objects, can desire Reform, or how R. Lowe, having his objects, can oppose Reform. I think that if he betrays Reform he is ruined. But I cannot believe, notwithstanding rumours, that this is possible.

Will you think me egotistical if I send you my two Edinburgh Lectures & a book of Notes which I have filled during the last few months? Please not to read more of them than you find amusing & skip the notes about the University.

Also I send a book of A. Coquerel.[3] Look at p. 170 which gave me pleasure & I hope will give you.

I was pleased with the Edinburgh people, who were very kind to me. There I saw my dear old friend Mr Erskine,[4] who came out before breakfast at the age of 77 in the frost to explain to me that I had not understood perfectly something that he had said about the personality of God. Also I saw another friend of mine, Mr Maitland, called in their language Lord Barcaple, the best & ablest of the Scotch Judges. And I made friends with a great leader of the Scotch Church, Dr Robert Lee, who has introduced a Liturgy[5] & whom I heard preaching the purest religion of reason to a delighted congregation in the Ch. of John Knox. His liturgy is decidedly good & very instructive. Upon second thoughts I send it you to look at & please, if you have never read them, to read the Psalms & Paraphrases at the end, taken from the Old Scotch Version—they always seem to me to be the best & most solemn hymns in the language.

On my way home on Monday I went to see the small estate of which I told you.[6] (It is a small matter & therefore I don't talk about it except to you). I think that it is worth about 5 or 6000£ being only 50 acres, but it has a river & a fine oak wood; very pretty, & my ancestors are believed to have lived there for hundreds of years. The old gentleman who left this to me was very rich & has

[2] On 12 Mar. Gladstone introduced the Reform Bill.
[3] Athanase Coquerel, *Des premières transformations historiques du Christianisme* (Paris, 1866). In a note to a passage on p. 170 about the harm done to the Church by the discipline of the convent, Coquerel deplores 'l'introduction d'institutions analogues au sein du protestantisme', and continues, 'les écoles laïques de gardes-malades, et l'œuvre sublime de Mademoiselle Florence Nightingale, démontrent pleinement qu'à s'enrégimenter dans les rangs d'une corporation monacale on ne gagne rien pour la bienfaisance véritable, tout en perdant beaucoup pour la religion et la société'.
[4] T. Erskine, *Remarks on the Internal Evidence for the Truth of Revealed Religion* (Edinburgh, 1820), went into many editions; *Letters*, ed. W. Hanna (2 vols., 1877).
[5] Dr Robert Lee, *The Reform of the Church in Worship, Government, and Doctrine* (1864).
[6] The property, Hirst Grove, came to BJ from his maternal grandmother via Mr Bilton Josephus Wilson, who died in 1866. The estate consisted of freehold and copyhold land. The freehold land bore a life interest, and came to BJ in 1870. BJ bought out his coheirs to the copyhold land, and then sold it for £5,505. The freehold land, Bishop Stubbs suggested, was worth more. *AC* i. 9, 375, *Faber*, p. 48.

left his property to 120 different persons. He was 88 years of age & is believed to have spent the last 13 years in making his will. I never saw him & did not know his name until last September.

I am afraid this gossip cannot be very interesting to you. Please to let me know when you write how you are; & how your plans prosper; and don't be discouraged if you get nothing this session, but lay your plans for next year or the year after, when politics are more settled....

FN to BJ [*draft*][1]

90   Good Friday, March 30, 1866

I would write a Sermon drawing *not* a contrast but a parallel—between the doctrine of Socrates, that this is life, to 'know thyself'—and the doctrine of the Evangelist, that this is life, to 'know God'.

... I would show how morality, religion, moral philosophy and politics are all, if not one and the same, at least different forms of the same.

Morality is bringing down heaven to earth (or bringing down God's will from heaven to earth).

Religion is bringing earth up to heaven.

Moral philosophy is the knowledge of the government of God over His worlds. Politics are the knowledge of His administration of this world (or bringing down God's government from heaven to earth).

... It is very easy to be religious, if religion is only the getting up to God (mysticism). It is very difficult to be religious—in the sense of incarnating Him upon earth—*either in "morality" or in politics*, or in any other practical embodiment of His will....

FN to BJ [*draft*][1]

91   [*n.d.*]

... take 'politics' as the realizing the eternal idea of God's administration of His world in the particular time and place of a nation—then there can be nothing with which a clergyman has *so much* 'to do' as with politics. *Nothing* except education, and the education of statesmen is the highest of all—because statesmen have the education of the world (to educate the nation) ... people are beginning to find out that the laws of nature are the laws of God. But they still shut Him out from the Houses of Parliament. He has no business there, except while the Chaplain reads prayers. The Crown is God the rest of the time....

[1] BL Add. MS 45783 fos. 74-7.

[1] BL Add. MS 45783 fos. 203-4.

92

Blenheim House
Shanklin until Thursday
afterwards Freshwater
[1 April 1866]

... I perceive that you will keep me living & thinking to the utmost of my power. And I am very glad to have a friend who can help me to do this.

And I want, if I can, to get you to help yourself to make the most of life (I thought of you & your work as you asked me at the Communion today). Twenty years of life probably remain to both of us & how much might be done in that time, with the experience that we already have & the increasing influence that time gives. You see that I am very ambitious for you as well as myself—& yet one ought to be conscious that any day one may be struck with palsy or other evils & still to labour on therefore with a feeling higher than ambition.

I am staying here with one of my best beloved pupils, Edmund Warre. He is a fine fellow—a real muscular Christian,[1] & is very likely to be Head Master of Eton some day. He is full of prejudices, aristocratic & other, but he is breaking out of them & has absolutely no other scheme of life but that of dedicating himself to the boys at Eton. In some respects these fellows are better than my free thinking friends of whom I told you. With best wishes on Easter Day which is a time of gladness (though not exactly for the reasons which the clergyman gave in his sermon today).

[*Postscript*]

I don't admit that Dr Stanley is dishonest. He is perfectly honest in his opinions but he has not the spirit of a hero or martyr. If you said to him, 'desert a friend & be made a Bishop', he would never desert his friend. ...

93

Address after Monday
Rectory
Bishopsgate
April 6 [1866]

I am sorry that I frightened you with 20 years of life. No wonder that you cannot wish for that, after surviving so many & amid such suffering. I sometimes think that I am very unfeeling towards you. For the truth is that when one is in health one has no continuous sense of another's pain though you may feel for them deeply at times. ...

Thank you for wishing me a long life. I think that I do desire that: sans tooth, sans eyes, sans ears, sans everything except mind. It seems to me that I have made so many mistakes & started so late in life, that I want, if I can, still to have

---

[1] Muscular Christianity was 'hearty or strongminded Christianity, which braces a man to fight the battle of life bravely and manfully', *Brewer's Dictionary of Phrase and Fable* (1953 edn.), p. 634.

my life before me. I think that I had hardly any idea of what sort of a place the world was until about 15 years ago. I see the same fault in the new generation of young men—they ought to be in character & judgement at 23 where they don't arrive until 33. And they take so long fermenting & clearing.

My friend here has your feeling, or rather he has the feeling that his life is past & that he will never do anything more; the Quarterly killed his great poem thirty years ago[1] & the retrospect of life, & all things in it, is sad to him— he is a very pained & melancholy nature with many troubles & few if any pleasures—little rejoicing in any praise & deeply grieved at the injustice of his critics. (He comes to London now & I am sure that he & his wife would be delighted to come & see you, if you were able to see them. She is a saint—a really good woman, with hardly enough of self in her to keep herself alive.) Browning on the other hand, who is about the same age as Tennyson, looks forward to writing more or less unintelligible verses for 30 years longer. I think that he has great enjoyment of life: he is a fine fellow.

I must thank you also for telling me about the Nightingale Fund.[2] I think I understand that you want quality rather than number in your new "order"— another sort of article, not the greatest quantity. The money was collected in your name & I think that the least which they can do is to leave your plan untouched during your life time.

What a poor speech Gladstone made at Liverpool.![3] He had no real reasons to give for Reform. I hear that he speaks contemptuously of the Bill as "not my bill": I think that both he & Lowe are in a very perilous position—as politicians, Lowe because he has insulted the people—& Gladstone because he is half hearted, & the least sign of faltering on his part will lead the Reformers to regard him as a traitor.

(I regret his political career, swelling & puffing out our Commerce—a good but a secondary object—and not providing for anything that required to be done at home, either Sanitary or Educational, or maintaining our position abroad.)

Will the end be a Conservative Reform Bill—redistribution of seats; 10£ occupying franchise in towns & counties alike, I wonder.

I don't much care about any fancy franchise. The best, if praticable, seems to me that of Mr Clay's Bill.[4]

I don't think that I shall defend Dr Stanley any more.... I think that you have got him, not in a wholly untrue but in a partial light, and woe to me & all of us if we are to be taken at our worst & in partial lights. I know that you are

[1] There was no 'great' poem in *Poems of Alfred Tennyson* (1832). BJ means that John Wilson Croker's unsigned review in the *Quarterly Review* for Apr. 1833 killed Tennyson's intention of writing one.
[2] See above, p. xv. Nightingale nurses were expected not to take private work, but to go as 'missionaries' into public institutions and train others.
[3] On 5 Apr. the South Lancs. Liberal Legislation Society gave a banquet to Mr Gladstone.
[4] On 20 Feb. 1866 Mr Clay (Kingston upon Hull) introduced a Bill to confer the franchise on those who submitted themselves for, and passed, an examination in writing, spelling, and the four first rules of arithmetic, to be conducted by the Civil Service Commissioners. The entry fee was to be one shilling, and the fee for a certificate one shilling and sixpence. *PD*, clxxxi. 825–32.

the most reasonable person in the world—in fact the only woman who can reason that I ever knew, & therefore I expect you to concede to me the bare possibility that I may be right about this. Let it be as 100:1 that your opinion is correct, still he ought to have the hundredth part of a doubt in his favour. Do you think that I can ask for less on behalf of a friend of about 30 years' standing?

I have been quarrelling with Tennyson tonight about Governor Eyre, and now I am beginning a quarrel with you. So that I had better leave off: Fare you well.

[*Postscript*]

Poor Mr Worsley is here—dying. Did you ever hear of him? He is a young Oxford man about 30 or 32 & the author of a better translation of Homer than Lord Derby's.[5]

94 [? April 1866][1]

. . . You are very good about Dr. Stanley. Indeed, I think that if you knew as much of him as I do, you would agree with me. Admitting what you feel about his conduct under peculiar circumstances, or rather about what his course may have been, I feel assured that the main tenour of his life has been truly upright and honorable. I am sure that I am impartial in this: as you know that there is something in the failings of one's best friends "not wholly displeasing to us", & also I am rather angry with him for leaving Oxford, & jealous of his great preferment.

About Miss Stanley I hardly know enough to form a judgement. I have been afraid of her for many years past as an intriguer—very weak yet with great strength of will, very clever under the mask of stupidity & with great power of reticence. I imagine that she has had a bad influence over her brother from his devoted & absurd attachment to her (in former days before he was married)— But I have lived among persons most of whom have a high opinion of her & I could hardly say on what (within my own experience) these impressions are founded. I fancied that there was a mixture of charity & benevolence & worldliness in her also. There are some persons to whom I am very well content in life to say "Fare well", but on condition of not renewing their acquaintance. Shall we do this with her? I hear that she is very miserable, poor creature. . . .

[*Postscript*]

Mr. Gladstone asked me to breakfast with him on Thursday.[2] He seemed in high spirits & told me that he would carry the bill. He asked me of his own accord to write him a letter for Lord Clarendon about the Public Schools.[3]

[5] P. S. Worsley published versions of the *Odyssey* (1861), and the first twelve books of the *Iliad* (1865).

[1] BL Add. MS 45783 fos. 80–1. [2] Not recorded in Gladstone's diary.
[3] The Clarendon Commission of inquiry into the major public schools was appointed in 1862 and

95 [end of April, 1866]

... I am quite well in health but I am aware that my mind is tired. It seems wrong to give up any man who is dependent on me—& it seems wrong to give up the Plato. And the end of that has been that every meal is utilized & every hour taken up in seeing the men or in lecturing or work. But I will manage better another term—I cannot resist such a remonstrance as yours. I think that you would batter the gates of heaven or hell....

And will you, dear friend, remember that nothing in this world would give me so much pleasure as to see you renewing your health & life & carrying on your work successfully.... "Nurse" nurse thyself....

And now I won't say more about health. But I must tell you something that will make you angry & also make you laugh.

Earl Russell appears to be of a poetical & sentimental turn: on the evening of the crisis he was not to be found—he had gone down to Richmond to hear the nightingales, your cousins!!! "And the provoking thing", as he wrote to a friend "was that they did not sing that night".[1]

Since I wrote the above I have been reading Mr Gladstone's speech.[2] It is fine in parts but also, I venture to think, mannered; he never knows how to speak of himself exactly in the unconscious way in which a gentleman should. Bright's speech struck me more. I liked the bold egotism of the ending.[3]

Lowe's was one of the most able speeches ever made against all Reform in all ages.[4] There was a sort of philosophical appeal to history & experience which in the H. of Commons neither Gladstone, nor any one seems able to answer....

If I am ever ill (which I never am) I shall come & be nursed by the Queen of the Nurses. I am so pleased always at having you for a friend; it seems to me such an honour.

---

reported in 1864. On 11 May 1866 Clarendon presented a Bill to the House of Lords to 'make further Provision for the good Government and Extension of certain Public Schools'. A similar Bill reached the Statute Book a year later as 31 and 32 Vict. c. 118.

[1] The story is plausible: see J. Prest, *Lord John Russell* (1972), p. 347.
[2] 27 Apr., *PD*, clxxxiii. 113–52.
[3] 23 Apr., *PD*, clxxxii. 1874–904; 'The political gains of the last twenty-five years ... are my political gains.... If now, in all the great centres of our population ... we do not find ourselves surrounded by hungry and exasperated multitudes ... have not I, as much as any living man, some claim to partake of that glory?'
[4] 26 Apr., *PD*, clxxxii. 2077–118.

96

Balliol College
Oxford
May 1, 1866

... I am glad that the Ministry have determined to stay in.[1] They would have been idiots to have done anything else. They would not have had the opportunity of proving the Adullamites[2] hypocrites if they had gone out. And this is surely a very important object. Besides they will gradually raise the country in their favour. Some persons say, & I am inclined to believe, that the working classes have a good deal of enthusiasm on behalf of America, but not much on the question of Reform or no Reform.

Mr Gladstone must have indiscreet female relatives....

A man's foes being those of his own household brings me to "family life"....

I agree with you about half & disagree the other half. 1st I feel strongly the healing power of the family; 2nd I don't think that you can cast it off without great suffering:

> "To be wroth with those we love
> Doth work like madness in the brain".[3]

3rd I don't think that you can judge of the family from its present artificial & degraded state.

4th the family is the beginning as of society so of individual life; & though we may get into wider spheres of political or philosophical interests there remains the original duty towards father, mother, brother, sister.

5thly I abhor the seven daughters tending the infirm mother, but then there comes the difficulty of what could the seven daughters do & what are they fit to do. They have been lowered by society & unless you could create society anew you could give them no new or upward impulse.

6thly I mix up counsels of prudence with counsels of perfection & do not insist on persons of dissimilar tastes & feelings living together. Did you ever observe how persons take refuge from family unhappiness in philanthropy?—this is a very curious & touching thing which I have had a good deal of opportunity of noticing.

I am always very much interested in this matter & think that I could write "A theory of the Family" some day. Will you help me? I am afraid that experience shows the widely spread unhappiness of families—so different from what they look when the wife appears of an evening, charmingly dressed, & the young gentlemen & ladies coming into the drawing room, "having their hair

---

[1] On 27 Apr., when thirty-five Liberals voted against the ministry on Grosvenor's amendment, the majority fell to five. The left wing of the Cabinet wanted to dissolve, as in 1831, and the right wing to resign. The leaders decided to stay on, and to introduce a Redistribution Bill, which was what Grosvenor had asked for.

[2] The name given by Bright, on 13 Mar. 1866, to the Palmerstonian Liberals who were preparing to vote against the Reform Bill, *PD*, clxxxii. 219.

[3] 'And to be wroth with one we love / Doth work like madness in the brain.' Coleridge, *Christabel*, ii. 414–15.

pleasingly combed on their foreheads", & a pandemonium underneath all this....

FN to BJ [*draft*]¹
97   [*n.d.*]

Men *and especially women* should never suffer themselves to be diverted from forming a real estimate of a man's character by what is termed 'respect for his office'....

It certainly requires great strength of mind for a woman to 'form a real estimate of her husband's character' and to behave the better, instead of the worse for it. Most women prefer to remain in an amiable fog thro' which they can see what they like about their husband's character.

But I believe half the misery in families would be done away with, if women could really rise to forming a true estimate of their husband's or their father's and brother's characters....

98   Balliol College
                                                                        Oxford
                                                                        [June 1866]

... I think that I should have answered your letters before, but the truth is that I have been feasting & entertaining people: first Mr. Browning & some friends, & then Mr. Coleridge. The latter is greatly improved by his H. of C. training & is really, I think, becoming liberal—considering what a hothouse of Puseyism &c. he has been brought up in this is very creditable to him. Also, though he is not a man of any force of mind, he has great gifts of speech & great kindness of nature. R. Palmer used to be a great idol with him—he told me how greatly disappointed he was with him in the House—he had every thing formalized & seemed incapable of reconciling contradicting lines of thought.

I am going to preach in the Abbey on July 1st & in Mr Davies's church, Ch. Ch., Marylebone next Sunday.¹ I thought of taking prayer for the last & family life for the W.A. one. It seems to me that I cannot think of anything else about which 4000 people can have any common notions.

Don't believe that we are all going to sink into positivism or Catholicism. Great changes of opinion may be in store for us; but the human race does not rise out of materialism only to go back to it....

¹ BL Add. MS 45785 fos. 181-2.

¹ J. L. Davies, *St Paul and Modern Thought, Remarks on Some of the Views Advanced in Professor Jowett's Commentary on St Paul* (1856); 'Although protesting against certain veins of thought running through it ... I may be allowed, however, to express ... my great admiration for many of its qualities. It seems to me the work of a most candid and honourable man, untainted by party spirit ... I believe, reverent also, in spite of much that may fairly shock reverence in others.'

There is a villainous bill, compounded by High Churchmen deluding the free Churchmen, called the Colonial Bishoprics bill, which I should like to try & stop.² The effect seems to be to preserve the Colonial Churches in all their properties [&] trusts, & give them all the power they can want, first of oppressing their own clergy & then of a United Clergy oppressing the laity....

[*Postscript omitted*]

99　　　　　　　　　　　　　　　　　　　　　　　　　　　Balliol College
　　　　　　　　　　　　　　　　　　　　　　　　　　　　　　　Oxford
　　　　　　　　　　　　　　　　　　　　　　　　　　　　　　[15 June 1866]

... I have got an heretical divine here staying with me, who has passed in five or six years from Dissenting Evangelicalism into Strauss—Dr Davidson. He has been turned out of a dissenting College & a subscription is being made for him as he is aged & has a family. We liberals ought to support our own poor, & though not a very able, he is a very learned & meritorious man....

100　　　　　　　　　　　　　　　　　　　　　　　　　　　Inglewood
　　　　　　　　　　　　　　　　　　　　　　　　　　　　　　　Torquay
　　　　　　　　　　　　　　　　　　　　　　　　　　　　　June 21 [1866]

... I fought with "beasts" in our College meeting on Tuesday, but these beasts (some of them *are* beasts) were tame & I got my way, & succeeded in reducing the estimate for the restoration of the Master's House from 6000£ to £4500.¹ Also I am going to try a plan for University Extension which will, as I hope, be the means of bringing up many more poor men.²

What a row this is? I think that it was very bad generalship to divide upon rating versus rental (I mean the reverse) which seems to be really a question of some doubt....³ They should have given a figure & made the issue distinct....

Will they go out, or dissolve, or will they stay in? Majesty, as Mr Carlyle would say, being dissolved in tears.⁴ (I am sorry to hear by the way that there is a foolish scandal going about respecting Majesty & a favourite gilly & attendant of Prince Albert called John Brown, & the common people call her Mrs

---

² The Colonial Bishops Bill was withdrawn on 16 July. It had been introduced by Cardwell.

¹ This was a running sore. CM 19 June 1866: '*Moved*, that as the sum of £6000 for the Master [Scott]'s house, seems to the College excessive, Mr. Waterhouse be requested to prepare a plan for it at a cost of not more than £4500.' CM, 26–7 Apr. 1867: '*Resolved*, that the College having already permitted an excess in the cost of the Master's House amounting to £250 beyond the original proposal of £4500, the College will not be justified in further exceeding that limit: & that for any such the Mastership shall pay a rent of 6 per cent.'

² See below, No. 115.

³ The final division on the ill-fated Reform Bill took place on 18 June on Dunkellin's amendment to substitute a rating for a net rental franchise in the boroughs. The ministry lost by 304 votes to 315.

⁴ Possibly a reference to the Bedchamber Crisis of 1839.

Brown—this has continued ever since last October—the great & good Augusta[5] in vain trying to hint that "Majesty must be careful".) But to return from this gossip to politics. I think that the best thing probably is that they should come back & try the bill another year. Meanwhile at the end of the session they will want something to make them popular and you might press upon them your poor law/hospital bill.[6]

I see that Lord Derby has succeeded in making the Public School Bill nearly useless by a majority of one.[7]

I find that Gladstone gave very great offence by his speech on Coleridge's Bill.[8] I had no idea that people cared so much about the matter.

I am sorry that you never have or know the joys of the country which, just now, is quite lovely. These late springs always have a flush of life & bloom. And this county has rare beauty. Next week I think that I shall wander about on Dartmoor & manufacture another sermon.

Did I ever thank you about Dr Davidson? I will send the money to him in the name of "Libertas". I should be strongly against your giving your own name in these sort of subscriptions.

The Colonial Bishops question appears to be fenced round by endless legal difficulties & there is no likelihood of the Bill being proceeded with at present. It is said that nothing can really be done in the Colonies which have legislatures, without the concurrence of the legislature & this is not likely to be very favorable to the A[nglican] Ch. Bishops.

101

address until Sunday
33 Alfred Place West
Thurlow Square[1]
[June 1866]

I shall certainly take your kind advice about health, for I have a great desire to live & get the better of my enemies. ...

But I am ashamed to talk to you about these trivialities when the Italians are lying dead & dying on the field of battle.[2]

I half incline to think that this war will put an end to kings & queens & aristocracies in Germany. You will ask why? Why because this is a war made

---

[5] Lady Augusta Stanley.
[6] See above, No. 66, n. 5.
[7] On 18 June Derby carried an amendment to the Public Schools Bill by 28 contents to 27 not contents, to prevent the Commissioners altering the governing bodies.
[8] Coleridge brought in a Bill to allow dissenters to proceed to the degree of MA, which they could already do at Cambridge, and to become members of the governing body of the University. He did not propose to interfere with the governing bodies of the colleges. Gladstone said University and colleges could not be separated, and argued against the Bill as unsettling a question which ought to be dealt with in due time by Government; *PD*, clxxxiv. 321-7.

---

[1] C. S. C. Bowen's address.
[2] The Italians were defeated by the Austrians at the battle of Custozza on 24 June.

by them—which but for them would never have taken place & a war of a most hateful kind which the people will one day attribute to them. The days are past when the Great Fritz[3] could butcher 200,000 unrepining victims because the great Theresa was indisposed to marry him. . . .

102

Address until Wednesday
At Mrs Wilson's
Hampsthwaite
nr Ripley
afterwards at Professor Nichol's
1 South Park Terrace
Glasgow
[August 1866]

I hope that the news about the war has brought peace to you, as well as to the rest of the world. I rejoice in the liberation of Italy & in the triumph of the Protestant power. But I wish that they had been effected by a democracy & not by the Prussian army under a "Junkerthum". England seems to get lower & lower in the world & is growing very Christian & humble. I think that some day one will have to set up as a Cosmopolite & not as an Englishman. And indeed, I cannot say that national feelings have any great attraction for me (any more than College feelings, or Church of England feelings at a University)—more than half of patriotism is dislike of other nations.

I gather that this ministry is not likely to stand (though I thought otherwise at first), because I find that the Adullamites are not inclined to support it. Lowe told me (in confidence) that it was all the selfishness of Lord Derby, who would not retire. He also said that he never dreamed of joining them—"Any stick is good enough to beat a dog & Derby is my stick with which I beat Gladstone". I asked him if he thought that they were likely to do anything about the workhouses. He thought "neither that nor anything else".

All religious people & the multitude hate & fear Lowe. All intellectual people & the upper classes of Society like him. I cannot help feeling that he is a very honest man (though people are saying all manner of things of him & his wife,[1] as they are also of Gladstone & his wife). And he puts his mind fairly to you in conversation. I hope he will see that he must do something if he really means to rival Gladstone. At present he $= 1/10$ of Gladstone in public services & yet (though I don't agree with him about Reform) he is more satisfactory to me in other ways. He said, "How can Gladstone be so absurd as to support Tests &c. & not see that they must be carried away in his deluge".

---

[3] Frederick the Great.

---

[1] 'She is rather loud and violent, not particularly attractive, but such a sketcher in pencil and colours both, that her volume of Australian sketches, is something well worth seeing.' *Letters of the Hon. Mrs Edward Twisleton Written to her Family, 1852-62* (1928), pp. 209–10.

1862–1866

I also saw Coleridge during the week of my stay in London. I liked him very much. Though I don't think him a first-rate intellect, he has certainly great gifts & is a thoroughly upright & good man.

I am told that Lord Russell is "full of fight", & lies on the floor playing with his one year old grandchild.[2] He told his daughter-in-law[3] that Walpole was the only honest man in the new Ministry. I am amused at Dizzy teaching Gladstone Christianity at the Mansion House....[4]

You said when I saw you last that you thought it possible the N[ew] Ministry might throw you off (you will have to make up to Lady Cranborne). I don't think that it is of the smallest consequence (to you) if they do. I believe that it would be better if you went out of office for a year & employed yourself in writing. Nothing that you have done has been more effectual than the book on nursing.[5] I am inclined to think that by writing letters in 'The Times' you might do more good than by working for Public Offices....

I expect that the Jamaica business will still make a row. I asked Mr Roundell what he thought about it. He said that they had certainly discovered nothing that convicted Gordon, who was a kind of fanatic—saying "The Lord is at hand" & having an extreme feeling of the wrongs of the Negroes—not guilty further than this. He said that what struck him most was the horrid professional spirit of some of the officers & that some of them, who under the influence of this had said the worst things, were really very good men. I think that there ought to be 1) an address to the Crown from the H. of C. requesting that Eyre should not be employed again: 2) a letter of censure of Col. Ellington & others from the Commander in Chief.[6]

Look at Stephen's two articles in Fraser on "Ecce Homo".[7] They are very interesting & powerful, but also wrongheaded: seven half legal, half ethical notions of Natural Theology patched with the Christianity of Butler's Analogy.[8] He, Stephen, knows the author[9] of this greatly overpraised book, which has almost converted Gladstone & R. Palmer.

I went to the Historical Portrait Exhibition on Friday. Splendid cartoons of Henry VIII & VII (quite a new idea of H. 8),[10] Sir T. More, the youthful Milton & Hobbes struck me most.

---

[2] The second Earl Russell.
[3] Lady Amberley.
[4] At the dinner given to ministers on 1 Aug. 1866, Disraeli said that 'there is some little mistake as to the character of the Session that is about to close ... a considerable portion of it has been employed in protracted discussions, but ... though they have terminated without any legislative result, I venture to think that they have not been in vain', *The Times*, 2 Aug. (9c).
[5] *Notes on Nursing: What It Is and What It Is Not* (1860).
[6] The Duke of Cambridge.
[7] Sir J. F. Stephen, *Frasers Magazine*, vol. 73, pp. 746–65, vol. 74, pp. 29–52.
[8] Joseph Butler, *The Analogy of Religion, Natural and Revealed* (1736).
[9] J. R. Seeley.
[10] In *The Catalogue of the First Special Exhibition of National Portraits ... on loan to the South Kensington Museum* one portrait only, no. 134, of Henry VIII, was called a cartoon.

103   Address until Friday
                                                                                         Professor Nichol's
                                                                                         1 South Park Terrace
                                                                                              Glasgow
                                                                                            [August 1866]

I don't think that I ever thanked you for the budget of news which you sent me—Well, is not the sky beginning to change already?—What if Russia should be at Constantinople, America at war, the Pope under English protection, this time next year, Louis Napoleon, perhaps, having left the world.

I cannot regard that hero in the dark colours which you & M. Mohl do. I think that he has no morality, no belief, but that he has political ideas. When I read his manifesto, I cannot help feeling that no other statesman in Europe could have written it.

Mind you live until next year, not only to reform the Workhouses but also to see the events that are coming upon the earth at home & abroad.

This is a splendid house in which I am staying with my old pupil, Lord Duncan. But the master of the house[1] is hopelessly out of his mind: he lives with us & is most assiduously tended by his family—he cannot speak, however, & seems to have only an occasional gleam of intelligence—he is continually having slight shocks of paralysis affecting the brain. You will be sorry to hear that my friend Dr John Brown (Rab) has been also suffering from mental troubles—I hope, however, that there is now a good prospect of his recovery. He had an insane wife whom he nursed for several years until at last his own mind has given way.

I read Max Schlesinger's article.[2] But I doubt whether Bismarck is your cat still. He has not been really tried, I think, & accidents have gone very much in his favour. Where would he have been had the battle of Sadowa turned out differently.

Is not all the mischief in the world done by conservatism & the world always cunningly pretends that it is really done by radicalism. Is not Austria ruined by being behind the world? I hope you have a little malicious pleasure in watching the fall of the Popedom—that seems to be very fair in Protestants—Rome shall perish—write the word in the blood that she has shed.

This letter is "like the breath of an unfee'd lawyer" good for nothing.[3] I always make you a very ungrateful return for your capital letters.

---

[1] The second Earl of Camperdown.
[2] 'Count Bismarck', *Fortnightly Review* vol. 5 (1866), pp. 385–405, 600–23.
[3] Fool, 'Then 'tis like the breath of an unfee'd lawyer; you gave me nothing for it.' *King Lear*, I. iv. 128–9.

104

Address for next month

Tummil Bridge
Pitlochry
Perthshire
[August 1866]

I have gone back to my old nest (or rather shall be there tomorrow) & am working on Plato who sends his compliments to you & desires to have a Platonic friendship with you. I trudge away along the road 4 miles a day which, if continued, will bring me to the end of the journey by next February. But this everlasting translation, which may perhaps be regarded in the light of a penance, takes away from me the power of doing much in the way of thinking.

What do you think of this foreign political world? I like the predominance of Protestant Prussia; I dislike the predominance of aristocratic, vulgar, military Prussia. And I doubt whether there is not a disadvantage to Germany in the work being done so fast by armies, instead of by Constitutional struggles. Is there not more of the "popular fibre" in Napoleon than in Prussian Junkerthum? ...

Will you get a book (I am out of the way of books or I would send it to you) called 'Essays on International Policy' by some Oxford disciples of Comte.[1] The book is not deep, nor is it knowing, but it is suggestive perhaps of impossibilities—but then I like to have impossibilities set before us. Read especially, in 'England & China', the striking account of the Peasant Empress.[2]

How do you fare with your new masters? I shall be curious to hear: "Got a new master, get a new man". I thought the letters which you sent me very creditable to both sets of ministers: upon the whole I look with more hope to Lord Stanley than to anyone else in the long run. There seems to be more a thread of continuity in his politics....

My friends here talk to me a great deal about Carlyle, whom they saw in the winter. I can't say that I altogether like him—a man of genius & in some respects the first man living, an independent man, a tenderhearted man—the most graphic of all painters, though in a sort of irregular, magic-lantern way. Yet on the other hand, a man totally regardless of truth, totally without admiration of any active goodness—a self-contradictory man who investigates facts with the most extraordinary care in order to prove his own preconceived notions. He has stirred up the minds of young men (those impressionable beings) but not really elevated them. I know that he can say things with a tenderness & power in conversation that no one else attains. But this does not atone at all to me for his utter recklessness & his habit of expressing his own personal fancies in the likeness of intellectual truths. If I were engaged in any work more than usually good (which I never shall be) I know that he would be the first person to utter a powerful sneer; or if I were seeking to know the truth

---

[1] *International Policy: Essays on the Foreign Relations of England* (1866).
[2] Ibid. 327–48, J. H. Bridges, 'England and China'.

he would ridicule the very notion of an "homunculus" discovering the truth. And therefore I like better living with Socrates & Plato than with Carlyle & Ruskin. (I hear that the two last are great allies & that "I will give unto this last" &c.³ is the inspiration of Carlyle). I don't think that Carlyle has any real insight, but only a great power of painting & embossing & crystallizing scenes real or imaginary. Nor is he a great doer, nor even a great artist. The really great men of the world are of a different stamp.

You see that I presume on your letting me gossip away to you in bad English upon anything that comes into my head. There are some charming little girls here whose great delight is to go with their brothers & cousins fishing, that is to say, collecting worms & holding the baskets for them. I remonstrate with them about this. But they say that it is quite right "because they are boys". You see how early public opinion teaches girls to know their place. I send this as a contribution to your "theory of daughters". . . .

[*Postscript*]

I have just been reading a poem of M. Arnold's on our poor friend Clough:⁴—not good. M.A., though he is not a bad fellow at all, has no real depth of feeling.

FN TO BJ [*draft*]¹

105 [?August 1866]

Socrates says, in the lesser Hippias that it is better to do or say what is bad and know it to be bad, than to do or say what is bad, not knowing it to be so.²

. . . If Plato had been writing [of] the state of England in 1866, he could not have been more exact.

It is the sin against the Holy Ghost.

Everybody, now, it seems to me, has a moral reason for doing what they like.

When I was a child, it did not use to be so among my grand-parents and the people of the last century. They did violent and wrong things—much more wrong things than are done now. But they never said they were right. On the contrary. They were very sorry afterwards and asked for forgiveness from God and man.

I see just the same thing in Government. . . .

It is perfectly well understood, perfectly well known by all and everyone of the actors, that the 'Reports' and the 'Enquiries' and the 'Minutes' and the

---

³ Ruskin's *Unto This Last* was published in 1860–2: the title came from Matt. 20: 14.

⁴ 'Thyrsis, a Monody, to Commemorate the Author's Friend, Arthur Hugh Clough, who died at Florence, 1861, by M. Arnold', *Macmillan's Magazine*, Apr. 1866, repr. in *New Poems* (1867).

---

¹ BL Add. MS 45783 fos. 84–7.
² It is the message of the dialogue.

'Correspondence' are not in order that anything may be done, but that anything may not be done.

... So nobody supposes that the Privy Council is going to enforce any sanitary measures on the local authorities—or that the local authorities are going to carry any, without their being enforced.... All these Boards and offices are nothing but a mechanism for enabling the persons responsible to do nothing. Now certainly the poor man who embezzles his employer's money, knowing it to be wrong, and goes and commits suicide, is much better, in a much more hopeful state, than these most respectable people— who are wilfully stupid—who cannot be saved—who commit the sin against the Holy Ghost every day.... I entirely agree with Socrates ... I have not a shadow of doubt, have you?—that I had rather die in the Workhouse Infirmary than live as I see those people do who drive in carriages in parks—with their dogs' heads out of window—taking everything they can out of this poor earth and giving nothing back. (If I kept a dog instead of a cat, I should have to keep a brougham for it to drive out in and a man-servant to take it out— whereas my cats are satisfied with a walk on the leads. But the cats of the next century will not be.) ...

106
Tummil Bridge
Pitlochry N.B.
Aug. 12 [1866]

... I don't say that the war was right, or the coup d'état right, or that Germany may not very likely become an odious military aristocracy. But I think that we must accept faits accomplis in politics or we become hopeless & isolated, antipathetic to all things, sympathetic with nothing. This is a state of great weakness, when all our ideas are dominated by antagonism to L.N.

These reflections are not made on Mon. Mohl for whom I have the greatest respect, though they may be suggested by his letter. The L.N. régime has fallen very hard on the press & on literary men; it was bad in its beginning & is immoral in its private ways. Still, it has some elements of real greatness which are wanting in other governments of Europe.

(Don't you sometimes feel how infinitely better & more blessed it is to be working at hospitals, which is undoubtedly right, than to be taking part in these debatable matters of Prussia v. Austria, & France against both, or indeed in any purely political matters. In a humble way I often feel that it is a real good that my own work, however imperfect, has no drawback or doubt about it. I only want to do it better & to do more of it.)

I am glad that "my Princess"[1] has made acquaintance with you. Shall I tell you my notion of her? She is extremely clever, has read infinite books, is very ambitious (it won't be her fault, the Queen said to a friend of mine one day, if

[1] Victoria.

she's not Empress of Germany)² and is also a real woman, quite la mère & la femme—& always in a mess with her money matters. She is full of politics but I doubt whether she has a real political head, & she has no reticence & very little power of gaining popularity & influence, except over her husband who is devoted to her. The reason is that she has such a tongue & also that she is subject to great alternations of spirits, now in wild excitement & then in depression. There are two things very interesting about her—her sympathy with human things quite apart from rank & the conventionalities of a court, & her devotion to the memory of her father. I am glad that you have got hold of her. It will do her a great deal of good & make her popular to have this hospital work to do. She was eating her heart out living alone in those great empty rooms of the Palace at Berlin.³ I think that I will write to her: I dare say that you will post my letter & get it sent through the Foreign Office.

... I am really taking care of my health for I never work more than 6 hours a day.... You see that I am obliged to go through this long mechanical labour of translating Plato—about 2100 pages—this will be finished next March. Then I have about half-finished a sketch of the history of the Early Greek Philosophy & of Plato. I fancy this to be important because the history of Greek ideas is the history of the ideas of the civilized world, & to most persons the very notion that ideas have a history is a new one. I want to throw my whole mind into this, when the translation is done. Then I have also an edition of the Republic with notes, which is likely to be used by students in the schools, in which I try to give in a condensed form modern views of the questions treated of, as well as explanations of the Greek. So that you see I have my hands full & am not idle, though people naturally think that I have gone to sleep or am dead.

I told my mother to send you one of my sermons....

Lord Lansdowne⁴ is here with me—he proposed to come immediately after his Father's death, which was very good of him, & he works away famously at Livy & Mommsen.⁵ (I suppose that you (who know everything) know that Niebuhr⁶ is now wholly discredited & that we have a new Roman History.) I have also Mr Newman with me, one of the fellows of our College: a remarkable man who has the greatest knowledge of history & the greatest power of thinking about it of any one whom I have known. I don't think that his judge-

---

² Queen Victoria was presumably referring to the difficulties she encountered in having Albert made Prince Consort (the title was not conferred until 1857), and the absolute refusal of successive ministries to contemplate his becoming King Consort. Their daughter will fare better.

³ Vicky's first home was the Berlin Schloss, 'a large, decaying, dreary palace which had not been lived in since Frederick William III had died there in 1840': 'that dark and dreadful prison'. Daphne Bennett, *Vicky, Princess Royal of England and German Empress* (1971), pp. 58, 79.

⁴ The fourth Marquis.

⁵ T. Mommsen, *Römische Geschichte*, vols. 1–3, and 5 (1854–6), *Die römische Chronologie bis auf Cäsar* (1858), *Geschichte des römischer Munzwesens* (1860), *Römische Forschungen* (1864–79), *Römische Staatsrecht* (1871–6).

⁶ B. G. Niebuhr, whose *Römische Geschichte* (3 vols., 1811–32), was based on the study of institutions rather than tradition.

ment is equal to his knowledge or genius, & he is one of those persons who appears to be absolutely without the religious sense, though he is a good man. Altogether I find him a most instructive companion. He was describing to me the other day, quite with excitement, the pleasure which he had in thinking.

...It is rather hard upon the Liberals that the Tories can always carry any of the measures which they would have opposed when out of office & therefore may seem to be great administrative Reformers. I wish they were out & that we had Lord Russell, though he never says or does anything right, in again.

That "fellow" Goldwin Smith hath the "finest mad devil of jealousy" in him that ever possessed the soul of any human being. People who know him & are not unfriendly tell me that he resigned under Lord Derby's government in order that he might not have a distinguished successor. He has succeeded in this....[7]

107
Tummil Bridge
Aug. 26 [1866]

...I leave here on (Monday) tomorrow week. The stay has been successful for I have done my tasks every day for five weeks & lectured my two young gentlemen.[1] I am certainly much better than when I came. What a bad thing the love of sport really is for the Upper Classes. These two youths are very much above the average in ability, but their souls as well as their bodies are absolutely given up to shooting & fishing, & more than half their conversation is on these subjects. It is quite weakening to them, this muscular Christianity of which Mr Kingsley is the prophet.[2] Mr Kingsley reminds me of Governor Eyre. I was glad that the common people made a row! I like to see them fighting their "betters" on such occasions....

[*Postscript*]

We have got a wise man staying here, Lord Kingsdown, the great light of the Privy Council. I look up to him with veneration.

FN to BJ's mother

108
35 South Street,
Park Lane
London W.
Aug. 28, 1866

Dear Madam,

May I trouble you with one line to thank you for sending me Mr. Jowett's sermon, & for the very kind note which accompanied it.

---

[7] His successor was Stubbs. In 1876, however, the college elected Stubbs to an Honorary Fellowship.

[1] Lansdowne was one, the other not identified.
[2] 'It is a school of which Mr. Kingsley is the ablest doctor', *Edinburgh Review* (Jan. 1858).

I am one of those many, to whom Mr. Jowett has shewn such extreme & graceful kindness—& for whom he has given himself so much trouble—that I feel as if I had a sort of claim to express my gratitude to you.

I think I am old enough, being a kind of Mother of the Army, to be permitted, without impertinence, to congratulate you upon having such a son. And, as I am quite sure that the kindnesses which he confers will be the last which you will hear of from him, this is my excuse for your hearing of them from me.

Pray believe me
dear Madam,
with great truth
Your respectful and faithful
Florence Nightingale

109

Brig of Tummil
Sept. 2 [1866]
Address until Sep. 11
Cortachy Castle
Kirriemuir, N.B.[1]

... About Elijah you must mean the Honble Elijah Pogram.[2] There is no other Elijah to whom I bear the least resemblance.

About my health I won't weary you with talking. I mean to take your advice—I shall have a few days entire rest & only four hours work for the next six weeks. Please not to be nervous about me. It is quite true that I have overworked during the last two years, but I repent & don't mean to offend again. I believe that I have not really injured myself, for you see, I sleep a great deal, which is a panpharmacon, & my work excludes care & I am particular about air & diet. You have done me a service for which I cannot be too grateful in drawing my attention to the matter.

I have been too much a drudge all my life; & I can hardly expect to be altogether my own master. For example, if I had gone abroad this vacation, Lord Lansdowne would probably, or very likely, have done nothing at the most critical time of his life. And our College is in such a shaky, slippery state that I dare not stay away. I have always had to work there against an opposite party who are partly bigots & partly inefficient & inert.

I went to church here today and heard the usual tale about Ahab & Jehu.[3] As we were coming out Lord Kingsdown affectionately greeted me. He said, 'I should have been sorry if you had preached such a sermon as that'. . . . As it is not absolutely [certain] that I may [not] be had up before him some day, as an

---

[1] Seat of Lord and Lady Airlie.
[2] Hon. Elijah Pogram in *Martin Chuzzlewit* (1843), an American Congressman who was not found amusing by Americans at the time.
[3] 'So Jehu slew all that remained of the house of Ahab in Jezreel', 2 Kgs 10: 11 *et seq.*

offender is had up before a magistrate, I was glad to hear him utter such liberal sentiments....

I hope that you don't countenance Carlyle, Kingsley, Ruskin & Co.... Governor Eyre is a good man—Granted. The Island was in some danger—Granted. The danger was of a peculiar kind from the small number of Whites being dispersed over the Island—Granted. But that is no sort of excuse for horrid barbarities, continued 3 weeks after the danger was over, or for the execution of Gordon without evidence. Governor Eyre will have the approval of the army, of all colonists, of all who judge questions of right & wrong on the gentleman versus snob principle—but no one can think him right, or regard his mistake as venial, considering the consequences....

CHAPTER 3

1866-1870

Address Linlathen
nr Dundee[1]
[September 1866]

I am very much grieved to hear that you are so ill. I often think that you have the greatest strength of mind of any woman that I have ever known. And I want you not to let this be clouded or shaken by physical suffering. . . .

(I am afraid that I say the same things to you over & over again. If you perceive this, I would ask you to set on the other side that there is nothing which I would not do for you if I could.)

You don't like having 20 years dealt out to you at a time. But suppose you have three years, the received time of Christ's ministry upon earth: how much may be done in that! As to your intrigues, I don't expect one fourth of them to succeed. But I think that you would be wrong in entering upon them if you did not mean to persevere with them. They seem to me to be "fery honest knaveries".

I don't think that Mr Hardy is a Puseyite; probably Evangelical as much as a country Squire ought to be.

Do you approve of Mr Simon? I made friends with him at Mr Lowe's who spoke very highly of him.

Do you know Mr Hozier? He is an old & I think attached pupil of mine (Lord Herbert's secretary): I hear of great people talking of his plan for the reorganization of the Army. . . .

FN to BJ [*draft*][1]

111 [*n.d.*]

You take the bread out of my mouth. I was to be appointed Professor of Sanitary Science to your disciples, the Medical Marquises.

And now you have gone over to Mr Simon.

I would not have gone over to Dr Pusey, not for a wilderness of Miss Sellons, tho' I am very much attached to her. I am always hating *your* enemies.

But you have been and "made friends" with Mr Simon because you like Mr Lowe. I have no objection to your liking Mr Lowe, but this is a treacherous act. And I am not there to defend myself. . . .

Mr Simon, not perhaps more than, but in common with, Doctors in general . . . has, during the last 10 years, brought down medicine, including Sanitary Science, from a profession to a trade. . . .

---

[1] Home of Thomas Erskine.

[1] BL Add. MS 45783 fos. 123-4.

FN to BJ [*draft*][1]

112   [*n.d.*]

... My doctrine about Education has no 'bad moral'.
It is the mistake of calling the 3 Rs 'Education', tho' Education should of course include the 3 Rs.

If the teaching of the 3 Rs does not prevent pauperism and crime, as sad experience clearly shows it does *not*, surely the *good* 'moral' is to show that the training of the moral faculties which leads to practical actions (and let your friends the 3 Rs come in too) is the sole Education which does prevent pauperism and crime.

Also about 'contagion'.
Surely the 'bad moral' is that of Simon Magus and G. which teaches there *is* 'Contagion' (no one is ever able to tell you what it is, where it is, how it is, and for a very good reason, because *it is not*). There is 'Contagion' and all you can do is to cut it off, to stamp it out, to kill or to segregate.... There is 'Infection', but from perfectly well known causes. Remove the causes and you remove the 'Infection'. There is no such thing as inevitable 'Infection'. Quarantine, segregating fever &c., above all concentrating them in Hospitals, these are all means expressly constructed to manufacture the best 'Infection'.

Killing the cows is exactly the same as killing the witches. O my Professor, are you a Doctor in Plato and not know these things! Depend upon it, if you can find out the facts in Science—Educational, Physical, or Sanitary—those *facts* will show a 'moral', the best moral, i.e. show best the Perfect God, leading man to perfection. 'Contagion' would show God a Devil. 'Infection' (facts and doctrine) leads man on to social improvement....

113   Balliol College
                                                                           Oxford
                                                                           [October 1866]

I now perfectly know & shall always remember the difference between contagion & infection. But, still, you do not mean to say, do you, that without infection, without contagion of any sort, Lord Granville's cows (probably) generated the cattle plague of their own free will in the bad cow house.... Would you further say that the cutting off contact between whole & diseased beasts had nothing to do with the stopping of the disease? That seems to an ignoramus like me the reverse of probable—that the cattle plague has stopped just as the cholera has stopped, either from some unknown reason or from the preventive measures of which it has been the occasion. But it may be so....

Who, do you think, is likely to be the chief opponent of the Extension

---

[1] BL Add. MS 45783 fos. 141–4.

Scheme? Goldwin Smith. He is going to write a pamphlet against it.[1] I am afraid that this is only the mad devil of jealousy again. This does not trouble me, however. He will write his pamphlet & the public will gradually discover that what he is attacking is a different thing from what I am proposing. He goes about saying, in his clever way, among the young liberals, "This is just what Pusey desires". What queer people there are in the world & there are no queerer people than some at Oxford.

You may have seen in the newspapers, perhaps, that three foolish fellows at our College & three at other Colleges have gone over to Rome.[2] There is no great harm in this really, for the youths are under much better guidance now than that of Pusey and Liddon. It is said that some more are going & those who, like Lady Castlemaine, don't like travelling in a crowd must make haste.

I think that an Ecclesiastical storm is getting up which, like a commercial panic, seems to return about once in seven years: Ecclesiastical titles—Essays & Reviews—Ritualism.... I quite agree with you in the comparison of this age & the last. The poor old drunken eighteenth century has great injustice done to it by the smooth, sleek religionism of this.[3]

114
Balliol College
Oxford
[October 1866]

Thank you for Mrs Clive's note. Her son[1] did write to tell me of his engagement. He is a youth whom I like very much; fair ability—but his strong point is his happy temperament.

She must be a woman of great genius. Unfortunately, she took it into her head to make a man who murdered his wife interesting. He may have been good & interesting & may have been perfectly justified in getting rid of an odious woman, but morality does not allow this to be said or thought. English people will not believe in murder of a wife with extenuating circumstances. There is something very droll in the poor lady not having seen this &, in the innocence of her heart, having perpetrated a worse than French novel.[2]

I think I see my way about the Extension Scheme. Hang the Hebdomadal Council & Goldwin Smith. If the application to the H.C. fails I mean to take a house & invite young gentlemen in needy circumstances to come & be lodged & taught free, & board themselves—if this answers, two houses &c., and so on.

I enclose a note of R. Lowe's which pleased me. I wish that you or I or some one could represent to that gentleman that he is driving full speed up a cul-de-sac, which leads no where. It is a thousand pities that such powers as his should

---

[1] Goldwin Smith, *The Reorganisation of the University of Oxford* (1868), pp. 47–56.
[2] Presumably, Gerard Manley Hopkins, W. E. Addis, and A. W. Garrett. The others included H. W. Challis, Merton, and A. Wood, Trinity.   [3] See above, No. 105.

---

[1] C. M. B. Clive.   [2] See above, No. 37, n. 4.

be wasted. For he has a mind whereas Gladstone has only a sort of madness akin to genius.

My pupil, Lord Lansdowne (the young Adullamite who owns Mr Lowe),[3] went up to town to see M. Lavalette a day or two ago. He seemed a good deal impressed by M. Lavalette telling him that there was a universal expectation in Europe that a great crisis was imminent in England—because, hitherto, we had been in advance of other countries & now we were falling behind them in the liberality of our institutions. (Lord Lansdowne works excellently &, as I really believe, will come to something.) I think this coming from the M. of the Interior in France is striking.

I am so glad about Lady Augusta's[4] writing to you—indeed I have nothing to do with that. She had probably heard of your friendship for Mrs Clough from Me Mohl, who is a great friend of her's. I find her a most upright, excellent, affectionate sort of woman, but difficult to talk to, for she is limited in her ideas, & though gifted with considerable administrative capacity, does not understand things & has no insight. How much superior the General[5] was in this respect! But she is a really good woman & I am glad that you keep up relations with her. You need not be at all afraid of her getting under the influences of which we once spoke;[6] nothing is less likely....

115
Balliol College
Oxford
Oct. 14, 1866

I had better success than I expected in my two days campaign with the fellows. I am opposed by two fools & a knave, but, as we are nearly two to one & all the disinterested part of the College is with me, that does not matter. The knave is a real knave & no mistake,[1] though the amount of his knavery I am not able precisely to determine. He is a very clever, dexterous sort of fellow. The two fools are the Master & the Senior Tutor,[2] who are very good men (in a sense) & gentlemen, but they are wholly incompetent & entirely without public spirit. I grudge them the large revenue which they get from the College, doing nothing but harm in return.

I found that my scheme of University Extension was very favorably received.[3] I want men, 1st to live in lodgings which we are to build & furnish & let at a rent of 10£ a year. 2nd to be allowed to attend the College lectures free. 3rdly to have small exhibitions of 25£ a year given away by examination among the successful candidates of the Middle Class Examination[4] & others. I reckon

---

[3] Lansdowne was the 'proprietor' of the borough of Calne for which Lowe sat.
[4] Lady Augusta Stanley.
[5] Robert Bruce, brother of Lady Augusta Stanley.
[6] Of Mary Stanley.

[1] Wall.
[2] Scott and Woollcombe.
[3] CM, 11–12 Oct.
[4] Oxford Local Examinations.

that paying 10£ a year rent & having nothing to pay for instruction, they could live for the academical year of 24 weeks on 50£ a year or, deducting the Exhibition, for 25 a year. 4thly I would allow the ordinary scholars & exhibitioners to live in the same way: & their expenses would be completely covered. The College would take the responsibility of the management & instruction of all these "lodgers out". At present not a 10th or a 20th part of the ability of the country comes to the University. This scheme is intended to draw from a new class, & with this object, I should propose that the subjects of examination be not confined to Latin & Greek, but embrace physical science, mathematics &c. The great difficulty in working it out is the present state of the Grammar Schools.

I think that this College, in 5 or 6 years time, would be able to give 600£ a year towards such a scheme. But a large outlay would be required for the building & the Exhibitions. I should hope to raise this by subscription.

I have been so full of this, & of the rebuilding of the College,[5] that I have not had time to write to "our" Princess.[6] But I will if I can....

[*Postscript omitted*]

116 Oct. 27, 1866

... Yesterday we had our first meeting, which was wholly occupied in getting rid of a resolution which the fellows passed in my absence,[1] the effect of which would have been to mulct the College of 3 or 400£ year, & so take away the funds which made the prosecution of the scheme of University Extension possible. This was effected with great difficulty but was at last accomplished. Today we proceeded to the other business. We first began by a row between the Bursar[2] & me about something which he had falsely said of me. After this was allayed I brought forward my scheme, which was entirely successful, every one of the six proposals being carried without a division, my friend the Bursar, who is a sort of rogue elephant, retiring sulkily into a corner & taking no part in the proceedings. The business is thus far prosperous enough. The College undertakes 1) to teach undergraduates gratuitously. 2) to petition the Hebdomadal Council to pass a Statute allowing them to lodge out. N.B. This puts the aforesaid Hebdomadal Council in a most invidious position if they refuse. 3) to apply 200£ a year of the College revenues to found small Exhibitions, if there is such a surplus. 4) to open a Subscription with the view of raising more money for the same objects.

The chief points now are 1) to raise money, 2) to get land & build lodgings,

---

[5] The old front of the college was demolished in 1867, and the Brackenbury buildings, designed by Alfred Waterhouse, were completed in 1868.

[6] Victoria.

---

[1] To reduce charges to undergraduates in general.   [2] Wall.

3rd to advertize & get the men.³ N.B. That this is not a Clerical (Keble) Hall, nor a poor hall, nor anything of that sort, but a Scotch University that we hope to add on to Oxford. Also that this is only the beginning & will very likely altogether fail—most likely—but so far good. . . .

P.S. The best way in which you can revenge yourself on me for writing such a letter as this, is by telling me of your arrangements in hospitals. I think that you will behave very ill if you don't contrive to live until your nurses & sisters are spread through all the hospitals & infirmaries. . . .

117
Balliol College
Oxford
[November 1866]

What do you think that we have been doing during the last week?—Electing two fellows[1] . . . I am sorry that we could not elect your friend, "the clean & singular youth", because I have a strong conviction that he was the ablest of all the candidates. But he broke down so much in the examination, & it is so dangerous to throw over the examination that I could not vote for him, nor could I have got others to vote if I had myself.

There were 7 candidates, all of them first classmen. They were probably more than half of the able young men in the University. What were their opinions? . . . Two of them were manifest Comtists; 4 of them were manifest democrats & liberals; 1 seemed to be balancing between his old Tory education & the new notions he had acquired at Oxford. The two Comtists were the poorest of the candidates; they seemed to have only their formulas and good powers of writing. There was not a word of the Church or Bp. Butler or anything of that sort, which was the staple of Oxford 30 years ago. One of the successful candidates wrote a very able English Essay with a wonderful judicial calmness (the subject was "The future internal condition of England judged of by the present"). But it was observed at the end that the only institution of the country which he had left standing was Fellowships. What is the far off event or state of opinion to which this is tending? It is nonsense to speak of the reaction at Oxford, at least among the able men—and the opinions of the able men must affect others in time. I wish life were a little longer that I might see the end.

The new election makes me stronger than ever in College:[2] I can never be annoyed again by the Master & the rascal Bursar & the incapable Senior Tutor[3] &, what is of more importance, I hope that I may be able to do many useful things.

---

³ See above, p. xxiv.

[1] J. Purves and James Leigh Strachan-Davidson.
[2] See above, p. xxiii.
[3] Scott, Wall and Woollcombe.

Much as I like Gorgias[4] I fear that there is a danger of his being regarded by all parties as a political bore. He has stopped the Reform Bill. But this is just the thing which the Conservatives will most bitterly regret two years hence. Nor can he come into any Conservative or Coalition ministry which deals with the question. The true policy of the Conservatives will be felt hereafter to be "getting the question out of the way"....

Last Sunday I spent with Mr. Coleridge, who is rapidly losing the remains of his High Church opinions. I liked him. He seems to me to have more sense of the value of truth than I expected. I was surprized to see what an evident dislike he has to Gladstone & his ways, which he seemed to think was shared by a great proportion of the Liberal party. This is a good thing in one way, but a bad thing in another. What a dislocated world of antagonism this political world is! Lord Russell feeble & superannuated; Gladstone & Lowe divided against themselves; Lord Stanley giving up political philosophy for party; Cardwell mum; Dizzy a wandering Jew perhaps destined to outlive them all; Lord Derby a schoolboy of magnificent proportions all his life. And then to think of America & foreign politics, or looking at home at Education & the Church & to see the utter helplessness to make organic changes. Don't you wish for a Bismarck to set the workhouses right? Does not the good last in politics & the evil disappear? Therefore by all means do evil that good may come, provided the good be greater. With which very immoral sentiment I am....

118 Private (B.J.)[1]

Nov. 28 [1866]

I think that I understood you about Dr. Stanley. Lady Augusta[2] is, I believe, quite aware of the danger to which you refer. At least I find that she has insisted on her sister-in-law[3] discontinuing to live with them for a part of the year, i.e. altogether.

He is not dishonest or sophistical, I assure you. But did you never come across a person (or a whole family) who has fallen under the torpedo touch of another? That I believe is the true account of the matter. He has behaved strangely to me at times & I have always imagined this to be the explanation. For I know from a long experience that his real nature is truthful & that he has very fine points of character.

I am very sorry about him for he always now looks ill & unhappy, and his sister, as I am told, is miserable. I tell you this that you may know the real state of matters.

[4] Gorgias, Plato's rhetorician, and BJ's name for Lowe.

---

[1] BL Add. MS 45783 fo. 60.
[2] Lady Augusta Stanley.
[3] Mary Stanley.

Lady Augusta asked me to say to you that if you ever could see her & would let her know she would greatly like to see you (they would never have known that I know you but for Madame Mohl asking about you at their house)....

119
Balliol College
Oxford
[November 1866]

... Gorgias[1] has been here & is just gone (he came after all), that kindly cynic, & has been charming everybody with his conversation—he is the very best "company". He will talk about anything to anybody ("Plautus is not too heavy for him nor Seneca too light"),[2] from the last lying gossip in London up to Plato & Hegel. Do you know I think that his visit has done some good? He has entirely & heartily agreed to take up the subject of University Reform (that part which is not in Mr Coleridge's hands) & thinks of putting all the principal points into an Act of Parliament.[3] (I perceive that he does this 3/4ths from his old interest in the place—he was a private Tutor here for 7 years—but also 1/4 from a desire "to have it out" with Gladstone.) This is agreed upon. Also he allowed me to have a long talk with him about primary education & he seems disposed to take that up also. He thought that it was impossible to get rid of the present system, but was inclined to try & supplement it, first by permissive rating aided, as at present, by grants from the Privy Council: 2ndly by compulsory rating in districts where education was disgraceful, without the aid of the P. Council. The great difficulty is to provide management for these.

I have heard about this education for the last 20 years from Temple & Lingen, & I want to make out from them & from Rogers what is best & practicable, & then urge it on Mr Lowe. I want him to see that this is the true answer to Bright's attack upon him. I find him very sensible to any warm appreciation of his abilities & character. Do you know that the Albino part of the business[4] has had a very serious effect upon him, beginning with a dislike on his mother's part? (You know I tell you things that I should tell no one else)....

---

[1] Lowe.

[2] 'Seneca cannot be too heavy, nor Plautus too light', *Hamlet*, II. ii. 396–7.

[3] The Oxford and Cambridge Universities Education Bill of 1867 was introduced by W. Ewart (Dumfries), who sought to open the Universities to students without obliging them to become members of colleges (*PD*, clxxxv. 1704–5, 12 Mar. 1867). He quoted Wall and Vaughan. Lowe spoke on 5 June (*PD*, clxxxvii. 1632–4), and served on the Select Committee nominated on 26 June.

[4] 'The peculiarity of my eyes consists in the total absence of colouring matter; this occasions ... a very marked peculiarity of complexion ... it necessarily occasions a great impatience of light. The eyelids must always be nearly closed, and so I have never been able to enjoy the luxury of staring anyone full in the face.' 'A Chapter of Autobiography' (1876) in A. P. Martin, *Life and Letters of... Viscount Sherbrooke* (2 vols., 1893), i. 4–5.

120   Balliol College
                                                           Oxford
                                                           [6 December 1866]

... Have you read the B. of London's charge? "Holiness is doing as I do"; "Truth is as much rhetoric as the Clergy are willing to bear." Still there is a great deal of kindliness & humanity in it.[1] Do you know that he has converted you into an English Churchwoman? He has.

121   address R. Lingen's Esq.,
Combe Hurst   6 Westbourne Crescent
Kingston   [December 1866]

I write to thank you for your most kind letter, which I have partly analysed & sent to Mr Roundell.... I always consider him to be one of the best of my pupils. For with good though not striking abilities he unites the most indomitable perseverance & force of character & is the most liberal & disinterested of men. He has really reformed Merton College.

I have been thinking a little more about the subject on which I bored you last Sunday. It seems to me that something very effective might be written on the present condition of the English soldier—his insufficient pay—his ruinously inactive life—his enforced celibacy—his miserable invalided state, winding up with the un-humane side of the question, the impossibility of having an efficient army which is made up of the dregs of the people, demoralized & uneducated. It would be a contribution to the subject of Army Reform which might strike upon people as with the sound of a trumpet. It should be also "an appeal to the feelings" about the Common Soldier. No one could do this so well as you, & from no one would it come so appropriately or command so much attention.

I would gladly give a fortnight at any time to helping you in this—I mean only in the way of criticism—verification & lightening the labour. For I should spoil it if I did anything more....

122   Balliol College
                                                           Oxford
                                                           [20 December 1866]

I am very grateful to you for your letter & will take your advice as far as I am able. I don't think that I am so unwell as you suppose.... I do work hard certainly and have a great deal of excitement from conversations & interviews

---

[1] Tait wrote, 'The time has, I think, come when the clergy generally and the heads of the Church must enter fully into the question how the help of Christian women living in community and holding themselves ready to act among the sick and poor is to be best arranged.' *The Times*, 4 Dec. 1866 (5def).

with old pupils & friends. But then, I eat & drink & sleep like a pig, & have no cares or anxieties in these latter days.

Don't you think that you might have been my half-sister in some former state of existence? Please therefore not to be anxious about me, my dear sister & friend....

I should like to talk to you about something which has been long on my mind about you. I want you, if possible, to see if you can find something else to do besides carrying on this incessant conflict with government offices. I don't think that you should allow all your great experience of life & religion & education & hospitals and army administration to pass away & make no sign. No one could say what you could say about many things, and though you are shattered in health & nerves, yet I am sure that your mind is as strong as ever.... Moreover, I fancy that I could really help you in this, & this would be a very pleasant tie between us....

I have prospered with my pupils this week. 12 of them have got first classes & one has just gained a studentship at Ch. Ch.[1]

123

Alderley Park[1]
Congleton
until Saturday
Jan. 1, 1867

I think that I ought to send my best wishes for all your undertakings on the first day of the new year. I must own that I don't quite like your way of keeping these festivities, while the rest of the world are eating & drinking. But then I regard you also as a superior being who is not to be required to do as other people.

I believe that you will get a great deal done in the ensuing year. Administrative reforms are in the air, either from the Conservatives to excuse themselves for not bringing forward a Reform Bill, or from your old friends the Whigs. There is certainly a sense of security & of possible advantage in having one's own party in, & though they are so foolish as to be almost too proud to speak to the Radicals there are no other people to do the work. (This is a Whig House & the most amusing squabbles go on between Lord Stanley & some of the younger members of the family, who are supposed to keep low company.)

Will you keep hope at the bottom of the Box? Although you have been jilted, deceived, & abominably used by every one, I really think that better times are coming & that some of the gentlemen's intentions are serious, though you can't expect to be married to four of them at once. Especially that

---

[1] de Paravicini.

[1] Home of E. J. Stanley, second Baron Stanley of Alderley. In his next letter (of Jan. 1867) BJ described him as 'a curious study of an old Whig, clear headed and able, who cannot be got to pass the limits of Whig Aristocratic tradition'.

Indian lover of your's,² I hope that you will not really cast off though there is no harm in fighting him a little. He is a good fellow really, and there is a great deal to be got out of him. . . .

124
Farringford
Address Inglewood Torquay
after Sat^y
[January, 1867]

. . . I am staying here with Tennyson who, I am afraid, is, like me, doing nothing. He repeated to me very impressively last night what, I think, I have told you before, his awful sense (he did not like to say God, for that was become hackneyed), of the great essence of all things holding communion with him. How unmanageable these strong creatures are! They do just what they like, & think as they like, & are, in a manner predestinated by their own characters to be what they are. I cannot imagine anyone saying anything to Tennyson that would exercise a rational influence over him, though he has been scared by the Quarterly out of writing his great poem on King Arthur. . . .¹

I wish you would tell me what you think Gorgias² might do. Some difficulty is springing up about our Oxford Bills, owing, I fear, to the jealousy which Coleridge has of Gorgias. My own idea about him is 1) that he should not trust the Tories, who will do nothing for him. 2) But try to make himself an independent position on a liberal conservative basis. 3) That he should take up some subject beforehand which may continue in a Reformed Parliament. 4) That the only subject of this class which Mr Lowe can take up is Education, & that the best form of treating this question is to bring forward a general permissive Bill for towns to rate themselves, receiving assistance from the Privy Council as at present. This would be the real answer (the proud man's answer) to the attacks of Bright & the Anti-Corn Law League.³ His wife, though a clever & warm hearted woman, is enough to sink anybody.⁴ She as good as told me, what I have no doubt she has told a hundred others, that he had been so ill-treated by the Aristocratic Whigs. But she did not seem to have the slightest notion how damaging it was to him to have this explanation given of his conduct.

The worst of planning anything for Gorgias is that the execution, even if he could be got to take it up, requires not more ability but more policy, more reticence & management of mankind than he seems to be capable of. He is the

---

² Possibly BJ is thinking of the Whigs returning to power, and of de Grey, but early in 1867 FN was also trying to capture the Conservative Secretary of State for India, Lord Cranborne, see F. B. Smith, *Florence Nightingale* (1982), p. 127.

¹ See above, No. 93, n. 1.   ² Lowe.
³ An anachronistic way of referring to Bright's political allies.
⁴ See above, No. 102, n. 1.

quickest, the clearest, the ablest & one of the most public spirited men (really) whom I have ever known (I wish you had had him instead of Lord de Grey), but he wants to do everything by force. He is the only man that I see who would fearlessly attempt great administrative reforms. But when he came to have a whole profession—the Army; Church—arrayed against him & he came to be deserted by his colleagues, he would be likely to sink under the load of unpopularity....

125
                 Inglewood,
                 Torquay.
                 Jan. 15 [1867]

... Shall I have the pleasure of coming to see you at 3 o'clock on Thursday week?—on my way from Mr Rogers, from whom I mean to gather all that I can learn about Education, to Mr Lowe to whom I mean to communicate it....

126
                 Private

                 Address until Monday
                 Rectory
                 Bishopgate[1]
                 afterwards Oxford
                 [January, 1867]

 I am staying with Mr Lowe whom I heartily like—though a little narrow from an excess of political economy & a deficiency of knowledge of the world, he is a most honest man. I wish you could get the situation of matron of all England under him.

 I thought that you might like to hear his views about the London poor.

 Shortly they are these:

1. The entire administration of the London poor to be transferred to the Poor Law Board. This he thinks necessary because of the incapacity of the guardians. And he thinks that there would be an additional gain in the office being brought more nearly into contact with the actual working of the law.
2. A general London rate: this he thinks a case in which the rights of property are overborn by the considerations of a public policy.
3. Casuals (Pall Mall Gazette)[2] & all that to be handed over to the police.
4. I think that he would try absolutely to suppress mendicancy.

 I don't know whether all this is practicable, but I thought you would like to hear his views. He has very strong sanitary interests.

[1] Rogers'.

[2] In Jan. 1866 the *Pall Mall Gazette* sent a reporter to spend a night in Lambeth workhouse 'there to learn by actual experience how casual paupers are lodged and fed, and what the 'casual' is like, and what the porter who admits him, and the master who rules over him'. *Pall Mall Gazette*, 12 Jan., pp. 137–8, 13 Jan., p. 150, 15 Jan., pp. 161–2, repr. in *The Times*, 13 Jan. (5ef), 15 Jan. (12de), and 16 Jan. (10de).

127   Balliol College
                                                                                              Oxford
                                                                                              [January 1867]

I hope to be in London on Sunday week & shall come & see you at 3 O'clock, if I may have that pleasure.

I had a very pleasant stay with Gorgias,[1] who is the best of friends with me, and I think that I have healed the rupture between Coleridge & him. I can hardly tell whether he will be induced to take up the subject of education. We had a sort of consultation about it, at which Lingen assisted, & he said that he would see what could be done if opportunity offered. Lingen & he both thought that it was useless for any one to bring forward the subject who was not in the Ministry. They agreed that the first step was to have educational districts on which the Inspectors could report; & that this would involve divesting the Inspectors of their denominational character. Lowe thought strongly that a general permissive Bill for rating should be introduced & was quite willing to support this. But he was against introducing any compulsion on parents.

I also saw our friends, the Trevelyans, & asked them about Sir J. Lawrence. They both said that they thought his government would be successful on the whole but that he was very unpopular. I asked 'Why' & they said for two reasons: partly his manners, & chiefly his distribution of patronage, wh. is almost entirely given by him to his old acquaintances in the Punjaub. When the Trevelyans remonstrated with him about this, he said that he must give to people whom he knew. Thus great heartburnings & jealousies have arisen & it is thought impossible for a man to get on in India unless he has been with Sir J. Lawrence in the Punjaub....

128   February 19 [1867]

Are not politics becoming a hopeless, impossible scrape? Everybody is divided from everybody & this wretched Convocation[1] & Church of England are adding to the troubles of the unfortunate nation. Men of much greater honesty & power are needed, & no one can see where they are to come from (not a divided power like Gladstone's). In a few years no one will much care about having a Parliament.

I hope you like your Poor Law Amendment Act[2] upon reflection—I think that it is a considerable gain.

Do you follow that "rampant lecturer", Mr Goldwin Smith? He is very

[1] Lowe.

---

[1] Convocation, which was revived in 1852, met on 12 Feb. 1867.
[2] The Metropolitan Poor Bill, later 30 and 31 Vict. c. 6, 'for the establishment in the Metropolis of Asylums for the Sick, Insane, and other classes of the Poor, and of Dispensaries, and for the distribution over the Metropolis of portions of the charge for Poor Relief'.

untrustworthy & full of honourable & dishonourable sentiments too. I think that he is a curious example of a man not having to trouble himself about his private character, provided he can make a good display in public. He is trying to act the part of the great man—But though he is a man of a good deal of erratic power, he is not really a great man. Nor can he write as vigorously as Junius, which is maintained by some of his admirers. He appears to me to be both reticent & often false—always self asserting, & hardly tolerating others. But I think that he may be a considerable instrument in doing something or other.

129
                                                      Balliol College
Oxford
[March 1867]

I shall hope to have the pleasure of coming to see you (if you are not yet tired of my visits, as you will some day be) on Sunday, March 24, at 3 o'clock.

I am afraid that your Poor Law Bill[1] is passing with fatal celerity into the serene atmosphere of the House of Lords, in which nothing that is bad has any chance of being stopped. But you will get something more done in a Reformed Parliament & with the help of Mr Mill & perhaps Mr Lowe.

I suppose that the Liberals will do all that they can to keep in the Ministry until the whole party has irretrievably lost their character. There is a curious "whirligig of revenges" in the business. Gladstone, being only half a Liberal, is not thought worthy (by Providence I mean) to pass a Reform Bill, just as David was not thought worthy to build the Temple.[2] The Liberals also, being only Conservatives in disguise, are to have the great measure taken from them by their opponents. Dizzy is destined to pass the bill (with some aid from Mephistopheles & the black art for which he will have to suffer hereafter). But then in accomplishing this feat he is doing 20 year's afterwards that for which he attacked Sir R. Peel. And all parties are doing what they don't want to do & what there was no reason, except their own folly, for their doing at all. Among political men perhaps at this moment Bright stands first & Lowe second & Gladstone third & Dizzy fourth & yet possibly within a year the Jew may outshine them all in the clear sky of fame—if, but this is a great if—he can persuade his party to sacrifice their character wholly for the sake of him who had no character....

Did you read the D. of Argyle's book?[3] It seemed to me like the work of a religious, orthodox mind partially getting under the dominion of science without the least idea of whither he was going, stating premises from which he would never venture to draw the self-evident conclusions. Does not the book

---

[1] See above, No. 128, n. 2.
[2] 1 Chr. 17: 4, 22: 8, 28: 3.
[3] G. D. Campbell, eighth Duke of Argyll, *The Reign of Law* (1867).

amount to this? He believes in the dominion of law as much as Professor Tyndal & others, but for the sake of a religious sound he prefers to state this under the name of design....

130

Balliol College
Oxford
[March 1867]

... I read today your pamphlet about India again.[1] Did it ever occur to you that you might write a short pamphlet or tract somewhat similar to that for the natives in India & get it translated? That would be a curious & interesting thing to do. When I saw the other day the account of Miss Carpenter in India (a terrible woman, but much to be respected) I felt half sorry that it was not you. They would have worshipped you like a divinity. A pretty reason! you will say. But then you might have gently rebuked the adoring natives, as St Paul did on a similar occasion, & assured them that you were only a washerwoman, & not a divinity at all; that would have had an excellent effect.

A friend of mine was telling me to-day that he had heard Mrs Lowe screaming, at the top of her voice, in a foreign railway carriage, 'Robert will be at 'em again, if they don't give him something good'. Is not this funny? I don't tell you this to depreciate them, who are two as honest people as breathe (in a sort, as Shakespeare says[2]), but because in this vale of tears nothing ludicrous should be lost. What would become of us if we were not laughing animals?...

131

[21 March 1867]

I am always pleased when I see any mention of you in the newspaper, like that in Lord Devon's speech.[1] I don't suppose that you care much, but I am sure that anything of that sort gives you an increased power of gaining your points.

Don't you think that you could get out of Lord Kimberley & their compliments some further improvements in Committee? N.B. (Lord Kimberley is a clever, popularity hunting, rather vulgar aristocrat, ambitious & energetic—he talked to me once about Plato—such long winded nonsense—he is not unlikely, however, some day to be Prime Minister).

Did you ever hear of the Baron Ward? He was an honest stable boy who was made a minister. He was very straight forward. He used to say, as he told

---

[1] *How People May Live and Not Die in India* (1863).

[2] Gonzalo: 'Is not, sir, my doublet as fresh as the first day I wore it? I mean, in a sort.' Antonio: 'That sort was well fish'd for'; *The Tempest*, II. i. 98–100.

---

[1] In the debate on the Metropolitan Poor Bill W. R. Courtenay said 'It would be improper on such an occasion to omit reference to the improved feeling on the subject which had resulted from the admiration the country must feel for that excellent and gifted woman, Miss Nightingale ...', *The Times*, 20 Mar. 1867 (6a).

a friend of mine, 'When anybody uses fine words to me', I say to him 'You be d——d'. As I know you are in the habit of privately swearing I recommend this anecdote (not) for your imitation....

132

Balliol College
Oxford
March 27 [1867]

I completed today the last page of my translation of Plato, & have revised rather more than two thirds....

I want to try & make people understand that they can only do justice to Plato by treating him historically as the natural growth of his age. I believe that the recognition of this historical point of view is the greatest difference between one man's mind & anothers. I hope to make people see that ideas have a history as well as nations, & that the greatest growth of ideas which there has ever been was in the century 450–350 B.C.

When that is done I have schemes beyond....

You see that the burden having partly slipped off my back makes me egotistical & talkative. Life seems to me perfectly swarming with interests, & I think that I get more interests as I get older. Don't you admit that the world is a very interesting place in which there is so much to be done & suffered? I am afraid that you often suffer terribly but I cannot believe that you are dull. Don't you know that you are one of the Queens of the Earth & ought to wear your crown lightly, & smile sometimes.

I see that the Poor Law Bill is actually through the House of Lords.[1] Politics seem to be getting out of their mess a little, owing to the general desire to pass the Reform Bill. What a good speech Dizzy made![2] You would not think that the mean looking Jew was a match, & more than a match, for Gladstone. But that is really the fact. I saw R. Lowe after I left you on Sunday. He prophesied that the Bill would not pass. But, I believe that it will, notwithstanding. He has broken 'the stick with which he beat the dog'. He will get into trouble if he does not mind—for he lives in a glass house, but wants to throw stones. It would be a great 'Mephistophelic' triumph for him if, after having thrown out the late ministry, he throws out this too.

I also saw some 'particular' friends of Lord Kimberley's who screamed at the idea of his being Prime Minister, & thought that his mother had been wanting in the common duties of life towards him in allowing him to grow up such a 'bore'. 'It might have been prevented'.

A very pretty, charming young lady favoured me with a visit yesterday—the same of whom you wrote to me—Lady Catherine Fielding, who is now married to Mr Clive. There could not be a happier or more pleasing pair than they are—neither very clever but most agreeable sort of natures....

[1] Passed third reading on 25 Mar. 1867.
[2] On the second reading of the Reform Bill, 26 Mar. 1867, *PD*, clxxxvi. 642–4.

133
Darmstadt
April 22 [1867]

... I am glad that you introduced Miss Carpenter to Sir John Lawrence. She has done real work in carrying on a Reformatory at Bristol with her own hands (though her enemies declare that she, in her enthusiasm for the cause, gets quite honest children out of the street). But she has shown great self-devotion & is a very good woman, & able & managing. On the other hand, she is ungainly in her appearance & rather a bore from her pertinacity & unintelligent Unitarianism (I should no more think of contradicting her on the subject of the comparative merits of Sir Joshua Jebb & Sir Walter Crofton—the latter is her oracle—than I should of contradicting you, 'dear Miss Nightingale', on the subject of contagion. 'Away, Sir, with your wheedling language!—don't you know that agreement on the subject of contagion is the only solid basis of friendship with me?' Well, but I do not believe in contagion after all.) To return, however, to Miss Carpenter. Her life, compared with that of most women, is admirable—still, however, leaving something to be desired & I find that she is the terror of Mr Lingen & others because they cannot get her out of their rooms.

I have spent the last week very pleasantly with my old friend [Morier] whose conversation I always find very instructive about foreign politics. He is full of ... the history of cooperation in Prussia which seems, under the presidency of Schulze Delitzsch, to have acquired enormous proportions. (It is based on Societies which borrow money collectively, and are responsible individually, with unlimited liability. The Society lends out this borrowed capital to individual workmen who are shareholders & are bound in their own security & that of two other shareholders. No failure or breakdown has, as yet, occurred among them.) Morier does not know what to think about the war—the time is now or never for France—& if the Prussians refuse to withdraw their garrison from Luxembourg he thinks that the war must go on.[1] He has the worst opinion of Bismarck, which I find is shared by the Princess & the Crown Princess[2] & all the German liberals, & thinks that the liberal cause in Germany, as distinct from the national, is far worse off than some years ago. But he & the Princess heartily acquiesce in the general result as better than the other alternative of Austria winning, I find the universal expectation here is that the war must come & both parties are arming, as they say, to the teeth. It is thought that Austria will stand aloof for the present, & perhaps come in at the end as mediator in the struggle. She seems to have a man in [von] Beust who knows what he means but is the reverse of a high character in another sense.

---

[1] 'If warlike rumours could bring about war, a pacific solution of the Luxemburg question would already be well-nigh hopeless', *The Times*, 22 Apr. 1867 (6b). See M. R. D. Foot, 'Great Britain and Luxemburg 1867' in *English Historical Review* (1952), pp. 352–79.

[2] Alice and Victoria.

134

Balliol College
Oxford
[April 1867]

... I have had my regular half yearly battle with the College, which was very successful & ended, I think, in a complete & final defeat of the Master & Senior Tutor,¹ & in a considerable improvement of the College. They have agreed to remodel the Divinity teaching which will hereafter be given in a freer manner,² & also to substitute a Lecturer for the Senior Tutor in a part of his work, which, as he is supposed to have 'a vested interest', is all that can be done with him.

The other day I cut Mr. Simon in the street, purely out of regard for you. I hear also that he is very unpopular in his Profession. But I am sometimes afraid that you carry your enmity to him further than is expedient. For he has a great deal of influence in these matters, & people always find out when you hate them.

Have you seen the article in the Quarterly on 'the Nightingale in the East'?³ Perhaps it may be disagreeable to have such verses made upon you: (they would call you 'Sweet Philomel', I am sure, if they knew that Philomel was the Latin for Nightingale). It gave me rather pleasure to find that you are a popular 'angel'. For it shows that these poor creatures have a sort of vague instinct that you are living for them. Therefore 'Be cheerful, lady'....

Will you get a 2nd vol. of Questions for a Reformed Parliament, which is much better than the first?⁴ (I can send you the book if you have not got it.) The two volumes are suggestive & if rather youthful, certainly enlarge the ordinary ideas of politics. I like one by my friend, Mr Newman,⁵ which is very characteristic of him, very able & thoughtful, but one-sided: there is also an interesting one by G. Lushington⁶ (Politics seem to be getting down into the region of trades unions), and not a bad one by C. S. Parker on Education.⁷ These essays won't produce a powerful effect, but they are important as showing the tendencies of younger minds.

Read also Dr Stanley's excellent article on Ritualism in the Edinburgh.⁸ These are the sort of writings in which he really shines much more than in his deeper ones....

¹ Scott and Woollcombe.
² CM, 26–7 Apr. 1867: undergraduates were still to be required to attend Divinity lectures in two terms out of three, but any of the Tutors or Lecturers could henceforth give lectures, and the undergraduates were to be allowed to choose which lectures they would attend.
³ 'The Poetry of Seven Dials' (1. *The Nightingale in the East*. Price One Half-penny (1854)), in the *Quarterly Review*, vol. 122 (1867), pp. 382–406.
⁴ The earlier volume was *Essays on Reform* (1867): the second was *Questions for a Reformed Parliament* (1867).
⁵ W. L. Newman, 'The Land Laws'.
⁶ G. Lushington, 'Workmen and Trade Unions'.
⁷ 'Popular Education'.
⁸ A. P. Stanley, 'Ritualism' in the *Edinburgh Review*, vol. 125 (Apr. 1867), pp. 439–69, repr. in *Essays Chiefly on Questions of Church and State from 1850 to 1870* (1870).

Says Bismarck to the Crown Princess.⁹ 'Gross Preussen I have seen & understand but I never saw German unity'. She replied 'You are orthodox; did you ever see the Holy Ghost?' She & her husband have the most bitter hatred of Bismarck.

Some one (supposed to be Herr von Rogenbach,¹⁰ who by the way is supposed to be making a mess of politics) said 'the Alliance between Prussia & the smaller states is like the alliance between a dog & his fleas'.

Von Beust, the Austrian Prime Minister, is greatly in debt. His creditors thought that it would be a good thing to set on foot a public subscription in honour of him & pay themselves out of the proceeds. However the subscription rather failed, being made up chiefly of the subscriptions of the Creditors. When they presented the subscription to V.B. he said that he could not think of taking money simply for doing his duty, & presented the whole to a charitable institution. May not this man also save a nation? Is he not of the class whom Carlyle would call "shifty"?

135
                                                                                      Balliol College
                                                                                            Oxford
                                                                                       [May 1867]

... At what a rate the chariot of democracy is driving.¹ It almost takes away one's breath. Last week the democratic movement might have been stopped; the Ministry driven from office, & a bill something like that of last session reintroduced. But all that is now impossible. Household suffrage, lodger franchise, one year's residence, are fairly given & cannot be withheld—and if the Conservatives are, as appears, really willing to give up principles which they held sacred a month ago, the Bill is certain to pass. For their opponents cannot, if they would, oppose them. And the Lords dare not.

Think of the effects on the Church of England (that of Ireland is gone anyhow)² & on the whole country. Think of the exultation of the Jew, who has revenged all his personal wrongs, triumphed over the virtue of Gladstone, made himself an historical name & really done a great service (not taking into account the means). He has got his pound of flesh out of these Tory magnates who have scoffed at him. People have often said that he would be the leader of the Radicals, but they never guessed that he would accomplish it by making the Tories Radicals. There is something that is not quite intelligible in his colleagues neither actively supporting nor opposing him. Think of all this also in connexion with the Conservative reaction of six years ago.

Goldwin Smith came to see me today, the first time for a great many years.

⁹ Victoria.
¹⁰ F. von Roggenbach.

¹ An amendment to reduce the residence qualification for compound householders from two years to twelve months was carried on 2 May by 278 votes to 197.
² The Irish Church was disestablished in 1869.

He looked, to my eye, very ill & not likely to live.³ He has a great head stuck upon a mere lath of a body....

Will you send me a volume of St Theresa or St John of the Cross that I may take my first draught of mysticism?⁴

136
Balliol College
Oxford
May 31, 1867

... There is a talk of the Ministry making the 'rascal' Bursar, Dean of Chester: they will do some good if they do.¹

After I left you I went back & dined at Mr Lowe's, who has become a warm friend of mine & is a 'lover' of yours: (He is very susceptible to female influences.) We were talking about Clough, & then he asked about Mr Nightingale & whether I knew anything about you. I gave him to understand (on the principle of pickpockets in a crowd) that I knew something & he said, "She's a noble minded woman & so charming". He also told me that you had written him what he in his wisdom was pleased to call "a rhapsody" about the removal of the hospitals, to which he by the aid of the devil, or rather of Simon Magus, contrived an answer. Why do I tell you this, which is a shameful breach of confidence? First, because I want you to know that I am not at all jealous of your having "lovers" & secondly, perhaps, to insinuate that you should not write rhapsodies to people who don't understand that sort of thing. He said that he did not show your letter because he thought that it would do you no good; he also said that he should like to come & call upon you.

Do you remember the line in Shakespeare:

"There is much matter in these convertites".²

... Would you like to know the list of persons whom Oxford is going to honour with Degrees? (This is another breach of confidence, which is the only reason why I tell you)

Sir H. Storks   D.C.L.
Lord Kingsdown
R. Browning
Abp. Trench
Mr Peabody

... How would you like to have one, in company with Colenso, Mazzini & Bright? That would make the honour worth having.

---

³ He lived till 1910.

⁴ The books FN sent were probably *The Life of St Theresa, Written by Herself*, trans. by J. Dalton (1851), and *The Spirit of St John of the Cross, Consisting of his Maxims, Sayings, and Spiritual Advice on Various Subjects*, trans. by J. Dalton (1863).

¹ Wall was not appointed: on 12 June the place went to J. S. Howson.

² 'Out of these convertites, there is much matter to be heard and learn'd', *As You Like It*, v. iv. 178–9.

What do you think that I have been doing during the last month—translating the Politics of Aristotle....[3]

137   [c. 3 June 1867][1]

I have a satisfaction in telling you that I did the Hebrew Conservative[2] today.

I got the Dean of Ch. Ch. to put up Lord Kingsdown for a D.C.L. degree; being a conservative he was carried. Pusey was furious & made a scene in the Council which will not soon be forgotten. I regret to say that they revenged themselves by throwing out Browning (which is a disgrace), but there is some chance of this being corrected. Do not mention about this until you see it in the paper.

I spent yesterday with Tennyson, not without regret. I doubt whether he will do much more; he seems to me to have lost his energy for writing. He is also so utterly unpractical, & (not altogether from selfishness) so intensely egotistical, as at times to be insupportable; you feel at the same time that there is a nobler element in him. She is a saint—a sacred person, who can never be spoken of as highly as she deserves, but she has not self love enough to keep herself alive. (Do you remember Bentham's proof that on principles of pure benevolence only, Adam & Eve must have died in Paradise in less than a month.[3]) Well that is her case. She is living in a house totally uninhabitable, in the worst sanitary state, because Tennyson has such a dislike to the house in the I. of Wight, & she is consequently always ill.

I think that the "pretty" Miss Agnes Jones is much better off with her own good sense than with the exalted ways of Mrs Butler or St. Theresa. Do you remember the place in St. Theresa's life when she speaks of the error she committed in forming a friendship with a very wicked man?[4] That is a mistake which Mrs Butler has made too, & has not yet discovered to be a mistake: & yet, I believe, for the best motives.

That you may not think me mad in translating the Politics I transcribe a short passage for you. "Now we ought to be careful of the health of the inhabitants & this will depend, first, on the situation & aspect of the place, secondly

---

[3] Vol. i and vol. ii, Pt. 1 of BJ's edition of the *Politics* were published in 1885: vol. ii, Pt. 2 was never published.

[1] BL Add. MS 45783 fos. 114–16.

[2] Pusey.

[3] 'Take any two persons, A and B, and suppose them the only persons in existence: call them, for example, *Adam* and *Eve*. *Adam* has no regard for himself: the whole of his regard has for its object *Eve*. *Eve* in like manner has no regard for herself: the whole of her regard has for its object *Adam* . . . at the end of an assignable length of time, greater or less according to accident, but in no case so much as a twelvemonth, both will unavoidably have perished.' F. Rosen and J. H. Burns (eds.), *Constitutional Code*, vol. i (1983), VI, 31, A9, p. 119. The point is discussed in F. Rosen, *Jeremy Bentham and Representative Democracy, A Study of the 'Constitutional Code'* (1983), pp. 206–11.

[4] *The Life of St Theresa, Written by Herself*, trans. by J. Dalton (1851), Chap. V.

on the use of good water, the care of which ought to be made a first object. For those things which we use most & oftenest have the greatest influence on health: & water & air are of this nature" &c Ar. Pol. VII, XI, 4.[5] And I could find similar passages in Plato's Laws.

I see that the memory of Lord Herbert is revived by the completion of his Statue. . . .[6]

[*Postscript omitted*]

138
Balliol College
Oxford
[June 1867]

. . . I sometimes think that you have not the temper of success. When you or Sir Bartle Frere think that you have done nothing, that may be in some degree true as a fact amid the difficulties & hindrances of human things. But is not the greater part a certain state of nerves, or a certain attitude of character, like the way which good people have of declaring that they are very miserable sinners.

I like to hear my friend Mr Browning say 'I have just finished a poem (I am ashamed to tell you the length—about 20,000 lines); I am sure that it is by far the best thing which I have yet done & when I have done that, I shall try to do something better still, & so on as long as I live! And I like to think of myself as beginning & not ending (though this may be a fancy) & I want you to let me think the same of you.

You kindly ask about Mr Browning's degree D.C.L. (Your friend Sir Bartle is to have a degree).[1] Stage 1st, A fortnight ago his degree was proposed in the Council but he failed to obtain the 2/3rds of the votes: Stage the 2nd, his friends in the hope partly of preventing this disgrace falling upon the University, memorialize the Council (about 100 residents signed) requesting that the degree might be conferred. Stage 3rd, The Council, being alarmed, & also unwilling to say that they had been wrong, agree that he shall have an Hon. M.A. degree. Did you ever hear of anything so idiotic? The last occurred today.

What do you think I have been doing for the last 2 days—entertaining a large party of folks—Mr. Browning, Lady Airlie, Mr. M. Arnold, Mr. Munro of Cambridge, Mr. Lecky, the Lingens &c. Mr. Lecky is an extremely tall & very thin man with a face expressive of a great deal of genius—a little thin in his intelligence too, but still a remarkable man. I like him & Mr. Munro of

---

[5] BJ's published translation runs: 'Special care should be taken of the health of the inhabitants, which will depend chiefly on the healthiness of the locality and of the quarter to which they are exposed, and secondly, on the use of pure water; this latter point is by no means a secondary consideration. For the elements which we use most and oftenest for the support of the body contribute most to health, and among these are water and air.'

[6] A statue by J. H. Foley was unveiled in front of the old War Office in Pall Mall on 1 June 1867.

[1] Frere received a DCL in 1867, and Browning an Honorary MA in 1868. Browning received a DCL in 1882.

Cambridge (who is a great scholar) very much. I give these entertainments once or twice a term in conjunction with Mr. Roundell at Merton: they give me an opportunity of introducing the undergraduates.

A. Peel (who was of the party) tells me that the Liberal Party are getting more & more demoralized—he despairs of Gladstone, "who has no sense". "Will you take our madman in exchange for your rogue?" was the address of a Liberal to a Conservative a few days ago. I was struck by what he said, as he is naturally allied to Gladstone.

About Mr Lowe, I think that he is likely to become a more important man, & therefore I would advise you to keep up a connexion with him. Could you not interest him about sanitary matters (notwithstanding Simon Magus)? He is full of the importance of such matters, but he belongs too much to the "impossible" school of Political Economists. When I next see him, if I have your leave, I shall tell him to call upon you.

I am very glad indeed, that you have got such an ally as Sir B. Frere—(don't let him break his heart or keep him company in doing so, but try & get him sent to India as Governor General). I judge of him partly from what you say & partly from what my old friend Sir A. Grant has told me about him....

139 Oxford
July 18, 1867

... I talked about Sir S. Northcote to some people who know him. They say, besides what I told you, that he works really hard at Indian affairs. Now you must get hold of him & fuse him & Sir Bartle Frere & Sir J. Lawrence into one by some alchemy or wicked wit of woman, & then something will be accomplished. I hear you bursting into a loud laugh but am I not right in telling you not to yield to the sympathetic fallacy, & never to give up a friend or patron while there is anything more to be got out of him? (I resign Sir C. Trevelyan to his fate.)

I went before the Committee on Monday & was examined for an hour, & then cross-examined for more than three hours on Tuesday.[1] Lowe, who was present, was quite satisfied & very much pleased, but I don't trust his judgement (any more than I do your's) of my performance, because he is partial to me. (And yet how often during the last four years have I been charmed & encouraged by your 'good words', which I did not believe, notwithstanding.) (As for Lowe, what an impulsive being he is! He cannot resist the impulse to make a good joke, or a classical allusion, or to fly out at anything or anybody.) To return to our Committee: I really believe that we shall succeed in getting free education at Oxford, independent of the Colleges, which will make an enormous difference. You have no idea what much greater liberality there is at

---

[1] See above, p. xxiv. BJ went before the Select Committee on University extension on 15–16 July. His evidence is in *PP* (1867), xiii. 324–48, Qu. 2380–699. The Committee also heard evidence from W. L. Newman, and from Scott.

Oxford than at Cambridge, about University matters. I read the Cambridge evidence;[2] it was quite miserable to see the adhesion, even of liberal men among them, to the old routine. My friend Mr Roundell & the Dean of Ch. Ch. (who is an excellent Reformer out of Ch. Ch.) gave capital evidence.

... Rogers has been getting into some trouble about his Schools with the Bishop & Mr G. Moore. The fact is that the secular people tug at Rogers, & the Clergy tug at the Bishop, & therefore the alliance between them is rather hollow. But I hope that they are coming to terms. I went to see the schools, which are a splendid institution. There are 700 boys in them already, & probably there will be twice the number in a year's time.

All his life Rogers will go on scheming & organizing. And when these schools are well established, I think that he will be very likely to take up the dwellings of the poor. Therefore, you were quite right in sending him Mr Rathbone's book.[3] The people in his own parish & the Alderman, merchants &c. entirely believe in him, but the Clergy are full of dark suspicions of him. He is very liberal but not farseeing, & he is apt to say anything which comes into his head—this makes people think him irreverent. He has the greatest practical originality, including the special gift of extracting money, of any one whom I have known.

... I think that you & I & Mr Rogers ought to do a great deal more in the rest of life than we have done in the past, as we have certainly more hold & influence (though I don't mean to compare us to you). I sometimes think that the work of Christ only lasted during 3 years & we have (probably) five, six or 7 times three years to live. ...

It seems probable to me that Dizzy & the Ministry will try to make Reforms next year, with a view to the elections, & will have this dying Parliament at their mercy. If this is true the opportunity should be seized.

140
Strathpeffer
Dingwall, N.B.
Aug. 4 [1867]

... I read St Theresa[1] yesterday. ... I know that the visions are all imagination, & I don't disagree with those who would say that the raptures are a sort of expansion or prolongation of earthly love. (It illustrates Plato's notions of love in some degree.) Still, the book has a great interest for me: I think that this is in some degree due to the style, for as a literary work it has very great merit: but much more, the attraction is the intensity of feeling, so far beyond

---

[2] W. H. Bateson, Master of St John's, J. L. Hammond, Bursar of Trinity, Revd. R. Burn, Fellow and Tutor of Trinity, Revd. H. Latham, Fellow and Tutor of Trinity Hall, and H. J. Roby of St John's, had already given evidence.

[3] William Rathbone, *Social Duties Considered with Reference to the Organization of Effort in Works of Benevolence and Public Utility* (1867).

[1] See above, No. 135. n. 4.

anything that is now to be found in this world. Some day I should like to draw out at length, in a sermon, how feeling & intellect ought to be combined. The secret seems to be lost in modern times....

I am glad to see that Sir Stafford Northcote has censured the Orissa mismanagement.² His relatives tell me that by convictions he ought to be a Liberal, as he was when secretary to Gladstone, but that the family blood of Toryism was too strong in him. His son was one of our undergraduates, who has hardly, if he has, been prevented from turning Roman Catholic like Sir C. Wood's eldest son.³

141   Aug 20, 1867
                                                                                                                      Strathpeffer
                                                                                                                      Dingwall
                                                                                                                      N.B.

I am delighted to hear that you are progressing in your Indian work, and that you are casting your toils about Sir S. Northcote.

Did you ever see him? Expect to see not a highborn aristocrat, but a sort of gentleman farmer with a touch of the Methodist parson. I believe him to be a very good man & not a fool—extremely quick & punctual in business, not at all inaccessible to new ideas but requiring to have them put into him, & not at all wanting in courage, but more wanting in the form of mind & character which would enable him to carry out difficult matters. He wants to be elevated, inspired, idealized—is a Liberal at heart in many ways, but has been drawn into Conservatism by family connexions. Fortunately for him Liberalism & Conservatism are now become one.

... May I talk to you as I would to one of the Undergraduates? Take care not to exaggerate to him ... he will have heard things said against you by the officials: & you will have to produce just the opposite impression to these reports....

142   Strathpeffer
                                                                                                                      Dingwall¹
                                                                                                                      [August 1867]

Socrates in the Symposium of Xenophon says that he likes to drink out of a full goblet but that he does not object to be "rained upon in little cups".²

---

² It was said that 750,000 perished in the Orissa famine of 1866, *PD*, clxxxix. 770. Northcote's dispatch criticized Sir Cecil Beadon, the Lieutenant-Governor of Bengal, who had, however, already returned to England in 1866. In his letter of 14 Aug. BJ said that Cranborne expressed FN's views best. Cranborne alleged that from the time the crop failed in 1865, the natives said there would be a famine, the merchants and missionaries tardily realized the natives were right, and the officials 'seemed all to have been walking in a dream', the Lieutenant-Governor at their head refusing to take any precautions. *PD*, clxxxix. 808–14, 2 Aug. 1867.

³ Sir C. L. Wood.

¹ BL Add. MS 45783 fos. 119–20.

² Here Socrates again interposed ... 'If we pour ourselves immense draughts, it will be no long

Do you object to being rained upon in little cups?

I am so glad to hear of your Indian prospects—perhaps you may be Governor General, who knows? And I think that you are quite right in keeping the treasure secret, for it really would be very likely to be lost, if it were talked about. There is no quality that I admire more or which is more rare or more potent than absolute reticence.

My young gentleman [Sir K. Muir Mackenzie] makes astonishing progress & I don't at all regret having taken him. I am going to finish off Lord Lansdowne at St. Andrews. You will attack me for this, but then, even on your theory, 100,000£ a year is of some value in the sight of God. I do not know whether I shall succeed with him for 'How hardly shall they that have riches &c.'³ I am going to have another youth, called Dick Grosvenor; Dick persuaded an Irish undergraduate called Lord Donoughmore to sham illness & go to the Derby with him—which they accordingly did, Dick of course winning & Lord D. losing, to a considerable amount. They were found out & rusticated, & I am now going to see if I can patch up Dick for heaven (he is a very unpromising subject), & then, if Dick (who is now penitent) can be patched up, he will patch up his inseparable friend, Lord D. This does not take up much time. But of late years especially I have felt personally responsible for all the Undergraduates, & am determined that, as far as I can, they shall none of them be lost. I see clearly that this is what I ought to do; not as the principal business, but as a sort of byeplay of life. Some of the things that have been most satisfactory to me have been the results of these sort of long vacation pupils (Morier was one of the first of them)....

143 [*c.* August 1867]

... You shall certainly be informed about 'Dick'. But I have not much expectations from him, for his family have not turned out well. I have another youth coming to stay with me who is very remarkable, one of the ablest young men living—W. Wallace. He is the son of a builder at Cupar, & through a Scotch University has been draughted into Oxford. He is quite a gentleman & yet always seems to have great social difficulties, never having a word to say to any human being, & being of too strong a nature readily to adapt himself to his new circumstances. In power & knowledge he is the best of our Balliol undergraduates & probably in Oxford.

... I am always impressed with the superiority of young men in character

---

time before both our bodies and our minds reel, and we shall not be able even to draw breath, much less to speak sensibly; but if the servants frequently "besprinkle" us—if I too may use a Gorgian expression—with small cups, we shall thus not be driven on by the wine to a state of intoxication, but instead shall be brought by its gentle persuasion to a more sportive mood'; *Xenophon's Banquet, with an English Translation by O. J. Todd* (1922), ii. 25–6.

³ Luke 17: 24.

& power. And yet how few of them come to much: the link with active life seems to be wanting.

144 [*pencil note written from the Tulchan*]
Address
Castle Mount
St Andrews[1]
[September 1867]

Shall I propose to you a study—the comparative merits of Governor Eyre, Sir Cecil Beadon & Mr William Broadhead? The latter has only, as far as I know, taken the life of one man: the two others have slain their thousands & tens of thousands.

... Lord Wodehouse has been staying here. Shall I give you a description of that rising statesman & intending prime minister? He is very clever & ready, & has an abundant armoury of words, & also excellent judgement & is not wanting in pertinacity & courage. His intellectual horizon is a good deal limited to that of the Whig aristocracy—he is liberal as against Church claims, but he does not understand much about such matters. He is intensely egotistical & selfish—affable but vulgar (with floods of talk)—and will only follow the public interest as far as goes with his own private interest. He has great energy & is determined to succeed, & very likely will succeed. Do you see the sort of man? He thought that the great mistake of last year was the 'not dissolving', & that after that mistake all that followed was irremediable & was foreseen by Gladstone.

On my way here I staid a day or two at Mr. G. Duff's, & there I made friends with Mr Thring, the Government Draughtsman, whom I found to have a great interest about sanitary questions, dwellings of the poor & the like, & very anxious to get things of that sort done. I liked him very much & believe you might find him very useful some day....

145 Castle Mount
St Andrews
until Sep. 9 [1867]
afterwards Oxford

... In the first place, though I am really afraid to say it, yet I must pluck up resolution to tell you that I don't believe Sir George Lewis to be Ahriman.[1] The little I knew of him I thought that he was a gentleman & a learned man

---

[1] BL Add. MS 45783 fos. 121-2.

[1] Ahriman, or Angra Mainyu, in the Zoroastrian system, the principle of evil, in perpetual conflict with Ormazd, the god of light.

& a ponderous thinker, weighty even in his jokes, but I believe that he was not fit to be a War Minister. If you will have an incarnation of Satan, take the Duke of Wellington, who had the greatest power & did the least good with it, either for the military or sanitary side of the Army. (People used to want him to introduce the Rifle—he would reply, 'Old muskets break a horse's leg; break a horse's leg, what do you want more?'—or again take the utter neglect of the sanitary state of the army—or of the preparation for another war—or the harbour at Alderney.) I don't think that Sir G. Lewis was nearly as bad as him.

Government is not the evil principle, but it is about $\frac{1}{2}$ or $\frac{1}{3}$ evil. The great evil is routine, & want of originality. (I agree with you quite about 'the trivial round &c.' which we sang in Church today[2]—it sounds pious & is really canting & mischievous—it soothes the minds of those who never intend to deny themselves anything.)

... Do you suppose that the Old India officials—Monros, Malcolms, Metcalfs, Morrisons (all their names begin with M)—were really great?[3] I think that they had singular opportunities in an unsettled state of the country, and in India 'one man does really chase a thousand', but I cannot think, judging either from the state of the finances, or of the health, or of the native army, that they were really great men—there was an element of limitation, I suspect, in all of them which prevented their doing much for the regeneration of the country.

... My stay here has been very prosperous: in the first place, "Dick" has been a good boy, & Lord Lansdowne has worked hard. Then I have here a dear friend, Professor Campbell (one of the best & most liberal & most disinterested of human beings; you see that I have a trick of introducing my friends to you), and we have planned out together his edition of Sophocles. . . .[4]

I am afraid that the B. of London[5] is getting himself entangled with the Pan-Anglican Synod & Conversazione.[6] Why should he express Christian sympathy with the B. of Capetown which he has not the courage to express with the B. of Natal? He has got a good name with the public, but he is not a man of principles, & will never stand up for right against public opinion, which is, after all, the real test of a man.

Look at an article of Mazzini in the 'Westminster'.[7] It is very sad but fine. I have a strong feeling for a man who has devoted his life in that way—whether he has used the 'moral' dagger or not.

[2] 'The trivial round, the common task, / Will furnish all we need to ask.' 'New Every Morning is the Love', S. Webbe (1740-1816).

[3] Probably Sir T. Munro, Governor of Madras, Sir H. Munro, General, Sir J. Malcolm, Governor of Bombay, C. T. Metcalfe, successively Resident of Delhi and Hyderabad, and possibly R. Morrison, translator to East Indian Company.

[4] Lewis Campbell, *Sophocles: The Plays and Fragments, Edited, with English Notes and Introductions, by Lewis Campbell* (2 vols., 1871-81).

[5] Tait.

[6] The first Lambeth Conference opened on 24 Sept. 1867. The Colonial Bishops were mustered by Grey, the Bishop of Cape Town, and much time was lost debating whether to do anything about the Colenso affair. A. M. G. Stephenson, *Anglicanism and the Lambeth Conferences* (1978).

[7] 'The Religious Side of the Italian Question', in the *Westminster Review*, vol. 88 (July 1867), pp. 226-43.

146 Address Oxford
Sep. 30 [1867]

I don't really think that there is any difference between us about "Whatever is, is best" & "Whatever is, is worst".... I would like to insist more on the perfectibility of the human race in the course of ages. Why should not this present state of 19th century civilization be merely the beginning—Clergy & Laity, Aristocracy, Employers & employed, Masters & Servants, perhaps diseases, may be regarded as mere barbarisms 5000 years hence....

I am not [at] all tired of hearing about Lord Herbert. That was one of the best friendships which there ever was upon earth. Shall I tell you why I say this? Because you were willing to have gone to India in 1857.[1] May God bless you & give you to see many times more, the fruit of your labours—I think that you will.

Mr. Senior is not a friend of mine & I am quite willing that he should be fried upon a gridiron, if you like. But are you quite sure that he is so bad as you imagine; is he a deliberate villain? I quite agree that you should be Pope,... but I don't like to be wholly deaf to the voice of humanity. Why don't you humbug him instead of quarrelling with him? That is much better & [a] more Christian policy....

147 [October 1867]

...I had a kind letter from Lord Russell which you may, perhaps, like to see. He is going to bring forward a resolution for an address to the Crown containing a triple proposal for improvement
1) in University Education
2) Grammar Schools
3) Primary Schools[1]....

[*Postscript omitted*]

148 [October 1867]

I am delighted to hear about your Indian victories.[1] You are quite right in thinking that nothing is done, while anything remains to be done.

The negociation with New College goes on very well,[2] but like Bismarck, we

---

[1] At the time of the mutiny, *Cook*, i. 370-1.

[1] The correspondence on this topic is printed in JCE.

[1] Northcote came to see FN on 23 Oct. and told her he had decided to appoint a Sanitary Committee at the India Office with Frere as Chairman; *Cook*, ii. 153.
[2] CM, 30 Nov. 1867, 'That it is desirable to enter into negotiations with New College with a view to frame a combined system of teaching and lectures.' CM, 24 Jan. 1868, Professor Müller and Mr D. B. Monro to give lectures on joint behalf of Balliol and New Colleges. CM, 17-18 Apr. 1868, the lecture arrangement with New College to be continued for one year.

proceed secretly. Also the disciple 'Dick' does well, except that he has got into a row with the Proctor for having supper at a Tavern.

I send you Abbott's letter (or rather two letters—the first that you may see he is worthy for whom you are doing this) I ought, perhaps, to add that he is a tall, muscular man, about six feet high. The upper half of him is thoroughly good & strong—the lower half is paralysed & nearly, though not quite, without feeling or power of motion (when I saw him with his books of comparative philology on the bed I thought of Mr Browning's Grammarian's funeral:

> 'thoroughly grounded οὖν
> Dead from the waist down'[3]

He used to be remarkably handsome. I like to tell this not as a matter of sentiment, but when a poor human creature is struck down in this way, he may as well have the benefit of former recollections of him.

149 [23 October 1867]

... I have written to Abbott, & sent him your book[1] & some books on Comparative Philology; also good advice about ventilation. He has a brother in London who might go & select the bed or chair at Ward's (I could not think of accepting your kind offer that you should bear half of the expence).

I had a charming visit to the Russells—Lord Russell said that he felt his time was short & he was determined to make a move about Education. (He asked me to draw him up a paper about it, which is a bore amid all my other work, but I must do it.) He talked about a great many political subjects—I always like him; he is so simple & natural. I wish that he had not done so many foolish things.

I had the pleasure of seeing your father for a few minutes yesterday.

150 [October 1867]

... Have you read the last number of the 'Quarterly'?[1] I have had another letter from Lord Russell about education. I am rather afraid that the effect of the Reform Bill will be to legislate about Education under a panic.

---

[3] 'He settled *Hoti's* business—let it be!— / Properly based *Oun*— / Gave us the doctrine of the enclitic *De*, / Dead from the waist down.' 'A Grammarian's Funeral', ll. 129–32.

---

[1] Presumably *Notes on Nursing* (1860).

---

[1] The reference is almost certainly to a review article by S. Baring-Gould in the October issue, dealing with the question of what Christ looked like. The two most recent works cited were Dr Legis Glückselig, *Christus Archaeologie: Studien über Jesus Christus und sein wahres Ebenbild* (1863), and Alfred Maury, *Croyances et légendes de l'antiquité* (1863).

151 [November 1867]

... Lord Russell has asked me to go & dine with him on the 20th to meet Mr Gladstone, Lowe, Bright & others. I hesitated a little because I have no real 'locus standi' among these gentlemen. But I thought it was better to pluck up courage & go.

He is intending to move an Address to the Crown on the subject of Education during the short session. He thinks that the subject can only be treated by a combination of parties in which he proposes to take the lead.

He is getting deaf, but otherwise he is as vigorous as ever. When you are alone with him & his shyness is over, he is one of the pleasantest persons to talk to that I have ever met with—he has a great memory & pleasant stories & will allow you to say anything to him (Yet the document which I saw at Berlin[1] comes unpleasantly into my mind when I think of him as a political leader)....

The New College scheme prospers & we are to have a meeting about it on Dec. 1. when we are invited to N.C. I contemplate getting, besides the Ball. & N.C. men, most of the men reading for honours in the rest of the University. The men are to choose their own lectures provided they go to a certain number.[2] This makes inefficiency in the Tutors impossible. It is a device for emptying Senior Tutors[3] who when they are deprived of pupils will soon be deprived of pay. I hope that we shall become in time a University in ourselves & then I shall try (in a sense) to have the appointment of Professors & Sub-professors.

Thank you for enquiring about our lodging house scheme.[4] It goes on very well & we are waiting for the decision about the Statute to make another move. Dr. Pusey has no idea of what is proper or not proper to be said in public. That was why I stopped him. He is utterly fanatical on the subject of morality, his ideas of which are derived from "penitents" filtered through a Sister of Charity. He is a pest here & does a great deal of harm & no good as far as I can make out. What force of character a man acquires from being a fanatic! Do you know that he is the descendant of Huguenots.

152 [November 21, 1867]

I went to Lord Russell's yesterday and had a very entertaining dinner. Lord R. made a very long speech to us about Education which was half prosy (going back to the reign of Henry IV) & half sensible. He then read us his resolutions. But the company, i.e., Lord Granville, Coleridge, Mr Bruce, Baines & Lowe were unanimously of opinion that he should wait & see what the Government intended.

[1] BJ went to Berlin in 1864 to christen Morier's child, Victor; *AC* i. 342.
[2] CM, 30 Nov. 1867, 'Undergraduates to be Allowed to Choose their own Lectures, under Conditions'.
[3] Woollcombe.
[4] See above, No. 115.

I went & took luncheon with Lowe, who appears to be profoundly in earnest about education & talked extremely well about it—I ventured to give him a sort of lecture about being more conciliatory & the necessity of uniting persons & classes if he means to do anything with Education. He quite agreed & thought that he would draw up a short Bill. I am more hopeful about him than I ever was before, notwithstanding his desertion of the Classics. ...

153

Balliol College
Oxford
Dec. 4 [1867]

... Lord Russell's resolutions[1] have passed over without any great harm, I think, & with some good. All the Editors of newspapers 'who have not been invited to Dinner' laugh at & ridicule general propositions, but they gradually sink into men's minds.

Mr Lowe was here on Sunday. He delighted us with his talk & his 'good natured' way of assailing every thing & person in this world. I think he is rather inclined to be penitent about his Edinburgh outbreak. His conscience had been awakened by a congratulatory letter from M. F. Tupper pointing out some pages in his works in which it was all to be found.

Both he & Goschen speak in despair of the strength of Dizzy & the ministry & of the utter disorganisation ('beyond anything that you can imagine', Goschen said) of the Liberal party. They are trying to screw Gladstone up to the point about the Universities & Education, & Goschen, who is very much his follower, thinks successfully. But I don't think that his account is very hopeful.

What a fool Selwyn is to give up his barbarians for the Bishopric of Lichfield. He will be mischievous because he is likely to be popular & I am afraid that he is hopelessly narrow—has learned nothing & forgotten nothing since he went out to N. Zealand. He had scruples at first, but when he found that there were 'barbarians' in the Midland Counties & more of them, he accepted.

154

A. Tennyson's Esqr.
Freshwater[1]
Jan. 8, 1868

(Excuse my writing in pencil as I happen to be in a steamer & have no pens.) I willingly agree to the compact with slight exceptions.

No. 1. Agreed (of course upon condition that you do the same).

No. 2. Say 12 o'clock; that will be a great improvement upon my present mode of proceeding.

[1] In the House of Lords, 2 Dec. 1867.
[1] Letter split between BCL and BL Add. MS 45783 fo. 127.

No. 3. (I am to insert myself.) To take a walk before breakfast when the weather is fine—to save eyes—& will you be disgusted?—not to eat & drink too much.

Every contract implies honourable dealing & I expect you to observe the 6 weeks cessation also—

"Do not, my dear Sister,
"Show me the steep & thorny path to heaven,
"Thyself a puffed & reckless libertine"[2]

working without rest for 13 months continuously. I am now quite convinced that you are really sane because I see that you will take some slight means towards self-preservation....

I have been staying at Alderley where, as usual, the family war is always raging. I think I will send you a Sermon which I preached them & which I am afraid that they did not much like. They said that I had given them a knock all round. (Though I don't think that there was anything really improper in the sermon but it was hasty & unconnected.) I have a great respect & love for them all; they are so characteristic & independent.

Last night I read 'A very simple story' (that is the title)—get it & read it (by Miss Florence Montomery);[3] it is the history of the feelings of a child of four years old, very touching & simple (I thought, but perhaps I am a fool in such matters). I also read Gladstone's article on Ecce Homo in Good Words:[4] it shows him quite hopeless & helpless in matters of theology. He is utterly devoid of the critical faculty, yet he has a sense that there ought to be criticism. He has the greatest power of living in words & formulas of any able man of the day.

Mr. Lowe is going to make his Edinburgh speech over again with improvements, to the Philomathic Society at Liverpool.[5] There is a great deal of unreasoning discontent about education at present & a great deal of folly talked about substituting things for words &c. But as Education is a very conservative thing I don't know that more will be gained by the agitation than a sufficient lever to move the world as much as it ought to be moved.

I am pleased with two Educational appointments which have been lately made of Balliol men who are old pupils of mine:

The Revᵈ J. J. Hornby Eton
The Revᵈ E. H. Bradby Haileybury—I dare say you have long ago observed

[2] 'But, good my brother, / Do not, as some ungracious pastors do, / Show me the steep and thorny way to heaven, / Whilst, like a puff'd, and reckless libertine, / Himself the primrose path of dalliance treads, / And recks not his own rede.' *Hamlet*, I. iii. 48–51.

[3] Florence Montomery, *A Very Simple Story: Being a Chronicle of the Thoughts and Feelings of a Child* (1867).

[4] '"Ecce homo" by the Rt. Hon. W. E. Gladstone', a review of J. R. Seeley, *Ecce homo: A Survey of the Life and Work of Jesus Christ*, in *Good Words*, 1 Jan., 1 Feb., and 1 Mar. 1868.

[5] 'Primary and Classical Education. An Address delivered before the Philosophical Institution of Edinburgh, 1 November 1867'. 'Middle Class and Primary Education. Two speeches by the Rt. Hon. Robert Lowe M.P. delivered at the Annual Dinner of the Liverpool Philomathic Society, and at the Conference on Education at the Town Hall, on 22 and 23 January 1868'; A. P. Martin, *Life and Letters of ... Viscount Sherbrooke* (2 vols., 1893), ii. 329.

that I tell you my vanities & I am pleased to see Ball. Coll. creeping over the world in this way.

The worst of Mr. Lowe in this matter of education is that though he really has a high type of education himself he is not willing to put forward a high type of education for people in general. What I want people to learn is that all education, even of the labouring classes, if it is to be worth anything must be liberal & not merely mechanical.

I hope that you will stay at Malvern as long as you possibly can. It was a happy thought going there. You never did your duty half so well before....

You will be amused to hear that I have got a young tuft, Lord Donoughmore, the companion of "Dick"[6] who is almost a friend of yours—to try & patch him up—But it is difficult. It seems like resisting the Order of Providence to try & prevent an Irish Lord from going to the Devil. The worst of him is that though clever he is awfully weak—quite puppy headed—in this respect his friend Dick is far superior to him & is the man of whom he is the monkey.

... Look at a curious account of the Comtist Service at Paris. Curious as a parody, in the Pall Mall of last night.[7]

155

Plumbleys' Hotel
Freshwater[1]
for ten days [1868]

...I have been talking about India with Mr. Cameron today, who is very much disposed to doubt whether the English have given India any sufficient compensation for the extinction of nationality, & the loss of their natural leaders. If you will add good health to good laws, perhaps this may be different....

156

Balliol College
Oxford
[17 February 1868]

[Agnes Jones died at Liverpool—F.N.]

I hope that you will let me hear about your friend. There are few persons like her in the world. What a self-indulgent life do I & many other Christian humbugs lead in comparison.

I trust that she will be spared to you: I am very anxious about that. But if not, we must leave her with God & go on & labour until the Evening....

---

[6] Grosvenor.

[7] The *Pall Mall Gazette* for 7 Jan. 1868, p. 10, told how the disciples of Comte met on New Year's Day for the eleventh time since his death 'to celebrate in common the annual ceremony of the worship of Abstract Humanity'. The good positivist looked forward to the time when 'Positivist ceremonies would be celebrated in suitable edifices, with ... music, painting, and sculpture'.

[1] BL Add. MS 45783 fo. 147.

I have never answered the remarks which you sent me about politics. In this country I don't see much more hope or good in one class than in another—nor in Centralization more than in local or self government. But I think that there might be some better proportions between them than there are in this country. When this is done you seem to want men—and it seems very difficult to say why we have not 'men' except that nature does not choose to produce them. In this place I see how many men run to seed. They have no high aim in life or knowledge, or they become useless, speculative radicals; also some of them are so very weak, men of genius, too. There is a notion among some of them that moral influence is no good, if not positively hurtful. A few of them have a kind of Goethe sort of speculative morality, trying new experiences & that sort of thing. In no place does a man more need force of character in order to make his way through the influences of the place than at Oxford. I am speaking not of the undergraduates but of the young Fellows. One reason is that they have so little natural sense of religion. They know that Puseyism is false & lying: (as one of them said to me the other day in Congregation, 'Dr. Pusey never speaks five minutes without telling a lie'), but they have no spring of new life in them. I am not in the least afraid of Puseyite reaction in the University, but much more of a lowering of life & character.

157   Balliol College
                                                             Oxford
                                                             [21 February 1868]

[Agnes Jones—F.N.]

I am very much grieved at the news contained in your note. I am afraid that this is one of the greatest trials that has ever happened to you....

Now that we are left we must not shrink, but do more & more. I suppose that the first thing is to try & find a successor for her. When people are engaged heart & soul in the work of life, the feeling about death should be only like that of a general who sees his Soldiers fall. Only that life is such a very long battle. Well, but, perhaps, the general would not object to be always fighting—he regrets that his battles are so few....

158   Balliol College
                                                             Oxford
                                                             [28 February 1868]

... The Free Divinity lectures go on very well.[1] I have had more men this term than last—about forty, I think. I take the Gospels by subjects, of course omitting one notable subject—that of miracles.

[1] See above, No. 134, n. 2.

I don't think that the men have been much offended hitherto. There is a Roman Catholic who comes. I have not kept back anything—except that I have not expressly stated my view about miracles.

I am astonished at the badness & folly in different ways of Trench[2] & Neander,[3] especially the first. . . .

159

March 4 [1868][1]

. . . I had a great deal of very interesting talk with Mr. Lowe on Sunday. He said, 'I am not like Dizzy an utter sceptic; I should like to believe if I could'. With all his bitter personalities & recklessness & impulsiveness, he always leaves on me the impression of being a very good man. He took me about in the afternoon to divers Whig houses, where I heard politicians talk. The hunger for office seemed to be prodigious; at the same time they appeared to be very disunited. Lowe & Cardwell are disposed to be cautious about the Irish Church & Land Question; it was thought that Gladstone & others would rush impulsively into them. They were full of Lord Chelmsford & Dizzy's quarrel, which is said by some to originate in a refusal on the part of Lord C to make Huddleston a Judge, while others declare that he insisted on making Hannen because he wanted his place for his own son. Others explain the affair by a quarrel between "May" & "Mary Ann",[2] who are ladies of temper & character. They also said, & appeared to believe, that Lord Stanley had taken to solitary drinking. You will see what an atmosphere I was in on Sunday afternoon.

I wonder whether the British lion will still roar at the Pope (apropos of the Irish Ch. Question), or whether he is reduced to the condition of a sucking dove.

Have you read Mill's pamphlet?[3] It seems to me very rash—ignores difficulties of climate & race—& turns the state into a huge collecting power—it ignores also the economical conditions of land in an old & rich country. In those countries where the peasantry live on plots of land does any one want to buy the land? . . . Dick[4] & Lord Donoughmore (who is an English as well as an Irish peer & therefore more worth regarding) are, or seem to be, amending their lives. Lord Donoughmore is my 'Irish' question. . . .

---

[2] R. C. Trench, *Notes on the Parables of Our Lord* (1841), and *Notes on the Miracles of Our Lord* (1846), went into many editions. See, too, *Commentary on the Epistles to the Seven Churches in Asia* (1861).

[3] J. A. W. Neander, *Das Leben Jesu Christi in seinem geschichtlichen Zusammenhange und seiner geschichtlichen Entwicklung* (1845).

[1] BL Add. MS 45783 fos. 128–30.

[2] May was Anna Maria, Lady Chelmsford, and Mary Ann was Mrs Wyndham Lewis, who married Disraeli.

[3] *England and Ireland* (1868), attacking England's self-satisfaction with her own institutions, and her failure to comprehend the social economy of Ireland.

[4] Grosvenor.

160 Balliol College
Oxford
[April 1868]

I return Mr. Mill's letter in which I only agree partly.

I think that he is right in supposing that the interests of women will be more cared about if they had political power. The mere fact of seeing them on an equality in one respect would lead men to regard them as equals in others. But I don't agree in what he says about delicacy, scruples &c. Each one must judge for themselves whether his or her conditions of life admit of public or private action. Although I agree that not among women, but among Clergymen & also among many men of the world, there is a great tendency to reserve, which is promoted by their interests & by public opinion.

I should not advise you to answer his letter, or at least only to answer it shortly & diplomatically, because I think that you may get into an interminable controversy in which he will never understand your position. But I think, if I were in your place, & if you approve, I should send my name to the female Suffrage petition.[1] If not, there is a danger that you who have done so much for 'Woman's mission' may seem indifferent to the efforts of others. . . .

The plan of allowing the undergraduates to choose their lectures, besides setting a good example in the University, has almost extinguished 'the rascal Bursar' & the Senior Tutor.[2] They have got about 4 men between them & though they are at present protected in their emoluments, I think that they must sooner or later resign & 'come down'. They are 'gone coons'. And if you knew how much harm the Senior Tutor, though a good man, has done for 30 year's past (or nearly) to his pupils you would not be displeased. He is a gentleman & a high principled man but utterly devoid of any sense of duty & obstinately imbecile. . . .

161 Inglewood,
Torquay
[c. Easter 1868]

My dear 'honoured' Miss or Mistress, or Madam, or 'Mermaid',
    or 'Sybil',

I am beginning to vegetate, which is worse than being a beast, & what can I do better than write to you? And first I must say to you not 'Give me an ounce of civet'[1] but 'Whence come these horrid imaginations'.[2] I don't like this talk of

---
[1] The pressure for female suffrage began with a petition signed by 1,499 women and presented by J. S. Mill and H. Fawcett on 7 June 1866: it was continued in 1867, and again in 1868 when the Reform Bill for Scotland was before Parliament. On 14 May Mill presented a petition with 21,757 signatures (*The Times*, 15 May 1868 (6b)).

[2] Wall and Woollcombe.

---
[1] 'Give me an ounce of civet, good apothecary, / to sweeten my imagination.' *King Lear*, IV. vi. 133–4.

[2] Possibly, 'What spirit, what devil suggests this imagination?' *Merry Wives of Windsor*, III. iii. 191.

'vampyres' & 'thigh bones'. It's such 'dreadful' nonsense. I know that you are a genius which you deny (& this proves the fact to me, for genius is always unconscious), (I wish I could make you believe it for then you might be induced to do something)—after two parentheses, how am I to go on? Well, I was going to say that genius should not extravaganze in that way.

This is folly (trying to be humour perhaps). But now I am going to say something serious which you shall think of, if you will, by day & by night. It is not true that you killed poor S. Herbert, or A.H.C., or Miss Jones. I think that you gave Lord Herbert & Miss Jones the idea which made life worth having to them; where would Lord Herbert's work or memory have been if he had died six years sooner? *You* made this difference to him. Will you not accept the natural consolation of this lifelong sorrow? And as for Una[3] & her paupers (I like that image), she is blessed in her death & that blessedness she owes to your example. A.H.C. was certainly not killed by you (that was the last thing he would have thought; never mind what wild people may have said in the violence of their grief). . . .

162　　　　　　　　　　　　　　　　　　　　　　　　　　　　Inglewood,
　　　　　　　　　　　　　　　　　　　　　　　　　　　　　　　　Torquay
　　　　　　　　　　　　　　　　　　　　　　　　　　　　　　　[April 1868]

. . . I am just finishing the printing of Plato Vol. 1. pp. 620. I think of publishing when I have got 3 vols printed[1]—the whole will be 5, or with the addition of the Text & Notes of the Republic 7 volumes. Two more volumes will take about 8 months. . . . You see that I am proud of having a large family of big books—I believe that they will sell, but that they will not be read.

Is it true, as I hear, that Sir S. Northcote is really going to make himself Governor General?[2] That will be good for you in some respects, but not upon the whole I think. He is too weak & flabby and does not seem to get stronger as he gets older. The lady who told me today said that his wife said so. She seemed to think it was a good thing because he had twelve children.

Do you think that Mr. Gladstone should kill the calf with his own hands? I fear that the blood of the victim will spurt over him & that he will contract a guilt not to be expiated.

I hope that they will do the thing completely & not leave the Clergy their houses & Churches.[3] The Churches are national property & should be used by all sects, at proper times, as Arnold proposed. This would do a great deal towards reconciling sects.

---

[3] FN's tribute to Agnes Jones, 'Una and the Lion', appeared in *Good Words* for June 1868, pp. 360–6. 'I do not give her name: were she alive, she would beg me not . . . I will, therefore, call her Una' (the heroine in Bk. I of Spenser's *Faerie Queene*). The notice was reprinted, without permission, as an introduction to *Memorials of Agnes Elizabeth Jones, by her sister* (1871).

[1] The first 4 vols. were published in 1871.　　　[2] Lawrence was succeeded in 1869 by Lord Mayo.
[3] The Act disestablishing the Irish Church did leave the clergy their houses and churches.

Have you seen Bunsen's 'Life'?[4] It seems very interesting, but not very true—he has the faculty of throwing a glow or haze of light over the most commonplace persons. He was that puzzling character, a weak good man of genius; omniscient, inventive, but entirely without judgement or reasoning power....

FN to BJ [*draft or copy*][1]
163
[1868]

... It is not quite easy to give an opinion on Bunsen. He has written at least 30 big volumes on very various subjects—he was rather coxcomby and vain than a humbug. He was learned and painstaking, but secondrate in his learning, because he wrote on too many subjects and was obliged to lean on other people's labours, on which he liked to build grand theories, but gradually the foundations give way and the whole crumbles away....

164
Balliol College, Oxford
May 3, 1868

(I enclose a blank cheque for Abbot[1] which please to fill up.... And if I want money at any time you are the first person of whom I shall come & beg. But Aristotle says, & I agree with him—I can quote Greek as well as you, like the devil quoting Scripture for his own purposes—that all true friendship is based on sound business principles[2]—therefore please take the money, or I shall never be able to ask you to do anything for me again.)

How rapidly the political atmosphere has changed since the meeting of Parliament. The glory of rascality is already beginning to fade away, (not that I consider Dizzy a rascal in the worst sense of the term by any means) and he is a rascal whom I rather like for his pluck & his cleverness (I don't dare to say this among Liberals or high principled people, because they would think me a rascal too: indeed, I know that a sound party man ought to believe & spread any lies about his opponents)—the latter half of this sentence has already forgotten the beginning so I shall go on to say that I think the Liberals are not out of the wood yet about the Irish Church, supposing they get over their own difficulties of jealousy & disunion. The legal difficulties are very great—then there is the difficulty of reconstructing the free Church—and there will be a shriek of Churchmen & of Protestants, which like a shriek of females, is very embarrassing. I think Dean

---

[4] Frances, Baroness Bunsen, *Memoir of Baron Bunsen; Chiefly from Family Papers* (2 vols., 1868).

[1] BL Add. MS 45783 fos. 158-9.

[1] For the chair which FN secured for the paralysed Abbott.
[2] *Nicomachean Ethics*, trans. by W. D. Ross (1925), 1163a, 'we must recognise that we were mistaken at the first and took a benefit from a person we should not have taken it from—since it was not from a friend...'.

144   CHAPTER 3

Stanley is right in urging that what is done ought to be done very carefully, because it is likely to be a precedent for the English Church. I would rather myself reduce the Irish Church to one fourth it's present dimension & leave it with the present restraints of the state....

165

Balliol College,
Oxford
May 24, 1868

May I have the pleasure of coming to see you on Sunday about 3 o'clock? I shall be staying with Mr. H. Taylor at East Sheen.

... we have carried with very slight opposition (I suppose in consequence of some intimation from Lord Derby)[1] the lodging out Statute which two years, or even a year, ago would have been rejected by a large majority.[2] Meanwhile the Hebrew Conservative[3] is trying to upset our whole system of education, which he has lately discovered to be very inimical to him (as any decent system of education would inevitably be).

Your friend Mr. Rathbone was here yesterday lamenting deeply the loss of poor Miss Jones: 'We' won't forget her.

I suspect that the opposition won't gain much by their resolutions on the Irish Church.[4] They are too hungry for office & they don't consider how vulnerable they all are (except Bright & Mill), and how terribly Dizzy may toss & gore them without either maintaining or giving up the Irish Church. There are all the objections to an abstract resolution—in a defunct parliament—nobody willing to commit themselves to any particular measure—while a Commission is sitting[5]—& where the issue will really be not the Irish Church but the comparative hatred of Gladstone & Dizzy. Irish grievances are: 1 loss of nationality; 2 tenure of Land; 3 Irish Church. This is the Irish order, but the Englishman takes them in the reverse order. Irishman wants really 1, 2: Englishman says 'You shall only have 3'....

166

Balliol College,
Oxford
May 25 [1868]

I have read the papers which you sent me & think that there will be no harm in signing the memorial.

---

[1] The Chancellor of the University.
[2] The change was accepted in the Hebdomadal Council on 8 May, in Congregation on 20 May, and in Convocation on 11 June.   [3] Pusey.
[4] The first of Gladstone's three resolutions for the disestablishment of the Irish Church was carried on 30 Apr. by a majority of sixty-five: the others, without a division, on 7 May.
[5] Commission for inquiring into the revenues and other matters relating to the Established Church in Ireland: the report is in *PP* (1867-8), xxiv.

I heard of the matter from Mr. Bryce & Miss Clough: I urged them to get the examination conducted by some regular authority such as the Universities & not by a voluntary association. I certainly think that Oxford ought to extend the examination to girls & that both Universities may fairly do what the petitioners request....[1]

I have not read Mr. Shaw Lefevre's bill,[2] but my own opinion is strongly in favour of giving married women control over their property—& therefore I signed the petition. And I am convinced that Plato would have agreed with me.

I think with you that Miss Clough is doing a good work in this matter of female education, & is deserving of every support & encouragement. I am a little puzzled about some other persons who are connected with it; & though I am very far from condemning them I do not wish to be mixed up with them.[3] (For which I am sorry as I believe that they have a kind feeling towards me, but I have not said this to anyone but you.)

167   Balliol College,
                                                                 Oxford.
                                                                 July 2, 1868.

... Let me tell you also how much I like 'Una & the Lion' in 'Good Words',[1] which Lady Augusta[2] gave me to read. It confirms me in my idea that you ought to write. I have no doubt that a great effect has been produced by it. I said a word or two upon the same subject in the Abbey.

I am looking forward to going to Lea Hirst about July 10 or 11 to stay till about the 15th. Will you consider it, as Pindar says, 'a matter higher than any business'[3] to go there at the same time? It will be a great pleasure & good to me to talk over with you my endless plans & to hear about your's.

I do not think that Spinoza had any conception of physical necessity. First he thought of an infinitely present God & then of a consecutive God—Spinoza's fatalism is a kind of prophecy of modern notions on the subject, just as Plato's conception of knowledge is a prophecy of Bacon & Hegel....

The dinner party on Monday was extremely interesting. Gladstone was very amiable but seemed hopelessly entangled about church matters—an impression

---

[1] In 1865 the Cambridge Local Examinations were opened to girls for an experimental period of three years, confirmed in 1868. Oxford Locals were opened to women in 1870, and this is what BJ appears to be referring to when he says 'Oxford ought to extend the examination to girls'. On this occasion 'the petitioners request' was for the Universities to establish some new 'recognised test of the capacity and attainments of women who desire to become teachers in families or schools'. Cambridge agreed to this in 1868, Oxford in 1875, and the new examinations became known as the Higher Local Examinations. J. Roach, *Public Examinations in England, 1850-1900* (1971), p. 120.

[2] A Bill to amend the law with respect to the Property of Married Women, introduced on 21 Apr. 1868.

[3] Presumably Josephine Butler and her husband.

---

[1] See above, No. 161, n. 3.   [2] Lady Augusta Stanley.

[3] 'Isthmian Odes', I. 1, 'O Mother, Thebe of the golden Shield, thy service will I set even above the matter that was in my hand', *The Extant Odes of Pindar*, trans. by Ernest Myers (1874).

which was rather confirmed by my going to his house on Tuesday & seeing there a plain, rather common looking man with an apron on—this was the Bp. of Cape Town.[4] Think of the Liberal P. Minister entertaining that bigot. I had a talk with him about Free Churches. He seems to be simply incapable of considering any question, as a matter of truth & falsehood. And yet he is perfectly honest.

I cannot look forward with any satisfaction to his being Prime Minister & I wish that some plan could be devised for putting Lord Granville in his place. He is the type of a Catholic statesman to the B. of Salisbury[5] & worshipped as an angel from heaven by Mr. S. Morley & the Dissenters. A free-thinking preacher in Palace Yard a few days ago was addressing a mob about the falsehood of miracles: One man he declared was above all that humbug of the supernatural = Mr. Gladstone. What manner of man can that be who produces all these extraordinary impressions of himself.

I saw the article on Characteristics of the Papacy[6] & quite agree in what you say. A.P.S. is very good in fighting Colenso's battle & very courageous. But he has no hold on deeper things. . . .

168 Hampsthwaite,
address Tummil Bridge,
Pitlochry, N.B.
[16 July 1868]

. . . I had great pleasure in seeing you at Lea Hurst. You speak of uncommon kindness. Why, anyone of common feeling would be kind to you, who have done so much for others. And I, now that other friends are gone, have that privilege. I am pleased also to think that you are at Lea Hurst, where there is the best chance of your, in some degree, recovering strength. It is a great benefit to me knowing you, & you must keep me up to the mark of spending my mind & time for others.

When you are writing about the Poor Law I will send you a homily (in return for your sermon). I can write it some day instead of going to Church, from which you always discourage me & to which I cannot say that I feel any strong inclination. In treating these questions it is necessary to show the strongest feeling of humanity combined with the strongest sense of the political economy requirements of the Case. I often doubt whether there ought to be any poor law because it tends to pauperize a large class & to diminish the sense of obligation about the poor. In a new country would one establish either a poor law or a Church?

. . . I had a most pleasant visit to the Gaskell's (a pleasant visit is one of the good things of this world). There is a great charm about him, great uprightness

[4] Robert Grey. [5] W. K. Hamilton.
[6] 'Some Characteristics of the Papacy', by the Dean of Westminster, in *Good Words*, Pt. I, 1 May 1868, pp. 304–9, Pt. II, 1 June 1868, pp. 350–4.

& natural liberality. He is an admirable critic, though he hardly seems to have any energy, & he is very kind (which, though I believe to be a common, is also a very pleasing virtue). *She* is a good sort of woman (though I hear her called very worldly; this seems to be a charge which women who have not succeeded in life bring against those who have). I see that I am getting into parentheses & also I ask myself what possible interest these people can have for you. I only hope that like myself you care about hearing of every human being who has a character at all. I forget to tell you, what may be more interesting, that Mr. Gaskell spoke with the greatest affection of Lord Herbert & also of Lord Canning.

I have been lounging at odd moments over a very old friend, Hegel's 'History of Philosophy'. You are quite right in thinking that Hegel mistakes history for truth. But I suspect that he could never have discovered the truth which he has if he had not believed it to be absolute—the ultimate of human knowledge. He fancied that he had passed criticism, while there he remains to be criticized still. Like many other errors his error may be summed up as a confusion of cause & effect. After all his efforts his ideas are 'nur' abstractions when exhibited in all the complexity of the 'idea'. I revere Hegel as the inventor of a new logical method & the greatest of methods, but liable, like all logical methods, to lead the mind astray. On the other hand I cannot imagine any one looking up at the Stars & being a Hegelian, any more than I can believe his maintaining the popular doctrine of the Atonement.

I found myself at H. de Bunsen's rather below the family temperature. For I feel that Bunsen, though he was a good man & a man of genius & learning & of the greatest kindness, was still a vie manquée both in politics & in literature. What a miserable thing for him to have been the intimate friend of the King of Prussia & yet powerless to exert any good influence over him? When I read his rhapsodies, either about the Jerusalem Bishopric or about his so-called Hippolytus, I lose respect for his mind & judgement. He was a simple man & not a tuft-hunter, and yet he seems to lose sight of things & get an exaggerated interest about persons. Also I am a little jealous of his appropriating you and your work....

169
Tummil Bridge,
Pitlochry.
Aug. 2 [1868]

... Since I wrote to you I spent a very pleasant ev^g with Dr. John Brown, whom I greatly like. (He is very much faded since his attack of insanity 2 years ago, & says that he has no inclination to read or write). He gave me a strange, I may say terrible account of the Howdie,[1] who appears to have the most extraordinary power of influencing people's minds & the most reckless way of

---
[1] Simpson: slang for a midwife.

performing clumsy operations: he said that Simpson would have been tried over & over again, if they had the Coroner's inquest in Scotland. (S. was not elected Principal because the Professors memorialized the electors against him & this changed the vote of Adam Black.) Dr. Brown also gave me a book to read which I admire in some respects very much—the life of Andrew Combe,[2] with whom I agree in his prophylactics better than in his phrenology. He seems to have been a very great character. Some one who has the knowledge & has also a philosophical turn of mind should write an account of the present state of medicine:—Why it makes no progress—what doctors know & what they don't. . . .[3]

Get Rossetti's edition of W. Whitman's poems.[4] He is a strange phenomenon & though not so great as his admirers pretend has some traces of real poetry. Read the 'voice from the sea',[5] which though strange seems to me to have a great deal of beauty; also the funeral hymn for Lincoln.[6]

My young Irish Lord[7] is a mixture of a child, a puppy & an Irish Squireen. He is clever & good natured but absolutely devoid of moral principle & only to be managed by fear. I never had to do with any one like him before. He has no conception of the meaning of gratitude. But he succumbs at once to a stronger will than his own. . . .

170
Tummil Bridge,
Pitlochry
Aug. 23 [1868]

. . . The Irish Lord[1] gets on rather better than I expected . . . & I have got another Scotch 'Scamp'[2] to keep him company, who, though a scamp, is one of a much better type. He is a big fellow who wears a kilt. . . . There is also a charming fellow with me named Raper, who comes here of his own accord to help me in Plato: and he is a real help for he is an excellent scholar & has very good taste.

I am sorry to see what a great impression Comte has made on his mind & that of some of his equals—not because I am jealous of Comte, or of the truth being taught by any one, but because I think that these young men fall blindly before Comte's generalizations. They have not been used to think & he supplies them with the elements of thought. Also his fanaticism, 'being dead still speaketh'.[3] Like some other persons who are nearly mad, he possesses the power of communicating his madness. I never shall think that either Comte or

---

[2] George Combe, *Life and Correspondence of Andrew Combe M.D.* (1850).
[3] The remainder of this letter is in BL Add. MS 45783 fo. 131.
[4] *Poems of Walt Whitman*, sel. and ed. by W. M. Rossetti (1868).
[5] 'A Word Out of the Sea', ibid., pp. 244–5.
[6] 'President Lincoln's Funeral Hymn', ibid., pp. 301–15. [7] Donoughmore.
[1] Donoughmore. [2] Probably R. J. Graham.
[3] 'By faith Abel offered unto God a more excellent sacrifice than Cain, by which he obtained witness that he was righteous, God testifying of his gifts: and by it he being dead yet speaketh', Heb. 11: 4.

Mill (whose character & power of writing I greatly respect) are great philosophers. But I think that Comte, passed through Mill (who does not exactly know the effect of him), has a great hold for the present on the intellectual world....

FN to BJ [*draft comments on BJ's Plato*]¹

171 24 August 1868

And I say that it is the absence of evil in the lives of Country gentlemen of fortune and their families, which makes their lives so bad—i.e. so little of a *heroic* struggle....

As to the 'Calvinists', I give them up to you. I really cannot call Calvin's God a God at all—for God = good.

As to the 'Hindoos' ditto....

As to the 'Romanists', I don't agree with you at all. On the contrary I believe ... that the only conception of *heroic* virtue is theirs. And as it is impossible to conceive of a moral God without morality, so without a capacity for *heroism* I believe it to be impossible to conceive of a Perfect God—of Him who 'sacrifices' not alone 'His own Son' but many, many sons for us to work out the perfection of mankind.

Instead of saying:—

'there is none to help us, no, not one', Surely the true thing to say is:—after all the 'help' that we have had from the 'New Testament writers' from 'the early Christians' (including the greatest of them all, Origen), from 'the best men of science', who have taught us the possibility of perfect law, from the great Roman Catholic and especially the Mystic writers, from the gallant fervour of the Puritans and later of John Wesley—is it not wonderful ... is it not shameful that we should sit down and waste all these noble materials ready to our hands, instead of building them up into the edifice, all but prepared for us, which contains the conception of the Perfect God?...

I don't *in the least* admit that 'we get no help even from a Savonarola'. On the contrary, I believe Savonarola to have been the very first preacher of Christianity who preached the inseparable tie between religion and politics, between religion and liberty, who showed that religion was nothing unless it embodied itself in politics—who created, in fact, the science of political religion.

With regard to p. 5, I should read it thus:—

'Plato' was the only founder of a religion or even of a philosophy, which has ever approached the conception of a *Perfect God*.... Surely, then, 'a Jowett' does the world a service by rendering 'Plato' accessible to them? (I say nothing of 'a Jowett' reforming a whole college, not to say two—nay, almost a whole University.)

¹ BL Add. MS 45783 fos. 134-8.

172 Tummil.
Aug. 24 [1868]

I must write a line to tell you how very glad I am to hear about the St. Pancras' workhouse, upon which 'preferment' I heartily congratulate you.[1] Thousands of poor creatures in the next ten years will have reason to be thankful for this. I suppose that you are already busy meditating the whole concern & the ways & means.

Thank you for the little book[2] for Mr. Abbott: I think that I must break my rule of never mentioning your name & tell him that you sent it, as it will please him & he will not talk about it. Also, for the same reason would you send one to my mother, although she has the book, no doubt.

I read a good part of it over today as I have often done & think it admirable—nothing could be better for it's purpose than the style. Also, it seems to me improved in several ways: I used to think that there was a little asperity or perhaps over-emphasis in the style. Not that 'I am one of those who would use the Devil himself with courtesy',[3] but over-emphasis comes to be under-emphasis. The chapter on 'minding baby' is excellent: only write tracts like that for the labouring poor & you will do an incalculable good. I particularly like the parenthesis (though he's not our baby), in which a world of morality is contained. . . .

So that restless, scheming Bp. of Peterborough is gone: I thought that he would have lived 20 years longer. He was as unlike the character given of him in 'The Times' as can well be imagined.[4]

[*Postscript omitted*]

173 St Andrews
Sep. 13 [1868]

. . . I send you a few generalities about the Poor law in which, as you know, I am not an expert.

[*Postscript*]

The leading idea, which I have ill expressed in the accompanying, is that the department of health & education may be transferred to the poor law board.

[1] The Liverpool experiment connected with Agnes Jones was being extended to London, and Mr William Wyatt 'entered into correspondence with Miss Nightingale with regard to the new Infirmary' at St Pancras, and suggested the introduction of Nightingale nurses. Miss Elizabeth Torrance was appointed Matron; *Cook*, ii. 192.

[2] *Notes on Nursing*: the new edition of 1868 was titled *Notes on Nursing for the Labouring Classes*, and contained a supplementary chapter on children, 'Minding Baby': 'And now, girls, I have a word for you. You and I have all had a great deal to do with "minding baby", though "baby" was not our own baby.'

[3] 'For I am one of those gentle ones that will use the Devil himself with courtesy', *Twelfth Night*, IV. ii. 32–3.

[4] Jeune. *The Times* said that he recommended the appointment of the Commission of Inquiry and wrote the greater part of the report, and that he bore the odium of the reform and saw others run off with the credit (22 Aug. (7e)).

[*Enclosed*]

The difficulties in the administration of the poor law seem to be:

1. The difficulty of administration: A central administration is needed to correct & prevent abuses:—this implies general & unvarying rules. On the other hand, a local administration is needed to meet particular circumstances, to provide for exceptional cases, & generally to deal with human beings who vary from the most worthless sot, rogue or drab up to the very ideal of decent poverty....

2. The difficulty of taxation....

3. The difficulty of local taxation leads to the further difficulty in the circulation of labour....

4. The accumulation of pauperism in the great towns....

Remedies suggested.

1. The local, personal, transient element should be left to local management.... The permanent element should be immediately under the control of the Poor Law Board.... By the transient element is meant the daily relief of the poor which may be safely left to the rate payers, who have an interest in keeping down the rates & are also most likely to have a personal knowledge of the paupers. If it be objected that they will be severe, it may be answered that this is not the evil to be feared most in the administration of the poor law. A good poor law must have a side of rigour & severity. The physical sufferings of the poor might almost be left to take care of themselves, if we could save them from their moral degradation. A hungry man, a wasted child, appeals to the sensibilities of almost any one. There seems to be no objection to giving property a greater influence in the administration of the rates. There is no reason why the landlord & the clergyman, who in country parishes contribute the greater part of the poor rate, should not have the greater part of the management.

By the permanent element of the poor law is meant that which affects posterity & the community at large, which appeals to no sensibilities for its working, is unseen, which is not liable to the abuse of extravagance & which is very liable to be neglected. This is that part of the poor law which relates to health & education. This should be placed more immediately under the Poor Law Board, or at least the Poor Law Board should possess larger powers over it than over the mere giving of relief. A pauper must continue a pauper in the second, in the third generation, unless he is placed under exceptionally good circumstances of health & education.... There should be political missionaries who would teach the poor (they are voters now) to be dissatisfied with their filthy piggish condition, & should create a class feeling about this similar to the class feeling about capitalists & hours of labour. They should teach them to hang together not as a trade but as a class, for such objects as the improvement of their dwellings & the education of their children.

(I am very much impressed when I go to see Mr. Rogers with the population of the East end of London; such miserable, half-grown, sottish, vicious looking people—I wish that some one would give a good description of this.)

The Poor Law is connected with at least four other great subjects: Emigration, Education, Management of Hospitals, Treatment of Crime....

174
Castle Mount,
St. Andrews[1]
[September 1868]

... I waited to send the abstract about the Poor Laws until I got to St. Andrews, when I could look at one or two books. I am afraid that such ideas as I have do not rest on any basis of fact or experience.

I have greatly enjoyed my holidays at the end of the world, far beyond highroads, crossroads &c., in Glen Isla. I am glad you approve of Lady Airlie as a friend of mine. She is a very fine creature gifted with great ability, who has had many conflicts & difficulties (not of the sentimental sort), & knowing the world, has got pretty well above it. She has been telling me how the Prince of Wales injures the higher sort of London Society, by creating a smart, noisy, fashionable set, who are congregated at a few houses to receive him.

I shall send you next week a MS. vol. of Divinity Lectures, or rather of notes for Divinity lectures, which I have been preparing for next Term. Please to add anything that occurs to you....

The great difficulty in the system of *theology* which you sometimes urge upon me, & in which I very much agree, is how to find vestiges of justice to the individual. That the human race are, or may be, in a progress towards finite perfection if they will attend to the laws of God is a true & consoling doctrine. The dark spot is the sacrifice of the individual, or rather of all but a very few, in this progress. It is said in reply that for every unit that ever was, however near the animals in his actual state, another life is reserved. That seems to me the most difficult point in rational religion to bring home to mankind, when the old traditional arguments for the resurrection of Christ are given up.... I shall confirm you in your conviction that I am only half a believer in the Immortality of the soul—and I acknowledge that, like Simmias & Cebes,[2] I do sometimes require to have my belief confirmed. I can easily get to the point of absolutely trusting God about another life for myself & others, but I feel difficulty when I have to make the next step, of asserting dogmatically that all these suffering millions shall certainly be reanimated. If an opponent like J. S. Mill asks for arguments & evidences what is to be the answer? Tell me that, Diotima prophetess of Mantinae....[3]

[1] The home of Mrs Margaret Farnie, who let lodgings. 'This season Mr. Jowett staid for some weeks at St. Andrews. He had several clever youths reading with him. The Marquis of Lansdowne was one, and another was Lord Francis Hervey ...'; A. K. H. Boyd, *Twenty-five Years of St Andrews* (2 vols., 1892), i. 101.   [2] Friends of Socrates who appear as interlocutors in Plato's *Phaedo*.
[3] Socrates' teacher mentioned in the *Symposium* (probably fictitious).

1866-1870

[*Postscript*]

I think that any one of my three Lords, Lansdowne, Morley or Camperdown, may make a respectable Governor-General 35 years hence.⁴ But you must promise to live & see them.

175 [21 September 1868]

... The Sophocles & Plato are quite partnership concerns with my dear friend Professor Campbell,¹ who is one of the best & most disinterested men I know.... We meet every day & talk over what we have done & this is a great support & help to me.

The lads here are the 'young Irish Scamp'² of a Lord; Lord F. Hervey, a most virtuous & promising scion of aristocracy; A. Taylor, son of H. Taylor; Mackenzie³ & Browning.⁴... I am quite happy here, for I feel that this is what I ought to be doing & there is nothing better in life than that....

FN to BJ [*draft*]¹
176 October 1868

... There is nothing I believe in so strongly as Immortality. It is never out of my thoughts. I believe in it much more than I do in anything in this world....

But I *cannot* bear to hear you say that you have sacrificed your life and you are not sure whether it was worth while. I think that gave me more pain than any one of the great misfortunes of my unfortunate life....

177 Balliol College,
Oxford
[Monday, 9 November 1868]

My dear Florence the first,
 Empress of Scavengers
 Queen of Nurses
 Maîtresse of drôlesses
 Governess of the Governors of India
 Reverend Mother Superior
 Mother of the British Army
 &c. &c. &c.
 ... I am much pleased to hear that Lord Mayo's education has proceeded

---

⁴ Lansdowne became Governor-General of Canada 1883-8, and Viceroy of India 1888-94.

¹ Campbell published his complete edition of Sophocles in 2 vols. (1875-81).
² Donoughmore.   ³ Muir-Mackenzie.   ⁴ The poet's son.

¹ BL Add. MS 45783 fos. 145-6.

satisfactorily. An Old Greek proverb says that he who knows is best; he who knows not & will learn is next best; he who knows not & will not learn is good for nothing.[1] Lord M. is in the 2nd class....

It seems to me that something should be said of the power of Individualism in practical life, as opposed to the necessity of Churches, Societies, Organizations. There is in the upper & middle classes quite a sufficient power, if people were not the slaves of custom & routine.... Suppose a person to say, 'I shall always consider 20 or 30 or 100 people dependent on me, through life; they shall be my care, my parish. I will see that the children go to school, that the parents hear the great truths of Sanitary reform, that in extreme distress they are not utterly overpowered, &c., &c. They shall be my people.' Why cannot persons do this off their own hook, without the interference of the Clergyman? I suppose because they have not the force or geniality of character.

What an extraordinary being Gladstone is! 1. At this time he is engaged in making an Index to Homer for the use of Schoolboys.[2] 2. I am told that he has been writing to Dr. Temple, whom he hardly knows, informing him, apropos of nothing, that he will not make him a Bishop....[3]

178
Balliol College,
Oxford
[20 November 1868]

I shall lose a great pleasure, if you give up writing to me....

Read Browning's 'A Ben Ezra'[1] & see if you do not wish to live a little longer yet....

179
Balliol College,
Oxford
[13 December 1868]

... I shall be curious to hear how you like the new Masters. I am sorry to see that you have not got my friend Lord Morley at the War Office. Pray make love to Mr. Grant Duff for my sake. His enemies call him 'Prig', partly because he is small, but I know him to be a man of considerable ability, of vast knowledge, of the best intentions & on one occasion (about Mr. Coleridge's Bill, which we took from him because he was unpopular in the House) he has behaved with uncommon magnanimity. I think that he is somewhat deficient in tact, but he is capable of learning & understanding anything. Also, though

---

[1] In the *Nicomachean Ethics*, 1095b, Aristotle quotes Hesiod, *Works and Days*, ll. 293–5: 'Far best is he who knows all things himself; / Good, he that hearkens when men counsel right; / But he who neither knows, nor lays to heart / Another's wisdom, is a useless wight.'

[2] *Juventus Mundi. The Gods and Men of the Homeric Age* (1869).

[3] Gladstone appointed Temple Bishop of Exeter in 1869.

[1] Rabbi Ben Ezra in *Dramatis Personae* (1864).

approaching the mature age of 40 he is too much (to me) like an undergraduate still, but this is probably an illusion. I think that Mr. Goschen is also good, though I am sorry to see Mr. Villiers out of the ministry & Lord Clarendon in it. Rogers says that Mr. Goschen greatly improves.

I took a walk today with Mr. Parker, an old friend of mine, now M.P. for Perthshire. He is a gentleman & an intelligent man, but too timid & too much a mere reflex of Gladstone. I think that I made him uneasy with my violent counsels.

I am ashamed to tell you how I am going to spend my vacation. Nearly three weeks will be passed in most pleasant country houses—e.g. your friend Mrs. Clive, Dr. Lushington's, the Tennysons, Lord Stanley of Alderley. I have always a great doubt whether this is right, but I cannot give up one without giving up all, which some day, as I foresee, I shall be compelled to do.

Do you remember Mr. Wright? He is a very good man, a tempestuous Radical, with very few beliefs, but with a great interest about the poor. He is trying to get up some sort of Association for the improvement of working men & asked me what subjects he should try to urge upon them. I said education & the dwellings of the poor....

Have you read Mr. Lowe on Endowments?[1] I don't agree with him in the least = some endowments are bad ∴ all endowments are bad....

Can you tell me whom you would consult in London for tendencies to brain disease, bad headache &c., declared by a Doctor at Manchester to be the beginning of congestion? The youth is one of the cleverest & best young men we have ever had here, the son of an Artisan.[2] He is naturally very strong, but enormously overworked about 2 years ago & is now almost unable to work at all.

180 [December 1868]

Don't be grieved about little things, my dear friend, like the disarrangement of the War Office....

FN to BJ [*draft*][1]

181 35 South Street, Park Lane, W.
[*end* 1868]

To any one who really knows and knowing feels what a great organisation like a Gov^t office is (the enormous stakes for weal or woe which a great Public Office like the W.O., the F.O., the P.L.B^d holds in its hands, working for

---

[1] Possibly his speech on being returned as Member for London University: 'Your degree...confers more honour on its recipient, than the ordinary degrees of either Oxford or Cambridge...you have done great things, and you have done them entirely without the usual aids of a University. You have hardly any endowments to bribe people to come here. You have no tests, imposed to conciliate the bigotry or the prejudices of any religious body'; *The Times*, 18 Nov. 1868 (6b–e).

[2] Edwin Harrison.

[1] BL Add. MS 45783 fos. 148–9.

eternity) the unutterable narrowmindedness of this cry for Retrenchment—Retrenchment pure & simple is ... painfully striking....

Do you believe that messrs Gladstone and Cardwell bring any other idea to the W.O. than that of economy.

Yet the W.O. is really the most gigantic Educational institution known in this world. Here are some hundred thousands of human beings absolutely in their hands, body, soul and mind....

At the P[oor] L[aw] reform of 1834, then economy was rightly the soul and principle of that movement, because England was rapidly going to destruction from pauperism. But very few men, except Mr Villiers, have advanced in the least beyond the principle of 1834....

Has Mr Lowe, with his surpassing powers, done, or has he any idea of doing, anything for his country in the same sense that Mr Cobden has, that Mr Villiers has, and I suppose Mr Bright has? Or is it to be only this stupid, brutal cry for economy? ...

182

Freshwater.
Dec. 28, 1868

Shall I write a line to wish you a happy new year? I cannot say with Cobbett in the 'Rejected Addresses', 'You are better off than you have been for many a year.'[1] But still, I think that in the coming year, there will be matters full of interest & better hopes than there have been during the last seven.

I staid two days more with Mr. Lowe who is a very warm friend to me & hoped that I would come as often as I liked & stay as long as I liked. He is full of initiatives & ready to talk about any thing. (By the way, I dined with Simon Magus[2] there—I hope that you don't think that this was very wrong.) He seems to agree in 'our' view of placing London more immediately under the Poor Law Board. Also he said that he thought the War Office should be simply administrative & give up all executive functions—guns & the like, I suppose. I do not know that I quite understood him, but he seems to me to have the notion of reorganizing offices. In fact he has a great notion of being Master of all the offices as far as expenditure goes. And I think that he has the force of mind to manage them, if he has only the self-control & perseverance.

Sir C. Trevelyan was at Lowe's, looking very wild & somewhat incoherent. He is possessed with a few ideas: he did not defend himself well against the objections which were made to his army schemes. He is a good man & a man of genius, but he is getting a little mad & entêté.

I have been looking through Janet's book on Materialism[3]—interesting, but

---

[1] 'I leave you better off than you have been this many a day'; James Smith and Horace Smith, *Rejected Addresses* (1812), 'Hampshire Farmer's Address, by W.C.'.

[2] Sir John Simon.

[3] Paul Janet, *Le Matérialisme contemporain en Allemagne: examen du système du docteur Büchner* (Paris, 1864).

not very good, and written with a party spirit against Materialists. I think a philosopher may very well ask himself whether he is writing for his own generation or for the ages. All flatter themselves that they are doing the last when they are really doing the first. And the beginning of philosophy is to be aware of this illusion. As Hegel, Kant, Sir W. Hamilton, Cousin have passed away, so also Comte & Mill will pass away, and what next? Anything that is to be permanent must recognize all facts & all our highest moral ideas & leave no sort of knowledge outside which may undermine the fabric. And it must begin again like Bacon by purging away inexact notions such as matter & mind, cause & effect, which to many seem to be the foundations of the faith. And it must avoid sentiments & sentimentalism, & must be aware how all classes, poets, prophets, metaphysicians, physicists, have all their narrow & limiting points of view....

[*Postscript omitted*]

183 [*Dated by FN*, 14 January 1869
35 S. St.]

I have read the greater part of the two chapters of the memoir which you gave me.[1] It does not lower your friend at all in my judgment. I was greatly affected by it, & this I think would be the feeling of many others.

But I would advise you strongly to dissuade the publication. Because, though it would be moderately (not very) popular as a religious biography, the book would do her memory harm. She had not much genius for writing & therefore is unequal to expressing what she felt about her own work. Besides she gossips to her own relations (as some persons do who think it a duty to write letters home about little things), and her relations will do her great injustice if they publish her 'trifles'. Hardly any of these letters would have been written if she could have foreseen their publication.... But this is not the lesson that her relations are able to draw. They take the accidents & leave the substance. If they objected to a statue, why do they raise this ill-conceived image of her?

There is too much about little things—'the wet'—'her poor feet'—'the governor', the time taken in decorating the wards....

If the publication cannot possibly be stopped, the life should be reduced to one-third of the original extracts. And a few passages should be written explaining her character & her work at Liverpool, to connect the better part of the letters & diary....

184 [17 January 1869]

I was very much pleased to stay at your house. The servants, especially the excellent Temperance, were most kind & attentive.

[1] *Memorials of Agnes Elizabeth Jones by her Sister*, published in 1871.

I do not expect that the new Ministers have forgotten you. But if they have, I should not so much regret that, because you would be delivered from the eternal routine of official work. All persons' thoughts seem to be turning towards the poor of London, and your thoughts should be in that direction too. The question is 'How is this perpetual flocking into the towns & accumulation of masses of pauperism in them to be prevented?' Is it practicable to say that food shall under no circumstances be given without a previous labour test? First, the Poor Law requires to be reorganized in London. Secondly, all private charity must be required to conform to certain regulations....

A dreadful thing has happened here which grieves me: Poor Ellis of Trinity, the Editor of Catullus,[1] a very faithful friend & pupil of mine, who gave me valuable assistance about a month ago in Plato, has been for the last 7 years really insane, living, as I think I told you, in a state of divided consciousness, & in the most aweful suffering. During the last year he appeared better because he never spoke of his misery. But on Friday night he could endure no longer & shot himself in the forehead, with a revolver. Alas, Alas—he is not killed & may possibly recover with the loss of one of his eyes—his mind never. This is concealed at present, but will, I suppose, come out sooner or later. I had just made an arrangement for him to have a large class in Latin Philology. It is just possible that this, which he had greatly desired, may have increased the trouble of his mind.

I have had Mr. Browning here this Sunday, who is charmed at his son having got into Ch. Ch. He himself is going to have rooms & reside at Ball. Coll.

I got through my battles pretty well with the M. & Fellows & am appointed College Preacher[2]—I begin my preaching on Sunday, Jan. 31. I see that I have undertaken a difficult enterprize, & if I do not succeed greatly shall fail greatly. What shall I begin preaching about? 'The truth makes free', or 'the nature of God', or 'in understanding be ye men'? I want to keep before myself that the work which I have to do in Oxford, both in the way of religion & education, is much greater than has been hitherto, now I have got a standing ground which is the College. The preliminaries are all well enough now, but a long time has been taken in attaining them. And I do not know whether life or power remains for all that I have to do—where I am now I ought to have been 10 years ago....

185

Balliol College,
Oxford
[*n.d.*]

... I am charmed that the Princess[1] appreciates you & your work. She is a very uncommon person, & if she had a little more steadiness might be the first lady in Europe. I am very glad you have got hold of her. Whether she 'pays' or

---

[1] *Catulli Veronensis liber recognovit*... R. Ellis (1867).
[2] CM, 15 Jan. 1869.

[1] Victoria.

not, in jest or in earnest, it is an excellent thing for her to take up hospitals & sanitary measures.

Do you know that poor Mr. Ellis appears to have fired a ball at the side of his right eye into his brain, & scarcely to have injured himself? He has partially lost the sight of his right eye but this so far appears to be all. He told me that he did it under the impression, which he has had for years, that some one was going to put him to a horrible & cruel death. When he found that he had not succeeded, he ran out to the Surgeon at 5 oClock in the m^g. He is wonderfully good & patient & perfectly rational....

I am trying to stimulate Rogers to interest himself & Dulwich College in Middle Class Female Education. Lady Stanley[2] urged me to this: I like her & respect her (I dare say you know how they talk about her in Society). This year she actually gave a course of twenty or twenty-five lectures in Physiology to her schoolchildren. This is pretty well for a fine lady.

186 [18 January 1869]

I write a line to tell you that I have had a talk with Harrison: your kindness & that of Sir James Clark seems to have entirely succeeded.

Dr. Reynolds[1] has taken the greatest pains with him: he has told him that he is to read only two hours a day, by half hours at a time—to take Strychnine &, if possible, to go to Schwalbach in the Summer....

There! you have done me a great service.

I read an interesting book at your house—the life of Mr. Gangooly.[2]

Browning said to me this morning—'the day I finish "The Ring & the Book"[3] I shall begin something else'. Can this ever be the white heat of poetry? He is going to have some rooms next to mine, & come & live here in the Summer....

187
Balliol College,
Oxford
Jan. 28, 1869

... Please not to suppose that I am thinking about the Mastership when I said that I ought to have been where I am, ten years ago. That used to trouble me in days long before I knew you, & when I was uncertain of the future of the College. But I have sometimes thought that I ought not to have spent so much time in lecturing & so little in writing. To lecture is a great strain & the effect is comparatively slight....

[2] Lady Stanley of Alderley.

[1] Sir J. R. Reynolds.
[2] Either *A Brief Account of Joguth Chundra Gangooly, a Brahmin of High Caste and a Convert to Christianity*, reprinted from the 'Christian Reformer' for August 1860, price one penny, or Joguth Chunder Gangooly, *Life and Religion of the Hindoos, with a Sketch of my Life and Experience* (1860).
[3] Published in four instalments (1868-9).

[*Postscript*]

I should like to hear whether you see anything of Mr. Peel or Mr. Goschen or G. Duff. Mr. Rogers is willing to take up the subject of female education.

188

Balliol College,
Oxford
[31 January 1869]

I send you my sermon, written (rather hastily) but never preached, through a ridiculous contretemps. The Catechetical lecturer[1] had forgotten that I was to preach on the last Sunday in every month & started to his legs before I could stop him. As the sermon is rather patchy & ill-expressed I was not very sorry. The fault of all my sermons is that they have many crude ideas, & jump from one to another, instead of a single one well developed. I wish that I had more time.

I tried the subject which you suggested, but got into a muddle about it & gave it up. I seem to have so little to say about this when I have once said that God works by fixed laws & that we have the power of co-operating with them.

I think that biographical sermons would be good, reading the lesson of individual lives. This is suited to mixed congregations & is new: Wesley, St. Bernard, &c.

I have been reading some of Newman's Sermons over again: I am rather surprized at their great reputation, for they are not really good, except here & there, as literary works. I think that South's are the best sermons in English.[2] In general the Puritan divines have a great deal more life in them than the Anglican. Robertson[3] is far better than Newman.

We have got an opinion from Mr. Mellish that the greater part of the Acts of the University, owing to an oversight, are illegal. I think this is probably correct & will strike a blow at the Chief Rabbi's[4] designs. The other party have rushed for an opinion to Roundell Palmer.

I think that there is something very touching in Mr. Ernest Jones's life & death—mistaken & foolish but quite unique for his disinterestedness.

189

[8 March 1869]

May I have the pleasure of coming to see you next Sunday at 3 oClock? I am going to stay with Mr. Goschen & to preach at Mr. Haweis's church.

I have read your article in Fraser's[1] on my return here this morning, with the

---

[1] See above, pp. xxiii, xxvi. The Lecturer was Edwin Palmer.
[2] Robert South, court preacher favoured by Charles II.
[3] F. W. Robertson.   [4] Pusey.

[1] 'A Note on Pauperism' in *Fraser's Magazine*, Mar. 1869, vol. lxxix, pp. 281–90. A very confused piece, bearing out BJ's strictures on FN's inability to write orderly to a theme.

greatest satisfaction. At first I thought that it was not connected. (Also I am a little doubtful about the depreciation of the 3 Rs, in which you will have some sympathizers whom you would rather not have had, e.g. Gorgias,[2] because, although the benefit of education is exaggerated, we cannot afford to give up or make light of any instrument.) But I am convinced that the whole is very powerful & effective & will do good....

The difficulties about the Poor Law are very great. I believe in Emigration, Education, Centralization, improvement of dwellings, a great extension of the system of annuities. I am afraid that the employment of the poor is more difficult than appears, because their labour would be irregular & the mass of paupers are best fitted either for working in the fields or in a mill. But this implies enormous outlay.

I think that I should try to combine the workhouse test with a system of wages & marks & with the opportunity of learning common trades. But this would fail if done in a mechanical spirit & could hardly be done in any other by officials....

[*Postscript omitted*]

190 [16 March 1869]

Private

After I left you I had a great deal of talk with Mr. Goschen about rating & about pauper children. He said that he was very much in favour of sending the children to private families (and against the schemes of Mr. Tufnell & others for large Schools) but that there were two difficulties. 1st, public opinion & the refusal of the parishes to give up their poor children, partly for the desire of jobbing & partly from a sort of fanciful humanity; 2ndly, the difficulty of applying such a system in London. What do you say to the last of these objections?

He said that partly the facilities of locomotion, & partly the changes in the law of settlement, also the love of the poor to hide themselves among the poor, had led to the great increases in London. The number he said was above 150,000. This will go on increasing & increasing. I suggested the possibility of breaking up pauperism by sending the paupers back to their parishes, or to other country parishes, paying for them partly out of the Consolidated fund. He answered that this would be difficult on grounds of humanity. He thought emigration only applicable to the class of ablebodied women.

I like him & her. He is very clever & knowing & a good political economist. But I doubt whether he has sufficient weight of character to carry difficult measures. He is not reticent enough. He told me that he was trying to get together every conceivable Statistic about the poor.

She is a very good & simple minded woman (rather High Church I am afraid) not in the least spoilt by her elevation.

[2] Lowe.

Now the hour of midnight is striking, so in accordance with our compact (having read Polybius), I will leave off. And some day I will make another compact with you, not to speak evil of any one, which I am always doing & which I always feel to be a great weakness & can often trace in myself to a personal motive: e.g. Gladstone, Goldwin Smith, R. Palmer, Tait & others to whom I feel a sort of antipathy. I think it is well to know people as they really are, but that it would be nobler & better to hold one's tongue about them. And you must help me to lead a higher life in this & in other ways.

I thought that you might like to hear about Mr. Goschen. Would you care to know him? . . .

[*Postscript*]

Mr. Goschen said that the teaching skilled trades in workhouses had failed, partly he thought from the trade unions, partly from bad management.

191

(*Private*)

Balliol College,
Oxford
[Good Friday, 26 March 1869]

. . . I am going to preach in Berwick Street[1] on May 2nd, & think that I must try the subject which you suggested, 'growth of character'. Will you tell me anything that occurs to you?

(After I left you on Sunday I went to see Mr. Hastings Russell.[2] He said, 'I want to prevent my son[3] from becoming a pest to Society: I don't think education can do much; it is mostly born with us'. This rather struck me: I shall try & consider in the sermon whether he is right.)

I saw in the papers an account of an interview between Mr. Goschen & some Poor Law Reformers.[4] Neither what he said, nor his manner of speaking seemed to me judicious. He is clever & clear-headed but too much like an Oxford undergraduate. Mr. Parker declares to me that Cardwell has more schemes about the War Office than he thinks fit to divulge to the House of Commons. He is not so clever as Goschen, but somehow there is more weight about him, & still more about Childers. I don't trust the reports of any one about any one, & I only half trust my own eyes so that I am unable to form any judgement.

. . . You are entirely mistaken about your not being a good writer. No one would write better than you, if you paid a little more attention to the connexions. For simplicity & force the writing is excellent. But the defect of

---

[1] At the Middlesex Hospital in Soho, which was built under the Metropolitan Poor Law Act of 1867 and staffed by Nightingale nurses; *Cook*, ii. 192.
[2] F. C. H. Russell.
[3] G. W. F. S. Russell.
[4] Goschen received a deputation from the Metropolitan Unions and Parishes asking for equalisation of the poor rates. He replied that 'he was thoroughly in favour of equal rating for the whole metropolis'. But 'Local Boards could not expect to have the pull at a common purse without supervision. . . . That point settled satisfactorily, the thing was done'; *The Times*, 23 Mar. 1869 (10a).

consecutiveness appears to me sometimes to interfere with the clearness. The strength does not lie sufficiently in the whole paragraph. (Though I preach this I cannot practise it; I always feel that I am unable to compose a paragraph). To be really strong nothing should be too strong.

I have a suspicious, unpleasant feeling about politics, that all things are going nobody knows where, directed by the impulses of Gladstone & Bright. I was glad to see Mr. Mundella exhorting the trade unions to take up Education. I am inclined strongly to think that the Spirit of Education, & the improvement of the dwellings & habits of the poor must come from some inspiration of their own.

I shall be in London at Lady Airlie's (Airlie Lodge, Campden Hill) on Easter Sunday. If you would like me to come to you I am always glad, but I did not offer for fear of wearying you.

192
Farringford
Freshwater
Isle of Wight

Address Inglewood Torquay until April 8.
[31 March 1869]

I am delighted with your Sapphics in which, however, there are some false quantities. Who told you that perfidjous might be a trisyllable? I remember in the days of my youth writing Sapphics addressed 'Ad lusciniam',[1] but the word 'luscinia' was a difficulty & we substituted 'Philomela'[2] instead.

And now my dear Philomela,[3] I have only to tell you that I will do all that you require and keep a book & follow your directions implicitly, if you will perform your part of the contract. Only you will be so good as remember that our object is not to do as little as we can but to do as much as we can, & if possible to complete the work which we have to do in life.

... Since I saw you I read through the Article on Pauperism[4] again. I retract what I said about it's being inconsecutive. But may I use an offensive word—it is 'jerky', & this gives persons the impression of it's being hard & unsympathizing, which is the reverse of the truth. I entirely agree with you that it does not matter whether it gives offence or not, provided it produces an impression & is suggestive. But then, as a personal matter, your friends are desirous that it should produce the right impression.

My kind friends here[5] are better than usual, I think. He gets harmonized as he gets older, & is less at war with life. I doubt his doing much more. Not that

---

[1] i.e. to a nightingale. [2] Poetical name for a nightingale.
[3] In Greek legend Philomela was the daughter of King Pandion of Athens, and sister of Procne who was married to Tereus, King of Thrace, and had a son. Tereus reported Procne was dead and sent for Philomela. When she arrived he raped her and cut out her tongue. Philomela embroidered the story of the outrage onto a cloth which she sent to Procne. Procne avenged her sister by serving her husband with the flesh of their son. When Tereus discovered what had happened he pursued the sisters with a sword. In order to escape, they turned, one into a swallow and the other into a nightingale. In order to continue the pursuit, which is still going on, Tereus became a hoopoe.
[4] See above, No. 189, n. 1. [5] The Tennysons.

he is exhausted, but he has nothing in him different in kind from what he has already put forth.

Lady Airlie told me that she always gave your book[2] to her housemaids. She is a 'fine' lady in more than the ordinary sense of the Term. She has endless activity of mind & unusual powers of administration....

193 [4 April 1869]

... Since I wrote I had the pleasure of seeing a little Prince,[1] the son of Theodore;[2] he is a little black boy about 7 years old. He seemed intelligent & asked me, 'Which were the best horses?' He is taken care of by Capt. Speedy,[3] an English officer ... who for a love of adventure, some years ago threw up his Commission & entered Theodore's service. The Queen,[4] when she was dying, entrusted the boy to him. At first he was 'a wee, timid, cowering beastie', but he has now recovered & begins to get on.

Captain Speedy had a great admiration for Theodore, whom he knew well. He thought that a few kind words would have settled the whole matter. He said that he was not mad but that in the latter years of his life he had taken to drinking 'Tedge'[5] & eating opium; this was owing to his matrimonial unhappiness. A little before his death he sent for his wife to speak to her. She was reading her Psalter & sent back word that 'she was conversing with a greater than he', viz. David. He told me of his rise & how during the early part of his reign the Clemency of Theodore was an 'adjuration among the Abyssinians'. He thought that the cruelty had been exaggerated, & arose out of the drinking. I am more grieved that a man of genius should have gone out of the world than Mr. Lowe can be at the ten millions.[6] Captain Speedy said that his memory & knowledge of men was wonderful. He did not blame Lord Napier for accepting the cattle,[7] because he did not know, but no doubt Theodore had built upon that.

Rogers is trying to get up a female Middle Class School[8] like his great boys

---

[6] *Notes on Nursing.*

[1] Prince Simyen.

[2] When Magdala was stormed by British troops on 13 Apr. 1868, Theodore II, Emperor of Ethiopia (born 1818), committed suicide with a revolver presented to him by Queen Victoria.

[3] Captain C. Speedy, had served in the 81st Regiment, in the Indian Army, and with King Theodore himself. He was appointed to Napier's staff as Amharic interpreter and met the British forces at Senafe. T. J. Holland and H. M. Hozier, *Record of the Expedition to Abyssinia* ... (2 vols., 1870), i. 181, 390.

[4] Teruwark, Princess of Simyen and Empress of Ethiopia, died in the British camp; ibid. ii. 93.

[5] Tedge or tej, the national drink of Ethiopia, based on honey.

[6] The cost of the expedition mounted by the Derby–Disraeli ministry against Theodore II.

[7] Theodore had already been defeated, and appears to have been ready to surrender his European captives. He begged his fellow Christian to accept an Easter present of a few cows (1,000 cows and 500 sheep). There is confusion as to whether Napier did accept. If he did, then, by Ethiopian usage, the war was over. Holland and Hozier, op. cit.; F. Myatt, *The March to Magdala: the Abyssinian War of 1868* (1970).

[8] R. H. Hadden, *Reminiscences of William Rogers* (1888), Chap. VI, 'The Middle-class schools', makes no reference to girls, but see below, No. 312.

school, & I am trying to help him. I should like to talk over this with you, especially with reference to the subjects of education, when we meet....

194 [12 April 1869]

[There never was a busier man than "Sir John Lawrence" in his "retirement". F.N. '95.]

... I am glad that you hold to Sir John Lawrence. I hope now he has returned that he will devote himself to public matters & at any rate to India. I doubt whether any body ought to be a retired statesman, unless he is absolutely paralyzed, & even then I would not if I could help. I hear that Sir John Lawrence likes retiring into the country & reading history. There is not much use in that.

He must be about 58 years of age & has an immense prestige. He ought to go on & on for 15 or 20 years longer. [He did. F.N.] Is not a person really responsible for not doing any thing which he can do? I want you to fire his imagination. A simple minded man like him is very likely to fail in his duty for fancying that he has done with active life.

One of my youths, Lord Camperdown, spent Sunday with me. He is a capital fellow—a little prosy & wanting in the power of expression—but very hardworking & clear headed & perfectly disinterested. He tells me that when he has nothing to do[1] he sends for one of the head Clerks & makes a peregrination through a dockyard, or a department in Somerset House.

... Thank you for asking about my terminal Battle: I succeeded pretty well. We deposed the Bursar[2] from his logic lectureship, which was a necessity for he had only two pupils. The feelings of the said Bursar towards me are much like those of the Hyena in the Zoological Gardens towards people who poke him.

I am glad to hear that you are consulted about measures. Forster's Bill[3] is too complicated to pass in the face of a very strong opposition of private interests. Dr. Temple who devised the scheme, though an excellent man, is wanting in knowledge of the world. The Scotch Education Bill[4] is also in difficulties. It's great merit is that it is undenominational. The Scotch want to have a Scotch Council & Inspectors. But everybody says that if this is allowed, the whole administration will fall into the hands of jobbers appointed by the great prince of jobbers who is the Lord Advocate.[5]

I had a very pleasant evening with Mr. Lowe after his Budget.[6] Though the

---

[1] At the Admiralty. [2] Wall, see above, p. xxiii.
[3] A Bill to amend the Law relating to Endowed Schools and other Educational Endowments in England, resulting from the Taunton Commission's inquiry into schools not comprised within the scope of Her Majesty's two former (Newcastle and Clarendon) Commissions; *PP* (1867-8), xxviii.
[4] Parochial Schools (Scotland) Bill, introduced in the House of Lords by the Duke of Argyll on 25 Feb. 1869.
[5] James Moncrieff, first Baron Moncrieff. [6] On 8 Apr. 1869, *PD*, cxcv. 363-400.

speech was ill delivered, owing to his eyesight, I think that it was a success. I perceive that there is a deep hatred towards him on the part of the younger Radicals, for he is & he is not one of them.

195 Oxford
April 25, 1869.

... To-day I dined with the Dean,[1] whom I like for his honesty & sincerity. He is a learned & clever man, but a fool. He has no force of character or will. He has a considerable hold on Oxford, none on Ch. Ch. Mrs. Dean is a clever, honest, half-vulgar sort of woman, very fond of tufts, and of finery of all sorts. She has character enough to make her way among great people though they privately speak of her as an âme damnée.

What makes me write you this Oxford gossip? Because I believe you to be a student of human nature 'femina sum, feminae nihil a me alienum puto'.[2] There is another Oxford Lady whom you might study, the Honble. Mrs. Cradock, a fanciful, capricious little woman with a good deal of originality who wrote a novel 35 years ago & still has some of the tricks & graces of her youth. But Oxford will not be saved by it's women.

... I have got a book which I shall send you to read: the memoirs of Miss Edgeworth[3] (not published)—a fine, simple nature & a charming picture of family life. I think that her books did us all a great deal of good in early days....

196

(*Strictly Private*) [19 May 1869]

... I think that no day passes in which I do not think of you & your work with pride & affection. But I did not write, because I don't like troubling your ladyship when I have nothing to say & also because Professor Campbell usually comes of an evening between the hours of 8 & 12—& as you sagaciously divine we do Plato & Sophocles together, a great deal of Plato & very little Sophocles; while his wife sits in the room & reads, a good little creature, very pious, who out of affection for him has become a sort of free thinker & is greatly improved & not at all injured by the process.

Thank you very much for what you say about R. Catholic conversions. I never connected what you said about Lady Herbert with my sister, any more than the remarks in my sermon are intended for you (I don't see where the cap

---

[1] Liddell.

[2] An adaptation of 'homo sum; humani nil a me alienum puto', I am a man, and I count nothing human foreign to me, Terence, *Heauton Timorumenos*, 77.

[3] *A Memoir of Maria Edgeworth with a Selection from her Letters by the late Mrs [Frances] Edgeworth* (3 vols., 1867), privately printed.

fits at all). I was annoyed at my sister becoming a Roman Catholic at the time but I have become reconciled; she leads a quiet, humble sort of life—takes care of my mother & goes about among the R. Catholic poor at Torquay, & though she might once have been fit for something more than this I don't think that she is now. She has been amusing herself with translating the memoirs of Cardinal Consalvi.[1]

I don't mind real prophetic denunciations of bad people, & I wish to keep my head clear about political people & their motives—Gladstone, Bright, my friend R. Lowe, &c. But I think if you ever mean to act in the world you should exercise great reticence in speaking of them. (This is my theory but has not been my practice hitherto.) I think that things are said against people chiefly for a want of self-control. And when you come to act with them or talk with them your influence over them seems to me to be taken away by the consciousness that you have not always spoken well of them, (perhaps deservedly). I think that the world requires infinitely more courage & infinitely more caution than it possesses at present.

I had a very nice party here on Saturday: some friends of yours I should think—the Nortons[2]—Mr. Morier, who whenever I see him seems to me to grow in mind as much as he does in body, & he is an extraordinarily stout man—Sir Louis Mallet, who is a most able man, I think, & like you terribly discontented with the state of the public offices.

The Hebrew Conservative has carried his Theological Statute.[3] We shall have an endless battle at Oxford.

197 May 28 [1869]
Oxford

I send a few books; Miss Edgeworth's life.... Also a vol. of Bentham about Poor Laws, &c. Do you possess Bentham? If not, I must give you one. With all his faults & monstrosities & unidealisms he is the greatest political philosopher of our time.

... We have three compacts; first that you are to give an hour a day to writing or some unprofessional occupation (& not to overwork) (I excuse the letter to the Presidencies,[1] but would rather it did not happen again) in return for which I will observe hours & days (I have only broken the hours once). All

---

[1] J. Crétineau-Joly, *Mémoires du cardinal Consalvi avec une introduction et des notes* (2 vols., Paris, 1864).
[2] C. E. Norton.
[3] Congregation agreed on 19 May 1869 to establish a School of Theology.

[1] 'The greater part' of the introduction to the *Report on Measures Adopted for Sanitary Improvements in India During the Year 1868 and up to the Month of June 1869*, was copied from a memorandum of FN's. 'Once the *Report* was published, Miss Nightingale took upon herself the task of ensuring its proper distribution. The 1868 *Report*, though sent to India in October of that year, had not been distributed to the several Presidencies till June 1869. She now saw to it that copies of the 1869 *Report* were sent separately to the various stations by book-post'; W. J. Bishop and S. Goldie, *A Bio-bibliography of Florence Nightingale* (1962).

this is to be strictly observed. Secondly we have a minor compact not to be observed so strictly; not to speak evil of others—even against Simon Magus[2] not to "bring a railing accusation";[3] this, however, may be occasionally broken when human nature can endure no longer. N.B. it does not rest on any religious ground but merely on expediency. Thirdly we will have a great compact that every year is to be calmer, happier, & more efficient & productive of results than the one which has preceded....

FN TO BJ [*draft*][1]

198 [June 1869]

... Sometimes a book and not even a clever book, is like a revelation (to one) of the whole of one's past life. I have lived 49 years in this world, and I never understood before, things which this Life of Miss Edgeworth makes me see quite plain....

She sums up her brother's perfect wife:— 'good sense, good manners, good conversation, good principles'.

That is like a new light to me.

What a fool I have been.

Now I see that that is really all that fathers want in their daughters, all that the world wants in his wife—good sense (meaning of course sense to think like him), good manners, *good conversation* (how enormous is the importance attached to that now-a-days—one would think the whole world was moved by talk!). Good principles (for they don't want their women to run away and get into the Divorce Court).

And with the four gs, even the better sort of people are satisfied—they *don't want* any deeper feeling, any higher purpose in life, any deeper hold on things....

199 Oxford June 11 [1869]

... the Senior Tutor[1] is dead, at which I greatly rejoice. "How inhuman, almost as bad as I am", is a reflection which some one makes. Well you see he is not physically dead, but only academically, if he can ever be said properly to have lived. This gives me a greater opportunity than I have ever had before: "The longest liver takes all."[2]

I entirely agree in what you say about J[eremy] B[entham], but I shall always

[2] Sir John Simon.
[3] 'Yet Michael the archangel, when contending with the devil he disputed about the body of Moses, durst not bring against him a railing accusation'; Jude, v. 9.

[1] BL Add. MS 45783 fos. 153-4.

[1] Woollcombe was forced to give up lecuring.
[2] See above, No. 79, n. 4.

think him a very great man, greater far than J. S. Mill or Comte. There is nothing like his perseverance in working out a great system. But he had a want of Sense and this was connected with his extreme egotism. I think it is worth observing that there are two classes of philosophers, the humble-minded & the egotists.

I wish that some one would write a logic of medicine—a first part about terminology, a second part about reasoning, with an appendix upon fallacies. Medicine will never be properly taught unless it is generalized in this way. Into all the physical sciences an element of general ideas & of logic should be introduced.

I am rather disposed to disagree with you about Mr. Huxley, whom I saw on Sat. ev^g. I am not quite sure whether he is always sound, but I certainly think him a remarkably able man & I like his character. He said that he did not consider Darwin's theory proved, because of the Sterility of Hybrids. I urged that even if the theory were 'true' it did not follow that it was "adequate". But he would not admit this....

200 [21 June 1869]

I saw Mr. Cordery yesterday....

He says that everywhere, as far as he knows, in India both in town & country, there is a local rate which is applied to the purposes of public & sanitary improvements (not to roads—these are provided for in another way). The payments are fixed by the Government, but the inhabitants are allowed to collect in their own way (at Umritza by an Octroi duty). He said that the fund was usually applied by the resident but that at Umritza & in some other places there was a local council of natives who assisted him.

He is a man of ability & judgement & a sanitary reformer & improver. He said that we could hardly estimate the difference in sanitary questions made by the heat of the sun; e.g. any kind of filth that was dried up by the heat of the sun was innoxious, while decaying vegetable or animal matter might be as injurious as in England. In great cities he said that there was scarcely any effluvium except just before sunrise. He said that he had written upon sanitary matters in the Hydrabad reports.[1]

I do not quite agree with you about Miss Edgeworth. I think that there is an absence of anything ideal in her, but I feel that we should make great allowance for the varieties of character in the world. May there not be room for the unideal as well as for the ideal?

I am not given to be an alarmist about you & have often quieted the fears of others. But I see that you are very ill, & may permanently break down. I shall

---

[1] Sir Richard Temple's Hyderabad Report for 1866-7 contains the first, brief report on 'Public Health and Sanitary Improvement', and a tribute to Cordery (India Office Records: L/P & S/6/572). Such reports later became a regular feature of the annual Reports.

not think it right to go away until I hear from you what arrangements you have made about leaving London—definitely....

Upon second thoughts I reflected that Jeremy Bentham would be dull & have therefore sent you

H. C. Robinson's diary.[2] ...

201   July 2, 1869

I am staying with my old friend, H. B. Wilson. Did you ever read his Bampton Lectures?[1] They were a remarkable work in their day. Mrs. Wilson,[2] who is a half-foolish woman with a kind of goodness & sense, has been reproaching us, & me in particular, with letting the Church go to ruin while I am busy with other things. Partly in consequence of her upbraidings, but more because we had previously determined, H. B. Wilson & I have sketched out a plan for a Vol. of Essays,[3] which I enclose. (Please to return.) Can you suggest other or better subjects? The Essays & the contributors are wholly hypothetical as yet.

I like your principle of getting a thing done & dying afterwards. The worst of it is that unless you are very prudent you will die first. And this is what I am particularly anxious that you will not do.

What a strange, unintelligible speech Gladstone made at the Mansion House.[4] The Lords are asking too much. They should stick to the Duke of Cleveland's amendment[5] & not completely unravel the web which the Commons have woven. I am better pleased with Gladstone since I see that he is really being forced along with his party to religious liberty. I do not know how he reconciles the Oxford Bill[6] to his conscience. But that is a matter which, in these days, it would be impertinent to enquire about.

[2] T. Sadler (ed.), *Diary, Reminiscences, and Correspondence of Henry Crabb Robinson* (3 vols., 1869).

---

[1] *The Communion of Saints: An Attempt to Illustrate the True Principles of Christian Union* (1851).
[2] His mother.
[3] This proposed successor volume to *Essays and Reviews* came to nothing.
[4] On 30 June: 'I may presume to say that I have not been unfortunate in the nature, in the qualities, and stamp of men whom I was not only enabled but constrained to associate with me in the work of government...'; *The Times*, 1 July 1869 (8cd, 9de).
[5] Salisbury wanted to take the glebes out of the scheme of disendowment and reserve them as private property for the clergy of the disestablished church. This was carried against the Government by 213 votes to 69. Cleveland's amendment was to offer residences with ten acres of glebe to Anglican, Roman Catholic, and Presbyterian clergy, i.e. concurrent endowment. The Archbishops of Canterbury and York voted with him, Tait saying that 'ever since I was able to think on politics I have conceived that the policy indicated by the noble Earl [Earl Russell]... was the only policy likely to bring peace to Ireland'. *PD*, cxcvii. 1026-32, 1077 (2 July 1868). *The Times*, too, favoured Cleveland's amendment as the best compromise, 8 July (8e).
[6] In 1869 Coleridge, who was Solicitor General, introduced a Bill 'to Repeal certain Tests and alter certain Statutes affecting the Constitution of the Universities of Oxford and Cambridge'. It went through all its stages in the House of Commons but the Session ended before it could be carried through the Lords.

202
                                                          Tummil Bridge,
Pitlochry
July 15, 1869

... I shall hope to have many conversations with you about the volume of Essays.[1] At present I have only spoken to Sir A. Grant, who is afraid that to join in our scheme will 'injure his usefulness'. I do not blame him. I believe he will be chairman of the new Education Board for Scotland.[2]

I will promise you, as you are so good to me, not to work after 11 o'Clock at night. I enjoy being here, & work with pleasure. Here is good air, good food, perfect retirement, & a pleasant stream which is always murmuring night & day—much better than the best society.

I met Mr. Wallace[3] at Edinburgh. He is probably the ablest man in the Scotch Established Church & appears to be an out & out free-thinker. I thought him very courageous & powerful, but not sufficiently recognising that freedom of thought in Clergymen must be supported by self sacrifice in life. I am to preach for him in the Kirk when I next go to Edinburgh.

I hear dreadful accounts of the state of the poor in Edinburgh—families living in the dark &c. There is a book by a Miss Bird,[4] which is a disclosure of the state of the Edinburgh poor, which you might find it worth while to get. There is a general approval of the lodging out of children.[5] But in other respects there is at least as much discontent with the management of the poor law here as in England, & many persons incline to the doctrine that you had better let the poor starve than be as they are at present.

I hope that you are already in the country & beginning to revive. ... I like your doctrine of getting the work done first & then dying, for that clearly conduces to length of life.

203
                                                           Tummil Bridge
July 18, 1869

... Mr. Gladstone appears to triumph & is certainly right in refusing the other additions of the Lords, if he refuses concurrent endowment.[1] So there will be a Collision—if the Lords were determined, he could never swamp them, but there seems to be a theory that the Lords ought not to resist, in which they acquiesce themselves.

---

[1] See above, No. 201, n. 3.
[2] Grant prepared the first Scottish education code.
[3] Robert Wallace.
[4] Isabella Lucy Bird, *Notes on Old Edinburgh* (1869).
[5] In Scotland the parishes sent orphan and destitute children out to foster parents.

[1] 'On all the changes made by the Lords from which Mr. Gladstone dissented the House of Commons has dissented also, by majorities of 80, 90, 100, and even 120'; *The Times*, 17 July 1869 (9b). Concurrent endowment was rejected without a division.

I liked what R. Palmer said that after all this is Protestant ascendancy. No statesman thinks that the Bill ought to have been in this form. Last year Mr. Bright told a friend of mine that he was for giving all denominations houses & glebes.

The measure is, upon the whole, barely right: (1) It is carried by the Dissenters who hope to attack the C. of E. (2) under the guidance of Mr. Gladstone, the High Church man, but who (3) is deceiving the Dissenters, for he says that he will not disestablish the C. of E., & who (4) very likely will do this when the necessities of practical statesmanship require this sacrifice at his hands; (5) the measure, though right in principle, is not of much value for any practical results. I am pleased to see that Mr. Gladstone is being educated & is not going in for denominational schools.

Mr. Harrison is with me here. He is getting better I think, & next week is to try reading 15 minutes at a time.... Did I tell you of Mr. Abbott? He has got 4 pupils of the best kind, & Murray[2] has agreed to take his translation of a German work on Philology....[3]

204
July 19, 1869

... I have got Dr. Stallard's book[1] here which makes me write to you about the poor. I am afraid that the whole of the New Poor Law was really a fatal error: 1. There are the 40 p.c. establishment expenses. 2. The system is not flexible—too ponderous for ordinary life—too feeble to meet great crises. 3. It ignores the family & the power of family affection. 4. It makes a caste of paupers. What shall we do with the workhouses?

I cannot help thinking that the Old law might have been sufficiently corrected by a strict system of inspection & periodical reports. I would have had the accounts printed & an annual report circulated in the parish.

I am still doubtful about the perfect equalisation of the poor rates, not so much on grounds of interference with property (though I think that this cannot be lightly set aside) but because all motive to economy is taken away. I would rather have over-burdened parishes relieved out of a general fund after a special investigation of the Poor Law Board.

I am very much annoyed to find that Lyulph Stanley has resigned his Fellowship, from conscientious scruples about the declaration of conformity. This is rather a blow to me for he was 'a Temple of Friendship', & most truly liberal in both senses of the word....

[2] John Murray.
[3] *Elucidations of the Student's Greek Grammar by Professor Curtius. From the German, with the Author's Sanction* (1870).

[1] J. H. Stallard. Up to 1869 Stallard had published: *Workhouse Hospitals* (1865); *London Pauperism among Jews and Christians* (1867), *Pauperism, Charity and Poor Laws* (1869), *The Scottish Poor Law* (1869, 1872). His other reports were: *Pauper Lunatics and their Treatment* (1870), *On the Sanitary Requirements of Liverpool: A Lecture* (1871).

205
                                                     Tummil Bridge,
                                                     N^r. Pitlochry,
                                                           N.B.
                                                   [23 July 1869]

Will you be tired of hearing my crude suggestions about the poor-law?

The great difficulty at present is administration. The guardians are a miserable low set (v. S. Pancras in the paper of today).[1]

I would have the number of elected guardians diminished & add a certain number of ex-officio guardians,

A Poor Law Inspector for chairman

All Magistrates

All Clergymen & Dissenting Ministers

... I wish a plan could be devised for gradually getting rid of the Poor Law by allowing parishes who undertook to support their poor to withdraw from its operation: of course there must be a strict system of inspection. ...

206
                                                      Tummil Bridge
                                                        Pitlochry[1]
                                                   [25 July 1869]

Alas, I must tell you the truth—I have not kept my engagement about 11 o'clock (about 12 I have) ... but the Timaeus is so exasperatingly troublesome that I have had to read it over & over again in the proof before I could get it right. I used rather to despise it, but now having read it about 20 times, I have a great admiration for it, & think it truly Platonic.

Dr. Acland is called 'Barnum' at Oxford. He is one of the vainest, rudest men that ever lived. He is also one of the greatest bores that ever lived. But against his boring must be set that he has got one or two good things done; & against his rudeness, that he is extremely kind to some persons. I believe him to be neither a man of science nor a good practitioner. He is an intolerable ass & an unendurable bore, yet a worthy man after a fashion. What could make you waste 8 hours upon him? This shows me how you are at the call of every one.

... I think that the House of Lords makes a very poor figure. Their fury on Tuesday & their weakness on Thursday are quite ludicrous.[2] And it was very mean of them on Monday to throw out the Oxford Bill without debating it.[3]

---

[1] A reference to the case of Mary Allen, who died after being turned out of the Infirmary by Mr Harley, the surgeon. *The Times*, 23 July 1869 (12c).

[1] BL Add. MS 45783 fos. 150–2.

[2] On 20 July the Lords debated the Commons' amendments to the Lords' amendments to the Irish Church Bill: on one point they voted 173 to 95 against the Government; two days later they gave way.

[3] On the second reading of the University Tests Bill, moved by Earl Russell on 19 July, there were 54 contents and 91 not-contents.

I see that Gladstone has voted for marrying his wife's sister.⁴ This is a secret which he has been compelled to keep in his bosom for 15 years, or he could never have been elected for Oxford. As a sign of the tendencies of his character it is important. I do not quite agree with your friend about him. I wait to see the end. But I cannot say that I like being ruled by a man who has such unsound views about Homer.⁵ As to the land question I expect that they will end by not doing much:—giving facilities for the sale of land—giving Tenant right, giving advantages to persons who have leases &c.

Thank you about the vol. of Essays.⁶ I should not wonder if the contributors are reduced to Mr. Wilson, Campbell & myself. We will have more talk about that some day. I really hope that the Plato may be completed in the Spring. And then I shall be devoured by the Cambridge Critics,⁷ just as people at an Inn are sometimes eaten up by ——.

Mr. Ellis has not come here—I asked him, but I fear he is offended—he wrote me a sort of half-mad epistle about the Fellows of Trinity. I told him that they had only acted from kindness to him, which is the case. Poor fellow, I fear he is on the road to destruction & cannot be stopped.

207   Tummil Bridge,
                                                                                     Pitlochry, N.B.
                                                                                     July 29, 1869

. . . I think that I see my way clearer than I used to do to saying what ought to be said without violating the Articles. No Church can control you—not even the R. Catholic. For you may always retire in greater generalities. No Church can attack you for always teaching that God is just & true, or for calling attention to facts of experience, or urging that the facts of Scripture & Ecclesiastical history must rest on evidence. Now I do not much want to say more than this. I do not [think] that this is a desirable state of things, but making allowance for all difficulties, it does not appear to me to be dishonest. . . .

---

⁴ The House of Commons debated the Marriage with a deceased wife's sister Bill on 20 July. There were divisions, but the House was in Committee, and no list was published in Hansard. Gladstone was of opinion that such marriages should be legalized, and that it should be left to each religious denomination to decide for itself the exact character of the service and ceremony; *The Times*, 21 July 1869 (9c).

⁵ Most recently expressed in *Juventus Mundi*; see above, No. 177, n. 2.

⁶ See above, No. 201, n. 3.

⁷ BJ may have had in mind, among others, Edward Meredith Cope (1818–73), who suffered a seizure in 1869 and never worked again. When the first part of the *Plato* was published in 1871, it was reviewed in *The Academy* (15 Apr., 1 May) by William Hepworth Thompson. In 1874 BJ went to stay with Thompson in Cambridge; see below, No. 351.

208
                                                                                Tummil Bridge,
Pitlochry, N.B.
Aug. 1, 1869

I have been looking at Clough's poems, which Harrison has brought with him. They always interest me very much, & I wonder that I did not appreciate them at the time more. As Harrison, who generally hits the truth, says, 'They show so much more of the character of the man than Tennyson or Browning'....

I was going to say about Clough's poems that I doubt whether Scepticism is the proper theme for poetry. Is there any use in expressing to men a pathetic sense of the doubts which crowd around every human thing, unless we give men some principle of life which stands firm. Poets are not prophets now but men of talent or imagination who express ideas a great deal better than other people. I have known Tennyson, Browning, the 'naughty' Swinburne & M. Arnold, but I have never seen any trace of the poet's life in his poetry or of his poetry in his life, except in Clough (& an occasional sensitiveness in Tennyson which is the expression of himself). I am sometimes inclined to think that Plato is right in banishing them.[1]

Why do not poets write hymns to the Gods to be sung in all Churches? This would be a suitable employment for a poet in his old age.

I have got two companions here besides Harrison. One of them, Liddell,[2] is a charming specimen of an Eton youth—excellent manners & a great deal of intellectual interest; the other, Graham, was inflicted upon me for my sins, a great kilted hero, with money in both pockets & slightly vulgar. We got on better without him, but I cannot send him off now....

Dr. Temple has done well in declining the Deanery of Durham. But I wish that he would speak out more plainly about theology. About 10 years ago I had a conversation with him about the Atonement, but the sum of his argument was that it seemed to give such comfort to his mother (who was an excellent person). I did not care to talk to him any more about Theology.

He is a good man & he has great powers, but he has neither caution nor courage. I got a great deal of good from him in early life, but I am always disappointed when I come back to him now. He might have written a great work of a sort like Whewell's[3] but better, or he could have administered a great office, but I do not think he produces much impression on human beings—he is so wanting in sympathy....

---

[1] *The Republic*, Bk. III, 398A. BJ's translation runs, 'when any one of these pantomimic gentlemen ... comes to us, and makes a proposal to exhibit himself and his poetry, we will fall down and worship him ... but we must also inform him that in our State such as he are not permitted to exist.... And so ... we shall send him away to another city.'

[2] A. G. C. Liddell.

[3] William Whewell, *History of the Inductive Sciences* (1837); *Philosophy of the Inductive Sciences* (1840).

209
                                                        Tummil Bridge,
Pitlochry, N.B.
Aug. 9 [1869]

... I agree with you very much about the Prayer book.... The making people repeat the Creed, prayer for fair weather & other relief for temporal calamities; also, in another way, the reading of parts of the Old Testament, is thoroughly demoralizing. And do but think of the hymns they sing. A good essay might be written on the Ideal of Public Worship.

You require α) Some common feeling concentrated in special acts or words; β the greatest latitude for individual thought or prayer; γ Every word should be true; δ Every word should be elevating.

You would have to select out of ancient liturgies & medieval prayers. For no one can write a prayer now, any more than he can compose an Epic poem. And in some ways antiquity has such a curious religious power—stronger perhaps than the belief in a future life....

210
                                                        Tummil Bridge,
Pitlochry, N.B.
Aug. 16 [1869]

I am sorry that you think we can never be perfectly friends until I agree with you on the subject of contagion. Have I not forsworn Simon Magus,[1] who thinks me perjured, because I invited him to Oxford, but when I found you had such a bad opinion of him I put him off.

... I wish that you did not feel things so much. You are always getting scalded & hurt. You, who live for others, never seem to gather any happiness from this as you ought....

211
                                          Cortachy Castle,
Kirriemuir[1]
until Sep. 7
afterwards Prof. Campbell, St. Andrew's
[30 August 1869]

We leave here (Tummil) the day after tomorrow having had a very happy & prosperous stay here. I have prepared 250 printed pages of my book while here, & am certainly a great deal better than when I came. And Mr. Harrison left me this morning saying that he had quite the feeling of health....

There is another poor man staying in the Hotel who interests me, Mr. de

---
[1] Sir John Simon.
[1] Lord and Lady Airlie's.

Salis. He appears to be a gentleman of large landed property, who has paralysed himself with intense study of the coins of the later Roman Empire. He has collected, deciphered and arranged in 14 years 40,000 of them, & here is the end. I am afraid he is not likely to recover, & he lives in great suffering, only brightening up occasionally when he talks about the 4 Greek mints of Ephesus, Alexandria &c. He seems pleased at the thought that he has done more than most people in his life. That is to say, I suppose, he may furnish some small materials for a future critic on Gibbon. This is rather pathetic—he is about 40 years of age. . . .

212

Castle Moat,
St. Andrews
Sep. 19 [1869]

. . . Did you know that the theory of rent is one of my favourite beliefs or doctrines? I am as fierce about it as you are about contagion. It is impossible to have any goodwill when there are two such fundamental points of disagreement. Therefore please to consider the following points:

1. Admitting all that you say, still I must ask you what is the reason why one sum is paid for rent rather than another, after the interest on Capital has been deducted, e.g. in a new colony, or an increasing town.

2. I readily grant that you may make any use of this rent which you please; but that does not alter the principle of rent, which is monopoly natural or artificial. . . .

I will not go on to 17^{thly}, do not fear. My feeling about land is to do away all restrictions, & even to impose restrictions which are required by the health of the people—have a registration, allow no land to be bequeathed encumbered, & leave the matter there for the present. I am inclined to think that the desirableness of great subdivision depends upon so many accidents of climate, national character, habit of life, tendency to early marriages, that I do not see my way in that direction.

I greatly enjoyed my ten days holidays. At the first I stayed with Lord Kimberley, of whom I have always heard an unpleasant character. But I was pleased with him; for though he pretends to be a Cynic &c., he is really a kind hearted man, of great energy & industry & therefore of great ability, though no touch of genius in him. He ought to make a good minister whenever hard work & not much regard for the feelings of others are required. He is very independent & inclined to republicanism. He did not say much, but I thought that he was quite aware of the nature of Gladstone.

How curious the childlike trust of the lower classes in Gladstone, & the deep distrust of him among the higher classes. ταλαίπωρος ἐγὼ ἄνθρωπος.[1] What I would, that I do not &c., all through his political life.

---

[1] 'O wretched man that I am', Romans 7: 24.

Some one said to him the other day that the Ch. of England would next be disestablished. 'Not while I live' was the reply. . . .

213   Not paralysis but the Railway.
[Birnam 1 October 1869]

Since I wrote last I passed a very interesting day at Camperdown, alone with Mr. Gladstone,[1] of whom I have a great deal to say when we meet. I wrote down hastily notes of the things which he said, & thought that you might like to see them. . . .

Ellis has been with me at St. Andrews. Since what he calls 'his accident' his mind appears decidedly better. . . . He is a curious character—an absolute heathen, whose ideas are framed entirely on the Classics, with a curiosity about Mesmerism & Dr. Home.[2]

214   Railroad.
                                                                       Address Oxford.
[Woburn, 8 October 1869]

. . . Though Mitres should rain from heaven as thick as hail, my dear friend, this head is so oddly shaped that not one of them would fit it!

I am both glad & sorry that Dr. Temple has been made a Bishop.[1] He has won & deserves the great prize of the profession, & his appointment will give a shadow or countenance to other free-thinkers. But, on the other hand, he could not have had it if he had spoken out, & he is not likely to speak out now.

I have had a good many talks about the land question with different people. I rather come to this conclusion:

1. A customary lease to be understood where there is no lease.

2. Compensation for improvements (to be retrospective), the improvements to be made under the control of a government officer, & the landlord to be allowed to sell part of the estates to pay them off.

3. Limitation of the amount or extent of incumbrances on estates, accompanied by a similar power of selling the estates, in spite of wills, deeds, &c.

I very much fear that the Government are going to give up the national system of education in Ireland,[2] which will probably lead to their not having a national system in England. . . .

---

[1] The details are not recorded in Gladstone's diary.   [2] D. D. Home.

[1] Reported unofficially in *The Times*, 8 Oct. 1869 (10b).

[2] The primary school system established in 1831, under which 107,000 children were receiving education in 1833, and over half a million in 1853. The system was intended to be undenominational, but this was honoured more in the breach than the observance. J. J. Auchmuty, *Irish Education* (1837); D. H. Akenson, *The Irish Education Experiment, the National System of Education in the Nineteenth Century* (1970).

215

(Rev^d. William Rogers,
Rectory
Devonshire Square,
Bishopsgate,
N.E.)

address Inglewood
Belgrave Road,
Torquay,
Sunday Ev^g.
[17 October 1869]

Since I saw you my dear mother has been taken from us. She was ill about ten days ago, but appeared to be getting better. I came to you intending to go on to her. I received a letter at Embley which made me think that there was no danger, & yesterday morning I received similar accounts. But on Friday night she passed into a sleep from which she could never be awakened. She died this morning early.

She was not a clever person, but she had great power of appreciation & the strongest affection I have ever known, not only to her own family but to every one whom she knew.

I am glad to think that she had every thing done for her that could be done by her friend Dr. Latham,[1] who happened to be staying in the house.

This is a great break—the only thing that I can hope is to lead a truer & deeper life. Meanwhile, I am thankful that I have such friends as you & Mr. Rogers & many others.

I would answer Mrs. Butler shortly, referring her to any reports on the subject about which she writes,[2] & saying firmly that you regret you have not time to pursue the matter further. And if she writes again I should repeat the answer.

She is thought to do good, but she is very excitable & emotional—of an over-sympathetic temperament, which leads her to take an interest about a class of sinners whom she had better have left to themselves. She is quite sincere & has a touch of genius....

216

Inglewood,
Belgrave Road,
Torquay Oct. 23 [1869]

... My dear mother was very much pleased at having heard from you: 'such a distinguished person', as she said. I have her face following me as she looked when she was alive. It was the pleasantest face when she was laid to rest, & the youngest for her age that I ever saw.

Thank you very much indeed about my sister.[1] I will remember what you say, if I have occasion. She is very resigned & sensible & does extremely well,

---

[1] P. M. Latham (1789–1875). On 12 Nov. BJ added that he was '80 years of age and long past work').
[2] The Contagious Diseases Acts.

[1] Emily.

and she has some good friends here. Though very intelligent, she is sensitive, & not efficient in the business of life. At present my plan for her is that she should live here quietly, & this she seems to wish. I should like to talk to you more about her when we meet.

I go on with my work here: 'the night cometh when no man shall work'.[2] I see that Professor Conington is taken. He was not a friend of mine, but I am very sorry that he is gone. He was eccentric, I think cracked, & to that I attribute some peculiarities of his character. His scholarship was a credit to the University.

I incline to think with you that Miss Clough is probably the best person who can be found to undertake the superintendence of the proposed female Schools. I will write to Mr. Rogers about it. She is a little too grave & solemn, but she has very good sense.

217
[Torquay
31 October 1869]

... I went to see my dear mother's resting place today. Her appearance seems to follow me about. I was pleased to find that some friends had put flowers on the grave....

My sister, who, as you know, is a R. Catholic, is very good & does me good.[1] I think that her religion has somehow enabled her to stand this blow in a way which she could not otherwise have done. Yet the religion is not the more true for that....

218
[Torquay
12 November 1869]

... Two things seem to me much wanted in Medicine. 1. A History of Medicine, describing the errors & phases through which it has passed during the last century, & 2nd a Logic of Medicine. As to the first, does it not really change every 25 years? As to the second, I do not expect that you can extend Medicine or anything else by Logic, but you can generalize the principles of medical evidence. It is, after all, on that intermediate ground between the exact & the inexact Sciences which render the application of Logic important. I would have general categories of disease & endless illustrations of true & false diagnosis & true & false remedies; also another head of the right mode of applying statistics to medicine. There should be an appendix on the nature of Quackery. I think that the Education of medical men has probably suffered greatly from not being generalized sufficiently. They have not had the powers of thinking which they might have had.

[2] 'I must work the works of him that sent me, while it is day: the night cometh when no man can work', John 11: 4.

[1] On 1 Dec. BJ wrote that he had 'no intention of having her to live with me at Oxford'.

You see I want to have a Logic of Medicine written similar in general form to Mill's Logic.¹ I think that this would greatly tend to improve Medical Education. . . .

219   Balliol.
                                Thurs. [18 November 1869]

. . . I never feel that I quite understand our dear friend A.H.C[lough]. There were a good many things—a sensitive nature overlaid, 1 by Dr. Arnold, 2nd by Mr. Ward;¹ family troubles in youth; a poet forced to be a philosopher & both crushed by a life of routine. That he was a real genius is shown by the amount of sympathy he has called forth in a certain class of minds as well as by the refusal to admit his claim to this in others. I did not see the article in 'The Times'.²

I do not feel very glad at Dr. Temple's Bishopric (though I perceive that a general joy is diffused among liberals) because though a very able & clear headed man he has done nothing for the cause of freedom of thought & has given up liberality in Theology for liberalism in Politics, which is a far easier game, and he will get less & less liberal, more absolutely silent on any point which will ruffle the feathers of High Ch. & Evangelical. He may, perhaps, afford a haven for a few liberal Clergymen, but I doubt even this. He is one of those minds who run away from truth into practical usefulness, which, if a man is capable of speculation, as he is, is a kind of treachery.

220   Inglewood,
                                Torquay
                                Dec. 26, 1869.

. . . I had a delightful visit to Mr. Lowe, who is a devoted friend to me. It is impossible to see him at home & not be charmed with him. . . .

Mr. Lowe said that he had been told by Gladstone to ask whether he could do anything for me. I told him that I did not intend to leave Oxford & therefore the only thing which could be done for me would be to make Scott a Dean or a Bishop. Mr. Lowe thought that this would be done & set about the matter with great zeal. But I do not expect this, nor much care (though I tell you because you are kindly interested about me.)

---

¹ John Stuart Mill, *System of Logic* (1843).

---

¹ W. G. Ward.
² Review of *The Poems and Prose Remains of Arthur Hugh Clough* in *The Times*, 27 Oct. 1869 (10a).

221 Inglewood,
Torquay.
Dec. 31 [1869]

... Did I ever tell you that I had sacrificed my life? I ought not to have said that; for the truth is rather that I have had many troubles & many compensations....

There was a time ten or twelve years ago when I was out of health & overworked & had only lukewarm help from friends. Then life did seem dark & miserable. But that has long passed away.

I do not anticipate much from Mr. Lowe's zeal & kindness. For Gladstone will surely say (if he has no mind to appoint Scott) that he cannot make a man a Bishop for the sake of doing me a favour, for which too he will never get any credit. I am quite happy to be as I am. Though I acknowledge that I should be glad to carry on the College without this perpetual strife.

I read Dr. Temple's sermon[1] without much satisfaction. Why should he make a declaration of the Doctrine of the Trinity in the first sentence? He knows that St. Paul would not have used this language, nor would he himself ten years ago. His notion of the conscience is utterly confused. I don't like a man publicly devoted to Christ on 5000£ a year & leaving Rugby to Haman[2] (that is the right way to spell his name). It seems to me that this is not the young man whom I knew twenty years ago who used to talk to me about 'Untruthfulness being the great Sin of the world'....

[*Postscript omitted*]

222 Torquay.
[12 January 1870]

The Bishopric with which I amused you & myself[1] is all a 'flan' as I suspected. Mr. Lowe says, 'Try again, better luck another time'....

I do not care about this matter at all. I have long seen that my main chance, either of usefulness or distinction, is writing.

I hope that you have made acquaintance with Maha Panthaka & Kulla Panthaka.[2]

The Dammapad seems to me very striking;[3] the fables are very amusing, but they are poor & make religion turn too much on relieving mendicants.

[1] At his enthronement on 29 Dec. 1869; *The Times*, 30 Dec. (10cde).
[2] Persian courtier at the court of Ahasuerus. He promoted a massacre of the Jews in Persia, but was hanged on the gallows he had caused to be erected for Mordecai, Esther 3–7. BJ is referring to Henry Hayman.

[1] See above, No. 220. The new Bishop of Manchester was James Fraser. Scott would not have been suited to Manchester.
[2] Brothers, disciples of Buddha.
[3] Probably *Buddha's Parables, Translated from Burmese by T. Rogers, with Buddha's Dhammapada, translated from Pali by F. Max Müller* (1870).

I am glad that you are making friends with Mr. Goschen. I agree with you about emigration—more than about waste lands because you have to consider the expense of this last. In emigration the chief thing to be considered is whether the people are fit, or can be made fit, to go.

I entirely agree with Dr. Guthrie about Compulsory Education.

Mr. Lowe would dwell very much on the pressure of the taxes on the smaller ratepayer as a reason for retrenchment. The question of local taxation ought to be taken up, or its injustice will interfere very much with any extension of the tax for educational or sanitary purposes, as they say the general taxes are taken on 600,000,000 & the local on 90 millions. . . .[4]

223

Inglewood
Torquay.
Jan. 14 [1870]

Our mad friend[1] has really been appointed at the London University—I suppose that they did not know. His mind has been far better since his attempt, now just a year ago. . . .

My hope of him is that his insanity belongs to a particular time of life.

How very good of you to write me a scrap of a note because you thought I should be grieved about the Bishopric of Manchester. Let me tell you that I value such a friendship as yours more than any Masterships of Balliol.

Fraser is a contemporary & acquaintance of mine—an honest, free spoken man—a good speaker & preacher—not much speculative intelligence, & what there is will probably disappear in the Episcopal swaddling.

There is a great deal both of comfort & serious meaning in that saying of Lord Melbourne's, "My dear fellow, would you wear such a dress as that for 10,000 a year."[2]

I wonder how long this organized hypocrisy will last—hypocrisy will always last, but few countries have such a magnificent organization for the encouragement of it.

I am reading a medical book, Hippocrates (for the Timaeus); he was a very wise old fellow with some superstitions. I like to hear that Iatrocles of Thasos had a pain in his foot.[3] It touches one with a near feeling of those old Greeks.

This is the best place in which I ever was for work, the only place in which I do my work. . . .

[4] Estimates (provided by Lowe?) of the annual taxable income of Great Britain and of the value of rateable property?

---

[1] Ellis.
[2] See above, No. 38, n. 1.
[3] It was not Iatrocles but Crito, who, while walking about in Thasos, 'was seized with a violent pain in the great toe. He took to bed the same day with shivering and nausea; regained a little warmth; at night was delirious. . . . He died on the second day from the commencement'; Hippocrates, *Epidemics* i, case ix, Loeb edn., ed. W. H. S. Jones (1923), vol. 1, p. 203.

224

Oxford
Jan. 30, 1870

... I am glad that you liked my sermons. They none of them seem to me at all good. I want boundless leisure to write really good sermons, if I could at all, & these are struck off rather at a haste & scamped towards the end.

I hope that you are pretty well & prospering in your works. I am always interested to hear about that more than about anything. I think that it must be a great good to you to have Lord Napier of Magdala in India.

Here I commence the old routine for the 90th time at least. I have a better chance now than formerly, having the whole entirely under my control—And I hope to take a particular & individual interest in every man in College. That is my aim.

The old, defunct Senior Tutor & the Master & Bursar[1] took occasion to testify against my sermons yesterday, but the College re-elected me.[2] They might make things troublesome, if they went to the Visitor.[3]

Some ladies whom I know more or less, Mrs. Butler[4] & Co., are getting excited about the Contagious disorders Bill. I hope that you have nothing to do with them,[5] for they are not wise people, & are, I think, on a wrong tack. The sole question for Sanitary Reformers is, I think, whether such measures are possible or successful. Miss Garratt's letter,[6] whether you agree with her or not, seemed to me written with great tact & propriety.

Tyndal's lecture[7] interested me very much. But I do not see that he gives much proof of germs of disease being retained in the air, and 'light being dirt' I am told is not new.

225

[Oxford
27 February 1870]

... I am afraid that Mr. Forster is making a mistake in leaving the school-boards elected by Town Councils to squabble over the religious question.[1] The

[1] Woolcombe, Scott, Wall.   [2] College preacher.   [3] Jackson.
[4] Glen Petrie says BJ 'disapproved of everything she stood for', and thinks this was because Josephine made fun of him. *A Singular Iniquity: the Campaigns of Josephine Butler* (1971), pp. 21, 37–8.
[5] BJ was speaking out of turn here, for FN (together with Mary Carpenter, Harriet Martineau and others) had already signed a protest against the Contagious Diseases Acts which was published in the *Daily News* on 1 Jan. 1870. For FN's views, see *Cook* ii. 75, 408.
[6] Advocating the extension of the Contagious Diseases Acts, appeared in the *Pall Mall Gazette* on 25 Jan. 1870 (6b–e). She asked, rhetorically, whether legislation would succeed, and whether it treated the sexes unequally. She answered that 'Success has everywhere been in proportion to the size of the area over which the Act could be brought into operation', and that since there was no parallel class among men, men and women were not being treated unequally. See, too, her *An Enquiry into the Character of the Contagious Diseases Acts of 1866-69*, p. 16, published by the Association for Promoting the Extension of the Contagious Diseases Acts (1870).
[7] For his lecture, see J. Tyndall, *Essays on the Floating Matter of the Air* (1881).

[1] 'Ought we to restrict the school Boards, in regard to religion, more than we do the managers of voluntary schools? We have come to the conclusion that we ought not.—Why do you not, then, pre-

demon of the old poor law, who is still walking about in dry places, i.e. in the minds of political economists, seems to have got the better of Mr. Goschen, when he throws the indoor relief on the Common rate.² And I am not sure that endless litigation & the consecration of bad customs is the best settlement of the Irish land question;³ nor do I see any reason for the new parliamentary undersecretary for war.⁴ For either you will have a better man (as Socrates would say) than Mr. Cardwell, or a worse. And to either alternative objections may be urged.

I shall send you a very pretty novel to read when an Oxford lady returns it— 'Lisa: A Russian Story'.⁵ It was given me by poor Mr. Bullock, the same who translated 'Resurrecturis',⁶ which I think that I showed you. He was married to Miss Cross, of whom you probably never heard. She was a woman of genius & character & he was absorbed in her. A few months ago she died. They had splendid prospects of wealth & happiness before them. An hour before her death she said that it seemed hard that God should take her now that she was so very happy. We all of us who knew her have a melancholy feeling about her, which makes me run on to you with this tale, apropos of nothing. And I have a sad feeling about one of my Scotch friends who has died last week, Lord Barcaple. He was one of the best men in Scotland & I think the most satisfactory lawyer & judge (except, perhaps, Lord Kingsdown) whom I have ever known. He died prematurely from overwork. When at the Bar he used to sit up night after night. And since he has been a judge, owing to his great eminence an unusual pressure of business came to him. He was a real solid man.

Mrs. Liddell, who is a pernicious, fine, vulgar woman, has invented a new way of demoralizing Oxford. She has taken a room at the Randolph Hotel & gives dances to undergraduates at 2. 6. a head every Monday evening.

Mr. Maine, now a Professor of Law at Oxford, came to see me today. He is an able & sensible man & will be an addition to the place. Unfortunately he is not required to reside.

Poor Mr. Harrison does not get much better, though he is cheerful. The passing of a slight examination last Term seems altogether to have overthrown

---

scribe that there shall be no doctrinal teaching? . . . Why, if we did so, out of the religious difficulty we should come to an irreligious difficulty.' *PD*, cxcix. 457, 17 Feb. 1870. But the Cowper–Temple clause, an amendment accepted by the Government, excluded all religious formularies from rate aided schools, and placed denominational schools outside the control of the local boards.

² Following the success of the Metropolitan Poor Law Act of 1867 (see above, No. 128, n. 2), Goschen introduced a Bill 'to provide for the equal distribution over the Metropolis of a further portion of the charge for Poor Relief'. He proposed that the Common Fund should contribute 3s. 6d. a week in respect of each inmate of a workhouse. In the Act, 33 and 34 Vict. c. 18, the figure was reduced to 5d. per day.

³ The Irish Land Bill provided for compensation for eviction to be settled in court, and arguably, by doing justice to outgoing tenants, burdened incoming ones. See E. D. Steele, *Irish Land and British Politics, Tenant Right and Nationality, 1865-70* (1974).

⁴ The overworked Cardwell introduced a Bill to provide for a new Financial Secretary at the War Office. *The Times*, 16 Feb. 1870 (7d).

⁵ I. S. Turgenev, *Liza*, trans. by W. R. S. Ralston (2 vols., 1869).

⁶ See above, 32, n. 2.

him—I am half inclined to think that he had better 'throw physic to the dogs',[7] & trust entirely to air & rest.

226 [7 March 1870]

I send back the notes on pauperism with many thanks. I hope that you will write something based upon them. I also send a Lay-Sermon of my friend, Mr. Green, to his pupils, which appears to me to be very good.

I am coming to town next Sunday to preach for Mr. Stopford Brooke. . . .

Mr. Lowe lives at Caterham on the top of a steep hill. He goes down this full speed, 20 or 30 miles an hour, on a Bicycle. I hope that he will not find himself in a ditch & in a better world.

If you write on the Poor Law, as I hope that you will, please to consider fairly the Political economy point of view—the refusal of people to do for themselves in sickness, in education, in taking care of parents, children &c. what they can do for themselves. 2) The difficulty of providing an organization suiting the poor laws to varying circumstances. . . .

227 [19 March 1870]

. . . I gain an increasing conviction that the Established Church must come down. It is so extremely unjust to those who are not members of it, socially, educationally & in every way. No wonder that the Church gains upon the Dissenters in the matter of education, when the one have their Churches & ministers found for them, the other have chapel & school to pay for & are themselves the poorer body. They are not equal to fighting their own battle; they are oppressed, vulgarized, denominationalized, & some of them will still compliment the Church for what it has done for them. They think that the Church helps to keep down the truth as some of themselves do. What an evil in a country a huge party, like the Church party, is. . . .

228 Inglewood, Torquay
April 7 [1870]

. . . On Monday I am going 'after strange women', i.e. Mrs. Lowe, who insists that I must come to the budget.[1] I did not intend to leave here so soon. But I do not like to seem indifferent to their kindness, especially as they have asked people to meet me.

Yet I feel rather out of humour with that potentate, after reading his speech

---

[7] 'Throw physic to the dogs; I'll none of it.' *Macbeth*, v. iii. 47.

[1] On 11 Apr. 1870, *PD*, cc. 1607–45.

of yesterday.² He seems to have no idea of consistency. The Irish Land Bill will do no good, but only complicate the disorder.

229 Oxford
April 18 [1870]

... I should advise you to write to Miss Jones's sister, or to the Bishop of Derry,¹ or both, & urge upon them plainly the great injury which will be done to her memory & to your work by the publication of this foolish memoir. They should be made to see that all people, & especially sanitary people, do not look at matters through their evangelical spectacles. And you, if any one, have a claim to be heard, because you introduced Miss Jones to the life to which she devoted herself.

Could you get the proofs & then write to the B. of Derry & point out your objections? Or I think that you might write to him at once as having a common interest in your friend & tell him what you fear. This appears to me to be the best plan. You have an additional claim upon them for writing Una & the lion....²

230 Oxford
May 29 [1870]

I am coming to London on Thursday—leaving these few sheep in the wilderness—to marry your cousin, Miss Gertrude Smith to Mr. Alexander Sellar. May I come & see you between five & six & tell you about the doings?

Thank you a thousand times about poor Greg. It is a sad story. He was a good & religious man, but he had gone wrong & he put an end to himself out of remorse. If I were more wide awake I could help these fellows a great deal more. But this & many other things have escaped me.

I preached about him today—not well, for I was hurried & tired—the only good thing which I said was taken out of your letters, for which many thanks....

The M. of Salisbury¹ has been making rather a fool of himself. He has proposed a list of 50 D.C.L.s among whom were Darwin, Tyndall, & Delitzsch. The Hebrew Conservative,² or some one, wrote threatening him & he has withdrawn the three last names (this is a secret). I dare say that you were not aware that there were fifty eminent persons in England....

---

² In his speech on the Irish Land Bill, Lowe poured scorn on 'The principles of political economy! Why we violate them every day ... you cannot settle all the complicated relations of mankind by the rules of political economy.' *The Times*, 5 Apr. 1870 (6c–f).

¹ William Alexander.
² See above, No. 161, n. 3.

¹ The Chancellor of the University.
² Pusey.

231 [6 June 1870]

... I agree to leave off work at 11.30 & to take 7 weeks of holiday in periods of not less than a week, and I will begin by taking a fortnight at the end of term. I think that you must allow me to correct the proofs in the fortnight—not to stop the press. But that is really no labour.

I am grieved that you should write so despondingly of yourself. Your's has been the best & greatest life of any woman's in this generation, & you must not allow yourself to leave it half-finished. I only wish that you would let me help you in writing. If you would write rough notes, on Education, on Sanitary improvement, on Theodice, I feel certain that I could put them into form & prepare them for the press. When you are somewhat better, will you try?

I have had 'doings' here,—Browning, & M. Arnold & Sir L. Mallet & Palgrave. M. Arnold gave me his St. Paul,[1] which I have been reading—very superficial, both in his account of St. Paul & in the application to the Dissenters. Mat. having eaten the mutton & drank the small beer of Dissenting ministers for 20 years is greatly exasperated at them. But as his wife, a most sensible ladylike woman, said to me, 'she was not sure about his writing on these subjects'.

We have also had Mrs. Lewis[2] here. Did I tell you of her? She is a very pleasing person in manners & has evidently great abilities. I am told that she has gone through some ceremony of marriage, though she can hardly be said, in the language of the Vicar of Wakefield, to 'be made an honest woman of'.[3] The ladies here don't seem to object to her. . . .

I am glad to find that they have snubbed me about the translation of the New Testament.[4] I should have done no good, & might have spent many weeks, 'fighting with beasts at Ephesus'. . . .[5]

232 [9 June 1870]

I please myself by thinking that you will be pleased to see that the M. of Balliol is made D[ean] of Rochester.[1] In the most lugubrious tones of voice he informed us of this at a College meeting today.

I suppose that I shall succeed him. If I do, I shall have the position best suited to me that I could have. But it will be only a pain & annoyance to me, if ten years hence I do not make the College a different sort of place—an ideal

---

[1] *St. Paul and Protestantism: with an Introduction on Puritanism and the Church of England* (1870).

[2] Lewes, George Eliot.

[3] '... my wife, too, kissed her daughter with much affection, as, to use her own expression, she was now made an honest woman of', Oliver Goldsmith, *The Vicar of Wakefield*, Chap. 31.

[4] The Committee to revise the English version of the *New Testament* began to sit in 1870. The selection rested with the Convocation of the English Clergy. The NT was published in 1881, the OT in 1885. When it appeared BJ said 'They seem to have forgotten that, in a certain sense, the Authorised Version is more inspired than the original'; *AC* i. 406.

[5] 'If, after the manner of men, I have fought with beasts at Ephesus . . .', 1 Cor. 15: 32.

---

[1] Gladstone made the offer to Scott on 27 May 1870. RSBJ, p. 20.

College. It will be very pleasant to me to have a large house in which I can collect my old pupils.

I cannot be too thankful for this. There is a great difference between doing as you please & constantly fighting a battle. Seventeen years ago I was all but elected & the first eight or ten years after that I had a bad time....

[*Postscript omitted*]

233

Aldworth,
Blackdown,
Haslemere.

address: Rev^d. W. Rogers,
Rectory,
Bishopsgate.
[1 July 1870]

Like a bad shilling I am returning to London next Saturday (tomorrow).... The reason is that a benevolent lady wants me to come & dine with her, and as she has carried off Mr. Abbot bodily to stay with her & see Mr. Paget, I do not like to refuse. She is Mrs. Baden Powell & I had sent her son to Mr. Abbot as a pupil.[1]

... Please to read a book which they have got here & which greatly delights Tennyson & me, "Ginx's Baby".[2] If you are not the authoress, which you might have been, I think that you will be disposed to say, 'Them's my sentiments'.

I have nothing to do tomorrow (I mean Sunday afternoon) & will gladly come & see you, if you are well enough to see me, at 4 oClock. Remember that it is always a pleasure to me to come, but put me off if you are engaged. It is rather an intrusion to come back again after saying 'Goodbye'.

This house is 900 feet above the sea & looks over 60 miles of Country. It is a beautiful house. Nevertheless, the owner, having spent 8000£ in building it, is already tired & says that he only looks into an 'Abyss' & into a 'void demon-haunted country'. This comes of being a poet: I am always surprized to find in him how disproportioned his powers as a philosopher are to his powers as a poet. And yet he is the philosopher-poet.

234

Inglewood,
Torquay
Monday Ev^g.
[11 July 1870]

... I spent last week at Sir H. Taylor's and at Marlborough with Mr. Bradley, the best of schoolmasters. The Taylors I greatly like; there is a sort of

---

[1] Mrs Baden Powell's fourth and third sons, Sir F. S. Baden Powell and Sir G. S. Baden Powell, came to Balliol (in that order).
[2] Anon. [*John Edward Jenkins*], *Ginx's Baby: His Birth and Other Misfortunes* (1870).

goodness & simplicity & mild philosophy about him & his family which makes their house refreshing. They appear to me only to have two friends but they are good ones, James Spedding & Aubrey de Vere. They take their great trouble[1] sadly but cheerfully, as I like to see sorrow taken. I made acquaintance with Aubrey de Vere there; do you know him? He is a bigoted papist, but a most excellent man & a man of genius. I wish there were people of his simplicity & self devotion among free thinkers.

My friend Dr. Symonds is dying (this is the fourth valuable friend whom I have lost in about 7 months).[2] I went to see him on Saturday, but they were afraid of exciting him by letting me see him. I heard that he was eagerly asking about the election at Balliol. He is very sceptical in the orthodox sense, but very peaceful & trustful. He appears to have had a mortal disease for some years past. He says 'O divine death' at the same time apologizing for the strangeness of the expression. I do not know what his merits were as a physician—he was a man of various culture. If I were to sum up his character in one word it would be 'Infinite in kindness'. . . .

235

Inglewood,
Torquay
[July 1870]

Have you read Faraday's life?[1] I have been skimming it today & yesterday with great interest. This is a distinct type of character—a genius for natural philosophy + extreme simplicity + the strongest kindness & affection. No one in our day has done more to ennoble science & scientific men. Yet there is also a certain limitation in his nature which interferes with greatness. There is a corner in this remarkable mind for Sandemanianism, which exerts a very great influence over him, & yet is absolutely irreconcileable with his philosophy. The two chambers are divided by an iron wall (not that Sandemanianism, by the way, seems to be a very bad thing). Mr. Home might retort upon Faraday, 'What more reason have you for believing in the Resurrection than I have for believing in Spirits &c., which you despise?' Faraday can only reply, 'One belongs to the province of faith'—& perhaps Mr. Home would say the same of the other. And an external observer would add 'that Faraday sprang from a strongly religious family & never laid aside his original constitution'. The external observer, like the intelligent foreigner, is very troublesome.

The simplicity & goodness of a man like Faraday does almost rob one of the first article of the Creed that truth is one. And I do strongly feel that Methodism, Evangelicalism &c. have an elevation & idealism in them for the lower

---

[1] Their eldest son, Aubrey died on 16 May 1870.
[2] See below, No. 237.

[1] Henry Bence Jones, *The Life and Letters of Faraday* (2 vols., 1870).

people with which we cannot afford to dispense, although it is a very difficult task to estimate the possible proportions of good & evil in them.

Faraday is not quite sufficiently impersonal for my ideal of greatness, & he did not know the world. Some one will say how much better his simplicity is. Well, I rather suspect that 'knowledge of the world' is simplicity + the power of observation, and that though the quality has a bad name there is none more necessary to enable a man to do any good. It is almost the opposite of the quality of readiness &c. which characterizes the so-called man of the world.

Faraday's early letters give the highest promise. He has noble ideas about friendship, which I would that any of us could realize in this world.

There is another reflection which is suggested to me by reading Faraday. What endless ability there must be among the poor, if one knew how to look for it & draw it out! At present it is wasted among skilled workers chiefly in drink &c. The greater part of the University & professional ability, $\frac{99}{100}$ths probably, comes from the upper 100,000, the rest is allowed to run to seed. This is different in Prussia, & Scotland to some degree.

Did you read Mr. Trevelyan's speech?[2] Not very good, but it interested me & I think is a severe reflection on the Ministry & my friend, R[obert] L[owe] &c.

[*Postscript omitted*]

FN to BJ [*draft or copy*][1]

236 July 12, 1870

I have only read the Life of Faraday in Extracts. I have now sent for it and will read it thoroughly.

What I am going to say is therefore quite general, on your letter and not on the Life....

He was absolutely without imagination. Bence Jones says he was remarkable for imagination, but he means by imagination the insight of genius into the scientific thing to be discovered which he sought to establish by his experiments, just as Newton imagined or guessed at the law of gravitation and then instituted experiments and calculations which decided his guess to be right. But in the imagination or conception which assimilates the higher spiritual or art impressions, Faraday was absolutely deficient. In Rome he finds nothing better to tell you of than the Horse-race in the Corso. His journals from Switzerland would disgrace a boy of 12 years old.... The Bible and the Bible alone was God's mind to *him*: of course he had nothing else to do but to quote, to

---

[2] Following the acceptance of the Cowper-Temple amendment (see above, No. 225, n. 1), Sir G. O. Trevelyan resigned and attacked the increase in the grant available to denominational schools. He argued that unsectarian schooling was the education of the future, and that the denominational grant was a shameful and unnecessary concession to the Church of England. *PD*, cciii. 75–7.

[1] BL Add. MS 45783 fos. 210–17.

study the Bible. On his system, he says truly that it is 'impious', 'blasphemous', to bring any methods of human inquiry into this.

237

Inglewood,
Torquay
July 18 [1870]

I have just been reading the debate in the French Chamber on the war. It certainly seems one of the greatest crimes that ever was committed—& the crime not of the Emperor so much as of the whole nation.[1] I feel on the other side that Prussia is not honestly where she is, & that her 'sin has now found her out' & probably that Bismarck cheated the Emperor about Luxembourg. It is the greatest & worst news for the world since 1815.

(Old Dr. Latham was describing to me this morning the news of the battle of Trafalgar—the half-muffled peals—'the nation would have given up the victory, if they could have got back Nelson'.)

I assure you that I am quite well.... The prospect of completing my work, & my changed circumstances, gives me a new spring of life.

I am afraid that this talk of war gives you more work. Our dear princesses[2] (not that I expect that they will do much good at it, they are not steady enough) will take to hospitals & nursing & write to you. I am grieved for Europe—to think of the places one knows so well, Mayence, Coblentz, Darmstadt, deluged with blood. In two months perhaps 500,000 men will have perished. I see that the C. Prince is to take the Command of the army in South Germany.[3] He is a good soldier-like man, but I can't imagine that he has a great military genius.

I hope that the tone of our newspapers will be neutral—at present they are taking on against France. But I don't think Prussia clean, any more than France. Hohenzollern &c. was very likely an intrigue of Bismarck's, & the King in refusing to see them should have remembered that this was the colour wh. would be put upon it. If the Prussians did not want war they should never [have] allowed the P[rince Leopold] of H[ohenzollern] to consent. But I suppose that the truth is that neither King nor Emperor dared to prevent the Prussian & French armies getting at one another.

You 'threaten' me with a gift & I know a way in which I could prevent you; I would at once break the treaty. But I have not the heart to do this & therefore I thankfully accept your great kindness; if you will give me some work of art good—but not expensive (no silver epergnes, which I could not accept). But as I am not elected until Sep. 7 let us put off the matter until then.

[1] On 18 July 1870 *The Times* (12a) reported votes of 240 to 1 in favour of credits, calling out the Garde Mobile, and of enlisting volunteers. Gambetta alone invited the Chamber to be cool and to deliberate.
[2] Victoria and Alice.
[3] Frederick commanded the Third Army in which the contingents from the South German states served.

The four friends about whom you kindly ask are Mr. Erskine, Lord Barcaple, Aubrey Taylor (who wrote from the Cape 3 months ago that 'I must always be the best-beloved of his friends—Alas, Alas'*) and now Dr. Symonds, who still lingers.

* As his mother said to me, he should have been alive to hear about Balliol.

238

Inglewood
July 23,
1870

I fear that you are terribly overworked: therefore do not write to me until you are quite at leisure. This war looks more wicked, more dangerous, more aweful the more you look at it. Both parties are equally to blame, but there is a sort of fate in great armies & national hatreds, which cannot be resisted. I do not see where the war is to end; when 200,000 Prussians are killed & 200,000 French they will be no nearer a solution. Then there is the mysterious Russia looming in the distance, ready to join either party who will allow her to get to Constantinople. Prussia would, if she were not afraid of England, & France would but for the glaring contradiction of the Crimean War. Here are two old men, F. William & Napoleon, ready to fight with one foot in the grave—and Frederick the Great & Napoleon 1st (for the real contest is between them) rejoicing in the world below.

I dare say the Princesses have written to you. I am sorry to see that the newspapers are calling the Crown Princess an infidel & a friend of Strauss—& I am afraid that she has got into not very good moral latitudes (though she does nothing wrong). This war will give her occupation & interest, & if you can stir her up you will do her a service. But take care of your own health first, & do not kill yourself because there is a war.

I dare say that you will have seen in the paper an event which causes me a great deal of sorrow—the death of poor Charteris.[2] I do not as yet make out whether it was by his own hand or an accident. If the first I suspect that his mind was impaired by long bodily illness. He was a charming fellow—good, I think, & clever, but idle—very handsome & not at all showy or fashionable. I used to think that he would come out some day. But that is all with the past now. I can hardly believe that that ringing laugh is now silent for ever.

I think that we English were very short sighted in not having the European conference 6 years ago.[3] We might have prevented this war if we had, & perhaps have restored Poland. We congratulate ourselves on non-interference

[1] Victoria and Alice.
[2] Hon. Francis Charteris.
[3] On 4 Nov. 1863, after the Powers had failed to intervene to help the Poles against the Tsar, Napoleon III invited the rulers of the principal states to join in a Congress to discuss all questions threatening to disturb the peace of Europe. The British refused, because the person most likely to try and upset the Treaties of 1815 was Napoleon himself.

in any cause, good or bad, & carry on our trade. But we may find some day that we are only a fat sheep about to be eaten by wolves.

Morier & his wife (who is an admirable woman) have gone back to Darmstadt to take care of the Princess Alice & to be in the thick of the battle. I think he will find an opportunity of distinguishing himself, but am a little afraid of his Prussian tendencies....

239
Inglewood,
Torquay
July 27 [1870]

It is a great relief to me to hear that you are going to Lea Hirst; I think that is better than going to Embley. There is youth & health in the Derbyshire hills & streams. If you will stay there until the middle of September I will come & see you there....

I am very glad to see that Mr. Lowe gives notice of a Bill for the Registration of Land....[1]

I had a very pleasing, sad letter from Lord Elcho a day or two ago. He is a warm hearted deep feeling man. Like another friend of mine, he has achieved great unpopularity by a certain spice of vanity in his composition, which is mistaken for aristocratic insolence, whereas he is not really an Aristocrat. He is brokenhearted about his poor son. He does not say—I do not know whether he suspects—that the deed was done by his own hand. The son was a fine creature. It grieves me to think of him.

240
Tummil Bridge,
Pitlochry, N.B.
Aug. 10 [1870]

... Do not these great battles take one's breath away.[1] I hope neither party will gain much. It would be a serious loss to Europe if either the German or French element were seriously weakened. Above all, I do not want to see the French pride humbled: that leaves a rankling sore & bequeathes a war to the next generation.

Nor do I at all wish that we should interfere on behalf of Belgium (from motives of honour—read interest) except in that innocent manner in which our ministry propose. It is not likely that either party will touch Belgium until the war is over, & then they may do what they like without our being able to

---

[1] The Land Registry Office had been founded in 1862 with a view to making 'the title to land as clear as the title to stock'. But Lord Westbury insisted that the title to land should show all the transactions that had taken place upon it. A new Bill had been prepared (*PD*, cciii. 997–8, 26 July 1870) but it was not brought in.

[1] At the battles of Weissenburg (4 Aug.) and Worth (6 Aug.), the Crown Prince defeated MacMahon. On 6 Aug. the Prussians drove the French out of the Saar after the battle of Spicheren.

prevent them. Do we really suppose that the prospective danger of the French possessing Antwerp is at all equal to the danger of an actual war with them?

What a strange thing this tendency to war is, which seems to become stronger & stronger as the reasons diminish. No one thinks of wars of conquest now; it is all the rectification of a frontier & the assertion of a nationality, & there is a certain discredit in not going to war. I suspect that the English people will want to go to war before long, that they may not become a byeword among the nations. I think that we are very aggravating to foreigners, with our great professions & high moral lessons, while secretly we care only for our trade.

Mr. Campbell is here with me, & we spend an hour or two a day over his Sophocles;[2] also Mr. Harrison who is certainly better, & Mr. Godley whose father you may have possibly known. The latter is a first-rate sort of young man & is covered with Oxford distinctions.

241　　　　　　　　　　　　　　　　　　　　　　　　Tummil Bridge,
　　　　　　　　　　　　　　　　　　　　　　　　　　　Pitlochry
　　　　　　　　　　　　　　　　　　　　　　　　　　　Aug. 14 [1870]

... At this place, being Sunday night, we have had no news for 36 hours, and the French Empire meanwhile may have come to an end. If we lose the Emperor I hope that we shall get rid of Bismarck, who is the greater rascal of the two. I sympathize with Prussia as the Protestant power, but I think that France even under the Emperor has done far more for the liberties of Europe & is likely to do more.

It seems to me that the great thing for England to aim at in the present state of European politics is the establishment of reserves, especially of a naval reserve, & to tie herself as closely as she can to America, removing causes of quarrel at any cost....

242　　　　　　　　　　　　　　　　　　　　　　　　Tummil
　　　　　　　　　　　　　　　　　　　　　　　　　　　Aug. 29 [1870]

... I entirely agree with you about the iniquity of the whole business beginning 4 years ago. This German nationality is a very delusive idea, meaning really the ascendancy of a military aristocracy. Germany has armed & France must arm & then England, & every other nation, & the end is that everybody having arms in their hands the military spirit is enormously developed & Europe blows up like a powder magazine. England will be slowest, but will at last fight, not in any good cause like Poland or Italy, but to show that she is not afraid, or because the Charivari makes a caricature of her.

[2] *Sophocles: the Plays and Fragments*, edited with English Notes and Introduction by L. Campbell (1871).

You are very good to think of me on Sep. 7.[1] I am ashamed to be happy when the rest of the world is so full of misery. No one has so vivid an impression of this as you have & no impression is a quarter of the truth. . . .

[1] The day of BJ's election as Master.

CHAPTER 4

1870-1875

243
Sep. 7 [1870]

I write a line to tell you that I have been elected Master of Balliol, only I cannot perform any of the duties of the office until, in accordance with an old Statute, I have been to see the Visitor,[1] who is said to be up in Scotland, & if this is true I shall have to go after him. I should have liked to tell you my hopes & fears about this new position, but Mr. Rogers, who has come from London to see me, is waiting for his dinner. So I will not inflict them upon you. . . .

244
Oxford
Oct. 3, 1870

I have been very negligent in not sending you back this letter of Mr. Lockhart's[1] & in not writing to you sooner. I think that you are never very long out of my thoughts, though I have a 'Cacoethes non scribendi',[2] which is very inexcusable. . . .

The journey to Scotland came to nothing, as we found the Visitor[3] at Malvern. He was kind & not troublesome, & rose in my estimation when he expressed a wish 'that God might give you grace to preside over that noble College'. I mean to try & keep on good terms with all men, or I shall get nothing done.

I enclose a letter from the Abp. of Canterbury[4]—kindly meant, although the tone does not please me.

I spent a day or two with Lingen at Brighton. I think very highly of him & believe that he will do good service to the State. He has greater experience of the public offices than anyone & speaks in the same way which you do. 'The War Office is the worst, except the Home Office'. Do not repeat this to any 'Temple to Friendship' or other person.

Let me hear from you, although I hardly deserve it. The truth is that I have had such multifarious things to do, that I have not had energy to answer my letters. Last week I had a partial holiday & spent two days with great pleasure at Woburn.[5] I like the people there. . . .

---

[1] Jackson.

---

[1] L. W. M. Lockhart.
[2] *Tenet insanabile multos scribendi cacoethes et aegro in corde senescit* (an inveterate itch of writing, now incurable, clings to many, and grows old in their distempered heart), Juvenal, *Satires*, vii. 51.
[3] Jackson.
[4] Tait.
[5] With William Russell the eighth Duke of Bedford.

245

Oct. 16, 1870
Ball. Coll.

... Will you tell me about yourself & what you are doing? I always like to hear about that. I never observed that poor Reginald Herbert had gone down in the 'Captain'.[1] I am sorry for him & sorry for you. There is something very painful in losing a young friend of such promise. I understand what you thought & felt about him, from the deaths of poor Taylor & Charteris which trouble me greatly.

I went to see Archbishop Euthyphro[2] on Wednesday at Addington (a most beautiful place), partly because I wanted to get his interest with the Bishop of London[3] to induce him to allow some changes to be made in the College. I have been fortunate since I returned here, at the College meeting. I succeeded in carrying several important matters almost unanimously & without any ill will.[4] The old Senior Tutor[5] behaved as he always does, like a simpleton & a gentleman. One thing he said rather touched me, "that he was aware the lectures had greatly improved since his day"....

Abp. Euthyphro says that he is nearly if not quite well & he appeared to be so. He is a gentleman & a shrewd man with a touch of humour, but absolutely devoid of any enlarged insight into things. His business is not with truth & right, but with the Church of England. He has a twang of Scotch Presbyterianism, and like a Scotchman, though a clever man does not readily see the point of a remark. He & Mrs. Tait were very kind—they like to see me because I knew their dead children (poor forgotten flowers)[6] and I liked them for a short time.

I entirely agree with you about this war which is making a Pandemonium of Europe. Morier said, O that he had been in Lord Granville's place[7] for 24 hours, knowing what he knew—he thought that he could have prevented the war by the facts respecting Germany which he could have laid before L. Napoleon. The French seem to be mad & their cause hopeless. I suspect that it is the desperate desire of the Republicans to retain the government, that renders them unwilling to yield. They know nothing in Paris of what is really going on. On the other hand, the Germans will be covered with infamy if they bombard Paris. London is said commonly to have food only for 3 days & Paris can hardly have it for three weeks....

---

[1] The *Captain*, a turret ship, sank off Cape Finisterre at 00.15 on 7 Sept. 1870.
[2] Tait.
[3] Jackson.
[4] CM, 13–14 Oct.: responsibility for buttery, shop, kitchen, and furniture was taken away from the Bursar and given to the Master, answers to questions upon the catechetical lecture were henceforth not to be enforced, and a committee was appointed to revise the Statutes with a view to reducing the number of clerical Fellowships and opening the way for Fellows to retain their Fellowships upon marriage. (See above, pp. xxvi–xxviii.)
[5] Woollcombe.
[6] Five out of their (then) seven children died in the space of a few weeks from scarlet fever in 1856.
[7] Clarendon died on 27 June 1870, and was succeeded as Foreign Secretary by Granville.

246 Oxford
Nov. 4, 1870

I am afraid that I must appear very negligent for not writing to you. I believe the real reason is that I have so much to do here: cook,[1] butler, shop, furniture of College, lectures, endless remonstrances of tradesmen whom I have been driving out of College, besides meagre attempts to finish Plato & enquiries of anxious parents. But the round of employments is very pleasant to me, & I hope soon to put the house in order (not my house), & then I shall have more time both for work & writing to you. . . .

You will rejoice about the armistice, which must, I think, lead to peace. How the French people need a man of genius to guide them! Without one or two such men they are nothing & with them may be anything. I was pleased with Lord Granville's letter;[2] it showed tact. But I have also the feeling that the English have never done anything for Europe which justifies them in opening their lips. John Bull is an infinite humbug. He wants to have all the virtue and all the money to himself, & all the power without being at the expense of an army.

A distinguished lady is coming to live at Oxford under the protection of Dr. Pusey—Miss Sellon—& has already taken a house, I am told. She seems to have great influence, but she has not solved the real question of sisterhoods, viz., how family relations can be reconciled with the work of an Order, or how such societies can be maintained without extravagant religious devotions. You must have often thought of that problem. The most probable solution seems to me a sisterhood living in their own homes or lodgings, but organized for a purpose, say under an engagement to devote 3 or 4 hours a day to some useful purpose, & meeting once a day at a religious service & perhaps for one meal.

It is curious to observe at Oxford, how the College system is breaking down; or rather, how people are becoming conscious that it was always breaking down & must break down. A College is a sham monastery—in the last century like the monastery in its idleness, luxury & religious services, & now rather refusing to be a sham & wanting to give up it's chapel services, & try education. Within the last ten years all the younger men have made the discovery that the head of the monastery is a sham & ought to be abolished. That is the reason why I want to make them terminable offices. . . .

---

[1] On 13 Dec. the Master was authorized to engage a cook at a salary not exceeding £120 p.a. For BJ's estimate of his success in all this housekeeping, see below, No. 269.
[2] In one intervention communicated to Tours and to Berlin Granville proposed an armistice and hoped to avoid a bombardment of Paris, and in a second he refuted German accusations of breaches of neutrality. *The Times*, 24 Oct. 1870 (8f, 9a) and 31 Oct. (5ef).

FN to BJ [*draft or copy*]¹

247
4 Nov., 1870

Serene Highness

Is it your Archbishop or your cook that you are looking after now?

Ah, Revd Sir, it's the poor old fogey, me, who's thrown overboard now by the Master who consorts with Archbishops in purple and fine linen, and Dukes, and teaches the sheep to laugh at Socrates, and goes to church on weekdays.

Nevertheless, you asked me to write, and I, obedient, write, tho' I've small stomach for it.

On this day, 16 years ago, I landed at Scutari—God be thanked! who would have thought that I should have lived to see the horrors of a war compared with which those were mere child's play?

... Is it not quite unknown in history that a philosophical, a deep thinking, the most highly and widely educated nation of Europe, these Germans, should plunge, head foremost, into this gulf and abyss, called military despotism, that they should not see ... that the real Devil, the true Mephistopheles is: Bismarck. . . .

248
Nov. 14 [1870]

I am coming to London on Wednesday to be examined by the Art & Science Commission.¹ May I have the pleasure of coming to see you about 4 oClock? ...

249
[2 December 1870]

... I hate the German oppressors. The rights & wrongs of the war have turned round, & the English people have begun to see this. I went to call on a German¹ here today. He informed me that Bismarck's plan was a close alliance of England & Germany, after Alsace & Lorraine had been ceded. They were then to keep the peace of the world together, against Russia & against France. I told him that I did not think English feeling would admit of this, upon which

---

¹ BL Add. MS 45783 fos. 223–6.

¹ On 16 Nov. 1870, by the Commissioners appointed to make Inquiry with regard to Scientific Instruction and the Advancement of Science. BJ's evidence is at *PP* (1872), xxv . 250–6. It is interesting that BJ was called before the Commission, for he argued that everyone should learn classics, and that scholarships, but not Fellowships, should be open to scientists. When asked whether his college had 'taken any measures for the promotion of scientific instruction' (Qn. 3892), he replied, 'Some years ago we had a laboratory at the College, and we made a beginning of teaching in physical science, but these things can be done so much better on a larger scale, that we have given up the laboratory, and the students who pursue physical science go to the new museum.' However, when the new Hall was built in 1875, the college included a chemistry laboratory (which remained in use until 1940).

¹ Not identified.

he went to war with me & would make peace upon no terms. He is dangerous & ought to be locked up; I shall not go near him again while the war lasts.

The term is nearly over & then comes seven weeks of vacation. I have got on pretty well & have had no approach to a quarrel. But I have been irregular with the men, which grieves me. Next term I shall not go out anywhere, & make real & serious efforts both with the undergraduates & theology.

Arthur Stanley, Lady Augusta & the Père Hyacinthe[2] spent the greater part of last week with me, & I was involved in a series of parties whom I invited to meet them. I heard him attacked at the Abp.'s the other day & I think that few persons understand him. The fact is that with all his attainments & high position he is like a child, impressible by any influence, & has never put away childish things. To the end of his life he will be the 'enfant gaté du monde' & yet be perfectly simple & free from vanity. I liked her very much. She is a fine creature with a love of truth & deep affection—also the père Hyacinthe, who is a true man, free from weakness. We talked a great deal about his future position. He is at present silenced & will remain in the R.C. church, if he is allowed to hold certain doctrines & to preach. But I expect that they want to get rid of him. And in that case I urged him to go on preaching—not, however, to make war on Romanism—but to preach as if he were still a member of some future or ideal Catholic Church.

... I hope to come & see you on Tuesday or Wednesday, when I come to London 'Cook-hunting' (for a College which is without a cook is not a College)....

250 Jan. 1, 1871

... I should have been sorry if you had not taken part in the Relief Fund.[1] I have no doubt that your knowledge & experience has soothed the hours of many an unconscious sufferer....

I had a rather remarkable letter from Morier which I will send you. I do not agree with him—he has been Germanized. I wish I could have a good talk with him. The Germans & he have a 'stupid' notion that they must crush the French, & in this instance certainly, Stupidity is 'the Sin against the Holy Ghost'.

I am at the Lushingtons for a day, according to an annual custom. The Doctor is feeble, & I hardly think that he can be with us long. But he is perfectly calm & intelligent & does not suffer. Two of the Sisters, Alice & Fanny, have a large school for 200 children & Laura has a convalescent home. This is about as much as women not gifted above the average can make of doing good to others.

[2] Charles Loison.

[1] A letter from FN was read to the public meeting at which the National Society for Aid to the Sick and Wounded in War, later the British Red Cross Society, was formed in 1870.

I wish some one would put forwards as the true solution of the poor Gentlewoman question is that they should become schoolmistresses of national schools, & not nuns. It is true that they would require more education, but they have also a good deal to give in the way of manners. . . .

251
Bowood,
Calne,
Wilts,

Jan. 12, 1871
Address
A. Tennyson's Esqre.,
Freshwater,
I. of Wight.

. . . I am at Lord Lansdowne's for a day & go away tomorrow, to Oxford. I have really enjoyed being here, in a way that I hardly thought I should enjoy Society. We have Lord Russell & have been talking to him most part of the day about his old parliamentary battles. He is very amiable: his memory & faculties, except a little deafness, quite perfect, & like many shy persons he is most agreeable when you are alone with him. I will tell you about the people I have seen here, if you care to hear, when we meet.

I always think him a good man of great reading & knowledge, & a good piece of a philosopher, but he has no sense & no knowledge of the world or of persons, & is perfectly ignorant of his own deficiencies.

252 [26 January 1871]

J'ai fini:—2700 pages, & am now in the hands of the Binders & shall soon be in the hands of the Critics. 'Do you know who the Critics are'? Cambridge men who have neither Logic nor style, but have a profound belief in Greek particles, & would like to see them sticking out in the English everywhere, regardless of the difference of idiom.[1]

I have no doubt that there are many mistakes left in, for I have found a great many at the last moment. Translation is a curious process; the mind wavers between the words of the Greek, & the English thought which seems to be parallel to them. . . .

Now that I have finished Plato I cannot help remembering with gratitude the constant interest you have taken in my work. In some places I think that you will find remarks wh. have been suggested by you, as there almost always are in my sermons. I send you another of those unsatisfactory performances.

Let me hear from you. The completion of Plato is as much to me as the Mastership—I am too prosperous & happy in these most evil times.

---

[1] See above, No. 206, n. 7.

253
Oxford Feb. 8, 1871

... I have told Macmillan to send you a copy of the book, which you have probably received by this time. It has, I think, a pleasing exterior. I am especially proud of the first vol., because it is so big & large, about 730 pages. Read the 'Republic' & the 'Timaeus' & the 'Theaetetus' & 'Gorgias' & 'Laws' Book V, if you read any of it.

You call me a breaker of pacts. But I am really mending my ways, going to bed at 11 oClock & getting up to chapel. Notwithstanding, you do not hit the right nail on the head—which is that I eat & drink too much. I mean to cure this if I can.

Now I am in a great scrape—will you help me? Tomorrow fortnight I am to have a public dinner given to me. I said & meant, 'No'—but Wright & Bowen wrote to several persons without my knowing, & I did not like to disavow what they had done.

The scrape I am in is that I do not know what to say to them, & something must be said. Will you tell me what to say which will be appropriate, & bring some good out of a foolish business?

... Will you look at a paper by Lady Amberley in the 'Fortnightly' for January?[1] Not bad, I think. She is a good woman, greatly impressed by Mill, who accepts woman's rights as the mission of her life.

Whom do you think I saw last week? You will frown & be displeased. But I was very much struck by him—Mazzini.[2] He is a visionary & a poet & a preacher, but a very noble sort of man. He was wonderfully moderate in his conversation & spoke strongly against Materialism, which he regarded as a transitive state not to be looked upon as too important. I talked to him for 3 or four hours. But I must not write about him now—& will tell you when we meet.

You will have heard that Miss Garrett is going to be married. O Lucifera, daughter of the morning, how art thou fallen: from being an historical personage to be a married woman!

254
Oxford[1]
[28 February 1871]

Our dinner went off well, or at least did no harm. Lord Westbury made an admirable speech.[2] I told them what you told me to say.

---

[1] Viscountess Amberley, 'The claims of women', in *Fortnightly Review*, New Ser., vol. 9 (Jan.–June 1871), pp. 95–110.

[2] The artist George James Howard, the ninth Earl of Carlisle, invited BJ to meet Mazzini at his home in London. His sketch of BJ and Mazzini in conversation is reproduced in *AC* ii. opp. p. 10.

[1] BL Add. MS 45783 fos. 232–6.

[2] The dinner took place in London on Friday, 24 Feb. 1871 at the Albion Hotel. The Dean of Westminster presided, and proposed the health of the Master. The Master replied. Arthur Hobhouse proposed the health of the visitors. Lord Westbury replied. Lowe, the Chancellor of the Exchequer,

I am so glad that you accept my proposal. I shall take as much pains with your works as I should with any of my own. When we meet we will talk over the form of the volume or volumes. Meanwhile, let me offer you the following considerations:

I think that you are quite right in not propounding schemes of Army Reform at the present time. But there remain a great many interesting subjects on which you have thought & had experience....

I Theology—α) you must work out your notion of Divine perfection, especially showing that this may be consistent with the appearances of evil in the world—β) of the vanity of free thinking & criticism, & their purely negative use.

II Social life—the ideal of the family: Education of women—Sisterhoods & their true principles. The employment of women; (you might rewrite in a more consecutive manner some part of those volumes which you used to call the 'Stuff').

III The poor law—beginning with a Study of Political Economy & shewing how there is still a place for humanity.

IV Sanitary or theological tracts for the poor, "How people may live & not die". These are the subjects which appear to me most suited to you. But if you will supply the outlines & materials of any others I will work them up for you, not in my own style but as far as I can in yours, which is much better & more striking.

You will find writing troublesome at first. The great point is to be moderate & consecutive.

I think that you should try the form of short papers or Essays, because these depend least upon the form, & admit even of an imperfect expression of the idea.

I am glad that you have given up drudging for the public offices.[3] The occupation was too servile & also too hazardous.

Would you like to publish 'the Essays' anonymously? I think that I could manage to have the secret kept perfectly....

You were quite right about Mrs Butler. She is really mad & has been in confinement (do not mention this) & is also, I fear, slightly demoralized. Hers is a sad story: she is a woman of genius & has missed a little of being a saint....

I have carried through, as far as the College assent is required, my scheme of Reform.[4] They only hesitated about making the Mastership terminable, but that was ultimately carried with the rest....

proposed 'Prosperity to Balliol College', and was followed by Temple, the Bishop of Exeter. Finally, Lansdowne proposed the health of the Chairman. There were nearly 200 diners, many of them lawyers. BJ's account of Westbury's speech is to be found in T. A. Nash, *Life of Lord Westbury* (2 vols., 1888), ii. 286-8.

[3] *Cook* (ii. 212) says that FN's influence at the War Office more or less came to an end with the departure of Captain Galton in 1869.

[4] The college accepted proposals made by the committee to revise the Statutes (see above, No. 245, n. 4). Henceforward nobody was to be disqualified from holding a Fellowship by reason of marriage (but see above p. xxvii), the Master was no longer to be required to be in Holy Orders, and the Mastership was to be terminable after twenty years.

The excellent Dr. Symonds is gone. About a month ago his daughter[5] was engaged to Mr. Green, 'my' Senior Tutor. She was his only care & he was very happy in the thought of this.

255

Inglewood, Torquay, until
Wed. mg. afterwards
Oxford April 9 [1871]

... I enjoy my holidays greatly, & shall take more of them. Having an eye to business as well as pleasure I went with Mr. Rogers to Brighton & visited 'my old lady', Miss Brakenbury,[1] who has given the College about 18,000£ & is giving 15,000£ for a Dispensary at Manchester. She is vain, like many other old ladies, but she is a fine creature & is bent upon doing all the good which she can with 200,000£ which came to her on the death of her brother.

Will you write to me? I always like a day which brings a letter from you....

I am staying here with my sister,[2] who goes on the even tenor of her way. In some respects she is like a nun, & is quite as helpless as a nun, though not at all ignorant of the world. She seems to be devoted to a few persons & they to her. She does some good & no harm, which is all that I can expect. I do not think that it would be of any use to suggest to her any literary or other course of life.

I have been reading Darwin & Wallace.[3] I should expect that there is quite as much in Lamarck's theory as in theirs, but that neither unlocked the mystery of animal life.

256

[Torquay 11 April 1871]

You complain that my note is short—here is another to make the last longer....

Your little Buddhist book is charming.[1] Do you know that I am going to have either the Son or the Nephew of the author as an undergraduate at Balliol,[2] if the Fellows will allow a Siamese to come to the College without a knowledge of Latin & Greek? The writer has more conception of true religion than all the Bishops put together. His difficulty is our difficulty, the amount of evil in the world, & this seems to lead him to the rejection of the Being of God.

---

[5] Charlotte.

[1] Hannah Brackenbury. [2] Emily.
[3] BJ was probably reading Darwin's *Origin of Species* (1859), and *Descent of Man* (1871), together with Wallace's *Contributions to the Theory of Natural Selection* (1870), Chap. IX, 'The Development of Human Races under the Law of Natural Selection', and Chap. X, 'The Limits of Natural Selection as Applied to Man'.

[1] *The Modern Buddhist; Being the Views of a Siamese Minister of State [Chao Phya Praklang] on his Own and Other Religions.* Translated, with Remarks, by Henry Alabaster (1870).
[2] Sootshai Bhanuwongsee.

I have really been doing very little, writing lazily a sermon about Darwin, & sending a commendatory epistle about our New Statutes to the Bishop of London.³ I think Darwin should be treated civilly, 1st because there is a religious interest against him & very likely the true Origin of Species would be as disagreeable to the Orthodox as Darwin's account of it; 2nd because he appears to be a very ingenious observer & a good man. The misfortune is that the whole subject is by it's nature speculative & inexact.

I am coming to the budget next week⁴ & shall hope to call & see you....

257 [16 May 1871]

I was delighted with your long letter. You & Morier (he is called by his familiars by the endearing but not very dignified name of Joe, supposed to be derived from the fat boy in Pickwick), you & 'Joe' write to me in the same way, full of indignation at most things that are—I do not think (myself) that you are always right. You idealize too much, or rather you want your ideals put into practice too soon—to make bricks without straw & houses without bricks—and you will not accept the world as it is. Yet I confess on the other hand, that both you & he often turn out to be right when I thought you wrong, i.e. when I was wrong myself.

I have been exhorting Mr. Lowe today to make a defence of himself & not to let judgement go by default.¹ He said that his justification would be the House of Commons' condemnation, & there is truth in this—also that he was not 'out of the wood' with the Income Tax & therefore could not venture to justify himself. He is one of the persons that I most regard, & I shall be very sorry when he & Gladstone pass away, & we come from 1st class men with all their faults to 2nd Class men—Forster, & Goschen, &c.

Now I must 'justify' myself for not writing to you. Do you not know that I write poor, miserable letters & that I dislike letter writing? But I will come & see you as often as you will have me, & if you will go into Derbyshire about the middle of July I shall be charmed to come & spend a week with you in perfect idleness. Is not that a fair offer?

You greatly misunderstand what I say to you. In the first place, I never 'snub' you. I am far too much afraid to do that. In the second place, I do not at all desire that you should go flirting or coquetting with M. P.ˢ. But I want to suggest to you that you should concentrate your life in some way & bring together the ravelled threads, & put in some permanent form of word or act what you have been aspiring to all your life. You have fancies like that of being old. I will not quote again 'To me, dear friend, you never can be old',² but the

---

³ Jackson.   ⁴ On 20 Apr. 1871, *PD*, ccv. 1391–419.

¹ On 11 May the ministry was obliged to withdraw part of its budget, the Income Tax and Inhabited House Duties Bill, because changes had been introduced into it without regard to the procedural rules of the House of Commons. Gladstone appears to have been as much at fault as Lowe.

² 'To me, fair friend, you never can be old', Shakespeare, *Sonnets*, 104.

truth is that, although you suffer greatly, you have as much energy & force of mind as you ever had. Whether you live few or many years you should look forward more to the future & not regretfully on the past, though that it is saddened with many memories of the loss of friends & the like. I am obliged to repeat nearly the same things to you which make me slow to write, for fear of boring you. There is nothing in this world that I would not do for you, as I think you know, if I could find out what was really for your good. But in this respect you do not seem able to help me, or to help yourself. So that I am obliged to stand by, sometimes offering you inappropriate advice—which I regret, for I am conscious that you are the best & kindest [of] friends to me. Only you glorify me & flatter me sometimes, which, I hope, does not deceive me, being very well aware that I am a poor, miserable creature, ambitious of doing much more than I shall ever compass.

[*Postscript omitted*]

258

Zermatt
Address (unpaid) Darmstadt
July 4 [1871]

Here I am, as you desire, doing nothing in the High Alps with Lyulph Stanley, who is an extremely good fellow & a true friend & pupil of mine, for a companion.[1] The worst of this country is that you depend wholly on weather—one day you take a long walk, get wet through & see nothing—another day the sky has the 'body of heaven in it's clearness'.[2] This is one of the dark, wet days & therefore I hope you will excuse me if I bestow some of the dullness on you.

I enjoy my holiday even on wet days & am a thorough believer in idleness. I cannot tell you how many good resolutions I have made in the last week, including one of going to bed for the future at ten oClock, but I will tell you if I keep them, so that you need not expect to hear much more about them. The tour has been a little spoilt by the excessive rain which has prevented us from going over the Monte Moro, a mild glacier pass suited to infirm 'pietons' like me, & we go to the Stats Glacier instead, thence to Milan for a day, & back to the Engadine & from there to Darmstadt.

S. is a very good companion & very amiable to me. He seems to me to know more than almost anyone whom I have been acquainted with—and to have a good deal of originality as well as practical ability. He is an extreme radical on some points, especially about land & the like. He is indolent & cannot write well; that is to say, not in proportion to his ability, & he has such a dislike to the law that he will do no good at it. I hope to see him in Parliament some day,

---

[1] For an account of the holiday see *AC* ii. 12.
[2] 'And they saw the God of Israel: and there was under his feet as it were a paved work of a sapphire stone, and as it were the body of heaven in his clearness', Exod. 24: 10.

& until then I think that he should occupy himself with commissions and making speeches.

I bore you with these young gentlemen who are the great interest of my life. Morier is going to Stuttard,³ & from there I suppose that he may go anywhere. I think that he has the ideas of a Statesman. He & you are the two persons whom I have ever known most abusive of public men, & you bring the same kind of charges against them. I dare say that you are both right, but I still maintain my doctrine against you, 'that you must work with such tools as you have'.

Did you ever come to this place? Here, or rather on the Riffel, which is 3,000 feet higher, is probably the finest mountain scenery in Europe, extending from Monte Rosa & the Monte Cervin to the Bernese Oberland. Yesterday was one of our heavenly days & we saw this wonderful scene in perfection. Below the snow line & in some places above it, the ground is covered with wild flowers. I think that such scenes do give you some real, though undefined, religious sense. You cannot quite justify this to reason, for of course there are greater wonders really in very common things, but the impression is natural to our age, & we ought, I suppose, to learn from that which is natural to us.

I think that it is a very curious question, 'What is the limit of the advantages to be gained from art & nature?' How far they educate & at what point they injure & weaken the mind as, e.g. in Ruskin? One of the phenomena of Sceptical times is the love of art, in which men fancy that they have a kind of rest. I see this in the musical & Esthetical revival in the Church, and also in a small knot of people at Oxford who preach art & necessity, & believe in a man named Pater, of Brasenose. Goethe did a great deal of harm to the world by turning all things, including human characters, into forms of art, & he is the great Apostle of the Sect. I often wonder that the race of poets, as Plato would have called them, have never understood that their calling was to be the great teachers of mankind. This is true of almost all of them, with the exception of the Hebrew prophets & some parts of the Greek tragedians. On the other hand, the writers of hymns are almost entirely without poetical feeling.

I saw your friend Madame Mohl in Paris (*He* was out). She is quite well & full of Parisian life, very bitter against the Communists.⁴ Paris is far less disfigured than I expected. You hear of all the places which have been destroyed, but do not consider that this is not a 1/50th part of an immense city. I should be the last person to defend the acts of the Communists, but still there is something painful to me in the manner in which all the upper classes of society denounce them from fear & weakness, & refuse (just as in the Jamaica question) to enquire into the acts of their opponents.

I send you as usual, unconnected remarks.... I believe that you may do

³ The capital of Würtemberg, which had been brought into the German empire in 1871.
⁴ Elections to the Paris Commune took place on 26 Mar. 1871. On 21 May the Versaillese entered Paris, and eight days of fighting followed, with artillery being used on both sides. BJ had previously gone to Paris after the revolution of 1848: on that occasion he went with A. P. Stanley, Palgrave, and Morier. AC i. 133, and R. E. Prothero, *Life of Dean Stanley* (2 vols., 1893), i. 390 ff.

more in the remaining years of life than in the preceding (like the Sibyls books).[5]

259 Tummil Bridge,
Pitlochry, N.B.
Aug. 5 [1871]

... I am gathering my sheep around me. Mr. Harrison has just come. He appears to be somewhat better & has taken to eating & drinking more and to smoking by advice of his doctor, which seems to suit him. His ability & cleverness strike me as much as ever, but his student's life at Oxford has been absolutely lost.

I shall send you some of the Children's Bible,[1] as you are kind enough to run your eye over it, & should like to hear what you have to say about it. I have laid it aside for a few days, being at work upon my Essay[2] & having to go to Glasgow on Wednesday &, I fear, to make a speech there on behalf of the Scott Bursaries,[3] which may be useful, if I can stir the liberality of the Scotch, but is not pleasant to me. Owing to the connexion of the College with Glasgow[4] I did not like to refuse.

Here am I fairly embarked on a 3 months' study of the religions of the world. What have you to say about them, my lady? I have read M. Müller's first vol. of 'Chips', & also his 'Sanscrit literature',[5] & he seems to me to deserve more credit than I thought. He is a real scholar & critic, but has a good deal of nonsense & weakness about him. I shall embark on Colebrook's 'Essays'[6] on Monday. He appears to me a really great scholar.

I mean to give a condensed sketch of each of the great religions & then make applications of them to ourselves. They are not absolutely false, & Xtianity absolutely true, but Xtianity is one among them. I intend also at the beginning to say something against Darwin & Tylor, & to show what appears to me to be the bearing of the antiquity of men on Theology. Does it not take our minds off the past, which is unknown to us, to fix them on the present & future. In a human history of 300,000 or 3,000,000 years there are infinite possibilities, but

---

[5] The Cumaean sibyl offered nine books for sale to Tarquin the Proud. He refused to buy them, whereupon she burned three, and offered the remaining six at the original price. When he refused a second time, she destroyed three more, and offered the remaining three at the original price. Tarquin bought the books which proved to contain directions as to the worship of the Gods and the policy of the Romans.

[1] Initiated by Rogers. BJ sought the assistance of friends, including Swinburne (*AC* ii. 36). He sent it off to Longmans in July 1872, and it was published in 1873 as *The School and Children's Bible*.
[2] On 'The Religions of the World', see below, No. 267.
[3] At the centenary of Sir Walter Scott's birth (15 Aug. 1771), BJ was asked to propose 'The University of Glasgow, and success to the Scott bursaries', *AC* ii. 14.
[4] Through the foundation of John Snell.
[5] *Chips from a German Workshop* by Max Müller (4 vols., 1867–75), and *A History of Ancient Sanskrit Literature* (1859).
[6] H. T. Colebrooke, *Essays on the Religion and Philosophy of the Hindus*, new edn. (1858).

that is all; no human ingenuity can fill up the chasm. I should like to put this in the true point of view. There is a fallacy, supposed to come from Newton, about nature working by the simplest causes, which is greatly misapplied, I think, by these modern speculators.

Why do you charge me with breaking treaties? Do I not go to bed every night at 10 oClock? & do I not forswear all reading after Dinner? You have no idea how I am mending my ways. But I get rather blind. This, however, is no matter, for I shall economize & read no more Newspapers. And if I am ever quite blind I shall try to compose a treatise on Moral Philosophy. . . .

[*Postscript*]

If anything occurs to you that I should say in proposing success to Glasgow University & the Scott Bursaries, please tell me. I mean to have a few words against Mr. Lowe's views of Education.

FN to BJ [*draft*]¹
260   Aug. 7, 1871

I am overjoyed that you are going to write an Essay on the 'religions of the world', and 'then make applications of them to ourselves'.

You ask me what I have to "say about it". And as I am naturally a patient and obedient beast (I do not look into your face for fear of seeing that you don't agree on this point), this is what I have to say.

1. Let what comes out of them all be: the search after a *Perfect* God.
2. Let what comes out of them all be: the search after Truth.

. . . In reading almost all Theological Essays of the present day, I feel constantly inclined to say: there is everything in this Theology, except God, there is everything except the belief that there *is* a Truth, and we have to find it out. As to a search after a *Perfect* God, there is nothing.

(Your man, M. Pattison, actually defines Theology to be: 'a speculative habit'. . . . Really, my dear soul, when you want to praise Pattison, the Dean of Ch. Ch.,² or Lord Overstone you must go and whisper it in a corn-field. Then, that poor man who is just dead, Mansel: his Bampton Lectures³ seemed to me to have nothing in them that they ought to have, and everything in them that they ought not to have. And the 'Times' calls him: 'One of the most successful leaders of original thought').⁴

But to return:— . . .

1. Is the condition, present, past and future . . . of mankind, consistent with any idea of Right in the Creator's mind . . .
2. . . . what is it possible for man to do towards making human existence *right* . . .

---

¹ BL Add. MS 45783 fos. 237–50.   ² Liddell.
³ *The Limits of Religious Thought Examined* (1858).   ⁴1 Aug. 1871 (12b).

3. is there evidence that there is a Perfect Being who, thro' those conditions which it is *not* possible for man to change, as thro' those conditions which it *is* possible for man to change, is working out a moral world that *shall* be satisfactory to a moral sense?... Surely these three are the fundamental questions of a real theology (or Theodike)....
(I read Dean Stanley's speech at the Centenary[5] and like him much better on Walter Scott than on Jesus Christ.)

Is it possible that a man, the ecclesiastical head of the greatest religious establishment in the most important Metropolis of the world, who has, within $\frac{1}{4}$ hr of his establishment, a population to be numbered by hundreds of thousands, ground down by vice and sin and pauperism and misery and physical deterioration, so that, to use the words of one pauper 'we have nothing but misery in this world, and those — clergy tell us we have nothing to look to but misery in the next.

Is it possible that this ecclesiatical head looks to the historical and geographical criticism of Palestine[6] as being the 'Gospel' which is to bring 'good news' to this wretched mass who, if they are not seething in hell already ... where are they? What is this but hell?

FN to BJ [*draft or copy*][1]
261   [*n.d.*]

He shows himself in the persons of our suffering fellow creatures—not, as in those legends, where Christ appears as a beggar and then flies away, but because He is really there. It is really Himself "descending into hell". For all those prisoners, those criminals, those sick, those infirm, are there by His laws. It is Himself we see, His word, His work, in them. I call this a part of the Inspiration of Error. Those people would not be there if mistakes had not been made in observing His laws—but not the less rather the more, are they Himself, His inspiration....

FN to BJ [*copy*][1]
262   Lea Hurst, Matlock. Aug. 8, 1871

Dear (tho' Perfidious) Professor,
I only write a word to say that I am glad you are going to make a speech, tho' I dare say it is 'not pleasant' to you.

---

[5] *The Times*, 10 Aug. 1871 (12cd).

[6] In 1856 Stanley published *Sinai and Palestine in Connection with their History*. In 1871 he wrote an introduction to Sir C. W. Wilson, *The Recovery of Jerusalem. A Narrative of Exploration and Discovery in the City and the Holy Land*. Perhaps FN ought to have recalled that he also contributed an introduction to J. I. Whitty, *Proposed Water Supply and Sewerage for Jerusalem* (1863).

---

[1] BL Add. MS 45783 fos. 179-80.

---

[1] BL Add. MS 45783 fos. 251-4.

What I feel about all these things, family life, social life, University life, political life, but quite *generally* ... is that:

1. Sermons, speeches, articles seems always made for happy people, at least for tolerably successful people, who have not to construct or alter their lives, sometimes to begin again life 'right from the bottom', but only to make themselves and others as happy as possible in their lives. It is taken for granted that life is to be as it is—in families, in Institutions, in Schools, Colleges and Universities, among the 'masses' as they are called.

... We are never lectured about the study of anything else in the weak, wishy-washy, womanish terms that we are preached to about *life*. (And this is thought Christian: as if Christ had not been the boldest preacher of all, about reforming or reconstructing life.) ...

5. I think there is great danger that we may run altogether into (a) universal toleration, (b) universal criticism....

There are some who see no difference between Sidney Herbert and Mr Cardwell.

There are some who see no difference between St Paul and a Saturday Reviewer.

There are some who see no difference between Ch. Ch. and Balliol. Or if they do, they think indifference and carelessness better than what they are pleased to call a 'hot-bed of nationalisation and infidelity'....

263
Tummil Bridge,
Pitlochry
Aug. 14 [1871]

Your letter came just in time, & I went to the dinner all the better for having read it. It was an immense dinner, more than 700 people. I sat by the Archbishop of Glasgow,[1] a weak, gentlemanlike man, who shirked all serious conversation. I think that the speech did fairly well & I make so few speeches that I was glad of the opportunity of making one.

Your letters always do me good. I shall preach them some day, and I do preach a good many things taken from them already.

I want you to tell me some day what is the 'Character of God' of which you often speak but, as appears to me, without coming to the point. Where do we get our knowledge of him? 1st answer: from nature & this leads to the recognition of fixed laws & tends to sanitary improvement. 2nd answer: from the human reason & conscience. But what do we definitely learn of him from these & on what grounds do we believe their anticipations? And how is the God revealed in nature to be reconciled with the God in reason & conscience?

Will you look at the accompanying scheme for Morning Service, & suggest

[1] W. S. Wilson.

any further improvements?² I am delighted that you take an interest about the Child's Bible.³ What have you to say about [it]? When I get the pasted sheets back ... I shall send them to you, if I may.

Harrison is with me & is certainly a great deal better. Though he cannot now get a first Class, I believe that he may get a Fellowship.⁴ He is a capital fellow & has great sense & force of character; but he is a Communist. He has changed his way of living & taken to Beer & stimulants, which seems to suit him.

Coming home on Thursday, about 8 miles from here whom should I meet but Mr. Browning. He is still 'wailing on the Mountains of Gilboa'.⁵ I said I hoped that he was getting over his trouble,⁶ & he replied, 'like the eels when they are skinned'.

Parliament is in it's dregs. How Mr. Gladstone must contrast now & the glory of 3 years ago. The retribution is not undeserved.

FN to BJ [*draft*]¹
264 Lea Hurst, Matlock.
Aug. 17, 1871

O Perfidious and Serene
    ... (You ought to be practising poenitential performances in dust and ashes for your conduct to me and the treaty, and instead of that, you are—perfidious and serene. But I shall treat of this farther on.)

I don't at all plead guilty to your accusation that I "speak of the character of God", without "coming to the point".

In one sense of course I *can* never "come to the point" because ... to know the character of God, we must know the history, past, present and future of the Universe. All mankind must contribute to it. And what part of mankind *is* contributing to it? We are told by the publishers that more religious and theological publications appear than any other.... And, amid all this paper & print about religion, I expect to find something about God. Not at all.

There are:—
in Germany volumes upon volumes of profound and admirable criticism ... there are, all over Europe, but especially in England, enormous masses of superficial controversy between Roman Catholicism, Protestantism and even the minor sects of Protestantism....

Then there is all the ecclesiastical controversy, the 'geography of Palestine' = the 'fifth Gospel'.

Then there is an extraordinary mass, even in matter-of-fact Scotland and

---

² On 13 May 1871 the College appointed a committee to make 'a selection of Prayers taken from the Prayer-Book, & also a selection of Psalms and Lessons' for use at Morning Prayer. The committee revised Evening Prayer too.
³ See above, No. 259, n. 1.   ⁴ He did not.   ⁵ 2 Sam. 1: 19.
⁶ Presumably the withdrawal of his son from Christ Church.

¹ BL Add. MS 45783 fos. 255–64.

England, but what it is in Roman Catholic countries you can have scarcely an idea, published of mere emotions and fancies.... And in this sense it is quite true that any one person thinking and speaking alone of the 'character of God' must think and speak "without coming to the point", (as H.S.H. the Master of Balliol so well observes). But in another sense it is "extremely not so" (A.H.C.'s phrase)....

What is the character of God? You say.

1. Not to create a world in order to forgive it
    or to damn it
    or to save it by a church
    or by the Sacraments
    or by the Atonement theory
    or by prayer
    or etc, etc, etc.
    or to be indifferent about it
    (the 'happiness enough' theory)
    the magazine-y theory of the present day;

but to create a world according to a certain definite plan by which each and every one of us is on the way to progress towards perfection, i.e. happiness. (What the end is ... we know so little that the Buddhists have actually invented a Word 'Nirvana' for it. But, if you translate that word 'Nirvana' to mean 'annihilation' or the like, I really must 'annihilate' *you*....)

2. ...God's Character is
    not to create an Eternity of which he alone is to be the spectator, merely for his own amusement as it were, but an Eternity in which each one will be on the way thro' his laws to progress towards perfection, the means and inducements by which such progress is brought about being the sins and sufferings as well as the virtues and enjoyments of human beings, the sinners and sufferers being also (it is needless to put in) on their way to perfection—being, in fact, the pioneers.

3. What is the character of God?
    Not to look to good intentions without requiring practical wisdom to allow blunders their full consequences in evil, as well as sins; to require, that is, the same search, study, earnest and wise endeavour, patient investigation of laws in discovering and reforming in the moral world as in the material....

Art thou a master in Israel and knowest not these things?

FN to BJ [*draft*][1]

265   Aug. 17, 1871.

My letter of Aug. 17 was to have gone on with

4. Not to create man in order to protect him from the consequences of his own

[1] BL Add. MS 45783 fos. 265-75.

Acts (as man so often desires). But to order such a Moral plan . . . as that there shall be inducement and means to bring man in eternity to think right, to will right, to act right—there being no such thing as *eternal* consequences for *evil* to anything poor, weak, ignorant 'we' can do, which would be a vengeance unworthy of, impossible to, a Perfect God.

FN to BJ [*draft*][1]
266 [*n.d.*]

. . . tho' you despise your pupil's Atalanta in Calydon,[2] allow me to observe that Atalanta herself, tho' she is only a sort of a Ginn and not a woman at all, yet there is more of reality, of character, of individuality (which is a stupid word) in her than in all the 'young women' of all the men novelists I ever read, with scarcely any exception. . . .

267
Address until Saturday
at the E. of Airlie's,
Glen Isla,
Alyth, N.B.
[11 September 1871]

. . . You have sent me a rich budget of letters, upon which I shall send you some commonplace reflections in a few days.

I have finished my 'party' with satisfaction, upon the whole. But I have only written thirty pages upon the 'religions of the world', and I begin to perceive (as I always do) that my essay will take 6 or 8 months instead of six or 8 weeks, and the second Essay nearly as long. Still I am quite satisfied (though not with myself) that I could not have chosen two more important or interesting subjects than the 'religions of the world' & the 'reign of law'. . . .[1]

I am greatly impressed with Swinburne's genius, though he has not got the one thing needful. I mean that he has not got deep feeling & thought—if he had he would be one of the greatest poets who ever lived. He took to Harrison greatly & they have started on a walking tour together (N.B. No beer or whisky to be drunk). If he could ever grow to be a man (he is only a child & sometimes a naughty child at present) his poetry would greatly improve. But at present he receives every impression from Rosetti & the painters, as well as from Mazzini. I believe that the best way of 'converting' him would be to get him to write on really noble themes, & so the good poet would become the good man. He appears to me to be one of the most learned persons whom I

---

[1] BL Add. MS 45783 fos. 55–6.   [2] Published in 1865.

[1] BJ selected these topics for the projected successor volume to *Essays and Reviews*. Neither was completed. *AC* i. 402–5, ii. 13, 15, 35.

have ever known, having a great appetite for reading & a perfect memory, not less wonderful, I should think, than Lord Macaulay. . . .

268 Inglewood, Torquay
Sep. 29 [1871]

I am sorry that I cannot accept your kind invitation to come to Lea Hirst & work at the Children's Bible,[1] but I must give up the remainder of the vacation to my sister,[2] & have accordingly come hither to rest after my wanderings.

I have been on 'the loose' now for nearly three weeks doing nothing but a little gentle correction of Thucydides,[3] on which I have been engaged. (It seems to me a duty to the Greek Professorship to keep something of this kind always simmering.) I like translation, although I do not intend to devote my life to is, and I feel such a much greater certainty that a translation of Plato or Th. will live & fructify than anything which I could write out of my own head.

I have to go to Manchester on Oct. 25[4] & shall hope to look in upon you by the way, when I will give an account of myself. . . .

I must answer your letters by driblets. When you admit that a part of the witness of the character of God is to be sought for in nature, how do you distinguish between the true & false witness of nature? For we cannot deny that physical good is sometimes at variance with moral—e.g. in marriage the sole or chief principle ought to be health & strength in the parents whether with or without a marriage ceremony—in other words Plato's Republic: (I mean on physical principles). Or again, the laws of physical improvement would require that we should get rid of sickly & deformed infants &c. And if, as Huxley would say, you reconstruct the world on a physical basis, you have to go to war with received principles of morality. . . .[5]

I cannot tell you how much I approve of your sentiments about Criticism & free thinking. I shall use my utmost efforts to make the Balliol youths do something & know something. The whole literary world is engaged in—dissection. And a very nasty operation it is, & not likely to lead to any sort of knowledge, anatomical or otherwise. I say with you 'do create something'. If it be the simplest thing which is wrong, set that right and you have done something; but by writing a thousand articles in reviews you have done nothing, & worse than nothing.

I made acquaintance at Glasgow with a man whom I greatly like: Sir William

---

[1] See above, No. 259, n. 1.   [2] Emily.
[3] *Thucydides translated into English* was published in 1881.
[4] To the opening of the new buildings of Manchester Grammar School, erected by F. W. Walker, High Master.
[5] T. H. Huxley, *Zoological Evidences as to Man's Place in Nature* (1863). Huxley served on the Royal Commission on the Administration and Operation of the Contagious Diseases Acts 1870-1.

Thomson, who (notwithstanding his foolish notion about life being thrown into this world)[6] belongs to the true breed of philosophers. He talked to me a great deal about Darwin whom he thinks entirely mistaken: 1. on the ground of time; 2. on the calculation of chances. It will be curious, if this bubble supported by so much genius & careful observation, breaks.

We are somewhat alarmed at Oxford about Small Pox.... I have sent a circular to the undergraduates telling them to be vaccinated, if they have not been vaccinated within 3 years; and shall send the Butler to the College Servants & their children, & to the laundresses. The lodging houses are also to be carefully inspected. Does your experience suggest anything else? The medical men are unanimously of opinion that we ought not to keep the Colleges down & I follow this opinion.

269

Inglewood. Torquay,
until Oct. 12.
Oct. 2 [1871]

... I have remodelled my Chapel Service & altered several of the Psalms,[1] in accordance with your suggestions. I am greatly struck with the poverty of the Liturgy. It is not nearly so good as Dr. Lee's service book[2] & that is not so good as might be, by a great deal, if a proper selection were made from the Fathers & mediaeval saints. I wonder that the High Churchmen, instead of busying themselves about externals, do not attend to the real improvement of the service....

Next week I begin my second year in Balliol. I have made money for the College by looking after things, I find—about 500£ which went into the wasteful maws of servants. And now I must set myself thoroughly to remodel the place from within, & work upon the characters of the men. There seem to me to be so many of them who might come to something good & even great if I could get rid of the flaws in them. There is a most clever monkey named Higgs, mad with vanity & Comtism, three 'minor' poets,[3] my 'Communist' friend Harrison, and also some fellows of sobriety as well as of ability. Whether I succeed or not, depends on what I can do with these people. The College is perfectly united—but I sometimes think that the teaching is not simple

---

[6] In his Address to the British Association at Edinburgh in 1871, Thomson said, 'I am ready to adopt as an article of scientific faith, true through all space and through all time, that life proceeds from life, and from nothing but life. How then did life originate on the Earth?... Every year thousands, probably millions, of fragments of solid matter fall upon the Earth.... Is it not possible... that the beginning of vegetable life on the Earth is to be similarly explained?', quoted in John Munro, *Lord Kelvin* (1902), pp. 74–5.

[1] See above, No. 263, n. 2.
[2] Robert Lee, *Prayers for Public Worship with Extracts from the Psalter and other parts of Scripture*, 2nd edn. (1858); *Prayers for Family Worship* (1861).
[3] Possibly A. C. Bradley, W. H. Mallock, and J. F. Rowbotham, who all came up in 1869.

enough—overphilosophized by the Hegelianism of Green & his pupils & by the tendencies to Comtism of an Historical Lecturer....[4]

FN to BJ[1]

270 Lea Hurst, Oct. 3 [1871]

I am quite scandalized at your materialism. (I shall shut up you and Plato for a hundred years in punishment in another world till you have both obtained clearer views.) Is it for an old maid like me to be preaching to you a Master in Israel that even "on physical principles" there are essential points in marriage (to turn out the best order of children), which, being absent, the perfection of "health and strength" in both parents is of no avail even for the physical part of the children? And might I just ask one small question: whether you consider man has a little soul? If he has ever such a little one, you can scarcely consider him as a simple body, an animal, or even as a twin, the soul being one twin and the body the other, but as all one, the soul and the body making one being (altho' only in this sense). If you *do*, at all events *God* does not. And consequently He makes a great many more things enter into the "physical" constitution even of the children than the mere "health and strength" of the parents. (My son, really Plato talked nonsense about this.) Take a much more material thing than the producing of a bad or degenerate family or race. Take a railway accident. What are the laws therein concerned? You have by no means only to consider the "physical" laws—the strength of iron, the speed of steam, the smoothness of rails, the friction &c., &c.—but you have to consider the state of mind of Directors, whether they care only for their dividends, so that the railway-servants are underpaid or overworked &c., &c. You quote Huxley. He is undoubtedly one of the prime educators of the age, but he makes a profound mistake when he says to Mankind: objects of sense are more worthy of your attention than your inferences and imaginations. On the contrary, the finest powers man is gifted with are those which enable him to infer from what he sees what he *can't* see. They lift him into truth of far higher import than that which he learns from the senses alone. I believe that the laws of nature all tend to improve the *whole* man, moral and physical, that it is absurd to consider man either as a body to be "improved," or as a soul to be "improved," separately.

As to the "laws of physical improvement requiring that we should get rid of sickly and deformed infants," they require that we should *prevent* or improve, not that we should *kill* them. *That* would be to get rid of some of the finest intellectual and moral specimens of our human nature that have ever existed. And, even were this not the case, the heroism, the patience, the wisdom of our

[4] Possibly W. L. Newman who retired in 1870.

[1] From *Cook*, ii. 224–5. Cook noted that he had 'somewhat compressed' the argument.

race have been more called forth by dealing with these and the like forms of evil than by almost anything else. The good of man in its highest sense cannot be attained by neglecting one set of laws or one aspect of man's nature and cultivating another.

I entirely therefore agree that "you must take man as a whole." But this seems at variance with a celebrated author's next sentence "and make morality and the mind the *limit* of physical improvement." If I were writing, I should use a word signifying the exact reverse; not limit, but expansion, enlargement, multiplication, master or informing spirit. As Plato says: the mind informs the body, owns the body, the body is the servant of the mind. How can the owner and the master be the limit? We must really pray for your conversion....

FN to BJ [*copy*][1]

271   Lea Hurst, Matlock
                                                                Oct. 3, 1871

Epidemic small-pox is at Oxford, notwithstanding vaccination. You have done all you can at present; but take good care that all the College rooms are thoroughly aired by open windows as much as the weather will permit. This epidemic is a new warning to the University to press forwards their sanitary works.

There is no reason for 'keeping down the Colleges'....

272   Inglewood,
                                                                Torquay. Oct. 4 [1871]

... And what have I said to deserve such an outburst? I have no wish to shake the foundations of Society. What I think about these matters is feebly expressed in a sort of Essay at the end of the introduction to the Republic.[1] But when I come to a 2nd Edition I will express it better. Shall I retort that some of your notions seem to me to be derived from Shakespeare?...

273   [30 October 1871]

... This has been a miserable day in consequence of the death of a poor undergraduate, Walker.[1] He was the best of creatures but seems to have shot himself from excess of pain in a fit of what is called temporary insanity.

[1] BL Add. MS 45784 fos. 1-2.

[1] *The Dialogues of Plato* (4 vols., 1871), ii. 137-63.

[1] F. J. C. Walker.

274

Ball. Coll.
Nov. 11 [1871]

Since I wrote to you I have been trying to put together an Evening Service as well as a Morning.[1] Will you look at the Versicles & see if any others strike you....

I am very busy as you may imagine—the last straw which breaks the Camel's back being the University Sermon for Nov. 26. I shall take the text which you suggest[2] & endeavour to work it out. The danger with this sort of subject is that it may be too bare & abstract.

The College appears to me prosperous, notwithstanding the sad event which has cast a gloom over us, not merely in word but in reality.

Tennyson was here at the beginning of the week. Another Idyll & another & another. He is caught in the vicious circle of the Arthur legend & seems as if he could only think or feel through this.

I should like to hear about yourself & what you are doing. I agree with you about the necessity of compiling a Bible on a different principle—& am ready to allow that although we may tell lies to children we may not tell 'bad lies'. I have been arranging the three Gospels again & will send them to you when they are pasted....

275

[21 November 1871]

... You think me a bad correspondent, which I am—letter-writing requires solitude, & I see 20 or 30 persons in a day.

The Americans have sent me a stereotyped Plato in 4 vols. & hold out a faint hope that I shall have some share in the profits hereafter....[1]

We have been carrying through this term a very good Reform of the University Examinations, which means a Reform of Education.[2] It will, I believe, make a great change in Oxford. If you care about such matters I will tell you about it. It appears to me to be the best thing which has been done since the old University Commission & has been done quite quietly & with an almost general consent. The Act of last session[3] has had a most excellent effect on the Puseyites. They feel that their old fighting ground is gone

---

[1] See above, No. 263, n. 2.
[2] From Luke 18: 8, 'When the son of Man cometh, shall he find faith on the earth?', Sermon V in *College Sermons*, ed. W. H. Fremantle (1895).

[1] See G. S. Nowell Smith, *International Copyright Law and the Publisher in the Reign of Queen Victoria* (1968). The stereotyped Plato is not listed in BJ's library catalogue.
[2] A liberalization of the examination required of all undergraduates in 'The Rudiments of Faith and Religion' to allow the Board of Studies to prescribe, in addition to the special study of some one or more books of the Old and New Testaments, 'some theological subject, such as one or more of the Three Creeds, or some period of ecclesiastical history'; *Oxford University Gazette*, 28 Nov. 1871.
[3] 34 and 35 Vict. c. 26, stated that persons taking lay degrees or holding lay academic or collegiate offices were not to be required, henceforth, to subscribe to any formulary of faith.

& Liddon, who will be their leader, is a much weaker & also a much better man than Pusey....

Shall I tell you one thing that strikes me? I see many persons from being superstitious become perfectly rational. But they seem to me in the process, e.g. my friend Pattison, to have lost the higher impulses & nothing but a keen & often very fanciful intellect remains.

276 [Oxford 9 December 1871]

... You have done me a great service about the Children's Bible & the other selections—I hope that you will some day allow me to do the like for you. But that is a small part of what you have done for me. Many new thoughts come into my mind after talking to you or receiving letters from you....

[*Postscript omitted*]

277 Oxford
Dec. 29 [1871]

I returned to-day from my pilgrimage—I think that the sermons & lectures were successful.

I send you the two lectures on Johnson,[1] but shall not expect you to read them, unless you chance to have an interest in the subject....

FN to BJ [*draft or copy*][1]
278 [*end* December 1871]

These lectures on Boswell seem to me like the 'tour de force' of a great man—as if St. Paul had delivered a lecture on Tents or St John written a General Epistle on Fishing.
While so many vital philosophical questions remain unsolved, while almost all vital religious questions remain untouched, I can hardly understand this interest in Boswell, except as the historical relaxation of an overstrained thought....

Johnson's Dictionary did more than anything else for half a century [to] prevent England's development in religious and philosophical thought.

Take his definition of Religion: Religion is virtue founded on a fear of future punishment and hope of future reward.... Is not this absolutely misleading people?

Might I not just as well say, under Philosophy, Philosophy is Study of

---

[1] The lectures, 'Boswell on Johnson' and 'The Writings and Character of Johnson', were delivered to the Edinburgh Philosophical Institution on 19 and 23 Dec. 1871. Printed in Gell.

[1] BL Add. MS 45784 fos. 43-4.

Aristotle and Herbert Spencer founded on emulation to be in the First Class at Final Examinations....

But, supposing that you and I were engaged on an English 'Scott and Liddell'[2] (Which God forbid—there are two things which would be indeed the 'fear of punishment': one is to be a Dean, the other, to write a Dictionary) do you not think that we should have hit upon a very different definition of 'Religion'....

What I can understand is this: in the follies and unphilosophical, unthoughtful, you may say absurdities of Ritualism, in the almost as great absurdities of Liberalism, among the nameless confusions of Church theories and Creed controversies and the idiocies of pinning one's faith upon an historical point, upon what an Athanasius or a Paulinus said, or a parcel of rascals like the Church Councils thought, there is something healthy in Johnson's manly, robust independence and hatred of cant and humbug which is like a good breeze from the sea blowing away Oxford fogs....

You quote two lines from 'Vanity of Human Wishes' as if the poem were generally not known. In my youth we all learnt it by heart, and I dare say I could say it now—and great part of Rasselas. Also, The Rambler.[3] But we none of us read Boswell. (I used to read the *Dictionary* for my amusement.)

I suppose it is just the contrary now. People read only Boswell.

279 address Monday at Lord Westbury's,
Hinton St. George, Taunton
Inglewood, Torquay
next week—Oxford

... I think that you once said D— Thucydides; there I don't agree with you. I believe that it is quite worth while, & not to me a work of very great labour, to put the best & noblest history which was ever written into a permanent English form—discussing the questions which arise out of it or about it & which have never been properly discussed. Another reason is that I am Greek Professor & ought to do something for the money; and lastly I have read Thucydides ever since I was a boy & do not want all this reading to be thrown away. Are you convinced? He is nearly half finished already.

I stayed with Mr. Lowe last week. The old story; he is the kindest & best of men to me—full of life & talk & the pleasantest of companions. He has a great deal of principle, but he has no political sense; & though he has a strong will he is incapable of criticizing himself or carrying out a purpose consistently. He is well-inclined to sanitary measures, but is in general more strenuous in resisting

---

[2] H. G. Liddell and R. Scott, *A Greek-English Lexicon* (1843).
[3] 'The Vanity of Human Wishes', a poem (1749), 'The History of Rasselas, Prince of Abbissinia', a didactic romance (1759), *The Rambler*, a periodical in 208 numbers issued between 20 Mar. 1750 and 14 Mar. 1752.

attacks upon the public purse than in doing any positive good. He seems to be on very good terms with his colleagues.

I am afraid I shall have some difficulties about the daily Chapel Service, for Woollcombe & his appeal[1] seem to have made some impression on the Visitor.[2] I foresee also that in some respects the College may not be so easy to manage in the future as in the past. Did I tell you that I am trying to inaugurate a scheme for establishing Lecturerships or Colleges in some of the large towns?[3] They would be for women as well as for men. I talked over the plan with Mr. Lowe, who strongly approved. The fact is that no adequate use can be made of the great wealth of the Universities without some extension of this sort....

Mr. Lowe said a curious thing to me coming from him: he asked whether it would not be possible to write a purely Ethical devotional work like St. Thomas a Kempis' 'Imitation of Christ'. He was very anxious that some effort should be made to place morality on a better foundation. When theology came in he thought that uncertainty began....

280 Inglewood,
Torquay Jan. 13 [1872]

I send you back the indenture duly signed, which I intend to observe and am doing so much against my inclination. But I must make two exceptions: 1st. I must be allowed to correct proofs, so as not to delay the press: 2. I must be allowed to read for amusement some Greek book for an hour a day. "Cupid is a child of conscience".[1] I read a book of the Odyssey every day for more than a fortnight & am greatly refreshed by it, & more than ever convinced that the Odyssey was not composed by one poet. You would not, I hope, deny me all amusement, or do you restrict me to newspapers & reviews? I cannot exist upon them....

I wish that you had ever known Lord Westbury. I hardly think that he can recover himself now, but he impresses me very much. He is the kindest & most considerate person & the best host that I ever staid with. He is always wanting sympathy & unfortunately there is no one in his own family who can give him this, & I believe that this is the real reason why he has fallen into the hands of strange folk. Also he appears to me to be a religious man, & has a great dislike to irreligious talk, but people in general think that this is all humbug....

---

[1] See below, No. 284.
[2] Jackson.
[3] See above, p. xxvii.

---

[1] 'Love is too young to know what conscience is; / Yet who knows not conscience is born of love.' Shakespeare, *Sonnets*, 151.

281

Oxford Jan. 21, 1872.

... I have been reading Middlemarch[1] this evening, which is, I fear, a failure. George Eliot takes more & more pains & loses, I think, her naturalness & power of drawing characters. Her prose is becoming strange & ill conditioned, like her poetry. For which I am sorry—there is a great charm of manner, & I think a wish to do good about her.

I had a very pleasant visit to Lord Westbury. He talks like you. You should have heard him discourse at great length in faultless sentences about the three tyrannies to which the world submits: 1 Theology, 2 Medicine, 3 Law. He did not lay on so heavily on the last as on the two first, and the ladies declared that I did not stand up properly for the Clergy.

282

Address: Oxford
Feb. 10 [1872]

I believe that you owe me a letter, of which I am really glad considering how many I owe you. I am away from Oxford for a day or two, having taken to walking about with two friends of mine among the Surrey hills. Yesterday I had a charming day with T. H. Farrer, one of my oldest friends whom I like about Leith Hill & Wootton. I find great pleasure in going about among such scenes, and without a book....

I have just finished the Children's Bible.[1] I blessed you every time I took the papers up, especially in the Prophets. I have adopted your selection almost entirely, with a slight abridgement, & it is further approved by Mr. Cheyne's authority. Knight, my amanuensis, has taken great interest in the work & discusses the reasons pro & con for keeping things or not, with a great deal of ability. He particularly pleads for Ezekiel, who he thinks 'must have been a very great man, though he may have written inferior Hebrew'.

Have you seen 'Middlemarch'? Not very good, I think, but quite interesting enough to read. I will send it to you, if you have not. George Eliot's natural genius is impaired by the talents of Mr. Lewis.[2] I know that you do not much like her, but I think that you would be softened if you knew her. She appears to me like a grave, gentle woman who has suffered a great deal, & has a great desire to do good, & with very pleasing manners....

I have been reading accounts of Mahomet—of whom I must write to you another time—a soldier, legislator, prophet, & not an impostor.

---

[1] Published in 1871-2: FN, on the other hand, described it as 'A novel of genius', in 'A "Note" of Interrogation', *Fraser's Magazine*, Jan.-June 1873, p. 567.

---

[1] See above, No. 259, n. 1.
[2] Lewes.

1870-1875

283   Oxford
                                                          Feb. 19 [1872]

... Your writing seems to me too abstract, & to turn too much upon the use of certain words, which have a meaning to yourself but not equally to others.

When I turn to the substance of the paper I agree very much. We want to form an idea of a millennium (not like the millennium of interpreters of prophecy), which shall represent to us the working out of the will of God upon earth, & the paths which lead thither. To realize this we must take the better mind of man, the highest conceptions which we can form of righteousness & holiness, & the like, & see how far in the past history of the world we can find recognitions of them, or tendencies towards them. In some respects this new moral world must be different from the highest morality which we have at present, especially in the religious importance attached to the consequences of actions, and in the positive as well as negative goodness which morality will require, + e.g. whether not doing good is not equivalent to doing evil. Neither is it synonymous with care of health, or with sanitary improvement. It should begin (I mean a new system of morality should) by clearing away those figments of necessity, the origin of evil & the like, which throw one powerless into the hands of the priests. . . .

I feel more difficulty about the College than I used to do. All the mechanical part is pretty well in order; the dinners are good, & the College & servants are well in hand. But I feel that men's characters are not easily trained or formed & I have not so much opportunity of influencing them as I had when I was only a Tutor. The tutors are very able men but they are not quite practical & vigorous. I take them out to walk & talk to them and they behave very well to me. Yet I doubt whether they are inspired with the real educational spirit. I can avoid some of the mistakes of Dr. Arnold,[1] but I cannot do what he did. I must go on hoping that I may one day accomplish more; at present the measure of external success is beyond the real success.

My friend & nearly contemporary, Arthur Hobhouse, is going to India as legal member of the Council. He is a good lawyer & most high principled man, of considerable ability, but I doubt whether he has the political experience or varied knowledge of the world which are required. . . .

284   Oxford
                                                          March 16, 1872

... Two things have occurred which rather please me & I know that you are good enough to be pleased at what pleases me. First, I have finished Thucydides—I mean the translation,[1] or rather I shall have done so in two days.

---
[1] T. Arnold.

[1] See above, No. 268, n. 3.

Secondly I was unanimously elected chairman of the Board of Studies for the Literae Humaniores Final Examinations—or rather not quite unanimously, for my old friend "the rascal Bursar", who is Professor of Logic (Henry Wall), attempted to jockey me, but was utterly discomforted. I mean to hold the office for life. I wish that you would tell me some good news of yourself.

I am very sorry for the death of Lord Mayo both because he was your friend & because he is a sort of man whom I like—a plain man who was found, when tried, to have better stuff in him than was supposed. There is another death which affects me still more, partly because I made his acquaintance a year ago, & that is Mazzini.[2] He was an enthusiast—a visionary, & may perhaps have recommended the 'moral' dagger in early life. But he was a very noble character & a genius—far beyond that of the ordinary statesman, though not a statesman. I think that his reputation will increase as time goes on when that of most statesmen disappears. One of our undergraduates (a clever man & religious) finds in his writings the stay & food of his life.

The Bishop[3] has disallowed our 'Versicles' & some other things on legal grounds—i.e. on the opinion of Sir Travers Twiss (poor man!). We will have them in a particular book of our own.[4] He says 'they are admirably selected'. The 'ci-devant' Senior Tutor[5] is much excited on this subject, & almost infuriated by a (very injudicious) sermon of Cheyne's. I try to kill him by an excess of civility, for if he brought Cheyne's Sermon before the Visitor, which he partly threatens, we should be [in] a row. These are mere breezes & there are many things to be thankful for in this place.

Am I to have an Undersecretary at War? Lord Lansdowne is a very good man for the post.[6]

[*Postscript omitted*]

285   Inglewood, Torquay
April 3, 1872

... You have worked for eternity; why should you be troubled at the Governor General[1] not coming to see you (as he most certainly ought to have done). Put not your trust in princes, or in princesses, or in the War Office, or in the India Office—all that sort of thing necessarily rests on a sandy foundation. I wonder that you have been able to carry on so long with them.

You have an endless work to do in your own sphere. And you must finish

---

[2] He died on 10 Mar. 1872 at Pisa.

[3] Jackson.

[4] On 19 Mar. 1872 college Meeting agreed upon a revised form of Morning and Evening Service to be submitted to the Visitor, and on 12 Apr. the Visitor's letter authorizing the college to use the abridged form of service on weekdays was read out.

[5] Woollcombe.

[6] Lansdowne was Under-secretary for War 1872–4.

---

[1] T. G. Baring, first Earl of Northbrook.

that & not fancy that life is receding from you. I always mean to cherish the illusion which is not an illusion that the last years of life are the most valuable & important—and every year I shall try in some way or other to do more than the year before....

[*Postscript omitted*]

286 Inglewood—Torquay
June 22 [1872]

... Something which you said on Sunday has rather disquieted me, & I hope that you will allow me to remonstrate with you about [it]. You said "that you were going to ask admission as a patient to St. Thomas Hospital". Do not do this; 1. because it is eccentric & we cannot strengthen our lives by eccentricity: 2. because you will not be a patient, but a kind of directress to the institution viewed with great alarm by the Doctors: 3. When a person is engaged in a great work I do not think the expense of living is to be much considered; the only thing is that you should live in such a way that you can do your work best: 4. I would not oppose your living at less expense if you wish, though I think that a matter of no moment, but I would live independently. 5. Do you mean really to live as a patient—it will kill you—I do not add the annoyance to your Father of a step which he can never be made to understand; I look at the matter solely from the point of view of your own work. I have cared about you for many years, & though I have little hope of prevailing with you I would ask you not to set aside these reasons without consideration....[1]

FN to BJ [*draft*][1]

287 35 South Street, Park Lane, W.
June, 1872

I think that seeing the present decline of administrative power in British Govt. offices ... and also seeing that the large majority of statesmen & of Parl^{ty} men come out of Oxford & chiefly, I suppose thro' your hands, the subject is one of such enormous, such intolerable importance, & so totally disregarded, that I venture once more to recall it.... But no one says anything about the stupendous, the increasing blunders & blank incapacity of British Gov^t Administration....

And men like you who have the great say in the future suggest as a panacea against unwise 'promotion' that all Gov^t Office Heads shall be paid alike.... It is much like saying all Oxford Professors should be paid alike, because otherwise the temptation will be irresistible of promoting the Geometry Professor

---

[1] Printed in *Cook*, ii. 211–12.

[1] BL Add. MS 45784 fos. 86–9.

at 300£ to the Greek Professorship at 500£.... What I said on Sunday was ... prompted solely by 1. interest in the Gov^t offices, 2. interest in Ld Lansdowne, (in whom I can *see* the interest Sidney Herbert would have taken, the pains he would have given to train him in every branch, had this been 11 years ago). 3. an absolute terror at the decline of administrative power in Gov^t & at men like you who almost hold the future of our youth in their hands joining in the reckless talk of men like Mr. Lowe & others.... As you think it a matter of no consequence what state an office or a College is in, provided a young man gets promotion in it. (I will not repeat my comparison of Dr. Scott, Mr. Woolcombe & a promising young Paravicini as Senior Tutor—*minus* you—because that makes you think that it is the W.O. being *minus* me which afflicts me. I assure you that it is 'extremely not so'.) ...

The first cause no doubt is the governing by majorities. Now majorities are more or less fools. At least no majority ever initiated reforms. No real Reformer ever began but with a minority.... Will you think what Balliol College would have been, if you had acted on the judgement of the majority in the College or in obedience to public criticism, instead of creating first your minority, then working it up into a majority? ...

288   Address: Oxford
[25 June 1872]

I think that you are right in principle, but do you not make too much of a chance thing which I said about Lord Lansdowne....

Also you exaggerate greatly any power which I may have of influencing others.

However you shall carry on the attack against me on Sunday, when I hope to come & see you....

FN to BJ [*draft or copy*][1]
289   [n.d.]

I think that your views of political good are becoming debased. I do not think that Mr. Lowe's views of political good ever were high, but when I knew him he had 'administrative indignation'. Now he has neither. And I think intercourse with his is pulling yours down. It may be that those are only 'chance words' which you have said to me.... But they signify very much.... It is far worse than it would be to repeat to me a vulgar gibe against S. Herbert personally....

[1] BL Add. MS 45784 fos. 107-8.

290 [?August 1872]

'You extraordinary—lady'. I see you know all about me by some species of second sight which you seem to possess, & therefore I have no need to write to you.

You are right about my reading party at Tummil—at least, as nearly right as an habitual spirit of exaggeration will ever allow you to be. I had no young Marquis—you see that I am going down in the world—& the poet was not drunk.¹

You are also right in supposing that I am not going to the Tyrol—which I only knew myself two days ago, but you, being gifted with prophecy, appear to have foreseen, O Delphian priestess of humanity. But why, alas? Because our Admiral, our Sir John, the hope of Europe & of the world,² has been ill in bed with the gout for six weeks & is not likely to move for some time to come. His mother died of rheumatism & I fear that may be his fate. I agree with you that he is one of the best fellows going & I have great hopes, if he could recover his health, that he might do something considerable.

You are also half right (as you always are) about Sophocles. About 12 years ago I made a set of notes on the Greek of the Republic of Plato. I thought that it would take me a year to finish them. Life is short & I had other things to do, so I handed them over to Mr. Campbell, who is to complete & work them over.³ Mr. Campbell is one of the most subtle & acute scholars anywhere, far better than I should ever be, but he has ingenious ways of doing things wrong, & therefore I have to look after him. . . .

[*Postscript*]

I have not been with Mr. Lowe & do not approve of the Chancellor of the Exchequer going about with the great Ex-pender. . . .⁴

FN to BJ [*draft*]¹

291 Aug. 9, 1872 (11 years)²

I write as soon as it is possible. You tell me to look back on the good that has been done. I cannot. It is not in me. I am just as much stripped of my past life,

---

¹ No new Lansdowne: the poet was Swinburne, and the reading party is described in *AC* ii. 34–40.

² Morier, 'Thine by yea and no—which is as much as to say, as thou usest him—Jack Falstaff with my familiars, John with my brothers and sisters, and Sir John with all Europe', *2 Henry IV*, II. ii. 124–8.

³ *Plato's Republic: the Greek Text*, edited, with notes and essays by the late B. Jowett and L. Campbell (3 vols., 1894).

⁴ The reference is almost certainly to Mr (later Sir) John Pender, an entrepreneurial pioneer in the laying of submarine telegraphs. Pender was MP (L) for Totnes 1862–6 until unseated for bribery. At the time BJ was writing, Pender was Chairman of the British Indian Submarine Telegraph Company, whose line was laid down the Red Sea to compete against the Government-owned line through Persia. Pender had been busy lobbying ministers for fair, or advantageous opportunities to do business in India; *PP* (1871), li. 361–406.

---

¹ BL Add. MS 45784 fos. 96–9.

² Since the death of Sidney Herbert.

'stand naked there' on the brink of the grave, as if it had really been done in another life.... I cannot remember, still less 'think of' my life in the Crimea, or my 5 years incessant work with S.H. or my 9 years Indian work, more than if it had been really the life of others, indeed much less for I am sure that I think much more of what Mr. Jowett had done than of what I have done. Rather it is absurd to say so. For I think every day of what he has done....

If I am forgotten it is no more than I have forgotten myself. If I am like a dead man, out of mind, it is not more than a dead man is out of his own mind.

And F.N. is not less stripped out of anyone else's mind than she is out of her own.... Such utter waste of time to finish this letter. [Man]y things which are real become *unreal* by [b]eing told. [']Hope'—to hope is for me like brandy, one feels all the weaker afterwards. I cannot & do not wish to 'hope' for what I know will not come. 'Pray fortune to finish your work'. You are at the pinnacle of your power, thank God. [You] only want time to *finish*. [I] with an utterly shattered body have to begin all over again.

292   John ffolliott's Esqr.,
                                     Hollybrook,
                                     Boyle [24 September 1872]
                                     until Sep. 30, afterwards Oxford

I am grieved that I can do so little for you. I think with pain on the contrast between my own enviable circumstances & your sad lot; I wish it were otherwise, or that I were able to make it so....

Do not give another thought to the War Office &c. I know that you have had to suffer a great deal (more than I can judge of) in seeing your work, which was once so promising, discontinued. But a great deal of good has been done, which is not lost upon the health & moral condition of the Army. The position which you held was always an unsatisfactory one, because dependent on 'Temples of friendship' & the goodwill of the Minister. I am glad that you have a straightforward work to do now, in which you are dependent on yourself. May God give you strength & life to do it.

If you can arouse people to the duty of sanitary improvement & general, as distinct from medical, care of health, you will have done a greater work than the administration of any public office....

My friend with whom I am staying[1] is very busy with the Irish Church & is a sort of leader among the laity of the Church. They seem to me to do nothing but dispute about the Athanasian Creed & the Ordination Service, & the High

---

[1] BJ met Ffolliott of University College through Morier, and visited him more than once in Ireland, *AC* i. 129, 136.

Church party get the better of them.² The popular election of their ministers appears to work badly & vulgarly among them (Omnibus covered with the name of the Candidate &c.). I am pleased with Ireland & the people. They all talk to you, which is a great merit, & poke fun—a nation which cannot laugh is not to be endured. They seem to me much more civilized than when I was here 20 years ago—reclaimed men, like the waste land, & I cannot doubt that the land bill³ has done good, though I suppose that it has transferred the improvement of the land from the landlord to the Tenant. I mean that you cannot expect the landlord to do what he used to do, now that they have tenant right.

I read the 2nd volume of Lord Palmerston's life⁴ this morning. I like him & his way of doing things. He was more of a man than any other statesman of his time, & though not equal to Peel on the whole, more natural & attractive in his character. His letters give you the idea of great ability—you see how he came to be the great War Minister of Europe.

293 Address: Oxford
Oct. 3 [1872]

Your letter made me quite happy for two days & more, & I shall always look back upon it with gratitude & thankfulness....

In your selection from the mystics¹ you will do a good work if you point out the kind of mysticism which is needed in this day—not mysticism at all, but as intense a feeling as the mystics had, of the power of truth & reason, & of the will of God that they should take effect in the world. The passion of the reason, the fusion of faith & reason, the reason in religion & the religion in reason—if you can only describe these you will teach people a new lesson. The new has something still to learn from the old—& I am not certain whether we ought not to retire into mysticism (though I should not use the word) when the antagonism with existing opinions becomes too great—the intense belief in we know not what....

294 Ball. Coll.
Oct. 16, 1872.

Why do you not write to me? I am afraid that you must be very ill.

Send me a line to say what this trouble is of which you spoke¹ & how you are. You must not lose heart whatever your difficulties may be....

² 32 and 33 Vict. c. 42, s. 19 removed all prohibitions on the holding of Synods and the framing in Synods of constitutions for the general management and good government of the Church.
³ Compare BJ's views above, Nos. 225, 228.
⁴ Sir Henry Lytton Bulwer, *The Life of ... Viscount Palmerston* (3 vols., 1870-4).

¹ Not published.

¹ The reorganization of the Nursing School when St Thomas's Hospital moved to its new site opposite the Houses of Parliament, *Cook*, ii. 246-9.

I cannot suppose you wanting in pluck under any circumstances. But you feel things too much, & this will wear you out.

I will come & see you whenever you like. . . .

295

Oxford
Oct. 31 [1872]

I like your abuse: please to let me have some more. Nothing does me so much good.

Still I shall venture to make two remarks by way of retaliation.

First, that you do not perceive that in the Introduction to the Phaedo,[1] I am speaking neither in my own nor in Plato's person, but in both, & am trying to prepare the mind of the modern reader for thinking that, after all, there may be something in the aforesaid Plato.

II. Please not to be offended. During the ten years & more that I have known you, you have repeated to me the expression 'character of God' about 1,000 times, but I cannot say that I have any clear [idea] of what you mean, if you mean anything more than divine perfection. . . .

The case of Shakespeare is not parallel to that of Plato, because no one ever supposed that Julius Caesar contains the real words of J.C., but many persons have supposed that the Phaedo is a real conversation: hence the necessity of pointing out that it goes beyond the speculation of Socrates.

Χαῖρε, vale, ὁ θεὸς μετὰ σοῦ.[2]

296

Balliol College
Dec. 1, 1872

. . . Why do you think that I have not written to you? Partly because I have been busy trying to improve the 'Phaedo' in accordance with your desires.

Dr. Pusey has been preaching a very impressive sermon today, the broadest liberality, the most Christian Charity—all intended to support the damnatory clauses of the Athanasian Creed.[1]

I am told that he has 94 daughters & that they give him a great deal of trouble, some by their Romish proclivities. Fanaticism is a catching thing & he seems to be gaining ground.

I would not have you suppose, dear Miss Nightingale, that I am indifferent to your troubles because I do not write: I feel equally anything that affects you. But I fear that I should only repeat what I have said before—I must trust you to God.

---

[1] *The Dialogues of Plato* (5 vols., 1875), i. 399–428.
[2] Farewell, farewell, God with you.

[1] On 30 Nov. Pusey preached before the University a sermon 'The responsibility of the intellect in matters of Faith' upon the proposal to remove the Athanasian creed from the services of the Church; H. P. Liddon, *Life of E. B. Pusey* (4 vols., 1893–7), iv. 253.

Please to let me hear how you are & whether the difficulties are clearing. I go on pounding away at Plato, & I fear that the mere revising of it will take nearly 18 months.² It will be a much better book & nobody will buy it.

297

Balliol Coll.
Dec. 15 [1872]

... I am in better heart about the College than I was when I last saw you. I am thinking about new buildings,¹ & have persuaded the Rev^d. Hegel Green to give up lecturing for a year & take to writing,² whereby the minds of our undergraduates will be greatly clarified.

Are you going to cut me? If you do, you shall see how well I will behave. That is the true test of friendship....

[*Postscript omitted*]

298

Inglewood Torquay
until Saturday Jan. 16 [1873]

I am right in not allowing you to be constantly using the expression, 'Character *of* God' (although I did not reclaim until I heard it about 1000 times) because it is anthropomorphic, and unless we change our words frequently in theology we shall be insensibly putting them in the place of ideas. 'Nature' is both better & worse than 'character': better because it is not affected by human associations, & worse because it is more dead & impersonal. No word will at all express the 'nature', 'being', 'substance', 'character' of God. We must describe it under many figures of speech, as well as we can.

I agree in general with your letter. We have never reconciled our abstract ideas of God with facts. Instead of attempting this we have turned our fears & hopes into logical forms called doctrines.

I should state your first argument in a different way. I should not like to apply the argument for probabilities, because God stands in an entirely different relation to the world from that in which any finite cause stands to any finite effect. We may get indefinitely nearer to the point at which mind works through the discovery of mechanical & physiological laws—much that we call design will be found to be the result of antecedent elements—I should not think that even the establishment of Darwinism would necessarily be inconsistent with the existence of God.

I am an enemy to the whole phraseology of cause & effect, which is full of

---

² Published in 1875.

---

¹ The new Hall was built in 1875–6.
² CM, 24 Jan. 1873, 'Mr. Abbott be appointed Lecturer after Easter.... That Mr. Tatton shall take over one of Mr. Green's lectures.'

illusion & is just talk without any enquiry into its true nature for the ancient philosophy.

I should say that God or mind worked in the world by various methods, mechanical, physiological, mental, & that the fact of order & the tendency to structure was a proof of the existence of mind.

(I have sometimes thought that the Comtists or Positivists might be brought round to become Theists, if we allowed them to use the language of Atheism, which they love—The difference even between Theists & Atheists is partly verbal.) . . .

I quite agree with you as to the second part of your letter: that we want to have God identified with the progress of good in the world, & instead of the favourite, Manicheism, to have shown to us over & over again the latent elements of Good, which are so many & mighty, of which we might if we would be partakers—that good is essential & evil, accidental only. Some higher creed than the present certainly needs to be taught, for that is all torn to shreds.

299 Oxford
[26 January 1873]

I am coming to London on Tuesday. . . . May I have the pleasure of coming to see you about 4 o'clock?

You do not tell me about your troubles now—(I do not mean about your family troubles, if you have any, for those a person had better keep to themselves)—I do not ask you about them, yet believe me, I shall not soon weary of anything which interests you.

[*Prepared by FN and signed by BJ*][1]

300 January 1873

I, *B. Jowett*,

I agree to take an entire holiday *doing nothing* for 3 weeks at the present time—for not less than 3 weeks at Easter—& for not less than six (6) weeks in the Long Vacation.

I agree to take 2 days in every week during Term Time (Sunday & one other day) of entire holiday, doing nothing except when I have a sermon to write.

I agree to give not more than two Lectures a week during the present year.

& to register all this in an Almanac

B. Jowett

---

[1] BL Add. MS 45784 fo. 123.

301
Balliol College
[Sunday], Feb. 9, 1873

I send you the Almanac....
... the compact is very well observed on the whole....
In consequence of these counsels of idleness I do nothing with the introduction to the 'Phaedrus'. You are quite right in thinking that it is lamely done. I have never had leisure to write well—this is the simple truth. I have sometimes thought that life would have been better spent in writing than in teaching. Teaching does some good but it is like the breath that goeth forth & returneth not, & writing is permanent. But you cannot do both.

I think that you are the best critic I ever had.

Poor Mr. Gaskell died quietly on Tuesday—a melancholy life, yet with a sort of gentleness & goodness that was very pleasing. The last time I saw him (ten days ago) he repeated a long passage from an unpublished poem of Arthur Hallam's.[1] What was melancholy to us in his life was never, I think, present to his mind—great talents & opportunities wasted.

I heard of Lord Westbury's marriage[2] from his grandson. Either his family are prejudiced, or he is in a state of self-delusion bordering on madness. I am afraid that we must give up seeing him do much more. Another 'vie manquée' with still greater powers & opportunities.

I quite understood what you said about caring for your work and not for the manner in which you were treated by persons. I dare say that I did you some injustice for, in my own case, I really cannot separate Benevolence from the Love of Power. Only, whichever is the motive, I mean to go on. And we must both go on for five or ten or twenty years, whatever is the appointed time, & carry out our work to the utmost. No doubt more might have been done by both of us, not by harder work, but by better considered work. (Christ only worked for 3 years, perhaps only for 15 months.) And the beginning of a higher & more considered work is rest, self-control, indifference to results....

I think that you are very intolerant & persecuting to George Elliott.[3] She has painted—what often takes place in real life—the failure of an ideal. Why should not this be described as well as any other chapter in the life of a family?

[*Postscript omitted*]

302
Bal. Col.
March 9, 1873

I have sometimes wished you at Embley: & now I wish you back again at your work in London. I know that your life is a sad one & have often desired to

---

[1] A. H. Hallam, betrothed to Tennyson's sister and subject of *In Memoriam*. His *Essays and Remains* were published in 1834.
[2] His second.
[3] Eliot.

make it lighter. I believe that the best thing for you is to be among hospitals & nurses.

What an absurd condition the Ministry have brought themselves into—framing a plan condemned by all parties about a question of no real importance.[1] They should have 1) reformed & thrown open Trinity College; 2) have strengthened with larger endowments the Queen's University & Colleges; & 3) allowed degrees to be taken at the Queen's, as at the London University, without residence.

Have you read M. Arnold's book?[2] And are you going to send it back to me ignominiously? (I will send you Joshua Dander,[3] if you like.) The fault of M.A.'s book is that he is flippant on a serious subject, & treats the whole question too much as a littérateur. Still, I think that his book is important 1) for many beautiful things which he says about Christ; & 2) because he is the first person who has urged in England that there is a real value in Christianity apart from miracle & legend. The world & the Church have been hitherto so anxious to keep the miracles, as to deny the possibility of the Christian faith being maintained without them.

I have sometimes a project in my head of going to London every year for about six weeks, & preaching courses of sermons (I should do nothing else for six weeks). Mr Stopford Brooke would, I think, be glad to take a holiday and lend me his chapel for six weeks. What do you think of this project? I rather shrink from the labour, & yet I do not like to let life slip away without saying what I think. Remember, if I write the sermons you must help me. . . .

303 Oxford
April 18 [1873]

I have read the translations with great interest. One or two things strike me about them.

1. St. Theresa, though shortened, I should shorten still more & reduce it to the pure Gold. To a modern reader it is too rhetorical & egotistical.

2 also I should leave out some of the allusions to herself & her own feelings. I should like better to have the impersonal soul rising to God.

3 I should not call the soul 'it', 'itself' (this is my old difficulty about the genders).

4 I think you should add a preface showing the use of such books. They are apt to appear unreal, & yet Thomas à Kempis has been one of the most influential books in the world. The subject of the preface should be the use of the

---

[1] In 1873 the ministry was unable to find a solution to the Irish university problem which would satisfy both the Roman Catholics and the Voluntaryist and secular groups of the Liberal party in Parliament. Forty-three Liberals voted against the second reading of the Irish University Bill on 11 Mar., and it was defeated by 287 votes to 284. Gladstone resigned, and returned, much weakened, to office one week later.

[2] *Literature and Dogma* (1873). [3] Not identified.

ideal, & especially the spiritual ideal. I do not say what may be the case with great saints themselves, but for us I think it is clear that this mystic state ought to be an occasional & not a permanent feeling—a taste of heaven in daily life.

Do you think it would be possible to write a mystical book, which would also be the essence of common sense? ...

[*Postscript*]

I hope that you are better. I get on pretty well, rising at 6 & doing nothing until after 1.P.M. That is my new plan.

304

Ball. Coll.
May 21 [1873]

I wanted to have written you a long letter but I have been overpowered by a stream of visitors. Mrs Grote & Co. I am glad to see for her husband's sake & because she is an inextinguishable old lady, 65 as she says, but really 81—though how much rather would I have seen him!

I am deeply grateful for your last letter.... I think that the truth is that I am a little overstrained with variety of things, persons, interests, & that the tasks before me look too great for my strength. The isolated life I lead here & the seeming failure of memory, a little depress me. But your words incline me to pluck up health & strength & to do my best.

I have read over your 'Notes On Nursing'[1] again—It always seems to me one of the most interesting books I ever read. The article in Fraser's is a little too much crowded.[2] I see that you have poured out your heart in it....

305

Ball. Coll.
Jun. 1 [1873]

> The age is out of joint
> O cursed spite
> That you should think me
> born to set it right[1]

instead of recognising that I am, & always have been, a feeble, rather worn out creature. However, as you prescribe three months idleness as a necessary preliminary to commencing the role of Reformer, I am not indisposed to take your advice & have already made a beginning by doing nothing to-day except

---

[1] *Notes on Nursing* (1860).
[2] *Fraser's Magazine* (Jan.–June 1873), pp. 567–77, 'A "Note" of Interrogation', ranges from George Eliot's Dorothea, who, FN suggests, ought to have joined the Charity Organization Society, to the character of God.

---

[1] 'The time is out of joint; o cursed spite, / That ever I was born to set it right! *Hamlet*, 1. v. 189–90.

reading Mrs. Grote's memoirs of her husband[2] (well done certainly), which with some other books I propose to send you in a parcel.

Individually I prosper better than I deserve, & have been successful (very) lately at some College & University meetings; nor do I doubt that I can maintain Ball. College as a decent academy for youth, as long as I live. But that is quite a different thing from having a heart or a head that will make a stir in the world.

... The span of life shortens, but there is more & more to be crammed into it—more work & greater interests—And you & I must do our part & help one another as we best can.

Thank you for Sir Bartle Frere's letters[3]—I always thought the Portuguese the greatest scoundrels in Europe.

Mr. Mohl has a very keen insight & great knowledge, but he always takes the dark view of things. I cannot think Ultramontanism so strong as he supposes; the fanaticism of a small minority of organised & concentrated wills is mistaken for popular strength. The Ultramontanism of the English & Roman Churches appears to me to be much the same, equally regardless of truth & equally disorganising of society. We Liberals are no match for their strength of will, which works like madness in the world. We are very loose & flabby in comparison with them. But we have the better mind of society on our side if we can only get hold of it, and we must fight with the same weapons as the Jesuits—Education.

The worst of taking the dark side of things is that it impairs the power of acting. I believe that those of us who mean to do anything (while looking facts in the face) ought to cherish inextinguishable hope....

306

June 25, 1873
Oxford

How can I thank you enough for all your care of me? I will take your advice: And do not you be anxious I shall get well enough when I have rested for a few months. I do not feel faintness or giddiness or headache, and I sleep fairly well—But I feel powerlessness. I cannot talk, I cannot remember. Yet sometimes strangely enough I have a sense of rest in doing Plato with Mr. [de] Paravicini. It soothes me....

You think that I do not take an interest in your writings; that is not so. I think that what you have written in 'Fraser'[1] will interest a great many persons.... It seems to me that your article has a great idea in that it expresses a real convic-

---

[2] Harriet Grote, *The Personal Life of George Grote* (1873).
[3] Frere was sent to Zanzibar in 1872 to negotiate the suppression of the slave trade.
[1] See above, No. 304, n. 2.

tion that the present methods of theology & moral science are erroneous.... Now I want you to begin where you leave off, & tell us not that we are ignorant of these moral & divine laws, but what they are—And when you speak of a 'perfect God' are you prepared to maintain that he governs the world with the least pain possible, consistently with his purposes of educating mankind? I want you to look the other side of the question in the face, & show how you reconcile this view of the perfect education with many of the appearances of 'wasteful' evil in the world.

I went to Mr. Mill's Committee[2] on Tuesday—a rather miserable scene—the object of a large section of the meeting appeared to be not to do honour to Mr. Mill, but to get the working man represented. Mr. Stansfield[3] showed good sense & spoke well, but I am sure that nothing can be done if they go on in that way.

Also I went to visit Mr. Lowe. He spoke of the Zanzibar packet business, which he said was a matter of honour, because the company had taken 2 contracts & would not have taken one only, without the other which is so much objected to.[4] He thought that the House of Commons was more & more undertaking administration, & that soon there would be standing Committees for the different offices & that the minister would be the delegate. In the midst of talking about this he broke off & said, 'Can you, as a theologian, tell me whether Adam is anywhere mentioned in the Old Testament except in the 3 or 4 first chapters of Genesis?'[5] You see his inference, which is perhaps true, that the beginning of the old Testament is very nearly, if not quite the end of it.

Also I went to stay a day with Dr. & Mrs. Butler at Harrow: I heartily like them; they are such good people & she has such extraordinary powers of sympathy with the Harrow boys & with every one. Very few persons do their duty as they do—what makes me speak to you about them? Because I respect them, & I like that you should know about them & about my other friends who are doing anything good or profitable in this world....

You & others have set a work before me which I am not really strong enough to accomplish. But I shall try, & go on cheerfully when I am up to the mark again, & if I fail, as I expect I shall, be resigned & willing to depart. There is certainly an *opportunity* in Moral Philosophy & Theology such as there has never been before. The wordy platitudes of Mr. H. Spencer[6] do not fill up the void. And I sometimes fear that our Hegelian friends, Professor Caird & Green, are resting on some metaphysical subtleties, & not on common sense or experience. Our undergraduates are constantly bringing me Kant in their essays which they derive from their aforesaid teachers. But Kant's idealism is

---

[2] BJ was added to the committee formed to establish a memorial to J. S. Mill, *The Times*, 20 May 1873 (10e).

[3] Stansfeld.

[4] Lowe had entered into an over-priced contract for the carriage of mails to Zanzibar, and this led to the appointment of a Select Committee.

[5] Deut. 32: 8; Job 31: 33.

[6] Herbert Spencer, *Principles of Psychology* (1855, repub. 1870–2), *First Principles* (1862), *Principles of Biology* (1864, repub. 1867), *Study of Sociology* (1873).

too abstract & vacant, & rests on his untenable hypothesis about space & time. I want to see a metaphysical philosophy which 1) deifies ideas or ideals (without any nonsense about space & time, or confusions of sensations with objects of sense); 2) which shows them to be the universal or common sense of mankind. . . .

307 Edinburgh
July 6, 1873

I have been reading your second Article,[1] which is very able & striking. Shall I say a provoking thing? It is a scream stile; but now you must tell us, quite calmly & consecutively, what we are to do.

I am never quite sure of your idea of "discovering more of God's laws" as if they were to be found inductively. . . . The great moral truths are well known & generally agreed upon, but nobody feels them.

100 women like your friends Miss Jones or Miss Berkely might change the face of England in all that belongs to women's mission to effect.

100 men like poor Luke might change the face of England in all that relates to Education Statesmanship etc.

Is it impossible that 100 such spirits should be created or renewed or go through some process which should fit them for such a work?

It is not our ignorance of moral laws, but our absolute insensibility to them which strikes me.

I hope that you will be very careful with your 3rd Article. . . .

308 Granttown
Invernesshire
July 10, 1873

I am settled here in a land where there are 'nae Christians, but only Grants & Gordons'. I like the place & the air is delightful—my four companions are Swinburne, Harrison, Higgs & Roe. I have taken to bullying them, which does them good & I think myself too.

I have read the preface, which I like, but (you know my prejudice) should also like it to be written more consecutively and with fewer jerks. To the flyleaf & to the remark at p. 3 about the Spanish Mystics, I decidedly object. It is only sounding a note of alarm beforehand. Why not . . . simply say:

These notes have been translated, some of them for the first time in English, from Spanish & other mystical writers. I have thought that they might have a fair chance of acceptance among Protestants if the names of their authors were concealed—or something of that sort.

---

[1] 'A sub-"Note" of Interrogation', *Fraser's Magazine* (July–Dec. 1873), pp. 25—36, what the religions of the world may be like by 1999. There is a subheading 'The Indian's Estimate of our Religion'.

309   Granton Invernesshire
                                                 July 11. 1873

I hope that you are not anxious about me for I really am a great deal better in this delightful air, & am beginning to be hopeful and determined not to be ill any more (are we not always to blame, as 'Erewhon' says, for being ill).[1] I sleep ten hours at least (as Goethe did) & am out in the air about 4 hours—I work very little & don't eat or drink much (for I do not need it). Is not this a satisfactory program? I have not got a pony, but I mean to have one at Oxford.

In the evening Swinburne reads over to us 'Marie Stuart'[2] & I think he begins to be aware of his defects—which are chiefly want of clearness & rhetorical phraseology. I wish he had more of the ideal in him—he is too much an imitator & dramatizer, immensely gifted in language & verse, & learned in poetry to a degree which destroys originality. This leads him constantly to introduce Archaisms.

I will send you my plan of life or rather of what remains of life when I have digested it. I shall make it carefully & not depart from it. No doubt I have a great opportunity, but have I the power? There is the rub. At present I am not satisfied with the position of the College—We have very clever able men, but half of them seem to me to have very little power of teaching or influencing others....

[*Postscript omitted*]

310   Grantown Invernesshire
                                                 July 22 [1873]

... I have no admiration of Carlyle, who has the gift of saying strong things without the least regard for truth. There is no human being for whom he would express any respect or admiration except Governor Eyre, & two or three hangers on of his own. For insolence & conceit he has really no equal. He takes poor Ruskin & squeezes him into a sort of pulp, never concerning himself with the consequences. Why should he? The poor creature gets feebler & feebler in his hands, ready to dilate upon any random remark of Carlyle's. He has become a lamentable wreck of a man of genius; & Carlyle instead of trying, as Goethe might have done, to 'minister to this mind diseased'[1] just inflames his folly.

He would be sure to say some word of detraction about any body who was doing anything.

I am grieved about the deaths of those two great men, especially about Lord Westbury; he was needed greatly & might still have had a future in the H. of

---

[1] Samuel Butler in *Erewhon* (1872), where physical ailment (not moral obliquity) was punished.
[2] *Mary Stuart* was published in 1881.

---

[1] 'cure her of that; / canst thou not minister to a mind diseas'd', *Macbeth*, v. iii. 40–1.

Lords & in the Courts of Law. He was unfortunate in his family, as the Public knows, but he was also unfortunate in another way: he had no one who could help him or guide him (though his daughter is an excellent person) and hence he got under strange influences. Any woman of ability & sense might have made his life different, & have found her life in doing so.

As for the Bishop of Winchester[2] I believe his disappearance from the world to be rather a good, but nevertheless I am sorry (You will probably be angry with me for this). In former days I went to stay with him. He was more sincere than the Dean of Westminster & others suppose—he had a natural kindness which made him like everybody when he was with them—this was mistaken for hypocrisy & to say the truth he did rather trade upon it. His deepest feeling I believe to have been sorrow for the death of his wife:[3] he never got over this, but tried to stifle the recollection with ambition & the world.

I have been reading Hume's 'Essays' (which the Revd. Hegel Green is to present to us in a new Edtn. with a Hegelian commentary of his own).[4] Did you ever read them? I wonder that people should think his argument about miracles set aside. It is really unanswerable, though in modern times it would be somewhat differently expressed. I always wonder what Hume really was, for I do not believe him to have been the mere Atheist & materialist, or wholly insincere in what he says here & there about God & the teaching of the Gospel....

[*Prepared by* FN][1]

311 August 13, 1873

I, B. Jowett, do hereby solemnly agree during the next twelve months to take five months' complete holiday & for the other seven months to work but three hours a day & not more than one hour at a time.

B. Jowett[2]

312 Inglewood Torquay
Aug. 18 [1873]

I send you the last part of the 'Phaedrus'.

I have found a 'Companion of my revels' & am going abroad with Rogers.... He fancies that he is stranded; he thinks that he has come to the end of education & does not much like the disguise of a Clergyman. He has

---

[2] Samuel Wilberforce.
[3] In 1841 after thirteen years together.
[4] *The Philosophical Works of David Hume*, ed. T. H. Green and T. H. Grose (4 vols., 1874).

---

[1] BL Add. MS 45784 fo. 197.
[2] The last nine words and the signature are in BJ's hand.

now established a Girls School:[1] he says that it goes on well but slowly. English people do not like a Public School for Girls, & their prejudices are with difficulty overcome.

I went to see Lady Westbury on Sat. I was very much pleased & interested with what she told me about Lord Westbury. She said that he died quite resigned & humble, like a great man, without a thought of repining. Her devotion to him & affection for him appeared to be quite extraordinary, & I do not think that she could have been acting. She said that she wished to die, but she hardly thought this would be granted, for she was very strong and if she lived she must try & do some good to others. I hear people speak against her as a worldly & designing woman, but I am not of this opinion. She told me that the family were very kind to her, & acknowledged gratefully that she had done for him what they could not have done, which is quite true. . . .

Lord Westbury's was a 'vie manquée' & a 'vie incomprise', but he was a great man. I think that I understand him now: I wish that I had done so in his life. His falsetto manner which never changed, was just the effect of his long practice as an advocate on his plastic nature. He was really simple & almost childlike, but was thought to be the greatest humbug in the world. He was courageous & even insolent in the highest degree, but also very weak & ignorant of the world when a woman or one of his own children was concerned. He was no sceptic but really religious, if not quite the 'eminent Christian' of the 'Saturday Review'.[2] He told me that he had never thought about theology until he had to sit upon the 'Essays & Reviews' case, & then he found the received views breaking down. I believe that when the book first appeared he expressed himself strongly against the writers of it.

Lord Russell told me that you could not 'believe a word that he said'. But this was a mistake. It seems to me that his life never could have been appreciated. Sincerity which always took the appearance of hypocrisy, could not be understood even by an intimate friend. Genius, industry, a heart as soft & foolish as a child's masked by a determination to succeed—with some vanity, not much, + the profession of an advocate make up a strange compound. . . .

FN TO BJ [*draft or copy on the Phaedrus*][1]

313 [*n.d.*]

... one of the highest relations in life possible is friendship (not love) between a *man* and a *woman*—*not* husband & wife, that where marriage is

---

[1] See above, No. 193, n. 8.

[2] The *Saturday Review* carried a double obituary of Lord Westbury and the Bishop of Winchester on 26 July 1873 (vol. XXXVI, pp. 98-9): 'It was felt that, if Lord Westbury had not been faultless, he had also made no Pharisaic pretensions to extraordinary virtue. Even his celebrated announcement that he owed his success in life to his practice of Christian doctrines was justly regarded as an outbreak of unconscious humour.'

---

[1] BL Add. MS 45784 fo. 160.

good its goodness is enhanced, enlarged, by the husband having *friendship* with other women, married or not, & also, I suppose, by the wife having friends among other men. Surely marriage should enlarge & strengthen all other ties, instead of cutting them off as in England. . . .

314

[Oxford]
Aug. 28 [1873]

I have been at work upon the 'Gorgias' which I find it difficult to do up to your ideas. What you suggest is always most useful to me: I mix it with water & make it drinkable for the English public. . . .

I send you a copy of the Bible[1]—not good in paper & print—object being to make it cheap—has the approbation of the Bp. of Gloucester & Bristol[2] ('our future Abp.' according to Messrs. Longman). But good upon the whole. I think though, it might have been better if the printer had taken more pains.

I met Mr. Froude in Devonshire[3] & had a good deal of talk with him. He is the same amiable, interesting, paradoxical, impressible sort of man that he always [was]. I like talking to him though his conversation appears to me to be a 'falsetto'. He is really liberal in religion & theology, & has a great horror of falsehood & priestcraft. With this he combines Carlyle's doctrine of the 'true ruler being the man of sense' who is strong enough to knock his opponents on the head.[4] He thought that Ruskin was going rather to ruin, wasting his property & talking of becoming a Roman Catholic. He said that Carlyle did all he could to keep him straight, but then surely C. has been the person who made him crooked.

315

Sep. 19 [1873]
Address
R. B. Morier Esqr. C.B.
Légation Britannique
Munich.

Will you not write & tell me how you are & what you are doing? I have had a very pleasant tour with Rogers, who is an excellent companion, but I cannot help remembering a friend at home who has never allowed herself any change or relaxation, who works on year after year with unswerving devotion to the good of her fellow creatures.

[1] *The School and Children's Bible*, prepared under the superintendence of William Rogers; see above, No. 259, n. 1.
[2] Ellicott.
[3] Froude came from Devon, and for many years after he moved to London he rented a house for the summer at Salcombe.
[4] Possibly, 'Surely of all "rights of man", this right of the ignorant man to be guided by the wiser, to be, gently or forcibly, held in the true course by him, is the indisputablest'; *Chartism*, Chap. VI, para. 5.

I saw your friend M. Mohl at Paris—I was very much struck & pleased by him. He appears to have excellent information about French politics. He thought that monarchy was a 'fait accompli' & yet admitted that it would cause a civil war. What a problem this is of the Government of France—how to combine hopelessly irreconcilable elements—it ought, I think, to make one more lenient to Louis Napoleon. There is something quite pathetic in the patient industry & cleverness of the French people, compared with their readiness to run headlong to destruction in a European war. I cannot agree with M. Mohl about the monarchy; I expect that the difficulties & jealousies will be found so great, in case any other course is followed, that they will fall back at last on M. Thiers's conservative Republic.

I have been delighted with Genoa & Florence. What a wonderful country is Italy: quite inexhaustible in works of art, & yet they have filled all Europe with their treasures. There is great appearance of prosperity, not only in Piedmont but at Bologna & Florence, although they are terribly taxed. Every where they are improving their towns, and the priests & beggars are disappearing. The people are certainly not asleep: indeed I think that the clerical element indicated by round black hats & long coats is far less obtrusive than in Oxford. Nor is there the least sign of a reaction, which seems to arise from the Reformation or revolution having been effected by the upper & middle classes & not by the people at large. The Churches are very thinly attended, whether this is to be regarded as a good sign or a bad one, & without much appearance either of reverence or of irreverence.

I went to St. Marks last Sunday & saw Savonarola's chapel & cell, & sat down in his chair. Seeing the places in which a great man lived helps you to think about him, but does not really tell you anything of his character. The portrait of him by Fr. Bartholomeus in the cell is a keen, intense face, which is completely filled up by the features and has a womanly expression. He was a Catholic Puritan, and Puritanism, though very exalted, seems always to fail in the struggle with human nature & to lead to a reaction, though I may, perhaps, be beaten for saying this (as for some things I have said about mysticism). I do not know whether George Eliot has caught him quite rightly[1]—she likes to draw mixed characters. My impression is that there was more of a simple, childlike enthusiasm about him for being good & great, & reforming the world, than she supposes.

[*Postscript omitted*]

316 Balliol Coll.
Oct. 20 [1873]

... I have had a great trouble during the last two days....

H. Smith, the most distinguished of our fellows, has suddenly announced

---

[1] In *Romola* (1863).

his intention of becoming a fellow of Corpus, the wily President,[1] without speaking to me, having offerred him a fellowship. We have offered to do all that they would do, but he persists that he cannot, chiefly for conscientious ! ! ! reasons, accept a sinecure Fellowship at a small College like ours. I cannot tell what his real motives are, but I suspect that he feels some kind of constraint in being here with me....

I send you the sketch of University Reform,[2] if you have time to look at it....

317

Saturday
Oct. 26, 1873

... Our great banquet[1] was rather commonplace, relieved however by the enthusiasm of the undergraduates, who I regret to say are fearfully High Church & Conservative. The worst speaker of the evening was the Lord Chancellor[2] by far, & the next worst was the Chancellor of the University.[3] The best was Manning & the next best was Coleridge.

I had my little banquet with the two archbishops[4] which went off very well. I made a speech to them about old times, which they seemed to like....

318

Ball. Coll.
Dec. 4, 1873

I see that 'like a ghost' you don't speak unless you are spoken to, and therefore I must write. I don't write oftener for 4 excellent reasons. 1st I have no time: 2nd I am a bad letter writer: 3rdly Oxford, just at present, is an uninteresting place, having a sort of leaden atmosphere: 4th because if I write I shall get directly or indirectly into talking about myself, & I have already drawn upon your sympathy & kindness far too much.

... The newly elected fellow, Mr. Forbes, is a very fine creature (perhaps the most learned young man living, & gifted with very considerable powers of thought). He is very religious, & very blameless & innocent. I hope that he will exercise a good influence over the Undergraduates. We gave this for an English Essay:

"What are our duties towards posterity?"

One of the Candidates (not Forbes) wrote about the duty of providing a religion for posterity, which touched me to the heart. I was very much pleased with the examination. They were equal, I think, to the best candidates we have ever had.

[1] J. M. Wilson.
[2] Presumably an early version of 'Suggestions for University Reform', published in L. Campbell (ed.), *On the Nationalisation of the Old English Universities* (1901), pp. 183–208.

---

[1] To celebrate the fiftieth anniversary of the Oxford Union.
[2] Lord Selborne.   [3] Lord Salisbury.   [4] Tait and Manning.

Not discouraged by the failure of our Siamese,[1] we are going, I believe, to have the son of the Japanese Prime Minister at Balliol.[2] I should like to govern the world (would not you?) through my pupils, but I find it impossible & rather expect to do less & less.

I never answered a letter of yours in which you attacked me about the position which we took up in the days of 'Essays & Reviews'. You are quite right, but do you fully appreciate the difficulties of the case? 1) We & all Liberal Theologians are really on sufferance in the Church of England: 2) we have to repeat services of which about one half appear to us to be monstrous & superstitious, like some parts of all the Creeds: 3) although we are in a false position in the Church we should be in a still more false position out of the Church (this Mr. Martineau appears to feel). These are great drawbacks, especially No 2. There is such a difficulty in saying to an ingenuous youth, 'Go & repeat what you don't believe, for the sake of doing good'. Even if it be right, am I sure that he has strength of character to take such a course without being demoralized? I suppose that the only way is to leaven the existing Church & the existing Creed, with a higher truth & a higher morality, & gradually change public opinion. That is why I want to write, before 'the time comes when no man shall write'.[3] You must help me; though I have great doubt whether I can do any good. I suspect that this High Church movement has nearly reached its limit.

In the days of 'Essays & Reviews' & of the Greek Professorship I held my tongue, & spoke to no one on the subject, except occasionally to the D. of Westminster[4] (who has great virtues as well as faults & weaknesses; and the virtues, I think, increase & the faults diminish as he gets older). I agree with you that this was not at all heroic or noble; but in looking back, considering the difficulties of the matter, & my own powerlessness & distraction with other things, I have been sometimes thankful that I did no worse. But you & my other friends will have good reason to say that I have utterly failed if the 'Essays & Reviews' are to be my last word on Theology.

I went to Ch.Ch. today to hear the Christmas Music of Bach got up by Mrs Liddell & the Choir. It is fine but rather monotonous; I should not place Bach in the first or the second class of musical composers. It seems to me that the really great masters are Beethoven & Handel, & in the second class Mozart, Haydn, Mendelssohn. Beethoven has done more to make the world lovelier than Shakespeare, & has perhaps had a greater influence. How did that dull 18th century come to produce music, & the Germans, who in the first half of the century were the dullest of all people? There is not really, as far as I can learn, any music of importance before the 18th century....

---

[1] Bhanuwongsee.
[2] Tomatsume Iwakura son of Tomomi Iwakura.
[3] See above, No. 216, n. 2.
[4] A. P. Stanley.

319 [December 1873]

... With whom do you think that I have been fraternizing today? You will never guess:—Dizzy ! ! !¹

[*Postscript omitted*]

320 Address   W. H. Hall Esqr.
Weybridge
Dec., 1873

I am very angry with you, & very grateful to you for writing to Sir James Paget about me. I must forgive you, *but please not to do it again*.

Indeed, you suppose me to be far worse than I am—You will make me ill if you frighten me. I have written, however, to Sir William Jenner to make an appointment for Tuesday.

I will come to you on Tuesday at 4, and will give you the communion on Wednesday. ...

321 Torquay
Jan. 4 [1874?]

... Will you give me some criticisms on the 'Republic'? I shall be at work upon that next Term. It is, of course, the greatest of Plato's works, & affords the greatest opportunity for modern applications of all sorts. You may show all your political feelings in commenting on the Republic. Have I not attacked Mr. Gladstone in several places?

I see that you hate to be reproved, my dear lady, and I am not going to reprove you any more. It is like pouring cold water upon red hot iron, & makes a terrible hissing. But you are mistaken if you suppose that I encourage G. Eliot. Have I not asked her to my house, & gone to see her, with the view of urging her to work at higher things, which she appears willing to do. She talks of writing a moral Philosophy, & told a friend of mine that she would like to write something specially for women, but she felt that there were certain parts of her own life which disqualified her. Only, I think that ... you ought not to be so much exasperated against her, for she has many troubles & is the only woman in this generation who can do much, besides yourself. ...

---

¹ *AC* ii. 108 record a meeting with Disraeli at Woburn, but give no date.

322
Inglewood
Torquay
Jan. 7, 1874.

I am very much grieved to hear of what has happened to you.[1] It is a great breaking up of family ties. I am as much surprized as you are—I certainly thought your father ... would last ten years longer. He was a fine old gentleman, full of liberal feelings, though he could not have been made to walk either in my ways or in yours. He simply would not have understood what we were doing or thought we were doing.

It is not unhappy for him to be taken as he has been. If you had had last words with him he would have had suffering & the pain of parting from you; though the regret is natural, I think it is better for you all as it is....

Do you observe that Lady Elcho has lost her 2nd son?[2] She said to me a few weeks ago, "whatever was the result, she was glad that he had volunteered".

323
Inglewood Torquay
Jan 8, 1874

... Your father was very proud & pleased about your work—though he did not understand it. I told him once that to have a daughter who would keep alive his name was better than to have many sons. He was greatly taken by this. And no doubt many persons will ask & talk about him, because he was your father.

It is painful (as I suppose that Christ found) that when a person undertakes an extraordinary work the family can do so little for them. The family is meant for ordinary life—Yet there may none the less be a deep affection & regard among its members....

324
Penzance
Jan. 15, 1874.

... You have had a heavy week of sorrow & suffering. The loss of a father or mother makes such a change in life. There is no longer a home, in the sense in which there used to be, & the survivors feel very lonely & isolated.

Yet you had long ago given up home for the good of others, & may now, as you have done, make a home everywhere where there is suffering to be relieved. People who live as you have done enter into a sort of larger family of which they become members.

Your father & mother, excellent people as they were, were not in the least

---

[1] FN's father died on 5 Jan. 1874 at Embley Park.
[2] Alfred Walter Charteris (1847–73), died at sea while returning from the Ashanti war. For the first son see above, No. 238, n. 2.

capable of aiding you in your work. This has been a matter of pain probably both to you & them, but it was unavoidable & therefore is only to be regretted because it was unavoidable.

325   not paralysis but the Railway
Address Oxford Jan. 21 [1874]

I have just finished my tour with Swinburne, & am on my way to Bristol, where I am going to stir up the question of a University College....[1]

S. behaved very well & showed no inclination to drink. The worst of him is that his moral nature is swallowed up in vanity & literature. But he is very considerate & affectionate.

We went to Penzance, then Land's End, the Lizard & Tintagel. By far the finest of the places which we saw is the Lizard. I never saw anything of the kind as fine as the huge Atlantic waves, with the sun glimmering through the tops of them, in a place called Kynance Cove.

... I have finished H. Spencer's 'First Principles'.[2] They are a strange mixture of the truisms of physics with metaphysics, & with some additional confusion of his own. They might be described as Sir W. Hamilton[3] padded with Physics.... Nevertheless, as the book is written clearly & systematically, it will probably have a great influence among persons who have had no metaphysical training, & do not perceive that so far as it differs from the ordinary inductive philosophy, it is a mass of assumptions & inconsistencies.

326   Oxford Jan. 25, 1874

... I have just had with me an ingenuous youth, Iwakura, the son of the Prime Minister of Japan, who has become an undergraduate of Balliol College. He seems very good & industrious, & rather above the average in intelligence. I hope that we shall succeed with him better than with the Siamese.[1] He tells me that his father was for several years in prison before he became Prime Minister.

[1] A proposal for a college of Science was made by Gilbert Elliot, the Dean of Bristol, and John Percival, Headmaster of Clifton College, who appealed to the colleges in Oxford for support. The support offered by Balliol and New Colleges (see above, p. xxvii) was conditional upon the Arts being included with the Sciences, and the college being open to women as well as men. The scheme was launched at a public meeting on 11 June 1874, with an appeal for £25,000, and the new college opened in Oct. 1876. J. G. Macqueen and S. W. Taylor (eds.), *University and Community, Essays to Mark the Centenary of the Founding of University College, Bristol* (1976), pp. 1–2.

[2] H. Spencer, *First Principles* (1862).

[3] Sir William Hamilton, *Lectures on Metaphysics and Logic*, ed. H. L. Mansel and J. Veitch (4 vols., Edinburgh, 1859–60).

---

[1] Bhanuwongsee.

This dissolution appears to me a move of despair. To go to the country without a principle will be the ruin of the Liberal party....²

327 Ball. Coll.
Feb. 5, 1874

...You are very good to offer me 100£ towards the new Hall.¹ I will accept it & shall be proud to put your name in the Subscription List. I shall pray for you (whether you give anything or not) in another sense from that in which I pray for the Duke of Bedford.² No one gives me 500£, we drop from 1000£ to 100£. The M. of Westminster³ is deterred by 'motives of economy' from sending me a reply until after Easter. Yet, with one strange exception (that of an old friend who is more deeply indebted to me than to almost anybody & who is very rich),⁴ the business of collecting subscriptions has been a very pleasant one....

It gives me pleasure to hear what you say of your mother—It is just what one would wish her last days on earth to be.... So the real mind clears up when the mechanical powers are beginning to pass away. Is this 'the better thing' which we may hope for as age grows upon us?...

328 Oxford March 4, 1874

...My schemes here seem to prosper; the Bristol scheme and the building of the Hall....

Goldwin Smith & Fawcett have been staying with me; also Sir Louis Mallet, whom I like. I tried to persuade G.S. to stay in this country, and I think that I almost persuaded him, if he was not persuaded before. He will probably take up the Education question & the disestablishment of the Church—though in a different sense from the Dissenters. Is it not clear that the Church will never be reformed without the co-operation of the Dissenters? They are a great organised political body already, whereas reformers within the Church are snuffed out before they come into existence. I have been urging this on G.S., & he seems to see that disestablishment, 'pur et simple', is nonsense. I should like to talk about this to you some day. He seems to me the only man at all likely to effect the required change in the Dissenting tactics.

I am very much pleased with my Japanese student¹—He is remarkably sagacious & intelligent. He tells me that the Japanese have lost their religion, &

---

² The Conservatives were returned with a majority of 83 in Great Britain, and of not less than 48 in the United Kingdom.

¹ Designed by Alfred Waterhouse, ready for use in Oct. 1876, and formally opened with a banquet on 16 Jan. 1877: *AC* ii. 102–3.
² The ninth Duke.
³ Hugh Lupus Grosvenor, first Duke of Westminster.
⁴ Not identified.

¹ Tomatsume Iwakura.

he is very anxious to know whether morality can exist without religion. He says that he talks about these matters with his father, the Prime Minister of Japan.² I enclose a paper which he brought me this morning which appears to me very remarkable.

The Great Tychoon³ & the little Tychoon have come to an agreement that the little Tychoon is to go on reading until Christmas. The little Tychoon was greatly excited about the matter, more than I ever saw him before, & has carried his point with his father. I am very anxious that this should turn out well.

329 Oxford
March 11 [1874]

... The Japanese movement is the most interesting thing going on in the world at present. My Japanese appears to be a most excellent & intelligent youth.¹

You have got an Under Secretary at War after your own heart.² I congratulate you & suspect that you had something to do with the appointment.

From what I hear from Hoare,³ I should think that he was a good fellow & well-gifted by nature, but undisciplined & quite unused to business. Will you train him. ...

330 Ball. Coll. March 23, 1874

... I enclose a very interesting letter of my friend, Arthur Hobhouse. He does not take the same view of the posibilities of India which you or I do, & he will not allow me to fire his imagination, as I endeavour to do with all my friends who get into high positions. Yet it is interesting to see how an able & conscientious man looks at things from the other side. The supineness of the natives is, I suppose, one of the difficult elements upon which we must reckon in all schemes for public works: also the half barbarism of vast tracts.

My old acquaintance, the B. of Manchester,¹ has made a mistake of feeling: I do not imagine that we do much towards relieving India by sending subscriptions, but we relieve ourselves. A subscription is an Englishman's mode of showing that he takes an interest in the subject. The conventional modes of raising money in charity (including appeals to the day of judgment) are very degrading, but people have become used to them & they seem to be a necessity. ...

---

² Tomomi Iwakura.   ³ Tycoon, i.e. great lord or prince.

¹ Tomatsume Iwakura.   ² G. R. C. Herbert.
³ Hamilton-Hoare.

---

¹ Fraser.

331   Westminster Arms Hotel,
                                                   West Malvern April 4, 1874

I am here playing at solitude, which I have enjoyed for 5 days, only interrupted by a call from another "Head of a house"¹ who appeared this morning. Will you not bestow a letter upon me? I go to bed early & work only 3 hours a day & obey the God Jenner in all matters of diet....

I have been reading Schleiermacher & Grote on the 'Republic'² with much dissatisfaction. Schleiermacher was the first who made a way in this country, & therefore we must not complain of him. But Grote appears to me utterly mistaken & misguided. He takes up the lowest level of philosophy which he can find (though he was far from being a bad or mean minded man himself), and applies this to Plato. He laboriously brings together far fetched contradictions from different parts of Plato's works, not knowing that Ancient philosophers never are or could be consistent. He is almost always paradoxical, even in defending Plato. In a word, he has no criticism & no imagination, though he has thought & read about a great number of subjects.

I feel that this book, which has been called the life of Mr. & Mrs. Grote,³ does him no justice. There were traits in his character that neither she nor Mr. Bain⁴ ever appreciated. He was the most ideal sort of man I have known, & yet his philosophy & his power of seeing the truth (through some accident of education—James Mill & the like) were as narrow as they could be. He was the reverse of clear-headed. But if he were truly described, no one would be pleased, as indeed is the case in all biographies.

Your old friend Lady Augusta⁵ is taking to your department of business. She has taken a house for nurses & is going, I believe, to nurse the Westminster Hospital—I have a very great respect & regard for her. She has lived about a court without becoming worldly; & she has got over her family difficulties & thoroughly maintained her position. Very few persons have so much strength & kindness combined.

The air of this place is charming. Will you not come & try it. I do not think that you can be very happy in a house which is no longer your own: although, occupied as you are, you have other things to think about. It is one of the greatest of women's wrongs that they do not succeed to estates....

---

¹ i.e. Iwakura's father.
² Schleiermacher's edition of *The Republic* was published in 1828, and Grote's *Plato and the Other Companions of Socrates* in 1865.
³ Harriet Grote, *The Personal Life of George Grote* (1873).
⁴ Alexander Bain assisted G. C. Robertson in editing Grote's *Aristotle* (1872), and Grote's *Minor Works* (1873).
⁵ Lady Augusta Stanley.

332

West Malvern
until Tuesday
[April, 1874]

Many thanks for two parcels of notes on the 'Republic'. It is not every one who has the advantage of being criticized by the Goddess Athene.

... But will you not let poor Middlemarch alone. She has gone wrong, not only in the literary way, but I have a respect & regard for her. And, moreover, she has more of the spirit which you want to introduce into literature than any one else in the present day. Let her be at peace: this is my request προσευχόμενος τῇ θεᾷ.[1]

I am not yet tired of solitude and am inclined to think that my present way of living alone is the best chance I have of doing anything. At Oxford there is no rest, & time is frittered away in a succession of interruptions....

333

Address
W. Malvern
April 27 [1874]

I ought to have acknowledged your valuable envelopes better than by 'two scampit Duds'. A thousand thanks for them....

I hope that I may make the Introduction the best thing that I have written—But I cannot tell. I greatly wish to satisfy you with my work....

Though you are not *always* right I am surprised at the manner in which you catch the Spirit of Plato....

Goldwin Smith came to dine with me 'tête à tête' last night. He has changed his mind about the Disestablishment of the Church, & he thinks that the Dissenters are beginning to change their minds also. His programme is: Repeal the Act of Uniformity—make Churches, Cathedrals, Schools &c. National property & allow the Parish or District to determine whether they will be Church or Dissent. He trusts to ritualism within & Dissent without the Church to accomplish this. He thinks that Dissenters should assert themselves in the Church & in legislation for the Church, as disestablishment has failed—I quite agree in all this.

There is a dark shadow over his life—madness I think—he talks of leaving England, never to return. Yet no one could do so much in many ways....

---

[1] Praying to the goddess.

334

W. Malvern
April 30, 1874

I have read your pamphlet,[1] & am all for irrigation & drainage....

You know I have no means of forming an independent judgement on the subject & can only criticize in a very superficial manner. I take a great interest in everything which you do & that makes me sometimes rather provoking. Are you quite sure that Sir Arthur Cotton is not a splendid dreamer? I have told you what I have heard of Lord Napier before, & shall therefore not provoke you with that again.

I cannot be too grateful to you for criticizing Plato (whom I perceive you quote) at the same time you are engaged in writing a pamphlet. I have adopted nearly all your hints as far as I have gone (however many hints I might give you, my belief is that you would never adopt any of them).

Morier is in England & goes about among Ministers & Ex-ministers & retails their conversations to me (I am always struck with his ability). Would you like to hear some of them? Lord Salisbury said that 'the mistake of the late Ministry had been following instead of leading the nation'; and the nation 'wanted to be led'—(in this I entirely agree). Gladstone is convinced that the High Church Clergy are not sacerdotalists, with the exception of a small fraction: they and the whole religious world want to unite in defence of historical Christianity—i.e. what he assumes to be historical Christianity. M. is very much afraid of Bismarck & thinks that he had better go off the scene, for he is probably bent on renewing the war with France. He says that the battle with the Clergy has been so ill-managed that he will probably fail. He fancies that such a battle should be short & decisive, like the French War. His character is quite unsuited to the sort of warfare which is required....

335

W. Malvern
May 15, 1874

... The 'School & Children's Bible' is all sold, and Longmans want me to revise it.[1] I shall make some alterations, but unfortunately it is electrotyped....

336

W. Malvern
May 20 [1874]

... I was at Oxford on Sunday. Your friend Mr. Rathbone came to dine with me. I may almost say that he came on a special mission to me, which was this.

---

[1] *Life or Death in India. A Paper Read at the Meeting of the National Association for the Promotion of Social Science, Norwich, October 1873. With an Appendix on 'Life or Death by Irrigation'* (1874).

[1] A second, revised, edition came out in Dec. 1874, AC ii. 36.

He wanted me to try & influence Goldwin Smith to remain in England. He, Mr. Rathbone, being willing to provide or guarantee to him an income of 1000£ a year (this is private). I liked him: there is great sincerity & some originality in his enthusiasm, & he rather carried me away. He wants G.S. to settle in Liverpool & found a University there, & finally to become member for the Borough.

He did not seem to be aware, & I did not tell him, that G.S. is not altogether right in his mind. Nevertheless, he is a great instrument & has many noble qualities & might be of much use in politics & Education at this time. I shall do what I can to assist Mr. Rathbone's plans.

337   Address Oxford
W. Malvern May 23, 1874

... I cannot thank you sufficiently for your help in the Plato. You are a first-rate Critic & you keep me up to a higher standard. I wish that I could [do] anything for you in return.

Some years ago you proposed to me that I should edit, what you called the 'Stuff'.[1] I was afraid that in the form in which they were written they were too unconnected, & might perhaps have seemed personal to your own family. This made me decline. But if you like to leave these or other papers for me to *select from* & arrange, if I outlive you, or would give them to me to arrange during your life time, I would do so with the greatest pleasure. There is always in your writings much that is original & of great value, but it is often not written in a manner suited for the Public & might lead to misconception. . . .

338   Ball. Coll.
May 29 [1874]

Will you, as you kindly proposed, arrange for me the last week of Christ's life?

I find that considerable alterations can be made, as the electrotypes are in pages, though I may very probably get the whole of that particular sheet reprinted.

For two reasons I rather wish that I had not drifted into doing this children's Bible. 1st, because it has taken up a great deal of your time (I am quite touched when I look upon the pages & pages which you wrote about it for me). 2nd, because I have not been able to give you any satisfaction about it, though it would have been far worse if I had not had your help. . . .

I sent you Swinburne's 'Bothwell'.[1] It is quite intelligible and it is free from

[1] See above, No. 1, n. 1.

[1] 'Bothwell, Act One', an early version, was privately printed in 1871, and *Bothwell* was published in 1874.

licentiousness. In parts I think it very striking & powerful though I fear that it does not come up to your ideal of the poetry which is only to do good. Still, it is something if he is kept from doing harm. I find him very affectionate & grateful, though I fear we shall have a deadly quarrel if he ever reads a passage which you induced me to insert in the Introduction to the 'Gorgias'.² He has gone on better during the last 4 months.

FN to BJ [*copy*]¹

339 35 South Street, Park Lane W.
June 13, 1874

I thank God, I thank God, who has given Irrigation the victory: in time, we may trust, to prevent more disastrous periodical famines: yet more to prevent a chronic state of half-starvation.

But for this we must yet set our hand to the plough & strike at the root of the Zemindary evil.² May God hasten his work.

I had had a hint of what was about to happen: but had no idea that a great Minister was going to nail his colours to the mast, or rather pass the Rubicon, in such a declaration to the House of Lords.³

Only let him *wisely* go on with his work, the work for one fifth of the human race. And let the Ho: of C. pass the Bill.

340 Ball. Coll.
June 14, 1874.

I see that you have a ray of comfort, for which I am truly thankful, & am most grateful to you for sending me the telegram. I rejoice with you.

Lord Salisbury must now prove to people that the money will not be wasted, which in Indian engineering it is very difficult to avoid. The mere mention of such a sum as 4,000,000£ will set the busy brains of thousands in a fever of speculation. . . .

---

² 'Modern poetry is often a sort of plaything . . . in which without any serious purpose, the poet just lends wings to his fancy and exhibits his gifts of language and metre.' *Dialogues of Plato* (5 vols., 1875), iii. 311.

---

¹ BL Add. MS 45785 fo. 44.
² The zemindar was the tax-collector rather than (as commentators were inclined to suppose) the landlord.
³ On 9 June 1874 Salisbury announced a proposed alteration 'in the constitution of the Council of the Governor General of India by appointing to it a Member of Council for Public Works'. *PD*, ccxix. 1262–3.

341

Malvern
July 5, 1874

Like a ghost you don't speak unless you are spoken to—you don't write unless you are written to, & not without the hope of getting an answer I write you a few lines. I should like to hear what you are doing & how you are. I have just sent off the last packet of the 'Children's' Bible to Longmans. I have followed your arrangement of the last week of Christ's life, except that I have not made the days & portions of days so precise. For I hardly think that we can determine this. There are several other changes for which I am indebted to you (though I despair of you ever thinking this, or any other book of mine, good enough to give your nurses or patients). Many thanks to you for this & many other helps: notwithstanding, I only expect you to 'beat me'.

Do you know (but perhaps I may displease you by saying this) I formed a very high opinion of Lord Lansdowne? His house is conducted admirably, both by him & his wife, & he is always ready for conversation on important subjects. I was very much struck with his knowledge of public affairs & his good judgement about them. There is a very uncommon maturity about him, & although he will never be a great Liberal he will always be an able & eminent statesman, possibly Prime Minister. I was also greatly pleased by their kindness & affection for me. But, perhaps, a wise lady like you may deduct a proportion from my previous eulogy of them. The manners of both of them are charming for their simplicity; he appears to me to have a great gift of expressing himself. . . .

We (that is to say I and some relations of theirs) are deeply grieved by the death of Lady Amberley & her poor little Rachel:[1] she had strange opinions, but she was greatly to be respected. She was a true believer in the Gospel according to J. S. Mill, which is far better than no Gospel at all. During the last four or five years she had carried out a regular plan of study with her husband & was greatly the better for it. I saw her last about a year ago: I am grieved to think that I shall never see her again.

I am wonderfully better for the air of this place. I obey the God Jenner & work between 3 & 4 hours a day. . . .

[*Postscript*]

. . . I began a new book today. I should be curious to know what you think of the Revd. Hegel Green's book,[2] which appears to me a remarkable performance, indicating great power.

---

[1] Lady Amberley died of diphtheria on 28 June, followed a few days later by Rachel. B. and P. Russell, *The Amberley Papers* (2 vols., 1937), ii, Chap. XIX.

[2] See above, No. 310, n. 4.

342 [August 1874]

... I wish you would contrive to fraternize with Fawcett. He is honest & impressible, & he is likely to be the most influential voice in the English H. of Commons raised about India in the next few years.

343 [August 1874?]

I think that a note should be: 1. an explanation, 2. a confirmation or quotation from authority which cannot be conveniently brought into the Text. Notes should be few: they generally arise out of some defect in the power of expression. The Ancients had no notes. If they are used they should be α) subordinate & β) not rhetorical.

References are perhaps best placed at the bottom of the page, but these are not notes. ...

344 Inglewood
Torquay Aug. 11 [1874]

I take a great interest about your Ryots[1] & will do all that I can to help you.

... You have a great deal of humour (I often laugh at things which you say in your letters), but it should be more continuous & connected. Humour is a great help in all writing but you must create an atmosphere in which it is appropriate.

Now you are not angry, I know, & therefore I shall go on & make some more criticisms—You & I have given up 'compliments' & we are going really to help each other.

The style of this pamphlet should be perfect—I have always thought that you would write capitally, if you would take more pains with the literary part of the work. The style is too jerky & impulsive, though I think it is logical & effective. You must avoid faults of taste & exaggeration. The more moderate any statement is, the stronger it is. Real strength lies in paragraphs, in pages, in the whole, not in single sentences. The force should appear to flow irresistibly from the facts & reasonings.

'What does the man mean by talking to me about style, when I am thinking only of the sufferings & oppression of 100,000,000 of Ryots?' Yes, but if you want to make the English people think about the Ryots you must be careful of the least indiscretion or exaggeration—you must make 'style' a duty—and then your book will last & somebody reading the book for the style will perhaps apply the meaning & nobody will poohpooh you. 'But can a person change their style as you suggest?' I think that any one who is fulfilled with a subject & has original force of mind can by some degree of labour write indefinitely well.

[1] Indian peasants.

You should have examples & authorities for everything which you say. I would not 'puff' Lord Salisbury & Sir George Campbell. In the first place, these men, if they are worth anything, do not like it themselves, & (2) it makes people reflect that 'this is a woman's writing'....

There are some facts which I should like to see stated. How far does the permanent settlement extend? And what is the state of other parts of India? What is the number of Zemindars,[2] & extent of acres owned by them? What of the Ryots, and what the size of their patches?

You know, I dare say, that Mill has written upon turning the Ryots into landed proprietors, I think in his 'Political Economy'.[3]

Might not something be said of the example of Prussia? . . .

of Japan?

The best pleading that I know, of the cause of a whole people, is the 'Drapier's letters'.[4] I will tell my 'fidus Achates'[5] to send you the volume of Swift which contains it.

345
address at Professor Campbell's
St. Andrews
Aug. 25, 1874
until Sep. 10

... I hope that the pamphlet will expand into a book. I am strongly against your writing hastily upon so large & important a subject. It is a positive duty, if you take up the question at all, to make the book as good as you can: and give the remedies....

346
In a railway
Sept. 25 [1874]

... The word which you & the printers could not read was 'po*m*pions'. *m*. Carlyle describes the negroes luxuriating 'up to their knees in pompions'.[1]

I suppose that one of the great Indian subjects which I did not talk of in the papers which I sent you, is coolie Emigration (excuse shaky writing)—labour wanted in the Western World—labour a drug in the East. The East to be civilized, partly by the west going to it partly by its going to the West. A black footman, if you contemplate him, if not a very magnificent is a very real product of civilization. Think of him quietly standing behind his master's chair, & of his grandfather a savage in Dahomey. This always seems to me instructive. It

---

[2] See above, No. 339, FN to BJ, n. 2.

[3] J. S. Mill, *Principles of Political Economy*, 1865 edn., Bk. II, Chap. IX, Sect. 4 'Ryot tenancy of India'. Mill approved his father's suggestion that the cultivators ought to be turned into owners.

[4] Jonathan Swift, *The Drapier's Letters* (1724).

[5] Matthew Knight.

---

[1] Not identified.

shows what can be done by individual European influence. And the Hindu is probably not less amenable to such influence.

Caste seems to me a terrible curse of India. I know that Mr. Mill & others would say that it was necessary for the organization of the country. It has overlived itself 2000 years, & the Hindus are in a far worse position than they were with regard to it in the time of Buddha. It is the way of everything in India, to last too long & overlive itself. Nothing can be worse than that, out of a population of 150,000,000, not more than one or two millions are, or ever can be, the respectable classes & that those should be wrapt up in an ideal pride & disdain of their fellow men who are not of the same class with them.

I have been spending a week with your cousin, Mrs. A. C. Sellar, in Morven where we had the benefit of V. Smith's yacht. The Sound of Mull, the Loch Linnhe & Loch Etive appear to me the most beautiful scenes which I ever saw, except the Lake of Como....

347 [6–9? October? 1874 *at Lea Hurst?*]

I have read Sir L. Mallet's paper....

I think that we must begin with what he calls "*imperial considerations*" viz., the staring fact that 50 or 60,000,000£ a year must be ground out of the poor people (poor & some rich) of India 1. for the maintenance of the government: 2 for the improvement of the people themselves. It is a hard truth, which we must look in the face, that they cannot have improved "standards of comfort" until this is supplied.

... No where so much as in India do you feel the truth of Adam Smith's text, "All taxation is an evil".[1] And no where do you need taxation so much, for more things have to be done in India by the government than anywhere else....

You must, with the assistance of others, create a public opinion about India in England....

[*Postscript omitted*]

348 Oxford
Oct. 13 [1874]

I send you ... Maine's 'Village Communities',[1] which appears to me to be a very good book.

---

[1] Even if Adam Smith did ever say this, it is a travesty of his views on taxation expressed in *The Wealth of Nations*, Bk. V, Chap. 2, where he accepts the desirability of raising taxes to defray 'the expense of defending the society and supporting the dignity of the chief magistrate'. Smith's interest lay in determining how the different methods of imposing taxation bore upon the various classes of society.

[1] Sir Henry Maine, *Village Communities in the East and West* (1871).

[*Postscript*]

I am up to the knees, not in 'pompions' but in bricks & mortar.

I have looked in vain for pompions in 'Past & Present'. There are many kindred sentiments but not that precise expression, which nevertheless I did not coin. . . .

349

Malvern until Thursday afternoon
afterwards
Ball. Coll.
Oct 27, 1874

My dear Cassandra

Are you really 'Cassandra', as I suspect when I see the title of Mr. Grant Duff's article in the 'Contemporary Review'?[1] I thought that Cassandra prophesied what was true but that nobody believed her. I am afraid that he may give you the labour of preparing an answer.

I have spoken to the Japanese, Iwakura, who will do what we want. He says that all the land of Japan now belongs to the Government, who let it out at a low rate to the peasants—the Daimios[2] receiving for the Government a tenth of their incomes in money. He will write an account of it for you, but says that he wishes to defer doing so until he can consult a friend of his who is coming to stay with him about the middle of next month & who perfectly understands the whole subject.

I cannot find the copy of Mr. Morier's report,[3] but I will write to him in a day or two & get another.

I was very successful with my College meeting. The fellows behaved excellently—they actually gave up the proceeds of a lease which has just been granted, which would have raised their incomes about 55£ a year each.[4] I have also got rid of the Anglo-Saxon student. . . .[5]

Have you returned to London? If so, I would endeavour to look in upon you for a few minutes on Saturday, when I have to attend a School Delegacy meeting[6] at the Langham Hotel.

Every body talks in an ominous way about the Church: more than I ever

---

[1] Three articles, 'Rocks ahead; or the Warnings of Cassandra', by W. R. Greg appeared in the *Contemporary Review* in May, June, and August. Cassandra's propositions were that (1) the working classes would achieve political supremacy, (2) the industrial power of Britain would decline, and (3) the intelligence of the country would be divorced from its religion. The articles were attacked by Arthur Arnold and by Lord Lyttelton in the September issue, and Greg replied in November.

[2] Feudal nobles.

[3] 'Agrarian Legislation of Prussia During the Present Century', in *Systems of Land Tenure in Various Countries. A Series of Essays Published Under the Sanction of the Cobden Club* (1870).

[4] CM, 15 Oct. 1874, 'That interest on £950 the price of the homestead sold at Benton now in the hands of the Copyhold Commissioners be paid to Domus at the rate of 4 p.c. . . . That the Rent received under the new lease of the Rood Lane Houses be allocated to Domus.'

[5] Henry Sweet.

[6] The Joint Oxford and Cambridge Schools Examining Board was established in 1873.

remember before. But the Bishops will be slow to be disestablished & the Puseyites hard to move out of the Church, which they have no intention of quitting unless they are forced. The age of enthusiasm has passed away with them [and] they are perfectly aware of the solid advantages of a good position. Some day I should like to make a short scheme of Church Reform & put it into people's heads—Abolition of Subscription—Option in the use of the Liturgy—intercommunion with the Protestant Dissenters—giving the right of using Church yards & pulpits, would be my programme.

350

Oxford
Nov. 16, 1874

Are you still at Lea Hirst? . . . It troubles me that in addition to your public work you should have this private care of watching over your mother. . . .

There is always a good deal of difficulty in reconciling public & private life. The family like to share in the fame & success & are really pleased at it. But they do not want to take part in the sacrifices necessary, and do not understand them. They have no idea of the effort required, and are shocked at any departure from the ways of the world. They are pleased to talk about the doings of a distinguished relative & do not see that they ought not to talk about them. I have often thought that you have had a great deal to bear in this way: I deeply sympathise with that though my trouble has been more, I think, in the want of persons about me who cared for what I was trying to do. And you have always shown such a deep & warm interest in it. I am afraid that sort of estrangement of which I was speaking (which I have not felt) is generally the lot of persons who choose an extraordinary life in this ordinary world.

. . . Mr. Gladstone has been at Oxford: he makes no secret of his conversion to disestablishment. Neither did he when I met him about six years ago,[1] but then it became a secret again, which no friend of the Ministry was allowed to question.

. . . Do you see that we have elected Mr. Abbott a fellow? It was all owing to you giving him that chair. Never did you & I [do] a better piece of work. He is still paralytic but in other respects well, & an admirable Tutor. We have not succeeded so well with Harrison, who is a fine fellow but still in a very sad state; though very cheerful, he is too sensitive to get well. He is one of the Candidates for the Fellowship.

Do you know that I had an enormous letter from Lord Radstock this morning, saying that I looked very ill & decrepit (which I do not think to be true), and that I must prepare to meet God & believe in the Atonement & not trust to my own speculations. He is an old pupil of mine. He evidently could not resist writing to me—I cannot bear him any grudge for wishing my salvation, but his letter is very strange & unmannerly. . . .

[1] See above, No. 213.

351

Dec. 12, 1874

... Do not kill yourself, even to save the Bengalese from starvation....

I am going to Cambridge to fulfill an old engagement of staying with the Master of Trinity.[1] Would not Dr. Johnson have said, 'Sir, it is a great thing to stay with the Master of Trinity?...

352

Inglewood
Torquay
Dec. 25, 1874

I do not like to think of you passing Christmas alone & in trouble.

Will you not sometimes consider that you have done more good, & have been allowed to do more good, than any woman living?...

I do not like your going on with the book on the Ryots at present, for you are not equal to it, and I think that it must be rewritten to produce the right effect. You & I cannot be sure, either of our facts or of our remedies, from personal knowledge—the subject is a dangerous one, & both Lord Lawrence & Sir G. Campbell seem to me in their letters to counsel prudence & caution.

Do not be grieved, if, as you would say, God told you to write the book by the advice of Sir G. Campbell, & now by the same advice he tells you to put it aside for a time.

You have a great position at the India office at present & can do much with Lord Salisbury & other friends, but if your book were deemed rash or inaccurate, you would be discredited & your other books would be discredited, & you would lose influence.

If the book is to be published & read in India I should hang over every word with anxiety....[1]

[*Postscript omitted*]

353

W. Malvern
Jan. 9, 1875

I am greatly pleased & touched by your New Year's Gift (How good & kind of you to think of it). But I cannot accept it, at least not at present, for I am getting on very well with the Subscription (6000£ and I hope 4000 more. I find begging letter writing a very fascinating occupation & profitable. I have taken to it again this year; 3 letters per diem until the whole Balliol world is

---

[1] W. H. Thompson.

[1] 'The Zemindar, the Sun, and the Watering Pot as Affecting Life or Death in India' (privately printed in draft, pp. 195), was never finished. *Cook*, ii. 449.

canvassed)—and therefore I have burnt your draft, but I will ask for it again if I am in want.

'My dear soul', what are you doing? You are often in my thoughts but you never keep me informed of that. And sometimes I think what is, I fear, true, that I am of no use or service to you at all, & sometimes that I ought never to oppose you, but let you do exactly what you think best. This last is a condition of friendship almost impossible to me, who greatly wish that you should succeed in your undertakings....

I have got Swinburne here with me. He is not at all worse, but rather better than last year, though he has not got rid of his animalisms. He is very grateful & pleased to be here; also I have with me Kent, a youth of 18 & a sort of youthful Swinburne, who has been sent away from Harrow & other places for 'nonconformity'. He is a remarkable youth & I am trying to 'hook' him.

I told you about Green—the other day I had a remarkable letter from him saying that he had been long aware that he was incapable of fitting his pupils for the world & for the schools, & proposing to give up his Tutorship. I have partly accepted his resignation. He is to give up lecturing almost entirely, but to continue to assist in the management of the College. Some day I should like you to see his Hume.[1] He is more likely than any Englishman to found a school of philosophy, if he can get out of the fangs of Kant & Hegel.

Let me tell you that I am very well here: & for me, getting on very well with my work. I have written the draft of my essay on Hegel,[2] which did not take very long, for I found old thoughts readily came back to my mind. I see that I must not try to grasp so much of the world, but must make everything subordinate to writing. The time is short.

[*Postscript omitted*]

FN to BJ [*draft or copy of notes on BJ's Plato*][1]

354   [*early* 1875]

I don't want to hear what Hegel thinks of God: nor what you think about what Hegel thinks of God: but what you think of God.

I don't want to hear the philosophy of Hegel: (I know it already) but the philosophy of God.

I don't want to know your Criticism of what Hegel thought that God thinks (at that rate Philosophy would be nothing but what the 19th century thinks of what the 18th century thinks of what the 17th century thinks ... of what the 5th century before Christ thinks), but what *you* think that God thinks....

---

[1] See above, No. 310, n. 4.
[2] In the introduction to the Sophist of Plato. *AC* ii. 250.

---

[1] BL Add. MS 45785 fo. 75.

355 Balliol College
Feb. 7, 1875

You made me promise to write & tell you the result of my visit to Dr Jenner. He examined me with the Stethoscope, & in various ways, & came to the conclusion that I was quite 'sound, wind & limb'. And I agreed to come & see him once a year.

So now having a prospect of life for 15 years about, I must try & make a good use of it. First I must finish the Plato, which will be accomplished by about June 1st. Then I shall take two months entire holiday—after which I think that I had better go somewhere with my 'fidus Achates',[1] & write out my sketch of early Greek philosophy while it is in my mind & I have Plato familiar to me. Then I shall set to work on the 3 first Gospels. And beyond that, if my life is spared, I have always had a vision of writing on Moral Philosophy. I am afraid you will think me too ambitious; I mean to keep up my practice of going to Malvern.

Sir W. Jenner says that as you get older it is much more important not to overwork than to have many holidays....

[1] Matthew Knight.

CHAPTER 5

1875–1893

356

W. Malvern
Aug. 1 [1875]

My dear 'Queen of the Nurses'

Will your Highness condescend to tell me how you are & where you are?

I am settled here with a party of friends & pupils, Swinburne, Harrison &c., & the faithful Knight, for about a month. My holidays in Germany turned out rather unfortunately, for I found Morier ill & he got worse & was in fact in a very critical state.[1] He is now out of danger, but still confined to bed. I hardly know of any one who, if he were taken, would be a greater loss.

He talked to me about foreign politics. He seems to think that Bismarck is always plotting to engage France in war. He says, 'No country has been more improved by the war than—France; or more deteriorated than—Germany'.

I also saw Döllinger several times: he impressed me as a very honest & liberal man,[2] but his aims are unmeaning. He is not a prophet or teacher, but only a Professor of Ecclesiastical History whose historical conscience has been violated. He never gets beyond the Ecclesiastical circle. When I saw him two years ago he had great hopes from the Falck laws.[3] Now, he considers that they have spoilt his own movement. He too, begins to feel some sympathy with his persecuted brethren. Morier thinks the Falck laws not wrong in themselves, but in the brutal manner in which the Prussians carry them out. Döllinger thought that there would be no successful resistance to them; 'The Bishops said that the only hope was a war with France'. I repeated this to Morier who said that this was one of the inventions which Bismarck spread abroad....

357

Ashfield House
W. Malvern.
[August 1875]

... You have no idea how indolent I have grown. We talk nothing but literature here, especially Shakespear & the English poets, about whom Swinburne pours forth floods of knowledge, and Red Republicanism, in which some of the youths indulge.

---

[1] BJ had intended to join Morier for a tour in Italy, but Morier fell ill and BJ remained in Munich for much of July reading Euripides; *AC* ii. 68.

[2] Döllinger opposed the decrees of the Vatican Council of 1869-70, and was excommunicated in 1871.

[3] A. Falk, Prussian minister of public worship and instruction 1872-9, introduced a series of anti-Catholic measures which came to be known as the May laws.

358

Oxford
Oct. 24, 1875

... I am coming up to a meeting of the Delegacy for examining schools[1] on Saturday, when we are going to discuss a question about which I should like to talk to you—the examination of ladies schools. It appears to be very important, because if the scheme grows, as it has done with boys schools, it will materially affect the education of women.

I will send you tomorrow a small pamphlet which contains our examination for boys. The question which we have to consider is—how far this will require modification when applied to girls. The principle of the scheme is to leave the schools as far as possible—merely requiring that they shall offer a certain amount & quality of knowledge to be presented for examination. In the case of girls, music & drawing would have to be added to the subjects. ...

359

Endsleigh
Torquay
Dec. 31 [1875]

... You know that I wish you every good in the coming year. ... May not life be like the Sibyl's books[1]—the value always doubling of what remains? At any rate, what one does & is in life does not count by time.

I begin to agree with you & Morier more than I did about the imbecillity with which this country is governed—no vestige of a purpose or plan carried on through many years, but political accidents & speechifying, necessities of the H. of Commons, are the great principles. It is very different from Pitt or Peel, or even Lord Palmerston. When there is a war the state of things will appear. Only I feel, on the other side: 1st, that those who have the opportunity should work with the present to the utmost amid all discouragements. 2ndly, that all of us, & not only the political world, are to blame for not having supplied mankind with better thoughts & ideas.

I had a very satisfactory visit to Lord Lansdowne (don't suppose that I go to great houses merely to idle & eat & drink; though not exactly a propagandist, I always have an eye to 'business' of some kind)—Mr Lowe says that he will be the last Prime Minister, & I think that he may attain to something like that position. He has a great deal of knowledge, & seems to me the most 'impartial' of any young men whom I know; he really makes up his mind upon facts, & has everything in the way of manner & character to recommend him. His mind, like that of his brother,[2] is in politics. Whether he has sufficient force & imagination I am not certain, but he has very right ideas about things, & an

---

[1] See above, No. 349, n. 6.

[1] See above, No. 258, n. 5.
[2] Petty-Fitzmaurice.

ambition to be something more than Lord Granville, whom in some respects he resembles.

The Liberals seem to be as far as ever from having any plan, or from being united among themselves. The London School Board appears to me to have done the best work during the last 3 years.

360 [7 January 1876]

I am grieved to see that you have lost a friend, one of the best & truest you ever had.[1] His death must bring back many old recollections. Your father told me of his fetching you away from the Convent when you were ill,[2] & as he thought, saving your life.

I remember meeting him about 10 years ago at Hampstead, when I had a great deal of talk with him. He was one of the most satisfactory scholars I have ever known because he was a great deal more than a scholar, & besides his vast learning had a penetrating insight into human affairs. The last time I saw him was in June 1873 when he talked about Politics in a very interesting manner. It was not in his nature to show outside what he was inside, & hence he was less known than he deserved to be by the many, though always respected by the few.

In criticism, I should imagine from what I saw of him (we talked about the mysteries &c.), that he had the greatest of all critical faculties, the faculty of being right. You felt that what he said was weighty & true & based upon great knowledge.

So great & valuable men pass away. Are there others to take their place? (I remember once more about M. Mohl that he struck me as being entirely above the jealousy & personality of scholars, & condemned strongly a recent example of that sort of thing.) ...

361
Oxford
Address Ashfield House
W. Malvern
April 5, 1876

I will not forget M. Mohl's library, though I fear that I cannot be of any real use in the matter. The only chance for it at Oxford would be that the Bodleian should purchase it, or a part of it. But, as I unfortunately know, the Bodleian is so much involved at present that it is not likely to make a large purchase. Madame Mohl will probably have a catalogue printed. She had better send it, either to the Librarian of the Bodleian, or to me. I should think that America

[1] M. Mohl.
[2] From La Maison de la Providence in Paris in June/July 1853, WS, 114-15.

might offer a good opportunity for disposing of an Oriental Library. Things of this sort, if left to a chance sale, are apt to fair badly, & therefore I would suggest to Madame Mohl that she should have the Library valued, & offered at a moderate price to some of the principal Libraries in Europe.[1]

Since I saw you I have a cold & cough which I cannot shake off, but shall go to Malvern tomorrow in the hope of improving there.

The Caps & Gowns are in a flutter about the University Bill. Lord Salisbury has changed his original Bill very much, & we shall probably get still more changes out of him.[2] I hardly see with what intention his original Bill was introduced. He seems to have very little insight or purpose, & has a great power of saying mischievous things like that about Fellows of Colleges not being Christians, which are specially unbecoming in the Chancellor of the University.[3] He has some mistaken notion of making a reaction in favour of the Ch. of England at Oxford.[4] The time for this has past. In the matter of University Reform, the majority of the Bishops are more liberal than he is, & voted against him.[5]

I have read 3 lives lately which are very interesting—Wm. Godwin, Miss Caroline Herschell & Mrs Fletcher, & which I commend to your notice.[6] Miss Herschell's is a very fine, feminine life & you forgive (or at least I do), when at 90 years of age, she no longer likes scientific discoveries because they are not made by her brother.

362   address W. Malvern
Dec. 31, 1876

I send you my best wishes on New Year's day. And best wishes to you means best wishes for your work—that in the next year you may be more

---

[1] Mohl's library was catalogued (1798 items), and advertised for sale in Paris from 15–23 May 1876.

[2] There was much dissatisfaction in the 1860s and '70s with the comparative wealth of the colleges and the poverty of the University. Following up the Duke of Cleveland's Commission of inquiry, Salisbury prepared to introduce an executive Commission to overhaul the finances of the colleges. He proposed to include among the Commissioners Selborne, and Burgon, the Dean of Chichester. Burgon had been vicar of the University Church, and had encouraged Scott to think himself ill-used by BJ. When the Commission was finally appointed, in 1877, Burgon, whose name had been ill received, was omitted.

[3] The Bishop of Oxford had 'told their Lordships . . . that there were Colleges in which some of the Fellows were not Christians. He [Lord Salisbury] . . . was afraid that was an undoubted fact.' *PD*, ccxxviii. 942, 31 Mar. 1876.

[4] Salisbury was suspected of wanting to reintroduce religious tests by insisting upon the retention of clerical Fellowships: 'If you had a certain element of clerical Fellowships in Colleges, you had security for a certain element of Christian government'; ibid.

[5] On 31 Mar. 1876, when the Earl of Airlie moved an amendment in order to extinguish Statutes requiring Heads of colleges to be members of the Church of England, Bangor, Chichester, Ely and Rochester voted with Salisbury, and Canterbury, Chester, Exeter, London, Oxford, and St Asaph with Airlie.

[6] C. Kegan Paul, *William Godwin, His Friends and Contemporaries, with Portraits* (2 vols., 1876); *Memoir and Correspondence of Caroline Herschel* (1876); *Autobiography of Mrs [Eliza] Fletcher, of Edinburgh, with Selections from her Letters and other Family Memorials. Compiled and Arranged by the Survivor of the Family [M.R., i.e. Lady Richardson]* 1st edn. (1874); 2nd edn. (1875).

successful than in the last, & in every year more than in the year preceding—that as life begins to fade away from you & me, we may both of us see the greater part, if not all, of our designs completed. This is a wish for myself as well as for you. I would not have you suppose that you have nothing to hope for in life. The last ten years are the best in experience, in freedom from care, in dispassionateness. I mean to 'die in harness' as I think that you do.

I have been thinking about your professorship.[1] What sort of an endowment do you propose? I should not advise you to give more than £400 a year: but then for this you would hardly expect to have an eminent man, if you required him to reside. I should therefore give up the condition of residence, and only require him to give a certain number of lectures, say 24, & to reside for a month in the year only. It would be a great advantage to the subject of the chair if an annual prize of fifty pounds could be given on some part of the subject.

The sort of person whom you might hope to get for such a chair would be a young physician. It is worth considering whether you would not make it terminable at the end of ten or seven years ... also whether you would confine the professorship to social physics, which I suppose to mean reasoning from statistics about the health & social state of man: or include, as an alternative, hygiene & sanitary knowledge generally. I should imagine that there are many more persons capable of teaching the second than the first. At any rate, there should be a provision that the chair should not be filled up if no able candidate appears; or that some alternative subject be chosen. Another question is, in whom shall the appointment be vested? The electors should, I think, be a board of five or seven, partly consisting of experts & partly of officials—persons such as the V. Chancellor, the Presidents of the College of Physicians & of the Royal Society. This, after a great deal of discussion of the matter, seems to be thought in Oxford the best way of regulating these appointments.

When I come to London next, we will go over these points, if you are still of the same mind, & I will draw out a short scheme which you can put in your desk & consider.

Do not grieve about the interruption of your Indian work. I do not mean the sanitary part of it, but the 'Zemindary' part. I have sometimes doubted whether it was a good thing for you to undertake it. Shall I tell you why? Because I observed that Lord Lawrence & others whom we most respected seemed to discourage it; and partly because, as you once said to me, it is dangerous writing about things which we do not know of our own personal knowledge. That there is a great deal wrong in the relations of Zemindars and Ryots in Bengal I do not doubt, but is it safe for any one who is not really familiar with them, to try & alter them? ...

---

[1] See John Bibby, *Notes towards a History of Teaching Statistics* (1986).

363

address W. Malvern
Weston House,[1]
Shipston-on-Stour
Dec 29 [1877?]

... I am going to Malvern with a party of youths for 3 weeks on Tuesday. You said something about wanting to slip away from London and not knowing where to go for quiet. Will you not go & take possession of my house in Oxford for 3 weeks, & stay over for a few days, that I may have the pleasure of seeing you on my return? The house is thoroughly warm & comfortable, and you would have drawing room & bedroom on the same floor. No one will know of your being there. This would be a great pleasure & honour to me.

364

Private
Oxford
May 22, 1878

I said I would talk to Sir Louis Mallet about the land question & tell you the result. He has been to see me & I was greatly pleased with him; he is perfectly disinterested & public spirited, very unofficial, with considerable powers of reflection on Indian Politics. But he is too much "sicklied o'er with the pale cast of thought",[1] and requires constant encouragement, which you must give him. He has 'fallen upon evil times', & 'the stars in their courses fight against him':[2] that is to say the stupidity of old Indian officials, the constant changes of Secretaries for India, who at their best only understand a quarter of the subject, the double, treble, quadruple government &c., &c.

He seemed to think that an intelligent Governor General + an intelligent Secretary of State might do a great deal; the Duke of Argyle & Lord Lytton (with all their faults) most likely to do good in India. Complained of want of public opinion in England—no force to make things move. Could a knot of young men like the old Westminster Reviewers of 50 years ago be got together to write upon the subject, the interest of England might be drawn to India.

His imagination might be fired, I think, & he might be induced to devote his life to India. He is quite in earnest about the land question & acknowledges the enormous mistake of the permanent settlement in Bengal, though he does not see how it can be altered without a revolution.[3] Nevertheless he would

---

[1] Belonging to Camperdown.

[1] 'And thus the native hue of resolution / Is sicklied o'er with the pale cast of thought', *Hamlet*, III. i. 84-5.

[2] 'The stars in their courses fought against Sisera.' Judg. 5: 20.

[3] The 'permanent settlement' of the revenues raised from land in Bengal dated from 1793. The argument in favour was that if the Government levied a fixed (traditional) amount it did at least receive some

introduce a permanent settlement of a different kind into the rest of India. He is quite aware of the indebtedness of the people, & of the manner in which our laws have stereotyped a vicious state of society.

I did not tell him of our acquaintance & friendship. It is better that we should be like pickpockets in a crowd, not known to be confederates, as far as I may claim to take a humble interest in your work.

He wants to be told that in spite of obstructions, taking the world as it is (a very troublesome place) & in spite of 'official cretinism', he must work on, & in the course of ten or twenty years he may produce, amid many disappointments, great results. He should write & talk & unite people; he has the entrée of society & should make the most of it for his purpose.

I don't agree, as I can judge, in his views about Russia—he wants us to make a partnership with Russia in the management of the East, leaving the 'rougher work', i.e. the greater crimes to Russia. This is really a crusade against Mahometanism & involves (though he does not intend it) the holding down India by force. Now there are 200,000,000 of Mahomedans & there may be a much closer combination among them, if Christians unite against them, than there has ever been yet. They are not dead, they are not decayed, but capable of a good deal of life & fanaticism.

The Northcotes stayed with me a few days ago. They seemed confident of peace, & this now seems to be the prevailing tone. I don't think we could have had peace unless we had made ready for war; for Russia, if let alone, would have demanded more than this country would have granted.

Lady Northcote told me that Count Schouvaloff said to her, "I might as well try to dance on your Turkey carpet, as get a decision of any sort out of Lord Derby"....

365

W. Malvern
Aug. 3, 1878

I have read your article[1] with the greatest interest: I often think of you toiling year after year for those whom nobody else seriously regards, & wish you a blessing on your labours.

Shall I descend to a very small matter—the criticism of style? The article is not consecutive enough, & therefore does not produce the clear, strong impression which such facts should. I was much more struck with it on reading it a second time, but most persons will not read it a second time. It is an awful revelation.

revenue. The argument against was that the Government could not participate in any increase in the production of the land. Neither, in practice, did the ryot, who was not protected by the Government from the rapacity of the zemindar with whom the bargain to collect the taxes was made.

[1] 'The People of India', in the *Nineteenth Century* (Aug. 1878), pp. 193–221, beginning 'We do not care for the people of India', was prompted by the famine in Madras, and went on to consider the problems of (1) money-lending, (2) irrigation, and (3) local representative government.

No one will measure it by the style, but by the intensity of feeling & by the facts. Still, your writings would be more effective if more consecutive & more studiously moderate in form.

I shall not lose the opportunity of coming to see you at some time.

My belief is that there are no usury laws in England. They were abolished about 35 years ago,[2] partly on account of the fraud to which they gave rise, & partly because they tended to raise the rate of interest, when it could not be recovered by law. This is very likely right in a country like England, but not in India. Though what are to be the remedies when a people have got into the habit of borrowing, it is difficult to see.

. . . . But as I am not a lawyer I have asked Albert Dicey, who is quite trustworthy on such a matter, to write & answer your question.

I shall be here for more than a month at work upon Thucydides & Aristotle.[3]

366

address until Sat. inclusive
West Malvern
Aug. 18, 1879

I return you the papers which you kindly lent me to read, and congratulate you on the opening of the Godavery Canal.[1] It is astonishing to me how much you have learned about India for the love of God & man. I believe that there are numberless good things which would never have been done in India, if you had not given the impulse to them. . . .

When I come to you (if you are able to have me), I shall ask you some Sanitary questions for my young Indians. They want to know where they are to read about the subject, which is, I suppose a difficult matter to answer. I like them. Most of them are a high class of men, who go out with a great wish to do something for their country. The discouraging point is that the government are so changeable that I do not know how long the system of their coming to the Universities will last. Already they are allowed to go anywhere else. The lowering of the age from 21 to 19 was a most serious error. . . .[2]

---

[2] The Bank of England was freed from the usury laws in 1833, for bills of less than three months (3 and 4 William IV c. 98), and the laws were abolished in 1854 (17 and 18 Vict. c. 21).

[3] Thucydides appeared in 1881, Aristotle's *Politics* in 1886.

---

[1] Making more of the Godaveri river delta, Madras, available for the cultivation of rice.

[2] See above, p. xxx.

367   Address by return
                                                 Brechin Castle[1]
                                                 Brechin
                                                 afterwards Skelmorlie[2]
                                                 Wemyss Bay
                                                 N.B.
                                                 Sep. 14, 1879

... I have thought about your work often during the last fortnight. If I understand rightly you wished me to make suggestions about it. I have a hesitation about this, because as I get older I see that persons should be left to work chiefly in their own way....

It is probable you might do more, if you could keep more 'en rapport', not only with those who are favourable to irrigation, canals &c., but to all honest persons who have an interest in India. I include in the above category the Duke of Argyle, Mr. Fawcett, Mr. Grant Duff, Sir Bartle Frere, & probably Lord Lytton &c., as well as Lord Lawrence, Sir Louis Mallet, Sir George Campbell. I do not suppose that any of these men, (though seen from a certain point of view they may have more or less grave defects) are actuated by motives of personal interest....

If one allows the mind to decompose itself into sympathy & antipathy, one falls too much under the influence of those who sympathize with us. We form a high opinion of them & then when they cease to sympathize with us we become alienated from them.... Thus a great deal of friction is created: & there is a good deal of mental pain & disappointment in finding that people are not what we supposed. As we get older we ought to expect this, & know how to meet it. When we find fault with others we may sometimes remember that they too, find fault with us, especially if we are making any considerable effort to act upon the world. This seems to me the true knowledge of mankind.

I run on telling you my own thoughts chiefly about myself. There is another thing which often occurs to me: I have drudged too much in private, & have found in this the excuse for doing too little in public. The latter is a kind of effort which it is difficult to make, and one readily listens to the excuse: "Here is this & the other duty which must not be neglected." And yet the only way to fight a cause, if you are not a Parliamentary leader, is by careful writing; and this requires rest & leisure & thought. It seems to me that no two years of your life (except the time in the Crimea), have produced as great an effect, or done as much for the health and well-being of mankind, as your little book on nursing.[3] And no cares or pains that can be bestowed on writing is too great. You said to

---

[1] Seat of George, the thirteenth Earl of Dalhousie (1806–80).
[2] Probably staying at Skelmorlie Castle which was owned by John Graham (1797–1886) a great uncle of R. J. Graham.
[3] *Notes on Nursing* (1860).

me once that the feeling which you would have in clearing out a drain was that you were doing the will of God—May we not feel this also in turning a sentence, i.e. in writing well & clearly about some truth that will be for the good of mankind? . . .

368 Oxford
Oct. 17, 1879

I received some days ago . . . your kind present of Dr Parke's Practical Hygiene,[1] which I shall deposit in the Library. I have another copy which I shall give to one of my Indian Candidates.

I hope your mother is at peace, during what are probably the last weeks of her life. If there are some appearances to the contrary you know better than any one that such appearances are due to physical causes & should not unduly disturb us, although they are painful to witness. She is not the less in the hands of God, though there may be a difficulty to us in realizing this.

369 West Malvern
Dec 31, 1879

I cannot let the New Year begin without sending my best & kindest wishes for you & for your work. I can only desire that you should go on as you are doing, in your own way, lessening human suffering and speaking for those who cannot make their voices heard, with less of suffering to yourself, if this, as I fear, be not a necessary condition of the life which you have chosen.

There was a great deal of romantic feeling about you 23 years ago when you came home from the Crimea (I really believe that you might have become a Duchess if you had played your cards better). And now you work on in silence, & nobody knows how many lives are saved by your nurses in hospitals (you have introduced a new era in nursing); how many thousand soldiers, who would have fallen victims to bad air, bad water, bad drainage & ventilation, are now alive owing to your forethought & diligence; how many natives of India (they might be counted probably in hundreds of thousands) in this generation & in generations to come, have been preserved from famine & oppression & their load of debt, by the energy of a sick lady who can scarcely rise from her bed. The world does not know all this, or think about it—But I know it & often think about it. . . .

I think that the romance too, which is with the past, did a great deal of good: Like D^r· Pusey you are a Myth in your own life time. Do you know that there are thousands of girls about the ages of 18 to 23 named after you? As you once

---

[1] E. A. Parkes, *A Manual of Practical Hygiene Prepared Especially for Use in the Medical Services of the Army* (1864, and many subsequent editions).

said to me, 'the world has not been unkind': every body has heard of you, & has a sweet association connected with your name.

It is about 18 years since you first sent me the 'Stuff'¹ to read, and about 17 years since we first became friends. How can I thank you properly for all your kindness & sympathy—never failing—when you had so many other things to occupy your mind? I have not been able to do so much as you expected of me, & probably never shall be, though I do not give up ambition. But I have been too much distracted by many things, and not 'strong enough for the place'. I shall go on as quietly & industriously as I can. If I ever do much more, it will be chiefly owing to you: Your friendship has strengthened & helped me, & never been a source of the least pain or regret.

Farewell. May the later years of your life be clearer & happier & more useful than the earlier! If you will believe it, this may be so:

370 West Malvern
Aug. 7, 1880

You kindly invited me to write to you, as I used to do years ago from Tummel Bridge and other places. A letter from you was quite an event in those days, & would set me thinking for some time afterwards....

... now that the years begin to become fewer, may every year be twice as successful as the last. For there is in these latter years from 60–70 & from 70 to 80, an extraordinary power latent, if we only knew how to call it forth. Greater experience, fewer mistakes, less personal antagonism, a more comprehensive view of the world.

I asked Mr Morier, as you wished to know, 'what he thought of the South Africa federation'—He thinks it an absurd scheme.¹ He says that the essence of federation is some sort of equality among its members, but here all the elements are unlike—Cape Representative Institutions, Natal, Crown Colony. The Orange Free State hardly constituted, the Transvaal a conquered country: no such federation could work. There seems to me reason in this: nor would it have appeared very likely that the Cape would have joined such a heterogeneous body. Morier thinks that Foreign Politics are very critical: 'Any day we may be involved in a war with Turkey out of our sentimental or Quixotic interest in the frontier of Hellas. The Turks will probably support the Albanians underhand, as the Russians did in the Servian War. And then what are we to do? Albanian & Turk will be too strong for the Greeks, and we must send

¹ See above, No. 1, n. 1.

---

¹ In 1877 the British annexed the Transvaal. In 1880 Sir Bartle Frere, the High Commissioner was promoting a federation of the four white communities (Cape Colony, Natal, the Transvaal, and the Orange Free State). The proposals were overthrown by the delegates (Kruger and Joubert) of the Transvaal independence committee. Frere was recalled, but the Transvaal was neither dis-annexed, nor given self-government, and in December the Boers rebelled.

soldiers to support them. But is this Government capable of conducting such a war? That is the way in which a very able man regards the matter.

I am staying at W. Malvern with the faithful Mr. Forbes and a succession of young Indians and one or two other friends—I began these vacation parties with Mr Morier in 1848 and, do you know, I think that it is the most successful thing that I have done & the most useful to the College....

371
            address Cambridge Terrace
            until Sat.
            afterwards Oxford
            July 21 [1881]

... I am invited to the D[ean] of Westminster's funeral.[1] I cannot bear to think of him as gone. He was my oldest friend, & I had no better. He had many more virtues than you sometimes imagine. But it was difficult for people to understand him. He was more of a child & of a genius in one than the world commonly supposes. He was perfectly simple yet very impressible by scenes & circumstances. He was impressed in this way by the court, yet not at all a courtier. I will tell you about him when we meet.

372
            address West Malvern[1]
            March 29, 1882

Will you kindly see Lady Tavistock? She wishes greatly to see you, but thought it 'not possible'. She is not likely to waste your time or to 'gossip' about you.

I gather, though she never told me so, that for some reason or other she is not happy at home. The Duke & Duchess of Bedford were opposed to the marriage & my friend, 'the lesser Tychoon',[2] wanted to withdraw from it (so I am told by Lady Airlie). I think that her beauty & her goodness will win him back some day. There was a prejudice against her, but she has made herself universally respected, and I have a great respect for her. She busies herself with hospitals and charities in a sensible manner, though she says she does not wish to be so absorbed in them as to withdraw from social life....

I have just returned from Prof. Green's funeral.[3] He is a terrible loss (notwithstanding his metaphysics). He was the only person who ever succeeded in uniting the University & the City. The Corporation attended the funeral.

[*Postscript omitted*]

[1] A. P. Stanley died on 18 July 1881, and was buried in Westminster Abbey on 25 July.
[1] BL Add. MS 45785 fos. 83–4.
[2] Tavistock, the Duke's heir.
[3] He died on 26 Mar. and was buried on 29 Mar.

373
West Malvern
July 16, 1882

... Will you not impress upon your own mind that all care & anxiety are wrong—that these family burdens are really (forgive me) a kind of illusion? It is hard to have no help from one's own kindred, or rather the reverse of help, but I suspect that it must generally be the case when the minds of persons are set upon great objects which are far beyond the limited ideas of their relatives. And we must not expect this to be otherwise.

For twenty years & more I have had the uninterrupted blessing of your friendship, & therefore you must not be grieved if I say what I think. I want to see you at peace in the years which remain to both of us.

Enclosed is Sir James Caird's letter. I have not yet seen Sir H. Maine but am going to see him on Thursday, when I hope also to get a sight of Morier, who has come over from Madrid, full of fire & fury against the Ministry for allowing the massacre of Alexandria.[1] He seems to me right, but there is something to be said on the other side. He is clearly right after the event & he wrote to me before the event.

I am satisfied that it was right to accept the V. Chancellorship[2] when I see how much there is to be done in it, I hope without much impairing the possibility of writing.

Look at some verses in the 'Fortnightly Review' for July—very striking—'A voice from the Nile'.[3] The unfortunate author, James Thomson, seemed to be a new poet, and now he is dead.[4]

[*Postscript*]

I have had staying with me here an Eton youth, Bolton King; very clever & of a serious character, full of cooperation & Land Leaguing—has been going off to Ireland to see Connemara with his own eyes. Meant to be a clergyman, but gives it up on account of subscription. I hope that he will come to good—he grew more rational after talking to him. He is full of enthusiasms & a man of property.

374
West Malvern
July 23, 1882.

... Lord Salisbury's conduct is rather bad. After having sat on the University's Committee (a judicial body) and never expressed any opinion,

---

[1] On 11 July 1882.

[2] BJ began his four year term at the beginning of Michaelmas Term 1882.

[3] 'A Voice from the Nile', by the Author of 'The City of Dreadful Night', James Thomson, in the *Fortnightly Review*, new ser., vol. 32, pp. 36–40 (July 1882). 'For man, this alien in my family, / Is alien most in this, to cherish dreams / And brood on visions of eternity, / And build religions in his brooding brain. . . .'

[4] BJ owned a copy of his best-known poem 'The City of Dreadful Night' (1880). An article by G. A. Simcox, 'A New Poet [James Thomson]' appeared in the *Fortnightly Review*, new ser., vol. 28 (July 1880), pp. 31–41.

he tries to get a Party Majority in the House of Lords to overthrow their decision. . . .[1]

375 *[early in August 1882]*

It was very kind of you to see Lady Tavistock: I think that your time was not wasted. I should like you to see a grateful epistle which she wrote to me (enclosed).

I have given up the hope of Lord Tavistock bestirring himself in Politics, but if he & his wife could be interested in their great London property, they might find a worthy employment for their time & do a great deal of good.

I have been at West Malvern a month, working with M. Knight successfully at the 'Politics' (I think).[1] On Monday I go to Oxford for a week; then to Davos for a fortnight to see J. A. Symonds[2] who, I rather fear, is beginning to sink in consumption. He is a man of genius & of immense knowledge, though he has not done anything equal to his powers, & I fear that it is becoming too late. Last year he had made up his mind to write a history of Italy, but his brain got excited & he took to wild poetry instead.

I should like to hear how you are getting on. This Egyptian business is a terrible affair & I am afraid presses upon your mind—a second Crimea & full of pitfalls & dangers.[3] When you fight with fanatics you have a war of a dreadful kind, not to [be] measured by differences of artillery. Europe looks on & rather laughs at John Bull having got into such a trouble—he so prosperous, who has not had a scratch for 25 years, nor a serious hurt for more than 60 years. Then there is the awful chance of great mismanagement, if not a certainty, and the possibility of a battle of Armageddon between Mohammedans and Christians extending to India in the distance. I do not think that these are imagination, but sober realities; and it is possible that Englishmen have a greater trial before them than any that has occurred in our lifetime. There is no concert among the Christian powers, or sense of honour. I suppose Germany wants to prop up Turkey against Russia: the interests change every year. Turkey is of course treacherous. No nation will do anything for another, & therefore can get nothing done for herself in the moment of trial. . . .

---

[1] The University Commissioners of 1877 created Boards of Faculties. The question then arose whether examiners were to be appointed, as hitherto, by the Vice-chancellor, the Senior Proctor, and the Junior Proctor in turn, or by a Board on which the Faculty Boards were represented. The question was argued before the Universities' Committee of the Privy Council, where Salisbury was in a minority of three to one. On 20 July 1882 he moved in the House of Lords to ask the Queen to withhold her assent 'from the proposed Statute . . . framed by the University of Oxford Commissioners, concerning the nomination of examiners'. He was defeated by 70 votes to 57, with Lansdowne and Camperdown acting as tellers for the majority.

---

[1] The translation was set up in type in 1882, but not revised and published until 1886.
[2] J. A. Symonds the younger.
[3] The British invaded and occupied Egypt, without French support, in order to recover European debts, and suppress a nationalist revolt which posed a threat to communications with India.

376

address Oxford
Davos
Aug. 22 [1882]

... The journey here was very pleasant for rather a strange reason: because I was alone. Solitude is better than company, not because I am specially fond of my own company, but because it is a rest, & in a cathedral or a beautiful scene so many thoughts arise in the mind about the past & the future. The stillness of this place is such as you cannot find in England. I am delighted with it & should like to stay here longer....

In another week or ten days we shall know whether we have a very serious or a comparatively slight war on hand. I incline to think the latter, if we strike hard at once & then offer easy terms to the defeated. The good government of Egypt, during the control & the professed disinterestedness of England, makes the case very different from that of the French at Tunis. The unpleasant side of the affair is, that we are in some degree fighting for the Egyptian bondholders, whose debt as far as the Egyptian people are concerned is not a 'bona fide' one, but spent on the extravagances of the late Khedive. Though I do not suppose there is any danger from India at present, yet I fancy that the Eastern question will wear more & more the appearance of a conflict between Mussulman & Christian or Catholic.

I find my friend here, Mr. Symonds, though very weak, somewhat better, & I do not despair of his being able to live some years longer in this climate. I have urged him to go on with a work which he has long had in view, the History of Italy. Today he showed me an excellent article on Machiavelli, the Patriot without morality, which he has been writing for the Encyc. Britannica.[1] It is very curious that in the excess of his really disinterested political feelings, the organ of morality should have dropped out....

377

Oxford
Nov. 6 1882.

I was very glad to see your handwriting again.

Sir James Caird paid me a visit yesterday & I think that I have nearly persuaded him to give two lectures on Indian agriculture....

He talked in a very interesting way about India: population increasing 1 p.c. per annum, notwithstanding the famine, equals 20,000,000 in 20 years. Productiveness of land diminishing, unless capital can be applied to it. Capital only to be had at interest of 20 or 25 p.c.. Remedy 1) loans from Government banks at reasonable rates of interest, paying off the Principal in a few years;

and 2) possible emigration of 20 millions to Queensland.

But probably this is a train of ideas familiar to you. He commends Indian

---

[1] *Encyclopaedia Britannica* 11th edn. (1910–11), xvii. 233—7.

Agriculture, & thinks the sinking of wells, which can be done almost anywhere at a depth of 30 feet, better than irrigation, or at least more important.

...I think that the V.C. business so far has been a success, but it hardly admits of anything else being done. It is all, I think, both interesting & important.

On Friday I went over to the Duke of Bedford's,[1] as I have done for 14 years at this time of the year. He said, 'I shan't be long here to keep Tavistock out of the H. of Lords'. I said, 'Why take such a melancholy view?' 'No', he replied, 'it is the most cheerful view'.[2] I saw Lady Tavistock there, rather sad & serious. She asked whether she might some day come & see you again. I said I thought that she might. Your 'friend' (?), Lord Napier of Ettrick was there, & the Duke de Broglie. . . .

378
56 Canyng's Square
Clifton, Bristol
[22 December 1882]

You are so kind a friend to me that I think I ought to write & tell you that my sister[1] has been taken from us. I came to see her on Tuesday, & found her looking much better than I had seen her since her illness began two years & a half ago, but the appearance was deceitful. She was seized with a fit on Wed. night, and never recovered consciousness.

She did not wish to live, & was prepared to die. She would say to me she had not thought it would be so long, and that though she feared she also hoped. She went on to the last, reading Shakespeare & Dante & Miss Austen. On the evening of her sudden attack she read with great admiration M. Arnold's last poem (one of his best—do read it) in a recent number of Macmillan.[2] She was a kind of saint in private life, perfectly disinterested, who lived for others only. Yet, for all her cultivation & curious knowledge of a world which she had never seen, she was nervous & inefficient except in the narrow circle of domestic charities.

I hardly wish her back; for it is better as it is. Now I have a few years more, & must make the most of them, not without your help & sympathy.

I was pleased with Rogers on Sunday; he was so courageous & full of spirit, notwithstanding his inability to walk, which I fear will never now be cured.

379
Oxford
Feb. 23 [1883]

... I hope that your sister is better. I have had a good deal of trouble lately from the death of two friends: H. Smith & Mrs. Montagu Butler. This loss of

---

[1] The ninth Duke.   [2] He shot himself on 14 Jan. 1891.

[1] Emily.
[2] 'Poor Matthias', *Macmillan's Magazine*, vol. 47 (Dec. 1882), pp. 81–5.

friends makes life sadder & poorer. Mr. Toynbee has also been very ill, away from Oxford.

[*Postscript omitted*]

380   Address
Emerald Bank
Newlands
nr. Keswick
June 28, 1883

You will be deeply grieved, as I am, at the death of William Spottiswoode.[1] He was one of the best &, I think, one of the greatest of living Englishmen; for if you consider his attainments, his energy, his great practical, as well as speculative qualities, and his extraordinary power of moderation & good temper, there was no superior or equal to him. He is the only person who lived amid many quarrelsome coteries of scientific men & was equally regarded by all of them. He probably never did a mean or weak thing in his life.

...I am writing this on the way to Newlands, a place near Keswick, where I have taken a house for a month. Do you know I have lost 7 friends, friends who cannot be replaced within two years. It must be so as we get on in life, & I suppose that as in a battle, when others fall, we should keep our heads clear & push on, until the night overtakes us.

Did you write to Lord Ripon?[2] I am sure that it will never do to give way. In the first place, the agitation is not real or powerful. And the English have behaved very badly & the natives very well; for they have been quiet. And to draw back would teach the natives the lesson that if they want to gain anything they must create a great agitation. I believe that the fury of the agitators has spent itself. Dr. Markby who is an excellent man [says] that the natives have great confidence in the administration of civil justice, but not equally of criminal justice, where native v. European is concerned.

I am not giving up my, or rather our, plans for the instruction of the Indian candidates in Agriculture. It can only be done, I think, by having lectures for them at Oxford. And an opportunity occurs for this in the existing vacancy of the Professorship of Agriculture, which will not, however, be filled up until the Court of Chancery authorizes some changes....[3]

[1] On 27 June 1883.
[2] As Governor-General Ripon was responsible for Ilbert's Bill to make Europeans submit to trial by natives. Ilbert was the law member of the Executive Council of the Governor-General of India from 1882–6. His 'Code of Criminal Procedure (Native Jurisdiction over British Subjects)' Bill angered the European British in India. Their resentment in turn stimulated Indian nationalism. In the end, jurisdiction was conferred on Sessions' Judges of whatever race, but a European British subject on trial before a district magistrate could claim a jury of which half were Europeans or citizens of the United States of America.
[3] The Chair was founded under the will of John Sibthorp, Professor of Botany 1784–96, and attached by him to the Sherardian Professorship of Botany. A Statute made by the University Commissioners of

381

Railway
address Newlands Keswick
July 6, 1883

It was not from any want of interest that I hurried away yesterday.

Shall I try to give you a considered opinion, always premising that I know nothing really about the subject, except what I pick up from persons in whom I have confidence?

1. If you write, I think that you will do harm rather than good by attacking anybody, or by wounding the 'esprit de corps' of the Civil Service. Let facts, in the quietest manner, speak for themselves about Lord Ripon & about every other subject. I have always admired the restless, untiring energy with which you pursue great objects. But to let this get into print is a mistake; it becomes a 'scream' & you are thought "wild". It is no use to try & make a popular movement about India; they are the few not the many who decide its fate and the appeal must be to 'thoughtful people'.

2. I think you might have a Royal Commission for certain definite objects, say respecting the Landlords of Bengal, the indebtedness of the Deccan, the improvement of agriculture &c.. But a roving commission to enquire generally into all things, & more especially into the past government of India, would not be tolerated—would be laughed at. You have already had an Agricultural Commissioner in Sir James Caird. And where would you find your Commissioners? Lord Dufferin has admirable popular qualities, but he is not a man of the necessary grasp. Mr. Goschen may some day do great service to India, but as Finance Minister rather or perhaps Governor General, not as head of a Commission. And what India Council, India Minister, or Governor General would tolerate such a Commission sitting in Calcutta & raising all sorts of fears & hopes?

You cannot anticipate or force public opinion by a Royal Commission. The only way is to work through the press—newspapers, Magazines, Books—especially through private & careful written letters to distinguished persons. There is no means more efficacious than this.

I know that you will not mind my saying what I think. I hope that you & I may never lose heart as long as life lasts. Can we say that the best years are still to come?

382

Boar's Hill
nr Abingdon

Aug. 23, 1883

... The agitation about the Ilbert Bill[1] seems to be quieting down, & I hear that the Government will leave Lord Ripon to do as he thinks best.

1877 separated the two Chairs. J. H. Gilbert, an agricultural chemist who had worked at Rothamsted, was the first holder of the separated Chair, from 1884 to 1890. He was knighted in 1893.

[1] See above, No. 380, n. 2.

I read a very interesting article of yours in 'Nineteenth Century'² & am glad that you are going to continue them.

I have been busy with Aristotle's 'Politics' during the last two months & begin to see the end in Print.³ A month I spent at the Lakes with some companions. Since then I have found a very nice house, about 4 miles from Oxford on a hill, where I have been staying, & rather think that I shall spend a considerable part of my remaining years there. If it were not too much like boasting I should say that I had been quite well & doing a good deal of work....

383

address until Tuesday:
Revd. Dr. Martineau, Aviemore N.B.
Gosford
Longniddry
N.B.¹
afterwards
A. Sellars'
Ardtornish
Oban
[September 1883]

You told me to write to you and I have great pleasure in doing so. But on the other hand do not write to me, if you have anything better to do, or if you need rest & do not feel in the humour. Or at least you need be under no obligation to send more than three lines saying how you are, & what you are about.

I have been very idle during the last week—having visited Lord Granville at Walmer where I saw Tseng & M. Waddington—the first seeming a very superior & the second a very inferior person in the opinion of us all. Lord Granville struck me by his extraordinary kindness & a sort of domestic goodness which one rarely meets among fashionable folk. He is not at all wanting in seriousness, and is the reverse of pretentious & egotistical. Whether he has the force of mind or the command of facts required in his position I do not know. But he certainly gives a high impression of his judgement & prudence. He did not tell us what Tseng & M. Waddington said to him but I think he was hopeful that France would get out or be got out of the war with China....

Here I am staying with my new friends, Lord & Lady Wemyss (you know I consider *her* a Prima Donna in my world—so true & simple), and here is your old acquaintance, Lord Houghton, looking very well—a sort of Cruda Senectus,² lamenting that the Doctors will not allow him to go to India. He has just

---

² 'Our Indian Stewardship', *Nineteenth Century* (Aug. 1883), vol. 14, pp. 329-38.
³ See above, No. 375, n. 1.

¹ BL Add. MS 45785 fos. 85-8.
² BJ has personified Vergil's line, in *The Aeneid*, Bk. VI, 304, to mean 'fresh (or lusty) old man'.

been letting me know he was on the point of marrying Lady Ashburton but it did not come off—& we told him, what he seemed to deny, that he had a fortunate escape. However, he clearly had not got this 'dream of a fat woman' at all out of his head. He is very much unchanged, very kind, goodhumoured, clever & vain. He asked about Lady Verney, and has not forgotten old times.

I tell you this gossip partly because I fancy you like to hear about the outside world. Into the outside world I do not intend to go much more, because I feel that it is distracting, though pleasant, and that if I am to do much more now that the years are fewer I must shut myself up as you do, & in that way find more time both for work & for rest. The V. Chancellorship has been a great happiness to me & has given me opportunities which it would be criminal to throw away. May I use them to the utmost! . . .

I go to see Dr. Martineau tomorrow & have just been reading his Spinoza,[3] which is very well done (at 78 too). It seems to me very doubtful whether what Spinoza evolved out of his own consciousness has done mankind much good. It is so confused & so isolated from experience. Even to understand it now requires you to go back into a metaphysical world which has ceased to have any reality to us. Yet there is a kind of metaphysical element in this age, which like the religious element needs to be drawn out & directed. The history of philosophy from Descartes to Hegel, and the history of the great religions of the world, is the preliminary to this sort of study or science, necessary to supply the elements & instruments of thought & also to place the mind above the metaphysical fallacies which through language beset us all. But the final result will be simpler & deeper & better balanced & more nearly connected with ordinary life. A curious sort of Neoplatonism or Neohegelianism is beginning to overspread both Britain & America—of which the two leading representatives have been Prof. Caird of Glasgow & Professor Green of Oxford, both men of great force of character. Their teaching has been, unconsciously to themselves, a self-contradictory eclecticism which they privately expound, but do not defend against attacks. It is too metaphysical & political & too little eternal & religious. They want to rescue the world from materialism & Darwinism & Utilitarianism. And they are right in their spirit, but not in their method, which is naught.

But I am running on about things which cannot be expected to interest you. We have a great number of Indian students now at Oxford, more than ever before. I hope, with the help of Dr. Markby & Prof. Marshall, we shall be able to do more for them. Next week I shall take the opportunity of being in Scotland to call on Sir John Lawes & talk to him about teaching agriculture, both to them & to students in general.

I am very sorry about your sister's illness & suffering, & the suffering it must cause to you. It is very hard to have a great public end interrupted by private trials. . . .

---

[3] J. Martineau, *A Study of Spinoza* (1882).

384

Boar's Hill
Wootton
Abingdon
Aug. 21 [1884]

... I rather want to speak to you about Mrs. Green, the daughter of Dr. Symonds & the widow of Professor Green. She is a lady for whom I have a great respect, as every one has in Oxford, and she has taken heart & soul to nursing. She is a very pleasing & refined person, has excellent abilities and many accomplishments, very quiet & absolutely free from feminine faults. At present she is only half trained & would come to London for another year of training. My impression is that, hereafter, there is no one who could be of more use to you in the nursing work, if you take her. I ought to mention—do not smile at the juxtaposition—that she is very strong & has a private fortune. She has been asked to stand for the headship of Girton but declines, because she thinks nursing her vocation.

At present she is in full work at the Radcliffe Infirmary, having given up her holiday to nurse a friend of hers & mine, Miss Alleyne, who has now gone to her rest. (Did you ever hear of her? I will tell you about her when we meet.) ...

385

address Oxford
Sep. 21 [1884]

You kindly told me that I might have the pleasure of writing to you in about a fortnight's time, a mode of communication which, though I consider it in every way greatly inferior to talking, I gladly accept, and I shall expect you, if you have nothing better to do (which is not likely) to answer me in about a week's time.

Shall we talk together about persons or about books? First about persons; secondly about books. Let me tell you then that I began my holiday by paying a short visit to my dear friends, the Lord Justice Bowen & his wife at their country place in Sussex. He is, as he always is, a most kind & delightful companion, though I question whether he does not give too much of his extraordinary powers of mind to literature & too little to law. I have rather come to the conclusion that a man of genius had better not go to the Bar. He does not find enough to satisfy him. At his house I met one of the candidates for Girton, Lady Pomeroy Colley, a very superior lady & I should think extremely well suited for the post by her goodness & intelligence & powers of conversation. She told me that she must make an effort to get rid of her 'selfish idleness' as she called it. She is not strong enough for nursing & has no special call for it, but I think she would do very well for education, in which she takes a great interest & is disposed to work on right lines: I mean, I think she would see that development of character & not mere attainments is the object at which to aim.

But I must go on my way. From the Lord Justice Bowen's I went to Mr. Ruskin, who gave me a very warm welcome at Coniston.... He lives with his cousin, Mrs. Severn & her husband the artist & their children. I have never been in so hospitable [a] house, for attention was paid to your least wants, & his conversation & kindness were a real rest to me. Of course, he is not rational, and it would be a mistake to oppose him: but there is a great 'sweetness & light' in his talk & he has very high aims, which are quite separable from his self conscious egotism. His moral influence over young men appears to me to be distinctly good, though on all subjects he talks extravagantly. He told me of signs which he had received in answer to prayer, the sun breaking through the clouds &c. I did not attempt to prove to him that this was a natural coincidence, nor was he quite capable of taking in the distinction between the natural & the supernatural. However, I feel that I can never say a word against him more.

Thence I went to Keswick & found my old pupil, the Neo Kantian & Hegelian Philosopher, Professor Edward Caird; also another old pupil, whom I used to think mad (Rawnsley) but is now Vicar of Keswick & a most energetic & valuable clergyman of the Liberal type. Thence I proceeded to pay a visit to my dear friends, Lord & Lady Wemyss, at Long Niddry in Scotland, where I fell ill for a day or two, I suspect from drinking impure water, & was nursed by them both with great care & affection & I did not deny them the pleasure of curing me (not a difficult matter) on homoeopathic principles. I wish you had known her, for she always appears to me one of the noblest women whom I have known—absolutely unworldly & indifferent to her great position. He is very unlike her but most excellent in his way, though in consequence of a certain Hibernian element he never does justice to himself.

But in the words of the Latin poet "Quo musa tendis"?[1] This is all interesting to you but how can it interest your friends? Well then, I will go on to the books. First, I have been reading Amiel's 'Diary'[2]—have you read it? I think it very interesting because it is the true picture of a man of genius whose nature led him to analyse himself until it became impossible for him to write. The book is really useful as a study in self knowledge, the man who makes the analysis being of a very noble nature, & it suggests to others what they ought to avoid in life, and deepens their views. Secondly, I read Maurice's life,[3] which appears to me very well done, but confirms the impression, which I already had, that he was a very elevated character, yet from the unconscious influence of two sets of impressions, Unitarian & Orthodox, he went on puzzling himself & others all his life long, which puzzle was greatly increased by a habit of idealising, or exaggerating, good & evil until he lost all sense of proportion or

---

[1] 'Non hoc iocosae conveniet lyrae; / Quo, Musa, tendis?' 'This will not suit a mirthful lyre, / Whither away my Muse?' Horace, *Odes* III. iii. 69.

[2] H. F. Amiel, *Fragments d'un journal intime* (1883–7). The first English translation of his journal, by Mrs Humphry Ward, was published in 1885.

[3] *The Life of Frederick Denison Maurice, Chiefly Told in His Own Letters, Edited by his son, F. Maurice* (2 vols., 1884).

distinctness. He lived in a luminous haze in which he succeeded in enveloping other minds. But such a haze cannot be permanent. He never had a conception of what a fact meant. Yet I am glad that the book was written & believe that it will do good.

Thirdly, I have been reading the translation of v. Hartmann's 'Philosophy of the Unconscious', *ninth* edition.[4] It is a very important book, not like Herbert Spencer, which seems to me verbiage & self satisfied phraseology, but one that should be grappled with. "This is not the worst of all possible words" as Schopenhauer maintained—that would be an exaggeration—but an extremely bad world, which can never be made any better. It seems to me fatal to morality, generalising the instincts & passions of men & setting them above the reason. The book is very interestingly written & contains many original psychological observations. In one respect I quite agree with it—in a steady opposition to Darwinism, which v. Hartmann truly regards as a great illusion which has taken in the scientific world.

I think that you must be tired both of persons & books, though I have omitted several of both (e.g. M. Arnold & Sir A. Grant of the first sort & a novel called 'The Amazon'[5] which I read when ill). So I will conclude, as I always do, with the warmest wishes for the success of your work, in which to you I believe that all other good is summed up.

[*Postscript omitted*]

386

Oxford
Oct. 31 [1884]

I should be very glad to see Lord Dufferin if he would like to see me amid the multitude of his engagements. But there is nothing about which I have a right to trouble him, except the age of the Candidates.

I entirely agree with you & Dr. Hunter that the Civil Servants should be men & not boys; they should have more experience, knowledge of the world, character, morals, powers of resistance than the youths whom we have sent out since Lord Salisbury's change.

Mr. Ilbert & Lord Ripon are in favour of 22 but they yielded to the Council's representation of 21. I may as well send you his letter once more.

I am in favour 1) either of 22, which has the advantage of selecting the candidates from the Universities, with a *two* years' probation at Oxford & Cambridge.

Or 2) of 20 with a *three* years' probation. This finds favour with the Schoolmasters & with the Civil Service Commissioners and has the advantage of a

---

[4] C. R. E. von Hartmann, *Philosophy of the Unconscious: Speculative Results According to the Inductive Method of Physical Science: Authorised Translation (from the seventh German edition) by W. C. Coupland* (3 vols., 1884).

[5] F. Dingelstedt, *The Amazon: A Tale* (1869).

more complete training & of a University Degree, which in the first case could not always be obtained.

The material point is to have older men, well selected & well trained.

We are making progress with the Scheme for an Indian School & hope to have it carried at the end of this term or the beginning of next.[1]

[*Postscript omitted*]

387   Oct. 31, 1884

The answer to Lord Dufferin's question (which writing in haste I did not observe) is:

1. That the 'lads' have three periodical examinations, conducted by the Civil Service Commissioners, in Indian Languages, Indian Law, & History, Political Economy &c. For these they are prepared at Oxford & examined in London. (I think this division is, upon the whole, right.)

2. That Oxford proposes to institute another examination in Indian Languages, Law, Political Economy &c., in which the Candidates will be allowed to specialise, as it is termed, i.e. in which the knowledge of one or two subjects will be carried to a higher point. The taking of honours in this examination & the B.A. Degree, which they seem to value, should be made compulsory.

[*Postscript*]

What a loss Mr. Fawcett is—no public man had more noble & generous feelings or more good sense, & no one except Mr. Gladstone greater ability & energy.

388   Oxford
                                                                                                                                 Nov. 6 [1884]

I must ask you not to shew the plan for the Indian School. I think that I shall be able to settle the matter satisfactorily, but at present there is a good deal of opposition to the scheme, on the ground that they want to have a "Scientific" School. Oxford is a curious place & is going through a strange phase of desire for Science—which means specialism without either learning or genius—thus, it seems to me—that higher subjects which are naturally connected tend to be depressed....

[*Postscript omitted*]

---

[1] An early plan of BJ's for a School of Oriental Studies is dated 28 Nov. 1876, Add. Jowett Papers, 11f. The final scheme emerged in the *Oxford University Gazette* for 23 Feb. 1886 as a new School of Oriental Studies in which undergraduates might study either Semitic or Indian Languages.

[*Enclosure*]

Plan for Indian School
(1) Classical Languages of India, viz. Persian, Arabic, Sanskrit.
(2) Vernacular Languages of India (Hindostanee, Mahratta, Telegu, etc.).
(3) Indian Law: Revenue System.
(4) Political Economy, including the Finance, Commerce & Agriculture of India.
(5) The History, Geography, and Religions of India.
    (a) The School to be for Candidates in Honours only;
        Every Candidate to offer one Classical and one Vernacular Language, and two out of subjects 3, 4, 5.
This is what I am going to propose, but shall ask opinions.

389

West Malvern
until Thursday mg. inclusive
Jan. 6, 1885.

... I am afraid that I cannot give a satisfactory answer to either of your questions.

1. The 'Politics' are not finished and they are becoming rather oppressive.[1] I have been hard at work upon them during the last 3 weeks.... I do not like to treat of very important subjects in a cursory manner... & can only wish that I had confined myself to a translation & notes, which might have been finished two years ago. The plague is a sort of running analysis & commentary & the length of the essays.

2. I do not know of any theological book that I should like to recommend to Lord Dunsany. My view of theology is independent of miracles & this, as you know, is shocking to most persons. Archdeacon Reichel is not known to me except by his writings,[2] which are very unsatisfactory. He is a good man, but he is not a critic or a philosopher. He had a son at Balliol,[3] extremely promising, who is now head of the N. Wales University College....

You are quite at liberty to mention that there is a scheme before the H. Council, which will probably be carried, for an Indian or Oriental School in which the Indian Candidates will be examined. But the scheme is already a good deal changed by the Council (not for the worse), & will be still further changed by the Board of Oriental Studies....

[*Postscript omitted*]

---

[1] See above, No. 375, n. 1.
[2] C. P. Reichel, *The Christian Miracles* (1861), *Modern Infidelity: With Special Reference to M. Renan's 'Life of Jesus'* (1864).
[3] H. R. Reichel.

390 Oxford
Jan. 10, 1885

... I have rather a sympathy with an old scout (though I should not express his thought in the same way) who says that he prayed "that he might not perish by the coldness of age, but be burned up with the fire of the divine Love."

I have been reading three books lately with great interest (I will send them to you). 1) The new series of the 'Greville Memoirs'[1]—excellent I think—the veritable history of our times. 2) Maine's 'Popular Government':[2] the contrast between the name & the reality. Also 3) the 'Teaching of the Apostles'[3]— probably the oldest Christian book after the New Testament—very like the three first Gospels—quite simple—written in the age of the church when prophets were the great teachers and Bishops very inferior persons. "Mais nous avons changé tout cela". There is no trace in the book of St. Paul or of St. John....

391 Oxford
May 20, 1885

You kindly take an interest in my plans & projects. Will you read the enclosed & if you feel disposed will you contribute to what we believe to be a great public benefit.[1]

The object is to provide 'good water & good air' for the city & University of Oxford. The first is to be obtained by bringing the water from a point 4 miles higher up the river, out of the way of the pollution of the Town. The second will be accomplished by getting rid of the floods—lowering the river & so the water in the subsoil of the valley about $2\frac{1}{2}$ feet. This latter measure will greatly contribute to the health of Oxford, especially of the poor in the lower & outlying parts of the town, who have the water in their cellars whenever the river is high.

Part of the cost of these undertakings cannot be imposed on any rates & must therefore be defrayed by voluntary subscriptions. We have raised 13,500£, & now comes the tug—to raise 4,500£ more, to enable us to fulfill our engagements with the Thames Commissioners. ...

---

[1] *The Greville Memoirs: Second Part, A Journal of the Reign of Queen Victoria, from 1837 to 1852*, by the Late Charles C. F. Greville (3 vols., 1885).

[2] Sir H. Maine, *Popular Government: Four Essays* (1885).

[3] P. Schaff, *The Oldest Church Manual Called 'The Teaching of the Twelve Apostles'* (1885). The text was discovered, as BJ added in Jan. 1886, by Philotheos Bryennios (1833–1914).

---

[1] The scheme was for a new mouth to the Cherwell, and the removal of Iffley lock. The first part was carried out, and is known as the Vice-chancellor's cut. But the second, which involved lowering the river, was opposed and had to be abandoned; *AC* ii. 219-21.

392

Boar's Hill
nr. Abingdon
Sep. 8 [1885]

... I hear that Lord Randolph [Churchill] is going to raise the age of native candidates for the Indian Civil Service. This, I suppose, will be followed by a similar change for the English. I had a very nice letter from Lord Reay this morning who tells me this. ...

393

Balliol College,
Feb. 23, 1886.

I send you a number of the Oxford University Gazette[1] containing two or three matters which may interest you:

1. A Statute containing provisions for a faculty of Medicine, which will give to medical study quite a new position in the University.
2. A Statute relating to Degrees & examinations in Medicine & Surgery. This statute will bring medical students to Oxford. We are at the same time providing teachers, laboratories, Dissecting Rooms &c. The London medical world and the Oxford, minus Dr. Acland, approve the Statute.
3. A Statute respecting Oriental Studies. The subject of Indian Agriculture will be included in the list of subjects issued by the Board of Studies.

I have also to tell you that at a meeting of the Associated Colleges who receive Indian students[2] it was also agreed to appoint a lecturer in Agriculture, which is now an optional subject in the Indian examinations. The stipend will, I fear, be small, for we have no money. Can you recommend any one? The Professor of Rural Economy here is a dry old gentleman & though rather eminent is not suitable (Dr. Gilbert). I hear named a Mr. Robinson of Cirencester College who is thought efficient.[3] We spoke of this some years ago, & I have forgotten the names which were suggested. Then there was no possibility of bringing the matter to bear. Now the Commissioners, or rather the India Office have added agriculture to the list of optional subjects & we are fairly afloat.

More than three fourths of the Indian Probationers have been trained at Oxford during the last 6 or 8 years; & more than half of them at Ball. Coll.[4] Formerly, the Indian civilians used to be very unpopular, & the whole

---

[1] Vol. XVI, no. 544, 23 Feb. 1886.
[2] In 1885, Balliol, Brasenose, Christ Church, Exeter, Keble, Magdalen, New, Oriel, Queen's, St John's, Trinity, University, and Worcester all made payments for lecturing and teaching; Add. Jowett Papers, 9b.
[3] M'Connell was appointed.
[4] See above, p. xxx-xxxi.

business disliked. Today we had seven heads of Houses sitting round the table & advising about their lectures &c.[5] This is a good sign. . . .

394
Oxford or rather Boar's Hill
Wootton
Abingdon
[April 1886]

I paid a visit to Mr. Godley, who always leaves on me the impression of a very able, considering, sort of a man.

He favoured the proposal of paying the agricultural teacher, but said that the Council were just now in a fit of economy. We agreed that I was to write a letter to Lord Kimberley. He also promised to do a very honest 'job' for me, i.e. to get Dr. Markby knighted, which he well deserves for his great services to India in many ways. I hope it may give my friends a passing pleasure to be Sir William & Lady Markby.

He told me, as you did, that the Government wanted to enlarge the Committee to 32 members, but that Lord Randolph insisted on preserving its purely official character. He did not value it, and was rather inclined to prophesy that it would never meet.

Everything seems to be in confusion, which will probably be increased after Thursday.[1] Ireland without a gentry, without capital, in a state of anarchy & perhaps of war, is all that we can expect, whatever measures are passed by Parliament.

Five years hence, if English Governments shew firmness & impartiality & moderation, it may be otherwise. I hear that the House of Commons are throwing off the ties of party and refuse to obey Whips. The Speaker[2] does not complain of them, but then he has only experienced the lull before the storm as yet. Do you know that he strikes me as one of the kindest & best of men—with good sense, combining firmness & the power of speech? . . .

395
Boar's Hill
Wootton Abingdon
July 19 [1886]

. . . A day or two ago Mrs. T. H. Green came to see me and to ask my advice, about giving up her hospital training and taking care of a niece (a very gifted

---

[5] Balliol (£918), Christ Church (£220), New (£217), Trinity (£126), Keble (£101), St John's (£77), Oriel (£69), and University (£64), made the largest payments to the Indian Civil Service Association for lectures and teaching; Add. Jowett Papers, 9b.

[1] The Home Rule Bill was introduced on 8 Apr. and defeated on 8 June.
[2] A. W. Peel.

young girl who has fallen into a consumption). Which was the more pressing duty? I told her that the public duty was to be preferred to the private duty. She then said that she would take care of the niece for a short time, and then return to the Hospital on which her whole heart is fixed.

I do not think that I have ever told you how highly I value her. She has admirable sense, power of sympathy, energy, quiet ability—is absolutely trustworthy & has a fortune of her own.

She is quite free from fancies, & could do more than any one whom I know to assist you & carry on your work. Do not let her slip if you can help it. It cannot be easy to find another lady equally gifted for the work.

She is about 42 years of age but she has great bodily strength, and thinks nothing of walking out to see us at Boar's Hill & back (4 miles from Oxford). Will you not get her perfectly educated & use her? . . .

396

address Boar's Hill
Wootton, Abingdon
Oxford
August 26, 1886

. . . I had a very pleasant three weeks in Switzerland & the north of Italy with Lyulph Stanley, who was a most considerate & kind companion. I like to sing his praises, for he does not appear to me to have justice done him by the world. He knows more about education, I should think, than anybody living, and he has a real interest in the lower classes. Yet he has lost his place, both on the School Board & in Parliament, and will continue out of Parliament, I fear, until this 'Irish' tyranny be overpast.[1]

I wish I could place before your eyes all the pleasant pictures which I saw on my tour, especially the sunrise on the whole range of the Alps from Monte Generoso. Will you never see any more beautiful scenes? They soothe & charm us & take us out of our own petty cares & irritations and give what Plato calls (a remarkable expression) a pleasure not to be repented of. One is the richer for every day spent on the Swiss & Italian Lakes.

I send you a little book called 'Country Conversations',[2] which may amuse you, as it has amused Mr. Gladstone, 'enormously'. It is a faithful report of what we never hear, the conversation of the poor among themselves. The book was not published but printed by a Miss Tollitt about 20 years ago. Will you let me have it again in about a fortnight, as I value it greatly & cannot get another—the authoress is, I believe dead. It shall be sent tomorrow.

Mr. Milner, a young political friend of mine who lives somewhere about the centre of news, thinks that the Ministry & the Union Liberals are getting on

---

[1] He did not return to Parliament.
[2] 'Country Conversations' [by Georgine Tollet] (privately printed by T. Richards, London, 1881).

very well, & that there is as yet (a month after the Honeymoon) no sign of a quarrel between them. I suppose that they will make a futile attempt to govern Ireland for six months without extraordinary powers & then apply for them.

I hope that Lady Verney is more at rest and not worse. She shows wonderful courage in writing under her sad circumstances.

Mr. Gladstone does not appear to me in his recent letter[3] to show any return of moral principles, if under moral principles are to be included the duty of a Government to enforce the payment of debt.

397 Boar's Hill
Sep. 2 [1886]

... I am glad that you wish to know Dr. Markby & will take care that you shall know him. He is a fine fellow & a noble character: undertakes our Indian Students for a miserable pittance of 200£ a year for the work's sake. The friend of mine & of poor Toynbee, whose name you could not read is A. Milner, a very remarkable person of great ability, who devotes himself to the study of social questions. I think that you would find him a valuable acquaintance (he is a charming person). The young scholar of Balliol I conclude, from your description, to be Elliot (I ought to have spelt his name with one l): he is also rather an extraordinary undergraduate & last Spring obtained both the Sanscrit & Ireland Scholarships. He is a nice creature, & I may say of him as Dr. Johnson, said of Chatterton, 'It is wonderful how the whelp has come to know such things'.[1]

With respect to the India Jurisdiction Bill[2] I see no reason to regret the time at which it was brought forward. It is evident that it will be carried, & whenever it was brought forward it would have produced a similar outbreak. These explosions are like epidemics: they have a tremendous force for a short time & then the air is cleared & the body is incapable of taking them again. I have often thought how completely the Ecclesiastical titles epidemic cured us of No Popery.[3] And so it will be in India. ...

---

[3] Gladstone wrote to his former secretary, George Leveson Gower, who had been defeated in North West Staffordshire, 'I advise you to take resolutely to the study of Irish history. I have done in that way what little I could, and I am amazed at the deadness of vulgar opinion to the blackguardism and baseness—no words are strong enough—which befoul the whole history of the Union'; *The Times*, 17 July 1886 (11f).

---

[1] 'Johnson said of Chatterton "This is the most extraordinary young man that has encountered my knowledge. It is wonderful how the whelp has written such things."' 29 Apr. 1776; *Boswell*, iii. 51.
[2] Ilbert's Bill of 1883, see above, No. 380, n. 2.
[3] Ecclesiastical Titles Act, 14 and 15 Vict. c. 60, repealed in 1871.

398

Oxford
Nov. 6 [1886]

... Many thanks for the Statistical Survey:[1] I am very glad to have it, as I had already given my own copy to the College Library. It is a capital work.

Will you accept of a little book which struck me a good deal when I read it last summer, "The Song Celestial"[2]—I think it expresses some of the deepest thoughts of the human heart.

399

Boar's Hill
Abingdon
Dec. 31, 1886

Many happy returns of the New Year to you & to your work. May you live to complete it!

Most persons are engaged in feasting & holiday making amid their friends & relations. You are alone in your room, devising plans for the good of the natives of India or of the English soldier, as you have been for the last thirty years, and always deploring your failures as you have been doing for the last thirty years, though you have had a far greater & more real success in life than any other lady of your time.

I think that you have chosen the better part.

But will you not thankfully & cheerfully acknowledge how much God has done by your means? It would be happier for you & better for your work....

I was extremely touched by Lord Sherbrooke[1] saying to me a few weeks ago, 'Of course I made endless mistakes'. That is my feeling too....

400

Oxford
April 22, 1887

I call to tell you that I had taken your kind advice & had consulted Sir William Gull.

He examined me very carefully and says that I am quite sound, & that there is nothing the matter with me. This is satisfactory. But I feel rather as I felt before, "therein the patient must minister to himself",[1] and I mean to do so. The treatment required is mental & moral, as well as medical. He said that I was below par & that this was the cause of a troublesome cough, which led me

---

[1] Sir William Wilson Hunter, *The Imperial Gazetteer of India* (9 vols., 1881).
[2] *The Song Celestial: or, Bhagavadgita, from Mahabharata*, trans. from the Sanskrit by Edwin Arnold (1885).

---

[1] Lowe.

---

[1] 'Therein the patient / Must minister to himself. Throw physic to the dogs; / I'll none of it.' *Macbeth*, v. iii. 45–7.

to go to him at this time. He has given me small doses of Arsenic to raise the system....

401 May 22, 1887

... I staid a week at Tennyson's, from Wed. to Wed., and was most kindly treated. The old poet softens with years—his powers otherwise are unchanged at about 78. He & Lady Tennyson, that sweet & aged saint, were extremely well & Hallam was pronounced safe from a dangerous illness.

My cough greatly improved by my stay at Freshwater, & on Friday I came home & gave my lecture without difficulty, but on Friday night I was seized with vertigo & lameness & began to be alarmed. I put off a party whom I had invited—I am now better, though still giddy & unable to walk freely. Acland promises me that I shall be well in a few days. I shall consider the attack as a warning. I am not now at all alarmed & must hope that you will not be, who so kindly take an interest in me. But I think it best to tell you the exact truth at all times.

Acland says that I ought to go away from Oxford for a few days more. The Lingens have kindly invited me to stay with them incog., and if I do I shall come & show myself to you, giving previous notice.

More than enough of myself—forgive so much. I agree with you that these are the worst times in which we have lived—with the least of purpose, spirit or principle. 'A plague on both your houses'. The only pleasing thing to me is the conduct of Lord Hartington & Chamberlain.

I have had a very good man staying with me today—one of the young men of the future who will be at work when we are gone, Welldon,[1] the Head Master of Harrow. He is a very able & eloquent man & not illiberal. He preached against eternal punishment, & quite agrees that the religion of Christ must be based upon a moral foundation—but he cannot give up miracles, because without them he cannot form a consistent idea of the character of Christ. He is not logical, but then he is young & is, perhaps, happy in his want of logic. He is a very fine young fellow, about 32 years of age, beginning life under the best auspices, & you will probably think it well that he is better accommodated than with a wife....

[*Postscript*]

Acland has been very kind & good to me & skilful, I think.

---

[1] Weldon.

402

13, Wetherby Gardens,
S.W.
address until Monday
at R. S. Wright's, Esq^e
Headley Park,
Hants.
May 31 [1887]

... I think that I am making progress, and was very much encouraged by Gull (who kept me for an hour & a half) assuring me this morning that there was nothing serious, only vertigo. He told me to do very much what I was intending to do—'short snatches of work, open air (Malvern), food rather inclining to stimulant and gave me a prescription of Nux Vomica.[1]

I had a great deal of conversation with Gull, who is a very clever man (a good rhetorician) and talked in a very interesting manner—Something of an actor, too....

403

Am Hof,
Davos Platz,
Switzerland
Aug. 19, 1887

... I am always interested to hear about your work & am extremely glad to know that you are taking part in the scheme for 'Free Nurses'. It is very wise of the Queen to use the Jubilee money in this way.[1] The difficulty of such a scheme seems to be that any relief, even medical relief, does tend to pauperize respectable persons. Might it not be better to have a very small payment to be remitted where necessary. The money would go further & there would not be the stigma of charity. It is quite fair that medical relief, like education, should be partly supported by endowments.

I hope you will spare your eyes.... I suspect that your way of reading & writing when lying down must be an additional trial to them.

You kindly ask about my health. I think that I am better, for I am beginning to sleep much better & to walk much better than I did a few weeks ago: and though not up to much I have done about 2 or 3 hours regular work every day. This place, owing to the rarification of the air, is trying until you become acclimatized (we have had very bad weather), but I am not so much discouraged as at first, & I believe the ultimate effect will be very good. Nothing could be better than my surroundings. I am staying with Mr. Symonds[2] who is a most

---

[1] Whose seeds yield strychnine.

[1] 'The Queen has decided that the surplus of the Women's Jubilee offering [about £70,000] shall be devoted to the benefit of nurses.' *The Times*, 19 Aug. 1887 (7f).

[2] The younger.

accomplished & in many ways remarkable man, & his girls (one of whom is my God-daughter)[3] take the greatest care of me. (Did you ever look at his writings?[4] His 'Greek poets' & his long work on the Renaissance are extremely interesting)....

[*Postscript omitted*]

404

The Pulchar,
Rothiemurchus,
Aviemore
address: Ball. Coll.
Sep. 22, 1887

It was very good of you to write & tell me about your Indian Affairs & Hospitals. I am delighted to hear that your "Masters are always kind and sometimes satisfactory".

I wish you would be rather more hopeful. To carry about with one the sense of failure always, is not the way to succeed. Will you consider this? ...

I am *sure*, especially as we get *older* that, while we go on working, we should leave the event with God. The lives of all of us will fall a great deal short of what we once hoped & perhaps might once have done. As the Indian poem says, 'Come to live with your failures'.[1] I think that Browning has expressed this very well in 'Rabbi Ben Ezra'[2] & several of his poems.

I am pleased to hear that Miss Pringle has taken the management of the Hospital. Women like her give a lesson in the art of government to us all—I am glad that she does not trouble you with her troubles. Any man or woman who does not need a confidant shows superiority of mind....

My host here, Dr. Martineau, remembers you in former days and greatly desires to be remembered by you. He is one of the best men whom I have ever known. At the age of 83 he has just finished printing a considerable work on the unchangeable elements of religion.[3] He appears to have no weakness of sight or hearing or mind. I am afraid that I don't read his writings with any great interest; they are too limited & unimaginative, but I may be to blame for that. This place, where he has a small house, is one of the loveliest parts in Scotland....

---

[3] Charlotte Mary, afterwards Mrs Walter Leaf (1867–1934).
[4] *Studies of the Greek Poets*, two series (1873–6), and *Renaissance in Italy* (7 vols., 1875–6).

---

[1] 'Better thine own work is, though done with fault, / Than doing others' work, ev'n excellently.' *The Song Celestial, or Bhagavadgita*, trans. from the Sanskrit by Edwin Arnold (1885), 3rd edn. (1886), p. 166.
[2] Included in *Dramatis Personae* (1864).
[3] *A Study of Religion: Its Sources and Contents* (2 vols., 1888); *The Seat of Authority in Religion* (1890).

405

Balliol College
Oct. 14, 1887

I was going to try & answer the question (according to my poor notions) which you & also Pilate asked when the Postman appeared this morning.

What is truth? Let me try & answer it still for my own satisfaction rather than your's, first premising that you must expect nothing which you do not know or which has any novelty or originality.

Truth is the sense of the highest within us: God the Good, the idea true conceived under many names & in various forms, personal & impersonal, intensive and extensive, acknowledged in some germ or seen in some ray of light, and capable of being developed by reason, from all regions and all the parts & infinitesimal particles of nature.

Truth is the sense of the Unity of God & nature which the true intelligence refuses to divide, a circle necessarily continuous, & necessarily vague & abstract, which we slowly fill up with a few particulars of knowledge.

Truth is the application of these two principles to our own lives that we may habitually dwell in them & appropriate them and become one with them.

(Of course I know that this is poor & meagre but I think that it points in the right direction.)

Truth in its negative form is the refusal to admit speculations & fancies about things which we are "always desirous to look into", but about which we can never attain certain or even probable knowledge, for such speculations only waste our time & draw us off from actual duties....

Also I want to prove to you that your words do sometimes affect my flighty or stony heart, & are not altogether cast to the winds; & therefore I send you the last report of the Indian students, in which you will perceive that Agricultural Chemistry has become a reality & that owing to you (though I fear that like so many other of your good deeds this will never be known to man) Indian students are reading about Agriculture, & that therefore Indian ryots may have a chance of being somewhat better fed than hitherto. We shall now make another move to get the India office to support us. How slowly the world moves....

406

Ball. Coll.
Nov. 3, 1887

I cannot help remembering the great trouble, & perhaps anxiety, which I caused you three weeks ago,[1] & the extraordinary kindness & affection which you showed me.

I think that I am getting better, for I have had no return of pain or vertigo—no need for opiates &c. I get up to Chapel every morning, but if the day is wet,

---

[1] He had been taken ill at her house.

or I have an inclination to cold, I return to a warm bed on coming out. (This is not known to the undergraduates.) But I am still rather weak & unable to walk far.

The translation of Plato (revision for new edition)[2] I find a very congenial and I hope not altogether useless work. It seems to be suited to a feeble brain & is rather a soothing occupation. My new Secretary, Fletcher, greatly pleases me—he is an excellent scholar and quite a gentleman: 'is he not the Carpenter's son'? . . .[3]

Have you read Mrs. Simpson's life of Madame Mohl?[4]—well done, I think, & giving a pleasant impression, chiefly through her own letters, of your old friend. She was a remarkable woman but he was a much more remarkable man. It is sad to think that so able & learned as he was he should have left so little behind him. I saw him chiefly at your lodgings at Hampstead 20 years ago.

Are you not rather touched by Jenny Lind's death? There was something about her, which no other singer ever had—she threw her character into her songs—and although really ugly she looked at times like an angel. She reminds one of old days at Norwich amid Stanleys & others who are now laid to rest. Peace be with them all & love with some of them. Do not the persons whom we knew 30 years ago seem on the whole superior to those whom we know now? But, perhaps, we were younger & therefore more hopeful about friends. And how some of them did impose upon us!

Do the defences of the country ever weigh upon your mind? They do upon mine though I am not an alarmist. We are the most unpopular nation in Europe: everybody is jealous of our wealth & would like to have a kick at us: we are too weak or too disunited to make a vigorous resistance, & the change in the weapons of war, both by land and sea is so great that we cannot form any judgment of the future from the past. We may add to this that nationality as a disintegrating force has enormously increased, as a uniting force it is lost in the war of classes, which is cosmopolitan. But no one thinks of these & similar considerations amid party strifes.

407 Ball. Coll.
Nov. 20, 1887

. . . I should like to give you the Sacrament whenever you would like to receive it. It is no fatigue & will do me good, I hope, as well as you. I sometimes gossip to you more than I ought to do—so it seems to me. It is due to your kindness & sympathy, and you know that I have no one else to gossip to. . . .

. . . Sir Harry & Mrs Verney came to see me on Thursday. . . .

Lord & Lady Wemyss also came to see me yesterday. They are quite

---

[2] 3rd edn. (1892).
[3] 'Is not this the carpenter's son?', Matt. 13: 55.
[4] M. C. M. Simpson, *Letters and Recollections of Julius and Mary Mohl* (1887).

delighted about the admission of their younger son[1] at Balliol, & he is doing very well there. Lord W. is a fine, frank person with a great flow of spirits & conversation. She is a 'schöne Seele', one in ten thousand, who does her part as a great lady but is altogether above the world & its ways. I have often wished that she knew you....

408   Ball. Coll.
                                                                            Dec. 2, 1887

It was very kind of you to write to me about Lord & Lady Dalhousie. As you may suppose, I have thought about them a great deal during the last week. He, with his noble disinterestedness & honesty (Gladstone thought him the best young man whom he had ever known), and she, with her striking beauty, a sort of queen in society. They were both of them very kind friends to me. This day they were buried in the same grave at Dalhousie near Edinburgh.

I am alarmed at finding that there is a Report in the newspapers that you are very ill.[1] I am only half believing it, but I should be glad if you would send me a line telling me without concealment the exact truth.

It is a very great pleasure to put the right man into the right hole; and I quite think Mr. Harford-Battersby has found the right hole, & that he will be a great good & blessing to Claydon & to its inhabitants. His father was a most excellent undergraduate here, who carried the ten commandments written on his forehead about 40 years ago, when I was first appointed Tutor. Do you know that the late Master of Balliol, Dr. Scott, who once caused me so much distress & trouble (I was not always in the right) is dying, or probably dead. He was a very good & conscientious man, but narrow. He did a good work in his half of the Greek Lexicon.

Yes, I have been fishing last week and brought up a number of large fish, rather of the coarser sort, but very able & likely to gain many University distinctions. It is about 46 years since I began to take part in these examinations,[2] and they show during that time a considerable change in the Higher English Education—more English, more Greek, & far more knowledge; much better teaching. But the candidates have not more ability or originality, probably less, than formerly. One subject in which there [is] a great change for the worse is knowledge of Scripture and of Theology....

[*Postscript omitted*]

[1] E. Charteris.

---

[1] Not found.
[2] The annual Balliol Fellowship and Scholarship examinations.

409

Ball. Coll.
Dec. 6, 1887

... I have just come from hearing a lecture in the Hall from Sir William Hunter about the rivers of India, or rather about the Hugli & the Ganges. He is a very clever & learned man & seems inclined to settle in Oxford. His coming here will be a great gain to the Indian students. Though a little affected & unreal, he is in the main a very honest & useful man.

The Barnets[1] came to see me since I saw you. They seem to be very happy & are very useful at the East End of London....

410

Six-Mile Bottom,[1]
Nr. Newmarket
address: Oxford
Dec. 30 [1887].

I hope that this note will reach you on New Year's day: I cannot let the beginning of the year pass without wishing you every good & blessing on your labours.

Do you know that it is more than 25 years since we first became acquainted? I may venture, perhaps, to call our's a silver friendship. It has been a great blessing to me: one of the best things in my life.

I do not believe in going down hill; the truer, the safer, the better years of life are the later ones. We must find new ways of using them, doing not so much but in a better manner. Economising because economy has become necessary: for bodily strength obviously grows less. That is the will of God & cannot be escaped or denied....

FN [*notes of a conversation*][1]

411 [1888]

Sermons (at Oxford) have quite changed in the last 4 years or so
   You never have a Sermon now on
   Miracles or on
   Atonement or on
   Everlasting Damnation
   Death-beds
You don't take your disciples to the Death-bed
Then what are they on?

---
[1] Barnetts.

---
[1] Home of W. H. Bullock-Hall.

---
[1] BL Add. MS 45785 fos. 90–1.

Chiefly on reconciling Science with Religion or Philosophy with Religion, or on good works, like Toynbee Hall, among the working classes.

412   West Malvern,
                                                                   March 22 [1888]

... I enclose a letter from Lord Lansdowne. Could you write me down, in single words only, the principal questions which a Governor General should consider & perhaps the titles of some books which he should read.
e.g. Irrigation
     Instruction in Agriculture
He is a very clear headed & disinterested man—in ability I should think a good deal beyond any one who has held his office since Lord Dalhousie.

[*Postscript omitted*]

413   Oxford
                                                                   May 22 [1888]

... I see that you think me very ridiculous in offering counsel to Lord Lansdowne.
Let me tell you what rather pleases me (but it is a secret until next Monday), that the Council have agreed to give him a D.C.L. Degree and also to Dr. Martineau. The latter is greatly delighted. ...

414   West Malvern[1]
                                                                   Dec. 31, 1888

Let me send you my best wishes for the New Year. May your health improve, may your work prosper, may your mind be at rest. ...
I can understand how great a trial to you is Miss Pringle's defection.[2] It is on those occasions that we most need force of character & the strength which comes from above. Miss Pringle is not really necessary to this work. Neither are you or I or any of us necessary to any work. ...

415   Ball. Coll.
                                                                   Feb. 10, 1889

I was very glad to hear from you again, though I think that you have asked me a very hard question, and not quite a fair one, for I have never used the

---

[1] BL Add. MS 45785 fos. 100–1.
[2] The Matron at Edinburgh Royal Infirmary, who accepted appointment as Matron at St Thomas's Hospital in 1887, and resigned less than two years later when she became a Roman Catholic.

words 'absorption' or 'annihilation'. I will try to answer you, though I do not expect to give you satisfaction, and even the attempt to speak on such a subject is a great presumption.

I think that you attach too much importance to the idea of personality—all that makes personality in a man is wanting in God, or to Man himself in another state of existence. The Greeks would not have understood the use of the term in either application. Therefore, though I use the ordinary mode of speech & thought I do not think it the only or necessary one. It is the faith in right, truth, goodness that is essential, whether in the form of a person or not in the form of person.

Any one who is thoroughly inspired with these, & who lives in them more & more, [But how is he "to live in them more and more"? F.N.], will have no doubts about either his present or future, and the more he becomes absorbed in them, the more he will recognise that he is doing the will of God, and ask no more questions. [That is what the R.C.Ch. says: You are to believe in me and ask no more questions. F.N.]

The world is not so evil as not to admit the utmost possibility of good. [But how to get it? F.N.]

What you say about organizations is true, but it is a secondary truth. We must almost always begin with the organization which is nearest—unless it be essentially bad & immoral. You & I would be foolish in trying to make a new one, like Robert Ellesmere[1] or Mr. Stopford Brook.

I think also that mysticism, if it be a true enlightenment, is a very important element of good. But considering the differences of human character I cannot say that it is attainable by all, or necessary to them. Nor can I allow that any church is a true one which excludes my dear old friend Godfrey Lushington, notwithstanding his adherence to the 'grotesque old French pedant'.[2]

I cannot see why persons should not be satisfied with devoting their lives to God in some very simple form. Provided the devotion is entire they will have no fears or doubts. If they have, let them increase their self-devotion. I cannot see how they can find a further safeguard or comfort in taking upon themselves the lies & the crimes of the R. Catholic Church. Why contaminate themselves with these when they can keep clear of them? I can compare it only to a pious and really good young lady falling in love with a man whom she knows to be a scamp.

I hope you will not let your friend make such an irretrievable mistake & will be able to prevent her. Cannot she be made to understand that she must make God & truth her support, & not this or that church. Will she not try for two years? ...

[*Postscript omitted*]

---

[1] Mrs Humphry Ward, *Robert Elsmere* (1888).
[2] Possibly Charles Loison, 'Père Hyacinthe'.

FN to BJ [*copy*]¹
416
10 South St.
May 16, 1889

Very many thanks for giving us Communion yesterday. I like the word 'Sacrament'—the Roman soldier's oath better. I may have something to say about our conversation another time.

I was rather aghast at hearing 'Mrs. Green knows about *Miss P*'. . . .

No one at St. Thomas' knows it, & *no one* but 2 or 3 knows it at all.

It would be absolute ruin to us if any one at St. Thomas' were to hear it. She would immediately declare herself. And then she *must* immediately resign.

It is precipitating the catastrophe.

The 2 or 3 who know it are Miss P's oldest friends, as earnest in their opposition as I.

Mrs. Green has never seen her, & would in no way understand the intensity of the case.

Please remember that it is life or death to me to keep it secret—to avert the catastrophe.

417
Ball. Coll.
May 28, 1889

I do not suppose that I can answer your question in a way that will do any good, but I have not forgotten.

It seems to me that a Christian may have perfect rest & satisfaction when he seeks out carefully the best & highest within him, & that this is far higher than the Creed or Standard of any Church.

To a person who has a constant sense of the presence or of the law of God the question of this or that Church sinks into insignificance.

The end "holiness" must be greater than any means such as the Sacraments or the Church. The Sabbath was made for man, not men for the Sabbath.

It is presumption to limit God to this or that Church, or to think that he so limits us or himself. There can be nothing arbitrary in the Divine Nature to any one who has a true conception of God which is worthy of Him.

The love or blind attachment to the Rom. Church can only be expelled by the inspiration of a higher & deeper affection for God, for the truth & for the good of mankind.

I mean & feel what I say, though I cannot put my meaning into any striking form of words which will arrest the fall from a precipice.

I had a very pleasant visit from Temple & his wife about a week ago. All his good qualities remain, but his defects have rather stiffened with the years. They are on the surface—but then the surface is what everybody sees.

¹ BL Add. MS 45785 fos. 117-18.

FN to BJ [copy]¹

418 June 12, 1889

Many thanks for your kind letter. But it was too late I fear. Miss Pringle had already seen Card. Manning, & the very day before your letter had written to the Treasurer of St. Thomas' Hosp^t· & to our Secretary her change of views. She is now in Jersey for a little rest, but returns this week.... She & many other persons of her intense temperament ... go off to philanthropy, or ... to the Ch. of Rome....

We have taken into counsel ... a former Surgeon of St. T's & great friend of hers.... He ... is very strongly of opinion that some loving & loyal soul to the Church of England should deal with her. "If Mr. Jowett would not undertake the duty could he not suggest the right man to do so? ..."

419 Ball. Coll.¹
July 23, 1889

I have seen Mr. Gore, who will write to you. I think that he quite understands Miss Pringle's case. I asked him to call & see you. I want him to become acquainted with you....

420 Ball. Coll.
Hurstbourne Park,
Whitchurch,
Hants.
Oct. 6, 1889

... I remember that it is exactly two years ago since I imposed myself upon you when I was ill; and you in your infinite kindness looked after me when I seemed to be in a bad way. I think I may say that I was nursed by the 'Queen of Nurses', though I hope never to trouble you again....

We have celebrations next week of two new colleges at Oxford: the Mansfield College & the Manchester Congregational College, (Unitarian).¹ I have tried to get them to call the latter "Martineau College", like Keble & Selwyn Colleges. But they have refused to do so—saying that it would be contrary to their principles—which seems to me a narrow answer.

Do you hear anything about Lord Lansdowne? I hope that he approves himself to your serene highness, as he appears to do to the rest of the world. I think

¹ BL Add. MS 45785 fos. 121–23.

¹ BL Add. MS 45785 fo. 127.

¹ Mansfield was Congregational, and moved from Spring Hill Birmingham. Manchester was a Unitarian foundation and a non-residential society having as its aim 'the free imparting of theological knowledge without insisting on the adoption of particular doctrines'.

he is superior to recent Governor Generals because he has more reflection & better manners. He wrote to me a few days ago & seems to be in good heart. Only there is a rascal Maharajah of Cashmere whom he has to coerce, & gets abused for it by the newspapers.² I think that he will do well—he has a great deal of conscience, and is above the ordinary views of politicians. And what influences me, perhaps too much, in my good opinion of him is that he is kind and loyal to me. . . .

421 Ball. Coll.
Feb. 15, 1890

Thank you for the small volume of Sir A. Lyall's poems.¹ I have been corresponding with him & Godley about the Indian probationers. They both appear to agree with me, but they are settling the matter in a bad way. Age of appointment: under 23 years & a half, probation one year. They say that the first was settled for them by the Government of India & that it necessitated the adoption of the second. I am still having one more shot at them, but I fear it is hopeless.

I send you Miss Margot's account of her and her sister's childhood.² Will you kindly forward it to her? Please to send it addressed to "the Glen, Inverleithie, N.B." I think her a fine creature.

I am rather well pleased with the report of the Parnell Commission.³ It clears Politics, acquits Mr. Parnell of immediate complicity with crime, but condemns his methods of leading into crime. But he is in a much worse scrape than the Commission (Mrs. O'Shea). I fancy that things will tend to a reconciliation of parties, which is much to be desired, or at any rate to a common ground upon which they can deal with Ireland.

Since I saw you we have had Mr. Gladstone here.⁴ He was very amiable & delighted us all. In social life there is much more of the old about him than of the new; still the old fondness for the aristocracy and the same irrational interest in Homer. His fascination is irresistible.

I think you sometimes see things out of proportion—shall I venture to say—and therefore you allow the St. Thomas' business to weigh upon you too much.⁵ You ought to let it pass and, with the 'patient tenacity of genius', only think of doing the best under the circumstances. 'Il n'y a pas une femme' any more than 'un homme nécessaire'.

Sir A. Lyall's poems are very good, but too much on one note. We are going

---

² A letter from William Digby in *The Times*, 7 Sept. 1889 (4ef).

¹ *Verses Written in India* (1889).
² An early version of Margot Tennant's *Autobiography*.
³ *PP* (1890), xxvii. 477–640.
⁴ A visit to All Souls. See J. Morley, *Life of W. E. Gladstone* (3 vols., 1903), iii. 420–1, and *Mr Gladstone at Oxford, 1890*, by C. R. L. F[letcher] (1908).
⁵ See above, No. 414, n. 2.

to perform Browning's 'Strafford'⁶ here & I have his son staying here for the performance.

422 Ball. Coll.
Oct. 26, 1890

... I want to talk to you upon two subjects.

First, about the scheme which Dr. Farr bequeathed to you.[1] I should be sorry to see it given up. If you would give or bequeath 2,000£ to the endowment I would bequeath, or perhaps give, a similar sum; and then we might go about begging of rich people in the world. 2. The other subject is Lord Lansdowne. I have to write to him in the course of the next three weeks; and I believe that I can, without being intrusive, say anything which is likely to be useful. But I do not know enough about India of my own knowledge to be sure that I can do good.

W. W. Hunter, an extreme Indophile, praises him highly without a word of disparagement, chiefly on account of his rearrangement of the native troups to whom, or rather to a select body of whom (about 25,000 or 30,000 men) he has given an English training, while leaving them permanently under their native officers. This measure, which has been entertained ever since Lord Mayo's time, has been finally carried out by Lord Lansdowne. W. W. H[unter] says that it will be a check on the rabble of the native princes and to themselves will give great satisfaction, because it removes the suspicion that the English ever mean to annex them. He thinks that Lord Lansdowne ought now to go on to deal in some way with the Wider Question & get rid of the Ecclesiastical Law;[2] and introduce more natives into the municipal Government of India, especially into the Provincial Councils.

Lord Lansdowne has now got the experience & a good deal of prestige. The three remaining years are the time in which he must make himself the Great Governor General. Something of that kind is what I want to tell him, but he must not, like Lord Ripon, excite the natives or arouse the alarm of the Civil Service by his manner of doing things.

FN to BJ [*copy*][1]

423 Claydon Ho. Winslow Bucks Jan. 3, 1891

I wish you all the blessings of a New Year & on your work.
Statistical Professorship
I think I cannot fully understand what you kindly tell me about Prof.

⁶ *Strafford*, a tragedy, first produced in 1837 at Covent Garden, with Macready in the title role, and Helen Faucit as Lady Carlisle.

[1] See above, No. 362, n. 1.   [2] Unexplained: what can BJ have meant?
[1] BL Add. MS 45785 fos. 144-5.

Marshall's answer.... He says that 'Govt. ought to do it'. I thought our chief point was that the enormous amount of Statistics at this moment at their disposal (or in their pigeon holes, which means *not* at their disposal) is almost absolutely useless. Why? Because the Cabinet Ministers, the army of their subordinates, the Houses of Parliament, the large majority of whom have received a University education, have received no education whatever on the point upon which all legislation & all administration must—to be progressive & not see-saw-y—ultimately be based. We do *not* want a *neat arithmetical sum*. We want to know *what we are doing*. We want experience & not experiment....
What we want first is, not so much an accumulation of facts (i.e. not at present) but to teach the men who are to govern the country what are the *uses* of facts, of 'Statistics'....

FN [*memo of a conversation*][1]

424 [n.d.]

During the last 40 years I have had about 1600 pupils at Ball. Coll.. Could I, or any one, draw up Statistical facts about them which would lead to trustworthy results, esp. of the proportion of length of life or of distinction in after life in University honours?

425 Balliol College
April 23, 1891

... Dr. Butler is a very kind & good friend of mine, an excellent man & an admirable scholar with a touch of genius. Speaking privately, I do not know that I should say he was a very sensible man in the higher meaning of the word, but he is quite sensible [enough] to be entrusted with the little scheme for establishing a Professor of Statistics & may have something to suggest about it.

426 Balliol College[1]
Aug. 14, 1891

I am glad to hear that you are at Embley....
We have hunted everywhere for Lord Landowne's typewritten letter & Miss Knight says that it is useless to make any further search. It was headed 'For your own eyes only'; nevertheless, I shall show it to you if we ever find it. Meanwhile let me tell you something about its contents. Lord Lansdowne is very liberal. He says that he agrees with 'our' letter in every respect. The

---

[1] BL Add. MS 45785 fos. 169-72.

[1] BL Add. MS 45785 fos. 179-80.

change of the age for marriage he acquiesces in,[2] but does not expect that much practical result will follow. In another letter he says that there has been an outcry about the change among the natives, but he does not think that any harm has been done. I have heard from another well informed & able person, Sir D. M. Wallace (do you know him? I am much struck with his knowledge of India), that the marriage question has divided the Congress: the natural feeling of the natives being against the change, but, on the other hand, they feel the necessity of making it, if they are to get the support of the English Radicals.

Lord Lansdowne is very strongly in favour of admitting the representative element to the Council of the Governor General. He has pressed it strongly upon Lord Cross, but without immediate effect....[3] The question is not about making up his own mind, but how he can force the hand of the Government. He is willing enough himself.

Since I saw you I have Lord Ripon here again, whom I get to like & to regard almost as a friend. Though he has not quite the style of a great man he is so simple & good that one cannot help respecting him. He comes here about University extension and has just made friends with the Common Room.

The College is very prosperous again, & that anxiety, which was great, has passed away. I am half ashamed to think of it, but I find that in the present state of the public schools it [is] as important that we should be among the first in Games as in University distinctions....

427

Heath's Court,[1]
Ottery S. Mary,
Devon.
Sep. 4, 1891
Address: Oxford

... Thank you for your kind suggestion that I should take about with me a companion in the likeness of a footman. I am afraid that I cannot comply because (1) I cannot afford to, (2) my man is away at a Hotel, (3) It would be of no use, as I have all my friend's servants & all the porters at the Railway at my disposal....

---

[2] The raising of the age of consent from ten to twelve.

[3] The Indian Councils Bill of 1890 favoured by Lansdowne was not pressed by the Government. Cross's Indian Councils Act of 1892 provided for the addition of another 10–16 members to the Governor-General's Council to represent different classes and interests. The new members were to be nominated, but they were given the right of interpellating ministers (along the lines of Question Time in the House of Commons). The provincial legislatures of Madras and Bombay were enlarged by twenty members each, nominated by municipalities, trade associations, and university senates.

---

[1] Seat of J. D. Coleridge.

428   Balliol College
                                                 Sep. 14, 1891

I am not very well, having been caught hold of by the Influenza and whatever it is which has got hold of me is not disposed to let me go for a few days. I am all for change of air.

... I should like to come & see you some day next week. I had no intention of being in Oxford at this time, but as I was not well after three or four visits to Coleridge, Ilbert, Tennyson, Jex-Blake, I thought it would be better to return home. My great trouble is sleeplessness—bad nights, bad days; not the effect of overwork, but of a virulent cough. The Doctors do not seem to understand the nature of it. I dare say that you do.

I was very much pleased with Mr. Morant & Prince Damrong.[1] The latter said that all educated people in Siam were rationalists in religion. There was no diversity of opinion. What a striking & perhaps encouraging fact! For the rest, Siam without literature, politics, religion, seems to be too much of a Doll's House to contain the elements of a great oriental nation. The account which they give of the late King,[2] who knew more than 20 languages, is very remarkable—like Akbar.

Did I tell you (this is private) that I have persuaded Tennyson to write a poem on Akbar—very grand, I think.[3]

I am quite willing to take good advice, & particularly your good advice. Please not to suppose that I am very ill: only I have a certain amount of malaise & discomfort.

This morning I heard news of the death of Mr. Warrack of Balliol at the age of 29, the progress of whose education kept nearly pace with the progress of consumption. He was a very poor man, but a gentleman & had very good & simple manners. He had a perfect genius for teaching & was the most popular private Tutor in Philosophy in Oxford. I think that his life was a happy one. He was greatly beloved by everyone. He was always thinking about philosophy. I will tell you more about him when we meet.

429   Langley Lodge,
                                                 near Oxford
                                                 Sep. 26 [1891]

I have been a good deal unwell but have got better by the help of my good friends, the Gells, who are admirable nurses & give me the best air about here. I am very penitent....

[*Postscript omitted*]

    [1] Signed BJ's Visitors Book on 13 Sept., together with three young sons of King Chulalongkorn.
    [2] Rama IV (called Maha Mongkut).
    [3] 'Akbar's Dream' appeared in *The Dream of Oenone and Other Poems* (1892), which included a poem 'To the Master of Balliol'.

430
(dictated to Miss Knight)

Balliol
[October 1891]

The physician here seems to think me very ill. I will not ask you to come to see me; perhaps it would be too much for both of us & not really wise; moreover, I am not at all certain that I am in so dangerous a state as I sometimes fancy. I only judge by this, that I have not eaten or slept, except by the help of anaesthetics, for several days. May God bless you & your work. I hope you will take care of yourself, & live as long as you can for the sake of the work.

[*Postscript*]

He could not sign this without fatigue, so he has asked me to do so.

(M. Knight)

FN to BJ

431

Oct. 8, 1891
Claydon House,
Winslow,
Bucks.

Words cannot say how grateful I am to you for your note.

You are thinking for us all. And we are thinking of you, who have fought the good fight in calmness and in love—& are fighting it still, to the good of all around you.

God is Love: & His light is around you.

432

Oct. 16, 1891[1]

Many interesting things have been revealed to me in my illness, of which I should like to talk to you. I never had an idea of what death was, or of what the human body was before, and am very far from knowing it now. I am always thankful for having known you. I try to go on to the end as I was. I hope you will do so too; it is best. I hope that you may continue many years, and that you may do endless kindnesses to others. Will you cast a look sometimes on my old friends, Miss Knight and Mrs. [T. H.] Green, and my two young friends, F. and J.? It would please me if you could say a word to them from time to time. But perhaps it is rather drivelling to try and make things permanent which are already passing away.

---

[1] From *Cook*, ii. 398.

FN to BJ
433
                                      Oct. 18. 1891
                                      Claydon House,
                                      Winslow,
                                      Bucks.

How good it was of you in this anxious, dear, never to be forgotten time to write to me again, a letter which seems to come straight from God's presence, and should maintain God's presence about us. . . .

How I should prize hearing from you of the "many interesting things revealed to you in your illness".

O Father, God of childhood & youth & middle age, but more especially God of *old age* & of what we can do in old age, teach us to do all in Thy name & for Thy sake. . . .

Do you remember at Lea Hurst in 1870 when you heard of your being Master praying aloud in my room, not thinking of any presence but God's: "O spare me that I may recover strength before I go hence & am no more seen"

Has He not done so? Is He not doing so?

FN to BJ
434
                                      Claydon House
                                      Winslow,
                                      Bucks.
                                      Nov. 10, 1891

. . . You live on your head for years. You entirely ignore the effect on the nerves, & the effect of the strained nervous system on the action of the heart and on sleep. . . .

Nature sends in her bill. And that bill always has to be paid. . . .

But if God wishes one to live, surely one ought to do all one can & all one knows to cooperate with Him. Else it is a kind of suicide. . . .

435   Nov. 18, 1891[1]

I am delighted to hear, that you will do me the honour to come to Balliol to see me. Acland will send his carriage for you to the station. It will be a great event for me to have a visit from you.

---

[1] From *Cook*, ii. 398.

FN to BJ

436

> Nov. 21, 1891
> Claydon House,
> Winslow,
> Bucks.

... Thank you for the list of trains.

I have not sate up to a meal for more than 30 years nor seen more than one at a time.

I think the best thing for us both will be for me to come for an hour or so by a train after luncheon.

But I will give you full notice that you may be able to decline me. For I am very much afraid of being one too many....

437

> at Mr. Justice Wright's,
> Headley Park,
> Hants.
> Dec. 30 [1891]

I want to send you my love on New Year's day if you won't think this language is too sentimental. I often think of the long years in which we have known one another & of the great piece in my life which this friendship has been.

I wish you a few more years of life, four or 5 perhaps, and when these have come to an end shall wish you 4 or 5 more, if I am alive. For I perceive that persons are terrified at having too long a life promised to them. I would not live always, but I think *life* always a blessing if we can find something real for its occupation. There have been so many gaps & omissions & waste of time by wrong methods, that we should like to have a little overtime to make up our deficiencies.

I hope you have health & strength to go on with your work, & do not feel discouraged; I know that some other persons would counsel you differently. But I shall always be of opinion, both respecting you and myself, that work is the law of our existence & that the best conditions of work are the best conditions for us, and the 'greatest happiness principle' of which we are capable....

I am staying with some friends of mine, Mr. Justice & Lady Wright—they are among the persons whom I like best in the world....

438

> Balliol College,
> May 26, 1892

Will you be surprized at receiving a letter from me? I want to write to you, because I so seldom see you & have many things to say. But I would not have you waste your time in answering me.

You are never out of my mind for long. I remember your extraordinary kindness to me during my illness and before when I was ill five years ago & for more than thirty years before that. You have taken an interest in the College & my work. I have never come to you for sympathy & failed to receive it. And how little or nothing have I done in return for all this!

I want to hold fast to you, dear friend, as I go down the hill. You and I are agreed that the last years of life are in a sense the best and that the most may be made of them even at the time when health & strength seem to be failing. I have been belated in life and have left many things undone which I still hope to finish, or if I do not finish them to be resigned to the will of God.

I hope that things prosper with you. A few days ago I had your friend, Mr Rathbone, with me who spoke of you and your work with great affection & interest. He is the sort of man whom I like: who having made a great deal of money lives above money. Also during the last 3 days there has been staying with me Mrs. Alexander Sellar & her children—very good & very cheerful & bent on doing good. Her son,[1] who is at this College is doing well & promises to be an intelligent & good man. She talked about you & spoke of her meeting you at the opening of the Law Courts.[2] She pleased me especially because she seemed to understand the meaning and purpose of your life and the necessity for your remaining in seclusion better than any of your relations whom I have known.

Some one told me that you were a good deal troubled about the proposals for registering nurses.[3] I agree with you, as far as I can understand the subject, that nurses cannot be registered & examined any more than mothers. But it may very well be that the measure cannot be carried out so as to cause any considerable effect on the position of those who are excluded. A good and skilful woman who is strongly recommended by a doctor will find room enough in which to carry on her profession. Since I have been ill I have a very high opinion of nurses. It seems to me a great thing that so many women should have an employment which is interesting to them & also inclines them to goodness & a good life. That is a point of view from which you ought sometimes to regard the movement which is associated with your name. . . .

FN to BJ [*copy*][1]

439 May, 1892

Thank you for your most kind letter.
'The proposal for registering Nurses' is no longer a 'proposal' but a stand up fight before the Privy Council—counsel engaged on both sides, all the petitions

---

[1] G. H. C. Sellar.
[2] Designed by G. E. Street, and opened in Dec. 1882.
[3] For the registration of nurses, *Cook*, ii. 269, 356, WS, 573.

---

[1] BL Add. MS 45785 fos. 183-90.

against the 'proposal' gone in, whose name is legion. The 'proposal' is for a R. Charter which would give the power to fix the conditions of training and certificate-ing tests and examinations for the whole profession.... There will be only one thing worse for us than a victory (because of the ill blood raised). And that is a defeat....

440 Jun. 26, 1892
Ball. Coll.

The bearer of this note is a young Indian lady, Miss Sorabji,[1] who is a friend of mine & for whom I have a great regard & esteem. She has been residing at Oxford during the last three years, & appears to me to have a very remarkable character. She desires to return to India with the view of assisting native ladies in their legal affairs. Would you kindly see her & talk to her for half an hour. I am very unwilling to take up your time in this way, but Miss Sorabji is starting on a mission something like your own fifty years ago, & you may perhaps feel a sympathy for her.

441 Balliol College
Dictated to Miss Knight Sept. 6th, 1893

Thank you for your most kind letter; it was a good, and a refreshment to me.

I am not very well at present, having some return of the old heart trouble, thought not so serious as two years ago. I shall fight through it.

I am glad that you have so high an opinion of Lord Lansdowne; both he and his wife are very simple, admirable people, though perhaps neither of them is gifted with sufficient force for a great position.

Could you tell me Mr. Higham's address? I wrote to Mrs. Verney, or rather to him, through Mrs. Verney, but have had no reply. I have sometimes thought that the Bishop of Ripon[1] might find a place for him. I don't like to leave him to the wiles of fortune.

Shall I tell you of two interesting books to read? Grant Duff's life of 'Ernest Renan'[2] and Captain Mahan's 'Influence of Sea Power on History'.[3] The latter is an excellent book—do get them and read them.

I have had a nurse staying in my house for the last three or four days, though I hope to get rid of her in a day or two. Of nurses, so far as I can speak, I have the highest opinion. They have a dignified position, and are made ladies of by force of circumstances. I wish there were more opportunities for persons to pass from one rank of society to another; it would be a great good. At present,

---

[1] The authority for the story that BJ proposed to FN: *India calling* (1934), p. 32.
[1] W. B. Carpenter.
[2] Sir M. E. G. Duff, *Ernest Renan, in memoriam* (1893).
[3] A. T. Mahan, *The Influence of Sea Power upon History, 1660-1783* (1890).

the dead level of the middle classes appears to me to be one of the most oppressive evils of society, there is no way out of it. No distinction can be attained but by literature and art, or by the way of making a fortune.

Will you write to me, I always like to hear from you? We used to be great correspondents in days gone past, but now, I suppose, that 'we have travelled over one another's minds.'

Let me tell you of two preferments which have given me great pleasure; Mr. Barnett's appointment to the Canonry of Bristol, and the elevation to the Peerage of Lord Justice Bowen,[4] probably the greatest lawyer in England, and now holding the post which is most likely to shew what he is. Does not half the good of the world (like the evils) arise from putting the best men in the best places?

Excuse my writing to you by a well known hand

442

Sept. 18, 1893[1]

We called upon you yesterday in South Street, but finding no one at home supposed you had migrated to Claydon. Fare you well! How greatly am I indebted to you for all your affection. How large a part has your life been of my life. There is only time I think for a few words.

FN[1]

443

In loving remembrance
of Rev[d] Professor Jowett
the genius of friendship
among many trials
Above all the friend of God
who has now received the crown of life.

Florence Nightingale
Oct 6, 1893[2]

---

[4] Created Baron Bowen of Colwood.
[1] From *Cook*, ii. 399.
[1] BL Add. MS 45785 fo. 204.
[2] These words appear at the close of the correspondence in the file in the British Library.

INDEX OF LETTERS FROM FLORENCE NIGHTINGALE TO BENJAMIN JOWETT

Letters, copies, and drafts of FN's letters to BJ selected for this volume, together with memos made by FN of conversations with BJ.

Document	Date
13	[16 July 1862]
43	[5 March 1865]
56	24 May 1865
59	1 June 1865
64	12 July 1865
68	n.d. (inserted at August 1865)
70	August 1865
90	30 March 1866
91	n.d. (inserted at March 1866)
97	n.d. (inserted at May 1866)
105	[? August 1865]
108	to BJ's mother, 28 August 1866
111	n.d. (inserted at September 1866)
112	n.d. (inserted at September/October 1866)
163	[1868]
171	24 August 1868
176	October 1868
181	[end 1868]
198	[June 1869]
236	12 July 1870
247	4 November 1870
260	7 August 1871
261	n.d. (inserted at 7 August 1871)
262	8 August 1871
264	17 August 1871
265	17 August 1871
266	n.d. (inserted at August 1871)
270	3 October [1871]
271	3 October 1871
278	[end December 1871]
287	June 1872

289	n.d. (inserted at June 1872)
291	9 August 1872
300	January 1873
311	13 August 1873
313	n.d. (inserted at August 1873)
339	13 June 1874
354	[early 1875]
411	memo [1888]
416	16 May 1889
418	12 June 1889
423	3 January 1891
424	memo, n.d. (inserted at January 1891)
431	8 October 1891
433	18 October 1891
434	10 November 1891
436	21 November 1891
439	May 1892
443	Valedictory, 6 October 1893

GENERAL INDEX

'A Ben Ezra' 154, 304
Abbott, Evelyn (1843–1901), Balliol 1862–70, paralysed while hurdling in 1866, master at Clifton 1870–3, Fellow and tutor of Balliol 1874–1901, edited, with L. Campbell, *Life and Letters of Benjamin Jowett*, 2 vols (1897) xii, xxvii, xxxiii, xxxiv, xxxv, xxxvi, xxxvii, 134, 143, 150, 172, 189, 235 n., 265
Abel 148 n.
Aberdeen, George Hamilton Gordon (1784–1860), fourth Earl of, Prime Minister 1852–5 x
abolition (of the slave trade) xiii
academic establishment xxvii
Acland, Sir Henry Wentworth (1815–1900), Regius Professor of Medicine 1858–94: 173, 297, 302, 319
Adam 125, 141
Addington 200
Addis, William Edward (1844–1917), Balliol 1861–6, joined Roman Catholic church in 1866, resigned priesthood 1888, minister of Unitarian chapel at Nottingham 1892, rejoined Church of England 1907: 43 n., 107 n.
administration 229, 241
administrative: details xxviii; indignation 230; power 229–30; reforms 114, 116
Adullamites 88, 92, 108
Agesilaus 44
Agricultural Chemistry 305
Agriculture, Professor of 287
Ahab 100
Ahriman 131
Airlie, David Graham Drummond (1826–81), seventh Earl of 72 n., 100 n., 274 n.; married Henrietta Blanche (1830–1921), daughter of Lord Stanley of Alderley 72 n., 126, 152, 163, 164, 282
Akbar 317
Albanians 281
Albert, Prince (1819–61) 17, 55, 90, 98
Albion Hotel 205 n.
Alderley *see* Stanley, Edward John
Alderley 137
Alderney 132
Alexander, William (1824–1911), Brasenose College, Bishop of Derry 1867–93, Archbishop of Armagh from 1893: 187
Alexandria 177, 283
Alice, Princess (1843–78), Queen Victoria's third child, married Ludwig of Hesse in 1862: 121, 192, 193, 194
All Souls College xxxvi, 313 n.
Alleyne, Sarah Frances (1836–84), organized courses of lectures for women, Secretary of Oxford Local Examinations at Clifton, translated E. Zeller's *Plato and the Older Academy* (1876), and M. Duncker's *History of Greece* (1883) 291
Alps, the 209, 299
Alsace 202
Amazon, The 293
Amberley, Katharine Louisa (1842–74), Lady, daughter of Lord Stanley of Alderley 93, 205, 260; married (1864) John Russell (1842–76), Viscount Amberley 260
Amberley, Rachel (1868–74), daughter of Lady Amberley 260
America xix, 59, 65, 67, 88, 94, 111, 195, 273, 290
Americans 46, 222
Amiel, Henri-Frédéric (1821–81), diarist and critic, Professor of Philosophy at Geneva 292
Analogy, Butler's 93
anatomy 57
Anderson, Elizabeth Garrett (1836–1917), pioneer female physician, qualified in 1865, opened dispensary for women and children, later the New Hospital for Women in Euston Road, senior physician 1866–92: 184, 205
annuity schemes 43, 65, 161
anti-clericalism xviii, xx
Anti-Corn Law League 115
antinomian 10
Antiochus Epiphanes 15
anti-slavery movement xx
Antwerp 195
Apology (Plato) 56
Apostles, Teaching of the 296
Arches, Court of 10 n., 16
Argyll, George Douglas Campbell (1823–1900), eighth Duke of, a 'cataclysmic' geologist, Lord Privy Seal 1853–5, 1859–60, 1860–6, Postmaster-General 1855–8, 1860, Secretary of State for India 1868–74, opposed Home Rule 118, 276, 279
aristocracy *see* classes
Aristophanes 11
Aristotle 56, 70, 125, 143, 224, 278, 284, 289
Armageddon 284
armies 28, 193
Armstrong, Sir William (1810–1900), pioneer of rifled-bore, breech loading guns favoured by General Peel and the Committee on rifled cannon in 1858: 31
Army, British xiv, xxi, xxxi, 17, 18, 19, 28, 29, 30, 42, 101, 105, 113, 114, 116, 132, 156, 201, 206, 232; FN the Mother of xiv, 100

Army: German 192; Indian xiv–xv, xviii, xxix, 17, 19, 28 n., 31, 314; Prussian 34, 92
Arnold, Matthew (1822–88), Balliol 1841–5, Fellow of Oriel 1845, private secretary to the Marquis of Lansdowne 1847, inspector of schools 1851, poet and critic 96, 126, 142, 175, 188, 238, 286, 293; married Frances Wightman 188
Arnold, Thomas (1795–1842), Headmaster of Rugby 1828–42 xii, 181, 227
Arnold, Thomas (1823–1900), younger son of Thomas Arnold (1795–1842) the Headmaster of Rugby, went to New Zealand, entered Roman Catholic church 1856, Professor of English Literature at the Catholic University in Dublin 1856–62, left Roman Church in 1865 and rejoined it in 1876, Professor of English Language and Literature at Dublin from 1882–1900: 59
Arthur, King 7, 115 222
articles of religion xi, 15, 16, 174
artisans *see* classes
Ashburton, Louisa Caroline (1827–1903), Lady, married William Bingham Baring, second Baron Ashburton (1799–1864) in 1858: 290
Ashley, Antony Ashley Cooper (1801–85), Lord Ashley and seventh Earl of Shaftesbury, champion of factory and mine workers, chimney sweeps, ragged schools, reform of the lunacy laws, and the improvement of public health ix, x
Atalanta in Calydon 217
Athanasian creed 232, 234
Athanasius 13, 224
Atheism xxv, 5, 236
Atheist 7, 244
Athene 256
Atonement, the xi, 27, 36, 41, 147, 175, 216, 265, 308
attraction, law of 9
Austen, Jane (1775–1817) 286
Austria 33, 94, 97
Aylesbury 62
'Aylmer's Field' 36

Bach, Johann Sebastian (1685–1750) 249
Bacon, Francis (1561–1626) 13, 46, 50, 70, 145, 157
Baden Powell, Mrs, widow of Baden Powell (1796–1860), Savilian Professor of Geometry 1827–60: 189
Baden Powell, Sir Frank Smyth (1850–1933), Balliol 1871–5: 189 n.
Baden Powell, Sir George Smyth (1847–98), Balliol 1871–5: 189 n.
Bain, Alexander (1818–1903), Professor of Logic at Aberdeen 255
Baines, Sir Edward (1800–90), MP (L) for Leeds 1859–74, served on Schools Inquiry Commission 1865: xxv, 135
Balfour, Arthur James (1848–1930), first Earl of, Prime Minister 1902–5: xxvi
Balliol College ix, x, xi, xii, xvi, xviii, xxiv, xxv, xxvi–xxviii, xxix, xxx–xxxi, xxxv, xxxvi, 40, 65, 74, 90, 100, 108–10, 110, 122, 130, 138, 149, 158, 159, 165, 182, 184, 188–9, 190, 193, 196, 199, 200, 201, 202, 202 n., 203, 206, 208, 214, 215 n., 218, 219, 222, 225, 227, 228, 230, 235, 240, 243, 249, 252, 253, 264, 266–7, 280, 282, 297, 298, 300, 301, 315, 316, 319, 321
Bampton lectures 16, 170, 212
Bar, the 54, 291
Barak 27
Barcaple, Edward Francis Maitland (1802–70), Lord Barcaple, Judge, Solicitor-General for Scotland 1855–8, 1859–62, and Lord of Session 1862–70: 82, 185, 193
Baring, Thomas George (1826–1904), first Earl of Northbrook, MP (L) Penryn and Falmouth 1857–65, Under-Secretary in India and War Offices 1859–65, Governor-General of India 1872–6: 228 n.
Barnett, Samuel Augustus (1844–1913), divine and social reformer who addressed himself to the housing problems of the working classes, first warden of Toynbee Hall 1884–96, Canon of Bristol 1893–1906, and of Westminster 1906–13: 308, 323; married (1873) Henrietta Octavia Weston (1851–1936), Dame, social reformer 308
Bartholomeo, Fr. (1472 or 75–1517), painter 247
Bateson, William Henry (1812–81), Master of St John's College, Cambridge 1857–81: 128 n.
Bath ix
Battersby, Revd Canon George Harford (1860–1921), Balliol 1879–84, Rector of Middle with East Claydon 1888–97: 307
Battersby, Revd Canon Thomas Dundas Harford (1823–83), Balliol 1841–4: 307
Baur, Ferdinand Christian (1792–1860), German biblical critic 40
Beadon, Sir Cecil (1816–81), Lieutenant-Governor of Bengal during the Orissa famine of 1866: 129 n., 131
Bedford, tenth Duke *see* Tavistock
Bedford, Francis Charles Hastings Russell (1819–91), ninth Duke, MP (L) Bedfordshire 1847–72, succeeded his cousin in 1872: 162, 253, 282, 286
Bedford, William Russell (1809–72), eighth Duke 199
Beethoven, Ludwig van (1770–1827) 249
Behmen, Jacob (1575–1624), German mystic 47
Belfast 63
Belgium 34, 194

INDEX 329

Bengal 129 n., 275, 276, 288; permanent settlement in 262, 276-7
Bengalese, the 266
Bentham, Jeremy 1748-1832: 125, 167, 168, 170
Berkely, Miss 242
Berlin 98, 135
Bermondsey ix
Bernard St 160
Bernard, Mountague (1820-82), of Trinity College, Oxford, first holder of the Chair of International Law and Diplomacy 1859: 25 n., 27 n.
Bethell, Richard (1800-73), first Baron Westbury, Fellow of Wadham College, QC 1840, MP (L) Aylesbury 1851, Wolverhampton 1852, Solicitor-General 1852, Attorney-General 1856, Lord Chancellor 1861-5, sat as member of Judicial Committee of Privy Council to hear appeals on *Essays and Reviews* cases and acquitted defendants on all counts xviii, 15 n., 60, 61, 62, 205, 225, 226, 237, 243, 245; married (2) (1873) Eleanor Margaret, daughter of Henry Tennant 245
Bethell, Hon. Richard (1830-75), son of Bethell, Richard 60 n.
Bethell, Slingsby (1831-96), son of Bethell, Richard 60 n.
Beust, Count Friedrich Ferdinand von (1809-86), Austrian statesman and principal opponent of Bismarck. Became Prime Minister 7 February 1867, and Chancellor, 23 June, of the Austrian Empire, instituted the Dual Monarchy 1868, dismissed 1871, Ambassador to London 1871 and to Paris 1878-82: 121, 123
Beveridge, William Henry (1879-1963), Balliol 1897-1902, sub-warden of Toynbee Hall 1903-5, civil servant and author of the Beveridge Report xxii
Bhanuwongsee, Sootshai (1851-1916), of Bangkok, Balliol 1871: 207, 249, 252
Bible, The xi, xxvi, 68, 191-2
Bible, The, quotations from 11, 27, 36, 73, 100, 118, 130, 168, 177, 180, 182, 188, 215, 222, 241, 276, 306
Bible, The School and Children's xxvi, 211, 215, 218, 222, 223, 226, 246, 257, 258, 260
Biglow Papers 39
biographies 255
Bird, Isabella Lucy (1831-1904), published *The Englishman in America* (1856), exposed poverty in *Notes on old Edinburgh* (1869), visited Australia and New Zealand 1872, Canada 1873, published *A lady's life in the Rocky Mountains* (1879). In 1881 she married Dr. Bishop. Following his death in 1886 she took up the study of medicine, went to India in 1889, and founded hospitals in Kashmir and the Punjab 171

bishops 16, 26, 207, 265, 274, 296
Bismarck, Otto (1815-98), Prince von xviii, 94, 111, 123, 133, 192, 195, 202, 257, 271
Black, Adam (1784-1874), politician and publisher, twice Lord Provost of Edinburgh, MP (L) Edinburgh 1856-65: 148
Blackheath ix
Blake, William (1757-1827) 33
'Boadicea' 36
Boars Hill 299
Bodleian Library xxix, 273
Bologna 247
Bonham Carter, Hilary (died 1865) 55, 71
Bonn ix
Bosanquet, George William (1845-69), Ensign 85th Foot 1864-6, author of *Essays and Stories by the Late G. W. Bosanquet* (1870) 58
Boswell, James (1740-95) 68, 223, 224
Bothwell 258
Bouverie, Edward Pleydell (1818-89) MP (L) Kilmarnock 1844-74, President of Poor Law Board 1855-8: 62
Bowen, Charles Synge Christopher (1835-94), Balliol 1854-8, Fellow 1858-62, barrister, Lincoln's Inn 1861, became a Judge in 1879, Visitor of Balliol in 1885, and a Baron in 1893: 91, 205, 291, 323; married (1862) Emily Frances, daughter of James Meadows Rendel 291
Brackenbury, Hannah (1795-1873), claimed descent from the Balliol family, founded scholarships at Balliol and contributed generously to the rebuilding of the Broad Street front designed by Alfred Waterhouse and erected in 1867-8. She also made large gifts to other institutions, in Manchester, where her brother had been a lawyer, in Durham, and in Brighton, where she spent the latter part of her life 207
Bradby, Edward Henry (1827-93), Balliol 1845-8, Headmaster of Haileybury 1868-83: 137
Bradford ix
Bradley, Andrew Cecil (1851-1935), Balliol 1869-73, Fellow 1874, first Professor of Literature and History at University College Liverpool 1882-90, Professor of English Language and Literature at Glasgow 1890-1900: 219 n.
Bradley, Revd George Granville (1821-1903), Fellow of University College, assistant master at Rugby School 1846-58, Master of Marlborough 1858-70, Master of University College 1870, Dean of Westminster 1881-1902: 189
Brasenose College xvi, 210, 297 n.
Bright, John (1811-89) 87, 112, 115, 118, 124, 135, 144, 156, 163, 167, 172
Brighton 199, 207
Bristol xvi, 121, 246, 252 n., 323

INDEX

Bristol University xxvii, 252, 253
Britain xix, 290
British institutions xix
British Lion 140
Broad Church *see* Church
Broadhead, William (1815–79), saw-grinder, explained to the Royal Commission on Trade Unions how gunpowder had been placed in the forges of non-union workmen 131
Brodie, Sir Benjamin Collins (1783–1862), surgeon 54
Brodie, Sir Benjamin Collins (1817–80), Balliol 1834–8, Professor of Chemistry 54
Brodrick, George Charles (1831–1903), Balliol 1850–4, joined *The Times* in 1860, Warden of Merton College 1881–1903: 77, 80
Broglie, Jacques Victor Albert (1821–1901), Duc de, statesman and historian, French Ambassador to London 1871, Prime Minister 1873–4, 1877: 286
Brooke, Stopford Augustus (1832–1916), Trinity College, Dublin, ordained 1857, chaplain to the British embassy at Berlin 1863–4, and to Queen Victoria 1872–80, minister of proprietary chapel of St James, York Street, London, 1866–76, and of Bedford Chapel, Bloomsbury 1876–95, seceded from Anglican church in 1880 to become a Unitarian 186, 238, 310
'Brotherhood of the Holy Trinity, the' 43
Brown, John (1826–83), servant to Queen Victoria 90
Brown, Dr John (1810–82), practised in Edinburgh, and published *Horae subsecivae*, three volumes of essays (1858–82), and *Rab and his friends* (1859) 95, 147, 148
Browning, Robert (1812–89), the poet. After his wife died at Florence in 1861, he returned to England with his son. In 1867, after the University had, in effect, snubbed him by offering him an Honorary MA rather than a higher degree, he was elected the first Honorary Fellow of Balliol 59, 85, 89, 124, 125, 126, 134, 154, 158, 159, 175, 188, 215, 304, 314
Browning, Robert Wiedemann Barrett (1849–1912), who, BJ feared, 'can never be made to pass his examination at Balliol' (to FN 15 Sept. 1868). He matriculated from Christ Church on 15 January 1869 and kept his name on the books until 24 June 1870: 59 n., 153, 158, 215 n., 314
Bruce, Henry Austin (1815–95), first Baron Aberdare, MP (L) Merthyr Tydvil 1852–68, Renfrewshire 1869, Under-Secretary of State for Home Department 1862–4, Vice-President Committee of Council on Education 1864, Home Secretary 1869–73, Lord President of Council 1873–4, Chairman of National African (Royal African) Company 1882–95, first President of University College, Cardiff 1883, first Chancellor of University of Wales 1894: xxv, 135
Bruce, Robert (1813–62), military secretary to his brother Lord Elgin in Jamaica 1841–7, in Canada 1847–54, Surveyor-General of the Ordnance 1855, governor to the Prince of Wales 1858–62: 108
Bryce, James (1838–1922), Fellow of Oriel 1862–89, served on Schools Enquiry Commission 1865–6, lectured at Manchester 1868–74, Regius Professor of Civil Law at Oxford 1870–93, MP (L) Tower Hamlets 1880–5, South Aberdeen 1885–1906, Chancellor of the Duchy of Lancaster 1892–4, President of the Board of Trade 1894–5, Ambassador at Washington 1907–13: 145
Bryennios, Philotheos (1833–1914), native of Constantinople, studied at German universities, Professor of Church History and Exegesis at Halki 1861, Director of the School in the Phanar at Constantinople 1867, Metropolitan of Serrae in Macedonia 1875, and of Nicomedia 1877: 296 n.
Buckinghamshire xv
Buddha 263
Bullock, William Henry, later W. H. Bullock-Hall (1837–1904), Balliol 1856–60, barrister 36, 185; married Elizabeth Dennistoun, daughter of William Cross of Champion Hill, Surrey 185
Bunsen, Baron Christian Carl Josias von (1791–1860), conducted the negotiations for the founding of the Anglo-Prussian bishopric at Jerusalem in 1841, and was Prussian Minister in London 1842–56. He published *Das evangelische Bisthum in Jerusalem. Geschichtliche Darlegung mit Urkunden* (1842), *Christianity and mankind, their beginnings and prospects*, 7 vols, including vols I and II, *Hippolytus and his age* (1854), *Gott in der Geschichte, oder der Fortschritt des Glaubens an eine sittliche Weltordung* (1857), transl. S. Winkworth, with a preface by A. P. Stanley, 3 vols (1868–70), 143, 147
Bunsen, Henry von, eldest son of Baron Christian von Bunsen (born 1818) 147
Burgon, John William (1813–88), Vicar of St Mary's Oxford 1864, and Dean of Chichester 1876: 274 n.
Burn, Revd R., Fellow and Tutor of Trinity College, Cambridge 128 n.
Burn, W. L., author of *The Age of Equipoise* (1964) xix
Busby, Dr Richard (1606–95), Headmaster of Westminster School, and Visitor of Balliol xxiii n.

INDEX

Butler, Revd Dr George (1818–90), examiner at Oxford 1850–2, Principal of Butler's Hall, Oxford 1856–8, Principal of Liverpool College 1866–82, Canon of Winchester 1882: 125, 145 n., 315; married Josephine Elizabeth (1828–1906), who went to Liverpool in 1866, set up homes for working girls and fallen women, supported campaign for higher education of women, and was secretary to Ladies National Association for Repeal of the Contagious Diseases Acts 1869–85: xxi, 125, 145 n., 179, 184, 206

Butler, Henry Montagu (1833–1918), Headmaster of Harrow School 1860–85, Dean of Gloucester 1885–6, Master of Trinity College, Cambridge 1886–1918: 241; married (1861) (1) Georgina Isabella Elliot 241, 286

Butler, Joseph (1692–1752), Bishop, author of *Analogy of Religion* (1736) 70, 93, 110

Butler, Samuel (1835–1902), author of *Erewhon* (1872) 243 n.

Cabinet, the x, xxv
Cain 148 n.
Caird, Edward (1835–1908), Balliol 1860–3, Fellow of Merton College 1864–6, Professor of Moral Philosophy at Glasgow 1866–93, Master of Balliol 1893–1907: 241, 290, 292
Caird, Sir James (1816–92), agriculturalist and author, MP (LC) Dartmouth 1857–9, Stirling Burghs 1859–65, member of Commission to inquire into Indian famine 1878–9: 283, 285, 288
Calcutta 19
Calne 108
Calvert, Frederick (1806–91), QC, brother of Sir Harry Verney 62 n.
Calvin, John (1509–64) 149
Calvinistic Church of Holland 17
Calvinists 149
Cambridge, George William Frederick Charles, Duke of (1819–1904), served in the Crimea, Commander-in-Chief 1856: 76, 93
Cambridge University xxx, 91 n., 126–7, 128, 145, 155 n., 174, 204, 266, 293
Cameron, Charles Hay (1795–1880), barrister, Commissioner on the administration of the law in Ceylon 1831, and on the Poor Laws 1833, law member of the Supreme Council of India 1835, returned to England in 1848. Married (1838) Julia Margaret Pattle (1815–79), the photographer, who took BJ's portrait at Freshwater 138
Campbell, Sir George (1824–92), wrote official account of the Mutiny, head of Commission to inquire into famine in Bengal 1866, DCL 1870, Lieutenant-Governor of Bengal 1871–4, KCSI 1873, MP (L) Kirkcaldy 1875–92: 262, 266, 279

Campbell, Lewis (1830–1908), Balliol 1850–5, Professor of Greek at St Andrews 1863–92: xxxv, xxxvi, xxxvii, 71, 72, 132, 153, 166, 174, 195, 231, 248 n., 262; married (1858) Frances Pitt Andrews 166

Camperdown, Adam Haldane-Duncan (1812–67), second Earl of Camperdown 94

Camperdown, Robert Adam Philips Haldane-Duncan (1841–1918), third Earl of Camperdown, Balliol 1859–63, Civil Lord of the Admiralty 1870–4: xxxi, 94, 153, 165, 276 n., 284 n.

Camperdown 178
Canada xxxi
Canning, Charles John (1812–62), Earl, MP (C) Warwick 1836, Under-Secretary for Foreign Affairs 1841–6, Postmaster-General 1853–5, Governor-General of India during the Mutiny, engaged in reorganizing the financial, legal and administrative systems in India 1859–62: 147

Cape Colony 281
Cape Town 146
Captain, the 200
Cardwell, Edward (1813–86), Balliol 1831–5, President of the Board of Trade 1852–5, Secretary for Ireland 1859–61, Chancellor of the Duchy of Lancaster 1861–4, Colonial Secretary 1864–6, and Secretary for War 1868–74: 90 n., 111, 140, 156, 162, 185, 214

careers for undergraduates xxxv
Carlisle, George James Howard (1843–1911), ninth Earl, artist 205 n.
Carlyle, Thomas (1795–1881) 11, 40, 90, 95, 96, 101, 123, 243, 246, 262, 264
Carpenter, Mary (1807–77), of Bristol, pioneer of reformatories for juvenile delinquents, visited India four times between 1866 and 1876 to investigate prison management and promote female education, published *Reformatory Schools* (1851), *Juvenile Delinquents, their Condition and Treatment* (1853), *Our Convicts*, 2 vols (1864), *Suggestions on Prison Discipline and Female Education in India* (1867), *Six Months in India*, 2 vols (1868) 119, 121

Carpenter, William Boyd, Bishop of Ripon, published 'Commentary on "Revelation"', in Bishop Ellicott ed., *New Testament Commentary for English readers* (1879), *Permanent elements of religion*, the Bampton lectures for 1887 (1889) 322

Cashmere 313
Cassandra 4, 8, 264
caste 263
Castlemaine, Lady 107
Catechetical Lectures xxiii, xxvi, 200 n.

332   INDEX

Catholic: Church, the 16; direction 64; esthetico 79; ideas 4; puritan 247; statesman 146
Catholicism 6, 89, 285
cattle plague 79, 106
Catullus 158
cause and effect 13
causes, external 10
Cavour, Camillo Benso, Count (1810–61) 33
Cebes 152
censorship xiv
centralization 139, 151, 161
centralized state xxii
Challis, Henry William (born 1841), of Merton College 107 n.
Chamberlain, Joseph (1836–1914) 302
Chancery, Court of 287
charges, bishops' 25, 69, 113
charities 282
charity 158, 254
Charity Commission xxi
Charity Organization Society xxii, 239
Charivari 195
Charles II (1630–85) 160 n.
Charles the Bold 33
Charteris, Alfred Walter (1847–73), 251
Charteris, Sir Evan (1864–1940), Balliol 1887–8, barrister, Chairman of National Portrait Gallery, Royal Commission on Museums 1927, Trustee of National Gallery 306
Charteris, Hon. Francis (1844–70), eldest son of Viscount Elcho, Balliol 1864, died of a revolver accident 22 July 1870 at 23 St James's Place 193, 194, 200
Chartists xix
Chatterton 300
Chelmsford *see* Thesiger
Cherwell, river 296 n.
Chester 124
Cheyne, Thomas Kelly (1841–1915), Worcester College and Göttingen, Vice-Principal of St Edmund Hall 1864–8, Fellow of Balliol 1868–82, Chaplain 1871, rector of Tendring 1880–5, joined Old Testament revision company in 1884, Oriel Professor of Interpretation of Scripture 1885–1908, Bampton Lecturer 1889: 226, 228
Chichester 274 n.
Childers, Hugh Culling Eardley (1827–96), inspector of schools at Melbourne 1851, and first Vice-Chancellor of Melbourne University, MP (L) Pontefract 1860–85, Financial Secretary to the Treasury 1865–6, First Lord of the Admiralty 1868–71, Chancellor of the Duchy of Lancaster 1872–3, Secretary of State for War 1880–2, Chancellor of the Exchequer 1882–5, MP South Edinburgh 1886, in favour of Home Rule 162
China 45, 95, 289

cholera 17, 18
Christ xvii, xviii, 6, 7, 11, 13–14, 23, 48, 55, 61, 71, 79, 105, 128, 134 n., 152, 182, 213, 214, 225, 237, 238, 251, 258, 260, 267, 302
Christ Church xii, 14, 43–4, 59 n., 66, 69, 114, 125, 128, 158, 212, 214, 215 n., 249, 297 n., 298 n.
Christian: book 296; charity 234; church 68; conduct xvii; doctrine 52; faith 238; feelings 65; humbugs 138; life 3; love 24; powers 284; sympathy 132
Christianity xvii, 3, 6, 35, 40, 52, 61, 79, 93, 149, 211, 238, 257
Christians xxv, xxxiv, 92, 245, 274, 277, 284, 285, 311
Church xviii, 16, 54, 56, 60, 63, 100, 110, 111, 116, 131, 132, 145, 146, 170, 174, 202, 216, 238, 253, 256, 264, 310, 311; authority of 35, 70; Broad xi, xvii, 15; High xiii, xxvi, 32, 38, 46, 60, 79, 82, 90, 111, 161, 172, 181, 219, 232–3, 248, 249, 257; Low 35
Church Discipline Act 10 n., 25
Church of England, Established Church xviii, xxxiii, xxxvii, 15, 16, 35, 65, 75, 79, 90–1, 92, 117, 123, 144, 172, 178, 186, 200, 240, 249, 274, 312; Convocation 16, 26, 117; Pan Anglican Synod 132
Church Party 186
churches 35, 154, 175, 186, 247
Churchill, Lord Randolph Henry Spencer (1849–94), Secretary of State for India 1885–6: 297, 298
churchyards 265
Civil Service x, xiv, xxii, 288, 297
Civil Service Commissioners 293, 294
Clarendon, George William Frederick Villiers (1800–70), fourth Earl of Clarendon, Lord Privy Seal 1839–41, President of the Board of Trade 1846, Lord Lieutenant of Ireland 1847–52, Foreign Secretary 1853–8, Chancellor of the Duchy of Lancaster 1864, Foreign Secretary 1865–6, 1868–70: 86, 155, 200 n.
Clark, Sir James (1788–1870), physician 159
class structure of society xxiv
classes and groups in society: agricultural labourers 30; aristocracies 91; aristocracy 63, 74, 131, 133, 153, 313; aristocracy, military 97, 195; aristocrats 119, 129, 194; aristocratic 28, 77, 84, 95, 115; artisans xii, xxiv, xxxiv, 13, 155; better class of soldiery xxi; bourgeoisie of the highest classes 74; capitalists 151; common people 35, 65; educated 13; employed 133; employers 133; farmers 66; gentlemen farmers 129; higher xxi, xxiv, xxxv, 13, 177; intelligent middle xix; labourers 59; labouring xx, 65, 80, 138; landed interest 65; lower 177, 299; lower people 191; lowest class 78; masses, the 214; masters 133; middle xxi, 108, 154, 247, 322; ouvriers 64; people at large 247; servants 133;

skilled workers 191; upper 92, 99, 154, 210, 247; upper ten thousand xvi; war of the 306; working 59, 88, 309; working man 64–5; workmen 58
classics, the x, xxviii, 27 n., 32, 76, 136, 178
Clay, Sir William (1791–1869), MP (L) for Tower Hamlets 1832–57: 85
Claydon xv, 307, 323
clergy xi, xvi, xvii, xviii, xx, xxi, xxxvii, 5, 16, 19, 26, 27, 30, 31, 35, 51, 61, 70, 81, 83, 84, 90, 113, 128, 133, 141, 151, 154, 160, 171, 173, 181, 213, 226, 244, 257, 283, 292; in Germany 257; orthodox 35
clerical: discipline xvii; fellowships xxiii, xxvi, 200 n., 274 n.; establishment xxvii; intolerance xvi
Cleveland, Harry George, Duke of (1803–91), MP (L) S. Durham 1841–59, Hastings 1859–64: 170, 274 n.
Clifton 57
Clive, Mrs Caroline Archer *née* Meysey-Wigley (1801–73), authoress who published mainly under the initial 'V' 39, 107, 155
Clive, Charles Meysey Bolton (1842–83), Balliol 1861–5: 107, 120; married 1867 Lady Katherine Fielding (died 1882), daughter of the seventh Earl of Denbigh 120
closed awards xxiii
Clough, Anne Jemima (1820–92), sister of A. H. Clough, Secretary 1867–70, and President 1873–4, of the North of England Council for promoting higher education of women, first Principal of Newnham College, Cambridge 1871: 145, 180
Clough, Arthur Hugh (1819–61), son of a Liverpool cotton merchant, educated at Rugby, Balliol 1837–40, Fellow of Oriel, Principal of University Hall, London, examiner in the Education Office, died at Florence xii, xiii, xvi, 13–14, 23, 37, 39 n., 55, 58, 59, 79, 96, 124, 142, 175, 181, 216; married Blanche, daughter of Samuel Smith, Examiner of Private Bills, of Combe Hurst, near Kingston, Surrey, and first cousin of FN, who played an important part in overcoming objections to the marriage 4, 13, 24, 108
Cobbett, William (1762–1835) 156
Cobden, Richard (1804–65) 34, 156
Coblentz 192
Colebrooke, Henry Thomas (1765–1837), published *Essays on the Religion and Philosophy of the Hindus* (1823–7, new edn. 1858) 211
Colenso, John William (1814–83), appointed Bishop of Natal 1853: 26, 27, 39, 56, 58, 124, 132, 146
Coleridge, Sir John Duke (1820–94), first Baron, Balliol 1838–42, QC 1861, MP (L) Exeter 1865–73, Solicitor-General 1868, Attorney General 1871, Chief Justice of Common Pleas 1873–80, Chief Justice of Queen's Bench 1880–94: xxv, 89, 91, 93, 111, 112, 115, 117, 135, 154, 170 n., 248, 316 n., 317
Coleridge, Samuel Taylor (1772–1834) 52, 88 n.
Coleridge's Bill 91, 154
college livings xvi, xxvii
Colley, Edith, daughter of Major-General H. Meade Hamilton married Sir George Pomeroy Colley (1835–81) in 1878: 291
Collins, Thomas (1825–84), MP (LC) for Knaresborough 1851–2, 1857–65, Boston 1868–74, Knaresborough 1881–4: 60
colonial: church 90–1; hospitals 31; prisons 52
Colonial Bishoprics Bill 90–1
Colonial Office 31
Combe, Andrew (1797–1847), phrenologist 148
Commander-in-Chief 17, 76 n., 93
commerce 85
Commissions: Army Hospitals and Health xiv, 62; Army in India xv, 17, 26, 28 n., 35, 62; Art and Science 202; Clarendon xx; Crimea xii; Devonshire xxv; Oxford University (executive) xii; Oxford University (inquiry) (1850) x, xxiii, 222 (1876) xxix; projected by FN on past government of India 288
committees: Macaulay's x, xxx; Oxford and Cambridge Universities 112 n.; University Extension xxiv, 127
communion/sacrament xvii, 19, 23, 24, 25, 26, 46, 84, 216, 250, 306, 311
communists 210, 215, 219
Como, Lake 263
compulsory chapel xxiii
Comte, Auguste (1798–1857), French positivist philosopher xxviii, 5–6, 95, 148, 157, 169
Comtism 219, 220
Comtist service 138
Comtists 6, 110, 236
confessions 32
Conington, John (1825–69), Fellow of University College, contributor to *Morning Chronicle*, Professor of Latin 1854–69: 180
Coniston 292
Connemara 283
Consalvi, Ercole (1757–1824), Secretary of State to Pope Pius VII 1800–6 and 1814–23: 38, 167
conscience 7, 16, 35, 40, 170, 182, 214, 271
conservatism xix, 94, 129
conservative 51, 125, 137
Conservatives 32, 82, 85, 111, 114, 118, 123, 127, 248
Constantinople 94, 193
contagion 106, 121, 176, 177
Contagious Diseases Acts xxi, 179, 184
Contemporary Review 264
convocation *see* Church of England

Cook, Sir Edward (1857–1919), biographer of Florence Nightingale xiii, xiv, xxxi, xxxii, xxxvi
co-operation 121
Cope, Edward Meredith (1818–73), Fellow of Trinity College, Cambridge 174 n.
Coquerel, Athanase (1795–1868) 82 n.
Cordery, John Graham (1833–1900), Balliol 1852–5, entered the Bengal Civil Service by the first competitive examinations held in 1855, served in the Punjab and Berar, then as assistant to the Resident at Hyderabad from 1864 to 1868 when he returned to England, went back to India, became Resident at Hyderabad in 1883, and retired in 1888: 169
Corn Laws 35
Corpus Christi College xxviii, 220 n., 248
Cortachy Castle 72, 100
cosmopolite 92
Cotton, Sir Arthur Thomas (1803–99), General, and irrigation engineer, worked in India 1821–62: 257
Cotton, Richard Lynch (1794–1880), Provost of Worcester College 1839–80, and Vice-Chancellor of Oxford University 1852–7: xi
Courtenay see Devon, Earl of
Cousin, Victor (1792–1867), French philosopher 157
Cradock, Revd Edward Hartopp Grove (1810–86), who took the name of Cradock in 1844, Balliol 1827–31, Principal of Brasenose College 1853–86: xvi, married (1844) Harriet Cradock (1809–84), the author of *Anne Grey* (1844), *The calendar of nature: or, the seasons of England* edited by Lord John Russell (1849), *Hulse House* (1860), *John Smith* (1878), *Rose* (1881): 166
Cranborne, Robert Arthur Talbot Gascoyne Cecil (1830–1903), Viscount Cranborne (1865) and Marquis of Salisbury (1868), MP (C) Stamford 1853–68, wrote for *Quarterly Review*, Secretary for India 1866–7, Chancellor of Oxford University 1869, Secretary for India 1874–8, and for Foreign Affairs 1878–80, Prime Minister and Foreign Secretary 1885–6, 1886–92, 1895–1900, resigned Foreign Secretaryship 1900 and Premiership 1902: 93, 115 n., 129 n., 170 n., 187, 248, 257, 259, 262, 266, 274, 283, 293; married Georgina Caroline Alderson 93
Cranbrook see Gathorne-Hardy
Cranworth see Rolfe
creed, the 176, 190, 224, 232, 234, 236, 249, 311
crime xxxii
Crimea xii, xiii, xiv, xv, xix, 13, 14, 62, 66, 76, 193, 232, 279, 280, 284
criticism 35, 42, 81, 137, 206, 218, 255, 273
Crito 56

Crofton, Sir Walter Frederic (1815–97), Chairman to the Directors of Convict Prisons in Ireland, knighted by the Lord Lieutenant in Dublin 1862: 121
Croker, John Wilson (1780–1857), Tory essayist, retired from parliament in 1832: 85 n.
Cross, Miss see Bullock, William Henry
Cross, Richard Assheton, first Viscount Cross (1823–1914), MP (C) Preston 1857–62, S. W. Lancs 1868, Home Secretary 1874–80, 1885–6, Secretary for India 1886–92: 316
crucifixion, the xvii, 52
Cupar 130
Cupid 225
custom and routine 68, 69, 154
Custozza, battle of 91

Dahomey 262
Daimios 264
Dalhousie, eleventh Earl (1801–74) see Panmure
Dalhousie, James Andrew Broun Ramsay (1812–60), ninth Earl, Governor-General of India 1848–56: 309
Dalhousie, Sir John William Ramsay (1847–87), thirteenth Earl, entered the navy 1861, Balliol 1875–6, toured with BJ in Switzerland in 1876: 279, 307; married (1877) Lady Ida Louise Bennet (died 1887) 307
Dammapad 182
Damrong, Prince (born 1862), half-brother of King Chulalongkorn (1853–1910) of Siam, and Minister of Education 317
Daniel 15
Dante (1265–1321) 286
Dartmoor 91
Darwin, Charles Robert (1809–82) xxviii, 169, 187, 207, 208, 211, 219
Darwinism 235, 290, 293
Davidson, Samuel (1806–98), Professor of Biblical Criticism at Belfast 1835–41, Professor of Biblical Literature and Ecclesiastical History at Lancashire Independent College, Manchester 1843–57, where the Committee objected to his views on the Old Testament 90, 91
Davies, John Llewellyn (1826–1916), Trinity College, Cambridge, Rector of Christ Church, Marylebone 1856–89: 89
Davos 284
deathbeds 308
Deborah 27
Deccan 288
defences of the country 306
Delane, John Thadeus (1817–79), editor of *The Times* 1841–77: 49 n.
Delitzsch, Franz (1813–90), a strict Lutheran, exegete and Hebraist, Professor of Theology

at Rostock in 1846, at Erlangen in 1850, and at Leipzig in 1867: 187
democracy 92, 123
democratic movement 123
democrats 110
Derby, Edward George Geoffrey Smith Stanley (1799-1869), fourteenth Earl, Prime Minister 1852, 1858-9, 1866-8: xxv, 41, 86, 91, 92, 99, 111, 144
Derby, Edward Henry Stanley (1826-93), fifteenth Earl, educated at Cambridge, Hon. DCL Oxford 1853, MP (C) King's Lynn 1848-69, Secretary for India 1858-9, Foreign Secretary 1866-8, succeeded as Earl 1869, Foreign Secretary 1874-8, left Conservatives, Colonial Secretary 1882-5, led Liberal Unionists in House of Lords 1886-91, Chancellor of London University 1891-3: xv, 17 n., 27, 61, 95, 111, 140, 277
Derbyshire xii, xiii, 194, 208
Descartes, René (1596-1650) 290
design (theol.) 119
devil 67, 106, 143, 150, 202
Devon, William Reginald Courtenay (1807-88), eleventh Earl, Secretary to the Poor Law Board 1850-9, and President 1867-8, Chancellor of the Duchy of Lancaster 1866-7: 119
Devonshire 246
Dicey, Albert Venn (1835-1922), Balliol 1854-60, barrister, Vinerian Professor of English Law and Fellow of All Souls 1882-1909, Official Fellow of Balliol for law students 1886-9: 278
dictionary 223, 224, 307
Diotima 152
Dipsychus 79
disestablishment 253, 256, 265; *see also* Irish Church
Disraeli, Benjamin (1804-81), first Earl of Beaconsfield, married (1839) Mary Anne, Mrs Wyndham Lewis (died 1872) xxv, xxvi, 38, 93, 111, 118, 120, 123, 128, 136, 140, 143, 144, 250
dissent 35, 75, 256
Dissenters xx, 146, 172, 186, 188, 253, 256, 265
dissenting: evangelicalism 90, 190; ministers 173, 188; tactics 253
divorce court 168
Döllinger, Johann Joseph Ignaz von (1799-1890), theologian 271
Donoughmore, John Luke George Hely-Hutchinson (1848-1900), fifth Earl, Balliol 1866-70, landowner 130, 138, 140, 148, 153
Dover ix
Drapier's Letters 262
Dublin, Co. 63
Duff, Sir Mountstuart Elphinstone Grant (1829-1906), Balliol 1847-50, barrister, MP (L) Elgin Burghs 1857-81, Lord Rector of Aberdeen

University 1866-72, Under-Secretary of State for India 1868-74, and for Colonies 1880-1, Governor of Madras 1881-6: 131, 154, 160, 264, 279, 322
Dufferin, Lady Helen Selina Sheridan *see* Gifford, Countess of
Dufferin and Ava, Frederick Temple Hamilton-Temple Blackwood (1826-1902), first Marquess, Under-Secretary for India 1864-6, and at War Office 1866-8, later Governor-General of Canada 1872-8, and Viceroy of India 1884-8: 73, 288, 293
Dulwich College 74, 159
Duncan, Lord *see* Camperdown
Dunkellin, Ulick de Burgh (1827-67), Adullamite 90 n.
Dunsany, Edward Plunkett (1808-89), sixteenth Baron, naval officer 295
Durham 175
dwellings of the poor 78, 128, 131, 151, 155, 161, 163

East, the 262, 277
East India Bill 18
'Easter poem' 39, 79
Eastern Question 285
Ecce Homo 79, 93, 137
ecclesiastical titles 107
Ecclesiastical Titles Act 300
Edgeworth, Maria (1767-1849), advocate of female education, published *Castle Rackrent* (1800), *Belinda* (1801), *Leonora* (1806), her father's *Memoirs* (1820), *Helen* (1834) 166, 167, 168, 169
Edinburgh 81-2, 136, 137, 171, 307
Edinburgh Review 122
Edinburgh Royal Infirmary 309 n.
Edinburgh University 82
educated classes 13
education ix, xvii, xviii, xix-xxi, xxii, xxxv, 27, 48, 79, 83, 106, 111, 112, 114, 115, 116, 117, 122, 134, 135, 136, 137, 138, 144, 151, 161, 162, 163, 186, 188, 201, 204, 222, 242, 244, 255, 258, 291, 299, 303, 317; at Oxford 32, 77, 127, 158; Board of 80; compulsory 183; department of 150; elementary xxv; female 180; higher English 307; in the Army 28; local Boards of xx; Lowe's views on 212; medical 58; middle class female 159, 160; military 28; national system of 178; of after life xxvii, 9; of Browning's son 59; of common people 35; of legislators and administrators 315; of Lord Mayo 153-4; of mankind 241; of the world 42; of women 7, 206, 272; old Tory 110; pauper 80; perfect 241; primary xx, xxi, xxiv, xxv, 112, 133; question 253; secondary xx, xxi; subjects of 7, 165; University xxi, xxiv, 133; weapon of the Jesuits 240

336   INDEX

Education: Act xxxii, 184–5; Board of 80; Office xii, xx; Privy Council Committee on xxv
educational: attainment xx; districts 117; improvement xxix; inspectors 117; movement 70; reform xxvii; science 106; spirit xxvii, 227; system xxiv
egotism 87, 169, 292
Egypt xiii, 67, 284, 285
Elcho *see* Wemyss, Francis
election (theol.) 67
electioneering question 62
elections (polit.) xxiv, 63, 128
electric telegraph xiv
Eliot, Sir Charles Norton Edgecumbe (1862–1931), Balliol 1880–3, diplomatic service, knighted 1900, resigned 1904, Vice-Chancellor of Sheffield University 1905–12, Principal of Hong Kong University 1912–18: 300
'Eliot, George', pseudonym of Mary Ann, or Marian Evans (1819–80) 188, 226, 237, 239 n., 247, 250, 256
Ellicot, Charles John (1819–1905), appointed Bishop of Gloucester and Bristol (1863): 246
Ellington, Colonel 93
Elliot, Revd Hon. Gilbert (1800–91), Dean of Bristol xvi, 252 n.
Elliot, Margaret, daughter of Gilbert Elliot xvi
Ellis, Robinson (1834–1913), Balliol 1852–7, Fellow of Trinity College 1858, Professor of Latin at University College, London 1870–6, Vice-President of Trinity 1879–93, Reader in Latin at Oxford 1883, Corpus Professor of Latin 1893: 158, 159, 174, 178, 183 n.
Elton, Charles (1839–1900), Balliol 1857–61: 44 n.
Embley xiii, 179, 194, 237, 315
emigration 152, 161, 183; coolie 262; from India 285
employers and employed 133
Encyclopedia Britannica 285
Endowed Schools: Act xxi; Bill 165
endowments 155
England xii, xiv, xix, 34, 59, 63, 67, 68, 92, 108, 110, 116, 156, 178, 193, 195, 216, 238, 242, 246, 257, 258, 276, 278, 285
English (people and affairs) 36, 47, 94, 96, 107, 110, 113, 140, 144, 193, 195, 201, 202, 204, 254, 284, 287, 298, 301, 307, 314, 316
'Enoch Arden' 36, 54
Ephesus 177, 188
Erewhon 243
Erskine, Thomas (1788–1870), of Linlathen, advocate and theologian, friend of Carlyle, A. P. Stanley and F. D. Maurice, 82, 105 n., 193
Essays and Reviews xi, xvi, xvii, xviii, 11, 15–17, 24, 27, 107, 245; proposed successor volume to 170, 171, 174, 249
Essays on International Policy 95
Essex xiii

Ethics, 70
Etive, Lake 263
Eton 56 n., 70, 77, 84, 175
Europe xix, 19, 34, 94, 97, 108, 158, 194, 195, 200, 201, 233, 240, 284, 306
European 193, 195
Europeans 19
Ewart, William (1798–1869), MP (Radical) for Dumfries boroughs 1841–68: 112 n.
Ewing, Alexander (1814–73), Bishop of Argyll, married (2) (1862) Lady Alice Douglas, daughter of the Earl of Morton 50
Eyre, Edward John (1815–1901), appointed Governor of Jamaica 1864, suppressed rebellion of 1865 and confirmed sentences of death in over 600 cases; supported by Carlyle, Kingsley, Ruskin, Tennyson, opposed by Thomas Hughes, Huxley, Mill, Goldwin Smith, Herbert Spencer 86, 93, 99, 101, 131, 243

Faber, Geoffrey (1876–1961), author of *Jowett* (1957) xvi, xxxiii, xxxvi
Fable of the Bees 56 n.
Factory Bill xx
faith 6, 14, 46, 48, 81, 190, 233, 238
Falk, Adalbert (1827–1900), Prussian minister of public worship and instruction 1872–9: 271
Falstaff 80
family relations xix, 4, 12, 78, 88–9, 107, 168, 186, 206, 214, 237, 251, 265, 283
fanaticism 12, 46, 64, 148, 234, 240, 277
Faraday, Michael (1791–1867) 190–1
farmers 66
Farr, William (1807–83), medical statistician, compiler of abstracts in Registrar General's office 1838–79: 314
Farrer, Sir Thomas Henry, first Baron Farrer (1819–99), Balliol 1836–41, barrister, Permanent Secretary to the Board of Trade 1865–86, member of London County Council 1889–98: 226
fatalism 145
fathers and daughters 168
Fawcett, Henry (1833–84), blinded in a shooting accident 1858, Professor of Political Economy at Cambridge 1863–84, MP (L) Brighton 1865–74, Hackney 1874–84, known as the 'Member for India', Postmaster-General 1880: 141 n., 253, 261, 279, 294
Ffolliott, John (1824–94), Sheriff of Sligo 1851 and of Leitrim 1882: 63 n., 232
Fielding *see* Clive, C.M.B.
Fitzgerald, Edward (1809–83), published the *Rubaiyat of Omar Khayyam* in 1859: 42
Fletcher, Mrs Eliza (1770–1858), her autobiography, edited by Lady Richardson, appeared in 1875: 274

INDEX 337

Fletcher, Frank (1867–1956), admitted as a library assistant and studied at Balliol 1886–9, literary secretary to BJ 1886–93, teacher in Mile End 1895–1900, and in Whitechapel 1901, Professor of Education 1904–6 and lecturer and later Professor of Classics at Exeter 1909–33: 306

Fliedner, Theodor (1800–64), Pastor, founded, 1836, an institute for nursing deaconesses at Kaiserswerth which was widely imitated in Europe and America xiii

Florence xvi, 247; as a Christian name 280

Forbes, William Henry (1851–1914), Balliol 1869–73, Fellow 1873–96, lecturer 1893–1902: 248, 282

Foreign Office 98, 155

formalisms 36

Forster, William Edward (1818–86), wool-trader, MP (L) Bradford 1861–86, Under-Secretary for the Colonies 1865, Vice-President of the Council 1868–74, carried the Elementary Education Act of 1870: 60, 165, 184, 208

Fortnightly Review 205, 283

Foundling Hospitals 79

Fowler, Thomas (1832–1904), Fellow of Lincoln College 1855–81, Wykeham Professor of Logic 1873–89, President of Corpus Christi College 1881: 25 n.

France xix, 34, 97, 121, 192, 193, 195, 202, 247, 257, 271, 289

Fraser, James (1818–85), Fellow of Oriel 1840–60, Chancellor of Salisbury diocese and Assistant Education Commissioner 1858, Commissioner to report on education in the United States and Canada 1865, and on employment of children in agriculture 1867, Bishop of Manchester 1870–85, arbitrated in trade disputes, seconded in Convocation the disuse of the Athanasian creed, supported in House of Lords the abolition of university tests 183, 254

Fraser's Magazine 93, 160, 239, 240

Frederick II, the Great (1712–86) 92, 193

free: agency xv, 5, 10, 29; thinkers 17, 166, 171, 178, 190; thinking 145, 206, 218; thought xi; trade xx, 64

Free Church 90, 146

freedom 9, 13, 16, 48, 181

freedom and necessity xv, 5, 10, 46

Freeman, Edward Augustus (1823–92), historian 44 n.

Frere, Sir Henry Bartle Edward (1815–84), Governor of Bombay 1862–7, accompanied the Prince of Wales to India 1875, Governor of the Cape 1877–80: 126, 127, 133 n., 240, 279

Freshwater 302

Froude, James Anthony (1818–94), historian, editor of *Fraser's Magazine* 1860–74, married

(2) Henrietta Elizabeth, daughter of John Ashley Warre, of West Cliff House, Ramsgate 33, 59, 246

Galileo (1564–1642) 41

Galton, Sir Francis (1822–1911), proved individuality and permanence of finger-prints, investigated heritability of genius, founded eugenics laboratory xxxi, xxxii

Game Laws 66, 67, 75

games 316

Gangooly, Mr 159

Garibaldi, Giuseppe de (1807–82) 33

Garrett, Alfred William (1844–1929), Balliol 1863–7, served in education departments in Bengal and Tasmania 107 n.

Garrett, Elizabeth *see* Anderson

Gaskell, James Milnes (1810–73), MP (C) for Wenlock 1832–68: 59, 146, 237; Mrs Gaskell 147

Gathorne-Hardy, Gathorne (1814–1906), first Earl of Cranbrook, MP (C) Leominister 1856–65, Oxford University 1865, Under-Secretary for Home Department 1858–9, President of Poor Law Board 1866, Home Secretary 1867–8, Secretary of State for War 1874–8, raised to the peerage 1878, Lord President of the Council 1885–92: 55 n., 63, 105

Gell, Philip Lyttelton (1852–1926), Balliol 1872–5, Secretary to the Delegates of the University Press 1883–97, first Chairman of Toynbee Hall 1884–96, literary executor of BJ, married (1889) Hon. Edith Mary Brodrick (1860–1944), daughter of the eighth Viscount Midleton 317

general election of 1865: 63

Genesis 46, 241

Genoa 247

gentlewoman, poor 204

German: nationality 195; oppressors 202; people 202, 203, 249; theology 35; unity 123

Germany xi, 63, 91, 95, 98, 195, 200, 202, 215, 271, 284

Gibbon, Edward (1737–94) 177

Gifford, Helen Selina Sheridan (1807–67), Countess of Dufferin and Countess of Gifford 73

Gilbert, Sir Joseph Henry (1817–1901), an agricultural chemist at Rothamsted, first holder of the Professorship of Rural Economy after its separation from the Chair of Botany 1884–90, knighted 1893: 288 n., 297

Gilboa 215

Ginx's baby 189

Girton College 291

Gladstone, William Ewart (1809–98) x, xxv, xxvi, 18, 28, 31, 34, 38, 41, 55, 57, 61, 63, 65, 75, 76, 82, 85, 86, 87, 88, 91, 92, 93, 108, 111, 112, 117, 118, 120, 123, 127, 129, 131, 135, 136, 137, 140,

Gladstone, William Ewart (cont.)
  142, 144, 145, 146, 154, 155, 156, 162, 163, 167, 170, 171, 172, 174, 177, 178, 181, 182, 208, 215, 250, 257, 265, 294, 299, 300, 307, 313; married (1839) Catherine Glynne (1812–1900) 92
Glasgow 214
Glasgow University xxvi, 211, 212, 218, 290
Glen Isla 152
Gloucester 246
God xii, xvii, xxii, xxxiii, 6, 15, 16, 18, 23, 24, 29, 33, 40, 43, 46, 47, 50, 51, 52, 55, 61, 62, 63, 66, 67, 69, 71, 81, 82, 83, 96, 106, 115, 130, 138, 145, 148 n., 149, 152, 158, 160, 174, 185, 199, 202, 207, 212, 214, 215, 216, 217, 218, 220, 224, 227, 232, 233, 234, 235, 236, 238, 241, 242, 244, 255, 259, 260, 265, 266, 267, 278, 280, 301, 304, 305, 308, 310, 311, 318, 319, 321, 323 *see also* Jehovah
Godavery Canal 278
Godley, John Arthur (1847–1932), first Baron Kilbracken, Balliol 1866–70, private secretary to Gladstone 1872 and 1880–2, Fellow of Hertford 1874–81, barrister, Commissioner of Inland Revenue 1882–3, Under-Secretary of State for India 1883–1909: 195, 298, 313
Godwin, William (1756–1836), Radical published *Enquiry concerning Political Justice* in 1793: 274
Goethe, Johann Wolfgang von (1749–1832) 139, 210, 243
Good Words 145
goodness 12, 38, 40, 111, 191, 221, 226, 227, 231, 236, 292, 310, 323
Goodwin, Alfred (1849–92), Balliol 1868–72, Fellow 1872–82, Professor of Greek at University College, London from 1882: xxvii
Gordon, George William, coloured member of the Jamaica Legislature, executed for his part in the rebellion at Morant Bay in 1865: 93, 101
Gordons 242
Gore, Charles (1853–1932), Balliol 1871–5, Bishop successively of Worcester, Birmingham and Oxford 312
Gorgias (Plato) 205, 246, 259
Gorham case 15
Goschen, George Joachim (1831–1907), MP (L) City of London 1863–80, Vice-President of Board of Trade 1865, Chancellor of Duchy of Lancaster 1866, President of Poor Law Board 1868–71, First Lord of the Admiralty 1871–4, MP Ripon 1880–5, East Edinburgh 1885–6, Liberal Unionist, Chancellor of the Exchequer 1886–92, MP (LU) for St George's Hanover Square 1887–1900, First Lord of the Admiralty 1895–1900, Viscount 1900, Chancellor of Oxford University 1903: 136, 155, 160, 161, 162, 183, 185, 208, 288; married (1857) Lucy Dalley (died 1898) 161
gospel history 35

Gospels, the xi, 139, 244, 260, 268
government 96, 132, 135, 178, 278, 315, 316; offices 114, 155, 229–30; *see also* ministry
governments xxxv, 298; Lord Derby's 99; of France 247; of Japan 264
Graham, Rutherford James (1850–72), Balliol 1868–71: 148 n., 175, 279 n.
grammar schools xx, xxi, 76, 109, 133
Grant, Sir Alexander (1826–84), Balliol 1844–9, Vice-Chancellor of Bombay University 1863–8 and director of public instruction, Principal of Edinburgh University 1868–84: 51, 127, 171, 293
Grants 242
Granville, Granville George Leveson-Gower (1815–91), second Earl, Foreign Secretary 1851–2, 1870–4, 1880–5, Lord Warden of the Cinque Ports 1865: xxv, 106, 135, 146, 200, 201, 273, 289
Gray, Robert (1809–72), Bishop of Cape Town 1847–72: 132, 146
Great Western Railway 59
Greece xiii, 50
Greek Professorship xi, xii, 218, 224, 249
Greek tragedians 210
Greeks 57, 183, 281, 310
Green, Thomas Hill (1836–82), Balliol 1855–9, Fellow 1861, Assistant Commissioner on middle class schools 1865, in charge of Balliol 'Hall' and of out-students, delegacy of Oxford 'Locals', President of Oxford Temperance Union 1876, member of Oxford Town Council 1876, Whyte's Professor of Moral Philosophy 1878: xxviii, 186, 207, 220, 235, 241, 244, 260, 266, 282, 290, 291; married Charlotte Byron (1842–1929), daughter of Dr Symonds 207, 291, 298–9, 311, 318
Greg, Favour James (1846–70), Glasgow University, and Balliol 1866–70: 187
Greville, Charles Cavendish Fulke (1794–1865), Clerk to the Council 296
Greville Memoirs 296
Grey, George Frederick Samuel Robinson de (1827–1909), succeeded his father as Earl of Ripon and his uncle as Earl de Grey in 1859, successively Under-Secretary at the War Office, June 1859, at the India Office, January 1861, and at the War Office, July 1861 to April 1863, Secretary for War 1863–6, Secretary for India 1866, Marquis of Ripon 1871, an erstwhile Christian Socialist who became a Roman Catholic in 1874, Governor-General of India 1880–4: 19, 27 n., 45, 115 n., 116, 287, 288, 293, 294, 314, 316
Grosvenor, Richard *see* Westminster
Grosvenor, Hon. Richard Cecil (1848–1919), Balliol 1866–9, later barrister and alderman 130, 132, 134, 138, 140

INDEX

Grote, George (1794-1871), historian 44, 56, 68, 69, 72, 239, 240, 255; married Harriet Lewin (1792-1878) 66, 239, 240, 255

Guizot, Francois Pierre Guillaume (1787-1874) 75

Gull, Sir William Withey (1816-90), tutor at Guy's Hospital, physician to Queen Victoria, Hon. DCL 1868: 301, 303

Guthrie, Dr Thomas (1803-73), preacher and philanthropist, minister at Old Greyfriars, Edinburgh 1837-40, and at St John's 1840-64, joined Free Church 1843, published *Plea for Ragged Schools* (1847-9), and *Plea on Behalf of Drunkards* (1851) 183

Halifax, Sir Charles Lindley Wood (1839-1934), second Viscount, leader of the Anglo-Catholics in face of the prosecutions following the Public Worship Regulation Act of 1874: his attempt to initiate conversations between Canterbury and Rome resulted in the latter condemning Anglican orders in 1896: 129

Hall, Sir John (1795-1866), army surgeon and principal medical officer in the Crimea 1854-6: xv

Hall, W. H. *see* Bullock, William Henry

Hallam, Arthur Henry (1811-33), betrothed to Tennyson's sister and the subject of *In Memoriam*, author of *Essays and Remains* (pub. 1834) 237

Hamilton, Walter Kerr (1808-69), Bishop of Salisbury 1854-69: 146 n.

Hamilton, Sir William (1788-1856), educated at Glasgow and Balliol, where he was an intimate of J. G. Lockhart, Professor of Civil History at Edinburgh 1821, and Professor of Logic and Metaphysics 1836: 157, 252

Hamilton-Hoare, Henry William (1843-1931), Balliol 1862-6, lecturer at Balliol and Worcester Colleges 1869, Education Department 1870, Chief Clerk 1893, Assistant Secretary Board of Education 1900-4, published *The Evolution of the English Bible* (1901), *The Question of Disestablishment* (1906) 254

Hammond, James Lempriere (1828-80), bursar of Trinity College, Cambridge 128 n.

Hampshire xiii

Hampstead 3, 273, 306

Handel, George Frederick (1685-1759) 249

Hannen, Sir James (1821-94), appointed a Judge of the Queen's Bench 1868: 140

'Hansard' 78

Hardy, Thomas (1840-1928), novelist and poet xxiv

Harris, James (1709-80), author of 'Hermes' 65

Harrison, Edwin (1844-99), Balliol 1867-72, career ruined by ill-health 155 n., 159, 172, 175, 176, 185, 195, 211, 215, 217, 219, 242, 271

Harrow 70, 241, 267, 302

Hartington, Spencer Compton Cavendish (1833-1908), Marquess, and eighth Duke of Devonshire, MP (L) North Lancs. 1857, Radnor Boroughs 1869, North-East Lancs. 1880, Rossendale 1885-91 when he succeeded his father, leader of the Liberal Unionists 302

Hartmann, Karl Robert Edouard von (1842-1906), German philosopher 293

Haweis, Hugh Reginald (1838-1901), incumbent of St James's Marylebone 1866-1901. Filled his church, and organized 'Sunday evenings for the people'; pioneer of Sunday opening of museums 160

Hawes, Sir Benjamin (1797-1862), MP (Whig) for Lambeth 1832-47, Kinsale 1848-52, Under-Secretary for War 1857-62: xv

Hawkins, Edward (1789-1882), Provost of Oriel College 1828-74: 52

Haydn, Franz Joseph (1732-1809) 249

Hayman, Henry (1823-1904), Fellow of St John's College, Oxford 1844-55, elected Headmaster of Rugby in spite of protests from masters 1869, instituted unsuccessful proceedings against governors for dismissal 1874, Hon. Canon of Carlisle 1884: 182

health, BJ's xxviii, xxxv, 46, 73, 87, 91, 98, 100, 113-14, 136-7, 162, 163, 167, 173, 182, 188, 192, 205, 212, 225, 236, 239, 240, 243, 244, 250, 255, 265, 268, 274, 292, 293, 301-2, 302, 303, 305-6, 312, 317, 318, 321, 322

health, FN's xiv, xxxii, xxxvii, 3-4, 5, 14, 18, 23, 24, 25, 26, 28-9, 39, 46, 49, 52, 53, 71, 81, 84, 105, 114, 137, 163, 167, 169-70, 188, 208-9, 233, 273, 303, 309, 320

Health Department 150

health of a Greek city 125-6

Health of Towns Movement xix

Heathcote, Sir William (1801-81), Oriel College, Fellow of All Souls 1822-5, MP (C) for Hants 1826-32, Hants N. 1837-49, and for Oxford University 1854-68: 55 n.

heaven 87

Hebrew prophets 47, 210

Hegel, Georg Wilhelm Friedrich (1770-1831) xi, 6, 47, 51, 52, 112, 145, 147, 157, 235, 244, 260, 267, 290

Hegelianism 220

hell 61, 68, 87, 213

Hellas 281

Henry IV (1367-1413) 135

Henry VII (1457-1509) 93

Henry VIII (1491-1547) 59, 93

Heraclitus 47

Herbert, George Robert Charles *see* Pembroke, Earl of

340   INDEX

Herbert, Reginald 200
Herbert, Sidney, first Baron Herbert of Lea
  (1810–61), Secretary at War 1852–5: xiii, xiv,
  xv, xvi, xxiii, xxxi, 11, 17, 18, 26, 29, 45, 47–8,
  49, 55, 66, 71, 72, 105, 126, 133, 142, 147, 214,
  230, 232; married Mary Elizabeth A'Court
  (1822–1911) 43, 50, 51, 77, 166
Hermes, The 65
Herschel, Caroline Lucretia (1750–1848), sister of
  Sir William Herschel (1738–1822) 274
Hervey, Lord Francis (1846–1931), Balliol 1865–9,
  Fellow of Hertford College 1874, MP (C) for
  Bury St Edmund's 1874–80 and 1885–92,
  London School Board 1876–9, Second Civil
  Service Commissioner 1892–1907, and First
  Commissioner 1907–9: 152 n., 153
Heurtley, Charles Abel (1806–95), Lady
  Margaret Professor of Divinity 25 n.
Hezekiah 73
Higgs, Arthur Hibble (1850–1915), Balliol 1869–
  74: 219, 242
Higham, Revd James Bellamy, incumbent of
  East Claydon, Bucks, 1888–93: 322
Hindus 45, 149, 263
Hippias Minor (Plato) 96
Hippocrates 183
Hirst Grove 82 n.
Historical Portrait Exhibition 93
history 6, 9, 40, 147, 165, 215, 224
Hobbes, Thomas (1588–1679) 93
Hobhouse, Arthur (1819–1904), Baron
  Hobhouse, Balliol 1836–40, barrister 1845, QC
  1862, Charity Commissioner 1866, one of
  three Commissioners for reorganizing
  endowed schools 1869–72, law member of
  Council of Governor General of India 1872–7,
  member of Judicial Committee of Privy
  Council 1881–1901, member of London
  School Board 1882–4, Alderman of London
  County Council 1889: 205 n., 227, 254
Home, Daniel Dunglas (1833–86), spiritualist
  medium descended from the tenth Earl of
  Home, returned to England from USA in
  1855, séances attended by Sir Edward Bulwer
  and the Brownings, became a Roman
  Catholic, held séances before sovereigns of
  France, Prussia and Holland 1857–8, expelled
  from Roman Church as a sorcerer 1864,
  followed German army from Sedan to
  Versailles 1870: 178, 190
Home Office 199
Homer 18, 41, 76, 86, 154, 174, 313
Hopkins, Gerard Manley (1844–89), Balliol
  1863–8: 107 n.
Horace 292 n.
Hornby, James John (1826–1909), Balliol 1845–9,
  Fellow of Brasenose 1849–69, Headmaster of
  Eton 1868–84, Provost of Eton 1884–1909: 137

Horse Guards, the 17
hospital: management 152; training 298; work 98
hospitals xiii, xiv, 23, 67, 78, 97, 98, 106, 110, 114,
  124, 152, 159, 192, 238, 280, 282, 299, 304;
  colonial 31–2
Hospitals: King's College xv; Middlesex 162; St
  Thomas's 229, 311, 312, 313; Westminster 255
Houghton *see* Milnes
House of Commons xix, 34, 62, 76, 87, 89, 93,
  154, 162, 170, 171 n., 174 n., 208, 241, 259, 261,
  272, 298
House of Lords 45, 49, 87 n., 118, 120, 123, 170,
  171, 173, 243–4, 259, 284, 286
Houses of Parliament 83, 117
Howard, George James *see* Carlisle
Howson, John Saul (1816–85), Dean of Chester
  124 n.
Hozier, J. W. (1834–1905), Balliol 1852–8: 105
Huddleston, Sir John Walter (1815–90), QC
  1857, MP (C) Canterbury 1865–8, Norwich
  1874–5, Judge Advocate of the Fleet 1865–75,
  Judge of Common Pleas 1875–80, and of the
  Queen's Bench 1880–90: 140
Huguenots 135
human: actions 9; beings 175; character 310;
  creatures xxv; history 211; ingenuity 212;
  nature 5, 6, 10, 12, 40, 46, 52, 166, 168, 220, 247;
  race 50, 133, 152, 259; reason 214; species 7;
  talents 12
Hume, David (1711–76) 244, 267
Hunt, George Ward (1825–77), MP (C) North
  Northants 1857–77, Financial Secretary to
  Treasury 1866–8, Chancellor of the Exchequer
  1868, First Lord of the Admiralty 1874–7: 62
Hunter, Sir William Wilson (1840–1900),
  educated at Glasgow University, studied
  Sanskrit at Paris and Bonn, entered Indian
  Civil Service in 1861, appointed by Lord
  Mayo in 1869 to organize statistical survey of
  Indian Empire which appeared as *The Imperial
  Gazetteer of India*, 9 vols (1881), LLD Glasgow
  1869, promoted by Balliol College for an MA
  by decree in 1889, examiner in Oriental
  Studies at Oxford 1889–90: 293, 301, 308, 314
husbands and wives xix, 245–6
Huxley, Thomas Henry (1825–95), scientist 169,
  218, 220
Hyacinthe, Père *see* Loison
Hyderabad 169

Iatrocles 183
ideal of public worship 176
idealism 72, 190, 241
'Idylls' 7
Iffley Lock 296 n.
Ilbert, Sir Courtenay Peregrine (1841–1924),
  Balliol 1860–4, Fellow 1864–74, barrister,
  Counsel to Education Department 1879–82,

law member of Executive Council of Governor General of India 1882-6, Vice-Chancellor of Calcutta University 1885-6, Counsel to the Treasury 1889-1901, Clerk to the House of Commons 1902-21, trustee of Jowett Memorial Fund, Honorary Fellow, married Jessie, daughter of Revd Charles Bradley xxiii, 287 n., 288, 293, 300 n., 317
illusions of language 13
immaculate conception 46
immortality xvii, 6, 7, 152, 153
improvement xxv, 4, 5, 41
income tax 76, 208
India ix, x, xiv, xv, xviii, xxix, xxx, xxxii, 19, 24, 54, 117, 119, 127, 133, 138, 153, 165, 262, 263, 266, 278, 284, 285, 289, 322
India: caste in 263; Civil Servants in 293; Civil Service in xxix, 314; Council 45, 288, 316; FN's article on 277 n.; FN as Governor-General of 130; FN's pamphlet on 119; government of xviii, 313; government of by Sir J. Lawrence 117; Governor-Generals of xxxi, 142, 228, 276, 288, 313, 314, 316; health of army in 31; Ilbert Bill for 288, 300; interest in 279; irrigation in xxix, 44 n., 259, 279, 309; justice in 287; land question in 276, 288; legal affairs of native ladies in 322; Minister for 288; municipal government in 314; native Princes in 314; native troops in 314; Office 228, 266, 297; old officials 132; permanent settlement in 277; possibilities of 254; Provincial Councils in 314; Report 26; rivers of 308; Sanitary Commission 35; sanitary condition of 73; sanitary regulations in large towns 19; sanitary state of army in 28 n.; Secretaries for 276; Secretary of State for xxx; service to 288; Writerships in 31
Indian: affairs 127, 304; agriculture 297; cadetships ix, x; candidates xxix-xxxi, 280, 287; Civil Service xxx, 297; Civil Service Association 298 n.; civilians 297; Commission 17; Councils Bill 316 n.; engineering 259; government xxix; hospitals 304; lover 115; Mutiny xiv; officials, old 276; poem 304; politics 276; population 285; Probationers 297; prospects, FN's 130; sanitary matters 19; School at Oxford 294, 295; students xxxii, 297; subjects 262; victories, FN's 133; work, FN's 129, 232, 275
Indians 282
industrial regiments 28
influences: external 10; internal 10
inspiration: of error 213; of scripture 47
Invalid Gentlewomen's Institution xiii
Inverleithie 313
Ireland 63, 233, 283, 300; denominational schools in 172; Union with 300 n.
Irish: church 75, 123, 140, 142, 143, 144, 170 n., 173 n., 232-3; Encumbered Estates Act 64 n.; Home Rule Bill 298; land 140, 144, 174, 185, 187, 233; Land League 283; national system of education 178; nationality 144; Universities Bill 238
irrigation xxix, 44 n., 257, 259, 309
Isaiah 15
Isle of Wight 125
Italian Lakes 299
Italians 91
Italy xiii, 33, 63, 92, 195, 247, 270, 284, 299; history of 285
Iwakura, Baron Tomatsume (1853-90), studied in America and Europe 1870-8; Balliol Hilary Term 1874, served in Japanese Foreign Service and imperial Household 249, 252, 253, 254, 264
Iwakura, Prince Tomomi (1835-83), Chief Councillor of State (Prime Minister) of Japan 249, 252, 254, 255

Jackson, John (1811-85), Pembroke College, Bishop of Lincoln 1853-68, and of London 1868-85, Visitor 1853-85: xxiii, xxvi, 184, 199, 200, 208, 225, 228
Jamaica 93, 101, 210
Janet, Paul (1823-99) 156
Japan 262, 264
Japanese, the 253
Japanese: movement 254; students xxvii
Jebb, Sir Joshua (1793-1863), Surveyor-General of convict prisons 31, 121
Jehovah 27
Jehu 100
Jenkyns, Richard (1782-1854), Master of Balliol College 1819-54: xi
Jenner, Sir William (1815-98), physician at University College Hospital 1854-76, Professor of Principles and Practice of Medicine 1863-72, established the distinct identities of typhus and typhoid fever 250, 255, 260, 268
Jersey 312
Jerusalem bishopric 147
Jesuits 70, 240
Jeune, Francis (1806-68), Master of Pembroke College 1843-64, Vice-Chancellor 1858-62, Bishop of Peterborough 1864-8: 50, 150
Jewish prophets 41, 47
Jews 77
Jex-Blake, Thomas William (1832-1915), Headmaster of Rugby 1874-87, Dean of Wells 1891-1910: 317
Jocelyn, Chronicle of 42
John, King 42
John of the Cross, St 124
Johnson, Samuel (1709-84) 55, 56, 65, 68, 75 n., 223, 224, 266, 300
Johnson's Dictionary 223

Jones, Agnes (died 1868), niece of Sir John Lawrence, followed in FN's footsteps to Kaiserswerth and as a probationer at St Thomas's. Selected by FN to reform workhouse nursing in Liverpool 61 n., 125, 138, 139, 142, 144, 150 n., 157 n., 187, 242
Jones, Bence 190 n., 191
Jones, Ernest Charles (1819–69), Chartist leader and poet, barrister 1844: 160
Jowett, Agnes, BJ's sister ix
Jowett, Alfred, BJ's brother (1821–58) MRCS 1846, obtained an Indian cadetship upon the recommendation of Lord Ashley ix, x, xxix, 19
Jowett, Benjamin (1788–1859), BJ's father ix, x
Jowett, Ellen, BJ's sister ix
Jowett, Emily, BJ's sister (1815–82) ix, x, 19 n., 45, 166, 179–80, 207, 218, 286
Jowett, Francis, BJ's brother ix
Jowett, Frederick, BJ's brother ix
Jowett, Isabella, BJ's mother, born Langhorne (1790–1869) ix, x, xxxv, 19 n., 45, 47, 49, 98, 99, 150, 179, 180
Jowett, Isabella, BJ's sister ix
Jowett, William Hudson, BJ's brother (1825–50), obtained an Indian cadetship upon the recommendation of Lord Ashley ix, x, xxix, 19
Jubilee 303
Judas 55
Jude the obscure xxiv
Judea 50
judge 16, 140
Judgement, Day of 254
judgement, legal 16
Julius Caesar 234
Junius 118
just, the 40
justice 11, 16, 41, 72, 152; of God 15

Kaiserswerth xiii
Kant, Immanuel (1724–1804) 157, 241, 267
Keble College 110, 297 n., 298 n., 312
Kelvin *see* Thomson, Sir William
Kempis, St Thomas of 225, 238
Kendall, Guy (1876–1960), author xxxvi
Kent, Armine Thomas (1856–1903), Balliol 1874–9, journalist 267
Keswick 287, 292
Khedive 285
Kilbracken *see* Godley
Kimberley *see* Wodehouse
Kinadon's conspiracy 44 n.
King, Bolton (1860–1937), Balliol 1879–83, Toynbee Hall 1884–92, Director of Education in Warwickshire 1904–20: 283
Kingsdown *see* Pemberton-Leigh
Kingsley, Charles (1819–75), Rector of Eversley, Regius Professor of Modern History at Cambridge 1860–9, author of *Yeast* (1848), *Alton Locke* (1850), *Westward Ho!* (1855), *Water Babies* (1863), *Hereward the Wake* (1865), etc. 99, 101
Kirk, J. F. 33
Knight, father of Martha and Matthew Knight, died 1880: 66 n.
Knight, Martha Jane (1847–1930) 315, 318, 322
Knight, Matthew John (died 1895 at age 42) 226, 262, 268, 271, 284
Knox, John (1505–72), 82
Krasinski, Sigismund (1812–59) 37
Kulla Panthaka 182
Kynance Cove 252

La Valette, Charles Jean Marie Felix (1806–81), Marquis de, Minister of the Interior 1865–7, and of Foreign Affairs 1868–9, Ambassador at London 1869: 108
Laity 133
Lakes, the 289
Lamarck, Jean Baptiste Pierre Antoine de Monet (1744–1829), French naturalist who argued in favour of the inheritance of acquired characteristics 207
Land Freehold Scheme 64–5, 66
Land Question 177–8
land registration 194
Land Tax 78
Land's End 252
Lankester, Edwin (1814–74), Coroner for Middlesex, and Medical Officer of Health for St James's Westminster 79
Lansdowne, Henry Charles Keith Petty-Fitzmaurice (1845–1927), fifth Marquess, Balliol 1863–7, succeeded father in 1866, junior Lord of Treasury 1869, Under-Secretary for War 1872–4, Under-Secretary of State for India 1880, resigned over Gladstone's Irish policy 1880, Governor-General of Canada 1883–8, Viceroy of India 1888–94, Secretary of State for War 1895–1900, and for Foreign Affairs 1900–5, joined first coalition government in 1915: xxxi, 67, 98, 100, 108, 130, 132, 152 n., 153, 204, 206 n., 228, 230, 231 n., 260, 272, 284 n., 309, 312, 314, 315, 316, 322, married (1869) Lady Maud Evelyn Hamilton, seventh daughter of the second Duke of Abercorn 260, 322
Lansdowne, Sir Henry Petty-Fitzmaurice (1780–1863), third Marquess 74
Lansdowne, Sir Henry Thomas Petty-Fitzmaurice (1816–66), fourth Marquess 67, 98
Latham, Revd Henry (1821–1902), Fellow and Tutor of Trinity Hall, Cambridge 1848–88, Master 1888–1902: 128 n.
Latham, Peter Mere (1789–1875), physician, educated at Brasenose and St Bartholomew's,

physician to the Middlesex Hospital 1815–24, and to St Bartholomew's 1824–41: 179, 192
law xv, 5, 9, 10, 12, 15, 16, 31, 47, 48, 50, 53, 56, 119, 226, 291; common 25; courts of 16, 25, 27, 39, 40, 62, 244, 287, 321; giver 50; reign of 217
Law, Universal 6, 9, 46
law and custom 16
Lawes, Sir John Bennet (1814–1900), first Baronet, resided on family estates at Rothamsted where he started the agricultural experiment station in 1843: 290
Lawrence, John Laird Mair (1811–79), first Baron Lawrence, went to India in 1830, Chief Commissioner for the Punjab 1853–7, KCB 1856, helped recapture Delhi from the mutineers, created Baronet 1858, at India Office 1859–62, Viceroy of India 1863–9, created Baron 1869, Chairman of the London School Board 1870–3, opposed Afghan War of 1878–9: 41, 54, 55, 117, 121, 127, 142 n., 165, 266, 275, 279
laws 205; fixed 160; of God 83, 152, 242; of nature 6, 18, 83, 220
lawyers xviii, 15, 24, 64, 81, 94, 323
Lecky, William Edward Hartpole (1838–1903), historian 72, 126
Lee, James Prince (1804–69), appointed Bishop of Manchester 1847: 26
Lee, Dr Robert (1804–68), minister of the Old Greyfriars Church, Edinburgh, 1843–68, and Professor of Biblical Criticism, published *The Reform of the Church in Worship, Government and Doctrine* (1864) 82, 219
legacy duties 76
legal judgement 16
Leith Hill 226
Leopold of Hohenzollern, whose candidature for the Spanish throne was exploited by Bismarck to bring on the war with France in 1870: 192
Lessing, Gotthold Ephraim (1729–81) 42
Lewes, George Henry (1817–78), lived with George Eliot from 1854 until his death 56, 226
Lewis, Sir George Cornewall (1806–63), Poor Law Commissioner for England and Wales 1839–47, MP (L) Herefordshire 1847, Under-Secretary at the Home Office 1848, Financial Secretary to the Treasury 1850–2, editor of the *Edinburgh Review* 1852–5, MP Radnor Boroughs 1855–63, Chancellor of the Exchequer 1855–8, Home Secretary 1859–61, Secretary for War 1861–3: 17, 18, 19, 27 n., 131, 132
liberal (persons, sentiments etc.) xi, xxi, xxii, xxiv, 25, 64, 72, 76, 89, 101, 113, 128, 131, 132, 138, 146, 172, 181, 246, 249, 251, 271, 274, 292, 315
Liberal: anti-democratic xxv; cause in Germany 121; conservative 115; leaders xxv; Party xxiv, xxvi, 111, 127, 136, 253; politics xxi; Unionist xxvi
Liberalism 129, 181, 224
liberality 127, 147, 181, 234
Liberals xxiv, 57, 62, 90, 99, 107, 110, 118, 127, 129, 143, 181, 240, 260, 273
Liberals, Union 299
Lichfield 136
Liddell, Adolphus George Charles (1846–1920), Balliol 1865–9, barrister 1871, assistant secretary to Lord Chancellor's department 1888–1919: 175
Liddell, Henry George (1811–98), Headmaster of Westminster School 1846–55, Dean of Christ Church 1855–91, published with Robert Scott *Greek-English Lexicon* (1843) xxx, 43–4, 125, 128, 166, 212, 224; married Lorina Reeve (1846) 166, 185, 249
Liddon, Henry Parry (1829–90), Vice-President of Cuddesdon Theological College 1854, and of St Edmund's Hall 1859, Ireland Professor of Exegesis 1870–82, Canon of St Paul's Cathedral 1870, left ready for publication three volumes of a life of Pusey 51, 64, 107, 223
Life of Mr Richard Savage 75
Lightfoot, John Prideaux (1803–87), Rector of Exeter College 1854–87, Vice-Chancellor 1862–6: 25 n.
Lincoln, Abraham (1809–65) 148
Lind, Jenny (1820–87), singer 306
Lindsay, Alexander Dunlop (1879–1952), Master of Balliol College 1924–49: xxxvi
Lingen, Ralph Robert Wheeler (1819–1905), first Baron Lingen, Trinity College, Oxford, Fellow of Balliol 1841, Secretary to the Education Office 1849–69, introduced Lowe's code of payment by results into the schools, Permanent Secretary to the Treasury 1869–85, married Emma (died 1908), daughter of Robert Hutton, MP (L) for Dublin 1837–41: xx, 112, 117, 121, 126, 199, 302
Linnhe, Loch 263
Li-Po 42, 50–1
Lisa, a Russian story 185
literary criticism 218
Liverpool xii, 85, 137, 150 n., 157; University 258
Lives of the Poets 75
Livy 98
Lizard, The 252
Locke, John (1632–1704) 5, 70
Lockhart, Laurence William Maxwell (1831–82), served at Sebastopol, *Times* correspondent in Franco-Prussian War 199
Loison, Charles, 'Père Hyacinthe' (1827–1912), French pulpit orator, excommunicated for refusing to accept the doctrine of Papal

Loison, Charles (cont.)
  infallibility, married in 1872, and became curate of a congregation of liberal Catholics in 1873, founded a Gallican congregation in Paris in 1879: 203, 310n.
London xvii, xxii, xxv, xxx, 26, 67, 69, 78, 85, 93, 112, 116, 134, 150n., 152, 155, 156, 158, 161, 163, 170, 187, 189, 200, 213, 236, 237, 238, 264, 275, 276, 284, 297, 308
London School Board 273
London University 155n., 183, 238
Long Niddry 292
Longley, Charles Thomas (1794–1868), appointed Archbishop of Canterbury 1862: 26
Longmans, publishers 246, 257, 260
Lorraine 202
Lowe, Robert (1811–92), first Viscount Sherbrooke, barrister 1842, went to Sydney and entered legislative council for New South Wales, returned to England and became a leader writer on *The Times* 1850, MP (L) Kidderminster 1852–9, Vice-President of the Board of Trade and Paymaster General 1855–8, MP Calne 1859–67, Vice-President of the Committee of Council on Education 1859–64, MP London University 1868–80, Chancellor of the Exchequer 1868–73, Home Secretary 1873–4, ennobled 1880: xx, xxv, xxvi, 66, 72, 76, 79, 82, 85, 87, 92, 105, 107, 108, 111, 112, 115, 116, 117, 118, 120, 124, 127, 135, 136, 137, 138, 140, 155, 156, 161, 164, 165, 167, 181, 182, 183, 186, 191, 194, 205 n., 208, 212, 224, 225, 230, 231, 241, 272, 301, married (1) (1836) Georgiana Orred (died 1884) 92, 115, 119, 186
Lucifera 205
Luffenham xii
Luke, George Rankine (1836–62), Balliol 1855–9, Student of Christ Church 1859–62: 14, 242
lunatic asylums 31
Lushington, Alice 46, 203
Lushington, Fanny 46, 203
Lushington, Godfrey (1832–1907), Balliol 1850–4, Permanent Under-Secretary at the Home Office 1885–95: 44, 46, 58, 122, 310; married Beatrice Ann Shore Smith, the daughter of FN's Aunt Mai, Mrs Samuel Smith 44, 46, 58
Lushington, Laura 203
Lushington, Dr Stephen (1782–1873), Fellow of All Souls, barrister, MP (Whig) Great Yarmouth 1806–8, Ilchester 1820–6, Tregony 1826–30, Winchelsea 1831, Ilchester 1831–2, Tower Hamlets 1832–41, Privy Councillor, Judge of the High Court of Admiralty 1838–67 and Dean of Arches 1858–67: 15, 16, 17, 39, 60, 74, 155, 203
Luther, Martin (1483–1546) 50
Luxemburg 121, 192
Lyall, Sir Alfred Comyn (1835–1911), Indian civil servant, successively Home Secretary and Foreign Secretary to the Indian Government, Lieutenant-Governor of the North West provinces and Oudh 1882–7, founded new University of Allahabad, member of India Council in London 1887–1902, published *Rise of British Dominion in India* (1893), Ford's Lecturer 1908: 313
Lytton, Edward Robert Lytton (1831–91), first Earl of, Minister to Portugal 1874–6, Governor General of India 1876–80, Ambassador to France 1887–91, wrote poetry under the name Owen Meredith 276, 279

Macaulay, Thomas Babington (1800–59), first Baron 218
M'Connell, Primrose (born 1856), Lecturer in Agriculture 297 n.
Machiavelli, Niccolò (1469–1527) 285
Macmillan, publisher 205
Macmillan's Magazine 286
McNeill, Sir John (1795–1883), MD Edinburgh, surgeon to the East India Company, Chairman of the Board of Supervision of the working of the Scottish Poor Law Act 1845–78, on commission of inquiry into the commissariat department and organization of troops in the Crimea xii
Madras famine 277 n.
Madrid 283
Magdalen College 297 n.
Maha Mongkut *see* Rama IV
Maha Panthaka 182
Mahan, Alfred Thayer (1840–1914), US naval officer and historian 322
Maine, Sir Henry James Sumner (1822–88), Regius Professor of Civil Law at Cambridge 1847–54, contributor to the *Saturday Review*, published *Ancient Law* 1861, legal member of the Council of India 1862–9, Corpus Professor of Jurisprudence at Oxford 1869–78, Master of Trinity Hall, Cambridge 1877–88: 185, 263, 283, 296
majority rule 230
Malcolm, Sir John (1769–1833), Governor of Bombay 1826–30: 132 n.
Mallet, Sir Louis (1823–90), civil servant in the Board of Trade, and after Cobden's death the spokesman of Free Trade, Permanent Under-Secretary of State for India 1874–83: 167, 188, 253, 263, 276, 279
Mallock, William Hurrell (1849–1923), Balliol 1869–74: 219 n.
Malvern 138, 199, 268, 274, 276, 282, 284, 303
Manchester 63, 78, 155, 183, 207, 218
Manchester College 312
Manchester Grammar School 218 n.

Mandeville, Bernard de (?1670–1733), author of *Fable of the Bees, or Private Vices made Public Benefits* (1705) 56
Manicheism 236
mankind 14, 18, 23, 30, 35, 41, 51, 68, 115, 149, 152, 220, 241, 242, 272, 279, 290, 311
Manning, Henry Edward (1808–92), Balliol 1827–30, nominated Roman Catholic Archbishop of Westminster in 1865, Cardinal 1875: 248, 312
Mansel, Henry Longueville (1820–71), strong Tory and High Churchman, Reader in theology at Magdalen College from 1855, Professor of Ecclesiastical History 1866–8, Dean of St Paul's 1868–71: 212
Mansfield College 312
Mansion House 93, 170
Maria Theresa (1717–80) 92
Markby, Sir William (1829–1914), barrister, Recorder of Buckingham 1865–6, Puisne Judge of High Court of Calcutta 1866–78, Vice-Chancellor of Calcutta University 1877–8, Reader in Indian Law at Oxford 1878–1900, Perpetual Curator of Indian Institute, Fellow of Balliol 1883–1914, tutor to Indian probationers xxxv, 287, 290, 298, 300; married Lucy, daughter of John Edward Taylor of Weybridge 298
Marlborough 70, 189
marriage 220, 245–6; among aristocracy 74; for BJ xvi, xviii, xxxii; for Fellows xvi, xxvii, 206 n.; for FN's sister xv; for soldiers xxi, 28, 30, 113; in India 316
Marshall, Alfred (1842–1924), first Principal of University College, Bristol 1877–81, Fellow and lecturer in political economy at Balliol 1883–5, Professor of Political Economy at Cambridge 1884–1908: 290, 315
Martineau, James (1805–1900), unitarian divine, Professor of Mental and Moral Philosophy and Political Economy at Manchester New College (which removed to London in 1853) 1840–57, Principal 1869–85: 249, 289, 290, 304, 309
Mary Stuart 243
Marylebone 89
masters and servants 133
materialism 89, 205, 220, 290
materialists 157, 244
mathematician xxviii
mathematics 32, 109
matron (nursing) xv, 116, 309 n.
mature students xxvii
Maule, Fox *see* Panmure
Maurice, Frederick Denison (1805–72), successively Professor of English Literature and History (1840) and of Theology (1846) at King's College, London, until obliged to resign in 1854, appointed Professor of Moral Philosophy at Cambridge 1866: 38, 292
Max Müller, Friedrich (1823–1900), educated at Leipzig, introduced to England by Baron Bunsen, settled at Oxford 1848, Taylorian Professor 1854, Professor of Comparative Philology 1868, Curator of the Bodleian Library and Fellow of All Souls xxiii, 133 n., 211
Mayence 192
Mayo, Richard Southwell Bourke (1822–72), sixth Earl, Chief Secretary for Ireland 1852, 1858 and 1866, Govenor-General of India 1869–72, assassinated by a convict on the Andaman Islands 142 n., 153–4, 228, 314
Mazzini, Giuseppe (1805–72), 58, 124, 132, 205, 217, 228
medical profession xiv
medicine xxxi, 54, 57, 105, 148, 169, 180, 226
Medicine, Faculty of 297
Melbourne, William Lamb (1779–1848), second Viscount 40, 183
Mellish, Sir George (1814–77), barrister 1848, QC 1861, Lord Justice of Appeal 1870, Hon. DCL 1874: 160
Mendelssohn-Bartholdy, Jakob Ludwig Felix (1809–47) 249
Merton College 113, 127
mesmerism 178
metaphysical: assumption 6; difficulty 40; element 290; fallacies 290; insight 6; philosophy 242; puzzles 46, 51; questions 52; subtleties 241; training 252; world 290
metaphysics 5, 52, 70, 252
Metcalfe, Charles Theophilus (1785–1846), first Baron, Resident of Delhi 1811–20, of Hyderabad 1820–7, Provisional Governor-General 1835–6: 132 n.
Methodism 190
Methodist parson 129
Methodistical fancies 6
Middlemarch 226, 256
Milan 209
militia 28
Mill, James (1773–1836) 255
Mill, John Stuart (1806–73), xii, 60, 63, 65, 69, 70, 118, 140, 141, 144, 149, 152, 157, 169, 181, 205, 241, 260, 262, 263
millenarianism 41
millenium 68, 71, 227
Milner, Alfred (1854–1925), Balliol 1873–6, journalist on the staff of the *Pall Mall Gazette*, contested Harrow (L) in 1885, helped form Liberal Unionist Association, secretary to Goschen as Chancellor of the Exchequer 1887–9, served in Egypt 1889–92, Chairman of Board of Inland Revenue 1892–7, High Commissioner for South Africa 1897–1905,

Milner, Alfred (*cont.*)
member of Lloyd George's war cabinet 1916–18, Secretary of State for Colonies 1918–21: 299, 300
Milnes, Richard Monckton (1809–85), first Baron Houghton, intimate of Tennyson and Hallam, advocate of mechanics' institutes and penny banks, supported the Florence Nightingale Fund, trustee of the British Museum, President of the London Library 1882–5: xii, 289
Milton, John (1608–74) 93
Ministers 27, 71, 119, 232, 241, 257, 259, 315
ministry 34, 61, 75, 88, 92, 93, 117, 118, 120, 123, 124, 191, 238, 257, 283, 299; *see also* government
Ministry, coalition 111
miracles xvii, xxxiv, 139, 140, 146, 238, 244, 295, 302, 308
Modern History 32, 70
Mohl, Julius von (1800–76), Professor at Tübingen 1826, went to Paris in 1834 where he taught Persian xxxiii, 15, 42, 53, 94, 97, 210, 240, 247, 273; married Mary Clarke (1793–1883), FN's 'Clarkey', salon hostess 108, 112, 210, 273, 274, 306
Mommsen, Theodor (1817–1903), German historian 98
Moncreiff, James (1811–95), first Baron, MP (L) Leith Burghs 1851–9, Edinburgh 1859–68, Glasgow and Aberdeen Universities 1868, Solicitor-General for Scotland 1850, Lord Advocate 1851–2, 1852–8, 1859–66, 1868–9: 165 n.
money xxxiv, 201, 321
monotheism 5
monotheists 7
Monro, David Binning (1836–1905), matriculated at BNC 1854 and migrated to Balliol 1854–9, Fellow of Oriel 1859–82, Provost 1882–1905: 133 n.
Montgomery, Florence 137
Moore, George (1806–76), philanthropist, distributed his charity to Commercial Travellers Schools, a reformatory for young men at Brixton, Warehousemen and Clerks' Schools etc. 128
moral: character 10, 38; corruption 68, 69; degradation 151; deterioration 9; evil 10; faculties 106; force 37; foundation 302; good 218; good of men 82; government xxxiv; governor xxxiv; greatness xvii; grounds 30; ideas 157; improvement in Italy 33; influence 139, 292; latitudes 193; laws 9, 241, 242; lessons 195; nature 252; new world 227; object 7; objection 31; order of nature 10; philosophy xxxiii, 83, 241, 250, 268; plan 217; preventives 30; principle 148; process 50; science 241;

sense 213; specimens 220; standard 38; treatment 301; truths 242; world 213, 216
morality 29, 31, 47, 48, 83, 94, 135, 225, 227, 249, 254, 285, 293; female 30; speculative 137
Morant, Sir Robert Laurie (1863–1920), tutor to the Prince of Siam, went into Education Department, responsible for the Education Act of 1902, Permanent Secretary at the Board of Education 1903–11, Chairman of National Health Insurance Commission 1911–19, First Secretary Ministry of Health 1919–20, knighted 1907: 317
More, Sir Thomas (1478–1535) 42, 93
Morier, Sir Robert Burnet David (1826–93), Balliol 1845–9, held various appointments at German courts 1853–76, opponent of Bismarck, Minister at Lisbon 1876–81, Madrid 1881–4, Ambassador at St Petersburg 1884–93: 32 n., 121, 130, 135 n., 167, 194, 200, 203, 208, 210, 231, 246, 257, 264, 271, 272, 282, 282, 283; married (1861) Alice, daughter of General Jonathan Peel 194
Morier, Victor Albert Louis (1867–92), Balliol 1886: 135 n.
Morley, Albert Edmund Parker (1843–1905), Viscount Boringdon, third Earl, Balliol 1861–5, Under-Secretary of State for War 1880–5, First Commissioner of Works 1886, Chairman of Committees and Deputy Speaker in the House of Lords 1889–1904, Chairman of Devon County Council 1901–4: 153, 154
Morley, Samuel (1809–86), proprietor of the *Daily News*, MP (L) Bristol 1868–85, member of the London School Board 1870–6, consistently supported dissenting, philanthrophic and temperance movements and Mr Gladstone 146
Mormon, Book of 46
Morrison, Robert (1782–1834), appointed translator to the East India Company 1819: 132 n., 153
Morven 263
Mozart, Wolfgang Amadeus (1756–91) 249
Müller *see* Max Müller
Muhammad 226
Muhammadans 277, 284, 285
Muir-Mackenzie, Kenneth Augustus (1846–1930), first Baron Muir-Mackenzie, Balliol 1864–8, Permanent Secretary to the Lord Chancellor 1880–1915: 130
Mull 263
Mundella, Anthony John (1825–97), hosiery manufacturer in Nottingham, interested in Boards of Conciliation and Arbitration, MP (Radical) Sheffield 1868–85, and Sheffield Brightside 1885–97, Vice-President of Committee of Council on Education 1880–5, President of Board of Trade 1886, 1892–4: 163

INDEX 347

Munich 270 n.
Munro, Sir Hector (1726–1805), General 132 n.
Munro, Hugh Andrew Johnstone (1819–85), Trinity College, Cambridge, first Kennedy Professor of Latin 1869–72: 126
Munro, Sir Thomas (1761–1827), Governor of Madras 132 n.
Murray, John (1808–92), publisher 172
muscular Christianity 79, 84, 99
mysticism 83, 124, 149, 233, 238–9
mystics, Spanish 242

Napier, Sir Francis (1819–98), first Baron Ettrick, Ambassador at St Petersburg 1860–4, Berlin 1864–6, Governor of Madras 1866, interested in public health, public works and irrigation 286
Napier, Robert Cornelis (1810–90), first Baron Napier of Magdala, distinguished himself at the siege of Lucknow 1857, took part in the Chinese War of 1860, Commander-in-Chief of the Bombay army 1865, Commander-in-Chief in India 1870: 164, 184, 257
Napier, Sir William Francis Patrick (1785–1860), fought in and wrote the history of the Peninsular War 72
Naples 33
Napoleon I: 38, 72–3, 193
Napoleon III: 38, 61, 63, 73, 94, 95, 97, 192, 193, 195, 247
Natal 281
Natal, Bishop of see Colenso
natural beauty 28, 34, 67, 68, 91, 210, 252, 263, 299
natural science 32
nature, laws of 6, 18, 83, 220
naval reserve 195
Neander, Johann August Wilhelm, originally David Mendel (1789–1850), German protestant church historian 13, 140
negroes 93, 262
Nehushtan 73
Nelson, Horatio (1758–1805) 192
neo-Hegelianism 290
neo-Kantian 292
neo-Platonism 290
Netley 45 n., 47, 49
Nettleship, Richard Lewis (1846–92), Balliol 1865–9, Fellow 1869–92, died climbing Mt. Blanc, edited the works of T. .H. Green xxvii
New College xxvii, 133, 135, 252 n., 297 n., 298 n.
New Testament xvii, 52, 70, 149, 188, 296
New Zealand 59, 136
Newlands 287
Newman, John Henry (1801–90) 37, 160
Newman, William Lambert (1834–1923), Balliol 1851–5, Fellow 1854, reitred 1870 to Cheltenham xxvii, 98–9, 122
newspapers xiv, 107, 136, 192, 212, 288, 307, 313;

Daily News 16; *The Record* 38; *The Times* xiv, 28, 35 n., 38, 44 n., 49, 77, 78, 80, 93, 150, 181, 212
Newton, Sir Isaac (1642–1727) 9, 191, 212
Nichol, John (1833–94), Glasgow University and Balliol 1855–9, Professor of English Language and Literature at Glasgow 1862–89, founded, with Professor Knight, the New Speculative Society 1867: 92, 94
Niebuhr, Barthold Georg (1776–1831), German historian xi, 98
Nightingale, Frances, FN's mother, daughter of William Smith, married 1818: xiii, 251–2, 253, 265, 280
Nightingale, Frances Parthenope (1819–90), elder daughter of William Edward Shore (from 1815 Nightingale) of Embley, married, 1858, Sir Harry Verney. Author of *Hints on Arithmetic addressed to a young governess* (1852), *Stone Edge* (anon. 1868), *Lettice Lisle* (anon. 1870), *The Verney family during the Civil War*, 2 vols (1892) xiii, xv, 286, 290, 300, 306
Nightingale, William Edward (1794–1874), FN's father xii, xiii, 24, 81, 124, 229, 251, 251–2, 273
Nightingale Fund xv, 85
'Nightingale in the East' 122
Nightingale Training School xv, xxii, 233
'Nile, a voice from the' 283
Nineteenth Century 289
Nirvana 216
'No Popery' 300
North Wales University College 295
Northcote, Sir Stafford Henry (1818–87), first Earl of Iddesleigh, Balliol 1836–42, private secretary to Gladstone 1842, President of the Board of Trade 1866, Secretary for India 1867, Chancellor of the Exchequer 1874–80: 127, 129, 133 n., 142, 277; married (1843) Cecilia Frances (1823–1910), daughter of Thomas Farrer of Lincoln's Inn Fields 142, 277
Northcote, Walter Stafford (1845–1927), second Earl of Iddesleigh, Balliol 1864, lost an eye and was unable to take a degree 129
'Northern Farmer, The' 36
Norton, Charles Eliot (1827–1908), born in Cambridge Mass., travelled abroad and met the Brownings (in Florence), Ruskin, the Cloughs, and many others. Married (1862) Susan Ridley Sedgwick (died 1872). Met Carlyle in 1869 and edited his letters, reminiscences, and notebooks 167
notes 261
Notes on Nursing 46, 93, 150, 164, 239, 279
nurses xiii, xiv, xix, xxii, xxix, 57, 78, 87, 110, 238, 255, 260, 280, 317, 321–2, 322; 'free' 303; registration of 321–2
nursing xiii, xiv, xv, xxix, 62, 192, 291; establishment 61

'Odyssey' 225
official cretinism 277
Official Secrets Act xiv
Ogilvie, Charles Atmore (1793–1873), Fellow of Balliol 1816–34, Regius Professor of Pastoral Theology 1842–73: 25 n.
Old Testament xvii, 42, 47, 176, 241
Open Awards x, xxiii, xxvi, 32
Opposition, the 34, 62, 144
Orange Free State 281
Orders, Holy 54
Ordination Service 232
Oriel College xii, 31, 52, 297 n.
Oriental Studies, School of see Indian School at Oxford
Origen 149
Orissa 129
Orthodox, the 208
Orthodoxy, old, the 39
O'Shea, Mrs Katharine, Parnell's lover, died 1921, aged seventy-six 313
out-residents xxiv, xxvii
Overstone, Samuel Jones Loyd (1796–1883), first Baron, succeeded to his father's banking business in 1844: 212
Oxford city x, 219, 221, 243, 247, 282, 289, 291, 296, 299
Oxford Movement xxxvi
Oxford University ix, xxvii, xxix, xxxv, 7, 13, 40, 42, 44–5, 47, 53, 57, 59, 63, 64, 65, 67, 70, 76, 79, 86, 95, 107, 109–10, 124, 127, 130, 135, 139, 141, 145, 149, 155 n., 158, 160, 162, 166, 167, 170, 173, 174, 176, 180, 181, 195, 201, 204, 210, 211, 221, 222, 224, 226, 229, 240, 248, 256, 257, 265, 273, 274, 276, 282, 284, 287, 293, 296, 297, 302, 308, 317
Oxford University: Board of Studies 70; Chancellor 274; Chancellor's Court 25 n., 27 n.; Committee on India candidates xxx; Congregation 32 n., 139, 144 n.; Convocation 32, 144 n.; Faculty Boards 284 n.; Gazette 297; Hebdomadal Council 107, 109, 125, 126, 144 n., 295, 309; Honorary Degrees 124, 125, 187, 309; Press 33; Proctors 25 n., 284 n.; Union 38; Vice-Chancellor xi, xxix, 25 n., 275, 283, 284 n., 286, 296 n.

paganism 68
Paget, Sir James (1814–99), trained at St Bartholomew's Hospital, surgeon-extraordinary to Queen Victoria 1858, baronet 1871, Vice-Chancellor of London University 1883–95: 189, 250
Palermo 43, 50
Palestine 213, 215
Palgrave, Francis Turner (1824–97), Balliol 1843–7, Fellow of Exeter College 1847, entered Education Department 1848, Vice-Principal of Kneller Hall, successively examiner and Assistant Secretary of Education Department 1855–84, Professor of Poetry at Oxford 1885–95: 188, 210 n.
Pall Mall Gazette 116, 138
Palmer, Edwin (1824–95), Balliol 1841–5, Fellow 1845–67, catechetical lecturer 160
Palmer, Sir Roundell (1812–95), first Earl of Selborne, Fellow of Magdalen College 1835, barrister 1837, QC 1849, MP (C) Plymouth 1847, passed over to Liberal party and joined Palmerston's ministry in 1861, MP Richmond 1861–72, Attorney-General 1863–6, opposed disestablishment of Irish Church, Lord Chancellor 1872–4, 1880–5, ennobled 1882, opposed Home Rule 60, 65, 89, 93, 160, 162, 172, 248, 274 n.
Palmerston, Henry John Temple (1784–1865), Viscount 74 n., 76, 233, 272; married (1839) Emily Mary (1787–1869), Countess Cowper 74
Pan-Anglican Synod 132
Panmure, Fox Maule (1801–74), second Baron, Secretary at War 1846–52 and 1855–8, succeeded as eleventh Earl of Dalhousie in 1860: xiv, xv, xvi, 19, 45, 47–8
papacy 146
papist 190
Paradise 125
Paravicini, Baron Francis de (1843–1920), Balliol 1862–6, Senior Student of Christ Church 1866–71, tutor of Balliol 1872–1908, Classical Lecturer 1872–8, Fellow 1878–1908: 114 n., 230, 240
parents and children xix, 12
Paris ix, xiii, 64, 67, 138, 200, 210, 247, 273, 274 n.
Parisian life 210
Parker, Charles Stuart (1829–1910), Fellow of University College 1854–68, organized University Volunteer Corps, private secretary to Cardwell 1864–6, MP (L) Perthshire 1868–74, Perth 1878–92, member of Commissions on public schools 1868–74, and military education 1869, published *Sir Robert Peel*, 3 vols (1891–9), *Sir James Graham*, 2 vols (1907) 122, 155, 162
Parkes, Dr Edmund Alexander (1819–76), author of *A Manual of Practical Hygiene for Use in the Medical Service of the Army* (1864) 280
parliament xix, 209, 215, 298, 299, 315
Parnell, Charles Stuart (1846–91) 313
Parnell Commission 313
Past and Present 264
Pater, Walter (1839–94), Fellow of Brasenose 1864, associated with the pre-Raphaelites and especially Swinburne. Published *Studies in the History of the Renaissance* (1873), and *Marius the Epicurean* (1885) 210
patients 260

patriotism xix, 92
Pattison, Mark (1813-84), Oriel College 1836-9, Fellow of Lincoln 1839, Rector 1861: 212, 223
Paul, St 11, 55, 119, 182, 188, 214, 223, 296; *Epistles* xi, 9
Paulinus 224
pauperism xxii, 106, 151, 156, 158, 161, 163, 186, 213
paupers 78, 80, 161, 172
Peabody, George (1795-1869), born in Massachusetts, banker and merchant in London, founded the low-rental Peabody Dwellings for workmen, benefactor of Harvard and Yale Universities 124
Peckham ix
Peel, Arthur Wellesley (1829-1912), Balliol 1848-52, MP (L) Warwick 1865-85, Warwick and Leamington 1885-95, Speaker of the House of Commons 1884-95, Visitor of Balliol 1894-1912: 63, 127, 160, 298
Peel, Sir Robert (1788-1850) 49, 63, 118, 233, 272
Peelites xxxi
Pemberton-Leigh, Thomas (1793-1867), first Baron Kingsdown, refused the Lord Chancellorship, strengthened the appellate tribunal of the House of Lords 99, 100, 124, 125, 185
Pembroke, George Robert Charles Herbert (1850-95), thirteenth Earl, son of Sidney Herbert, Under-Secretary for War 1874-5, published *Letters and Speeches* (1896) 77, 254
Pender, Sir John (1815-96), promoter and director of submarine telegraph companies, MP (L) Totnes 1862-6 (unseated on petition) and Wick Boroughs (1872-85) 231
Pentateuch 27, 35
Penzance 252
Percival, John (1834-1918), Headmaster of Clifton College 252 n.
'personality' 12
Perthshire 155
Peterborough 150
Petty-Fitzmaurice, Edmond George (1846-1935), first Baron Fitzmaurice of Leigh, Wilts, barrister, MP (L) Calne 1868-85, N. Wilts 1898-1905, Under-Secretary of State for Foreign Affairs 1883-5, 1905-8, Chancellor of the Duchy of Lancaster 1908-9, biographer of Shelburne and Granville 272
Phaedo (Plato) 56, 234
Phaedrus (Plato) 237, 244, 245
philanthropic persons 12
philanthropy 61, 88
Phillimore, Sir Robert Joseph (1810-85), QC 1858, succeeded Dr Stephen Lushington as Judge of the High Court of Admiralty and Dean of Arches 1867: 24
philology 134, 158, 172

Philomathic Society 137
Philomel 122
Philomela 163
philosophers 54, 60, 75, 149, 157, 169, 181, 189, 204, 219, 292, 295; ancient 255; political 167
philosophical: appeal 87; interests 88; nation 202; notions 76; positions 53; questions 223; thought 223
philosophy x, 5, 47, 68, 69, 149, 157, 190, 223, 255, 267, 290, 293, 309, 317; ancient x, 70; early Greek 98, 268; ethical 75; inductive 252; moral 212; natural 54, 190; of history 6; political 75, 111, 167
physical: basis 218; constitution 220; deterioration 213; good 218; improvement 218, 220, 221; laws 220; misery 68; necessity 145; part 220; preventive 30; principles 218, 220; sciences 57, 70, 106, 109, 169; world 6
Physicians, College of 275
physics 5, 6, 252
Physics (Aristotle) 56
physiological laws 9, 235
physiologist 54
physiology 57, 159
Pickwick 208
Piedmont 247
Pilate, Pontius xxxiv, 305
Pindar 145
Pitt, William (1759-1806) 272
Plato xxiv, xxxiii-xxxiv, 7, 28, 32, 34, 36, 41, 56, 58, 63, 67, 68, 69, 70, 72, 76, 87, 95, 96, 98, 106, 111 n., 112, 119, 120, 126, 128, 142, 145, 148, 149, 152 n., 153, 158, 166, 173, 174, 175, 201, 204, 210, 218, 220, 221, 222, 231, 234, 235, 240, 250, 255, 256, 257, 258, 268, 299, 306
Plautus 112
plutocracy 63
poetical insight 6
Pogram, Hon. Elijah 100
Poland 193, 195
police 28, 29, 30, 31, 116
Polish travels 36
political: accidents 272; atmosphere 143; bore 111; careeer of Gladstone 85; economy xxii, 28, 58, 75, 78, 80, 116, 127, 146, 161, 186, 206, 294; experience 227; feelings 250, 285; friend xxvi; good 230; ideas 94; influence xxvi; interests 88; issue xxi; leader 135; life 214; matters 97; men 118; missionaries 151; parties xxv, xxvi; people 167; philosophy 75, 111, 167; question 78; sense 224; subjects 134; system xxxvi; tactics 35, world 95, 111, 272
politicians 18, 27, 85, 140
politics xxiv, xxvi, 34, 83, 91, 97, 98, 111, 117, 120, 122, 139, 147, 149, 163, 181, 258, 272, 273, 284, 313, 317; foreign 111, 121, 271, 281; French 247; German 123; Indian 276
Politics (Aristotle) 284, 289, 295

Polybius 162
polytheism 5
polytheist 76
pope 94, 110, 133, 140
popedom 94
popery 63
poor xxii, xxxv, 43, 60, 70, 78, 80, 146, 151, 155, 161, 171, 172, 191, 206, 296, 299; aged 78; destitute children 78; dwellings of the 78, 128, 131, 151, 155, 161, 163; incurable 78; mad 78; sick 78
Poor Law 65, 75, 78, 146, 150, 151, 152, 158, 161, 173, 186; administration 151; Amendment Act 117; Bill 118, 120; Board 80, 116, 150, 151, 155, 156, 172; Hospital Bill 91; Inspector 173; London 116, 156, 158, 161; Metropolitan xxii, 65 n., 117, 118, 119 n., 120, 162 n., 185 n.; New xxii; Old 172, 185; Rates 43, 78, 80, 81, 151, 161, 172, 185; Reform of (1834) 156, 172
Portuguese 240
positivism xxv, 5, 89
positivists 236
Potter, George (1832–93), prominent in the lockout in the building trades in London 1859, founded the *Beehive* 1861, opened first Trade Union Congress 1868: 58
prayer 18, 50, 176, 216, 292
prayer book 176
Presbyterianism 200
Prime Ministers 65, 119, 120, 146, 260, 272; of Japan 252, 254
Prince of Wales, the, later Edward VII (1841–1910) 152
Pringle, Miss A. L., trained at the Nightingale School, known to FN as 'little sister' and 'the Pearl', matron of the Edinburgh Royal Infirmary 1873–87. Appointed matron of St Thomas's Hospital in 1887, but resigned, despite FN's protests, a year later when she became a Roman Catholic 304, 309, 310, 311, 312
Privy Council 15 n., 80, 97, 99, 112, 115, 321; Education Committee xxv; Judicial Committee 38; Universities Committee 283, 284 n.
prophecies 36, 41, 145
prophets 27, 157, 296; Hebrew 46, 226; Jewish 41
Protestantism 215
Protestants xiii, 25 n., 92, 94, 95, 143, 172, 215, 242, 265
Prussia 67, 77, 95, 97, 121, 123, 147, 191, 192, 193, 195, 262, 271
Prussian Army 34, 92
psalms 27, 82, 219
public health xii, xix, xxi, xxxi
Public Health Act xv
public opinion 10, 11, 14, 16, 30, 96, 132, 141, 161, 249

punishment xxxii
Punjab 117
purchase system 28
Puritans 149, 160, 247
Purves, John (1840–89), Balliol 1860–5, Fellow 1866, published *Selections from Plato* (1883), translated the *Iliad* (1891) xxiii, 110 n.
Pusey, Edward Bouverie (1800–82), Fellow of Oriel 1822, studied oriental languages and biblical criticism at Göttingen, Berlin, and Bonn, Regius Professor of Hebrew 1828, worked with Keble and Newman on *Tracts for the Times* 1833, leader of the 'Oxford Movement' from 1841, commenced the establishment of Anglican sisterhoods in 1845, opposed reform of the University in 1854; his efforts, from 1865, to bring about union of the Roman and Anglican communions were frustrated by the Vatican Council in 1870: xviii, 25 n., 27 n., 32, 44, 63, 64, 70, 105, 107, 125, 135, 139, 144, 160, 167, 187, 201, 223, 234, 280
Puseyism 17, 89, 139
Puseyites xviii, 43, 105, 139, 222, 265

Quarterly Review 85, 115, 122, 134
Queen of the Nurses 45, 87, 153, 271, 312
Queen's College 297 n.
Queen's University, Belfast 238
Queensland 285
Questions for a Reformed Parliament 122
quietism 4

Rs, the three 106
Radcliffe Infirmary 291
radicalism xix, 63, 94
Radicals 114, 123, 139, 155, 166, 209, 316
Radstock, Granville Augustus William Waldegrave (1833–1913), third Baron Radstock, Balliol 1851–4: 265
railway: accident 220; employees 30
Raleigh, Sir Walter (?1552–1618) 74
Rama IV, Maha Mongkut (1804–68), King of Siam 317
Rambler, The 224
Raper, Robert William (1842–1915), Balliol Trinity Term 1861, migrated to Trinity College 1861–5, Fellow of Queen's College 1865, and of Trinity College 1871–1915: 148
Rasselas 224
Rathbone, William (1819–1902), partner in a Liverpool firm, established Liverpool training school for nurses 1862, and London and National Association for providing trained nurses 1874, MP (L) Liverpool 1868–80, Caernarvonshire 1880–5, North Caernarvonshire 1885–95: 128, 144, 257, 258, 321

INDEX   351

rationalists 317
Rawnsley, Revd Hardwicke Drummond (1851–
  1920), Balliol 1870–4, Hon. Canon of Carlisle
  1893–1909, residentiary Canon 1909–20, a
  founder and Hon. Secretary of the National
  Trust 292
real presence 46
Reay, Donald James Mackay (1839–1921),
  eleventh Baron, born at the Hague, educated
  at Leyden, naturalised 1877, Governor of
  Bombay 1885–90, Under-Secretary of State for
  India 1894–5, first President of the British
  Academy 1902–7: 297
Red Cross Society 203 n.
red republicanism 271
Reform Act of 1832: xix
Reform of Parliament: in 1866: 75, 82, 85, 87, 88,
  90, 91, 111; in 1867: 118, 120, 123, 134; for
  Scotland in 1868: 141 n.
Reform Party xix
Reformation 68, 247
reformers xi, 128, 230, 239; administrative 99;
  political 85; theological 16
Reichel, Revd Charles Parsons (1816–94),
  Professor of Latin at Queen's College, Belfast,
  Bishop of Meath 1885–94: 295
Reichel, Sir Harry Rudolf (1856–1931), Balliol
  1875–9, Fellow of All Souls 1880–94, first
  Principal of the University College of North
  Wales 1884: 295
religion xii, xvii, xviii, 3, 11, 12, 13, 35, 41, 44, 46,
  47, 48, 52, 65, 71, 75, 83, 114, 139, 149, 158, 180,
  182, 215, 223, 224, 246, 253–4, 304, 309, 317;
  natural 35, 56; of Christ 302; of reason 82;
  popular 41; rational 36, 152; rationalists in 317;
  sham 40; true 207
religionism 107
Religions: of the East xxiii; of the world 210, 212,
  217, 290
Religious: act 18; approach xix; belief 14;
  biography 157; books 35–6; denominations xx;
  devotions 201; element 290; family 190;
  ground 168; ideas 4; interest 208; liberty 170;
  life of the people 35; man xxxv, 187, 225, 228,
  245, 248; movement 70; orthodox mind 118;
  parties xvii; people 92; persons 12; poem 7;
  power 176; publications 215; question 62, 184,
  223; sense 99, 210; service 201; sound 119;
  standards xxxiv; state of the world 4; teaching
  35, 68; tests xi, 91, 92; thought 223; truth 48;
  truths 7; want 32; world 11, 27, 257
Renan, (Joseph) Ernest (1823–92), returned from
  a mission to the East in 1861 and was called to
  the Chair of Hebrew in the Collège de France.
  In *La vie de Jesus* (1863), he denied the divinity
  of Christ, and was forced to resign his Chair
  in 1864: 81, 322
rent 177

Republic 7, 98, 142, 205, 218, 221, 231, 250, 255,
  256
republic in France 247
republicanism 177
resurrection, the xvii, 52, 152, 190
retrenchment 156
Reynolds, Sir John Russell (1828–96), Professor
  of Medicine in University College, London
  1865, Physician in Ordinary to the Queen's
  household 1878, President of the BMA 1895,
  Baronet 1895: 159
Rhine provinces 34
Richmond 87
Richter, Jean Paul (1763–1825), German
  humorist 7
Riddell, James (1823–66), Balliol 1840–5, Fellow
  1845–66: xxiii, 25 n.
rifle movement 28
right 310
Ring and the Book, The 159
Ripon *see* de Grey
Ripon 322
ritualism xxv, 107, 122, 224, 256
Robert Elsmere 310
Robertson, Frederick William (1816–53),
  Edinburgh University and Brasenose,
  incumbent of Trinity Chapel, Brighton 1847.
  His sermons were published in five series, and
  his *Life and Letters*, ed. A. Stopford Brooke
  (1865) 160
Robinson, Henry (1842–94), lecturer on
  agriculture at Cirencester College, farmer in
  Lincolnshire, lecturer on agriculture for the
  Cambridge and Counties Agricultural
  Education Committee 297
Robinson, Henry Crabb (1775–1867), newspaper
  correspondent, barrister, helped to found both
  London University and the Athenaeum 170
Roby, Henry John (1830–1915), Fellow of St
  John's College, Cambridge 1854–61, second
  Master at Dulwich College, first secretary to
  the Cambridge Local Examinations, secretary
  to the Schools Inquiry Commission of 1864,
  secretary, and from 1872 member, of the
  Endowed Schools Commission of 1869, later
  businessman and MP (L) Eccles division of
  Lancs 1890–5: 128 n.
Rochester 188
Roe, Reginald Heber (1850–1926), Balliol 1869–
  74, Headmaster of Brisbane Grammar School
  1876–1909, first Vice-Chancellor of
  Queensland University from 1910: 242
Rogers, William (1819–96), Balliol 1837–42,
  appointed Perpetual Curate of St Thomas's,
  Charterhouse 1845, and rector of St.
  Botolph's, Bishopsgate 1863, educational
  reformer xxvi, 74, 112, 116, 128, 151, 155, 159,
  160, 164, 179, 180, 189, 199, 207, 244, 246, 286

352   INDEX

Roggenbach, Franz von (1825–1907), Liberal minister of Grand Duchy of Baden, signed his letters to Morier 'Ryebrook' 123
Rolfe, Robert Monsey (1790–1868), Lord Cranworth, Lord Chancellor 1852, 1865–6: 60 n.
Roman Catholic Church 75, 174, 203, 215, 240, 310, 311
Roman Catholics ix, xiii, xxxiii, 6, 37, 52, 59, 76, 129, 140, 149, 166, 167, 180, 216, 246
Romanism 203
Romanists 149
Rome xiii, 67, 94, 107
Romish proclivities 234
Roper, William (1496–1576), biographer of Sir T. More 42
Rossetti, Dante Gabriel (1828–1882) 148, 217
Rothamsted 288 n.
Roundell, Charles Savile (1827–1906), Balliol 1845–50, Fellow of Merton 1851–74, Secretary to the Jamaica Commission 1865, and to the Commission of Inquiry into Oxford and Cambridge Universities 1872, MP (L) Grantham 1880–5: 93, 113, 127, 128
Rousseau, Jean Jacques (1712–78) xxv
Rowbotham, John Frederick (1850–1925), Balliol 1869–73: 219 n.
Royal Institution xxxii
Royal Society 275
Rugby School xii, 70, 182
Rural Economy, Chair of 297
Ruskin, John (1819–1900) 96, 101, 210, 243, 246, 292
Russell, Francis Charles Hastings (1819–91) *see* Bedford, ninth Duke
Russell, George William Francis Sackville (1852–93) *see* Tavistock
Russell, John Francis Stanley (1865–1931), eldest son of Viscount Amberley, succeeded his grandfather as second Earl Russell 93
Russell, Lord John (1792–1878), first Earl Russell x, xix, xxi, xxiv, xxv, 61, 74, 76, 87, 93, 99, 111, 133, 134, 135, 136, 170 n., 173 n., 204, 245; married (2) Frances Anna Maria Elliot (1815–98), daughter of the second Earl of Minto 61, 76
Russia 63, 94, 193, 202, 277, 281, 284
ryots (peasants) xxix, 261, 262, 266, 275, 277 n., 305

sabbath 311
sacrament *see* communion
Sadowa 94
St Andrews 130, 152, 178
St James's Street xvi, 67
St Mark's 247
St Pancras workhouse 150, 173
St Paul's School ix, x

Salis, John Francis William de (1825–71), Count of the Holy Roman Empire, attaché to the British Legation at Turin 1845–9, frequented medal room at the British Museum, where he perfected the arrangement of Roman coins on a system of his own 176–7
Salisbury Plain xiv
Samuel 27, 49
Sandemanianism 190
sanitary 85; improvement 188, 214, 227, 232; improvement in Italy 33; knowledge 275; matters 127; measures 97, 159, 224; purposes 183; questions 131; reform 154; reformers 184; science 105, 106; state of the army 132; tracts 206; works in the University 221
Sanskrit scholarship 300
Satan 132
Saturday Review 78, 214, 215
Savonarola, Girolamo (1452–98) 149, 247
scepticism 175
Schleiermacher, Friedrich Daniel Ernst (1768–1834), German theologian and philosopher 255
Schlesinger, Max 94
Schleswig-Holstein 34
School: for training nurses xv; for working men's children 17–18
School Boards 184, 273, 299; Delegacy 264, 272
schoolmasters 293
schools xxv, xxx, 46, 154, 186, 203; commercial xxi; elementary xx; endowed 165 n.; grammar xx, xxi, 76, 109, 133; middle class xx; middle class female 159, 160, 180, 245; national 204; parish xxiv; pauper 161; primary xxi; provision of xix; public xx, 86; ragged 67; Rogers's 128, 159, 160, 180, 245; teaching in 70; voluntary xx
Schopenhauer, Arthur (1788–1860) 293
Schouvaloff, Peter Andreivich (1827–89), Count, came to London in 1873 to negotiate the marriage of the Duke of Edinburgh to the Grand Duchess Marie Alexandrovina, Ambassador in London during the Eastern crisis of 1877–8: 277
Schulze-Delitzsch, Hermann (1808–83), founder of working men's co-operatives in Germany, including the People's Bank 121
Schwalbach 159
science 3, 48, 118, 180, 190, 191, 252 n., 294, 309; men of 173, 190
scientific: people 12; world 293
Scottish: Church 82; Education Bill 165; Education Board 171; judge 185; Poor Law 171; Presbyterianism 200; Reform Act of 1868: 141 n.; universities xxiv, xxvi, 110, 130
Scotland 185, 191, 199, 215, 304
Scots, the 211
Scott, Revd Robert (1811–87), Fellow of Balliol

1835, Rector of Duloe 1840, of South Luffenham 1850, Master 1854-70, Professor of Exegesis 1861-70, Dean of Rochester from 1870, published, with H. G. Liddell, *Greek-English Lexikon* (1843) xii, xvi, xviii, xxiii, xxv, xxvi, xxvii, 74, 90, 108, 110, 122, 181, 182, 184, 188, 224, 230, 274 n., 307
Scott, Sir Walter (1771-1832) 211, 213
Scott Bursaries 211, 212
scripture xi, xvii, 15, 16
Seeley, Sir John Robert (1834-95), Professor of Latin at University College, London 1863-9, Professor of Modern History at Cambridge from 1869: 79 n., 93, 137 n.
Selborne *see* Palmer, Roundell
Sellar, Alexander Craig (1835-90), Balliol 1854-8, advocate, Scottish bar 1862, legal secretary to the Lord Advocate 1870-4, MP (L) Haddington 1882-5, and (LU) Partick division of Lanarkshire 1885-90: 187, 289; married Gertrude, daughter of FN's uncle Octavius Smith, of Ardtornish, Argyllshire 187, 263, 321
Sellar, Gerard Henry Craig (1871-1929), Balliol 1889-93, served in Boer War, Member of LCC 1907-10, MP (U) West Derbyshire 1908-18, senator of Irish Free State 1922-9: 321
Sellon, Priscilla Lydia (1821-76), founder of Society of Sisters of Mercy of the Holy Trinity, Devonport 105, 201
Selwyn, George Augustus (1809-78), Bishop of New Zealand 1841, attended first Lambeth Conference 1867, Bishop of Lichfield 1868: 136
Selwyn College 312
Seneca 112
Senior, Nassau William (1790-1864), Professor of Political Economy 1825-30, 1847-52, wrote Poor Law Commission Report of 1834: 133
sentimentalism 7, 17, 157
Serbian War 281
sermons xxxiv, 70, 91, 98, 137, 146, 160, 162, 184, 186, 208, 214, 222, 234 n., 238, 308-9
services, the 54
Seven Dials 80
Severn, Mrs Joan Ruskin Agnew (died 1924) 292; married Arthur Severn, cousin and ward of Ruskin 292
Shakespeare, William (1564-1616) 7, 38, 119, 124, 221, 234, 249, 271, 286; quotations from 38, 61, 74, 80, 94, 112, 119, 124, 137, 141, 168, 186, 208, 225, 239, 243, 276, 301
Shaw Lefevre, George John (1831-1928), Baron Eversley, MP (L) Reading 1863-85, Central Bradford 1886-95, founder of Commons Preservation Society, Postmaster General 1883, First Commissioner of Works 1892-4, President Local Government Board 1894-5: 145

Sherbrooke *see* Lowe, Robert
Shore, W. E. *see* Nightingale, William Edward
Short, Thomas Vowler (1790-1872), appointed Bishop of St Asaph 1846: 26
Shuttleworth, Sir James (1804-77), Secretary to the Manchester Board of Health, Vice-Chairman of Central Relief Committee during Lancashire cotton famine 1861-5: 50
Siam 317
Sibyl's books 211, 272
Sidney, Sir Philip (1554-86) 74
Simmias 152
Simon, Sir John (1816-1904), medical officer of health for the City of London 1848, for the General Board of Health 1855-8, and for the Privy Council 1858-71, Chief Medical Officer of Local Government Board 1871-6, published *Public Health Reports*, 2 vols (1887), *English Sanitary Institutions* (1890) xv, 105, 106, 122, 124, 127, 156, 168, 176
Simpson, Mrs, author of á life of Madame Mohl 306
Simpson, Sir James Young (1811-70), Professor of Midwifery at Edinburgh from 1839, Hon. DCL 1866: 147, 148
Simyen, Prince Palamayu (1861-79), son of Theodore II, Emperor of Ethiopia, ward under the British government of Dr Jex-Blake, School House, Rugby from 1872-7, Sandhurst 1878, died at Headingley, Leeds 164
Simyen, Princess Teruwark, Empress of Ethiopia, died in the British camp in 1867: 164
Sin xxvi, 9, 30, 36, 38, 68, 97, 182, 216
Sisera 27
sisterhoods 201, 206
sisters (nursing) 110
slave trade xiii
smallpox 219
Smith, Adam (1723-90) 263
Smith, Beatrice Ann Shore *see* Lushington, Godfrey
Smith, F. B., author of *Florence Nightingale, reputation and power* (1982) xiii, xxxvi-xxxvii
Smith, Fanny, FN's mother *see* Nightingale, W. E.
Smith, Gertrude *see* Sellar, A. C.
Smith, Goldwin (1823-1910), Regius Professor of Modern History 1858-66: xii n., 99, 107, 117-18, 123-4, 162, 253, 256, 258
Smith, Henry John Stephen (1826-83), Balliol 1844-8, Fellow 1849-73, Fellow of Corpus Christi College 1873-83, Savilian Professor of Geometry from 1860, served on University Commission 1877: xxviii, 247, 286
Smith, Joseph (1805-44), founder of the Mormon sect 46
Smith, Robert Payne (1819-95), Fellow of Pembroke College 1843, Regius Professor of

Smith, Robert Payne (cont.)
  Divinity 1865–70, Dean of Canterbury 1870–95: 76
Smith, Mr Samuel, brother of FN's mother xii, 19, 58 n.; married FN's Aunt Mai, sister of FN's father, who lived with FN and looked after her 1857–60: 19, 58 n.
Smith, V., unidentified 263
Smith, William (1756–1835), MP for Sudbury 1784–90, 1796–1802, Norwich 1802–30, a follower of Fox, opposed war with France, campaigned for abolition of slave trade and emancipation of slaves xiii
Smith, William Henry (1825–91), newsagent, MP (C) Westminster 1868, member of London School Board 1871, First Lord of the Admiralty 1877, Leader of the House of Commons 1886: 60
Snell, John (1629–79), founded scholarships linking Glasgow University and Balliol 211 n.
Snell Exhibitions xxvi
social: improvement 106; life 206, 214, 282; physics 275; question 78; questions 66, 300; science 6; state of man 275; state of the world 4; system xxxi
socialism xxii
society xxiv, 88, 162, 204, 221, 323; constitution of xxii
Socrates 6, 9, 47, 81, 83, 96, 97, 129, 152 n., 185, 202, 234
Soldiers xiv, xv, xviii, xxi, 18, 28, 29, 30, 31, 58, 66, 113, 139, 226, 280, 282, 301
Soldiers' Club 18
soldiery xxi, 28
Somerset House 165
Song Celestial, The 301
Sophocles 132, 153, 166, 195, 231
Sorabji, Cornelia (1867–1954), Somerville College 1888–92, first woman to take the BCL examination, Indian feminist xxxii, 322
South, Robert (1634–1716), preacher 160
South African Federation 281
Spanish marriages 75
Spedding, James (1808–81), editor of Bacon's *Works*, 7 vols (1857–9), and of his *Life and Letters*, 7 vols (1861–74) 190
Speedy, Captain C., interpreter with the British forces in Ethiopia 164
Spencer, Herbert (1820–1903) 224, 241, 252, 293
Spinoza, Benedictus de (1632–77) 39, 42, 46, 50, 61, 145, 290
Spottiswoode, William (1825–83), Balliol 1842–6, mathematician and physicist, President of the Royal Society 1878–83, DCL 1878, Queen's printer, married, 1861, a daughter of William Urquhart Arbuthnot, member of the Council for India 287

Stallard, JH 172
Stanley, Arthur Penrhyn (1815–81), Balliol College 1834–8, Fellow of University College, helped to promote petition for relief of clergy from subscription to damnatory clauses of Athanasian creed, Secretary of Oxford University Commission 1850–2, published *Commentary on the epistles to the Corinthians* 1855, Professor of Ecclesiastical History and Canon of Christ Church, examining chaplain to Archbishop Tait, defended *Essays and Reviews*, accompanied Prince of Wales on eastern tour in 1862, stood up for Bishop Colenso, Dean of Westminster 1864–81: x, xi, xviii, 32 n., 40, 84, 86, 111, 122, 144, 146, 203, 205 n., 210 n., 213, 244, 249, 282; married (1862) Lady Augusta Bruce (1822–76), fifth daughter of the seventh Earl of Elgin 91, 108, 111, 112, 145, 203, 255
Stanley, Edward Henry, Lord Stanley see Derby, fifteenth Earl
Stanley, Edward John (1802–69), second Baron Stanley of Alderley, President of Board of Trade 1855–8, Postmaster-General 1860–6, promoter between 1865 and 1874 of Girton college, the Girls Public Day-school Company, and the Medical College for Women 114, 155; married Henrietta Maria (1807–95), daughter of Viscount Dillon 159
Stanley, Edward Lyulph (1839–1925), fourth Baron Sheffield of Roscommon and fourth Baron Stanley of Alderley, Balliol 1857–61, member of the London School Board 1876–85 and 1888–1904, resisted all efforts to strengthen the position of denominational bodies within the public system, MP (L) Oldham 1880–5: 172, 209, 299
Stanley, Mary, sister of AP Stanley, and FN's rival in the Crimea and critic afterwards 86, 111
Stanleys 306
Stansfeld, Sir James (1820–98), MP (L) Halifax 1859–95, intimate of Mazzini, President of Local Government Board 1871–4: 241
state, the xx, xxii, 199
statistical: averages 5; facts 315; inquiries 31; survey 301
statistics xiv, 57, 80, 161, 275
Statistics, proposed Chair of xxxi–xxxii, 275, 314–15
Stephen, Sir James Fitzjames (1829–94), counsel for Rowland Williams in the *Essays and Reviews* case, chief writer on *Pall Mall Gazette* 1865–9, acted for 'Jamaica Committee' against Governor Eyre, legal member of Council of India 1869–72, Judge 1879–91: 93
Stockmar, Christian Friedrich (1787–1863),

Baron, private secretary to King Leopold of the Belgians and confidential adviser to Queen Victoria and Prince Albert 49

Stockmar, Ernst Alfred Christian (1823–86), Baron 77

Stopford Brooke *see* Brooke

Storks, Sir Henry Knight (1811–74), Major-General in charge of British establishments in Turkey during the Crimean War, member of the Commission of inquiry into the Jamaica rebellion of 1865 and its suppression 124

Strachan-Davidson, James Leigh (1843–1916), Balliol 1862–7, Fellow 1866–1907, Classical tutor 1872–1907, Senior Dean 1874–1907, Master 1907–16: xxiii, 110 n.

Strafford 314

Strauss, David Friedrich (1808–74), successively Lecturer at Tübingen, and Professor of Dogmatics and Church History at Zurich, encountered much opposition to his view that gospel history is mythical in character xi, 33 n., 76, 81, 82, 90, 193

Street, George Edmund (1824–81), architect 321 n.

strong and the weak, the 24

Stubbs, William (1825–1901), Regius Professor of Modern History 1866–84, Bishop of Chester 1884–7, and of Oxford 1888–1901: 82 n., 99

'Stuff', the *see* theodicy

Stuttgart 210

Surrey 226

Sussex 291

Sutherland, John (1808–91), MD Edinburgh 1831, inspector under the General Board of Health 1848, investigated sanitary conditions in the Crimea, and co-operated with FN xv, 31

Sweet, Henry (1845–1912), gained experience of German philology at Heidelberg before coming to Balliol in 1869, did not adapt to study at Oxford, and was placed in the fourth class in *Lit. Hum.* in 1873. Published a succession of major philological works beginning with *History of English sounds from the earliest period* (1874), not appointed a University Reader until 1901: 264

Swift, Jonathan (1667–1745) 262 n.

Swinburne, Algernon Charles (1837–1909), Balliol 1856–9: 175, 211 n., 217, 231 n., 242, 243, 252, 258, 267, 271

Swiss Lakes 299

Symonds, Charlotte Mary, daughter of JA Symonds the younger, afterwards Mrs Walter Leaf (1867–1934), BJ's god-daughter 304

Symonds, John Addington (1807–71), physician (whose daughter Charlotte married TH Green) 57, 80, 190, 193, 207, 291

Symonds, John Addington (1840–93), Balliol 1858–62. At BJ's suggestion collaborated with Mrs Clough to produce the 2 volume edition of Clough's works (1869) 284, 285, 303

sympathy and antipathy 23

Symposium, The 129

Tait, Archibald Campbell (1811–82), Balliol 1830–3, Fellow 1834–42, Bishop of London 1856–69, Archbishop of Canterbury 1869–82: xvii, xviii, 25, 26, 69, 70, 113, 128, 132, 162, 170 n., 199, 200, 248; married (1843) Catherine (1819–78), daughter of William Spooner, Archdeacon of Coventry and Rector of Elmdon 200

Tatton, Robert Grey (1848–1934), Balliol 1867–71, Fellow, lecturer and tutor 1872–87: xxvii, 235 n.

Tavistock, George William Francis Sackville Russell (1852–93), Viscount, later tenth Duke of Bedford, Balliol 1870–4, MP (L) Bedford 1875–85: 162, 282, 284, 286; married (1876) Lady Adeline Marie (died 1920), daughter of the third Earl Somers 282, 284, 286

Taylor, Aubrey Charles Ashworth (1845–70), Balliol 1864–8, son of Sir Henry Taylor 153, 193, 200

Taylor, Sir Henry (1800–86), author of *Philip van Artevelde* (1834), friend of Mill and JF Stephen, approved of Governor Eyre's actions 144, 153, 189; married (1839) Theodosia Alice, daughter of Thomas Spring Rice, Lord Monteagle 193

teaching 70, 161, 237

tedge 164

Teignmouth ix

Temperance, a maid of FN's 157

Temple, Frederick (1821–1902), Balliol 1839–42, Fellow 1842–8, Headmaster of Rugby School 1857–69, contributed 'The education of the world' to *Essays and Reviews*, Bishop of Exeter 1869, and of London 1885, Archbishop of Canterbury 1896–1902: xviii, 11–12, 112, 154, 165, 175, 178, 181, 182, 206 n., 311; married Beatrice Blanche (1845–1915), fifth daughter of William Saunders Sebright Lascelles and Lady Caroline Georgina Howard 311

Temple, Sir Richard (1826–1902), assistant to Sir John Lawrence, Chief Commissioner Central Provinces 1862–7, Lieutenant-Governor of Bengal 1874–7, Governor of Bombay 1877–80: 169 n.

Tenby ix

Tennant, Emma Alice Margaret 'Margot' (1864–1945), married H. H. Asquith as his second wife in 1894: 313

Tennyson, Alfred, first Baron Tennyson (1809–92), the poet xvi, 7, 36, 41, 42, 45, 51, 59, 85, 86,

Tennyson, Alfred (*cont.*)
  115, 125, 155, 163 n., 175, 189, 222, 237 n., 302, 317; married (13 June 1850) Emily, *née* Sellwood (1813–96) 85, 125, 302
Tennyson, Hallam (1852–1928), second Baron 302
Thames Commissioners 296
Theaetetus, The (Plato) 205
theists 236
theodicy, the 'Stuff' xii, xv, xxxiii, 3, 4, 8–9, 112, 14, 17, 40–1, 46, 53, 152, 188, 206, 213, 258, 281
Theodore II, Emperor of Ethiopia (1818–68) 164
theologians 6, 16, 50, 241, 249
theological: book 295; controversy xv; publications 215; radicals xxvi; statute 167; tracts 206
Theological Prize xxvi
theology 5, 16, 32, 42, 46, 137, 152, 175, 181, 203, 206, 211, 212, 213, 225, 226, 235, 241, 245, 246, 249, 295, 307; German 35; natural 93
Thesiger, Frederick (1794–1878), first Baron Chelmsford, KC 1834, MP (C) Woodstock 1840, Abingdon 1844, Stamford 1852, Lord Chancellor 1858–9, 1866–8, married Anna Maria 140
Thiers, Louis Adolphe (1797–1877) 247
Thirlwall, Connop (1797–1875), appointed Bishop of St David's 1840: 26
Thompson, William Hepworth (1810–86), Master of Trinity College, Cambridge 1866–86: 174 n., 266
Thomson, James (1834–82), poet, educated at the Royal Caledonian Asylum, lived a sad and isolated life in London 283
Thomson, William (1819–90), appointed Archbishop of York 1862: 26
Thomson, Sir William (1824–1907), first Baron Kelvin, Glasgow University and Peterhouse, Professor of Natural Philosophy in Glasgow 1846–99, formulated (1851–4) the two great laws of thermodynamics 218–19
Thrale, Mrs (1741–1821) 55 n.
Thring, Henry (1818–1907), first Baron Thring, parliamentary draughtsman, brother of Godfrey Thring, Balliol 1842–4, author of *Practical Legislation* (1902) 131
Thucydides 218, 224, 227, 278
'Thyrsis' 96
Timaeus (Plato) 173, 183, 205
Tintagel 252
Tollet, Georgine, author of *Country Conversations* 299
Tories xxv, 99, 110, 115, 123, 129
Torquay x, 167
Tory magnates 123
Toryism 129
Toynbee, Arnold (1852–83), Pembroke College, Oxford 1873–4, migrated to Balliol 1875–8,

appointed Tutor to India candidates 1878: xxx, xxxiv n., 287, 300
Toynbee Hall xxxiv, 309
Tractarians xi
trade 194, 195
Trade Unions 43, 58, 122, 162, 163
Trafalgar, battle of 192
Transvaal 281
Trench, Richard Chenevix (1807–86), Archbishop of Dublin, opposed disestablishment of Irish Church 124, 140
Trevelyan, Sir Charles Edward (1807–86), Governor of Madras 1859, recalled 1860, and returned to India as Finance Minister 1862: 24, 31, 50, 117, 127, 156; married (1834) Hannah Moore (died 1871), sister of Lord Macaulay 117
Trevelyan, Sir George Otto (1833–1928), financial member of Governor General's Council in India 1863, MP (L) Tynemouth 1865–8, Border Burghs 1868–86, Bridgeton (Glasgow) 1887, Civil Lord of the Admiralty 1868–70, Parliamentary Secretary to the Admiralty 1881, Chief Secretary for Ireland 1882–4, Chancellor of Duchy of Lancaster 1884, Secretary for Scotland 1886, 1892–5: 191
Trinity, the 46, 182
Trinity College 174, 297 n., 298 n.
Trinity College, Cambridge 266
Trinity College, Dublin 238
true, the 40
truest idea 50
truth xii, xxxiv, 3, 4, 6, 11, 12, 23, 35, 48, 68, 82, 111, 113, 181, 190, 212, 220, 233, 249, 255, 305, 310
Tseng, Chi-Tse (1839–90), Chinese diplomat, successively ambassador at Paris, London and St Petersburg 289
Tuckwell, W., author of *Reminiscences of Oxford* (1900) xxiii n.
Tübingen School 40
Tufnell, Edward Carleton (1806–86), Eton and Balliol, Assistant Poor Law Commissioner 1835, supported half-time system of industrial education, retired 1874: 161
Tummil Bridge 281
Tummil Loch 68
Tunis 285
Tupper, Martin Farquhar (1810–89), published *Proverbial Philosophy* (1838); his name became a synonym for the commonplace 136
Turgenev, Ivan Sergeyevich (1818–83) 185 n.
Turkey 281, 284
Twiss, Sir Travers (1809–97), Regius Professor of Civil Law 1855–70, Chancellor of London diocese 1858: 228
Tylor, Sir Edward Burnett (1832–1917), Keeper of the University Museum 1883, Professor of

Anthropology 1896–1909, published *Researches into the early history of mankind and the development of civilisation* (1865, second edn. 1870), *Primitive culture: researches into the development of mythology, philosophy, religion, art and custom* (1871) 211

Tyndall, John (1820–93), friend of Huxley and colleague of Faraday, noted for his investigations into electricity and magnetism, radiant heat, light, acoustics and glaciers, and for his advocacy of a doctrine of materialism 119, 184, 187

Tyrol 231

Ulrich von Hutten 33
ultramontanism 240
'Una and the Lion' 142, 145, 187
Uniformity, Act of 256
Union Liberals 299
Unitarianism 35, 121
Unitarians xiii, 16–17, 292, 312
United Kingdom xix
United States of America xix, 60, 287 n.; Civil war in 36
Universal Law 5–6, 9–10, 46
universe, God's 61
University: Bill 274; extension xxvii, 77, 90, 107, 108–10, 135, 144, 225, 316; Reform 112, 248; Reform Bill, draft x; reformers xxi; tests xi, 75, 77; Tests Act 77 n., 222 n.; Tests Bill 170, 173
Unto this last 96
untruthfulness 182
Urquhart, Edward William (1839–1916), Balliol 1857–61: 43 n.
utilitarianism 290

'Vanity of Human Wishes' 224
Vaughan, Charles John (1816–97), Headmaster of Harrow 1844–59, Vicar of Doncaster 1860–9: 8 n., 112 n.
venereal disease, 'the disease' xxi, 30–1
Vere, Aubrey Thomas de (1814–1902), poet and author, educated at Trinity College, Dublin, joined Roman Church in 1851, Irish sympathizer 190
Verney, Sir Harry (Calvert) (1801–94), MP (Whig) for Buckingham 1832–41, Bedford 1847–52, Buckingham 1857–85: xv, 306; married FN's sister Parthenope *see* Nightingale
Verney, Mrs 322
Vicar of Wakefield 188
vice 18, 31
Vice-Chancellor, BJ as xxix, 283, 286, 296 n.
Victoria, Queen (1819–1901) 90–1, 97, 303
Victoria Adelaide Mary Louise (1840–1901), eldest child of Queen Victoria 32, 77, 97, 109, 121, 123, 158, 192, 193; married (1858)

Frederick William, Crown Prince of Prussia 98, 192
Vienna Conference 61
Village Communities 263
Villiers, Charles Pelham (1802–98), disciple of Bentham, barrister, MP (L) Wolverhampton 1835–98, President of the Poor Law Board 1859–66: 61, 69, 80, 155, 156
Vincent, J. L. Samuel 40, 50
Vishnu 46
volunteers 14

Waddington, William Henry (1826–94), French statesman and archaeologist, entered the National Assembly in 1871 and the Senate in 1876, Minister of Public Instruction 1873 and 1876–7, Foreign Minister 1877–9, Prime Minister 1879, and Ambassador to Great Britain 1883–93: 289
Walker, Francis John Chesshyre (1851–71), Balliol 1868–71 (Oct.) 221
Walker, Frederick William (1830–1910), Corpus Christi College, High Master of Manchester Grammar School 1859–76, and of St Paul's 1876–1905: 218 n.
Wall, Revd Professor Henry (1810–73), Fellow of Balliol 1839–71, Bursar, Professor of Logic 1849–73, Vicar of Huntspill 1870: xvi, xviii, xxiii, xxvii, xxviii, 65 n., 108 n., 109, 110, 112 n., 124, 141, 165, 184, 200 n., 228
Wallace, Alfred Russell (1823–1913), naturalist 207
Wallace, Sir Donald Mackenzie (1841–1919), foreign correspondent of *The Times* at Constantinople 1878–84, private secretary to Lord Dufferin in India 1884–8, director of *The Times* foreign department 1891–9: 316
Wallace, Robert (1831–99), Trinity College Church, Edinburgh 1860–71, and Old Greyfriars 1871, Professor of Church History at Edinburgh 1872, left the church in 1876 and became editor of *The Scotsman* 1876–80, MP (Radical) East Edinburgh 1886–99: 171
Wallace, William (1844–97), Balliol 1865–7, Fellow of Merton 1867, Whyte's Professor of Moral Philosophy 1882: 130
Walmer 289
Walpole, Spencer Horatio (1806–98), Home Secretary 1852, 1858–9, 1866–7 (May), when he resigned following criticism of his handling of the Reform meetings in Hyde Park 93
war 195, 272, 281, 282, 285; American 36; of 1866: 91–2; of 1870: 192, 193–4, 194, 195, 200, 201, 257; Crimean *see* Crimea; Serbian 281
War: ministers 76, 132, 133; Secretaries of xiv, 18, 49
War Office xv, xvi, xviii, 17, 40, 61, 62, 74, 154, 155, 156, 162, 199, 228, 230, 232

Ward, Mary Augusta, Mrs Humphry (1851–1920), novelist 310 n.
Ward, Thomas (1809–58), created Baron Ward of the Austrian Empire 1849, a Yorkshireman who went as a jockey to Hungary in 1823, entered the service of Charles Louis of Bourbon, Duke of Lucca, 1827, and became Chief Minister of Parma 1847–54: 119
Ward, William George (1812–82), Fellow of Balliol 1834–45, deprived of his degree for heresy 1845: 181
Wardroper, Mrs xv
Ward's (shop) 134
Warrack, Charles (1861–91), Balliol 1882–6, Lecturer in Philosophy at Balliol 1890–1: 317
Warre, Edmond (1837–1920), Balliol 1855–9, Headmaster of Eton 1884–1905, Provost 1909–18: 84
Warwick 63
Waterhouse, Alfred (1830–1905), architect 90 n., 253 n.
Weldon, James Edward Cowdell (1854–1937), successively Headmaster of Dulwich 1883–5 and Harrow 1885–98, Bishop of Calcutta 1898–1902, Dean of Manchester 1906–18 and Durham 1918–33: 302
Wellington, Arthur Wellesley (1769–1852), first Duke of 72–3, 132
Wemyss and March, Francis Wemyss-Charteris-Douglas (1818–1914), tenth Earl, MP (C) E. Gloucestershire 1841–6, Haddingtonshire 1847–83: 194, 289, 292, 306–7; married Lady Anne Frederica Anson (died 1896), second daughter of the first Earl of Lichfield 251, 289, 292, 306–7
Wensleydale 34
Wesley, John (1703–91) 70, 149, 160
Westbury *see* Bethell, Richard
Western world 262
Westminster, Hugh Lupus Grosvenor (1825–99), first Duke, Balliol 1843–5, MP (L) Chester 1847–69, opposed government's Reform Bill 1866, succeeded as Marquis of Westminster 1869, created a Duke by Gladstone in the dissolution honours 1874, opposed Home Rule 1886: 88 n., 253
Westminster, Richard Grosvenor (1795–1869), second Marquis 69
Westminster 60
Westminster Abbey 89, 145
Westminster Hospital 255
Westminster Review 132, 276
Whewell, William (1794–1866), Master of Trinity College, Cambridge 1841–66: 175
Whigs xvi, xxxi, 114, 115, 131, 140
White, Joseph Blanco (1775–1841), born at Seville, successively Roman priest, unbeliever, and clergyman of the Church of England. Settled at Oriel College in 1826, later adopted Unitarian views and went to Liverpool 13
Whitman, Walt (1819–92) 148
Wilberforce, Samuel (1805–73), Bishop of Oxford 1845–69, and of Winchester 1869–73: 26, 244; married (1828) Emily (died 1841), daughter of John Sargent, Rector of Lavington, Sussex 244
William I of Prussia and Emperor of Germany (1797–1888) 192, 193
Williams, Pownoll Toker (1850–1911), Balliol 1867–71, landscape painter 56, 59
Williams, Rowland (1817–70), Professor of Hebrew at St David's, Lampeter, contributor to *Essays and Reviews* xviii, 10, 15 n., 16
Wilson, Mrs, mother of H. B. Wilson 170
Wilson, Bilton Josephus, benefactor of BJ 82 n.
Wilson, H. B. (1803–88), contributor to *Essays and Reviews* xviii, 10 n., 15 n., 16, 170, 174
Wilson, John Matthias (1813–81), President of Corpus Christi College, Oxford 1872–81: 248 n.
Wilson, William Scot (1806–88), incumbent of Holy Trinity, Ayr 1832–84, synod clerk of united diocese of Glasgow and Galloway 1840–5, Dean 1845–59, Bishop of Glasgow and Galloway 1859–88: 214
Winchester 70, 244
Wodehouse, John (1826–1902), first Earl of Kimberley, British Minister at St Petersburg after the Crimean War, Lord-Lieutenant of Ireland 1864–6, created Earl 1866, Lord Privy Seal 1868–70, Colonial Secretary 1870–4, 1880–2, India Office 1882–5, 1886, Secretary for India and Lord President of the Council 1892–4, Foreign Secretary 1894–5, Chancellor of London University 1899–1907: 119, 120, 131, 177, 298
women xix, xx, xxiii–xxiv, 4, 5, 6–7, 42, 56, 60, 61–2, 63, 67, 88–9, 96, 121, 141, 145, 159, 160, 164, 168, 203, 205, 206, 225, 242, 245, 250, 252 n., 255, 262, 272, 321, 322
Wood, Alexander, of Trinity College, matriculated 1863: 107
Wood, Sir Charles (1800–85), first Viscount Halifax, Secretary of State for India 1859–66: 74
Wood, Sir Charles Lindley *see* Halifax
Wood, John (1793–1871), factory reformer ix
Woodham-Smith, Mrs Cecil, author of *Florence Nightingale, 1820-1910* (1950) xiii
Woollcombe, Edward Cooper (1816–80), Fellow of Balliol 1838–80, tutor 1840–69, senior Tutor, Dean 1841–74, Rector of Tendring 1879: xviii, xxiii, xxvi, 108, 110, 122, 135, 141, 168, 184, 200, 225, 228, 230
Wooton, Surrey 226
Worcester College 297 n.

workhouses xxii, xxxii, 69, 78, 92, 94, 111, 150, 161, 162, 172
Working Men's Children's School 17–18
world, the xxxv, 13, 56, 85; ignorance and knowledge of 12, 116, 165, 191, 204, 227, 286, 295
Worsley, Philip Stanhope (1835–66), Fellow of Corpus Christi College, Oxford, published versions of the *Odyssey* (1861), and the first twelve books of the *Iliad* (1865) 86
Wright, Robert Samuel (1839–1904), Balliol 1856–60, Fellow of Oriel 1861–80, Judge xviii, 31, 44, 52, 155, 205, 303, 320; married (1891) Merriel, daughter of Revd. R. S. Chermside 320
Wyndham-Lewis, Mrs *see* Disraeli

Xenophon 129

Zanzibar 240 n., 241
zemindars (tax collectors) xxix, 262, 266 n., 275, 277 n.
zemindary evil 259
Zoological Gardens 165